THE BELIEF IN IMMORTALITY

THE

BELIEF IN IMMORTALITY

AND THE WORSHIP OF THE DEAD

BY

J. G. FRAZER, D.C.L., LL.D., Litt.D.

FELLOW. OF TRINITY COLLEGE, CAMBRIDGE
PROFESSOR OF SOCIAL ANTHROPOLOGY IN THE UNIVERSITY OF LIVERPOOL

VOL. I

THE BELIEF AMONG THE ABORIGINES OF AUSTRALIA,
THE TORRES STRAITS ISLANDS, NEW GUINEA
AND MELANESIA

THE GIFFORD LECTURES, ST. ANDREWS
1911–1912

1968
DAWSONS OF PALL MALL
London

First published by Messrs Macmillan & Co. Ltd.
© This edition Trinity College, Cambridge, 1913.
Reprinted 1968
Dawsons of Pall Mall
16 Pall Mall, London, S.W.1.
SBN: 7129 0246 5

Printed in Great Britain
by Photolithography
Unwin Brothers Limited
Woking and London

"*Itaque unum illud erat insitum priscis illis, quos cascos appellat Ennius, esse in morte sensum neque excessu vitae sic deleri hominem, ut funditus interiret; idque cum multis aliis rebus, tum e pontificio jure et e caerimoniis sepulchrorum intellegi licet, quas maxumis ingeniis praediti nec tanta cura coluissent nec violatas tam inexpiabili religione sanxissent, nisi haereret in eorum mentibus mortem non interitum esse omnia tollentem atque delentem, sed quandam quasi migrationem commutationemque vitae.*"

CICERO, *Tuscul. Disput.* i. 12.

PREFACE·

THE following lectures were delivered on Lord Gifford's Foundation before the University of St. Andrews in the early winters of 1911 and 1912. They are printed nearly as they were spoken, except that a few passages, omitted for the sake of brevity in the oral delivery, have been here restored and a few more added. Further, I have compressed the two introductory lectures into one, striking out some passages which on reflection I judged to be irrelevant or superfluous. The volume incorporates twelve lectures on " The Fear and Worship of the Dead " which I delivered in the Lent and Easter terms of 1911 at Trinity College, Cambridge, and repeated, with large additions, in my course at St. Andrews.

The theme here broached is a vast one, and I hope to pursue it hereafter by describing the belief in immortality and the worship of the dead, as these have been found among the other principal races of the world both in ancient and modern times. Of all the many forms which natural religion has assumed none probably has exerted so deep and far-reaching an influence on human life as the belief in immortality and the worship of the dead ; hence an historical survey of this most momentous creed and of the practical consequences which have been deduced from it can hardly fail to be at once instructive and impressive, whether we regard the record with complacency as a noble testimony to the aspiring genius of man, who claims to outlive the sun and the stars, or whether we view it with pity as a melancholy monument of fruitless labour and barren ingenuity expended in prying into that great mystery of which fools profess their knowledge and wise men confess their ignorance.

J. G. FRAZER.

CAMBRIDGE,
9th February 1913.

CONTENTS

Natural theology, three modes of handling it, the dogmatic, the philosophical, and the historical, pp. 1 *sq.* ; the historical method followed in these lectures, 2 *sq.* ; questions of the truth and moral value of religious beliefs irrelevant in an historical enquiry, 3 *sq.* ; need of studying the religion of primitive man and possibility of doing so by means of the comparative method, 5 *sq.* ; urgent need of investigating the native religion of savages before it disappears, 6 *sq.* ; a portion of savage religion the theme of these lectures, 7 *sq.* ; the question of a supernatural revelation dismissed, 8 *sq.* ; theology and religion, their relations, 9 ; the term God defined, 9 *sqq.* ; monotheism and polytheism, 11 ; a natural knowledge of God, if it exists, only possible through experience, 11 *sq.* ; the nature of experience, 12 *sq.* ; two kinds of experience, an inward and an outward, 13 *sq.* ; the conception of God reached historically through both kinds of experience, 14 ; inward experience or inspiration, 14 *sq.* ; deification of living men, 16 *sq.* ; outward experience as a source of the idea of God, 17 ; the tendency to seek for causes, 17 *sq.* ; the meaning of cause, 18 *sq.* ; the savage explains natural processes by the hypothesis of spirits or gods, 19 *sq.* ; natural processes afterwards explained by hypothetical forces and atoms instead of by hypothetical spirits and gods, 20 *sq.* ; nature in general still commonly explained by the hypothesis of a deity, 21 *sq.* ; God an inferential or hypothetical cause, 22 *sq.* ; the deification of dead men, 23-25 ; such a deification presupposes the immortality of the human soul or rather its survival for a longer or shorter time after death, 25 *sq.* ; the conception of human immortality suggested both by inward experience, such as dreams, and by outward experience, such as the resemblances of the living to the dead, 26-29 ; the lectures intended to collect evidence as to the belief in immortality among certain savage races, 29 *sq.* ; the method to be descriptive rather than comparative or philosophical, 30.

LECTURE IV.—THE BELIEF IN IMMOR-TALITY AMONG THE ABORIGINES OF CENTRAL AUSTRALIA . . . Pp. 87-106

LECTURE V.—THE BELIEF IN IMMOR-TALITY AMONG THE ABORIGINES OF CENTRAL AUSTRALIA (*continued*) . Pp. 107-126

LECTURE VI.—THE BELIEF IN IMMORTALITY AMONG THE OTHER ABORIGINES OF AUSTRALIA . . . Pp. 127-149

Lecture XIII.—The Belief in Immortality among the Natives of German New Guinea (*continued*) . Pp. 276-295

Lecture XIV.—The Belief in Immortality among the Natives of German and Dutch New Guinea Pp. 296-323

LECTURE I

INTRODUCTION

THE subject of these lectures is a branch of natural theology. By natural theology I understand that reasoned knowledge of a God or gods which man may be supposed, whether rightly or wrongly, capable of attaining to by the exercise of his natural faculties alone. Thus defined, the subject may be treated in at least three different ways, namely, dogmatically, philosophically, and historically. We may simply state the dogmas of natural theology which appear to us to be true: that is the dogmatic method. Or, secondly, we may examine the validity of the grounds on which these dogmas have been or may be maintained: that is the philosophic method. Or, thirdly, we may content ourselves with describing the various views which have been held on the subject and tracing their origin and evolution in history: that is the historical method. The first of these three methods assumes the truth of natural theology, the second discusses it, and the third neither assumes nor discusses but simply ignores it: the historian as such is not concerned with the truth or falsehood of the beliefs he describes, his business is merely to record them and to track them as far as possible to their sources. Now that the subject of natural theology is ripe for a purely dogmatic treatment will hardly, I think, be maintained by any one, to whatever school of thought he may belong; accordingly that method of treatment need not occupy us further. Far otherwise is it with the philosophic method which undertakes to enquire into the truth or falsehood of the belief in a God: no method could be more appropriate at a time like the present, when the

Natural theology, and the three modes of handling it, the dogmatic, the philosophical, and the historical.

S   I   B

opinions of educated and thoughtful men on that profound topic are so unsettled, diverse, and conflicting. A philosophical treatment of the subject might comprise a discussion of such questions as whether a natural knowledge of God is possible to man, and, if possible, by what means and through what faculties it is attainable; what are the grounds for believing in the existence of a God; and, if this belief is justified, what may be supposed to be his essential nature and attributes, and what his relations to the world in general and to man in particular. Now I desire to confess at once that an adequate discussion of these and kindred questions would far exceed both my capacity and my knowledge; for he who would do justice to so arduous an enquiry should not only be endowed with a comprehensive and penetrating genius, but should possess a wide and accurate acquaintance with the best accredited results of philosophic speculation and scientific research. To such qualifications I can lay no claim, and accordingly I must regard myself as unfitted for a purely philosophic treatment of natural theology. To speak plainly, the question of the existence of a God is too deep for me. I dare neither affirm nor deny it. I can only humbly confess my ignorance. Accordingly, if Lord Gifford had required of his lecturers either a dogmatic or a philosophical treatment of natural theology, I could not have undertaken to deliver the lectures.

The method followed in these lectures is the historical. But in his deed of foundation, as I understand it, Lord Gifford left his lecturers free to follow the historical rather than the dogmatic or the philosophical method of treatment. He says: "The lecturers shall be under no restraint whatever in their treatment of their theme: for example, they may freely discuss (and it may be well to do so) all questions about man's conceptions of God or the Infinite, their origin, nature, and truth." In making this provision the founder appears to have allowed and indeed encouraged the lecturers not only to discuss, if they chose to do so, the philosophical basis of a belief in God, but also to set forth the various conceptions of the divine nature which have been held by men in all ages and to trace them to their origin: in short, he permitted and encouraged the lecturers to compose a history of natural theology or of some part of it. Even when it is thus limited to its historical aspect the theme is too vast to be mastered completely by any one man : the most that a single enquirer can do is to take a general but necessarily superficial survey of the whole and to devote himself especially to the investigation of some particular branch or aspect of the subject. This I have done more or less for many years, and accordingly I think that without being presumptuous I may attempt, in compliance with Lord Gifford's wishes and directions, to lay before my hearers a portion of the history of religion to which I have paid particular attention. That the historical study of religious beliefs, quite apart from the question of their truth or falsehood, is both interesting and instructive will hardly be disputed by any intelligent and thoughtful enquirer. Whether they have been well or ill founded, these beliefs have deeply influenced the conduct of human affairs ; they have furnished some of the most powerful, persistent, and far-reaching motives of action ; they have transformed nations and altered the face of the globe. No one who would understand the general history of mankind can afford to ignore the annals of religion. If he does so, he will inevitably fall into the most serious misconceptions even in studying branches of human activity which might seem, on a superficial view, to be quite unaffected by religious considerations.

Therefore to trace theological and in general religious ideas to their sources and to follow them through all the manifold influences which they have exerted on the destinies of our race must always be an object of prime importance to the historian, whatever view he may take of their speculative truth or ethical value. Clearly we cannot estimate their ethical value until we have learned the modes in which they have actually determined human conduct for good or evil : in other words, we cannot judge of the morality of religious beliefs until we have ascertained their history : the facts must be known before judgment can be passed on them : the work of the historian must precede the work of the moralist. Even the question of the validity or truth of religious creeds cannot, perhaps, be wholly dissociated from the question of their origin. If, for example, we discover that doctrines which we had accepted with implicit faith

An historical enquiry into the evolution of religion prejudices neither the question of the ethical value of religious practice nor the question of the truth or falsehood of religious belief.

from tradition have their close analogies in the barbarous superstitions of ignorant savages, we can hardly help suspecting that our own cherished doctrines may have originated in the similar superstitions of our rude forefathers ; and the suspicion inevitably shakes the confidence with which we had hitherto regarded these articles of our faith.   The doubt thus cast on our old creed is perhaps illogical, since even if we should discover that the creed did originate in mere superstition, in other words, that the grounds on which it was first adopted were false and absurd, this discovery would not really disprove the beliefs themselves, for it is perfectly possible that a belief may be true, though the reasons alleged in favour of it are false and absurd : indeed we may affirm with great probability that a multitude of human beliefs, true in themselves, have been accepted and defended by millions of people on grounds which cannot bear exact investigation for a moment.   For example, if the facts of savage life which it will be my duty to submit to you should have the effect of making the belief in immortality look exceedingly foolish, those of my hearers who cherish the belief may console themselves by reflecting that, as I have just pointed out, a creed is not necessarily false because some of the reasons adduced in its favour are invalid, because it has sometimes been supported by the despicable tricks of vulgar imposture, and because the practices to which it has given rise have often been in the highest degree not only absurd but pernicious.

Yet such an enquiry may shake the confidence with which traditional beliefs have been held.

Thus an historical enquiry into the origin of religious creeds cannot, strictly speaking, invalidate, still less refute, the creeds themselves, though it may, and doubtless often does weaken the confidence with which they are held.   This weakening of religious faith as a consequence of a closer scrutiny of religious origins is unquestionably a matter of great importance to the community ; for society has been built and cemented to a great extent on a foundation of religion, and it is impossible to loosen. the cement and shake the foundation without endangering the superstructure. The candid historian of religion will not dissemble the danger incidental to his enquiries, but nevertheless it is his duty to prosecute them unflinchingly.   Come what may, he must ascertain the facts so far as it is possible to do so ; having done that, he may leave to others the onerous and delicate task of adjusting the new knowledge to the practical needs of mankind. The narrow way of truth may often look dark and threatening, and the wayfarer may often be weary ; yet even at the darkest and the weariest he will go forward in the trust, if not in the knowledge, that the way will lead at last to light and to rest ; in plain words, that there is no ultimate incompatibility between the good and the true.

Now if we are indeed to discover the origin of man's conception of God, it is not sufficient to analyse the ideas which the educated and enlightened portion of mankind entertain on the subject at the present day ; for in great measure these ideas are traditional, they have been handed down with little or no independent reflection or enquiry from generation to generation ; hence in order to detect them in their inception it becomes necessary to push our analysis far back into the past. Large materials for such an historical enquiry are provided for us in the literature of ancient nations which, though often sadly mutilated and imperfect, has survived to modern times and throws much precious light on the religious beliefs and practices of the peoples who created it. But the ancients themselves inherited a great part of their religion from their prehistoric ancestors, and accordingly it becomes desirable to investigate the religious notions of these remote forefathers of mankind, since in them we may hope at last to arrive at the ultimate source, the historical origin, of the whole long development.

To discover the origin of the idea of God we must study the beliefs of primitive man.

But how can this be done ? how can we investigate the ideas of peoples who, ignorant of writing, had no means of permanently recording their beliefs ? At first sight the thing seems impossible ; the thread of enquiry is broken off short ; it has landed us on the brink of a gulf which looks impassable. But the case is not so hopeless as it appears. True, we cannot investigate the beliefs of prehistoric ages directly, but the comparative method of research may furnish us with the means of studying them indirectly ; it may hold up to us a mirror in which, if we do not see the originals, we may perhaps contemplate their reflections. For a comparative study of the various races of mankind demonstrates,

The beliefs of primitive man can only be understood through a comparative study of the various races in the lower stages of culture.

or at least renders it highly probable, that humanity has everywhere started at an exceedingly low level of culture, a level far beneath that of the lowest existing savages, and that from this humble beginning all the various races of men have gradually progressed upward at different rates, some faster and some slower, till they have attained the particular stage which each of them occupies at the present time.

Hence the need of studying the beliefs and customs of savages, if we are to understand the evolution of culture in general.
If this conclusion is correct, the various stages of savagery and barbarism on which many tribes and peoples now stand represent, broadly speaking, so many degrees of retarded social and intellectual development, they correspond to similar stages which the ancestors of the civilised races may be supposed to have passed through at more or less remote periods of their history. Thus when we arrange all the known peoples of the world according to the degree of their savagery or civilisation in a graduated scale of culture, we obtain not merely a comparative view of their relative positions in the scale, but also in some measure an historical record of the genetic development of culture from a very early time down to the present day. Hence a study of the savage and barbarous races of mankind is of the greatest importance for a full understanding of the beliefs and practices, whether religious, social, moral, or political, of the most civilised races, including our own, since it is practically certain that a large part of these beliefs and practices originated with our savage ancestors, and has been inherited by us from them, with more or less of modification, through a long line of intermediate generations.

The need is all the more urgent because savages are rapidly disappearing or being transformed.
That is why the study of existing savages at the present day engrosses so much of the attention of civilised peoples. We see that if we are to comprehend not only our past history but our present condition, with all its many intricate and perplexing problems, we must begin at the beginning by attempting to discover the mental state of our savage forefathers, who bequeathed to us so much of the faiths, the laws, and the institutions which we still cherish ; and more and more men are coming to perceive that the only way open to us of doing this effectually is to study the mental state of savages who to this day occupy a state of culture analogous to that

of our rude progenitors. Through contact with civilisation these savages are now rapidly disappearing, or at least losing the old habits and ideas which render them a document of priceless historical value for us. Hence we have every motive for prosecuting the study of savagery with ardour and diligence before it is too late, before the record is gone for ever. We are like an heir whose title-deeds must be scrutinised before he can take possession of the inheritance, but who finds the handwriting of the deeds so fading and evanescent that it threatens to disappear entirely before he can read the document to the end. With what keen attention, what eager haste, would he not scan the fast-vanishing characters? With the like attention and the like haste civilised men are now applying themselves to the investigation of the fast-vanishing savages.

Thus if we are to trace historically man's conception of God to its origin, it is desirable, or rather essential, that we should begin by studying the most primitive ideas on the subject which are accessible to us, and the most primitive ideas are unquestionably those of the lowest savages. Accordingly in these lectures I propose to deal with a particular side or aspect of savage religion. I shall not trench on the sphere of the higher religions, not only because my knowledge of them is for the most part very slight, but also because I believe that a searching study of the higher and more complex religions should be postponed till we have acquired an accurate knowledge of the lower and simpler. For a similar reason the study of inorganic chemistry naturally precedes the study of organic chemistry, because inorganic compounds are much simpler and therefore more easily analysed and investigated than organic compounds. So with the chemistry of the mind ; we should analyse the comparatively simple phenomena of savage thought into its constituent elements before we attempt to perform a similar operation on the vastly more complex phenomena of civilised beliefs.

Savage religion is to be the subject of these lectures.

But while I shall confine myself rigidly to the field of savage religion, I shall not attempt to present you with a complete survey even of that restricted area, and that for more reasons than one. In the first place the theme, even

But only a part of savage religion will be dealt with.

with this great limitation, is far too large to be adequately set forth in the time at my disposal; the sketch—for it could be no more than a sketch—would be necessarily superficial and probably misleading. In the second place, even a sketch of primitive religion in general ought to pre-suppose in the sketcher a fairly complete knowledge of the whole subject, so that all the parts may appear, not indeed in detail, but in their proper relative proportions. Now though I have given altogether a good deal of time to the study of primitive religion, I am far from having studied it in all its branches, and I could not trust myself to give an accurate general account of it even in outline; were I to attempt such a thing I should almost certainly fall, through sheer ignorance or inadvertence, into the mistake of exaggerat-ing some features, unduly diminishing others, and omitting certain essential features altogether. Hence it seems to me better not to commit myself to so ambitious an enterprise but to confine myself in my lectures, as I have always done in my writings, to a comparatively minute investigation of certain special aspects or forms of primitive religion rather than attempt to embrace in a general view the whole of that large subject. Such a relatively detailed study of a single compartment may be less attractive and more tedious than a bird's-eye view of a wider area; but in the end it may perhaps prove a more solid contribution to knowledge.

Introduc-tory obser-vations. The ques-tion of a super-natural revelation excluded.

But before I come to details I wish to make a few general introductory remarks, and in particular to define some of the terms which I shall have occasion to use in the lectures. I have defined natural theology as that reasoned know-ledge of a God or gods which man may be supposed, whether rightly or wrongly, capable of attaining to by the exercise of his natural faculties alone. Whether there ever has been or can be a special miraculous revelation of God to man through channels different from those through which all other human knowledge is derived, is a question which does not concern us in these lectures; indeed it is expressly excluded from their scope by the will of the founder, who directed the lecturers to treat the subject " as a strictly natural science," " without reference to or reliance upon any supposed special exceptional or so-called miraculous revelation." Accordingly, in compliance with these directions, I dismiss at the outset the question of a revelation, and shall limit myself strictly to natural theology in the sense in which I have defined it.

I have called natural theology a reasoned knowledge of a God or gods to distinguish it from that simple and comparatively, though I believe never absolutely, unreasoning faith in God which suffices for the practice of religion. For theology is at once more and less than religion: if on the one hand it includes a more complete acquaintance with the grounds of religious belief than is essential to religion, on the other hand it excludes the observance of those practical duties which are indispensable to any religion worthy of the name. In short, whereas theology is purely theoretical, religion is both theoretical and practical, though the theoretical part of it need not be so highly developed as in theology. But while the subject of the lectures is, strictly speaking, natural theology rather than natural religion, I think it would be not only difficult but undesirable to confine our attention to the purely theological or theoretical part of natural religion: in all religions, and not least in the undeveloped savage religions with which we shall deal, theory and practice fuse with and interact on each other too closely to be forcibly disjoined and handled apart. Hence throughout the lectures I shall not scruple to refer constantly to religious practice as well as to religious theory, without feeling that thereby I am transgressing the proper limits of my subject.

Theology and religion, how related to each other.

As theology is not only by definition but by etymology a reasoned knowledge or theory of a God or gods, it becomes desirable, before we proceed further, to define the sense in which I understand and shall employ the word God. That sense is neither novel nor abstruse; it is simply the sense which I believe the generality of mankind attach to the term. By a God I understand a superhuman and supernatural being, of a spiritual and personal nature, who controls the world or some part of it on the whole for good, and who is endowed with intellectual faculties, moral feelings, and active powers, which we can only conceive on the analogy of human faculties, feelings, and activities, though we are bound to suppose

The term God defined.

that in the divine nature they exist in higher degrees, perhaps in infinitely higher degrees, than the corresponding faculties, feelings, and activities of man.   In short, by a God I mean a beneficent supernatural spirit, the ruler of the world or of some part of it, who resembles man in nature though he excels him in knowledge, goodness, and power.   This is, I think, the sense in which the ordinary man speaks of a God, and I believe that he is right in so doing.   I am aware that it has been not unusual, especially perhaps of late years, to apply the name of God to very different conceptions, to empty it of all implication of personality, and to reduce it to signifying something very large and very vague, such as the Infinite or the Absolute (whatever these hard words may signify), the great First Cause, the Universal Substance, " the stream of tendency by which all things seek to fulfil the law of their being," [1] and so forth.   Now without expressing any opinion as to the truth or falsehood of the views implied by such applications of the name of God, I cannot but regard them all as illegitimate extensions of the term, in short as an abuse of language, and I venture to protest against it in the interest not only of verbal accuracy but of clear thinking, because it is apt to conceal from our-selves and others a real and very important change of thought: in particular it may lead many to imagine that the persons who use the name of God in one or other of these extended senses retain certain theological opinions which they may in fact have long abandoned.   Thus the misuse of the name of God may resemble the stratagem in war of putting up dummies to make an enemy imagine that a fort is still held after it has been evacuated by the garrison.   I am far from alleging or insinuating that the illegitimate extension of the divine name is deliberately employed by theologians or others for the purpose of masking a change of front ; but that it may have that effect seems at least possible.   And as we cannot use words in wrong senses without running a serious risk of deceiving ourselves as well as others, it appears better on all accounts to adhere strictly to the common meaning of the name of God as signifying a powerful super-

---

[1] Matthew Arnold, *Literature and Dogma*, ch. i., p. 31 (Popular Edition, London, 1893).

natural and on the whole beneficent spirit, akin in nature to man ; and if any of us have ceased to believe in such a being we should refrain from applying the old word to the new faith, and should find some other and more appropriate term to express our meaning. At all events, speaking for myself, I intend to use the name of God consistently in the familiar sense, and I would beg my hearers to bear this steadily in mind.

You will have observed that I have spoken of natural theology as a reasoned knowledge of a God or gods. There is indeed nothing in the definition of God which I have adopted to imply that he is unique, in other words, that there is only one God rather than several or many gods. It is true that modern European thinkers, bred in a monotheistic religion, commonly overlook polytheism as a crude theory unworthy the serious attention of philosophers ; in short, the champions and the assailants of religion in Europe alike for the most part tacitly assume that there is either one God or none. Yet some highly civilised nations of antiquity and of modern times, such as the ancient Egyptians, Greeks, and Romans, and the modern Chinese and Hindoos, have accepted the polytheistic explanation of the world, and as no reasonable man will deny the philosophical subtlety of the Greeks and the Hindoos, to say nothing of the rest, a theory of the universe which has commended itself to them deserves perhaps more consideration than it has commonly received from Western philosophers ; certainly it cannot be ignored in an historical enquiry into the origin of religion.

Monotheism and polytheism.

If there is such a thing as natural theology, that is, a knowledge of a God or gods acquired by our natural faculties alone without the aid of a special revelation, it follows that it must be obtained by one or other of the methods by which all our natural knowledge is conveyed to us. Roughly speaking, these methods are two in number, namely, intuition and experience. Now if we ask ourselves, Do we know God intuitively in the same sense in which we know intuitively our own sensations and the simplest truths of mathematics, I think most men will acknowledge that they do not. It is true that according to Berkeley the world exists only as it is perceived, and that our perceptions of it are produced by the

A natural knowledge of God can only be acquired by experience.

immediate action of God on our minds, so that everything we perceive might be described, if not as an idea in
the mind of the deity, at least as a direct emanation from
him.   On this theory we might in a sense be said to have
an immediate knowledge of God.   But Berkeley's theory
has found little acceptance, so far as I know, even among
philosophers ; and even if we regarded it as true, we should
still have to admit that the knowledge of God implied by it
is inferential rather than intuitive in the strict sense of the
word : we infer God to be the cause of our perceptions
rather than identify him with the perceptions themselves.
On the whole, then, I conclude that man, or at all events the
ordinary man, has, properly speaking, no immediate or
intuitive knowledge of God, and that, if he obtains, without
the aid of revelation, any knowledge of him at all, it can
only be through the other natural channel of knowledge,
that is, through experience.

The nature of experience.   In experience, as distinct from intuition, we reach our
conclusions not directly through simple contemplation of the
particular sensations, emotions, or ideas of which we are at
the moment conscious, but indirectly by calling up before
the imagination and comparing with each other our
memories of a variety of sensations, emotions, or ideas of
which we have been conscious in the past, and by selecting
or abstracting from the mental images so compared the
points in which they resemble each other.   The points of
resemblance thus selected or abstracted from a number of
particulars compose what we call an abstract or general
idea, and from a comparison of such abstract or general
ideas with each other we arrive at general conclusions, which
define the relations of the ideas to each other.   Experience
in general consists in the whole body of conclusions thus
deduced from a comparison of all the particular sensations,
emotions, and ideas which make up the conscious life of the
individual.   Hence in order to constitute experience the
mind has to perform a more or less complex series of
operations, which are commonly referred to certain mental
faculties, such as memory, imagination, and judgment.
This analysis of experience does not pretend to be philosophically complete or exact ; but perhaps it is sufficiently

accurate for the purpose of these lectures, the scope of which
is not philosophical but historical.

Now experience in the widest sense of the word may
be conveniently distinguished into two sorts, the experience
of our own mind and the experience of an external world.
The distinction is indeed, like the others with which I am
dealing at present, rather practically useful than theoretically
sound ; certainly it would not be granted by all philosophers,
for many of them have held that we neither have nor with
our present faculties can possibly attain to any immediate
knowledge or perception of an external world, we merely
infer its existence from our own sensations, which are as
strictly a part of our mind as the ideas and emotions of
our waking life or the visions of sleep. According to them,
the existence of matter or of an external world is, so far as
we are concerned, merely an hypothesis devised to explain
the order of our sensations ; it never has been perceived by
any man, woman, or child who ever lived on earth ; we have
and can have no immediate knowledge or perception of anything but the states and operations of our own mind. On this
theory what we call the world, with all its supposed infini-
tudes of space and time, its systems of suns and planets,
its seemingly endless forms of inorganic matter and organic
life, shrivels up, on a close inspection, into a fleeting, a
momentary figment of thought. It is like one of those
glass baubles, iridescent with a thousand varied and delicate
hues, which a single touch suffices to shatter into dust. The
philosopher, like the sorcerer, has but to wave his magic
wand,

> " And, like the baseless fabric of this vision,
> The cloud-capped towers, the gorgeous palaces,
> The solemn temples, the great globe itself,
> Yea, all which it inherit, shall dissolve
> And, like this insubstantial pageant faded,
> Leave not a rack behind. We are such stuff
> As dreams are made on, and our little life
> Is rounded with a sleep."

It would be beyond my province, even if it were within
my power, to discuss these airy speculations, and thereby to
descend into the arena where for ages subtle dialecticians
have battled with each other over the reality or unreality of

Two kinds of experience, the experience of our own mind and the experience of an external world.

The distinction rather popular and con- venient

than philo-
sophically
strict. an external world.   For my purpose it suffices to adopt the popular and convenient distinction of mind and matter and hence to divide experience into two sorts, an inward experience of the acts and states of our own minds, and an outward experience of the acts and states of that physical universe by which we seem to be surrounded.

The
knowledge
or concep-
tion of God
has been
attained
both by
inward and
by outward
experience.   Now if a natural knowledge of God is only possible by means of experience, in other words, by a process of reasoning based on observation, it will follow that such a knowledge may conceivably be acquired either by the way of inward or of outward experience ; in other words, it may be attained either by reflecting on the processes of our own minds or by observing the processes of external nature. In point of fact, if we survey the history of thought, mankind appears to have arrived at a knowledge, or at all events at a conception, of deity by both these roads.   Let me say a few words as to the two roads which lead, or seem to lead, man to God.

The
conception
of God is
attained by
inward
experience,
that is, by
the obser-
vation of
certain
remarkable
thoughts
and feel-
ings which
are attri-
buted to
the inspira-
tion of a
deity.   In the first place, then, men in many lands and many ages have experienced certain extraordinary emotions and entertained certain extraordinary ideas, which, unable to account for them by reference to the ordinary forms of experience, they have set down to the direct action of a powerful spirit or deity working on their minds and even entering into and taking possession of their bodies ; and in this excited state—for violent excitement is characteristic of these manifestations — the patient believes himself to be possessed of supernatural knowledge and supernatural power.   This real or supposed mode of apprehending a divine spirit and entering into communion with it, is commonly and appropriately called inspiration.   The pheno-menon is familiar to us from the example of the Hebrew nation, who believed that their prophets were thus inspired by the deity, and that their sacred books were regularly composed under the divine afflatus.   The belief is by no means singular, indeed it appears to be world-wide ; for it would be hard to point to any race of men among whom instances of such inspiration have not been reported ; and the more ignorant and savage the race the more numerous, to judge by the reports, are the cases of inspiration.   Volumes

might be filled with examples, but through the spread
of information as to the lower races in recent years the
topic has become so familiar that I need not stop to
illustrate it by instances. I will merely say that among
savages the theory of inspiration or possession is commonly
invoked to explain all abnormal mental states, particularly
insanity or conditions of mind bordering on it, so that
persons more or less crazed in their wits, and particularly
hysterical or epileptic patients, are for that very reason
thought to be peculiarly favoured by the spirits and are
therefore consulted as oracles, their wild and whirling words
passing for the revelations of a higher power, whether a
god or a ghost, who considerately screens his too dazzling
light under a thick veil of dark sayings and mysterious
ejaculations.[1] I need hardly point out the very serious Practical
dangers which menace any society where such theories dangers of
the theory
are commonly held and acted upon. If the decisions of inspira-
tion.
of a whole community in matters of the gravest importance
are left to turn on the wayward fancies, the whims and
vagaries of the insane or the semi-insane, what are likely
to be the consequences to the commonwealth? What, for
example, can be expected to result from a war entered upon
at such dictation and waged under such auspices? Are cattle-
breeding, agriculture, commerce, all the arts of life on which a
people depend for their subsistence, likely to thrive when they
are directed by the ravings of epilepsy or the drivellings of
hysteria? Defeat in battle, conquest by enemies, death by
famine and widespread disease, these and a thousand other
lesser evils threaten the blind people who commit themselves
to such blind guides. The history of savage and barbarous
tribes, could we follow it throughout, might furnish us with
a thousand warning instances of the fatal effects of carrying
out this crude theory of inspiration to its logical conclusions;
and if we hear less than might be expected of such instances,
it is probably because the tribes who consistently acted up
to their beliefs have thereby wiped themselves out of exist-

---

[1] For a single instance see L.
Sternberg, "Die Religion der Gil-
jaken," *Archiv für Religionswissen-
schaft*, viii. (1905) pp. 462 *sqq.*, where
the writer tells us that the Gilyaks
have boundless faith in the supernatural
power of their shamans, and that the
shamans are nearly always persons who
suffer from hysteria in one form or
another.

ence : they have perished the victims of their folly and left no record behind. I believe that historians have not yet reckoned sufficiently with the disastrous influence which this worship of insanity,—for it is often nothing less—has exercised on the fortunes of peoples and on the development or decay of their institutions.

The belief in inspiration leads to the worship of living men as gods.

To a certain extent, however, the evil has provided its own remedy. For men of strong heads and ambitious temper, perceiving the exorbitant power which a belief in inspiration places in the hands of the feeble-minded, have often feigned to be similarly afflicted, and trading on their reputation for imbecility, or rather inspiration, have acquired an authority over their fellows which, though they have often abused it for vulgar ends, they have sometimes exerted for good, as for example by giving sound advice in matters of public concern, applying salutary remedies to the sick, and detecting and punishing crime, whereby they have helped to preserve the commonwealth, to alleviate suffering, and to cement that respect for law and order which is essential to the stability of society, and without which any community must fall to pieces like a house of cards. These great services have been rendered to the cause of civilisation and progress by the class of men who in primitive society are variously known as medicine-men, magicians, sorcerers, diviners, soothsayers, and so forth. Sometimes the respect which they have gained by the exercise of their profession has won for them political as well as spiritual or ghostly authority ; in short, from being simple medicine-men or sorcerers they have grown into chiefs and kings. When such men, seated on the throne of state, retain their old reputation for being the vehicles of a divine spirit, they may be worshipped in the character of gods as well as revered in the capacity of kings ; and thus exerting a two-fold sway over the minds of men they possess a most potent instrument for elevating or depressing the fortunes of their worshippers and subjects. In this way the old savage notion of inspiration or possession gradually develops into the doctrine of the divinity of kings, which after a long period of florescence dwindles away into the modest theory that kings reign by divine right, a theory familiar to our ancestors not long ago, and perhaps not wholly obsolete among us even now. However, inspired men need not always blossom out into divine kings; they may, and often do, remain in the chrysalis state of simple deities revered by their simple worshippers, their brows encircled indeed with a halo of divinity but not weighted with the more solid substance of a kingly crown. Thus certain extraordinary mental states, which those who experience and those who witness them cannot account for in any other way, are often explained by the supposed interposition of a spirit or deity. This, therefore, is one of the two forms of experience by which men attain, or imagine that they attain, to a know-ledge of God and a communion with him. It is what I have called the road of inward experience. Let us now glance at the other form of experience which leads, or seems to lead, to the same goal. It is what I have called the road of outward experience.

Outward experience as a source of the idea of God.

When we contemplate the seemingly infinite variety, the endless succession, of events that pass under our observa-tion in what we call the external world, we are led by an irresistible tendency to trace what we call a causal connexion between them. The tendency to discover the causes of things appears indeed to be innate in the constitution of our minds and indispensable to our continued existence. It is the link that arrests and colligates into convenient bundles the mass of particulars drifting pell-mell past on the stream of sensation; it is the cement that binds into an edifice seemingly of adamant the loose sand of isolated perceptions. Deprived of the knowledge which this tendency procures for us we should be powerless to foresee the succession of phenomena and so to adapt ourselves to it. We should be bewildered by the apparent disorder and confusion of every-thing, we should toss on a sea without a rudder, we should wander in an endless maze without a clue, and finding no way out of it, or, in plain words, unable to avoid a single one of the dangers which menace us at every turn, we should inevitably perish. Accordingly the propensity to search for causes is characteristic of man in all ages and at all levels of culture, though without doubt it is far more highly developed in civilised than in savage communities. Among savages

Tendency of the mind to search for causes, and the necessity for their discovery.

it is more or less unconscious and instinctive ; among civilised men it is deliberately cultivated and rewarded at least by the applause of their fellows, by the dignity, if not by the more solid recompenses, of learning. Indeed as civilisation progresses the enquiry into causes tends to absorb more and more of the highest intellectual energies of a people ; and an ever greater number of men, renouncing the bustle, the pleasures, and the ambitions of an active life, devote themselves exclusively to the pursuit of abstract truth ; they set themselves to discover the causes of things, to trace the regularity and order that may be supposed to underlie the seemingly irregular, confused, and arbitrary sequence of phenomena. Unquestionably the progress of civilisation owes much to the sustained efforts of such men, and if of late years and within our own memory the pace of progress has sensibly quickened, we shall perhaps not err in supposing that some part at least of the acceleration may be accounted for by an increase in the number of lifelong students.

The idea of cause is simply that of invariable sequence suggested by the observation of many particular cases of sequence. Now when we analyse the conception of a cause to the bottom, we find as the last residuum in our crucible nothing but what Hume found there long ago, and that is simply the idea of invariable sequence. Whenever we say that something is the cause of something else, all that we really mean is that the latter is invariably preceded by the former, so that whenever we find the second, which we call the effect, we may infer that the first, which we call the cause, has gone before it. All such inferences from effects to causes are based on experience ; having observed a certain sequence of events a certain number of times, we conclude that the events are so conjoined that the latter cannot occur without the previous occurrence of the former. A single case of two events following each other could not of itself suggest that the one event is the cause of the other, since there is no necessary link between them in the mind ; the sequence has to be repeated more or less frequently before we infer a causal connexion between the two ; and this inference rests simply on that association of ideas which is established in our mind by the reiterated observation of the things. Once the ideas are by dint of repetition firmly welded together, the one by sheer force of habit calls up the other, and we say that the two things which are represented by those ideas stand to each other in the relation of cause and effect. The notion of causality is in short only one particular case of the association of ideas. Thus all reasoning as to causes implies previous observation: we reason from the observed to the unobserved, from the known to the unknown ; and the wider the range of our observation and knowledge, the greater the probability that our reasoning will be correct.

All this is as true of the savage as of the civilised man. *The savage draws his ideas of natural causation from observation of himself.* He too argues, and indeed can only argue on the basis of experience from the known to the unknown, from the observed to the hypothetical. But the range of his experience is comparatively narrow, and accordingly his inferences from it often appear to civilised men, with their wider knowledge, to be palpably false and absurd. This holds good most obviously in regard to his observation of external nature. While he often knows a good deal about the natural objects, whether animals, plants, or inanimate things, on which he is immediately dependent for his subsistence, the extent of country with which he is acquainted is commonly but small, and he has little or no opportunity of correcting the conclusions which he bases on his observation of it by a comparison with other parts of the world. But if he knows little of the outer world, he is necessarily somewhat better acquainted with his own inner life, with his sensations and ideas, his emotions, appetites, and desires. Accordingly it is natural enough that when he seeks to discover the causes of events in the external world, he should, arguing from experience, imagine that they are produced by the actions of invisible beings like himself, who behind the veil of nature pull the strings that set the vast machinery in motion. For example, he knows by experience that he can make sparks fly by knocking two flints against each other ; what more natural, therefore, than that he should imagine the great sparks which we call lightning to be made in the same way by somebody up aloft, and that when he finds chipped flints on the ground he should take them for thunder-stones dropped by the maker of thunder and lightning from the clouds?[1] Thus *Hence he explains the phenomena of nature by supposing that they are produced by beings like himself. These beings may be called spirits or gods of nature to distinguish them from living human gods.*

[1] As to the widespread belief that flint weapons are thunderbolts see Sir E. B. Tylor, *Researches into the Early History of Mankind*, Third Edition

arguing from his limited experience primitive man creates a multitude of spirits or gods in his own likeness to explain the succession of phenomena in nature of whose true causes he is ignorant; in short he personifies the phenomena as powerful anthropomorphic spirits, and believing himself to be more or less dependent on their good will he woos their favour by prayer and sacrifice. This personification of the various aspects of external nature is one of the most fruitful sources of polytheism. The spirits and gods created by this train of thought may be called spirits and gods of nature to distinguish them from the human gods, by which I mean the living men and women who are believed by their worshippers to be inspired or possessed by a divine spirit.

In time men reject polytheism as an explanation of natural processes and substitute certain abstract ideas of ethers, atoms, molecules, and so on. But as time goes on and men learn more about nature, they commonly become dissatisfied with polytheism as an explanation of the world and gradually discard it. From one department of nature after another the gods are reluctantly or contemptuously dismissed and their provinces committed to the care of certain abstract ideas of ethers, atoms, molecules, and so forth, which, though just as imperceptible to human senses as their divine predecessors, are judged by prevailing opinion to discharge their duties with greater regularity and despatch, and are accordingly firmly installed on the vacant thrones amid the general applause of the more enlightened portion of mankind. Thus instead of being peopled with a noisy bustling crowd of full-blooded and picturesque deities, clothed in the graceful form and animated with the warm passions of humanity, the universe outside the narrow circle of our consciousness is now conceived as absolutely silent, colourless, and deserted. The cheerful sounds which we hear, the bright hues which we see, have no existence, we are told, in the external world: the voices of friends, the harmonies of music, the chime of falling waters, the solemn roll of ocean, the silver splendour of the moon, the golden glories of sunset, the verdure

(London, 1878), pp. 223-227 ; Chr. Blinkenberg, *The Thunderweapon in Religion and Folklore* (Cambridge, 1911); W. W. Skeat "Snakestones and Thunderbolts," *Folk-lore*, xxiii. (1912) pp. 60 *sqq.* ; and the references in *The Magic Art and the Evolution of Kings*, ii. 374.

of summer woods, and the hectic tints of autumn—all these subsist only in our own minds, and if we imagine them to have any reality elsewhere, we deceive ourselves. In fact the whole external world as perceived by us is one great illusion: if we gave the reins to fancy we might call it a mirage, a piece of witchery, conjured up by the spells of some unknown magician to bewilder poor ignorant humanity. Outside of ourselves there stretches away on every side an infinitude of space without sound, without light, without colour, a solitude traversed only in every direction by an inconceivably complex web of silent and impersonal forces. That, if I understand it aright, is the general conception of the world which modern science has substituted for polytheism.

When philosophy and science by their combined efforts have ejected gods and goddesses from all the subordinate posts of nature, it might perhaps be expected that they would have no further occasion for the services of a deity, and that having relieved him of all his particular functions they would have arranged for the creation and general maintenance of the universe without him by handing over these important offices to an efficient staff of those ethers, atoms, corpuscles, and so forth, which had already proved themselves so punctual in the discharge of the minor duties entrusted to them. Nor, indeed, is this expectation altogether disappointed. A number of atheistical philosophers have courageously come forward and assured us that the hypothesis of a deity as the creator and preserver of the universe is quite superfluous, and that all things came into being or have existed from eternity without the help of any divine spirit, and that they will continue to exist without it to the end, if end indeed there is to be. But on the whole these daring speculators appear to be in a minority. The general opinion of educated people at the present day, could we ascertain it, would probably be found to incline to the conclusion that, though every department of nature is now worked by impersonal material forces alone, the universe as a whole was created and is still maintained by a great supernatural spirit whom we call God. Thus in Europe and in the countries which have borrowed their civilisation, their

But while they commonly discard the hypothesis of a deity as an explanation of all the particular processes of nature, they retain it as an explanation of nature in general.

philosophy, and their religion from it, the central problem of natural theology has narrowed itself down to the question, Is there one God or none? It is a profound question, and I for one profess myself unable to answer it.

Whether attained by inward or outward experience, the idea of God is regularly that of a cause inferred, not perceived.

If this brief sketch of the history of natural theology is correct, man has by the exercise of his natural faculties alone, without the help of revelation, attained to a knowledge or at least to a conception of God in one of two ways, either by meditating on the operations of his own mind, or by observing the processes of external nature: inward experience and outward experience have conducted him by different roads to the same goal. By whichever of them the conception has been reached, it is regularly employed to explain the causal connexion of things, whether the things to be explained are the ideas and emotions of man himself or the changes in the physical world outside of him. In short, a God is always brought in to play the part of a cause; it is the imperious need of tracing the causes of events which has driven man to discover or invent a deity. Now causes may be arranged in two classes according as they are perceived or unperceived by the senses. For example, when we see the impact of a billiard cue on a billiard ball followed immediately by the motion of the ball, we say that the impact is the cause of the motion. In this case we perceive the cause as well as the effect. But, when we see an apple fall from a tree to the ground, we say that the cause of the fall is the force of gravitation exercised by the superior mass of the earth on the inferior mass of the apple. In this case, though we perceive the effect, we do not perceive the cause, we only infer it by a process of reasoning from experience. Causes of the latter sort may be called inferential or hypothetical causes to distinguish them from those which are perceived. Of the two classes of causes a deity belongs in general, if not universally, to the second, that is, to the inferential or hypothetical causes; for as a rule at all events his existence is not perceived by our senses but inferred by our reason. To say that he has never appeared in visible and tangible form to men would be to beg the question; it would be to make an assertion which is incapable of proof and which is contradicted by a multitude of contrary affirmations recorded in the traditions or the sacred books of many races ; but without being rash we may perhaps say that such appearances, if they ever took place, belong to a past order of events and need hardly be reckoned with at the present time. For all practical purposes, therefore, God is now a purely inferential or hypothetical cause ; he may be invoked to explain either our own thoughts and feelings, our impulses and emotions, or the manifold states and processes of external nature ; he may be viewed either as the inspirer of the one or the creator and preserver of the other ; and according as he is mainly regarded from the one point of view or the other, the conception of the divine nature tends to beget one of two very different types of piety. To the man who traces the finger of God in the workings of his own mind, the deity appears to be far closer than he seems to the man who only infers the divine existence from the marvellous order, harmony, and beauty of the external world ; and we need not wonder that the faith of the former is of a more fervent temper and supplies him with more powerful incentives to a life of active devotion than the calm and rational faith of the latter. We may conjecture that the piety of most great religious reformers has belonged to the former rather than to the latter type ; in other words, that they have believed in God because they felt, or imagined that they felt, him stirring in their own hearts rather than because they discerned the handiwork of a divine artificer in the wonderful mechanism of nature.

Thus far I have distinguished two sorts of gods whom man discovers or creates for himself by the exercise of his unaided faculties, to wit natural gods, whom he infers from his observation of external nature, and human gods or inspired men, whom he recognises by virtue of certain extraordinary mental manifestations in himself or in others. But there is another class of human gods which I have not yet mentioned and which has played a very important part in the evolution of theology, I mean the deified spirits of dead men. To judge by the accounts we possess not only of savage and barbarous tribes but of some highly civilised peoples, the worship of the human dead has been one of the commonest and most influential forms of natural religion,

Besides the two sorts of gods already distinguished, namely natural gods and living human gods, there is a third sort which has played an important part in history, namely, the spirits of deified dead men.

perhaps indeed the commonest and most influential of all. Obviously it rests on the supposition that the human personality in some form, whether we call it a soul, a spirit, a ghost, or what not, can survive death and thereafter continue for a longer or shorter time to exercise great power for good or evil over the destinies of the living, who are therefore compelled to propitiate the shades of the dead out of a regard for their own safety and well-being. This belief in the survival of the human spirit after death is world-wide ; it is found among men in all stages of culture from the lowest to the highest ; we need not wonder therefore that the custom of propitiating the ghosts or souls of the departed should be world-wide also. No doubt the degree of attention paid to ghosts is not the same in all cases ; it varies with the particular degree of power attributed to each of them ; the spirits of men who for any reason were much feared in their lifetime, such as mighty warriors, chiefs, and kings, are more revered and receive far more marks of homage than the spirits of common men ; and it is only when this reverence and homage are carried to a very high pitch that they can properly be described as a deification of the dead. But that dead men have thus been raised to the rank of deities in many lands, there is abundant evidence to prove. And quite apart from the worship paid to those spirits which are admitted by their worshippers to have once animated the bodies of living men, there is good reason to suspect that many gods, who rank as purely mythical beings, were once men of flesh and blood, though their true history has passed out of memory or rather been transformed by legend into a myth, which veils more or less completely the real character

Euhemer-
ism.

of the imaginary deity. The theory that most or all gods originated after this fashion, in other words, that the worship of the gods is little or nothing but the worship of dead men, is known as Euhemerism from Euhemerus, the ancient Greek writer who propounded it. Regarded as a universal explanation of the belief in gods it is certainly false ; regarded as a partial explanation of the belief it is unquestionably true ; and perhaps we may even go further and say, that the more we penetrate into the inner history of natural religion, the larger is seen to be the element of truth contained in Euhemerism. For the more closely we look at many deities of natural religion, the more distinctly do we seem to perceive, under the quaint or splendid pall which the mythical fancy has wrapt round their stately figures, the familiar features of real men, who once shared the common joys and the common sorrows of humanity, who trod life's common road to the common end.

When we ask how it comes about that dead men have so often been raised to the rank of divinities, the first thing to be observed is that all such deifications must, if our theory is correct, be inferences drawn from experience of some sort ; they must be hypotheses devised to explain the unperceived causes of certain phenomena, whether of the human mind or of external nature. All of them imply, as I have said, a belief that the conscious human personality, call it the soul, the spirit, or what you please, can survive the body and continue to exist in a disembodied state with unabated or even greatly increased powers for good or evil. This faith in the survival of personality after death may for the sake of brevity be called a faith in immortality, though the term immortality is not strictly correct, since it seems to imply eternal duration, whereas the idea of eternity is hardly intelligible to many primitive peoples, who nevertheless firmly believe in the continued existence, for a longer or shorter time, of the human spirit after the dissolution of the body. Now the faith in the immortality of the soul or, to speak more correctly, in the continued existence of conscious human personality after death, is, as I remarked before, exceedingly common among men at all levels of intellectual evolution from the lowest upwards ; certainly it is not peculiar to adherents of the higher religions, but is held as an unquestionable truth by at least the great majority of savage and barbarous peoples as to whose ideas we possess accurate information ; indeed it might be hard to point to any single tribe of men, however savage, of whom we could say with certainty that the faith is totally wanting among them.

Hence if we are to explain the deification of dead men, we must first explain the widespread belief in immortality ;

The deification of dead men presupposes the immortality of the human soul, or rather its survival for a longer or shorter time after death.

The question of immortality is a fundamental problem of natural theology in the wider sense.

we must answer the question, how does it happen that men in all countries and at all stages of ignorance or knowledge so commonly suppose that when they die their consciousness will still persist for an indefinite time after the decay of the body? To answer that question is one of the fundamental problems of natural theology, not indeed in the full sense of the word theology, if we confine the term strictly to a reasoned knowledge of a God; for the example of Buddhism proves that a belief in the existence of the human soul after death is quite compatible with disbelief in a deity. But if we may use, as I think we may, the phrase natural theology in an extended sense to cover theories which, though they do not in themselves affirm the existence of a God, nevertheless appear to be one of the deepest and most fruitful sources of the belief in his reality, then we may legitimately say that the doctrine of human immortality does fall within the scope of natural theology. What then is its origin? How is it that men so commonly believe themselves to be immortal?

If there is any natural knowledge of immortality, it must be acquired either by intuition or by experience: it is apparently not given by intuition; hence it must be acquired, if at all, by experience.

If there is any natural knowledge of human immortality, it must be acquired either by intuition or by experience; there is no other way. Now whether other men from a simple contemplation of their own nature, quite apart from reasoning, know or believe themselves intuitively to be immortal, I cannot say; but I can say with some confidence that for myself I have no such intuition whatever of my own immortality, and that if I am left to the resources of my natural faculties alone, I can as little affirm the certain or probable existence of my personality after death as I can affirm the certain or probable existence of a personal God. And I am bold enough to suspect that if men could analyse their own ideas, they would generally find themselves to be in a similar predicament as to both these profound topics. Hence I incline to lay it down as a probable proposition that men as a rule have no intuitive knowledge of their own immortality, and that if there is any natural knowledge of such a thing it can only be acquired by a process of reasoning from experience.[1]

---

[1] Wordsworth, who argues strongly, almost passionately, for "the consciousness of a principle of Immortality in the human soul," admits that "the

What then is the kind of experience from which the The idea of immortality seems to have been suggested to man both by his inward and his outward experience, notably by dreams, which are a case of inward experience. theory of human immortality is deduced? Is it our experience of the operations of our own minds? or is it our experience of external nature? As a matter of historical fact—and you will remember that I am treating the question purely from the historical standpoint—men seem to have inferred the persistence of their personality after death both from the one kind of experience and from the other, that is, both from the phenomena of their inner life and from the phenomena of what we call the external world. Thus the savage, with whose beliefs we are chiefly concerned in these lectures, finds a very strong argument for immortality in the phenomena of dreams, which are strictly a part of his inner life, though in his ignorance he commonly fails to discriminate them from what we popularly call waking realities. Hence when the images of persons whom he knows to be dead appear to him in a dream, he naturally infers that these persons still exist somewhere and somehow apart from their bodies, of the decay or destruction of which he may have had ocular demonstration. How could he see dead people, he asks, if they did not exist? To argue that they have perished like their bodies is to contradict the plain evidence of his senses; for to the savage still more than to the civilised man seeing is believing; that he sees the dead only in dreams does not shake his belief, since he thinks the appearances of dreams just as real as the appearances of his waking hours. And once he has in this way gained a conviction that the dead survive and can help or harm him, as they seem to do in dreams, it is natural or necessary for him to extend the theory to the occurrences of daily life, which, as I have said, he does not sharply distinguish from the visions of slumber. He now explains many of these occurrences and many of the processes of nature by the direct interposition of the spirits of the departed; he traces their invisible hand in many of the misfortunes and

sense of Immortality, if not a co-existent and twin birth with Reason, is among the earliest of her offspring." See his *Essay upon Epitaphs*, appended to *The Excursion* (*Poetical Works*, London, 1832, vol. iv. pp. 336, 338).

This somewhat hesitating admission of the inferential nature of the belief in immortality carries all the more weight because it is made by so warm an advocate of human immortality.

ɪ

in some of the blessings which befall him ; for it is a common feature of the faith in ghosts, at least among savages, that they are usually spiteful and mischievous, or at least testy and petulant, more apt to injure than to benefit the survivors. In that they resemble the personified spirits of nature, which in the opinion of most savages appear to be generally tricky and malignant beings, whose anger is dangerous and whose favour is courted with fear and trembling. Thus even without the additional assurance afforded by tales of apparitions and spectres, primitive man may come in time to imagine the world around him to be more or less thickly peopled, influenced, and even dominated by a countless multitude of spirits, among whom the shades of past generations of men and women hold a very prominent, often apparently the leading place. These spirits, powerful to help or harm, he seeks either simply to avert, when he deems them purely mischievous, or to appease and conciliate, when he supposes them sufficiently good-natured to respond to his advances. In some such way as this, arguing from the real but, as we think, misinterpreted phenomena of dreams, the savage may arrive at a doctrine of human immortality and from that at a worship of the dead.

It has also been suggested by the resemblance of the living to the dead, which is a case of outward experience.

This explanation of the savage faith in immortality is neither novel nor original : on the contrary it is perhaps the commonest and most familiar that has yet been propounded. If it does not account for all the facts, it probably accounts for many of them. At the same time I do not doubt that many other inferences drawn from experiences of different kinds have confirmed, even if they did not originally suggest, man's confident belief in his own immortality. To take a single example of outward experience, the resemblances which children often bear to deceased kinsfolk appear to have prompted in the minds of many savages the notion that the souls of these dead kinsfolk have been born again in their descendants.[1] From a few cases of resemblances so

[1] For instance, the Kagoro of Northern Nigeria believe that "a spirit may transmigrate into the body of a descendant born afterwards, male or female ; in fact, this is common, as is proved by the likeness of children to their parents or grand-parents, and it is lucky, for the ghost has returned, and has no longer any power to frighten the relatives until the new body dies, and it is free again " (Major A. J. N. Tremearne, "Notes on some

explained it would be easy to arrive at a general theory that all living persons are animated by the souls of the dead ; in other words, that the human spirit survives death for an indefinite period, if not for eternity, during which it undergoes a series of rebirths or reincarnations.   However it has been arrived at, this doctrine of the transmigration or reincarnation of the soul is found among many tribes of savages ; and from what we know on the subject we seem to be justified in conjecturing that at certain stages of mental and social evolution the belief in metempsychosis has been far commoner and has exercised a far deeper influence on the life and institutions of primitive man than the actual evidence before us at present allows us positively to affirm.

Be that as it may—and I have no wish to dogmatise on so obscure a topic—it is certain that a belief in the survival of the human personality after death and the practice of a propitiation or worship of the dead have prevailed very widely among mankind and have played a very important part in the development of natural religion.   While many writers have duly recognised the high importance both of the belief and of the worship, no one, so far as I know, has attempted systematically to collect and arrange the facts which illustrate the prevalence of this particular type of religion among the various races of mankind.   A large body of evidence lies to hand in the voluminous and rapidly increasing literature of ethnology ; but it is dispersed over an enormous number of printed books and papers, to say nothing of the materials which still remain buried either in manuscript or in the minds of men who possess the requisite knowledge but have not yet committed it to writing.   To draw all those stores of information together and digest them into a single treatise would be a herculean labour, from which even the most industrious researcher into the dusty annals of the human past might shrink dismayed.   Certainly I shall make no attempt to perform such a feat within the narrow compass of these lectures.   But it seems to me that I may make a useful, if a humble, contribution to the history

The aim of these lectures is to collect a number of facts illustrative of the belief in immortality and of the customs based on it among some of the lower races.

Nigerian Head-hunters," *Journal of the R. Anthropological Institute*, xlii. (1912) p. 159).   Compare *Taboo and* the *Perils of the Soul*, pp. 88 *sq.* ; *The Dying God*, p. 287 (p. 288, Second Impression).

of religion by selecting a portion of the evidence and sub-mitting it to my hearers. For that purpose, instead of accumulating a mass of facts from all the various races of mankind and then comparing them together, I prefer to limit myself to a few races and to deal with each of them separately, beginning with the lowest savages, about whom we possess accurate information, and gradually ascending to peoples who stand higher in the scale of culture. In short the method of treatment which I shall adopt will be the descriptive rather than the comparative. I shall not absolutely refrain from instituting comparisons between the customs and beliefs of different races, but for the most part I shall content myself with describing the customs and beliefs of each race separately without reference to those of others. Each of the two methods, the comparative and the descriptive, has its peculiar advantages and disadvantages, and in my published writings I have followed now the one method and now the other. The comparative method is unquestionably the more attractive and stimulating, but it cannot be adopted without a good deal of more or less conscious theorising, since every comparison implicitly involves a theory. If we desire to exclude theories and merely accumulate facts for the use of science, the descrip-tive method is undoubtedly the better adapted for the arrangement of our materials : it may not stimulate enquiry so powerfully, but it lays a more solid foundation on which future enquirers may build. It is as a collection of facts illustrative of the belief in immortality and of all the momentous consequences which have flowed from that belief, that I desire the following lectures to be regarded. They are intended to serve simply as a document of religious history ; they make no pretence to discuss philosophically the truth of the beliefs and the morality of the practices which will be passed under review. If any inferences can indeed be drawn from the facts to the truth or falsehood of the beliefs and to the moral worth or worthlessness of the practices, I prefer to leave it to others more competent than myself to draw them. My sight is not keen enough, my hand is not steady enough to load the scales and hold the balance in so difficult and delicate an enquiry.

LECTURE II

THE SAVAGE CONCEPTION OF DEATH

LAST day I explained the subject of which I propose to treat and the method which I intend to follow in these lectures. I shall describe the belief in immortality, or rather in the continued existence of the human soul after death, as that belief is found among certain of the lower races, and I shall give some account of the religion which has been based upon it. That religion is in brief a propitiation or worship of the human dead, who according to the degree of power ascribed to them by the living are supposed to vary in dignity from the humble rank of a mere common ghost up to the proud position of deity. The elements of such a worship appear to exist among all races of men, though in some they have been much more highly developed than in others.

But before I address myself to the description of particular races, I wish in this and the following lecture to give you some general account of the beliefs of savages concerning the nature and origin of death. The problem of death has very naturally exercised the minds of men in all ages. Unlike so many problems which interest only a few solitary thinkers this one concerns us all alike, since simpletons as well as sages must die, and even the most heedless and feather-brained can hardly help sometimes asking themselves what comes after death. The question is therefore thrust in a practical, indeed importunate form on our attention ; and we need not wonder that in the long history of human speculation some of the highest intellects should have occupied themselves with it and sought to find an answer to the riddle. Some of their solutions of the problem, though dressed out in all the beauty of exquisite language and poetic imagery, singularly resemble the rude guesses of savages. So little, it would seem, do the natural powers even of the greatest minds avail to pierce the thick veil that hides the end of life.

The problem of death is one of universal interest.

In saying that the problem is thrust home upon us all, I do not mean to imply that all men are constantly or even often engaged in meditating on the nature and origin of death. Far from it. Few people trouble themselves about that or any other purely abstract question : the common man would probably not give a straw for an answer to it. What he wants to know, what we all want to know, is whether death is the end of all things for the individual, whether our conscious personality perishes with the body or survives it for a time or for eternity. That is the enigma propounded to every human being who has been born into the world : that is the door at which so many enquirers have knocked in vain. Stated in this limited form the problem has indeed been of universal interest : there is no race of men known to us which has not pondered the mystery and arrived at some conclusions to which it more or less confidently adheres. Not that all races have paid an equal attention to it. On some it has weighed much more heavily than on others. While some races, like some individuals, take death almost lightly, and are too busy with the certainties of the present world to pay much heed to the uncertainties of a world to come, the minds of others have dwelt on the prospect of a life beyond the grave till the thought of it has risen with them to a passion, almost to an obsession, and has begotten a contempt for the fleeting joys of this ephemeral existence by comparison with the hoped-for bliss of an eternal existence hereafter. To the sceptic, examining the evidence for immortality by the cold light of reason, such peoples and such individuals may seem to sacrifice the substance for the shadow : to adopt a homely comparison, they are like the dog in the fable who dropped the real leg of mutton from his mouth in order to snap at its reflection in the water. Be that as it may, where such beliefs and hopes are entertained in full force, the whole activity of the mind and the whole energy of the body are apt to be devoted to a preparation for a blissful or at all events an untroubled eternity, and life becomes, in the language of Plato, a meditation or practising of death.   This excessive preoccupation with a problematic future has been a fruitful source of the most fatal aberrations both for nations and individuals.   In pursuit of these visionary aims the few short years of life have been frittered away : wealth has been squandered : blood has been poured out in torrents : the natural affections have been stifled ; and the cheerful serenity of reason has been exchanged for the melancholy gloom of madness.

> " *Oh threats of Hell and Hopes of Paradise !*
> *One thing at least is certain—*This *Life flies ;*
> *One thing is certain and the rest is Lies ;*
> *The Flower that once has blown for ever dies.*"

The question whether our conscious personality survives after death has been answered by almost all races of men in the affirmative.   On this point sceptical or agnostic peoples are nearly, if not wholly, unknown.   Accordingly if abstract truth could be determined, like the gravest issues of national policy, by a show of hands or a counting of heads, the doctrine of human immortality, or at least of a life after death, would deserve to rank among the most firmly established of truths ; for were the question put to the vote of the whole of mankind, there can be no doubt that the ayes would have it by an overwhelming majority. The few dissenters would be overborne ; their voices would be drowned in the general roar.   For dissenters there have been even among savages.   The Tongans, for example, thought that only the souls of noblemen are saved, the rest perish with their bodies.[1]   However, this aristocratic view has never been popular, and is not likely to find favour in our democratic age.

The belief in immortality general among mankind.

But many savage races not only believe in a life after death ; they are even of opinion that they would never die at all if it were not for the maleficent arts of sorcerers who cut the vital thread prematurely short.   In other

Belief of many savages that they would never die if their lives were not cut short by sorcery.

[1] W. Martin, *An Account of the Natives of the Tonga Islands*, Second Edition (London, 1818), ii. 99.

words, they disbelieve in what we call a natural death ; they think that all men are naturally immortal in this life, and that every death which takes place is in fact a violent death inflicted by the hand of a human enemy, though in many cases the foe is invisible and works his fell purpose not by a sword or a spear but by magic. Thus the Abipones, a now extinct tribe of horse Indians in Paraguay, used to allege that they would be immortal and that none of them would ever die if only the Spaniards and the sorcerers could be banished from America ; for they were in the habit of attributing every death, whatever its cause, either to the baleful arts of sorcerers or to the firearms of the Spaniards. Even if a man died riddled with wounds, with his bones smashed, or through the exhaustion of old age, these Indians would all deny that the wounds or old age was the cause of his death ; they firmly believed that the death was brought about by magic, and they would make careful enquiries to discover the sorcerer who had cast the fatal spell on their comrade. The relations of the deceased would move every stone to detect and punish the culprit ; and they imagined that they could do this by cutting out the heart and tongue of the dead man and throwing them to a dog to be devoured. They thought that this in some way killed the wicked magician who had killed their friend. For example, it happened that in a squabble between two men about a horse a third man who tried to make peace between the disputants was mortally wounded by their spears and died in a few days. To us it might seem obvious that the peacemaker was killed by the spear-wounds which he had received, but none of the Abipones would admit such a thing for a moment. They stoutly affirmed that their comrade had been done to death by the magical arts of some person unknown, and their suspicions fell on a certain old woman, known to be a witch, to whom the deceased had lately refused to give a water-melon, and who out of spite had killed him by her spells, though he appeared to the European eye to have died of a spear-wound.[1]

Belief of the Abipones.

---

[1] M. Dobrizhoffer, *Historia de Abi-ponibus* (Vienna, 1784), ii, 92 *sq.*, 240 *sqq.* The author of this valuable work lived as a Catholic missionary in the tribe for eighteen years.

Similarly the warlike Araucanians of Chili are said to disbelieve in natural death. Even if a man dies peaceably at the age of a hundred, they still think that he has been bewitched by an enemy. A diviner or medicine-man is consulted in order to discover the culprit. Some of these wizards enjoy a great reputation and the Indians will send a hundred miles or more to get the opinion of an eminent member of the profession. In such cases they submit to him some of the remains of the dead man, for example, his eyebrows, his nails, his tongue, or the soles of his feet, and from an examination of these relics the man of skill pronounces on the author of the death. The person whom he accuses is hunted down and killed, sometimes by fire, amid the yells of an enraged crowd.[1] Belief of the Araucanians.

When the eminent German anthropologist was questioning a Bakaïri Indian of Brazil as to the language of his tribe, he gave the sentence, "Every man must die" to be translated into the Bakaïri language. To his astonishment, the Indian remained long silent. The same long pause always occurred when an abstract proposition, with which he was unfamiliar, was put before the Indian for translation into his native tongue. On the present occasion the enquirer learned that the Indian has no idea of necessity in the abstract, and in particular he has no conception at all of the necessity of death. The cause of death, in his opinion, is invariably an ill turn done by somebody to the deceased. If there were only good men in the world, he thinks that there would be neither sickness nor death. He knows nothing about a natural end of the vital process ; he believes that all sickness and disease are the effects of witchcraft.[2] Belief of the Bakaïri.

Speaking of the Indians of Guiana, an English missionary, who knew them well, says that the worst feature in their character is their proneness to blood revenge, "by which a succession of retaliatory murders may be kept up for a long time. It is closely connected with Belief of the Indians of Guiana in sorcery as the cause of sickness and death.

---

[1] C. Gay, "Fragment d'un Voyage dans le Chili et au Cusco," *Bulletin de la Société de Géographie* (Paris), Deuxième Série, xix. (1843) p. 25 ; H. Delaporte, "Une visite chez les Araucaniens," *Bulletin de la Société de Géo-graphie* (Paris), Quatrième Série, x. (1855) p. 30.

[2] K. von den Steinen, *Unter den Naturvölkern Zentral - Brasiliens* (Berlin, 1894), pp. 344, 348.

their system of sorcery, which we shall presently consider. A person dies,—and it is supposed that an enemy has secured the agency of an evil spirit to compass his death. Some sorcerer, employed by the friends of the deceased for that purpose, pretends by his incantations to discover the guilty individual or family, or at any rate to indicate the quarter where they dwell. A near relative of the deceased is then charged with the work of vengeance. He becomes a *kanaima*, or is supposed to be possessed by the destroying spirit so called, and has to live apart, according to strict rule, and submit to many privations, until the deed of blood be accomplished. If the supposed offender cannot be slain, some innocent member of his family—man, woman, or little child—must suffer instead."[1] The same writer tells us that these Indians of Guiana attribute sickness and death directly to the agency of certain evil spirits called *yauhahu*, who delight in inflicting miseries upon mankind. Pain, in the language of the Arawaks (one of the best-known tribes of Guiana), is called *yauhahu simaira* or "the evil spirit's arrow."[2] It is these evil spirits whom wicked sorcerers employ to accomplish their fell purpose. Thus while the demon is the direct cause of sickness and death, the sorcerer who uses him as his tool is the indirect cause. The demon is thought to do his work by inserting some alien substance into the body of the sufferer, and a medicine-man is employed to extract it by chanting an invocation to the maleficent spirit, shaking his rattle, and sucking the part of the patient's frame in which the cause of the malady is imagined to reside. "After many ceremonies he will produce from his mouth some strange substance, such as a thorn or gravel-stone, a fish-bone or bird's claw, a snake's tooth, or a piece of wire, which some malicious *yauhahu* is supposed to have inserted in the affected part. As soon as the patient fancies himself rid of this cause of his illness his recovery is generally rapid, and the fame of the sorcerer greatly increased. Should death, however, ensue, the blame is laid upon the evil spirit whose power and malignity have prevailed over the counteracting charms. Some rival sorcerer

[1] Rev. W. H. Brett, *The Indian Tribes of Guiana* (London, 1868), p. 357.
[2] W. H. Brett, *op. cit.* pp. 361 *sq.*

will at times come in for a share of the blame, whom the
sufferer has unhappily made his enemy, and who is supposed
to have employed the *yauhahu* in destroying him.   The
sorcerers being supposed to have the power of causing, as
well as of curing diseases, are much dreaded by the common
people, who never wilfully offend them.   So deeply rooted
in the Indian's bosom is this belief concerning the origin of
diseases, that they have little idea of sickness arising from
other causes.   Death may arise from a wound or a contu-
sion, or be brought on by want of food, but in other cases it
is the work of the *yauhahu*"[1] or evil spirit.

In this account it is to be observed that while all
natural deaths from sickness and disease are attributed to
the direct action of evil spirits, only some of them are
attributed to the indirect action of sorcerers.   The practical
consequences of this theoretical distinction are very important.   For whereas death by sorcery must, in the
opinion of savages, be avenged by killing the supposed
sorcerer, death by the action of a demon cannot be
so avenged; for how are you to get at the demon?
Hence, while every death by sorcery involves, theoretically at least, another death by violence, death by a
demon involves no such practical consequence.   So far,
therefore, the faith in sorcery is far more murderous than
the faith in demons.   This practical distinction is clearly
recognised by these Indians of Guiana; for another writer,
who laboured among them as a missionary, tells us
that when a person dies a natural death, the medicine-
man is called upon to decide whether he perished through
the agency of a demon or the agency of a sorcerer.   If he
decides that the deceased died through the malice of an evil
spirit, the body is quietly buried, and no more is thought
of the matter.   But if the wizard declares that the cause of
death was sorcery, the corpse is closely inspected, and if a
blue mark is discovered, it is pointed out as the spot where
the invisible poisoned arrow, discharged by the sorcerer,
entered the man.   The next thing is to detect the culprit.
For this purpose a pot containing a decoction of leaves
is set to boil on a fire.   When it begins to boil over, the

Some deaths attributed to sorcery and others to evil spirits: practical conse- quence of this distinction.

---

[1] Rev. W. H. Brett, *op. cit.* pp. 364 *sq.*

side on which the scum first falls is the quarter in which the supposed murderer is to be sought. A consultation is then held : the guilt is laid on some individual, and one of the nearest relations of the deceased is charged with the duty of finding and killing him. If the imaginary culprit cannot be found, any other member of his family may be slain in his stead. " It is not difficult to conceive," adds the writer, " how, under such circumstances, no man's life is secure ; whilst these by no means unfrequent murders must greatly tend to diminish the number of the natives." [1]

Among the Indians of Guiana death is oftener attributed to sorcery than to demons. However, it would seem that among the Indians of Guiana sickness and death are oftener ascribed to the agency of sorcerers than to the agency of demons acting alone. For another high authority on these Indians, Sir Everard F. im Thurn, tells us that " every death, every illness, is regarded not as the result of natural law, but as the work of a *kenaima*" or sorcerer. " Often indeed," he adds, " the survivors or the relatives of the invalid do not know to whom to attribute the deed, which therefore perforce remains unpunished ; but often, again, there is real or fancied reason to fix on some one as the *kenaima*, and then the nearest relative of the injured individual devotes himself to retaliate. Strange ceremonies are sometimes observed in order to discover the secret *kenaima*. Richard Schomburgk describes a striking instance of this. A Macusi boy had died a natural death, and his relatives endeavoured to discover the quarter to which the *kenaima* who was supposed to have slain him belonged. Raising a terrible and monotonous dirge, they carried the body to an open piece of ground, and there formed a circle round it, while the father, cutting from the corpse both the thumbs and little fingers, both the great and the little toes, and a piece of each heel, threw these pieces into a new pot, which had been filled with water. A fire was kindled, and on this the pot was placed. When the water began to boil, according to the side on which one of the pieces was first thrown out from the pot by the bubbling of the water, in that direction would the *kenaima* be. In thus looking round to see who did the deed, the Indian thinks it

---

[1] Rev. J. H. Bernau, *Missionary Labours in British Guiana* (London, 1847), pp. 56 *sq.*, 58.

by no means necessary to fix on any one who has been with or near the injured man. The *kenaima* is supposed to have done the deed, not necessarily in person, but probably in spirit."[1] For these Indians believe that each individual man has a body and a spirit within it, and that sorcerers can despatch their spirits out of their bodies to harm people at a distance. It is not always in an invisible form that these spirits of sorcerers are supposed to roam on their errands of mischief. The wizard can put his spirit into the shape of an animal, such as a jaguar, a serpent, a sting-ray, a bird, an insect, or anything else he pleases. Hence when an Indian is attacked by a wild beast, he thinks that his real foe is not the animal, but the sorcerer who has transformed himself into it. Curiously enough they look upon some small harmless birds in the same light. One little bird, in particular, which flits across the savannahs with a peculiar shrill whistle at morning and evening, is regarded by the Indians with especial fear as a transformed sorcerer. They think that for every one of these birds that they shoot they have an enemy the less, and they burn its little body, taking great care that not even a single feather escapes to be blown about by the wind. On a windy day a dozen men and women have been seen chasing the floating feathers of these birds about the savannah in order utterly to extinguish the imaginary wizard. Even the foreign substance, the stick, bone, or whatever it is, which the good medicine-man pretends to suck from the body of the sufferer "is often, if not always, regarded not simply as a natural body, but as the materialised form of a hostile spirit."[2]

Beliefs and practices of the same general character are reported to have formerly prevailed among the Tinneh or Déné Indians of North-west America. When any beloved or influential person died, nobody, we are told, would think of attributing the death to natural causes ; it was assumed that the demise was an effect of sorcery, and the only difficulty

Belief of the Tinneh Indians in sorcery as the cause of death.

---

[1] (Sir) E. F. im Thurn, *Among the Indians of Guiana* (London, 1883), pp. 330 *sq.* For the case described see R. Schomburgk, *Reisen in Britisch-Guiana,* i. (Leipsic, 1847) pp. 324 *sq.* The boy died of dropsy. Perhaps the mode of

divination adopted, by boiling some portions of him in water, had special reference to the nature of the disease.

[2] (Sir) E. F. im Thurn, *op. cit.* pp. 332 *sq.*

was to ascertain the culprit. For that purpose the services of a shaman were employed. Rigged out in all his finery he would dance and sing, then suddenly fall down and feign death or sleep. On awaking from the apparent trance he would denounce the sorcerer who had killed the deceased by his magic art, and the denunciation generally proved the death-warrant of the accused.[1]

Belief of the Australian aborigines in sorcery as the cause of death. Again, similar beliefs and customs in regard to what we should call natural death appear to have prevailed universally amongst the aborigines of Australia, and to have contributed very materially to thin the population. On this subject I will quote the words of an observer. His remarks apply to the Australian aborigines in general but to the tribes of Victoria in particular. He says : " The natives are much more numerous in some parts of Australia than they are in others, but nowhere is the country thickly peopled ; some dire disease occasionally breaks out among the natives, and carries off large numbers. . . . But there are two other causes which, in my opinion, principally account for their paucity of numbers. The first is that infanticide is universally practised ; the second, that a belief exists that no one can die a natural death. Thus, if an individual of a certain tribe dies, his relatives consider that his death has been caused by sorcery on the part of another tribe. The deceased's sons, or nearest relatives, therefore start off on a *bucceening* or murdering expedition. If the deceased is buried, a fly or a beetle is put into the grave, and the direction in which the insect wings its way when released is the one the avengers take. If the body is burnt, the whereabouts of the offending parties is indicated by the direction of the smoke. The first unfortunates fallen in with are generally watched until they encamp for the night ; when they are buried in sleep, the murderers steal quietly up until they are within a yard or two of their victims, rush suddenly upon and butcher them. On these occasions they always abstract the kidney-fat, and also take off a piece of the skin of the thigh. These are carried home as trophies, as the American Indians take the scalp. The murderers anoint

---

[1] Father A. G. Morice, " The Canadian Dénés," *Annual Archaeolo-* *gical Report, 1905* (Toronto, 1906), p. 207.

their bodies with the fat of their victims, thinking that by
that process the strength of the deceased enters into them.
Sometimes it happens that the *bucceening* party come suddenly
upon a man of a strange tribe in a tree hunting opossums ;
he is immediately speared, and left weltering in his blood at
the foot of the tree.   The relatives of the murdered man at
once proceed to retaliate ; and thus a constant and never-
ending series of murders is always going on. . . . I do not
mean to assert that for every man that dies or is killed
another is murdered ; for it often happens that the deceased
has no sons or relatives who care about avenging his death.
At other times a *bucceening* party will return without having
met with any one ; then, again, they are sometimes repelled
by those they attack." [1]

Again, speaking of the tribes of Western Australia, *Belief of the*
Sir George Grey tells us that " the natives do not *natives of*
Western
allow that there is such a thing as a death from natural *Australia*
causes ; they believe, that were it not for murderers or *in sorcery*
as a cause
the malignity of sorcerers, they might live for ever ; hence, *of death.*
when a native dies from the effect of an accident, or
from some natural cause, they use a variety of superstitious
ceremonies, to ascertain in what direction the sorcerer
lives, whose evil practices have brought about the death
of their relative ; this point being satisfactorily settled
by friendly sorcerers, they then attach the crime to some
individual, and the funeral obsequies are scarcely concluded, ere they start to revenge their supposed wrongs." [2]
Again, speaking of the Watch-an-die tribe of Western
Australia, another writer tells us that they " possess the
comfortable assurance that nearly all diseases, and consequently deaths, are caused by the enchantments of hostile
tribes, and that were it not for the malevolence of their
enemies they would (with a few exceptions) live for ever.
Consequently, on the first approach of sickness their first
endeavour is to ascertain whether the *boollia* [magic] of their
own tribe is not sufficiently potent to counteract that of

[1] Albert A. C. Le Souëf, "Notes
on the Natives of Australia," in R.
Brough Smyth's *Aborigines of Victoria* (Melbourne and London, 1878),
ii. 289 *sq.*

[2] (Sir) George Grey, *Journals of
two Expeditions of Discovery in North-
west and Western Australia* (London,
1841), ii. 238.

their foes. Should the patient recover, they are, of course, proud of the superiority of their enchantment over that of their enemies : but should the *boollia* [magical influence] within the sick man prove stronger than their own, as there is no help for it, he must die, the utmost they can do in this case is to revenge his death."[1] But the same writer qualifies this general statement as follows : " It is not true," he says, " that the New Hollanders impute *all* natural deaths to the *boollia* [magic] of inimical tribes, for in most cases of persons wasting visibly away before death, they do not entertain the notion. It is chiefly in cases of sudden death, or when the body of the deceased is fat and in good condition, that this belief prevails, and it is only in such contingencies that it becomes an imperative duty to have revenge."[2] Similarly, speaking of the tribes of Victoria in the early days of European settlement among them, the experienced observer Mr. James Dawson says that " natural deaths are generally—but not always—attributed to the malevolence and the spells of an enemy belonging to another tribe."[3] Again, with regard to the Encounter Bay tribe of South Australia we read that " there are but few diseases which they regard as the consequences of natural causes ; in general they consider them the effects of enchantment, and produced by sorcerers."[4] Similarly of the Port Lincoln tribes in South Australia it is recorded that " in all cases of death that do not arise from old age, wounds, or other equally palpable causes, the natives suspect that unfair means have been practised ; and even where the cause of death is sufficiently plain, they sometimes will not content themselves with it, but have recourse to an imaginary one, as the following case will prove :—A woman had been bitten by a black snake, across the thumb, in clearing out a well ; she began to swell directly, and was a corpse in twenty-four hours ; yet, another woman who had been

Belief of the tribes of Victoria and South Australia.

[1] A. Oldfield, " The Aborigines of Australia," *Transactions of the Ethnological Society of London*, N.S. iii. (1865) p. 236.

[2] A. Oldfield, *op. cit.* p. 245.

[3] J. Dawson, *Australian Aborigines*

(Melbourne, Sydney and Adelaide, 1881), p. 63.

[4] H. E. A. Meyer, "Manners and Customs of the Aborigines of the Encounter Bay Tribe," *Native Tribes of South Australia* (Adelaide, 1879), p. 195.

present when the accident occurred, stated that the deceased had named a certain native as having caused her death. Upon this statement, which was in their opinion corroborated by the circumstance that the snake had drawn no blood from the deceased, her husband and other friends had a fight with the accused party and his friends ; a reconciliation, however, took place afterwards, and it was admitted on the part of the aggressors that they had been in error with regard to the guilty individual ; but nowise more satisfied as to the bite of the snake being the true cause of the woman's death, another party was now suddenly discovered to be the real offender, and accordingly war was made upon him and his partisans, till at last the matter was dropped and forgotten. From this case, as well as from frequent occurrences of a similar nature, it appears evident that thirst for revenge has quite as great a share in these foul accusations as superstition." [1]

However, other experienced observers of the Australian aborigines admit no such limitations and exceptions to the native theory that death is an effect of sorcery. Thus in regard to the Narrinyeri tribe of South Australia the Rev. George Taplin, who knew them intimately for years, says that "no native regards death as natural, but always as the result of sorcery." [2] Again, to quote Mr. R. Brough Smyth, who has collected much information on the tribes of Victoria : " Mr. Daniel Bunce, an intelligent observer, and a gentleman well acquainted with the habits of the blacks, says that no tribe that he has ever met with believes in the possibility of a man dying a natural death. If a man is taken ill, it is at once assumed that some member of a hostile tribe has stolen some of his hair. This is quite enough to cause serious illness. If the man continues sick and gets worse, it is assumed that the hair has been burnt by his enemy. Such an act, they say, is sufficient to imperil his life. If the man dies, it is assumed that the thief has choked his victim and taken away his kidney-fat.

Other testimonies as to the belief of the natives of South Australia and Victoria.

---

[1] C. W. Schürmann, "The Aboriginal Tribes of Port Lincoln in South Australia," *Native Tribes of South Australia*, pp. 237 *sq.*

[2] Rev. G. Taplin, "The Narrinyeri," *Native Tribes of South Australia* (Adelaide, 1879), p. 25.

When the grave is being dug, one or more of the older men —generally doctors or conjurors (*Buk-na-look*)—stand by and attentively watch the laborers ; and if an insect is thrown out of the ground, these old men observe the direction which it takes, and having determined the line, two of the young men, relations of the deceased, are despatched in the path indicated, with instructions to kill the first native they meet, who they are assured and believe is the person directly chargeable with the crime of causing the death of their relative. Mr. John Green says that the men of the Yarra tribe firmly believe that no one ever dies a natural death. A man or a woman dies because of the wicked arts practised by some member of a hostile tribe ; and they discover the direction in which to search for the slayer by the movements of a lizard which is seen immediately after the corpse is interred." [1] Again, speaking of the aborigines of Victoria, another writer observes : " All deaths from natural causes are attributed to the machinations of enemies, who are supposed to have sought for and burned the excrement of the intended victim, which, according to the general belief, causes a gradual wasting away. The relatives, therefore, watch the struggling feet of the dying person, as they point in the direction whence the injury is thought to come, and serve as a guide to the spot where it should be avenged. This is the duty of the nearest male relative ; should he fail in its execution, it will ever be to him a reproach, although other relatives may have avenged the death. If the deceased were a chief, then the duty devolves upon the tribe. Chosen men are sent in the direction indicated, who kill the first persons they meet, whether men, women, or children ; and the more lives that are sacrificed, the greater is the honour to the dead." [2] Again, in his account of the Kurnai tribe of Victoria the late Dr. A. W. Howitt remarks : " It is not difficult to see how, among savages, who have no knowledge of the real causes of diseases which are the common lot of humanity,

[1] R. Brough Smyth, *The Aborigines of Victoria* (Melbourne and London, 1878) i. 110.

[2] W. E. Stanbridge, "Some Particulars of the General Characteristics, Astronomy, and Mythology of the Tribes in the Central Part of Victoria, Southern Australia," *Transactions of the Ethnological Society of London*, New Series, i. (1861) p. 299.

the very suspicion even of such a thing as death from disease should be unknown. Death by accident they can imagine; death by violence they can imagine; but I question if they can, in their savage condition, imagine death by mere disease. Rheumatism is believed to be produced by the machinations of some enemy. Seeing a Tatungolung very lame, I asked him what was the matter? He said, 'Some fellow has put *bottle* in my foot.' I asked him to let me see it. I found he was probably suffering from acute rheumatism. He explained that some enemy must have found his foot track, and have buried in it a piece of broken bottle. The magic influence, he believed, caused it to enter his foot. . . . Phthisis, pneumonia, bowel complaints, and insanity are supposed to be produced by an evil spirit—Brewin—'who is like the wind,' and who, entering his victims, can only be expelled by suitable incantations. . . . Thus the belief arises that death occurs only from accident, open violence, or secret magic; and, naturally, that the latter can only be met by counter-charms." [1]

The beliefs and practices of the aborigines of New South Wales in respect of death were similar. Thus we are told by a well-informed writer that "the natives do not believe in death from natural causes; therefore all sickness is attributed to the agency of sorcery, and counter charms are used to destroy its effect. . . . As a man's death is never supposed to have occurred naturally, except as the result of accident, or from a wound in battle, the first thing to be done when a death occurs is to endeavour to find out the person whose spells have brought about the calamity. In the Wathi-Wathi tribe the corpse is asked by each relative in succession to signify by some sign the person who has caused his death. Not receiving an answer, they watch in which direction a bird flies, after having passed over the deceased. This is considered an indication that the sorcerer is to be found in that direction. Sometimes the nearest relative sleeps with his head on the corpse, which causes him, they think, to dream of the murderer. There is, however, a good deal of uncertainty about the proceedings,

Belief of the aborigines of New South Wales in sorcery as the cause of sickness and death.

[1] Lorimer Fison and A. W. Howitt, *Kamilaroi and Kurnai* (Melbourne, Sydney, Adelaide, and Brisbane, 1880), pp. 250 *sq.*

which seldom result in more than a great display of wrath, and of vowing of vengeance against some member of a neighbouring tribe. Unfortunately this is not always the case, the man who is supposed to have exercised the death-spell being sometimes waylaid and murdered in a most cruel manner."[1] With regard to the great Kamilaroi tribe of New South Wales we read that "in some parts of the country a belief prevails that death, through disease, is, in many, if not in all cases, the result of an enemy's malice. It is a common saying, when illness or death comes, that some one has thrown his belt (*boor*) at the victim. There are various modes of fixing upon the murderer. One is to let an insect fly from the body of the deceased and see towards whom it goes. The person thus singled out is doomed."[2]

Belief of the aborigines of Central Australia in sorcery as the cause of death.

Speaking of the tribes of Central Australia, Messrs. Spencer and Gillen observe that "in the matter of morality their code differs radically from ours, but it cannot be denied that their conduct is governed by it, and that any known breaches are dealt with both surely and severely. In very many cases there takes place what the white man, not seeing beneath the surface, not unnaturally describes as secret murder, but, in reality, revolting though such slaughter may be to our minds at the present day, it is simply exactly on a par with the treatment accorded to witches not so very long ago in European countries. Every case of such secret murder, when one or more men stealthily stalk their prey with the object of killing him, is in reality the exacting of a life for a life, the accused person being indicated by the so-called medicine-man as one who has brought about the death of another man by magic, and whose life must there-fore be forfeited. It need hardly be pointed out what a potent element this custom has been in keeping down the numbers of the tribe ; no such thing as natural death is realised by the native ; a man who dies has of necessity been killed by some other man, or perhaps even by a woman, and sooner or later that man or woman will be

[1] A. L. P. Cameron, " Notes on some Tribes of New South Wales," *Journal of the Anthropological Institute* xiv. (1885) pp. 361, 362 *sq.*
[2] Rev. W. Ridley, *Kamilaroi,* Second Edition (Sydney, 1875), p. 159.

attacked.   In the normal condition of the tribe every death
meant the killing of another individual." [1]

Passing from Australia to other savage lands we learn
that according to the belief of the Torres Straits Islanders
all sickness and death were due to sorcery. [2]   The natives of
Mowat or Mawatta in British New Guinea "do not believe
in a natural death, but attribute even the decease of an old
man to the agency of some enemy known or unknown." [3]
In the opinion of the tribes about Hood Peninsula in British
New Guinea no one dies a natural death.   Every such death
is caused by the evil magic either of a living sorcerer or of a
dead relation. [4]   Of the Roro-speaking tribes of British New
Guinea Dr. Seligmann writes that "except in the case of old
folk, death is not admitted to occur without some obvious
cause such as a spear-thrust.   Therefore when vigorous and
active members of the community die, it becomes necessary
to explain their fate, and such deaths are firmly believed to
be produced by sorcery.   Indeed, as far as I have been able to
ascertain, the Papuasian of this district regards the existence
of sorcery, not, as has been alleged, as a particularly terri-
fying and horrible affair, but as a necessary and inevitable
condition of existence in the world as he knows it." [5]
Amongst the Yabim of German New Guinea "every case
of death, even though it should happen accidentally, as by
the fall of a tree or the bite of a shark, is laid at the door of
the sorcerers.   They are blamed even for the death of a child.
If it is said that a little child never hurt anybody and therefore cannot have an enemy, the reply is that the intention
was to injure the mother, and that the malady had been
transferred to the infant through its mother's milk." [6]

Belief of the natives of the Torres Straits Islands and New Guinea in sorcery as the cause of death.

[1] Baldwin Spencer and F. J. Gillen, *Native Tribes of Central Australia* (London, 1899), pp. 46-48.
[2] *Reports of the Cambridge Anthropological Expedition to Torres Straits*, v. (Cambridge, 1904) pp. 248, 323.
[3] E. Beardmore, "The Natives of Mowat, British New Guinea," *Journal of the Anthropological Institute*, xix. (1890) p. 461.
[4] R. E. Guise, "On the Tribes inhabiting the Mouth of the Wanigela River, New Guinea," *Journal of the*

Anthropological Institute, xxviii. (1899) p. 216.
[5] C. G. Seligmann, *The Melanesians of British New Guinea* (Cambridge, 1910), p. 279.
[6] K. Vetter, *Komm herüber und hilf uns! oder die Arbeit der Neuen-Dettelsauer Mission*, iii. (Barmen, 1898) pp. 10 *sq.* ; *id.*, in *Nachrichten über Kaiser-Wilhelms-Land und den Bis-marck-Archipel, 1897*, pp. 94, 98. Compare B. Hagen, *Unter den Papuas* (Wiesbaden, 1899), p. 256 ; *Verhand-*

Belief of
the Melan-
esians in
sorcery as
the cause
of sickness
and death.
Again, in the island of Malo, one of the New Hebrides, a Catholic missionary reports that according to a belief deeply implanted in the native mind every disease is the effect of witchcraft, and that nobody dies a natural death but only as a consequence of violence, poison, or sorcery.[1] Similarly in New Georgia, one of the Solomon Islands, when a person is sick, the natives think that he must be bewitched by a man or woman, for in their opinion nobody can be sick or die unless he is bewitched ; what we call natural sickness and death are impossible.   In case of illness suspicion falls on some one who is supposed to have buried a charmed object with intent to injure the sufferer.[2]   Of the Melanesians who inhabit the coast of the Gazelle Peninsula in New Britain it is said that all deaths by sickness or disease are attributed by them to the witchcraft of a sorcerer, and a diviner is called in to ascertain the culprit who by his evil magic has destroyed their friends.[3]   " Amongst the Melan-esians few, if any, are believed to die from natural causes only ; if they are not killed in war, they are supposed to die from the effects of witchcraft or magic.   Whenever any one was sick, his friends made anxious inquiries as to the person who had bewitched (*agara'd*) him.   Some one would generally be found to admit that he had buried some portion of food or something belonging to the sick man, which had caused his illness.   The friends would pay him to dig it up, and after that the patient would generally get well.   If, however, he did not recover, it was assumed that some other person had also *agara'd* him." [4]

Speaking of the Malagasy a Catholic missionary tells us that in Madagascar nobody dies a natural death.   With the

lungen der Berliner Gesellschaft für Anthropologie, Ethnologie, und Urgeschichte, 1900, p. (415).

[1] Father A. Deniau, "Croyances religieuses et mœurs des indigènes de l'île Malo," *Missions Catholiques*, xxxiii. (1901) pp. 315 *sq.*

[2] C. Ribbe, *Zwei Jahre unter den Kannibalen der Salomo-Inseln* (Dresden-Blasewitz, 1903), p. 268.

[3] P. A. Kleintitschen, *Die Küstenbewohner der Gazellehalbinsel* (Hiltrup

bei Münster, N.D.), p. 344.   As to beliefs of this sort among the Sulka of New Britain, see *P.* Rascher, "Die Sulka," *Archiv für Anthropologie*, xxix. (1904) pp. 221 *sq.* ; R. Parkinson, *Dreissig Jahre in der Südsee* (Stuttgart, 1907), pp. 199-201.

[4] G. Brown, D.D., *Melanesians and Polynesians* (London, 1910), p. 176. Dr. Brown's account of the Melanesians applies to the natives of New Britain and more particularly of the neighbour-ing Duke of York islands.

possible exception of centenarians everybody is supposed to die the victim of the sorcerer's diabolic art. If a relation of yours dies, the people comfort you by saying, "Cursed be the sorcerer who caused his death!" If your horse falls down a precipice and breaks its back, the accident has been caused by the malicious look of a sorcerer. If your dog dies of hydrophobia or your horse of a carbuncle, the cause is still the same. If you catch a fever in a district where malaria abounds, the malady is still ascribed to the art of the sorcerer, who has insinuated some deadly substances into your body.[1]   Again, speaking of the Sakalava, a tribe in Madagascar, an eminent French authority on the island observes: "They have such a faith in the power of talismans that they even ascribe to them the power of killing their enemies. When they speak of poisoning, they do not allude, as many Europeans wrongly suppose, to death by vegetable or mineral poisons; the reference is to charms or spells. They often throw under the bed of an enemy an *ahouli* [talisman], praying it to kill him, and they are persuaded that sooner or later their wish will be accomplished. I have often been present at bloody vendettas which had no other origin but this. The Sakalava think that a great part of the population dies of poison in this way. In their opinion, only old people who have attained the extreme limits of human longevity die a natural death."[2]

In Africa similar beliefs are widely spread and lead, as elsewhere, to fatal consequences. Thus the Kagoro of Northern Nigeria refuse to believe in death from natural causes; all illnesses and deaths, in their opinion, are brought about by black magic, however old and decrepit the deceased may have been. They explain sickness by saying that a man's soul wanders from his body in sleep and may then be caught, detained, and even beaten with a stick by some evil-wisher; whenever that happens, the man naturally falls ill. Sometimes an enemy will

The belief of the Malagasy in sorcery as a cause of death.

Belief of African tribes in sorcery as the cause of sickness and death.

[1] Father Abinal, "Astrologie Malgache," *Missions Catholiques*, xi. (1879) p. 506.

[2] A. Grandidier, "Madagascar," *Bulletin de la Société de Géographie* (Paris), Sixième Série, iii. (1872) pp. 399 *sq.*. The talismans (*ahouli*) in question consist of the horns of oxen stuffed with a variety of odds and ends, such as sand, sticks, nails, and so forth.

abstract the patient's liver by magic and carry it away to a
cave in a sacred grove, where he will devour it in company
with other wicked sorcerers.   A witch-doctor is called in to
detect the culprit, and whomever he denounces is shut up in
a room, where a fire is kindled and pepper thrown into it ;
and there he is kept in the fumes of the burning pepper till
he confesses his guilt and returns the stolen liver, upon
which of course the sick man recovers.   But should the
patient die, the miscreant who did him to death by kid-
napping his soul or his liver will be sold as a slave or
choked.[1]   In like manner the Bakerewe, who inhabit the
largest island in the Victoria Nyanza lake, believe that all
deaths and all ailments, however trivial, are the effect of
witchcraft ; and the person, generally an old woman, whom
the witch-doctor accuses of having cast the spell on the
patient is tied up, severely beaten, or stabbed to death
on the spot.[2]   Again, we are told that " the peoples
of the Congo do not believe in a natural death, not
even when it happens through drowning or any other
accident.   Whoever dies is the victim of witchcraft or of a
spell.   His soul has been eaten.   He must be avenged by
the punishment of the person who has committed the crime."
Accordingly when a death has taken place, the medicine-
man is sent for to discover the criminal.   He pretends to be
possessed by a spirit and in this state he names the wretch
who has caused the death by sorcery.   The accused has to
submit to the poison ordeal by drinking a decoction of the
red bark of the *Erythrophloeum guiniense.*   If he vomits up
the poison, he is innocent ; but if he fails to do so, the
infuriated crowd rushes on him and despatches him with
knives and clubs.   The family of the supposed culprit has
moreover to pay an indemnity to the family of the supposed
victim.[3]   " Death, in the opinion of the natives, is never due
to a natural cause.   It is always the result either of a crime

[1] Major A. J. N. Tremearne, *The Tailed Head-hunters of Nigeria* (London, 1912), pp. 171 *sq.* ; *id.*, " Notes on the Kagoro and other Head-hunters," *Journal of the Royal Anthropological Institute*, xlii. (1912) pp. 160, 161.

[2] E. Hurel, " Religion et vie domestique des Bakerewe," *Anthropos*, vi. (1912) pp. 85-87.

[3] Father Campana, " Congo Mission Catholique de Landana," *Missions Catholiques*, xxvii. (1895) pp. 102 *sq.*

or of sorcery, and is followed by the poison ordeal, which has to be undergone by an innocent person whom the fetish-man accuses from selfish motives." [1]

Evidence of the same sort could be multiplied for West Africa, where the fear of sorcery is rampant.[2]   But without going into further details, I wish to point out the disastrous effects which here, as elsewhere, this theory of death has produced upon the population.   For when a death from natural causes takes place, the author of the death being of course unknown, suspicion often falls on a number of people, all of whom are obliged to submit to the poison ordeal in order to prove their innocence, with the result that some or possibly all of them perish.   A very experienced American missionary in West Africa, the Rev. R. H. Nassau, the friend of the late Miss Mary H. Kingsley, tells us that for every person who dies a natural death at least one, and often ten or more have been executed on an accusation of witchcraft.[3]   Andrew Battel, a native of Essex, who lived in Angola for many years at the end of the sixteenth and beginning of the seventeenth century, informs us that " in this country none on any account dieth, but they kill another for him : for they believe they die not their own natural death, but that some other has bewitched them to death.   And all those are brought in by the friends of the dead whom they suspect ; so that there many times come five hundred men and women to take the drink, made of the foresaid root *imbando*.   They are brought all to the high-

Effect of such beliefs in thinning the population by causing multitudes to die for the imaginary crime of sorcery.

---

[1] Th. Masui, *Guide de la Section de l'État Indépendant du Congo à l'Exposition de Bruxelles - Tervueren en 1874* (Brussels, 1897), p. 82.
[2] See for example O. Lenz, *Skizzen aus Westafrika* (Berlin, 1878), pp. 184 *sq.* ; C. Cuny, " De Libreville au Cameroun," *Bulletin de la Société de Géographie* (Paris), Septième Série, xvii. (1896) p. 341; Ch. Wunenberger, " La mission et le royaume de Humbé, sur les bords du Cunène," *Missions Catholiques*, xx. (1888) p. 262 ; Lieut. Herold, " Bericht betreffend religiöse Anschauungen und Gebräuche der deutschen Ewe-Neger," *Mittheilungen aus den deutschen Schutzgebieten*, v.

(1892) p. 153 ; Dr. R. Plehn, " Beiträge zur Völkerkunde des Togo-Gebietes," *Mittheilungen des Seminars für Orientalische Sprachen zu Berlin*, ii. Dritte Abtheilung (1899), p. 97 ; R. Fisch, " Die Dagbamba," *Baessler-Archiv*, iii. (1912) p. 148.   For evidence of similar beliefs and practices in other parts of Africa, see Brard, " Der Victoria-Nyanza," *Petermann's Mittheilungen*, xliii. (1897) pp. 79 *sq.* ; Father Picarda, " Autour du Mandéra," *Missions Catholiques*, xviii. (1886) p. 342.
[3] Rev. R. H. Nassau, *Fetichism in West Africa* (London, 1904), pp. 241 *sq.*

street or market-place, and there the master of the *imbando* sits with his water, and gives every one a cup of water by one measure ; and they are commanded to walk in a certain place till they make water, and then they are free. But he that cannot urine presently falls down, and all the people, great and small, fall upon him with their knives, and beat and cut him into pieces. But I think the witch that gives the water is partial, and gives to him whose death is desired the strongest water, but no man of the bye-standers can perceive it. This is done in the town of Longo, almost every week throughout the year." [1] A French official tells us that among the Neyaux of the Ivory Coast similar beliefs and practices were visibly depopulating the country, every single natural death causing the death of four or five persons by the poison ordeal, which consisted in drinking the decoction of a red bark called by the natives *boduru*. At the death of a chief fifteen men and women perished in this way. The French Government had great difficulty in suppressing the ordeal ; for the deluded natives firmly believed in the justice of the test and therefore submitted to it willingly in the full consciousness of their innocence.[2] In the neighbour-hood of Calabar the poison ordeal, which here consists in drinking a decoction of a certain bean, the *Physostigma venenosum* of botanists, has had similar disastrous results, as we learn from the testimony of a missionary, the Rev. Hugh Goldie. He tells us that the people have firm faith in the ordeal and therefore not only accept it readily but appeal to it, convinced that it will demonstrate their innocence. A small tribe named Uwet in the hill-country of Calabar almost swept itself off the face of the earth by its constant use of the ordeal. On one occasion the whole population drank the poison to prove themselves pure, as they said ; about half perished, " and the remnant," says Mr. Goldie, " still continuing their superstitious prac-tice, must soon become extinct." [3] These words were

---

[1] "Strange Adventures of Andrew Battel," in John Pinkerton's *Voyages and Travels*, xvi. (London, 1814) p. 334.

[2] *Gouvernement Général de l'Afrique Occidentale Française, Notices publiées par le Gouvernement Général à l'occasion* *de l'Exposition Coloniale de Marseille, La Côte d'Ivoire* (Corbeil, 1906), pp. 570-572.

[3] Hugh Goldie, *Calabar and its Mission*, New Edition (Edinburgh and London, 1901), pp. 34 *sq.*, 37 *sq.*

written a good many years ago, and it is probable that by this time these poor fanatics have actually succeeded in exterminating themselves. So fatal may be the practical consequences of a purely speculative error ; for it is to be remembered that these disasters flow directly from a mistaken theory of death.

Much more evidence of the same kind could be adduced, but without pursuing the theme further I think we may lay it down as a general rule that at a certain stage of social and intellectual evolution men have believed themselves to be naturally immortal in this life and have regarded death by disease or even by accident or violence as an unnatural event which has been brought about by sorcery and which must be avenged by the death of the sorcerer. If that has been so, we seem bound to conclude that a belief in magic or sorcery has had a most potent influence in keeping down the numbers of savage tribes ; since as a rule every natural death has entailed at least one, often several, sometimes many deaths by violence. This may help us to understand what an immense power for evil the world-wide faith in magic or sorcery has been among men. General conclusion as to the belief in sorcery as the great cause of death.

But even savages come in time to perceive that deaths are sometimes brought about by other causes than sorcery. We have seen that some of them admit extreme old age, accidents, and violence as causes of death which are independent of sorcery. The admission of these exceptions to the general rule certainly marks a stage of intellectual progress. I will give a few more instances of such admissions before concluding this part of my subject. But some savages have attributed death to other causes than sorcery.

In the first place, certain savage tribes are reported to dissect the bodies of their dead in order to ascertain from an examination of the corpse whether the deceased died a natural death or perished by magic. This is reported by Mr. E. R. Smith concerning the Araucanians of Chili, who according to other writers, as we saw,[1] believe all deaths to be due to sorcery. Mr. Smith tells us that after death the services of the *machi* or medicine-man " are again required, especially if the deceased be a person of distinction. The body is dissected and examined. If the liver be found in a Some savages dissect the corpse to ascertain whether death was due to natural causes or to sorcery.

---

[1] Above, p. 35.

healthy state, the death is attributed to natural causes; but if the liver prove to be inflamed, it is supposed to indicate the machinations of some evil-intentioned persons, and it rests with the medicine-man to discover the conspirator. This is accomplished by much the same means that were used to find out the nature of the disease. The gall is extracted, put in the magic drum, and after various incantations taken out and placed over the fire, in a pot carefully covered; if, after subjecting the gall to a certain amount of roasting, a stone is found in the bottom of the pot, it is declared to be the means by which death was produced. These stones, as well as the frogs, spiders, arrows, or whatever else may be extracted from the sick man, are called *Huecuvu*—the 'Evil One.' By aid of the *Huecuvu* the *machi* [medicine-man] throws himself into a trance, in which state he discovers and announces the person guilty of the death, and describes the manner in which it was produced." [1]

Again, speaking of the Pahouins, a tribe of the Gaboon region in French Congo, a Catholic missionary writes thus: " It is so rare among the Pahouins that a death is considered natural! Scarcely has the deceased given up the ghost when the sorcerer appears on the scene. With three cuts of the knife, one transverse and two lateral, he dissects the breast of the corpse and turns down the skin on the face. Then he grabbles in the breast, examines the bowels attentively, marks the last muscular contractions, and thereupon pronounces whether the death was natural or not." If he decides that the death was due to sorcery, the suspected culprit has to submit to the poison ordeal in the usual manner to determine his guilt or innocence. [2]

The possibility of natural death admitted by the Melanesians.

Another savage people who have come to admit the possibility of merely natural death are the Melanesians of the New Hebrides and other parts of Central Melanesia. Amongst them " any sickness that is serious is believed to be brought about by ghosts or spirits; common complaints such as fever and ague are taken as coming in the course of nature.

[1] E. R. Smith, *The Araucanians* (London, 1855), pp. 236 *sq.*
[2] Father Trilles, " Milles lieues dans l'inconnu; à travers le pays Fang, de la côte aux rives du Djah," *Missions Catholiques*, xxxv. (1903) pp. 466 *sq.*, and as to the poison ordeal, *ib.* pp. 472 *sq.*

To say that savages are never ill without supposing a super-natural cause is not true of Melanesians ; they make up their minds as the sickness comes whether it is natural or not, and the more important the individual who is sick, the more likely his sickness is to be ascribed to the anger of a ghost whom he has offended, or to witchcraft.   No great man would like to be told that he was ill by natural weakness or decay.   The sickness is almost always believed to be caused by a ghost, not by a spirit. . . . Generally it is to the ghosts of the dead that sickness is ascribed in the eastern islands as well as in the western ; recourse is had to them for aid in causing and removing sickness ; and ghosts are believed to inflict sickness not only because some òffence, such as a trespass, has been committed against them, or because one familiar with them has sought their aid with sacrifice and spells, but because there is a certain malignity in the feeling of all ghosts towards the living, who offend them by being alive." [1] From this account we learn, first, that the Melanesians admit some deaths by common diseases, such as fever and ague, to be natural ; and, second, that they recognise ghosts and spirits as well as sorcerers and witches, among the causes of death ; indeed they hold that ghosts are the commonest of all causes of sickness and death.

The same causes of death are recognised also by the Caffres of South Africa, as we learn from Mr. Dudley Kidd, who tells us that according to the beliefs of the natives, " to start with, there is sickness which is supposed to be caused by the action of ancestral spirits or by fabulous monsters. Secondly, there is sickness which is caused by the magical practices of some evil person who is using witchcraft in secret. Thirdly, there is sickness which comes from neither of these causes, and remains unexplained.   It is said to be ' only sickness, and nothing more.'   This third form of sickness is, I think, the commonest.   Yet most writers wholly ignore it, or deny its existence.   It may happen that an attack of indigestion is one day attributed to the action of witch or wizard ; another day the trouble is put down to the account of ancestral spirits ; on a third occasion the people may be at a loss to account for it, and so may dismiss the problem

The possibility of natural death admitted by the Caffres of South Africa.

[1] R. H. Codrington, *The Melanesians* (Oxford, 1891), p. 194.

by saying that it is merely sickness.   It is quite common to hear natives say that they are at a loss to account for some special case of illness.   At first they thought it was caused by an angry ancestral spirit ; but a great doctor has assured them that it is not the result of such a spirit. They then suppose it to be due to the magical practices of some enemy ; but the doctor negatives that theory.   The people are, therefore, driven to the conclusion that the trouble has no ascertainable cause.   In some cases they do not even trouble to consult a diviner ; they speedily re- cognise the sickness as due to natural causes.   In such a case it needs no explanation.   If they think that some friend of theirs knows of a remedy, they will try it on their own initiative, or may even go off to a white man to ask for some of his medicine.   They would never dream of doing this if they thought they were being influenced by magic or by ancestral spirits.   The Kafirs quite recognise that there are types of disease which are inherited, and have not been caused by magic or by ancestral spirits.   They admit that some accidents are due to nothing but the patient's carelessness or stupidity.   If a native gets his leg run over by a waggon, the people will often say that it is all his own fault through being clumsy.   In other cases, with delightful inconsistency, they may say that some one has been working magic to cause the accident.   In short, it is impossible to make out a theory of sickness which will satisfy our European conception of consistency." [1]

The admission that death may be due to natural causes, marks an intellectual advance.

From the foregoing accounts we see that the Melanesians and the Caffres, two widely different and widely separated races, agree in recognising at least three distinct causes of what we should call natural death.   These three causes are, first, sorcery or witchcraft; second, ghosts or spirits; and third, disease.[2]   That the recognition of disease in itself as a cause of death, quite apart from sorcery, marks an intellectual

[1] Dudley Kidd, *The Essential Kafir* (London, 1904), pp. 133 *sq.*

[2] In like manner the Baganda generally ascribed natural deaths either to sorcery or to the action of a ghost ; but when they could not account for a person's death in either of these ways they said that Walumbe, the God of Death, had taken him.   This last ex- planation approaches to an admission of natural death, though it is still mythical in form.   The Baganda usually attributed any illness of the king to ghosts, because no man would

advance, will not be disputed.   It is not so clear, though I believe it is equally true, that the recognition of ghosts or spirits as a cause of disease, quite apart from witchcraft, marks a real step in intellectual, moral, and social progress. In the first place, it marks a step in intellectual and moral progress ; for it recognises that effects which before had been ascribed to human agency spring from superhuman causes ; and this recognition of powers in the universe superior to man is not only an intellectual gain but a moral discipline : it teaches the important lesson of humility.   In the second place it marks a step in social progress because when the blame of a death is laid upon a ghost or a spirit instead of on a sorcerer, the death has not to be avenged by killing a human being, the supposed author of the calamity.   Thus the recognition of ghosts or spirits as the sources of sickness and death has as its immediate effect the sparing of an immense number of lives of men and women, who on the theory of death by sorcery would have perished by violence to expiate their imaginary crime.   That this is a great gain to society is obvious : it adds immensely to the security of human life by removing one of the most fruitful causes of its destruction.

It must be admitted, however, that the gain is not always as great as might be expected ; the social advantages of a belief in ghosts and spirits are attended by many serious drawbacks.   For while ghosts or spirits are commonly, though not always, supposed to be beyond the reach of human vengeance, they are generally thought to be well within the reach of human persuasion, flattery, and bribery ; in other words, men think that they can appease and propitiate them by prayer and sacrifice ; and while prayer is always cheap, sacrifice may be very dear, since it can, and often does, involve the destruction of an immense deal of valuable property and of a vast number of human lives.   Yet if we could reckon up the myriads who have been slain in sacrifice to ghosts and gods, it seems probable

---

dare to practise magic on him.   A much-dreaded ghost was that of a man's sister ; she was thought to vent her spite on his sons and daughters by visiting them with sickness.   When she proved implacable, a medicine-man was employed to catch her ghost in a gourd or a pot and throw it away on waste land or drown it in a river.   See Rev. J. Roscoe, *The Baganda* (London, 1911), pp. 98, 100, 101 *sq.*, 286 *sq.*, 315 *sq.*

that they would fall far short of the untold multitudes who have perished as sorcerers and witches. For while human sacrifices in honour of deities or of the dead have been for the most part exceptional rather than regular, only the great gods and the illustrious dead being deemed worthy of such costly offerings, the slaughter of witches and wizards, theoretically at least, followed inevitably on every natural death among people who attributed all such deaths to sorcery. Hence if natural religion be defined roughly as a belief in superhuman spiritual beings and an attempt to propitiate them, we may perhaps say that, while natural religion has slain its thousands, magic has slain its ten thousands. But there are strong reasons for inferring that in the history of society an Age of Magic preceded an Age of Religion. If that was so, we may conclude that the advent of religion marked a great social as well as intellectual advance upon the preceding Age of Magic : it inaugurated an era of what might be described as mercy by comparison with the relentless severity of its predecessor.

LECTURE III

MYTHS OF THE ORIGIN OF DEATH

IN my last lecture I shewed that many savages do not believe in what we call a natural death ; they imagine that all men are naturally immortal and would never die, if their lives were not cut prematurely short by sorcery. Further, I pointed out that this mistaken view of the nature of death has exercised a disastrous influence on the tribes who entertain it, since, attributing all natural deaths to sorcery, they consider themselves bound to discover and kill the wicked sorcerers whom they regard as responsible for the death of their friends. Thus in primitive society as a rule every natural death entails at least one and often several deaths by violence ; since the supposed culprit being unknown suspicion may fall upon many persons, all of whom may be killed either out of hand or as a consequence of failing to demonstrate their innocence by means of an ordeal.

Yet even the savages who firmly believe in man's natural immortality are obliged sorrowfully to admit that, as things are at the present day, men do frequently die, whatever explanation we may give of so unexpected and unnatural an occurrence. Accordingly they are hard put to it to reconcile their theory of immortality with the practice of mortality. They have meditated on the subject and have given us the fruit of their meditation in a series of myths which profess to explain the origin of death. For the most part these myths are very crude and childish ; yet they have a value of their own as examples of man's early attempts to fathom one of the great mysteries which

Belief of savages in man's natural immortality.

Savage stories of the origin of death.

59

encompass his frail and transient existence on earth ; and accordingly I have here collected, in all their naked simplicity, a few of these savage guesses at truth.

Four types of such stories.

Myths of the origin of death conform to several types, among which we may distinguish, first, what I will call the type of the Two Messengers ; second, the type of the Waxing and Waning Moon ; third, the type of the Serpent and his Cast Skin ; and fourth, the type of the Banana-tree. I will illustrate each type by examples, and will afterwards cite some miscellaneous instances which do not fall under any of these heads.

I. The tale of the Two Messengers.

First, then, we begin with the type of the Two Messengers. Stories of this pattern are widespread in Africa, especially among tribes belonging to the great Bantu family, which occupies roughly the southern half of the continent. The best-known example of the tale

Zulu story of the chameleon and the lizard.

is the one told by the Zulus. They say that in the beginning Unkulunkulu, that is, the Old Old One, sent the chameleon to men with a message saying, " Go, chameleon, go and say, Let not men die." The chameleon set out, but it crawled very slowly, and it loitered by the way to eat the purple berries of the *ubukwebezane* tree, or according to others it climbed up a tree to bask in the sun, filled its belly with flies, and fell fast asleep. Meantime the Old Old One had thought better of it and sent a lizard posting after the chameleon with a very different message to men, for he said to the animal, " Lizard, when you have arrived, say, Let men die." So the lizard went on his way, passed the dawdling chameleon, and arriving first among men delivered his message of death, saying, " Let men die." Then he turned on his heel and went back to the Old Old One who had sent him. But after he was gone, the chameleon at last arrived among men with his glad tidings of immortality, and he shouted, saying, " It is said, Let not men die ! " But men answered, " O ! we have heard the word of the lizard ; it has told us the word, ' It is said, Let men die.' We cannot hear your word. Through the word of the lizard, men will die." And died they have ever since from that day to this. That is why some of the Zulus hate the lizard, saying, " Why did he run first and say, ' Let

people die?'"   So they beat and kill the lizard and say,
"Why did it speak?"   But others hate the chameleon and
hustle it, saying, "That is the little thing which delayed to
tell the people that they should not die.   If he had only
brought his message in time we should not have died; our
ancestors also would have been still living; there would
have been no diseases here on the earth.   It all comes from
the delay of the chameleon."[1]   The same story is told in   The same
nearly the same form by other Bantu tribes, such as the   story
among
Bechuanas,[2] the Basutos,[3] the Baronga,[4] and the Ngoni.[5]   other
To this day the Baronga and the Ngoni owe the chameleon   Bantu
tribes.
a grudge for having brought death into the world, so when
children find a chameleon they will induce it to open its
mouth, then throw a pinch of tobacco on its tongue, and
watch with delight the creature writhing and changing
colour from orange to green, from green to black in the
agony of death; for thus they avenge the wrong which the
chameleon has done to mankind.[6]

A story of the same type, but with some variations, is   Akamba
told by the Akamba, a Bantu tribe of British East Africa;   story of the
chameleon
but in their version the lizard has disappeared from the legend   and the
and has been replaced by the *itoroko*, a small bird of the   thrush.
thrush tribe, with a black head, a bluish-black back, and a
buff-coloured breast.   The tale runs thus:—Once upon a
time God sent out the chameleon, the frog, and the thrush to
find people who died one day and came to life again the next.

[1] H. Callaway, *The Religious System
of the Amazulu*, Part i. pp. 1, 3 *sq.*,
Part ii. p. 138 ; Rev. L. Grout, *Zulu-
land, or Life among the Zulu-Kafirs*
(Philadelphia, N.D.), pp. 148 *sq.* ;
Dudley Kidd, *The Essential Kafir*
(London, 1904), pp. 76 *sq.* Compare
A. F. Gardiner, *Narrative of a Journey
to the Zoolu Country* (London, 1836),
pp. 178 *sq.* ; T. Arbousset et F.
Daumas, *Relation d'un voyage d'Ex-
ploration au Nord-Est de la Colonie
du Cap de Bonne-Espérance* (Paris,
1842), p. 472 ; Rev. J. Shooter, *The
Kafirs of Natal and the Zulu Country*
(London, 1857), p. 159 ; W. H. I.
Bleek, *Reynard the Fox in South Africa*
(London, 1864), p. 74 ; D. Leslie,
Among the Zulus and Amatongas,

Second Edition (Edinburgh, 1875), p.
209 ; F. Speckmann, *Die Hermanns-
burger Mission in Afrika* (Hermanns-
burg, 1876), p. 164.

[2] J. Chapman, *Travels in the Interior of South Africa* (London, 1868),
i. 47.

[3] E. Casalis, *The Basutos* (London,
1861), p. 242 ; E. Jacottet, *The
Treasury of Ba-suto Lore*, i. (Morija,
Basutoland, 1908), pp. 46 *sqq.*

[4] H. A. Junod, *Les Ba-Ronga*
(Neuchâtel, 1898), pp. 401 *sq.*

[5] W. A. Elmslie, *Among the Wild
Ngoni* (Edinburgh and London, 1899),
p. 70.

[6] H. A. Junod and W. A. Elmslie,
ll.cc.

So off they set, the chameleon leading the way, for in those days he was a very important personage. Presently they came to some people lying like dead, so the chameleon went up to them and said, *Niwe, niwe, niwe.* The thrush asked him testily what he was making that noise for, to which the chameleon replied mildly, " I am only calling the people who go forward and then came back again," and he explained that the dead people would come to life again. But the thrush, who was of a sceptical turn of mind, derided the idea. Nevertheless, the chameleon persisted in calling to the dead people, and sure enough they opened their eyes and listened to him. But here the thrush broke in and told them roughly that dead they were and dead they must remain. With that away he flew, and though the chameleon preached to the corpses, telling them that he had come from God on purpose to bring them to life again, and that they were not to believe the lies of that shallow sceptic the thrush, they obstinately refused to pay any heed to him ; not one of those dead corpses would budge. So the chameleon returned crestfallen to God and reported to him how, when he preached the gospel of resurrection to the corpses, the thrush had roared him down, so that the corpses could not hear a word he said. God thereupon cross-questioned the thrush, who stated that the chameleon had so bungled his message that he, the thrush, felt it his imperative duty to interrupt him. The simple deity believed the thrush, and being very angry with the chameleon he degraded him from his high position and made him walk very slow, lurching this way and that, as he does down to this very day. But the thrush he promoted to the office of wakening men from their slumber every morning, which he still does punctually at 2 A.M. before the note of any other bird is heard in the tropical forest.[1]

In this version, though the frog is sent out by God with the other two messengers he plays no part in the story ; he is a mere dummy. But in another version of the story, which is told by the negroes of Togoland in German West Africa, the frog takes the place of the

Togo story of the dog and the frog.

[1] C. W. Hobley, *Ethnology of A-Kamba and other East African Tribes* (Cambridge, 1910), pp. 107-109.

lizard and the thrush as the messenger of death. They
say that once upon a time men sent a dog to God to say
that when they died they would like to come to life again.
So off the dog trotted to deliver the message. But on the
way he felt hungry and turned into a house, where a man
was boiling magic herbs. So the dog sat down and thought
to himself, " He is cooking food." Meantime the frog had
set off to tell God that when men died they would like not
to come to life again. Nobody had asked him to give that
message ; it was a piece of pure officiousness and impertinence
on his part. However, away he tore. The dog, who still
sat watching the hell-broth brewing, saw him hurrying past
the door, but he thought to himself, " When I have had
something to eat, I will soon catch froggy up." However,
froggy came in first and said to the deity, " When men die,
they would like not to come to life again." After that, up
comes the dog, and says he, " When men die, they would
like to come to life again." God was naturally puzzled and
said to the dog, " I really do not understand these two
messages. As I heard the frog's request first, I will comply
with it. I will not do what you said." That is the real
reason why men die and do not come to life again. If the
frog had only minded his own business instead of meddling
with other people's, the dead would all have come to life
again to this day.[1] In this version of the story not only are
the persons of the two messengers different, the dog and the
frog having replaced the chameleon and the lizard of the
Bantu version, but the messengers are sent from men to God
instead of from God to men.

In another version told by the Ashantees of West Africa
the persons of the messengers are again different, but as in
the Bantu version they are sent from God to men. The
Ashantees say that long ago men were happy, for God
dwelt among them and talked with them face to face. For
example, if a child was roasting yams at the fire and wanted
a relish to eat with the yams, he had nothing to do but to

Ashantee story of the goat and the sheep.

[1] Fr. Müller, " Die Religionen
Togos in Einzeldarstellungen," *Anthropos*, ii. (1907) p. 203. In a version of the story reported from Calabar
a sheep appears as the messenger of
mortality, while a dog is the messenger
of immortality or rather of resurrection.
See "Calabar Stories," *Journal of the
African Society*, No. 18 (January
1906), p. 194.

throw a stick in the air and say, " God give me fish," and God gave him fish at once.   However, these happy days did not last for ever.   One unlucky day it happened that some women were pounding a mash with pestles in a mortar, while God stood by looking on.   For some reason they were annoyed by the presence of the deity and told him to be off; and as he did not take himself off fast enough to please them, they beat him with their pestles.   In a great huff God retired altogether from the world and left it to the direction of the fetishes ; and still to this day people say, " Ah, if it had not been for that old woman, how happy we should be ! " However, after he had withdrawn to heaven, the long-suffering deity sent a kind message by a goat to men upon earth to say, " There is something which they call Death.   He will kill some of you.   But even if you die, you will not perish completely.   You will come to me in heaven."   So off the goat set with this cheering intelligence.   But before he came to the town he saw a tempting bush by the wayside and stopped to browse on it.   When God in heaven saw the goat thus loitering by the way, he sent off a sheep with the same message to carry the glad tidings to men without delay.   But the sheep did not give the message aright.   Far from it: he said, " God sends you word that you will die and that will be an end of you."   Afterwards the goat arrived on the scene and said, " God sends you word that you will die, certainly, but that will not be the end of you, for you will go to him."   But men said to the goat, " No, goat, that is not what God said.   We believe that the message which the sheep brought us is the one which God sent to us."   That was the beginning of death among men.[1]   However, in another Ashantee version of the tale the parts played by the sheep and the goat are reversed. It is the sheep who brings the tidings of immortality from God to men, but the goat overruns him and offers them death instead.   Not knowing what death was, men accepted the seeming boon with enthusiasm and have died ever since.[2]

So much for the tale of the Two Messengers.   In the last versions of it which I have quoted, a feature to be

---

[1] E. Perregaux, *Chez les Achanti* (Neuchâtel, 1906), pp. 198 *sq.*

[2] E. Perregaux, *op. cit.* p. 199.

noticed is the perversion of the message by one of the II. The
story of the
Waxing
and Wan-
ing Moon. messengers, who brings tidings of death instead of life eternal to men. The same perversion of the message re- appears in some examples of the next type of story which I shall illustrate, namely the type of the Waxing and Waning Moon. Thus the Namaquas or Hottentots say that once the Moon charged the hare to go to men and say, " As I die and rise to life again, so shall you die and rise to life again." So the hare went to men, but either out of forget- fulness or malice he reversed the message and said, " As I die and do not rise to life again, so you shall also die and not rise to life again." Then he went back to the Moon, and she asked him what he had said. He told her, and when she heard how he had given the wrong message, she was so angry that she threw a stick at him and split his lip, which is the reason why the hare's lip is still split. So the hare ran away and is still running to this day. Some people, however, say that before he fled he clawed the Moon's face, which still bears the marks of the scratching, as anybody may see for himself on a clear moonlight night. So the Hottentots are still angry with the hare for bringing death into the world, and they will not let initiated men partake of its flesh.[1] There are traces of a similar story among the Bushmen.[2] In another Hottentot version two messengers appear, an insect and a hare; the insect is charged by the Moon with a message of immortality or rather of resurrection to men, but the hare persuades the insect to let him bear the tidings, which he perverts into a message of annihilation.[3] Thus in this particular version the type of the Two Messengers coincides with the Moon type.

A story of the same type, though different in details, is told by the Masai of East Africa. They say that in the Masai
story of
the moon
and death. early days a certain god named Naiteru-kop told a man named Le-eyo that if a child were to die he was to throw

[1] Sir J. E. Alexander, *Expedition of Discovery into the Interior of Africa* (London, 1838), i. 169; C. J. Ander- sson, *Lake Ngami*, Second Edition (London, 1856), pp. 328 *sq.* ; W. H. I. Bleek, *Reynard the Fox in South Africa* (London, 1864), pp. 71-73 ; Th. Hahn, *Tsuni-||Goam, the Supreme* *Being of the Khoi-Khoi* (London, 1881), p. 52.

[2] W. H. I. Bleek, *A Brief Account of Bushman Folk-lore* (London, 1875), pp. 9 *sq.*

[3] W. H. I. Bleek, *Reynard the Fox in South Africa*, pp. 69 *sq.*

away the body and say, " Man, die, and come back again ;
moon, die, and remain away." Well, soon afterwards a child
died, but it was not one of the man's own children, so when
he threw the body away he said, " Man, die, and remain
away ; moon, die, and return." Next one of his own
children died, and when he threw away the body he said,
" Man, die, and return ; moon, die, and remain away." But
the god said to him, " It is of no use now, for you
spoilt matters with the other child." That is why down to
this day when a man dies he returns no more, but when the
moon dies she always comes to life again.[1]

Another story of the origin of death which belongs to
this type is told by the Nandi of British East Africa. They
say that when the first people lived upon the earth a dog
came to them one day and said : " All people will die like the
moon, but unlike the moon you will not return to life again
unless you give me some milk to drink out of your gourd,
and beer to drink through your straw. If you do this, I
will arrange for you to go to the river when you die and to
come to life again on the third day." But the people
laughed at the dog, and gave him some milk and beer to
drink off a stool. The dog was angry at not being served
in the same vessels as a human being, and though he put
his pride in his pocket and drank the milk and the beer
from the stool, he went away in high dudgeon, saying, " All
people will die, and the moon alone will return to life."
That is the reason why, when people die, they stay away,
whereas when the moon goes away she comes back again
after three days' absence.[2] The Wa-Sania of British East
Africa believe that in days gone by people never died, till
one unlucky day a lizard came and said to them, " All of you
know that the moon dies and rises again, but human beings
will die and rise no more." They say that from that day
people began to die and have persisted in dying ever since.[3]

        With these African stories of the origin of death we may
compare one told by the Fijians on the other side of the

[1] A. C. Hollis, *The Masai* (Oxford,
1905), pp. 271 *sq.*

[2] A. C. Hollis, *The Nandi* (Oxford,
1909), p. 98.

[3] Captain W. E. H. Barrett, " Notes
on the Customs and Beliefs of the Wa-
Giriama, etc., British East Africa,"
*Journal of the R. Anthropological Insti-
tute*, xli. (1911) p. 37.

world. They say that once upon a time the Moon con- Fijian story of the moon, the rat, and death.
tended that men should be like himself (for the Fijian moon
seems to be a male); that is, he meant that just as he grows
old, disappears, and comes in sight again, so men grown old
should vanish for a while and then return to life. But the
rat, who is a Fijian god, would not hear of it. "No," said
he, "let men die like rats." And he had the best of it
in the dispute, for men die like rats to this day.[1] In the Caroline Islands story of the moon, death, and resurrection.
Caroline Islands they say that long, long ago death was
unknown, or rather it was a short sleep, not a long, long
one, as it is now. Men died on the last day of the waning
moon and came to life again on the first appearance of the
new moon, just as if they had awakened from a refreshing
slumber. But an evil spirit somehow contrived that when
men slept the sleep of death they should wake no more.[2]
The Wotjobaluk of south-eastern Australia relate that, when Wotjobaluk story of the moon, death, and resurrection.
all animals were men and women, some of them died and
the moon used to say, "You up-again," whereupon they
came to life again. But once on a time an old man said,
"Let them remain dead"; and since then nobody has ever
come to life again except the moon, which still continues to
do so down to this very day.[3] The Chams of Annam and Cham story of the moon, death, and resurrection.
Cambodia say that the goddess of good luck used to resus-
citate people as fast as they died, till the sky-god, tired of
her constant interference with the laws of nature, transferred
her to the moon, where it is no longer in her power to bring
the dead to life again.[4]

These stories which associate human immortality with Cycle of death and resurrection after three days, like the monthly disappearance and reappearance of the moon.
the moon are products of a primitive philosophy which,
meditating on the visible changes of the lunar orb, drew
from the observation of its waning and waxing a dim
notion that under a happier fate man might have been
immortal like the moon, or rather that like it he might have
undergone an endless cycle of death and resurrection, dying
and then rising again from the dead after three days. The

[1] Th. Williams, *Fiji and the Fijians,* Second Edition (London, 1860), i. 205.
[2] *Lettres Édifiantes et Curieuses,* Nouvelle Édition, xv. (Paris, 1781) pp. 305 *sq.*
[3] A. W. Howitt, *Native Tribes of South-East Australia* (London, 1904), pp. 428 *sq.*
[4] Antoine Cabaton, *Nouvelles Recherches sur les Chams* (Paris, 1901), pp. 18 *sq.*

same curious notion of death and resurrection after three
days is entertained by the Unmatjera and Kaitish, two
savage tribes of Central Australia.   They say that long ago
their dead used to be buried either in trees or underground,
and that after three days they regularly rose from the dead.
The Kaitish tell how this happy state of things came to an
end.   It was all through a man of the Curlew totem, who
finding some men of the Little Wallaby totem burying a
Little Wallaby man, fell into a passion and kicked the body
into the sea.   Of course after that the dead man could not
come to life again, and that is why nowadays nobody rises
from the dead after three days, as everybody used to do
long ago.[1]   Although no mention is made of the moon in
this Australian story, we may conjecture that these savages,
like the Nandi of East Africa, fixed upon three days as the
normal interval between death and resurrection simply
because three days is the interval between the disappearance
of the old and the reappearance of the new moon.   If that
is so, the aborigines of Central Australia may be added to the
many races of mankind who have seen in the waning and
waxing moon an emblem of human immortality.   Nor does
this association of ideas end with a mere tradition that in some
former age men used to die with the old moon and come to
life again with the new moon.   Many savages, on seeing the
new moon for the first time in the month, observe ceremonies
which seem to be intended to renew and increase their life
and strength with the renewal and the increase of the lunar
light.   For example, on the day when the new moon first
appeared, the Indians of San Juan Capistrano in California
used to call together all the young men and make them run
about, while the old men danced in a circle, saying, " As the
moon dieth and cometh to life again, so we also having to
die will again live." [2]   Again, an old writer tells us that at
the appearance of every new moon the negroes of the Congo
clapped their hands and cried out, sometimes falling on their
knees, " So may I renew my life as thou art renewed." [3]

[1] Baldwin Spencer and F. J. Gillen, *Northern Tribes of Central Australia* (London, 1904), pp. 513 *sq.*

[2] Father G. Boscana, "Chinig-chinich," in *Life in California, by an* American [A. Robinson] (New York, 1846), pp. 298 *sq.*

[3] Merolla, "Voyage to Congo," in J. Pinkerton's *Voyages and Travels*, xvi. (London, 1814) p. 273.

Another type of stories told to explain the origin of death is the one which I have called the type of the Serpent and his Cast Skin. Some savages seem to think that serpents and all other animals, such as lizards, which periodically shed their skins, thereby renew their life and so never die. Hence they imagine that if man also could only cast his old skin and put on a new one, he too would be immortal like a serpent. Thus the Melanesians, who inhabit the coast of the Gazelle Peninsula in New Britain, tell the following story of the origin of death. They say that To Kambinana, the Good Spirit, loved men and wished to make them immortal; but he hated the serpents and wished to kill them. So he called his brother To Korvuvu and said to him, " Go to men and take them the secret of immortality. Tell them to cast their skin every year. So will they be protected from death, for their life will be constantly renewed. But tell the serpents that they must thenceforth die." But To Korvuvu acquitted himself badly of his task; for he commanded men to die and betrayed to the serpents the secret of immortality. Since then all men have been mortal, but the serpents cast their skins every year and are immortal.[1] In this story we meet again with the incident of the reversed message; through a blunder or through the malice of the messenger the glad tidings of immortality are perverted into a melancholy message of death. A similar tale, with a similar incident, is told in Annam. They say that Ngoc hoang sent a messenger from heaven to men to say that when they had reached old age they should change their skins and live for ever, but that when serpents grew old they must die. The messenger came down to earth and said, rightly enough, " When man is old, he shall cast his skin; but when serpents are old, they shall die and be laid in coffins." So far, so good. But unfortunately there happened to be a brood of serpents within hearing, and when they heard the doom pronounced on their kind they fell into a fury and said to the messenger, " You must say it over again and just the contrary, or we will bite you." That frightened the messenger and he repeated his message, changing the

III. Story of the Serpent and his Cast Skin.

New Britain story of immortality, the serpent, and death.

Annamite story of immortality, the serpent, and death.

¹ P. A. Kleintitschen, *Die Küstenbewohner der Gazellehalbinsel* (Hiltrup bei Münster, N.D.), p. 334.

words thus : " When he is old, the serpent shall cast his skin ; but when he is old, man shall die and be laid in the coffin." That is why all creatures are now subject to death, except the serpent, who, when he is old, casts his skin and

Vuatom story of immortality, the lizard, the serpent, and death. lives for ever.[1] The natives of Vuatom, an island in the Bismarck Archipelago, say that a certain To Konokonomiange bade two lads fetch fire, promising that if they did so they should never die, but that if they refused their bodies would perish, though their shades or souls would survive. They would not hearken to him, so he cursed them, saying, " What ! You would all have lived ! Now you shall die, though your soul shall live. But the iguana (*Goniocephalus*) and the lizard (*Varanus indicus*) and the snake (*Enygrus*), they shall live, they shall cast their skin and they shall live for evermore." When the lads heard that, they wept, for bitterly they rued their folly in not going to fetch the fire for To Konokonomiange.[2]

Nias story of immortality, the crab, and death. Other peoples tell somewhat different stories to explain how men missed the boon of immortality and serpents acquired it. Thus the natives of Nias, an island off the coast of Sumatra, say that, when the earth was created, a certain being was sent down by God from heaven to put the last touches to the work of creation. He should have fasted for a month, but unable to withstand the pangs of hunger he ate some bananas. The choice of food was most unlucky, for had he only eaten river-crabs instead of bananas men would have cast their skins like crabs and

Arawak and Tamanachier stories of immortality, the serpent, the lizard, the beetle, and death. would never have died.[3] The Arawaks of British Guiana relate that once upon a time the Creator came down to earth to see how his creature man was getting on. But men were so wicked that they tried to kill him ; so he deprived them of eternal life and bestowed it on the animals which renew their skin, such as serpents, lizards, and beetles.[4] A somewhat different version of the story is told by the Tamanachiers,

[1] A. Landes, "Contes et Légendes Annamites," *Cochinchine française, Excursions et Reconnaissances*, No. 25 (Saigon, 1886), pp. 108 *sq.*

[2] Otto Meyer, " Mythen und Erzählungen von der Insel Vuatom (Bismarck-Archipel, Südsee),"*Anthropos*, v. (1910) p. 724.

[3] H. Sundermann, " Die Insel Nias und die Mission daselbst," *Allgemeine Missions-Zeitschrift*, xi. (1884) p. 451 ; E. Modigliani, *Un Viaggio a Nías* (Milan, 1890), p. 295.

[4] R. Schomburgk, *Reisen in Britisch-Guiana* (Leipsig, 1847-1848), ii. 319.

an Indian tribe of the Orinoco. They say that after residing among them for some time the Creator took boat to cross to the other side of the great salt water from which he had come. Just as he was shoving off from the shore, he called out to them in a changed voice, "You will change your skins," by which he meant to say, "You will renew your youth like the serpents and the beetles." But unfortunately an old woman, hearing these words, cried out "Oh!" in a tone of scepticism, if not of sarcasm, which so annoyed the Creator that he changed his tune at once and said testily, "Ye shall die." That is why we are all mortal.[1]

The natives of the Banks' Islands and the New Hebrides believe that there was a time in the beginning of things when men never died but cast their skins like snakes and crabs and so renewed their youth. But the unhappy change to mortality came about at last, as it so often does in these stories, through an old woman. Having grown old, this dame went to a stream to change her skin, and change it she did, for she stripped off her wizened old hide, cast it upon the waters, and watched it floating down stream till it caught on a stick. Then she went home a buxom young woman. But the child whom she had left at home did not know her and set up such a prodigious squalling that to quiet it the woman went straight back to the river, fished out her cast-off old skin, and put it on again. From that day to this people have ceased to cast their skins and to live for ever.[2] The same legend of the origin of death has been recorded in the Shortlands Islands[3] and among the Kai of German New Guinea.[4] It is also told with some variations by the natives of the Admiralty Islands. They say that once on a time there was an old woman and she was frail. She had two sons, and they went a-fishing, and she herself went to bathe. She stripped off her wrinkled old skin and came forth as young as she had been long ago.

(marginal note: Melanesian story of the old woman who renewed her youth by casting her skin.)

[1] R. Schomburgk, *op. cit.* ii. 320.
[2] R. H. Codrington, *The Melanesians* (Oxford, 1891), p. 265; W. Gray, "Some Notes on the Tannese," *Internationales Archiv für Ethnographie*, vii. (1894) p. 232.
[3] C. Ribbe, *Zwei Jahre unter den Kannibalen der Salomo-Inseln* (Dresden-Blasowitz, 1903), p. 148.
[4] Ch. Keysser, "Aus dem Leben der Kaileute," in R. Neuhauss's *Deutsch Neu-Guinea* (Berlin, 1911), iii. 161 *sq.*

Her sons came home from the fishing, and very much astonished were they to see her. The one said, " It is our mother," but the other said, " She may be your mother, but she shall be my wife." Their mother heard them and said, " What were you two saying?" The two said, " Nothing! We only-said that you are our mother." " You are liars," said she, " I heard you both. If I had had my way, we should have grown to be old men and women, and then we should have cast our skin and been young men and young women. But you have had your way. We shall grow old men and old women and then we shall die." With that she fetched her old skin, and put it on, and became an old woman again. As for us, her descendants, we grow up and we grow old. And if it had not been for those two young men there would have been no end of our days, we should have lived for ever and ever.[1]

Samoan story of the shell-fish, two torches, and death. The Samoans tell how the gods held a council to decide what was to be done with men. One of them said, " Bring men and let them cast their skin; and when they die, let them be turned to shellfish or to a coco-nut leaf torch, which when shaken in the wind blazes out again." But another god called Palsy (*Supa*) rose up and said, " Bring men and let them be like the candle-nut torch, which when it is once out cannot be blown up again. Let the shellfish change their skin, but let men die." While they were debating, a heavy rain came on and broke up the meeting. As the gods ran for shelter to their houses, they cried, " Let it be according to the counsel of Palsy! Let it be according to the counsel of Palsy!" So men died, but shellfish cast their skins.[2]

IV. The Banana story. The last type of tales of the origin of death which I shall notice is the one which I have called the Banana type. We have already seen that according to the natives of Nias human mortality is all due to eating bananas instead of crabs.[3] A similar opinion is entertained by other people in that Poso story of immor-tality, region of the world. Thus the natives of Poso, a district of Central Celebes, say that in the beginning the sky was very

[1] Josef Meier, " Mythen und Sagen der Admiralitätsinsulaner," *Anthropos*, iii. (1908) p. 193.

[2] George Brown, D.D., *Melanesians and Polynesians* (London, 1910), p. 365; George Turner, LL.D., *Samoa* (London, 1884), pp. 8 *sq.*

[3] See above, p. 70.

near the earth, and that the Creator, who lived in it, used to the stone, the banana, and death.
let down his good gifts to men at the end of a rope. One
day he thus lowered a stone; but our first father and mother
would have none of it and they called out to their Maker,
"What have we to do with this stone? Give us something
else." The Creator complied and hauled away at.the rope;
the stone mounted up and up till it vanished from sight.
Presently the rope was seen coming down from heaven again,
and this time there was a banana at the end of it instead of
a stone. Our first parents ran at the banana and took it.
Then there came a voice from heaven, saying: "Because
ye have chosen the banana, your life shall be like its life.
When the banana-tree has offspring, the parent stem dies;
so shall ye die and your children shall step into your place.
Had ye chosen the stone, your life would have been like the
life of the stone changeless and immortal." The man and
his wife mourned over their fatal choice, but it was too late;
that is how through the eating of a banana death came into
the world.[1] The Mentras or Mantras, a shy tribe of savages Mentra story of immortality, the banana, and death.
in the jungles of the Malay Peninsula, allege that in the
early days of the world men did not die, but only grew thin
at the waning of the moon and then waxed fat again as she
waxed to the full. Thus there was no check whatever on
the population, which increased to a truly alarming extent.
So a son of the first man brought this state of things to his
father's notice and asked him what was to be done. The
first man said, "Leave things as they are"; but his younger
brother, who took a more Malthusian view of the situation,
said, "No, let men die like the banana, leaving their offspring
behind." The question was submitted to the Lord of the
Underworld, and he decided in favour of death. Ever since
then men have ceased to renew their youth like the moon
and have died like the banana.[2]

Thus the three stories of the origin of death which
I have called the Moon type, the Serpent type, and the

[1] A. C. Kruijt, "De legenden der
Poso - Alfoeren aangaande de erste
menschen," *Mededeelingen van wege
het Nederlandsche Zendelinggenootschap*,
xxxviii. (1894) p. 340.
  [2] D. F. A. Hervey, "The Mĕntra

Traditions," *Journal of the Straits
Branch of the Royal Asiatic Society*,
No. 10 (December 1882), p. 190;
W. W. Skeat and C. O. Blagden,
Pagan Races of the Malay Peninsula
(London, 1906), ii. 337 *sq.*

Primitive
philosophy
in the
stories of
the origin
of death. Banana type appear to be products of a primitive philosophy which sees a cheerful emblem of immortality in
the waxing and waning moon and in the cast skins of
serpents, but a sad emblem of mortality in the banana-tree,
which perishes as soon as it has produced its fruit.   But, as
I have already said, these types of stories do not exhaust
the theories or fancies of primitive man on the question how
death came into the world.   I will conclude this part of my
subject with some myths which do not fall under any of the
preceding heads.

Bahnar
story of im-
mortality,
the tree,
and death.   The Bahnars of eastern Cochinchina say that in the
beginning when people died they used to be buried at the
foot of a tree called Lông Blô, and that after a time they
always rose from the dead, not as infants but as full-grown
men and women.   So the earth was peopled very fast, and
all the inhabitants formed but one great town under the
presidency of our first parents.   In time men multiplied to
such an extent that a certain lizard could not take his walks
abroad without somebody treading on his tail.   This vexed
him, and the wily creature gave an insidious hint to the
gravediggers.   " Why bury the dead at the foot of the Lông
Blô tree ? " said he ; " bury them at the foot of Lông Khung,
and they will not come to life again.   Let them die outright
and be done with it."   The hint was taken, and from that
day the dead have not come to life again.[1]   In this story
there are several points to be noticed.   In the first place the
tree Lông Blô would seem to have been a tree of life, since
all the dead who were buried at its foot came to life again.
Rivalry for
the boon
of immor-
tality
between
men and
animals
that cast
their skins,
such as
serpents
and lizards. In the second place the lizard is here, as in so many African
tales, the instrument of bringing death among men.   Why
was that so ?   We may conjecture that the reason is that
the lizard like the serpent casts its skin periodically, from
which primitive man might infer, as he infers with regard to
serpents, that the creature renews its youth and lives for
ever.   Thus all the myths which relate how a lizard or a
serpent became the maleficent agent of human mortality
may perhaps be referred to an old idea of a certain jealousy
and rivalry between men and all creatures which cast their

[1] Guerlach, " Mœurs et Superstitions des sauvages Ba-hnars," *Missions
Catholiques*, xix. (1887) p. 479.

III MYTHS OF THE ORIGIN OF DEATH 75

skin, notably serpents and lizards ; we may suppose that in all such cases a story was told of a contest between man and his animal rivals for the possession of immortality, a contest in which, whether by mistake or by guile, the victory always remained with the animals, who thus became immortal, while mankind was doomed to mortality.

The Chingpaws of Upper Burma say that death originated in a practical joke played by an old man who pretended to be dead in the ancient days when nobody really died. But the Lord of the Sun, who held the threads of all human lives in his hand, detected the fraud and in anger cut short the thread of life of the practical joker. Since then everybody else has died ; the door for death to enter into the world was opened by the folly of that silly, though humorous, old man.[1] The natives about the Murray River in Australia used to relate how the first man and woman were forbidden to go near a tree in which a bat lived, lest they should disturb the creature. One day, however, the woman was gathering firewood and she went near the tree. The bat flew away, and after that death came into the world.[2] Some of the Fijians accounted for human mortality as follows. When the first man, the father of the human race, was being buried, a god passed by the grave and asked what it meant, for he had never seen a grave before. On learning from the bystanders that they had just buried their father, " Do not bury him," said he, " dig the body up again." " No," said they, " we cannot do that. He has been dead four days and stinks." " Not so," pleaded the god ; " dig him up, and I promise you that he will live again." Heedless of the divine promise, these primitive sextons persisted in leaving their dead father in the grave. Then said the god to these wicked men, " By disobeying me you have sealed your own fate. Had you dug up your ancestor, you would have found him alive, and

Chingpaw story of the origin of death.

Australian story of the tree, the bat, and death.

Fijian story of the origin of death.

[1] (Sir) J. G. Scott and J. P. Hardiman, *Gazetteer of Upper Burma and the Shan States*, Part i. vol. i. (Rangoon, 1900) pp. 408 *sq.*

[2] R. Brough Smyth, *The Aborigines of Victoria* (Melbourne and London, 1878), i. 428. On this narrative the author remarks : " This story appears to bear too close a resemblance to the Biblical account of the Fall. Is it genuine or not ? Mr. Bulmer admits that it may have been invented by the aborigines after they had heard something of Scripture history."

you yourselves, when you passed from this world, should have been buried, as bananas are, for the space of four days, after which you should have been dug up, not rotten, but ripe. But now, as a punishment for your disobedience, you shall die and rot." And still, when they hear this sad tale told, the Fijians say, "O that those children had dug up that body!"[1]

Admiralty Islanders' stories of the origin of death.

The Admiralty Islanders tell various stories to explain why man is mortal. One of them has already been related. Here is another. A Souh man went once to catch fish. A devil tried to devour him, but he fled into the forest and took refuge in a tree. The tree kindly closed on him so that the devil could not see him. When the devil was gone, the tree opened up and the man clambered down to the ground. Then said the tree to him, "Go to Souh and bring me two white pigs." He went and found two pigs, one was white and one was black. He took chalk and chalked the black pig so that it was white. Then he brought them to the tree, but on the way the chalk fell off the black pig. And when the tree saw the white pig and the black pig, he chid the man and said, "You are thankless. I was good to you. An evil will overtake you ; you will die. The devil will fall upon you, and you will die." So it has been with us as it was with the man of Souh. An evil overtakes us or a spirit falls upon us, and we die. If it had been as the tree said, we should not have died.[2] Another story told by the Admiralty Islanders to account for the melancholy truth of man's mortality runs thus. Kosi, the chief of Moakareng, was in his house. He was hungry. He said to his two sons, "Go and climb the breadfruit trees and bring the fruit, that we may eat them together and not die." But they would not. So he went himself and climbed the breadfruit tree. But the north-west wind blew a storm, it blew and threw him down. He fell and his body died, but his ghost went home. He went and sat in his house. He tied up his hair and he painted his face with red ochre.

---

[1] Th. Williams, *Fiji and the Fijians*, Second Edition (London, 1860), i. 204 *sq.* For another Fijian story of the origin of death, see above, p. 67.

[2] Josef Meier, " Mythen und Sagen der Admiralitätsinsulaner," *Anthropos*, iii. (1908) p. 194.

Now his wife and his two sons had gone after him into the wood. They went to fetch home the breadfruits. They came and saw Kosi, and he was dead. The three returned home, and there they saw the ghost of Kosi sitting in his house. They said, " You there! Who's that dead at the foot of the breadfruit tree? Kosi, he is dead at the foot of the breadfruit tree." Kosi, he said, " Here am I. I did not fall. Perhaps somebody else fell down. I did not. Here I am." " You're a liar," said they. " I ain't," said he. " Come," said they, " we'll go and see." They went. Kosi, he jumped into his body. He died. They buried him. If his wife had behaved well, we should not die. Our body would die, but our ghost would go about always in the old home.[1]

The Wemba of Northern Rhodesia relate how God in the beginning created a man and a woman and gave them two bundles; in one of them was life and in the other death. Most unfortunately the man chose " the little bundle of death." [2] The Cherokee Indians of North America say that a number of beings were engaged in the work of creation. The Sun was made first. Now the creators intended that men should live for ever. But when the Sun passed over them in the sky, he told the people that there was not room enough for them all and that they had better die. At last the Sun's own daughter, who was with the people on earth, was bitten by a snake and died. Then the Sun repented him and said that men might live always; and he bade them take a box and go fetch his daughter's spirit in the box and bring it to her body, that she might live. But he charged them straitly not to open the box until they arrived at the dead body. However, moved by curiosity, they unhappily opened the box too soon; away flew the spirit, and all men have died ever since.[3] Some of the North American Indians informed the early Jesuit missionaries that a certain man had received the gift of immortality

Stories of the origin of death : the fatal bundle or the fatal box.

---

[1] Josef Meier, *op. cit.* pp. 194 *sq.*

[2] C. Gouldsbury and H. Sheane, *The Great Plateau of Northern Rhodesia* (London, 1911), pp. 80 *sq.* A like tale is told by the Balolo of the Upper Congo. See *Folk-lore*, xii. (1901) p. 461 ; and below, p. 472.

[3] J. Mooney, " Myths of the Cherokee," *Nineteenth Annual Report of the Bureau of American Ethnology*, Part i. (Washington, 1900) p. 436, quoting " the Payne manuscript, of date about 1835." Compare *id.*, pp. 252-254, 436 *sq.*

in a small packet from a famous magician named Messou, who repaired the world after it had been seriously damaged by a great flood. In bestowing on the man this valuable gift the magician strictly enjoined him on no account to open the packet. The man obeyed, and so long as the packet was unopened he remained immortal. But his wife was both curious and incredulous; she opened the packet to see what was in it, the precious contents flew away, and mankind has been subject to death ever since.[1]

Baganda story how death came into the world through the forget-fulness and imprud-ence of a woman.

As these American Indians tell how death came through the curiosity and incredulity of one woman, the Baganda of Central Africa relate how it came through the forgetfulness and imprudence of another. According to the Baganda the first man who came to earth in Uganda was named Kintu. He brought with him one cow and lived on its milk, for he had no other food. But in time a woman named Nambi, a daughter of Gulu, the king of heaven, came down to earth with her brother or sister, and seeing Kintu she fell in love with him and wished to have him for her husband. But her proud father doubted whether Kintu was worthy of his daughter's hand, and accordingly he insisted on testing his future son-in-law before he would consent to the marriage. So he carried off Kintu's cow and put it among his own herds in heaven. When Kintu found that the cow was stolen, he was in a great rage, but hunger getting the better of anger, he made shift to live by peeling the bark of trees and gathering herbs and leaves, which he cooked and ate. In time his future wife Nambi happened to spy the stolen cow among her father's herds and she told Kintu, who came to heaven to seek and recover the lost animal. His future father-in-law Gulu, Lord of Heaven, obliged him to submit to many tests designed to prove his fitness for marriage with the daughter of so exalted a being as the Lord of Heaven. All these tests Kintu successfully passed through. At last Gulu was satisfied, gave him his daughter Nambi to wife, and allowed him to return to earth with her.

The coming of Death.

But Nambi had a brother and his name was Death (*Walumbe*). So before the Lord of Heaven sent her away with her husband he called them both to him

[1] *Relations des Jésuites*, 1634, p. 13 (Canadian reprint, Quebec, 1858).

and said, "You must hurry away before Death comes, or he will wish to go with you. You must not let him do so, for he would only cause you trouble and unhappiness." To this his daughter agreed, and she went to pack up her things. She and her husband then took leave of the Lord of Heaven, who gave them at parting a piece of advice. "Be sure," said he, "if you have forgotten anything, not to come back for it ; because, if you do, Death will wish to go with you, and you must go without him." So off they set, the man and his wife, taking with them his cow and its calves, also a sheep, a goat, a fowl, and a banana tree. But on the way the woman remembered that she had forgotten the grain to feed the fowl, so she said to her husband, "I must go back for the grain to feed the fowl, or it will die." Her husband tried to dissuade her, but in vain. She said, "I will hurry back and get it without any one seeing me." So back she went in an evil hour and said to her father the Lord of Heaven, "I have forgotten the grain for the fowl and I am come back to fetch it from the doorway where I put it." Her father said sadly, "Did I not tell you that you were not to return if you had forgotten anything, because your brother Death would wish to go with you? Now he will accompany you." The woman fled, but Death saw her and followed hard after her. When she rejoined her husband, he was angry, for he saw Death and said, "Why have you brought your brother with you? Who can live with him?"

When they reached the earth, Nambi planted her garden, and the bananas sprang up quickly and formed a grove. They lived happily for a time till one day Death came and asked for one of their daughters, that she might go away with him and be his cook. But the father said, "If the Lord of Heaven comes and asks me for one of my children, what am I to say? Shall I tell him that I have given her to you to be your cook?" Death was silent and went away. But he came back another day and asked again for a child to be his cook. When the father again refused, Death said, "I will kill your children." The father did not know what that meant, so he asked Death, "What is that you will do?" However, in a short time one of the children fell ill and

The importunity of Death.

died, and then another and another. So the man went to
the Lord of Heaven and complained that Death was
taking away his children one by one. The Lord of Heaven
said, " Did I not tell you, when you were going away, to go
at once with your wife and not to return if you had forgotten anything, but you let your wife return to fetch the
grain ? Now you have Death living with you. If you had
obeyed me, you would have been free from him and not lost
any of your children."

The hunt for Death.

However, the man pleaded with him, and the Lord
of Heaven at last consented to send Death's brother
Kaikuzi to help the woman and to prevent Death from
killing her children. So down came Kaikuzi to earth, and
when he met his brother Death they greeted each other
lovingly. Then Kaikuzi told Death that he had come to
fetch him away from earth to heaven. Death was willing
to go, but he said, " Let us take our sister too." " Nay," said
his brother, " that cannot be, for she is a wife and must
stay with her husband." The dispute waxed warm, Death
insisting on carrying off his sister, and his brother refusing
to allow him to do so. At last the brother angrily ordered
Death to do as he was bid, and so saying he made as
though he would seize him. But Death slipped from
between his hands and fled into the earth. For a long
time after that there was enmity between the two brothers.
Kaikuzi tried in every way to catch Death, but Death always
escaped. At last Kaikuzi told the people that he would
have one final hunt for Death, and while the hunt was
going on they must all stay in their houses ; not a man,
a woman, a child, nor even an animal was to be allowed
to pass the threshold ; and if they saw Death passing
the window, they were not to utter a cry of terror but
to keep still. Well, for some days his orders were obeyed.
Not a living soul, not an animal, stirred abroad. All
without was solitude, all within was silence. Encouraged
by the universal stillness Death emerged from his lair, and his
brother was just about to catch him, when some children,
who had ventured out to herd their goats, saw Death and
cried out. Death's good brother rushed to the spot and
asked them why they had cried out. They said, " Because

we saw Death." So his brother was angry because Death had again made good his escape into the earth, and he went to the first man and told him that he was weary of hunting Death and wished to return home to heaven. The first man thanked him kindly for all he had done, and said, " I fear there is nothing more to be done. We must only hope that Death will not kill all the people." It was a vain hope. Since then Death has lived on earth and killed everybody who is born into the world ; and always, after the deed of murder is done, he escapes into the earth at Tanda in Singo.[1]

If this curious tale of the origin of death reveals no very deep philosophy, it is at least interesting for the distinctness with which Death is conceived as a personal being, the son of the Lord of Heaven, the brother of the first man's wife. In this personification of Death the story differs from all the others which we have examined and marks an intellectual advance upon them ; since the power of picturing abstract ideas to the mind with all the sharpness of outline and vividness of colour which are implied by personification is a faculty above the reach of very low intelligences. It is not surprising that the Baganda should have attained to this power, for they are probably the most highly cultured and intellectual of all the many Bantu tribes of Africa. The same conception of Death as a person occurs in a story of the origin of death which is told by the Hos, a negro tribe in Togoland, a district of West Africa. These Hos belong to the Ewe-speaking family of the true negroes, who have reached a comparatively high level of barbarism in the notorious kingdom of Dahomey. The story which the Hos tell as to the origin of death is as follows. Once upon a time there was a great famine in which even the hunters could find no flesh to eat. Then Death went and made a road as broad as from here to Sokode, and there he set many snares. Every animal that tried to pass that way fell into a snare. So Death had much flesh to eat. One

In the preceding story Death is distinctly personified.

Death personified in a West African story of the origin of death.

Death and the spider and the spider's daughter.

[1] Sir Harry Johnston, *The Uganda Protectorate* (London, 1904), ii. 700-705 (the story was taken down by Mr. J. F. Cunningham) ; Rev. J. Roscoe, *The Baganda* (London, 1911), pp. 460-464. The story is briefly told by Mr. L. Decle, *Three Years in Savage Africa* (London, 1898), pp. 439 *sq.*

day the Spider came to Death and said to him, " You have so much meat ! " and she asked if she might have some to take home with her.   Death gave her leave.   So the Spider made a basket as long as from Ho to Akoviewe (a distance of about five miles), crammed it full of meat, and dragged it home.   In return for this bounty the Spider gave Death her daughter Yiyisa to wife.   So when Death had her for his wife, he gave her a hint.   He said, " Don't walk on the broad road which I have made.   Walk on the footpath which I have not made.   When you go to the water, be sure to take none but the narrow way through the wood."   Well, some time afterwards it had rained a little ; the grass was wet, and Yiyisa wished to go to the watering-place.   When she tried to walk on the narrow path through the forest, the tall damp grass wet her through and through, so she thought to herself, " In future I will only go on the broad road."   But scarce had she set foot on the beautiful broad road when she fell into a snare and died on the spot.   When Death came to the snare and saw his wife in it dead, he cut her up into bits and toasted them on the fire.   One day the Spider paid a visit to her son-in-law Death, and he set a good meal before her.   When she had eaten and drunk her fill and had got up to go home, she asked Death after her daughter. " If you take that meat from the fire," said Death, " you will see her."   So the Spider took the flesh from the fire and there, sure enough, she found her dead daughter.   Then she went home in great wrath and whetted her knife till it was so sharp that a fly lighting on the edge was cut in two. With that knife she came back to attack Death.   But Death shot an arrow at her.   She dodged it, and the arrow whizzed past her and set all the forest on fire.   Then the Spider flung her sharp knife at Death, but it missed him and only sliced off the tops of the palms and all the other trees of the wood.   Seeing that her stroke had failed, the Spider fled away home and shut herself up in her house.   But Death waited for her on the edge of the town to kill her as soon as she ventured out.   Next morning some women came out of the town to draw water at the watering-place, and as they went they talked with one another.   But Death shot an arrow among them and killed several.   The rest ran

ran away home and said, "So and so is dead." Then
Death came and looked at the bodies and said, "That
is my game. I need go no more into the wood to hunt."
That is how Death came into the world. If the Spider
had not done what she did, nobody would ever have
died.[1]

Again, the Melanesians of the Banks Islands tell a
story of the origin of Death, in which that grim power is
personified. They say that Death (*Mate*) used to live
underground in a shadowy realm called Panoi, while men
on earth changed their skins like serpents and so renewing
their youth lived for ever. But a practical inconvenience of
immortality was that property never changed hands; new-
comers had no chance, everything was monopolised by the
old, old stagers. To remedy this state of things and secure
a more equitable distribution of property Death was induced
to emerge from the lower world and to appear on earth
among men; he came relying on an assurance that no
harm would be done him. Well, when they had him, they
laid him out on a board, covered him with a pall as if he
were a corpse, and then proceeded with great gusto to
divide his property and eat the funeral feast. On the fifth
day they blew the conch shell to drive away the ghost, as
usual, and lifted the pall to see what had become of Death.
But there was no Death there; he had absconded leaving only
his skeleton behind. They naturally feared that he had made
off with an intention to return to his home underground,
which would have been a great calamity; for if there were no
Death on earth, how could men die and how could other
people inherit their property? The idea was intolerable ;
so to cut off the retreat of the fugitive, the Fool was set
to do sentinel duty at the parting of the ways, where one
road leads down to the underworld, Death's home, and the
other leads up to the upper world, the abode of the living.
Here accordingly the Fool was stationed with strict orders
to keep his eye on Death if he should attempt to sneak past
him and return to the nether world. However, the Fool,
like a fool as he was, sat watching the road to the upper
world, and Death slipped behind him and so made good his

*Death
personified
in a Melan-
esian story
of the
origin of
death.*

[1] J. Spieth, *Die Ewe-Stämme* (Berlin, 1906), pp. 590-593.

retreat.   Since then all men have followed Death down that fatal path.[1]

Thus according to savages death is not a necessary part of the order of nature.

So much for savage stories of the origin of death.   They all imply a belief that death is not a necessary part of the order of nature, but that it originated in a pure mistake or misdeed of some sort on somebody's part, and that we should all have lived happy and immortal if it had not been for that disastrous blunder or crime.   Thus the tales reflect the same frame of mind which I illustrated in the last lecture, when I shewed that many savages still to this day believe all men to be naturally immortal and death to be nothing but an effect of sorcery.   In short, whether we regard the savage's attitude to death at the present day or his ideas as to its origin in the remote past, we must conclude that primitive man cannot reconcile himself to the notion of death as a natural and necessary event; he persists in regarding it as an accidental and unnecessary disturbance of the proper order of nature.

A similar view is held by some eminent modern biologists.

To a certain extent, perhaps, in these crude speculations he has anticipated certain views of modern biology.   Thus it has been maintained by Professor August Weissmann that death is not a natural necessity, that many of the lowest species of living animals do in fact live for ever ; and that in the higher animals the custom of dying has been introduced in the course of evolution for the purpose of thinning the population and preventing the degeneration of the species, which would otherwise follow through the gradual and necessary deterioration of the immortal individuals, who, though they could not die, might yet sustain much bodily damage through hard knocks in the hurly-burly of eternal existence on earth.

Weissmann's view that death is not a natural necessity but an adaptation acquired in the course of evolution for the advantage of the race.

On this subject I will quote some sentences from Professor Weissmann's essay on the duration of life.   He says, " The necessity of death has been hitherto explained as due to causes which are inherent in organic nature, and not to the fact that it may be advantageous.   I do not however believe in the validity of this explanation ; I consider that death is not a primary necessity, but that it has been secondarily acquired as an adaptation.   I believe that life is endowed with a fixed duration, not because it is

[1] R. H. Codrington, *The Melanesians* (Oxford, 1891), pp. 265 *sq.*

contrary to its nature to be unlimited, but because the unlimited existence of individuals would be a luxury without any corresponding advantage. The above-mentioned hypothesis upon the origin and necessity of death leads me to believe that the organism did not finally cease to renew the worn-out cell material because the nature of the cells did not permit them to multiply indefinitely, but because the power of multiplying indefinitely was lost when it ceased to be of use. . . . John Hunter, supported by his experiments on *anabiosis*, hoped to prolong the life of man indefinitely by alternate freezing and thawing ; and the Veronese Colonel Aless. Guaguino made his contemporaries believe that a race of men existed in Russia, of which the individuals died regularly every year on the 27th of November, and returned to life on the 24th of the following April. There cannot however be the least doubt, that the higher organisms, as they are now constructed, contain within themselves the germs of death. The question however arises as to how this has come to pass ; and I reply that death is to be looked upon as an occurrence which is advantageous to the species as a concession to the outer conditions of life, and not as an absolute necessity, essentially inherent in life itself. Death, that is the end of life, is by no means, as is usually assumed, an attribute of all organisms. An immense number of low organisms do not die, although they are easily destroyed, being killed by heat, poisons, etc. As long, however, as those conditions which are necessary for their life are fulfilled, they continue to live, and they thus carry the potentiality of unending life in themselves. I am speaking not only of the Amoebae and the low unicellular Algae, but also of far more highly organized unicellular animals, such as the Infusoria." [1]

A similar suggestion that death is not a natural necessity but an innovation introduced for the good of the breed, has been made by our eminent English biologist, Mr. Alfred Russel Wallace. He says : " If individuals did not die they would soon multiply inordinately and would interfere with each other's healthy existence. Food would become scarce,

Similar view expressed by Alfred Russel Wallace.

[1] A. Weissmann, *Essays upon Problems,* vol. i. (Oxford, 1891) pp. *Heredity and Kindred Biological* 25 *sq.*

and hence the larger individuals would probably decompose or diminish in size. The deficiency of nourishment would lead to parts of the organism not being renewed; they would become fixed, and liable to more or less slow decomposition as dead parts within a living body. The smaller organisms would have a better chance of finding food, the larger ones less chance. That one which gave off several small portions to form each a new organism would have a better chance of leaving descendants like itself than one which divided equally or gave off a large part of itself. Hence it would happen that those which gave off very small portions would probably soon after cease to maintain their own existence while they would leave a numerous offspring. This state of things would be in any case for the advantage of the race, and would therefore, by natural selection, soon become established as the regular course of things, and thus we have the origin of *old age, decay, and death*; for it is evident that when one or more individuals have provided a sufficient number of successors they themselves, as consumers of nourishment in a constantly increasing degree, are an injury to their successors. Natural selection therefore weeds them out, and in many cases favours such races as die almost immediately after they have left successors. Many moths and other insects are in this condition, living only to propagate their kind and then immediately dying, some not even taking any food in the perfect and reproductive state." [1]

Savages and some men of science agree that death is not a natural necessity.

Thus it appears that two of the most eminent biologists of our time agree with savages in thinking that death is by no means a natural necessity for all living beings. They only differ from savages in this, that whereas savages look upon death as the result of a deplorable accident, our men of science regard it as a beneficent reform instituted by nature as a means of adjusting the numbers of living beings to the quantity of the food supply, and so tending to the improvement and therefore on the whole to the happiness of the species.

[1] A. R. Wallace, quoted in A. Weissmann's *Essays upon Heredity*, i. (Oxford, 1891) p. 24 note.

LECTURE IV

THE BELIEF IN IMMORTALITY AMONG THE ABORIGINES OF CENTRAL AUSTRALIA

IN previous lectures we have considered the ideas which savages in general entertain of death and its origin. To-day we begin our survey of the beliefs and practices of particular races in regard to the dead. I propose to deal separately with some of the principal races of men and to shew in detail how the belief in human immortality and the worship of the dead, to which that belief naturally gives rise, have formed a more or less important element of their religion. And in order to trace as far as possible the evolution of that worship in history I shall begin with the lowest savages about whom we possess accurate information, and shall pass from them to higher races until, if time permitted, we might come to the civilised nations of antiquity and of modern times. In this way, by comparing the ideas and practices of peoples on different planes of culture we may be able approximately to reconstruct or represent to ourselves with a fair degree of probability the various stages through which this particular phase of religion may be supposed to have passed in the great civilised races before the dawn of history. Of course all such reconstructions must be more or less conjectural. In the absence of historical documents that is inevitable; but our reconstruction will be more or less probable according to the degree in which the corresponding stages of evolution are found to resemble or differ from each other in the various races of men. If we find that tribes at approximately the same level of culture in different parts of the world have

Proposed survey of the belief in immortality and the worship of the dead, as these are found among the various races of men, beginning with the lowest savages.

87

approximately the same religion, we may fairly infer that religion is in a sense a function of culture, and therefore that all races which have traversed the same stages of culture in the past have traversed also the same stages of religion ; in short that, allowing for many minor variations, which flow inevitably from varying circumstances such as climate, soil, racial temperament, and so forth, the course of religious development has on the whole been uniform among mankind. This enquiry may be called the embryology of religion, in as much as it seeks to do for the development of religion what embryology in the strict sense of the word attempts to do for the development of life. And just as biology or the science of life naturally begins with the study of the lowest sorts of living beings, the humble protozoa, so we shall begin our enquiry with a study of the lowest savages of whom we possess a comparatively full and accurate record, namely, the aborigines of Australia.

Savagery a case not of degeneracy but of arrested or rather retarded development.

At the outset I would ask you to bear in mind that, so far as the evidence allows us to judge, savagery in all its phases appears to be nothing but a case of arrested or rather retarded development. The old view that savages have degenerated from a higher level of culture, on which their forefathers once stood, is destitute alike of evidence and of probability. On the contrary, the information which we possess as to the lower races, meagre and fragmentary as it unfortunately is, all seems to point to the conclusion that on the whole even the most savage tribes have reached their low level of culture from one still lower, and that the upward movement, though so slow as to be almost imperceptible, has yet been real and steady up to the point where savagery has come into contact with civilisation. The moment of such contact is a critical one for the savages. If the intellectual, moral, and social interval which divides them from the civilised intruders exceeds a certain degree, then it appears that sooner or later the savages must inevitably perish ; the shock of collision with a stronger race is too violent to be withstood, the weaker goes to the wall and is shattered. But if on the other hand the breach between the two conflicting races is not so wide as to be impassable, there is a hope that the weaker may assimilate enough of the higher culture of the other to survive. It was so, for example, with our barbarous forefathers in contact with the ancient civilisations of Greece and Rome ; and it may be so in future with some, for example, of the black races of the present day in contact with European civilisation. Time will shew. But among the savages who cannot permanently survive the shock of collision with Europe may certainly be numbered the aborigines of Australia. They are rapidly dwindling and wasting away, and before very many years have passed it is probable that they will be extinct like the Tasmanians, who, so far as we can judge from the miserably imperfect records of them which we possess, appear to have been savages of an even lower type than the Australians, and therefore to have been still less able to survive in the struggle for existence with their vigorous European rivals.

The causes which have retarded progress in Australia and kept the aboriginal population at the lowest level of savagery appear to be mainly two ; namely, first, the geographical isolation and comparatively small area of the continent, and, second, the barren and indeed desert nature of a great part of its surface ; for the combined effect of these causes has been, by excluding foreign competitors and seriously restricting the number of competitors at home, to abate the rigour of competition and thereby to restrain the action of one of the most powerful influences which make for progress. In other words, elements of weakness have been allowed to linger on, which under the sterner conditions of life entailed by fierce competition would long ago have been eliminated and have made way for elements better adapted to the environment. What is true of the human inhabitants of Australia in this respect is true also of its fauna and flora. It has long been recognised that the animals and plants of Australia represent on the whole more archaic types of life than the animals and plants of the larger continents ; and the reason why these antiquated creatures have survived there rather than elsewhere is mainly that, the area of competition being so much restricted through the causes I have mentioned, these comparatively weak forms of animal and vegetable life have not been killed off by

Physical causes which have retarded progress in Australia.

stronger competitors.   That this is the real cause appears to be proved by the rapidity with which many animals and plants introduced into Australia from Europe tend to over-run the country and to oust the old native fauna and flora.[1]

I have said that among the causes which have kept the aborigines of Australia at a very low level of savagery must be reckoned the desert nature of a great part of the country. Now it is the interior of the continent which is the most arid, waste, and barren.   The coasts are comparatively fertile, for they are watered by showers condensed from an atmosphere which is charged with moisture by the neighbouring sea ; and this condensation is greatly facilitated in the south-eastern and eastern parts of the continent by a high range of mountains which here skirts the coast for a long distance, attracting the moisture from the ocean and precipitating it in the form of snow and rain.   Thus the vegetation and hence the supply of food both animal and vegetable in these well-watered portions of the continent are varied and plentiful.   In striking contrast with the fertility and abundance of these favoured regions are the stony plains and bare rocky ranges of the interior, where water is scarce, vegetation scanty, and animal life at certain seasons of the year can only with difficulty be maintained.   It would be no wonder if the natives of these arid sun-scorched wildernesses should have lagged behind even their savage brethren of the coasts in respect of material and social progress ; and in fact there are many indications that they have done so, in other words, that the aborigines of the more fertile districts near the sea have made a greater advance towards civilisation than the tribes of the desert interior.   This is the view of men who have studied the Australian savages most deeply at first hand, and, so far as I can judge of the matter without any such first-hand acquaintance, I entirely agree with their opinion.   I have given my reasons elsewhere and shall not repeat them here.   All that I wish to impress on you now

---

[1] On the zoological peculiarities of Australia regarded as effects of its geographical isolation, see Alfred New-ton, *Dictionary of Birds* (London, 1893-96), pp. 317-319.   He observes (p. 318) that "the isolation of Australia is probably the next oldest in the world to that of New Zealand, having pos-sibly existed since the time when no mammals higher than marsupials had appeared on the face of the earth."

is that in aboriginal Australia a movement of social and intellectual progress, slow but perceptible, appears to have been setting from the coast inwards, and that, so far as such things can be referred to physical causes, this particular movement in Australia would seem to have been initiated by the sea acting through an abundant rainfall and a consequent abundant supply of food.[1]

Accordingly, in attempting to give you some account of the belief in immortality and the worship of the dead among the various races of mankind, I propose to begin with the natives of Central Australia, first, because the Australian aborigines are the most primitive savages about whom we have full and accurate information, and, second, because among these primitive savages the inhabitants of the central deserts are on the whole the most primitive. Like their brethren in the rest of the continent they were in their native condition absolutely ignorant of metals and of agriculture; they had no domestic animals except the dog, and they subsisted wholly by the products of the chase and the natural fruits, roots, and seeds, which the ground yielded without cultivation of any sort. In regard to their intellectual outlook upon the world, they were deeply imbued, as I shewed in a former lecture, with a belief in magic, but it can hardly be said that they possessed any religion in the strict sense of the word, by which I mean a propitiation of real or imaginary powers regarded as personal beings superior to man: certainly the Australian aborigines appear to have believed in no beings who deserve to be called gods. On this subject Messrs. Spencer and Gillen, our best authorities on these tribes, observe as follows: "The Central Australian natives— and this is true of the tribes extending from Lake Eyre in the south to the far north and eastwards across to the Gulf of Carpentaria—have no idea whatever of the existence of any supreme being who is pleased if they follow a certain line of what we call moral conduct and displeased if they do not do so. They have not the vaguest idea of a personal individual other than an actual living member of the tribe who approves or disapproves of

Marginal notes:

Backward state of the Central Australian aborigines.

They have no idea of a moral supreme being.

---

[1] For details see *Totemism and Exogamy*, i. 314 *sqq.*

their conduct, so far as anything like what we call morality is concerned. Any such idea as that of a future life of happiness or the reverse, as a reward for meritorious or as a punishment for blameworthy conduct, is quite foreign to them. . . . We know of no tribe in which there is a belief of any kind in a supreme being who rewards or punishes the individual according to his moral behaviour, using the word moral in the native sense." [1]

Central Australian theory that the souls of the dead survive and are afterwards reborn as infants.

But if the aborigines of Central Australia have no religion properly so called, they entertain beliefs and they observe practices out of which under favourable circumstances a religion might have been developed, if its evolution had not been arrested by the advent of Europeans. Among these elements of natural religion one of the most important is the theory which these savages hold as to the existence and nature of the dead. That theory is a very remarkable one. With a single exception, which I shall mention presently, they unanimously believe that death is not the end of all things for the individual, but that the human personality survives, apparently with little change, in the form of a spirit, which may afterwards be reborn as a child into the world. In fact they think that every living person without exception is the reincarnation of a dead person who lived on earth a longer or shorter time ago. This belief is held universally by the tribes which occupy an immense area of Australia from the centre northwards to the Gulf of Carpentaria.[2] The single exception to which I have referred is furnished by the Gnanji, a fierce and wild-looking tribe who eat their dead enemies and perhaps also their dead friends.[3] These savages deny that women have spirits which live after death ; when a woman dies, that, they say, is the end of her. On the other hand, the spirit of a dead man, in their opinion, survives and goes to and fro on the earth visiting the places where his forefathers camped in days of old and destined to be born again of a woman at some future time, when the rains have fallen and bleached his bones.[4] But why these

[1] Baldwin Spencer and F. J. Gillen, *Northern Tribes of Central Australia* (London, 1904), p. 491.
[2] Spencer and Gillen, *Northern*
[3] Spencer and Gillen, *op. cit.* p. 545.
[4] Spencer and Gillen, *op. cit.* p. 546.
Tribes of Central Australia, p. xi.

primitive philosophers should deny the privilege of immortality to women and reserve it exclusively for men, is
not manifest.   All other Central Australian tribes appear
to admit the rights of women equally with the rights of
men in a life beyond the grave.

With regard to the state of the souls of the dead in the
intervals between their successive reincarnations, the opinions
of the Central Australian savages are clear and definite.
Most civilised races who believe in the immortality of
the soul have found themselves compelled to confess
that, however immortal the spirits of the depaited may
be, they do not present themselves commonly to our eyes
or ears, nor meddle much with the affairs of the living ;
hence the survivors have for the most part inferred that the
dead do not hover invisible in our midst, but that they
dwell somewhere, far away, in the height of heaven, or in
the depth of earth, or in Islands of the Blest beyond the
sea where the sun goes down.   Not so with the simple
aborigines of Australia.   They imagine that the spirits of
the dead continue to haunt their native land and especially
certain striking natural features of the landscape, it may be
a pool of water in a deep gorge of the barren hills, or a
solitary tree in the sun-baked plains, or a great rock that
affords a welcome shade in the sultry noon.   Such spots
are thought to be tenanted by the souls of the departed
waiting to be born again.   There they lurk, constantly on
the look-out for passing women into whom they may enter,
and from whom in due time they may be born as infants.
It matters not whether the woman be married or unmarried,
a matron or a maid, a blooming girl or a withered hag :
any woman may conceive directly by the entrance into her
of one of these disembodied spirits ; but the natives have
shrewdly observed that the spirits shew a decided preference
for plump young women.   Hence when such a damsel is
passing near a plot of haunted ground, if she does not
wish to become a mother, she will disguise herself as an
aged crone and hobble past, saying in a thin cracked
voice, " Don't come to me. I am an old woman."   Such
spots are often stones, which the natives call child-stones
because the souls of the dead are there lying in wait for

Central Australian theory as to the state of the dead.

Certain conspicuous features of the landscape supposed to be tenanted by the souls of the dead waiting to be born again.

women in order to be born as children. One such stone, for example, may be seen in the land of the Arunta tribe near Alice Springs. It projects to a height of three feet from the ground among the mulga scrub, and there is a round hole in it through which the souls of dead plum-tree people are constantly peeping, ready to pounce out on a likely damsel. Again, in the territory of the Warramunga tribe the ghosts of black-snake people are supposed to gather in the rocks round certain pools or in the gum-trees which border the generally dry bed of a water-course. No Warramunga woman would dare to strike one of these trees with an axe, because she is firmly convinced that in doing so she would set free one of the lurking black-snake spirits, who would immediately dart into her body. They think that the spirits are no larger than grains of sand and that they make their way into women through the navel. Nor is it merely by direct contact with one of these repositories of souls, nor yet by passing near it, that women may be gotten with child against their wish. The Arunta believe that any malicious man may by magic cause a woman or even a child to become a mother : he has only to go to one of the child-stones and rub it with his hands, muttering the words, " Plenty of young women. You look and go quickly." [1]

As a rule, only the souls of persons of one particular totemic clan are thought to congregate in one place.

A remarkable feature in these gathering-places of the dead remains to be noticed. The society at each of them is very select. The ghosts are very clannish ; as a rule none but people of one particular totemic clan are supposed to forgather at any one place. For example, we have just seen that in the Arunta tribe the souls of dead people of the plum-tree totem congregate at a certain stone in the mulga scrub, and that in the Warramunga tribe the spirits of deceased persons who had black snakes for their totem haunt certain gum-trees. The same thing applies to most of the other haunts of the dead in Central Australia. Whether the totem was a kangaroo or an emu, a rat or a bat, a hawk or a cockatoo,

[1] Baldwin Spencer and F. J. Gillen, *Native Tribes of Central Australia* (London, 1899), pp. 119-127, 335-338, 552; *id., Northern Tribes of* *Central Australia*, pp. 145-153, 162, 271, 330 *sq.*, 448-451, 512-515. Compare *Totemism and Exogamy,* i. 188 *sqq.*

a bee or a fly, a yam or a grass seed, the sun or the moon, fire or water, lightning or the wind, it matters not what the totem was, only the ghosts of people of one totemic clan meet for the most part in one place; thus one rock will be tenanted by the spirits of kangaroo folk only, and another by spirits of emu folk only; one water-pool will be the home of dead rat people alone, and another the haunt of none but dead bat people; and so on with most of the other abodes of the souls.   However, in the Urabunna tribe the ghosts are not so exclusive; some of them consent to share their abode with people of other totems.   For example, a certain pool of water is haunted by the spirits of folk who in their lifetime had for their totems respectively the emu, rain, and a certain grub.   On the other hand a group of granite boulders is inhabited only by the souls of persons of the pigeon totem.[1]

Perhaps for the sake of some of my hearers I should say a word as to the meaning of totems and totemism. The subject is a large one and is still under discussion.   For our present purpose it is not necessary that I should enter into details; I will therefore only say that a totem is commonly a class of natural objects, usually a species of animals or plants, with which a savage identifies himself in a curious way, imagining that he himself and his kinsfolk are for all practical purposes kangaroos or emus, rats or bats, hawks or cockatoos, yams or grass-seed, and so on, according to the particular class of natural objects which he claims as his totem.   The origin of this remarkable identification of men with animals, plants, or other things is still much debated; my own view is that the key to the mystery is furnished by the Australian beliefs as to birth and rebirth which I have just described to you; but on that subject I will not now dwell.[2]   All that I ask you to remember is that in Central Australia there is no general gathering-place for the spirits of the departed; the souls are sorted out more or less strictly according to their totems and dwell apart each in their own little pre- serve or preserves, on which ghosts of other totems are

Totemism defined.

---

[1] Spencer and Gillen, *Northern Tribes of Central Australia*, p. 147.

[2] See *Totemism and Exogamy*, i. 155 *sqq.*, iv. 40 *sqq.*

supposed seldom or never to trespass. Thus the whole
country-side is dotted at intervals with these spiritual parks
or reservations, which are respected by the natives as the
abodes of their departed kinsfolk. In size they vary from
a few square yards to many square miles.[1]

Tradition-
ary origin
of the local
totem
centres
(*oknani-
killa*)
where the
souls of
the dead
are sup-
posed to
assemble.The way in which these spiritual preserves originated is
supposed to be as follows. In the earliest days of which
the aborigines retain a tradition, and to which they give the
name of the *alcheringa* or dream times, their remote ancestors
roamed about the country in bands, each band composed of
people of the same totem. Thus one band would consist
of frog people only, another of witchetty grub people only,
another of Hakea flower people only, and so on. Now in
regard to the nature of these remote totemic ancestors of the
alcheringa or dream times, the ideas of the natives are very
hazy ; they do not in fact clearly distinguish their human
from their totemic nature ; in speaking, for example, of a
man of the kangaroo totem they seem unable to discriminate
sharply between the man and the animal : perhaps we may
say that what is before their mind is a blurred image, a sort
of composite photograph, of a man and a kangaroo in one :
the man is semi-bestial, the kangaroo is semi-human. And
similarly with their ancestors of all other totems : if the
particular ancestors, for example, had the bean-tree for their
totem, then their descendants in thinking of them might,
like the blind man in the Gospel, see in their mind's eye
men walking like trees and trees perambulating like men.

The sacred
sticks or
stones
(*churinga*)
which the
totemic
ancestors
carried
about with
them.Now each of these semi-human ancestors is thought to have
carried about with him on his peregrinations one or more
sacred sticks or stones of a peculiar pattern, to which the
Arunta give the name of *churinga* : they are for the most
part oval or elongated and flattened stones or slabs of wood,
varying in length from a few inches to over five feet, and
inscribed with a variety of patterns which represent or have
reference to the totems. But the patterns are purely conventional, consisting of circles, curved lines, spirals, and dots
with no attempt to represent natural objects pictorially.
Each of these sacred stones or sticks was intimately
associated with the spirit part of the man or woman who

<hr />

[1] Spencer and Gillen, *Native Tribes of Central Australia*, pp. 123, 126.

carried it ; for women as well as men had their *churinga*.
When these semi-human ancestors died, they went into the
ground, leaving their sacred stones or sticks behind them on
the spot, and in every case some natural feature arose to
mark the place, it might be a tree, a rock, a pool of water,
or what not.   The memory of all such spots has been carefully preserved and handed down from generation to
generation by the old men, and it is to these spots that
down to the present day the souls of all the dead regularly
repair in order to await reincarnation.   The Arunta call the
places *oknanikilla*, and we may call them local totem centres,
because they are the centres where the spirits of the departed
assemble according to their totems.[1]

But it is not merely the remote forefathers of the
Central Australian savages who are said to have been
possessed of these sacred sticks or stones : every man and
woman who is born into the world has one of them, with
which his or her spirit is believed to be closely bound up.
This is intelligible when we remember that every living
person is believed to be simply the reincarnation of an
ancestor ; for that being so he naturally comes to life with
all the attributes which belonged to him in his previous
state of existence on earth.   The notion of the natives is
that when a spirit child enters into a woman to be born, he
immediately drops his sacred stick or stone on the spot,
which is necessarily one of what we have called the local
totem centres, since in the opinion of the natives it is only
at or near them that a woman can conceive a child.   Hence
when her child is born, the woman tells her husband the
place where she fancies that the infant entered into her, and
he goes with some old men to find the precious object, the
stick or stone dropped by the spirit of the infant when it
entered into the mother.   If it cannot be found, the men
cut a wooden one from the nearest hard-wood tree, and
this becomes the sacred stick or *churinga* of the newborn
child.   The exact spot, whether a tree or a stone or what
not, in which the child's spirit is supposed to have tarried in

Every living person has also his or her sacred stick or stone (churinga), with which his or her spirit is closely bound up.

---

[1] Spencer and Gillen, *Native Tribes
of Central Australia*, pp. 119 - 127,
128 *sqq.*, 513 ; *id., Northern Tribes*
of Central Australia, pp. 145 *sqq.*,
257 *sqq.*

the interval between its incarnations, is called its *nanja* tree or stone or what not. A definite relation is supposed to exist between each individual and his *nanja* tree or stone. The tree or stone and any animal or bird that lights upon it is sacred to him and may not be molested. A native has been known earnestly to intercede with a white man to spare a tree because it was his *nanja* or birth-tree, and he feared that evil would befall him if it were cut down.[1]

Sanctity of the *churinga*. Thus in these Central Australian tribes every man, woman, and child has his or her sacred birth-stone or stick. But though every woman, like every man, has her sacred birth-stone or stick, she is never allowed to see it under pain of death or of being blinded with a fire-stick. Indeed none but old women are aware even of the existence of such things. Uninitiated men are likewise forbidden under the same severe penalties ever to look upon these most sacred objects.[2] The sanctity ascribed to the sticks and stones is intelligible when we remember that the spirits of all the people both living and dead are believed to be intimately associated with them. Each of them, we are told, is supposed to be so closely bound up with a person's spirit that it may be regarded as his or her representative, and those of dead people are believed to be endowed with the attributes of their former owners and actually to impart them to any one who happens to carry them about with him. Hence these apparently insignificant sticks and stones are, in the opinion of the natives, most potent instruments for conveying to the living the virtues and powers of the dead. For example, in a fight the possession of one of these holy sticks or stones is thought to endow the possessor with courage and accuracy of aim and also to deprive his adversary of these qualities. So firmly is this belief held, that if two men were fighting and one of them knew that the other carried a sacred birth-stone or stick while he himself did not, he would certainly lose heart and be beaten. Again, when a man is sick, he will sometimes have one of these sacred stones brought to him and will scrape a little

[1] Spencer and Gillen, *Native Tribes of Central Australia*, pp. 132-135; id., *Northern Tribes of Central Australia*, pp. 258, 268 *sqq.*

[2] Spencer and Gillen, *Native Tribes of Central Australia*, pp. 128, 134.

dust off it, mix the dust with water, and drink it.   This is
supposed to strengthen him.   Clearly he imagines that with
the scrapings of the stone he absorbs the strength and other
qualities of the person to whom the stone belonged.[1]

All the birth-stones or sticks (*churinga*) belonging to
any particular totemic group are kept together, hidden away
from the eyes of women and uninitiated men, in a sacred
store-house or *ertnatulunga*, as the Arunta and Unmatjera
call it.   This store-house is always situated in one of the local
totem centres or *oknanikilla*, which, as we have seen, vary in
size from a few yards to many square miles.   In itself the
sacred treasure-house is usually a small cave or crevice in
some lonely spot among the rugged hills.   The entrance is
carefully blocked up with stones arranged so artfully as to
simulate nature and to awake no suspicion in the mind of
passing strangers that behind these tumbled blocks lie
concealed the most prized possessions of the tribe.   The
immediate neighbourhood of any one of these sacred store-
houses is a kind of haven of refuge for wild animals, for
once they have run thither, they are safe ; no hunter would
spear a kangaroo or opossum which cowered on the ground
at one of these hallowed spots.   The very plants which
grow there are sacred and may not be plucked or broken or
interfered with in any way.   Similarly, an enemy who
succeeds in taking refuge there, is safe from his pursuer, so
long as he keeps within the sacred boundaries : even the
avenger of blood, pursuing the murderer hot-foot, would not
dare to lift up his hand against him on the holy ground.
Thus, these places are sanctuaries in the strict sense of the
word ; they are probably the most primitive examples of
their class and contain the germ out of which cities of refuge
for manslayers and others might be developed.   It is
instructive, therefore, to observe that these rudimentary
sanctuaries in the heart of the Australian wilderness derive
their sacredness mainly, it would seem, from their association
with the spirits of the dead, whose repose must not be
disturbed by tumult, violence, and bloodshed.   Even when
the sacred birth-stones and sticks have been removed from
the store-house in the secret recesses of the hills and have

Sacred store-houses (ertnatulunga) of the churinga.

---

[1] Spencer and Gillen, *Native Tribes of Central Australia*, pp. 134 *sq.*

been brought into the camp for the performance of certain solemn ceremonies, no fighting may take place, no weapons may be brandished in their neighbourhood : if men will quarrel and fight, they must take their weapons and go elsewhere to do it.[1]   And when the men go to one of the sacred store-houses to inspect the treasures which it contains, they must each of them put his open hand solemnly over the mouth of the rocky crevice and then retire, in order to give the spirits due notice of the approach of strangers ; for if they were disturbed suddenly, they would be angry.[2]

Exhibition of the *churinga* to young men.

It is only after a young man has passed through the severe ceremonies of initiation, which include most painful bodily mutilations, that he is deemed worthy to be introduced to the tribal arcana, the sacred sticks and stones, which repose in their hallowed cave among the mountain solitudes. Even when he has passed through all the ordeals, many years may elapse before he is admitted to a knowledge of these mysteries, if he shews himself to be of a light and frivolous disposition.   When at last by the gravity of his demeanour he is judged to have proved himself indeed a man, a day is fixed for revealing to him the great secret. Then the headman of his local group, together with other grave and reverend seniors, conducts him to the mouth of the cave : the stones are rolled away from the entrance : the spirits within are duly warned of the approach of visitors ; and then the sacred sticks and stones, tied up in bundles, are brought forth.   The bundles are undone, the sticks and stones are taken out, one by one, reverently scrutinised, and exhibited to the novice, while the old men explain to him the meaning of the patterns incised on each and reveal to him the persons, alive or dead, to whom they belong.   All the time the other men keep chanting in a low voice the traditions of their remote ancestors in the far-off dream times.   At the close the novice is told the secret and sacred name which he is thenceforth to bear, and is warned never to allow it to pass his lips in the hearing

---

[1] Spencer and Gillen, *Native Tribes of Central Australia*, pp. 133, 135; *id.*, *Northern Tribes of Central Australia*,   p. 269.

[2] Spencer and Gillen, *Northern Tribes of Central Australia*, p. 267.

of anybody except members of his own totemic group.[1]
Sometimes this secret name is that of an ancestor of whom
the man or woman is supposed to be a reincarnation: for
women as well as men have their secret and sacred names.[2]

The number of sacred birth-stones and sticks kept Number of
churinga
in any one store-house naturally varies from group to in a store-
group; but whatever their number, whether more or less, house.
in any one store-house they all normally belong to the
same totem, though a few belonging to other totems may
be borrowed and deposited for a time with them. For
example, a sacred store-house of the honey-ant totem
was found to contain sixty-eight birth-sticks of that totem
with a few of the lizard totem and two of the wild-cat
totem.[3] Any store-house will usually contain both sticks
and stones, but as a rule perhaps the sticks predominate
in number.[4] Time after time these tribal repositories
are visited by the men and their contents taken out and
examined. On each examination the sacred sticks and
stones are carefully rubbed over with dry and powdered
red ochre or charcoal, the sticks being rubbed with red
ochre only, but the stones either with red ochre or
charcoal.[5] Further, it is customary on these occasions
to press the sacred objects against the stomachs and thighs
of all the men present; this is supposed to untie their
bowels, which are thought to be tightened and knotted
by the emotion which the men feel at the sight of these
venerated sticks and stones. Indeed, the emotion is
sometimes very real: men have been seen to weep on
beholding these mystic objects for the first time after a
considerable interval.[6] Whenever the sacred store-house Signifi-
cance
is visited and its contents examined, the old men explain of the
to the younger men the marks incised on the sticks and *churinga*.
stones, and recite the traditions associated with the dead
men to whom they belonged;[7] so that these rude objects

[1] Spencer and Gillen, *Native Tribes
of Central Australia*, pp. 139 *sq.*

[2] Spencer and Gillen, *Northern
Tribes of Central Australia*, p. 273.

[3] Spencer and Gillen, *Native Tribes
of Central Australia*, p. 141.

[4] Spencer and Gillen, *op. cit.* p.
140.

[5] Spencer and Gillen, *Native Tribes,*
pp. 144, 145.

[6] Spencer and Gillen, *Native Tribes,*
pp. 164 *sq.* ; *id., Northern Tribes,*
pp. 261, 264.

[7] Spencer and Gillen, *Native Tribes,*
p. 145.

of wood and stone, with the lines and dots scratched on them, serve the savages as memorials of the past; they are in fact rudimentary archives as well as, we may almost say, rudimentary idols; for a stone or stick which represents a revered ancestor and is supposed to be endowed with some portion of his spirit, is not far from being an idol. No wonder, therefore, that they are guarded and treasured by a tribe as its most precious possession. When a group of natives have been robbed of them by thoughtless white men and have found the sacred store-house empty, they have tried to kill the traitor who betrayed the hallowed spot to the strangers, and have remained in camp for a fortnight weeping and wailing for the loss and plastering themselves with pipeclay, which is their token of mourning for the dead.[1] Yet, as a great mark of friendship, they will sometimes lend these sacred sticks and stones to a neighbouring group; for believing that the sticks and stones are associated with the spiritual parts of their former and present owners, they naturally wish to have as many of them as possible and regard their possession as a treasure of great price, a sort of reservoir of spiritual force,[2] which can be turned to account not only in battle by worsting the enemy, but in various other ways,

Use of the *churinga* in magic.

such as by magically increasing the food supply. For instance, when a man of the grass-seed totem wishes to increase the supply of grass-seed in order that it may be eaten by people of other totems, he goes to the sacred store-house, clears the ground all around it, takes out a few of the holy sticks and stones, smears them with red ochre and decorates them with birds' down, chanting a spell all the time. Then he rubs them together so that the down flies off in all directions; this is supposed to carry with it the magical virtue of the sticks or stones and so to fertilise the grass-seed.[3]

Elements of a worship of the dead.

On the whole, when we survey these practices and beliefs of the Central Australian aborigines, we may perhaps conclude that, if they do not amount to a worship of the

[1] Spencer and Gillen, *Native Tribes*, p. 136.

[2] Spencer and Gillen, *Native Tribes*,

pp. 158 *sq.*

[3] Spencer and Gillen, *Northern Tribes*, pp. 271 *sq.*

dead, they at least contain the elements out of which such a
worship might easily be developed.   At first sight, no doubt,
their faith in the transmigration of souls seems and perhaps
really is a serious impediment to a worship of the dead in
the strict sense of the word.   For if they themselves are the
dead come to life again, it is difficult to see how they can
worship the spirits of the dead without also worshipping each
other, since they are all by hypothesis simply these worshipful spirits reincarnated.   But though in theory every living
man and woman is merely an ancestor or ancestress born
again and therefore should be his or her equal, in practice
they appear to admit that their forefathers of the remote *Marvellous*
alcheringa or dream time were endowed with many marvel- *powers*
attributed
lous powers which their modern reincarnations cannot lay *by the*
claim to, and that accordingly these ancestral spirits were *Central*
Australians
more to be reverenced, were in fact more worshipful, than *to their*
their living representatives.   On this subject Messrs. Spencer *remote*
ancestors
and Gillen observe : " The Central Australian native is firmly *of the*
convinced, as will be seen from the accounts relating to their *alcheringa*
or dream
alcheringa ancestors, that the latter were endowed with *time.*
powers such as no living man now possesses.   They could
travel underground or mount into the sky, and could make
creeks and water-courses, mountain-ranges, sand-hills, and
plains.   In very many cases the actual names of these
natives are preserved in their traditions, but, so far as
we have been able to discover, there is no instance of any
one of them being regarded in the light of a ' deity.'
Amongst the Central Australian natives there is never any
idea of appealing for assistance to any one of these Alcheringa ancestors in any way, nor is there any attempt made in
the direction of propitiation, with one single exception in the
case of the mythic creature called Wollunqua, amongst the
Warramunga tribe, who, it may be remarked, is most
distinctly regarded as a snake and not as a human being."[1]
Thus far Messrs. Spencer and Gillen.   From their testimony
it appears that with a single possible exception, to which I
will return immediately, the Central Australian aborigines
are not known to worship any of their dead ancestors ;
they indeed believe their remote forefathers of the *alcheringa*

[1] Spencer and Gillen, *Northern Tribes of Central Australia*, pp. 490 *sq.*

age to have been endowed with marvellous powers which they themselves do not possess ; but they do not regard these ancestral spirits as deities, nor do they pray and sacrifice to them for help and protection.   The single possible exception to this general rule known to Messrs. Spencer and Gillen is the case of the mythical water-snake called Wollunqua, who is in a sense revered and propitiated by the Warramunga tribe.   The case is interesting and instructive as indicative of an advance from magic towards religion in the strict sense of the word.   Accordingly I propose to consider it somewhat fully.

The Wol-
lunqua, a
mythical
water-
snake,
one of the
Warra-
munga
totems.

The Wollunqua is one of the many totems of the Warramunga tribe.   It is to be borne in mind that, though every Australian tribe has many totems which are most commonly animals or plants and more rarely other natural objects, all the totems are not respected by all the members of the tribe ; each totem is respected only by a particular group of men and women in the tribe, who believe themselves to be descended from the same totemic ancestor.   Thus the whole tribe is broken up into many groups or bodies of men and women, each group knit together by a belief in a common descent from the totem, by a common respect for the totemic species, whether it be a species of animals or plants, or what not, and finally by the possession of a common name derived from the totem.   Thus, for example, we have a group of men and women who believe themselves descended from an ancestor who had the bandicoot for his totem ; they all respect bandicoots ; and they are all called bandicoot people.   Similarly with all the other totemic groups within the tribe.   It is convenient to have a name for these totemic groups or tribal subdivisions, and accordingly we may call them clans, provided we remember that a totemic clan in this sense is not an independent political community such as the Scottish Highland clans used to be ; it is merely a subdivision of the tribe, and the members of it do not usually keep to themselves but live more or less interfused with members of all the other totemic clans which together compose the tribe.   Now amongst the Warramunga the Wollunqua or mythical water-snake is the totem of such a clan or tribal subdivision, the members of which believe

themselves to be descended from the creature and call themselves by its name.   So far, therefore, the Wollunqua is
merely a totem of the ordinary sort, an object of respect
for a particular section of the tribe.   Like other totemic
ancestors the Wollunqua is supposed to have wandered
about the country leaving supplies of spirit individuals at
various points, individuals who are constantly undergoing
reincarnation.   But on the other hand the Wollunqua differs
from almost all other Australian totems in this, that whereas
they are real objects, such as animals, plants, water, wind,
the sun and moon, and so on, the Wollunqua is a purely
mythical creature, which exists only in the imagination of
the natives ; for they believe it to be a water-snake so
huge that if it were to stand up on its tail, its head would
reach far up into the sky.   It now lives in a large pool
called Thapauerlu, hidden away in a lonely valley of the
Murchison Range ; but the Warramunga fear that it may at
any moment sally out and do some damage.   They say that
it actually killed a number of them on one of its excursions,
though happily they at last succeeded in beating it off.   So
afraid are they of the creature, that in speaking of it
amongst themselves they will not use its proper name of
Wollunqua but call it instead *urkulu nappaurinnia*, because,
as they told Messrs. Spencer and Gillen, if they were to
name it too often by its real name they would lose control
over the beast and it would rush forth and devour them.[1]
Thus the natives do not distinguish the Wollunqua from
the rest of their actually existing totems, as we do : they
have never beheld him with their bodily eyes, yet to them he
is just as real as the kangaroos which they see hopping along
the sands, as the flies which buzz about their heads in the
sunshine, or as the cockatoos which flap screaming past in
the thickets.   How real this belief in the mythical snake is
with these savages, was brought vividly home to Messrs.
Spencer and Gillen when they visited, in company with some

---

[1] Spencer and Gillen, *Northern Tribes of Central Australia*, pp. 226 *sq.*   Another mythical being in which the Warramunga believe is the *pau-wa*, a fabulous animal, half human and somewhat resembling a dog.   See Spencer and Gillen, *op. cit.* pp. 195, 197, 201, 210 *sq.*   But the creature seems not to be a totem, for it is not included in the list of totems given by Messrs. Spencer and Gillen (*op. cit.* pp. 768-773).

natives, the deep and lonely pool among the rocky hills in which the awful being is supposed to reside. Before they approached the spot, the natives had been talking and laughing freely, but when they drew near the water their voices were hushed and their demeanour became solemn. When all stood silent on the brink of the deep still pool, enclosed by a sandy margin on one side and by a line of red rocks on the other, two old men, the leaders of the totemic group of the Wollunqua, went down to the edge of the water and, with bowed heads, addressed the Wollunqua in whispers, asking him to remain quiet and do them no harm, for they were mates of his, and had brought two great white men to see where he lived and to tell them all about him. "We could plainly see," add Messrs. Spencer and Gillen, "that it was all very real to them, and that they implicitly believed that the Wollunqua was indeed alive beneath the water, watching them, though they could not see him." [1]

Religious character of the belief in the Wollunqua.

I need hardly point out what a near approach all this is to religion in the proper sense of the word. Here we have a firm belief in a purely imaginary being who is necessarily visible to the eye of faith alone, since I think we may safely assume that a water-snake, supposed to be many miles long and capable of reaching up to the sky, has no real existence either on the earth or in the waters under the earth. Yet to these savages this invisible being is just as real as the actually existing animals and men whom they perceive with their bodily senses; they not only pray to him but they propitiate him with a solemn ritual; and no doubt they would spurn with scorn the feeble attempts of shallow sceptics to question the reality of his existence or the literal truth of the myths they tell about him. Certainly these savages are far on the road to religion, if they have not already passed the Rubicon which divides it from the common workaday world. If an unhesitating faith in the unseen is part of religion, the Warramunga people of the Wollunqua totem are unquestionably religious.

[1] Spencer and Gillen, *Northern Tribes of Central Australia*, pp. 252 *sq.*

LECTURE V

THE BELIEF IN IMMORTALITY AMONG THE ABORIGINES OF CENTRAL AUSTRALIA (*continued*)

IN the last lecture we began our survey of the belief in immortality and the practices to which it has given rise among the aboriginal tribes of Central Australia. I shewed that these primitive savages hold a very remarkable theory of birth and death. [They believe that the souls of the dead do not perish but are reborn in human form after a longer or shorter interval. During that interval the spirits of the departed are supposed to congregate in certain parts of the country, generally distinguished by some conspicuous natural feature, which accordingly the natives account sacred, believing them to be haunted by the souls of the dead. From time to time one of these disembodied spirits enters into a passing woman and is born as an infant into the world.] Thus according to the Central Australian theory every living person without exception is the reincarnation of a dead man, woman, or child. At first sight the theory seems to exclude the possibility of any worship of the dead, since it appears to put the living on a footing of perfect equality with the dead by identifying the one with the other. But I pointed out that as a matter of fact these savages do admit, whether logically or not, the superiority of their remote ancestors to themselves : they acknowledge that these old forefathers of theirs did possess many marvellous powers to which they themselves can lay no claim. In this acknowledgment, accordingly, we may detect an opening or possibility for the development of a real worship of ancestors. Indeed, as I said at the close of last lecture, something

Beliefs of the Central Australian aborigines concerning the re-incarnation of the dead.

107

closely approaching to ancestor worship has actually grown up in regard to the mythical ancestor of the Wollunqua clan in the Warramunga tribe. The Wollunqua is a purely fabulous water-snake, of gigantic dimensions, which is supposed to haunt the waters of a certain lonely pool called Thapauerlu, in the Murchison Range of mountains. Unlike the ancestors of the other totemic clans, this mythical serpent is never reborn in human form; he always lives in his solitary pool among the barren hills; but the natives think that he has it in his power to come forth and do them an injury, and accordingly they pray to him to remain quiet and not to harm them. Indeed so afraid of him are they that speaking of the creature among themselves they avoid using his proper name of Wollunqua and call him by a different name, lest hearing himself called by his true name he should rush forth and devour them. More than that they even endeavour to propitiate him by the performance of certain rites, which, however childish and absurd they may seem to us, are very solemn affairs for these simple folk. The rites were witnessed by Messrs. Spencer and Gillen, whose description I will summarise. It offers an interesting and instructive example of a ritual observed by primitive savages, who are clearly standing on, if they have not already crossed, the threshold of religion.

Like all other totemic ancestors the Wollunqua is said to have arisen at a particular spot, to have wandered about the country, and finally to have gone down into the ground. Starting from the deep rocky pool in the Murchison Range he travelled at first underground, coming up, however, at various points where he performed ceremonies and left many spirit children, who issued from his body and remained behind, forming local totemic centres when he had passed on. It is these spirit children who have formed the Wollunqua clan ever since, undergoing an endless series of reincarnations. Now the ceremonies which the clan perform in honour of their mythical ancestor the Wollunqua all refer to his wanderings about the country. Thus there is a particular water-hole called Pitingari where the great old water-snake is said to have emerged from the ground and looked about him. Here, accordingly, two

The mythical water-snake Wollunqua.

Wanderings of the Wollunqua.

Dramatic ceremonies in honour of the Wollunqua.

men performed a ceremony. Each of them was decorated with a broad band of red down, which curved round both the front and the back of the performer and stood sharply out from the mass of white down with which all the rest of the upper part of his body was covered. These broad red bands represented the Wollunqua. Each man also wore a tall, conical helmet adorned with a curved band of red down, which, no doubt, likewise symbolised the mythical serpent. When the two actors in the little drama had been attired in this quaint costume of red and white down, they retired behind a bush, which served for the side scenes of a theatre. Then, when the orchestra, composed of adult men, struck up the music on the ceremonial ground by chanting and beating boomerangs and sticks together, the performers ran in, stopping every now and then to shake themselves in imitation of the snake. Finally, they sat down close together with their heads bowed down on a few green branches of gum-trees. A man then stepped up to them, knocked off their head-dresses, and the simple ceremony came to an end.[1]

The next ceremony was performed on the following day at another place called Antipataringa, where the mythical snake is said to have halted in his wanderings. The same two men acted as before, but this time one of them carried on his head a curious curved bundle shaped like an enormous boomerang. It was made of grass-stalks bound together with human hair-string and decorated with white down. This sacred object represented the Wollunqua himself.[2] From this spot the snake was believed to have travelled on to another place called Tjunguniari, where he popped up his head among the sand-hills, the greater part of his body remaining underground. Indeed, of such an enormous length was the serpent, that though his head had now travelled very many miles his tail still remained at the starting-point and had not yet begun to take part in the procession. Here accordingly the third ceremony, perhaps we may say the third act in the drama, was performed on the third day. In it one of

Ceremony in honour of the Wollunqua.

---

[1] Spencer and Gillen, *Northern Tribes of Central Australia*, pp. 228 *sq.*

[2] Spencer and Gillen, *Northern Tribes of Central Australia*, pp. 229 *sq.*

the actors personated the snake himself, while the other stood for a sand-hill.[1]

Further ceremony in honour of the Wollunqua: the white mound with the red wavy band to represent the mythical snake.

After an interval of three days a fourth ceremony was performed of an entirely different kind. A keel-shaped mound was made of wet sand, about fifteen feet long by two feet high. The smooth surface of the mound was covered with a mass of little dots of white down, except for a long wavy band of red down which ran all along both sides of the mound. This wavy red band represented the Wollunqua, his head being indicated by a small round swelling at one end and his tail by a short prolongation at the other. The mound itself represented a sand-hill beside which the snake is said to have stood up and looked about. The preparation of this elaborate emblem of the Wollunqua occupied the greater part of the day, and it was late in the afternoon before it was completed. When darkness fell, fires were lighted on the ceremonial ground, and as the night grew late more fires were kindled, and all of the men sat round the mound singing songs which referred to the mythical water-snake. This went on for hours. At last, about three o'clock in the morning, a ring of fires was lit all round the ceremonial ground, in the light of which the white trunks of the gum-trees and the surrounding scrub stood out weird and ghastly against the blackness of darkness beyond. Amid the wildest excitement the men of the Wollunqua totem now ranged themselves in single file on their knees beside the mound which bore the red image of their great mythical forefather, and with their hands on their thighs surged round and round it, every man bending in unison first to one side and then to the other, each successive movement being accompanied by a loud and simultaneous shout, or rather yell, while the other men, who were not of the Wollunqua totem, stood by, clanging their boomerangs excitedly, and one old man, who acted as a sort of choregus, walked backwards at the end of the kneeling procession of Wollunqua men, swaying his body about and lifting high his knees at every step. In this way, with shouts and clangour, the men of the totem surged twice round the mound on their knees. After that, as the fires died down, the men rose from their knees, and

---

[1] Spencer and Gillen, *op. cit.* pp. 230 *sq.*

for another hour every one sat round the mound singing incessantly.   The last act in the drama was played at four o'clock in the morning at the moment when the first faint streaks of dawn glimmered in the east.   At sight of them every man jumped to his feet, the smouldering fires were rekindled, and in their blaze the long white mound stood out in strong relief.   The men of the totem, armed with spears, boomerangs, and clubs, ranged themselves round it, and encouraged by the men of the other totems attacked it fiercely with their weapons, until in a few minutes they had hacked it to pieces, and nothing was left of it but a rough heap of sandy earth.   The fires again died down and for a short time silence reigned.   Then, just as the sun rose above the eastern horizon, the painful ceremony of subincision was performed on three youths, who had recently passed through the earlier stages of initiation.[1]

This remarkable rite is supposed, we are informed, " in some way to be associated with the idea of persuading, or almost forcing, the Wollunqua to remain quietly in his home under the water-hole at Thapauerlu, and to do no harm to any of the natives.   They say that when he sees the mound with his representation drawn upon it he is gratified, and wriggles about underneath with pleasure.   The savage attack upon the mound is associated with the idea of driving him down, and, taken altogether, the ceremony indicates their belief that, at one and the same time, they can both please and coerce the mythic beast.   It is necessary to do things to please him, or else he might grow sulky and come out and do them harm, but at the same time they occasionally use force to make him do what they want." [2]   In fact the ritual of the mound with its red image of the snake combines the principles of religion and magic.   So far as the rite is intended to please and propitiate the mythical beast, it is religious ; so far as it is intended to constrain him, it is magical.   The two principles are contradictory and the attempt to combine them is illogical ; but the savage is heedless, or rather

The rite aims both at pleasing and at co-ercing the mythical snake.

---

[1] Spencer and Gillen, *Northern Tribes of Central Australia*, pp. 231-238.

[2] Spencer and Gillen, *op. cit.* p. 238.

totally unaware, of the contradiction and illogicality: all that concerns him is to accomplish his ends : he has neither the wish nor the ability to analyse his motives. In this respect he is in substantial agreement with the vast majority of mankind. How many of us scrutinise the reasons of our conduct with the view of detecting and eliminating any latent inconsistencies in them? And how many, or rather how few of us, on such a scrutiny would be so fortunate as to discover that there were no such inconsistencies to detect? The logical pedant who imagines that men cannot possibly act on inconsistent and even contradictory motives only betrays his ignorance of life. It is not therefore for us to cast stones at the Warramunga men of the Wollunqua totem for attempting to propitiate and constrain their mythical serpent at the same time. Such contradictions meet us again and again in the history of religion : it is interesting but by no means surprising to find them in one of its rudimentary stages.

Thunder the voice of the Wollunqua.
On the evening of the day which succeeded the construction of the emblematic mound the old men who had made the emblem said they had heard the Wollunqua talking, and that he was pleased with what had been done and was sending them rain. What they took for the voice of the Wollunqua was thunder rumbling in the distance. No rain fell, but a few days later thunder was again heard rolling afar off and a heavy bank of clouds lay low on the western horizon. The old men now said that the Wollunqua was growling because the remains of the mound had been left uncovered ; so they hastily cut down branches and covered up the ruins. After that the Wollunqua ceased to growl : there was no more thunder.[1]

Ground drawings of the Wollunqua.
On the four following days ceremonies of an entirely different kind from all the preceding were performed in honour of the Wollunqua. A space of sandy ground was smoothed down, sprinkled with water, and rubbed so as to form a compact surface. The smooth surface was then overlaid with a coat of red or yellow ochre, and on this coloured background a number of designs were traced, one after the other, by a series of white dots, which together

---

[1] Spencer and Gillen, *op. cit.* pp. 238 *sq.*

made up a pattern of curved lines and concentric circles.
These patterns represented the Wollunqua and some of his
traditionary adventures. The snake himself was portrayed
by a broad wavy band, but all the other designs were purely
conventional; for example, trees, ant-hills, and wells were
alike indicated by circles. Altogether there were eight such
drawings on the earth, some of them very elaborate and
entailing, each of them, not less than six or seven hours'
labour : one of them was ten feet long. Each drawing was
rubbed out before the next one was drawn. Moreover, the
drawings were accompanied by little dramas acted by
decorated men. In one of these dramas no fewer than
eight actors took part, some of whom wore head-dresses
adorned with a long wavy band to represent the Wollunqua.
The last drawing of all was supposed to portray the
mythical snake as he plunged into the earth and returned
to his home in the rocky pool called Thapauerlu among the
Murchison Ranges.[1]

I have dwelt at some length on these ceremonies of the Religious importance of the Wollunqua.
Wollunqua totem, because they furnish a remarkable and
perhaps unique instance in Australia of a totemic ancestor
in the act of developing into something like a god. In the
Warramunga tribe there are other snake totems besides the
Wollunqua ; for example, there is the black snake totem
and the deaf adder totem. But this purely mythical water-
snake, the Wollunqua, is the most important of them all
and is regarded as the great father of all the snakes. " It
is not easy," say Messrs. Spencer and Gillen, " to express
in words what is in reality rather a vague feeling amongst
the natives, but after carefully watching the different series
of ceremonies we were impressed with the feeling that the
Wollunqua represented to the native mind the idea of a
dominant totem." [2] Thus he is at once a fabulous animal
and the mythical ancestor of a human clan, but his animal
nature apparently predominates over his semi-human nature,
as shewn by the drawings and effigies of him, all of which
are in serpent form. The prayers offered to him at the pool

---

[1] Spencer and Gillen, *Northern Tribes of Central Australia*, pp. 239-247.

[2] Spencer and Cillen, *op. cit.* p. 248.

which he is supposed to haunt, and the attempt to please him by drawing his likeness can only be regarded as propitiatory rites and therefore as rudimentary forms of worship. And the idea that thunder is his voice, and that the rain is a gift sent by him in return for the homage paid to him by the people, appears to prove that in course of time, if left to himself, he might easily have been elevated to the sky and have ranked as a celestial deity, who dwells aloft and sends down or withholds the refreshing showers at his good pleasure. Thus the Wollunqua, a rude creation of the savage Australian imagination, possesses a high interest for the historian of religion, since he combines elements of ancestor worship and totem worship with a germ of heaven worship ; while on the purely material side his representation, both in plastic form by a curved bundle of grass-stalks and in graphic form by broad wavy bands of red down, may be said in a sense to stand at the starting-point of that long development of religious art, which in so many countries and so many ages has attempted to represent to the bodily eye the mysteries of the unseen and invisible, and which, whatever we may think of the success or failure of that attempt, has given to the world some of the noblest works of sculpture and painting.

Possible religious evolution of totemism.

I have already pointed out the difficulty of seeing how a belief in the reincarnation of the dead, such as prevails universally among the aborigines of Central Australia, could ever be reconciled with or develop into a worship of the dead ; for by identifying the living with the dead, the theory of reincarnation seems to abolish that distinction between the worshipper and the worshipped which is essential to the existence of worship. But, as I also indicated, what seems a loophole or mode of escape from the dilemma may be furnished by the belief of these savages, that though they themselves are nothing but their ancestors come to life again, nevertheless in their earliest incarnations of the *alcheringa* or dream times their ancestors possessed miraculous powers which they have admittedly lost in their later reincarnations ; for this suggests an incipient discrimination or line of cleavage between the living and the dead ; it hints that perhaps after all the first ancestors, with their marvellous endowments, may have been entirely different persons from their feebler descendants, and if this vague hint could only grow into a firm conviction of the essential difference between the two, then the course would be clear for the development of ancestor worship: the dead forefathers, viewed as beings perfectly distinct from and far superior to the living, might easily come to receive from the latter the homage of prayer and sacrifice, might be besought by their descendants to protect them in danger and to succour them in all the manifold ills of life, or at least to abstain from injuring them.   Now, this important step in religious evolution appears to have been actually taken by the Wollunqua, the mythical water-snake, who is the totem of one of the Warramunga clans.   Unlike all the other totems he is supposed to exist only in his invisible and animal form and never to be reincarnated in a man.[1]   Hence, withdrawn as he is from the real world of sense, the imagination is free to play about him and to invest him more and more with those supernatural attributes which men ascribe to their deities. And what has actually happened to this particular totemic ancestor might under favourable circumstances happen to many others.   Each of them might be gradually detached from the line of his descendants, might cease to be reincarnated in them, and might gradually attain to the lonely pre-eminence of godhead.   Thus a system of pure totemism, such as prevails among the aborigines of Central Australia, might develop through a phase of ancestor worship into a pantheon of the ordinary type.

Although none of the other totemic ancestors of the Central Australian aborigines appears to have advanced so far on the road to religion as the Wollunqua, yet they all contain in germ the elements out of which a religion might have been developed.   It is difficult for us civilised men to conceive the extent to which the thoughts and lives of these savages are dominated by the memories and traditions of the dead.   Every conspicuous feature in the landscape is

Conspicuous features of the landscape associated with ancestral spirits.

[1] "On the other hand there is a great difference between the Wollunqua and any other totem, inasmuch as the particular animal is purely mythical, and except for the one great progenitor of the totemic group, is not supposed to exist at the present day" (Spencer and Gillen, *Northern Tribes of Central Australia*, p. 248).

not only associated with the legendary doings of some
ancestors but is commonly said to have arisen as a direct
result of their actions.   The mountains, the plains, the rivers,
the seas, the islands of ancient Greece itself were not more
thickly haunted by the phantoms of a fairy mythology than
are the barren sun-scorched steppes and stony hills of the
Australian wilderness; but great indeed is the gulf which
divides the beautiful creations of Greek fancy from the crude
imaginings of the Australian savage, whose legendary tales
are for the most part a mere tissue of trivial absurdities
unrelieved by a single touch of beauty or poetry.

A journey through the Warramunga country.

To illustrate at once the nature and the abundance of these
legends I will quote a passage in which Messrs. Spencer and
Gillen describe a journey they took in company with some
Warramunga natives over part of their country :—" For the
first two days our way lay across miserable plain country
covered with poor scrub, with here and there low ranges rising.
Every prominent feature of any kind was associated with
some tradition of their past.   A range some five miles away
from Tennant Creek arose to mark the path traversed by
the great ancestor of the Pittongu (bat) totem.   Several
miles further on a solitary upstanding column of rock represented an opossum man who rested here, looked about the
country, and left spirit children behind him ; a low range of
remarkably white quartzite hills indicated a large number of
white ant eggs thrown here in the *wingara* [1] by the Mungamunga women as they passed across the country.   A solitary
flat-topped hill arose to mark the spot where the Wongana
(crow) ancestor paused for some time to pierce his nose ;
and on the second night we camped by the side of a water-
hole where the same crow lived for some time in the
wingara, and where now there are plenty of crow spirit
children.   All the time, as we travelled along, the old men
were talking amongst themselves about the natural features
associated in tradition with these and other totemic ancestors
of the tribe, and pointing them out to us.   On the third
day we travelled, at first for some hours, by the side of a

[1] The *wingara* is the equivalent of
the Arunta *alcheringa*, that is, the
earliest legendary or mythical times of
which the natives profess to have
knowledge.

river-bed,—perfectly dry of course,—and passed the spot
where two hawks first made fire by rubbing sticks together,
two fine gum-trees on the banks now representing the place
where they stood up.   A few miles further on we came to a
water-hole by the side of which the moon-man met a bandicoot woman, and while the two were talking together the
fire made by the hawks crept upon them and burnt the
woman, who was, however, restored to life again by the
moon-man, with whom she then went up into the sky.   Late
in the afternoon we skirted the eastern base of the Murchison Range, the rugged quartzite hills in this part being
associated partly with the crow ancestor and partly with
the bat.   Following up a valley leading into the hills we
camped, just after sunset, by the side of a rather picturesque
water-pool amongst the ranges.   A short distance before
reaching this the natives pointed out a curious red cliff,
standing out amongst the low hills which were elsewhere
covered with thin scrub.   This, which is called Tjiti, represents the spot where an old woman spent a long time
digging for yams, the latter being indicated by great heaps
of stones lying all around.   On the opposite side of the
valley a column of stone marks the spot where the woman
went into the earth.   The water-hole by which we were
camped was called Wiarminni.   It was in reality a deep
pool in the bed of a creek coming down from the hills.
Behind it the rocks rose abruptly, and amongst them there
was, or rather would have been if a stream had been flowing,
a succession of cascades and rocky water-holes.   Two of the
latter, just above Wiarminni, are connected with a fish totem,
and represent the spot where two fish men arose in the
alcheringa, fought one another, left spirit children behind, and
finally went down into the ground.   We were now, so to
speak, in the very midst of *mungai* [*i.e.* of places associated
with the totems], for the old totemic ancestors of the tribe,
who showed a most commendable fondness for arising and
walking about in the few picturesque spots which their
country contained, had apparently selected these rocky
gorges as their central home.   All around us the water-
holes, gorges, and rocky crags were peopled with spirit individuals left behind by one or other of the following totemic

ancestors :—Wollunqua, Pittongu (bat), Wongana (crow), wild dog, emu, bandicoot, and fish, whose lines of travel in the *alcheringa* formed a regular network over the whole countryside." [1]

Dramatic ceremonies to commemorate the doings of ancestors.

Similar evidence could be multiplied, but this may suffice to teach us how to the minds of these Central Australian savages the whole country is haunted, in the literal sense, not merely by the memories of their dead, but by the spirits which they left behind them and which are constantly undergoing reincarnation. And not only are the minds of the aborigines preoccupied by the thought of their ancestors, who are recalled to them by all the familiar features of the landscape, but they spend a considerable part of their time in dramatically representing the legendary doings of their rude forefathers of the remote past. It is astonishing, we are told, how large a part of a native's life is occupied with the performance of these dramatic ceremonies. The older he grows, the greater is the share he takes in them, until at last they actually absorb the greater part of his thoughts. The rites which seem so trivial to us are most serious matters to him. They are all connected with the great ancestors of the tribe, and he is firmly convinced that when he dies his spirit will rejoin theirs and live in communion with them until the time comes for him to be born again into the world. With such solemnity does he look on the celebration of these commemorative services, as we may call them, that none but initiated men are allowed to witness them ; women and children are strictly excluded from the spectacle. These sacred dramas are often, though by no means always, associated with the rites of initiation which young men have to pass through before they are admitted to full membership of the tribe and to participation in its deepest mysteries. The rites of initiation are not all undergone by a youth at the same time ; they succeed each other at longer or shorter intervals of time, and at each of them he is privileged to witness some of the solemn ceremonies in which the traditions of the tribal ancestors are dramatically set forth before him, until, when he has passed through the last of the rites and ordeals, he is free to behold and to take part in the whole

[1] Spencer and Gillen, *Northern Tribes of Central Australia*, pp. 249 *sq.*

series of mystery plays or professedly historical dramas. Sometimes the performance of these dramas extends over two or three months, during which one or more of them are acted daily.[1] For the most part, they are very short and simple, each of them generally lasting only a few minutes, though the costumes of the actors are often elaborate and may have taken hours to prepare. I will describe a few of them as samples.

We will begin with a ceremony of the Hakea flower totem in the Arunta tribe, as to which it may be premised that a decoction of the Hakea flower is a favourite drink of the natives. The little drama was acted by two men, each of whom was decorated on his bare body by broad bands of pearly grey edged with white down, which passed round his waist and over his shoulders, contrasting well with the chocolate colour of his skin. On his head each of them wore a kind of helmet made of twigs, and from their ears hung tips of the tails of rabbit-bandicoots. The two sat on the ground facing each other with a shield between them. One of them held in his hand some twigs representing the Hakea flower in bloom ; these he pretended to steep in water so as to brew the favourite beverage of the natives, and the man sitting opposite him made believe to suck it up with a little mop. Meantime the other men ran round and round them shouting *wha ! wha !* This was the substance of the play, which ended as usual by several men placing their hands on the shoulders of the performers as a signal to them to stop.[2] *Ceremony of the Hakea flower totem.*

Again, to take another Arunta ceremony of a fish totem called *interpitna*. The fish is the bony bream (*Chatoessus horni*), which abounds in the water-holes of the country. The play was performed by a single actor, an old man, whose face was covered with a mass of white down contrasting strongly with a large bunch of black eagle-hawk feathers which he wore on his head. His body was decorated with bands of charcoal edged with white down. Squatting on the ground he moved his body and extended his arms *Ceremony of a fish totem.*

---

[1] Spencer and Gillen, *Northern Tribes of Central Australia*, pp. 33 *sq.*, 177 *sq.*

[2] Spencer and Gillen, *Native Tribes of Central Australia*, pp. 297 *sq.*

from his sides, opening and closing them as he leaned forwards, so as to imitate a fish swelling itself out and opening and closing its gills. Then, holding twigs in his hands, he moved along mimicking the action of a man who drives fish before him with a branch in a pool, just as the natives do to catch the fish. Meantime an orchestra of four men squatted beside him singing and beating time with a stick on the ground.[1]

Ceremony of a plum-tree totem.

Again, another Arunta ceremony of the plum-tree totem was performed by four actors, who simply pretended to knock down and eat imaginary plums from an imaginary plum-tree.[2] An interesting point in this very simple drama is that in it the men of the plum-tree totem are represented eating freely of their totem, which is quite contrary to the practice of the present day, but taken along with many similar ceremonies it goes far to prove that in the ancient days, to which all these dramatic ceremonies refer, it was the regular practice for men and women of a totem to eat their totemic animals or plants. As another example of a drama in which the performers are represented eating their totem we may take a ceremony of the ant totem in the Warramunga tribe. The legendary personages who figure in it are two women of the ant totem, ancestresses of the ant clan, who are said to have devoted all their time to catching and eating ants, except when they were engaged in the performance of ceremonies. The two men who personated these women in the drama (for no woman is allowed to witness, much less to act in, these sacred dramas) had the whole of the upper parts of their bodies, including their faces and the cylindrical helmets which they wore on their heads, covered with a dense mass of little specks of red down. These specks stood for the ants, alive or dead, and also for the stones and trees on the spots where the two women encamped. In the drama the two actors thus arrayed walked about the ground as if they were searching for ants to eat. Each of them carried a wooden trough and stooping down from time to time he turned over the ground and picked up small stones which he placed in the trough

[1] Spencer and Gillen, *Native Tribes of Central Australia*, pp. 316 *sq.*   [2] Spencer and Gillen, *op. cit.* p. 320.

till it was full. The stones represented the masses of ants which the women gathered for food. After carrying on this pantomime for a time the two actors pretended to discover each other with surprise and to embrace with joy, much to the amusement of the spectators.[1]

In all these ceremonies you will observe that the action of the drama is strictly appropriate to the totem. In the drama of the Hakea flower totem the actors pretend to make and drink the beverage brewed from Hakea flowers ; in the ceremony of the fish totem the actor feigns to be a fish and also to catch fish ; in the ceremony of the plum-tree totem the actors pretend to knock down and eat plums ; and in the ceremony of the ant totem the actors make believe to gather ants for food. Similarly, to take a few more examples, in a ceremony of the witchetty grub totem of the Arunta tribe the body of the actor was decorated with lines of white and red down, and he had a shield adorned with a number of concentric circles of down. The smaller circles represented the bush on which the grub lives first of all, and the larger circles represented the bush on which the adult insect lays its eggs. When all was ready, the performer seated himself on the ground and imitated the grub, alternately doubling himself up and rising on his knees, while he extended his arms and made them quiver in imitation of the insect's wings ; and every now and then he would bend over the shield and sway to and fro, and up and down, in imitation of the insect hovering over the bushes on which it lays its eggs.[2] In another ceremony of the witchetty grub totem, which followed immediately the one I have just described, the actor had two shields beside him. The smaller of the shields was ornamented with zigzag lines of white pipe-clay which were supposed to indicate the tracks of the grub ; the larger shield was covered with larger and smaller series of concentric circles, the larger representing the seeds of a bush on which the insect feeds, while the smaller stood for the eggs of the adult insect. As before, the actor wriggled and flapped his arms in imitation of the fluttering of the insect when it first

In these ceremonies the action is appropriate to the totem.

Ceremony of the witchetty grub totem.

---

[1] Spencer and Gillen, *Northern Tribes of Central Australia*, pp. 199-204.

[2] Spencer and Gillen, *Northern Tribes of Central Australia*, pp. 179 *sq.*

leaves its chrysalis case in the ground and attempts to fly. In acting thus he was supposed to represent a celebrated ancestor of the witchetty grub totem.[1]

Ceremony of the emu totem.   The last example of such ceremonies which I shall cite is one of the emu totem in the Arunta tribe. The body of the actor was decorated with perpendicular lines of white down reaching from his shoulders to his knees ; and on his head he supported a towering head-piece tipped with a bunch of emu feathers in imitation of the neck and head of an emu. Thus arrayed he stalked backwards and forwards in the aimless fashion of the bird.[2]

These dramatic ceremonies were probably at first magical rites intended to supply the people with food and other necessaries.   What are we to think of the intention of these little dramas which the Central Australian aborigines regard as sacred and to the performance of which they devote so much time and labour? At first sight they are simply commemorative services, designed to represent the ancestors as they lived and moved in the far-past times, to recall their adventures, of which legend has preserved the memory, and to set them dramatically before the eyes of their living descendants. So far, therefore, the dramas might be described as purely historical in intention, if not in reality. But there are reasons for thinking that in all cases a deeper meaning underlies, or formerly underlay, the performance of all these apparently simple historical plays ; in fact, we may suspect that originally they were all magical ceremonies observed for the practical purpose of supplying the people with food, water, sunshine, and everything else of which they stand in need. This conclusion is suggested first of all by the practice of the Arunta and other Central Australian tribes, who observe very similar ceremonies with the avowed intention of thereby multiplying the totemic animals and plants in order that they may be eaten by the tribe, though not by the particular clan which has these animals or plants for its totem. It is true that the Arunta distinguish these magical ceremonies for the multiplication of the totems from what we may call the more purely commemorative or historical performances, and they have a

[1] Spencer and Gillen, *Northern Tribes of Central Australia*, pp. 179 sq.

[2] Spencer and Gillen, *Native Tribes of Central Australia*, pp. 358 sq., and p. 343, fig. 73.

special name for the former, namely *intichiuma*, which they do not bestow on the latter. Yet these *intichiuma* or magical ceremonies resemble the commemorative ceremonies so closely that it is difficult to suppose they can always have been wholly distinct. For example, in the magical ceremonies for the multiplication of witchetty grubs the performers pretend to be the insects emerging from their chrysalis cases,[1] just as the actors do in the similar commemorative ceremony which I have described; and again in a magical ceremony for the multiplication of emus the performers wear head-dresses to represent the long neck and small head of the bird, and they mimic its gait,[2] exactly as the actors do in the commemorative ceremony. It seems reasonable, therefore, to conjecture that the ceremonies which now are, or seem to be, purely commemorative or historical were originally magical in intention, being observed for the practical purpose of multiplying edible animals and plants or supplying other wants of the tribe.

Now this conjecture is strongly confirmed by the actual usage of the Warramunga tribe, amongst whom the commemorative or historical dramas are avowedly performed as magical rites: in other words, the Warramunga attribute a magical virtue to the simple performance of such dramas: they think that by merely acting the parts of their totemic ancestors they thereby magically multiply the edible animals or plants which these ancestors had for their totems. Hence in this tribe the magical ceremonies and the dramatic performances practically coincide: with them, as Messrs. Spencer and Gillen say, the *intichiuma* or magical ceremonies (called by the Warramunga *thalamminta*) "for the most part simply consist in the performance of a complete series representing the *alcheringa* history of the totemic ancestor. In this tribe each totemic group has usually one great ancestor, who arose in some special spot and walked across the country, making various natural features as he did so,—creeks, plains, ranges, and water-holes,—and leaving behind him spirit individuals who have since been reincarnated. The *intichiuma* [or magical] ceremony of the totem really consists in tracking

Among the Warramunga these dramatic ceremonies are avowedly performed as magical rites.

---

[1] Spencer and Gillen, *Native Tribes of Central Australia*, p. 176.

[2] Spencer and Gillen, *op. cit.* pp. 182 *sq.*

these ancestors' paths, and repeating, one after the other, ceremonies commemorative of what are called the *mungai* spots,
the equivalent of the *oknanikilla* amongst the Arunta—that
is, the places where he left the spirit children behind."[1]
Apparently the Warramunga imagine that by imitating a
totemic ancestor at the very place where he left spirit children
of the same totem behind him, they thereby enable these
spirit children to be born again and so increase the food
supply, whenever their totem is an edible animal or plant;
for we must always remember that in the mind of these
savages the idea of a man or woman is inextricably confused
with the idea of his or her totem; they seem unable to distinguish between the two, and therefore they believe that
in multiplying human beings at their local totemic centres
(*mungai* or *oknanikilla*) they simultaneously multiply their
totems; and as the totems are commonly edible animals
and plants, it follows that in the opinion of the Warramunga
the general effect of performing these ancestral plays is to
increase the supply of food of the tribe. No wonder, therefore, that the dramas are sacred, and that the natives attribute
the most serious significance to their performance: the neglect
to perform them might, in their judgment, bring famine and
ruin on the whole tribe. As Messrs. Spencer and Gillen,
speaking of these ceremonies, justly observe: "Their proper
performance is a matter of very great importance in the eyes
of the natives, because, not only do they serve to keep alive
and hand down from generation to generation the traditions
of the tribe, but they are, at least amongst the Warramunga,
intimately associated with the most important object of main-
taining the food supply, as every totemic group is held
responsible for the maintenance of the material object the
name of which it bears."[2]

General view of the attitude of the Central Australian natives towards their dead.

To sum up the attitude of the Central Australian natives
towards their dead. They believe that their dead are constantly undergoing reincarnation by being born again of
women into the world, in fact that every living man, woman,
and child is nothing but a dead person come to life again,
that so it has been from the beginning and that so it will be

[1] Spencer and Gillen, *Northern Tribes of Central Australia*, p. 297.

[2] Spencer and Gillen, *Northern Tribes of Central Australia*, p. 197.

to the end.   Of a special world of the departed, remote and
different from the material world in which they live and from
the familiar scenes to which they have been accustomed from
infancy, they have no conception ; still less, if that is possible,
have they any idea of a division of the world of the dead
into a realm of bliss and a realm of woe, where the spirits of
the good live ineffably happy and the spirits of the bad live
unspeakably miserable.   To their simple minds the spirits of
the dead dwell all about them in the rocky gorges, the barren
plains, the wooded dells, the rustling trees, the still waters of
their native land, haunting in death the very spots where they
last entered into their mothers' wombs to be born, and where
in future they will again enter into the wombs of other women
to be born again as other children into the world.   And so,
they think, it will go on for ever and ever.   Such a creed
seems at first sight, as I have pointed out, irreconcilable
with a worship of the dead in the proper sense of the word ;
and so perhaps it would be, if these savages were strictly
consistent and logical in their theories.   But they are not.
They admit that their remote ancestors, in other words, that
they themselves in former incarnations, possessed certain
marvellous powers to which in the present degenerate days
they can lay no claim ; and in this significant admission we
may detect a rift, a real distinction of kind, between the living
and the dead, which in time might widen out into an impassable gulf.   In other words, we may suppose that the
Central Australians, if left to themselves, might come to hold
that the dead return no more to the land of the living, and
that, acknowledging as they do the vast superiority of their
remote ancestors to themselves, they might end by worshipping them, at first simply as powerful ancestral spirits, and
afterwards as supernatural deities, whose original connexion
with humanity had been totally forgotten.   In point of fact
we saw that among the Warramunga the mythical water-
snake Wollunqua, who is regarded as an ancestor of a
totemic clan, has made some progress towards deification ;
for while he is still regarded as the forefather of the clan
which bears his name, it is no longer supposed that he is
born again of women into the world, but that he lives eternal
and invisible under the water of a haunted pool, and that he

has it in his power both to help and to harm his people, who pray to him and perform ceremonies in his honour. This awful being, whose voice is heard in the peal of thunder and whose dreadful name may not be pronounced in common life, is not far from godhead; at least he is apparently the nearest approach to it which the imagination of these rude savages has been able to conceive. Lastly, as I have pointed out, the reverence which the Central Australians entertain for their dead ancestors is closely bound up with their totemism; they fail to distinguish clearly or at all between men and their totems, and accordingly the ceremonies which they perform to commemorate the dead are at the same time magical rites designed to ensure an abundant supply of food and of all the other necessaries and conveniences which savage life requires or admits of; indeed, we may with some probability conjecture that the magical intention of these ceremonies is the primary and original one, and that the commemorative intention is secondary and derivative. If that could be proved to be so (which is hardly to be expected), we should be obliged to conclude that in this as in so many enquiries into the remote human past we detect evidence of an Age of Magic preceding anything that deserves to be dignified with the name of religion.

That ends what I have to say at present as to the belief in immortality and the worship of the dead among the Central Australian aborigines. In my next lecture I propose to pursue the enquiry among the other tribes of Australia.

LECTURE VI

THE BELIEF IN IMMORTALITY AMONG THE OTHER
ABORIGINES OF AUSTRALIA

IN the last lecture I concluded my account of the beliefs Customs and practices of the Central Australian aborigines in regard to the dead. To-day I propose to consider the customs and beliefs concerning the dead which prevail among the native tribes in other parts of Australia. But at the outset I must warn you that our information as to these other tribes is far less full and precise than that which we possess as to the tribes of the centre, which have had the great advantage of being observed and described by two highly qualified scientific observers, Messrs. Spencer and Gillen. Our knowledge of all other Australian tribes is comparatively fragmentary, and accordingly it is impossible to give even an approximately complete view of their notions concerning the state of the human spirit after death, and of the rites which they observe for the purpose of disarming or propitiating the souls of the departed. We must therefore content ourselves with more or less partial glimpses of this side of native religion.

The first question we naturally ask is whether the belief in the reincarnation of the dead, which prevails universally among the Central tribes, reappears among tribes in other parts of the continent. It certainly does so, and although the evidence on this subject is very imperfect it suffices to raise a presumption that a similar belief in the rebirth or reincarnation of the dead was formerly universal among the Australian aborigines. Unquestionably the belief is entertained by some of the natives of Queensland, who have been

Customs
and beliefs
concerning
the dead in
the other
tribes of
Australia.

Belief in
the re-
incarnation
of the dead
among the
natives of
Queens-
land.

described for us by Mr. W. E. Roth. Thus, for example, the aborigines on the Pennefather River think that every person's spirit undergoes a series of reincarnations, and that in the interval between two reincarnations the spirit resides in one or other of the haunts of Anjea, a mythical being who causes conception in women by putting mud babies into their bodies. Such spots, haunted by the fabulous being Anjea and by the souls of the dead awaiting rebirth, may be a tree, a rock, or a pool of water; they clearly correspond to the local totem centres (*oknanikilla* among the Arunta, *mungai* among the Warramunga) of the Central Australian tribes which I described in former lectures. The natives of the Pennefather River observe a ceremony at the birth of a child in order to ascertain the exact spot where its spirit tarried in the interval since its last incarnation; and when they have discovered it they speak of the child as obtained from a tree, a rock, or a pool of water, according to the place from which its spirit is supposed to have passed into its mother.[1]   Readers of the classics can hardly fail to be reminded of the Homeric phrase to be "born of an oak or a rock," [2] which seems to point to a similar belief in the possibility of human souls awaiting reincarnation in the boughs of an oak-tree or in the cleft of a rock. In the opinion of the Pennefather natives all disembodied human spirits or *choi*, as they call them, are mischief-makers and evil-doers, for they make people sick or crazy; but the medicine-men can sometimes control them for good or evil. They wander about in the bush, but there are certain hollow trees or clumps of trees with wide-spreading branches, which they most love to haunt, and they can be heard in the rustling of the leaves or the crackling of the boughs at night. Anjea himself, who puts babies into women, is never seen, but you may hear him laughing in the depths of the forest, among the rocks, in the lagoons, and along the mangrove swamps; and when you hear his laugh you may be sure that he has got a baby.[3]   If a native happens to hurt himself near a tree, he imagines that the spirit of some dead

---

[1] W. E. Roth, *North Queensland Ethnography*, Bulletin No. 5, *Superstition, Magic, and Medicine* (Brisbane, 1903), pp. 18, 23, §§ 68, 83.
[2] Homer, *Odyssey*, xix. 163.
[3] W. E. Roth, *ll.cc.*

person is lurking among the branches, and he will never
cut that tree down lest a worse thing should befall him at
the hands of the vengeful ghost.[1] A curious feature in the
beliefs of these Pennefather natives is that apart from the
spirit called *choi*, which lives in a disembodied state between
two incarnations, every person is supposed to have a spirit
of a different sort called *ngai*, which has its seat in the
heart; they feel it beating within their breast; it talks to
them in sleep and so is the cause of dreams. At death a
man's *ngai* spirit does not go away into the bush to await
reincarnation like his *choi* spirit; on the contrary, it passes
at once into his children, boys and girls alike; for before
their father's death children are supposed not to possess
a *ngai* spirit; if a child dies before its father, they think
that it never had a *ngai* spirit at all. And the *ngai* spirit
may leave a man in his lifetime as well as at death; for
example, when a person faints, the natives think that he does
so because his *ngai* spirit has departed from him, and they will
stamp on the ground to make it return. On the other hand
the *choi* spirit is supposed never to quit a man during life;
it is thought to be in some undefined way related to the
shadow, whereas the *ngai* spirit, as we saw, manifests itself
in the beating of the heart. When a woman dies, her *ngai*
spirit goes not into her children but into her sisters, one
after the other; and when all the sisters are dead, the
woman's *ngai* spirit goes away among the mangroves and
perishes altogether.[2]

Thus these savages explain the phenomena of birth and
death, of conscious and unconscious life, by a theory of a
double human spirit, one associated with the heart and the
other with the shadow. The psychology is rudimentary,
still it is interesting as an attempt to solve problems which
still puzzle civilised man.

Other Queensland aborigines associate the vital principle
not with the heart but with the breath. For example, at
Cape Bedford the natives call it *wau-wu* and think that it
never leaves the body sleeping or waking till death, when it

---

[1] W. E. Roth, *North Queensland
Ethnography, Bulletin No. 5* (Brisbane,
1903), p. 29, § 116.

[2] W. E. Roth, *op. cit.* p. 18,
§ 68.

haunts its place of burial for a time and may communicate with the living.   Thus, like the ghost of Hamlet's father, it will often appear to a near kinsman or intimate friend, tell him the pitiful tale how he was done to death by an enemy, and urge him to revenge.   Again, the soul of a man's dead father or friend may bear him company on a journey and, like the beryl-stone in Rossetti's poem *Rose Mary*, warn him of an ambuscade lurking for him in a spot where the man himself sees nothing.   But the spirits of the dead do not always come with such friendly intent ; they may drive the living distracted ; a peculiar form of mental excitement and bewilderment is attributed to their action.   Further, these aborigines at Cape Bedford, in Queensland, believe that all spirits of nature are in fact souls of the dead.   Such spirits usually leave their haunts in the forests and caves at night.   Stouthearted old men can see and converse with them and receive from them warnings of danger ; but women and children fear these spirits and never see them.   But some spirits of the dead, when they have ceased to haunt their places of burial, go away eastward and are reincarnated in white people ; hence these savages often look for a resemblance to some deceased tribesman among Europeans, and frequently wonder why it is that the white man, on whom their fancy has pitched, remembers nothing about his former life as a black man among blacks.[1]

Beliefs of the natives of the Tully River in Queensland. The natives of the Tully River in Queensland associate the principle of life both with the breath and with the shadow.   It departs from the body temporarily in sleep and fainting-fits and permanently in death, after which it may be heard at night tapping on the top of huts or creaking in the branches of trees.   It is everlasting, so far as these savages have any idea of eternity, and further it is intangible ; hence in its disembodied state it needs no food, and none is set out for it.   The disposition of these disembodied spirits of the dead is good or bad, according to their disposition in life.   Yet when a man is alone by himself, the spirit even of one of his own dead kinsfolk will sometimes come and do him a mischief.   On the other hand it can do nothing to several people together ; there is safety in numbers.   They may all

---

[1] W. E. Roth, *op. cit.* pp. 17, 29, §§ 65, 116.

see and hear the ghost, but he will not attack them.   Hence
these savages have been taught from childhood to beware of
going alone : solitary people are liable at any moment to be
assailed by the spirits of the dead.   The only means they
know of warding off these ghostly assailants is by lighting
good fires.[1]

I have mentioned the belief of the Cape Bedford natives
that the spirits of their dead are sometimes reincarnated in
white people.   A similar notion is reported from other and
widely separated parts of Australia, and wherever it exists
may be taken as evidence of a general belief as to the
rebirth or reincarnation of the dead, even where such a belief
is not expressly recorded.   This superstition has sometimes
proved of service to white people who have been cast among
the blacks, for it has ensured them a hospitable and even
affectionate welcome, where otherwise they might have
encountered suspicion and hostility, if not open violence.
Thus, for example, the convict Buckley, who escaped from
the penal settlement on Port Phillip Bay in 1803, was
found by some of the Wudthaurung tribe carrying a piece
of a broken spear, which he had abstracted from the grave
of one of their people.   So they took him to be the dead
man risen from the grave ; he received the name of the
deceased, was adopted by his relations, and lived with the
tribe for thirty-two years without ever conversing with a
white man ; when at last he met one, he had forgotten the
English language.[2]   Again, a Mr. Naseby, who lived in the
Kamilaroi country for fifty years, happened to have the
marks of cupping on his back, and the natives could not be
persuaded that he was not one of themselves come to life
again with the family scars on his body,[3] for the Australian
aborigines commonly raise scars on the bodies of young
men at initiation.   The late Sir George Grey was identified
by an old Australian woman as her dead son come to
life again.   It may be worth while to quote his account
of this unlooked-for meeting with his long-lost mother ; for

[1] W. E. Roth, *op. cit.* p. 17, § 65.
[2] J. Dawson, *Australian Aborigines*
(Melbourne, Sydney, and Adelaide,
1881), pp. 110 *sq.* ; A. W. Howitt,

Native Tribes of South-East Australia
(London, 1904), p. 442.

[3] A. W. Howitt, *op. cit.* p. 445.

it will impress on you, better than any words of mine could do, the firmness of the faith which these savages repose in the resurrection of the body, or at all events in the reincarnation of the soul. Grey writes as follows:—

Experience of Sir George Grey.

"After we had tethered the horses, and made ourselves tolerably comfortable, we heard loud voices from the hills above us: the effect was fine,—for they really almost appeared to float in the air; and as the wild cries of the women, who knew not our exact position, came by upon the wind, I thought it was well worth a little trouble to hear these savage sounds under such circumstances. Our guides shouted in return, and gradually the approaching cries came nearer and nearer. I was, however, wholly unprepared for the scene that was about to take place. A sort of procession came up, headed by two women, down whose cheeks tears were streaming. The eldest of these came up to me, and looking for a moment at me, said,—' Gwa, gwa, bundo, bal,' —' Yes, yes, in truth it is him'; and then throwing her arms round me, cried bitterly, her head resting on my breast; and although I was totally ignorant of what their meaning was, from mere motives of compassion, I offered no resistance to her caresses, however disagreeable they might be, for she was old, ugly, and filthily dirty; the other younger one knelt at my feet, also crying. At last the old lady, emboldened by my submission, deliberately kissed me on each cheek, just in the manner a Frenchwoman would have done; she then cried a little more, and at length relieving me, assured me that I was the ghost of her son, who had some time before been killed by a spear-wound in his breast. The younger female was my sister; but she, whether from motives of delicacy, or from any imagined backwardness on my part, did not think proper to kiss me. My new mother expressed almost as much delight at my return to my family, as my real mother would have done, had I been unexpectedly restored to her. As soon as she left me, my brothers, and father (the old man who had previously been so frightened), came up and embraced me after their manner,—that is, they threw their arms round my waist, placed their right knee against my right knee, and their breast against my breast, holding me in this way for several minutes.   During the time that the ceremony lasted, I, according to the native custom, preserved a grave and mournful expression of countenance.   This belief, that white people are the souls of departed blacks, is by no means an uncommon superstition amongst them ; they themselves never having an idea of quitting their own land, cannot imagine others doing it ;—and thus, when they see white people suddenly appear in their country, and settling themselves down in particular spots, they imagine that they must have formed an attachment for this land in some other state of existence ; and hence conclude the settlers were at one period black men and their own relations.   Likenesses, whether real or imagined, complete the delusion ; and from the manner of the old woman I have just alluded to, from her many tears, and from her warm caresses, I feel firmly convinced that she really believed I was her son, whose first thought, upon his return to earth, had been to re-visit his old mother, and bring her a present." [1]

On the whole then we may conclude that a belief in the reincarnation of the dead has not been confined to the tribes of Central Australia, but has been held by the tribes in many, perhaps at one time in all, other parts of the continent.   Yet, if we may judge from the imperfect records which we possess, this faith in the return of the dead to life in human form would seem to have given way and been replaced to some extent by a different creed among many tribes of South - eastern Australia.   In this part of the continent it appears to have been often held by the natives that after death the soul is not born again among men, but goes away for ever to some distant country either in the sky or beyond the sea, where all the spirits of the dead congregate.   Thus Lieutenant-Colonel Collins, who was Governor of New South Wales in the early days of the colony, at the end of the eighteenth century, reports that when the natives were often questioned " as to what became of them after their decease, some answered that they went either on or beyond the great water ; but by far the greater number signified,

In South-eastern Australia the natives believed that the souls of the dead were not reborn but went up to the sky.

---

[1] (Sir) George Grey, *Journals of Two Expeditions of Discovery in North-*   *West and Western Australia* (London, 1841), i. 301-303.

that they went to the clouds." [1]   Again, the Narrinyeri tribe
of South Australia believed that all the dead went up to the
sky and that some of them at least became stars. We
possess an excellent description of the beliefs and customs
of this tribe from the pen of a missionary, the Rev. George
Taplin, who lived among them for many years. His account
of their theory of the state of the dead is instructive. It
runs thus :—

Beliefs
of the
Narrinyeri
concerning
the dead.

"The Narrinyeri point out several stars, and say that
they are deceased warriors who have gone to heaven
(*Wyirrewarre*). There are Wyungare, and Nepalle, and the
Manchingga, and several others. Every native expects to
go to *Wyirrewarre* after death. They also believe that the
dead descend from thence, and walk the earth ; and that
they are able to injure those whom they dislike. Consequently, men who have been notorious in life for a
domineering and revengeful disposition are very much
dreaded after death. For instance, there is Karungpe, who
comes in the dead of night, when the camp fire has
burned low, and like a rushing wind scatters the dying
embers, and then takes advantage of the darkness to rob
some sleeper of life ; and it is considered dangerous to
whistle in the dark, for Karungpe is especially attracted
by a whistle. There is another restless spirit—the deceased
father of a boy whom I well know—who is said to rove
about armed with a rope, with which he catches people.
All the Narrinyeri, old and young, are dreadfully afraid of
seeing ghosts, and none of them will venture into the scrub
after dark, lest he should encounter the spirits which are
supposed to roam there. I have heard some admirable
specimens of ghost stories from them. In one case I
remember the ghost was represented to have set fire to a
wurley [hut], and ascended to heaven in the flame. The
Narrinyeri regard the disapprobation of the spirits of the
dead as a thing to be dreaded ; and if a serious quarrel takes
place between near relatives, some of the friends are sure to
interpose with entreaties to the contentious parties to be
reconciled, lest the spirits of the dead should be offended

---

[1] Lieutenant-Colonel David Collins, *An Account of the English Colony in*   *New South Wales*, Second Edition (London, 1804), p. 354.

at unseemly disputes between those who ought to be at peace. The name of the dead must not be mentioned until his body has decayed, lest a want of sorrow should seem to be indicated by the common and flippant use of his name. A native would have the deceased believe that he cannot hear or speak his name without weeping." [1]

From this account it would appear that the Narrinyeri have no belief in the reincarnation of the dead ; they suppose that the souls of the departed live up aloft in the sky, from which they descend at night in the form of ghosts to haunt and trouble the living. On the whole the attitude of the Narrinyeri towards their dead kinsfolk seems to be dominated by fear ; of affection there is apparently little or no trace. It is true that like most Australian tribes they indulge in extravagant demonstrations of grief at the death of their kinsfolk. A great lamentation and wailing is made by all the relations and friends of the deceased. They cut off their hair close to the head and besmudge themselves with oil and pounded charcoal. The women besmear themselves with the most disgusting filth. All beat and cut themselves and make a violent show of sorrow ; and all the time that the corpse, rubbed over with grease and red ochre, is being dried over a slow fire in the hut, the women take it by turns to weep and wail before it, so that the lamentation never ceases for days. Yet Mr. Taplin was persuaded " that fear has more to do with most of these exhibitions than grief " ; and he tells us that " for one minute a woman will appear in the deepest agony of grief and tears ; a few minutes after, the conventional amount of weeping having been accomplished, they will laugh and talk with the merriest." [2] The principal motive, in fact, for all this excessive display of sorrow would seem to be a fear lest the jealous ghost should think himself slighted and should avenge the slight on the cold-hearted relatives who do not mourn sufficiently for the irreparable loss they have sustained by his death. We may conjecture that the same train of thought explains the ancient and widespread

Narrinyeri fear of the dead.

Mourning customs.

[1] Rev. G. Taplin, "The Narrin-yeri," in *Native Tribes of South Australia* (Adelaide, 1879), pp. 18 *sq.*

[2] Rev. G. Taplin, "The Narrinyeri," *op. cit.* pp. 20 *sq.*

custom of hiring professional mourners to wail over the dead ; the tears and lamentations of his kinsfolk are not enough to soothe the wounded feelings of the departed, they must be reinforced by noisier expressions of regret.

Deaths attributed by the Narrinyeri to sorcery. But there is another powerful motive for all these violent demonstrations of grief, into the secret of which we are let by Mr. Taplin. He says that " all the relatives are careful to be present and not to be wanting in the proper signs of sorrow, lest they should be suspected of complicity in causing the death." [1] In fact the Narrinyeri, like many other savages, attribute all, or most, natural deaths to sorcery. When a person dies, they think that he or she has been killed by the evil magic of some ill-wisher, and one of the first things to be done is to discover the culprit in order that his life may be taken in revenge. For this purpose the Narrinyeri resort to a form of divination. On the first night after the death the nearest relation of the deceased sleeps with his head on the corpse, hoping thus to dream of the sorcerer who has done the mischief. Next day the corpse is placed on a sort of bier supported on men's shoulders. The friends of the deceased gather round and call out the names of suspected persons to see whether the corpse will give any sign. At last the next of kin calls out the name of the person of whom he has dreamed, and if at the sound the corpse makes a movement towards him, which the bearers say they cannot resist, it is regarded as a clear token that the man so named is the malefactor. It only remains for the kinsfolk of the dead to hunt down the culprit and kill him.[2] Thus not only the relations but everybody in the neighbourhood has the strongest motive for assuming at least an appearance of sorrow at a death, lest the suspicion of having caused it by sorcery should fall upon him.

Pretence made by the Narrinyeri of avenging the death of their friends on the guilty sorcerer. It deserves to be noted, that while the Narrinyeri nominally acknowledged the duty of killing the sorcerer who in their opinion had caused the death of their friend, they by no means always discharged the duty, but sometimes contented themselves with little more than a pretence of revenge. Mr. Taplin's account of the proceedings ob-

[1] Rev. G. Taplin, *op. cit.* p. 20.   [2] Rev. G. Taplin, *op. cit.* pp. 19 *sq.*, 21.

served on such an occasion is instructive. It runs thus:
"The spirit of the dead is not considered to have been
appeased until his relatives have avenged his death. They
will kill the sorcerer who has caused it if they can catch
him ; but generally they cannot catch him, and often do
not wish it. Most probably he belongs to some other tribe
of the Narrinyeri. Messengers pass between the tribes
relative to the affair, and the friends of the accused person
at last formally curse the dead man and all his dead
relatives. This constitutes a *casus belli.* Arrangements are
forthwith made for a pitched battle, and the two tribes meet
in company with their respective allies. The tribe to which
the dead man belongs weep and make a great lamentation
for him, and the opposing tribe sets some fellows to dance
about and play antics in derision of their enemies. Then
the whole tribe will set up a great laugh by way of further
provocation. If there is any other cause of animosity
between the tribes besides the matter of avenging the dead
there will now be a pretty severe fight with spears. If,
however, the tribes have nothing but the dead man to fight
about, they will probably throw a few spears, indulge in
considerable abuse of each other, perhaps one or two will
get slightly wounded, and then some of the old men will
declare that enough has been done. The dead man is considered to have been appeased by the efforts of his friends
to avenge his death by fighting, and the two tribes are
friendly again. In such a case the fight is a mere ceremony." [1] Thus among the Narrinyeri the duty of blood
revenge was often supposed to be sufficiently discharged by
a sham fight performed apparently for the satisfaction of
the ghost, who was supposed to be looking on and to be
gratified by the sight of his friends hurling spears at the
author of his death. Merciful pretences of the same sort
have been practised by other savages in order to satisfy the
vengeful ghost without the effusion of blood. Examples of
them will come before us later on. [2]

However, the attitude of the Narrinyeri towards their
dead was not purely one of fear and aversion. They
imagined that they could derive certain benefits from their

Magical virtue ascribed to the hair of the dead.

---

[1] Rev. G. Taplin, *op. cit.* p. 21.   [2] See below, pp. 235 *sqq.*, 327 *sq.*

departed kinsfolk, and the channel through which these benefits flowed was furnished by their hair. They cut off the hair of the dead and spun it into a cord, and this cord was commonly worn by the men as a head-band. They said that thereby they "smelled the dead," and that the smell made their eyes large and their sight keen, so that in a fight they could see the spears coming and could parry or avoid them.[1] Similar magical virtues are ascribed to the hair of the dead by the Arunta. Among them the hair of a dead man is cut off and made into a magic girdle, which is a valued possession and is only worn when a man is going out to engage in a tribal fight or to stalk a foe for the purpose of destroying him by witchcraft. The girdle is supposed to be endowed with magic power and to impart to its possessor all the warlike qualities of the dead man from whose hair it was made ; in particular, it is thought to ensure accuracy of aim in the wearer, while at the same time it destroys that of his adversary.[2] Hence the girdle is worn by the man who takes the lead in avenging the death of the deceased on his supposed murderer ; the mere sight of it, they think, so terrifies the victim that his legs tremble under him, he becomes incapable of fighting, and is easily speared.[3]

Belief that the souls of the dead go up to the sky.

Among the tribes of South-eastern Australia the Narrinyeri were not alone in holding the curious belief that the souls of the dead go up into the sky to live there for ever, but that their ghosts come down again from time to time, roam about their old haunts on earth, and communicate with the living. This, for example, was the belief of the Dieri, the Buandik, the Kurnai, and the Kulin tribes.[4] The Buandik thought that everything in skyland was better than on earth ; a fat kangaroo, for example, was compared to a kangaroo of heaven, where, of course, the animals might be expected to abound.[5] The Kulin imagined

[1] Rev. G. Taplin, *op. cit.* p. 21.

[2] Spencer and Gillen, *Native Tribes of Central Australia*, pp. 538 *sq.*

[3] Spencer and Gillen, *Northern Tribes of Central Australia*, pp. 544 *sq.*

[4] A. W. Howitt, *Native Tribes of South-East Australia*, pp. 434, 436, 437, 438. Compare E. J. Eyre, *Journals of Expeditions of Discovery into Central Australia* (London, 1845), ii. 357.

[5] A. W. Howitt, *op. cit.* p. 434.

that the spirits of the dead ascended to heaven by the bright rays of the setting sun.[1] The Wailwun natives in New South Wales used to bury their dead in hollow trees, and when they dropped the body into its place, the bearers and the bystanders joined in a loud whirring sound, like the rush of the wind. They said that this represented the upward flight of the soul to the sky.[2]

With regard to the ghosts on earth, some tribes of South-eastern Australia believe that they can be seen by the living, can partake of food, and can warm themselves at a fire. It is especially the graves, where their mouldering bodies are deposited, that these restless spirits are supposed to haunt; it is there that they shew themselves either to people generally or to such as have the second sight.[3] But it is most commonly in dreams that they appear to the living and hold communication with them. Often these communications are believed to be helpful. Thus the tribes of the Wotjobaluk nation thought that the ghosts of their dead relations could visit them in sleep to protect them. A Mukjarawaint man told Dr. Howitt that his father came to him in a dream and warned him to beware or he would be killed. This, the man believed, was the saving of his life; for he afterwards came to the place which he had seen in his dream; whereupon, instead of going on, he turned back, so that his enemies, who might have been waiting for him there, did not catch him.[4] Another man informed Dr. Howitt that his dead uncle appeared to him in sleep and taught him charms against sickness and other evils; and the Chepara tribe similarly believed that male ancestors visited sleepers and imparted to them charms to avert evil magic.[5]

Such notions follow naturally from the savage theory of dreams. Almost all savages appear to believe firmly in the truth of dreams; they fail to draw the distinction, which to us seems obvious, between the imaginary creations of the mind in sleep and the waking realities of the

Appearance of the dead to the living, especially in dreams.

Savage faith in the truth of dreams.

[1] A. W. Howitt, *op. cit.* p. 438.
[2] Rev. W. Ridley, *Kamilaroi* (Sydney, 1875), p. 160.
[3] A. W. Howitt, *Native Tribes of South-East Australia*, pp. 434, 438, 439; J. Dawson, *Australian Aborigines*, p. 50.
[4] A. W. Howitt, *op. cit.* p. 435.
[5] A. W. Howitt, *op. cit.* p. 437.

physical world. Whatever they dream of must, they think, be actually existing; for have they not seen it with their own eyes? To argue that the visions of sleep have no real existence is, therefore, in their opinion, to argue against the plain evidence of their senses; and they naturally treat such exaggerated scepticism with incredulity and contempt. Hence when they dream of their dead friends and relations they necessarily conclude that these persons are still alive somewhere and somehow, though they do not commonly appear by daylight to people in their waking hours. Un-questionably this savage faith in the reality of dreams has been one of the principal sources of the widespread, almost universal, belief in the survival of the human soul after death. It explains why ghosts are supposed to appear rather by night than by day, since it is chiefly by night that men sleep

and dream dreams. Perhaps it may also partly account for the association of the stars with the souls of the dead. For if the dead appear to the living mainly in the hours of dark-ness, it seems not unnatural to imagine that the bright points of light which then bespangle the canopy of heaven are either the souls of the departed or fires kindled by them in their home aloft. For example, the Central Australian aborigines commonly suppose the stars to be the camp-fires of natives who live on the banks of the great river which we civilised men, by a survival of primitive mythology, call the Milky Way. However, these rude savages, we are told, as a general rule " appear to pay very little attention to the stars in detail, probably because they enter very little into anything which is connected with their daily life, and more especially with their food supply." [1] The same observation which Messrs. Spencer and Gillen here make as to the natives of Central Australia might be applied to most savages who have remained in the purely hunting stage of social development. Such men are not much addicted to star-gazing, since the stars have little or nothing to tell them that they wish to know. It is not till people have betaken themselves to sowing and reaping crops that they begin to scan the heavens more carefully in order to determine the season of sowing by observation of the great celestial

---

[1] Spencer and Gillen, *Northern Tribes of Central Australia*, p. 628.

time-keepers, the rising and setting of certain constellations, above all, apparently, of the Pleiades.[1]   In short, the rise of agriculture favours the rise of astronomy.

But to return to the ideas of the Australian aborigines concerning the dead, we may say of the natives of the south-eastern part of the continent, in the words of Dr. Howitt, that " there is a universal belief in the existence of the human spirit after death, as a ghost, which is able to communicate with the living when they sleep.   It finds its way to the sky-country, where it lives in a land like the earth, only more fertile, better watered, and plentifully supplied with game." [2]   This belief is very different from that of the Central Australian natives, who think that the souls of the dead tarry on earth in their old familiar haunts until the time comes for them to be born again into the world. Of the two different creeds that of the south-eastern tribes may be regarded as the more advanced, since it admits that the dead do not return to life, and that their disembodied spirits do not haunt perpetually a multitude of spiritual parks or reservations dotted over the face of the country.

Creed of the South-eastern Australians touching the dead.

But how are we to account for this marked difference of belief between the natives of the Centre and the natives of the South-east ?   Perhaps the most probable explanation is that the creed of the south-eastern tribes in this respect is part of a general advance of culture brought about by the more favourable natural conditions under which they live as compared with the forlorn state of the rude inhabitants of the Central deserts.   That advance of culture manifests itself in a variety of ways.   On the material side it is seen in more substantial and permanent dwellings and in warmer and better clothing.   On the social side it is seen in an incipient tendency to the rise of a regular chieftainship, a thing which is quite unknown among the democratic or rather oligarchic savages of the Centre, who are mainly governed by the old men in council.[3]   But the rise of chieftainship is a great step in political progress ; since a

The creed seems to form part of a general advance of culture in this part of the continent.

---

[1] As to the place occupied by the Pleiades in primitive calendars, see *Spirits of the Corn and of the Wild,* i. 309-319.

[2] A. W. Howitt, *Native Tribes of South-East Australia,* pp. 439 *sq.*

[3] See *Totemism and Exogamy,* i. 314 *sqq.*

monarchical government of some sort appears to be essential to the emergence of mankind from savagery.   On the whole, then, the beliefs of the South-eastern Australian aborigines seem to mark a step on the upward road towards civilisation.

Possible influence of European teaching on native beliefs.

At the same time we must not forget that these beliefs may have been influenced by the lessons which they have learned from white settlers with whom in this part of Australia they have been so long in contact.   The possibility of such a transfusion of the new wine of Europe into the old bottles of Australia did not escape the experienced Mr. James Dawson, an early settler in Victoria, who has given us a valuable account of the natives of that region in the old days when they were still comparatively little contaminated by intercourse with the whites.   He describes as follows the views which prevailed as to the dead among the tribes of Western Victoria :—" After the disposal of the body of a good person, its shade walks about for three days ; and although it appears to people, it holds no communication with them.   Should it be seen and named by anyone during these three days, it instantly disappears.   At the expiry of three days it goes off to a beautiful country above the clouds, abounding with kangaroo and other game, where life will be enjoyed for ever.   Friends will meet and recognize each other there ; but there will be no marrying, as the bodies have been left on earth.   Children under four or five years have no souls and no future life.   The shades of the wicked wander miserably about the earth for one year after death, frightening people, and then descend to Ummekulleen, never to return."   After giving us this account of the native creed Mr. Dawson adds very justly : " Some of the ideas described above may possibly have originated with the white man, and been transmitted from Sydney by one tribe to another." [1]   The probability of white influence on this particular doctrine of religion is increased

---

[1] J. Dawson, *Australian Aborigines*, p. 51.   A man of the Ta-ta-thi tribe in New South Wales informed Mr. A. L. P. Cameron that the natives believed in a pit of fire where bad men were roasted after death.   This reported belief, resting apparently on the testimony of a single informant, may without doubt be ascribed to the influence of Christian teaching.   See A. L. P. Cameron, " Notes on some Tribes of New South Wales," *Journal of the Anthropological Institute*, xiv. (1885) pp. 364 *sq.*

by the frank confession which these same natives made of the religious deterioration (as they regarded it) which they had suffered in another direction through the teaching of the missionaries.   On this subject, to quote again from Mr. Dawson, the savages are of opinion that " the good spirit, Pirnmeheeal, is a gigantic man, living above the clouds ; and as he is of a kindly disposition, and harms no one, he is seldom mentioned, but always with respect.   His voice, the thunder, is listened to with pleasure, as it does good to man and beast, by bringing rain, and making grass and roots grow for their benefit.   But the aborigines say that the missionaries and government protectors have given them a dread of Pirnmeheeal ; and they are sorry that the young people, and many of the old, are now afraid of a being who never did any harm to their forefathers." [1]

However, it is very difficult to ascertain the exact beliefs of savages as to the dead.   The thought of the savage is apt to be vague and inconsistent ; he neither represents his ideas clearly to his own mind nor can he express them lucidly to others, even if he wishes to do so.   And his thought is not only vague and inconsistent ; it is fluid and unstable, liable to shift and change under alien influence. For these and other reasons, such as the distrust of strangers and the difficulty of language, which often interposes a formidable barrier between savage man and the civilised enquirer, the domain of primitive beliefs is beset by so many snares and pitfalls that we might almost despair of arriving at the truth, were it not that we possess a clue to guide us on the dark and slippery way.   That clue is action.   While it is generally very difficult to ascertain what any man thinks, it is comparatively easy to ascertain what he does ; and what a man does, not what he says, is the surest touchstone to his real belief.   Hence when we attempt to study the religion of backward races, the ritual which they practise is generally a safer indication of their actual creed than the loudest profession of faith. In regard to the state of the human soul after death the beliefs of the Australian aborigines are clearly reflected in many of the customs which they observe at the death and

Vagueness and inconsistency of native beliefs as to the state of the dead.

Custom or ritual as the interpreter of belief.

---

[1] J. Dawson, *Australian Aborigines,* p. 49.

burial of their friends and enemies, and it is accordingly with an account of some of these customs that I propose to conclude this part of my subject.

Burial customs of the Australian aborigines as evidence of their beliefs concerning the state of the soul after death.

Food placed on the grave for the use of the ghost and fires kindled to warm him.

Now some of the burial customs observed by the Australian savages reveal in the clearest manner their belief that the human soul survives the death of the body, that in its disembodied state it retains consciousness and feeling, and can do a mischief to the living ; in short, they shew that in the opinion of these people the departed live in the form of dangerous ghosts. Thus, for example, when the deceased is a person of importance, the Dieri place food for many days on the grave, and in winter they kindle a fire in order that the ghost may warm himself at it. If the food remains untouched on the grave, they think that the dead is not hungry.[1] The Blanch-water section of that tribe fear the spirits of the dead and accordingly take steps to prevent their resurrection. For that purpose they tie the toes of the corpse together and the thumbs behind the back, which must obviously make it difficult for the dead man to arise in his might and pursue them. Moreover, for a month after the death they sweep a clear space round the grave at dusk every evening, and inspect it every morning. If they find any tracks on it, they assume that they have been made by the restless ghost in his nocturnal peregrinations, and accordingly they dig up his mouldering remains and bury them in some other place, where they hope he will sleep sounder.[2] The Kukata tribe think that the ghost may be thirsty, so they obligingly leave a drinking vessel on the grave, that he may slake his thirst. Also they deposit spears and other weapons on the spot, together with a digging-stick, which is specially intended to ward off evil spirits who may be on the prowl.[3] The ghosts of the natives on the Maranoa river were also thirsty souls, so vessels full of water were sometimes suspended for their use over the grave.[4] A custom of lighting a fire on the

[1] A. W. Howitt, *Native Tribes of South-East Australia*, p. 448.
[2] A. W. Howitt, *op. cit.* p. 449. Compare E. M. Curr, *The Australian Race*, i. 87 : " The object sought in tying up the remains of the dead is to prevent the deceased from escaping from the tomb and frightening or injuring the survivors."
[3] A. W. Howitt, *op. cit.* p. 451.
[4] A. W. Howitt, *op. cit.* p. 467.

grave to warm the poor shivering ghost seems to have been not uncommon among the aboriginal Australians. The Western Victorians, for example, kept up large fires all night for this purpose.[1] In the Wiimbaio tribe two fires were kept burning for a whole month on the grave, one to the right and the other to the left, in order that the ghost might come out and warm himself at them in the chill night air. If they found tracks near the grave, they inferred, like the Dieri, that the perturbed spirit had quitted his narrow bed to pace to and fro in the long hours of darkness ; but if no footprints were visible they thought that he slept in peace.[2] In some parts of Western Australia the natives maintained fires on the grave for more than a month for the convenience of the ghost ; and they clearly expected him to come to life again, for they detached the nails from the thumb and forefinger of the corpse and deposited them in a small hole beside the grave, in order that they might know their friend at his resurrection.[3] The length of time during which fires were maintained or kindled daily on the grave is said to have varied, according to the estimation in which the man was held, from a few days to three or four years.[4] We have seen that the Dieri laid food on the grave for the hungry ghost to partake of, and the same custom was observed by the Gournditch-mara tribe.[5] However, some intelligent old aborigines of Western Victoria derided the custom as " white fellow's gammon." [6]

Further, in some tribes of South-eastern Australia it was customary to deposit the scanty property of the deceased, usually consisting of a few rude weapons or implements, on the grave or to bury it with him. Thus the natives of Western Victoria buried all a dead man's orna-ments, weapons, and property with him in the grave, only reserving his stone axes, which were too valuable to be thus

Property of the dead buried with them.

[1] J. Dawson, *Australian Aborigines*, p. 50.
[2] A. W. Howitt, *Native Tribes of South-East Australia*, p. 452.
[3] R. Salvado, *Mémoires historiques sur l'Australie* (Paris, 1854), p. 261 ; *Missions Catholiques*, x. (1878) p. 247. For more evidence as to the lighting of fires for this purpose see A. W. Howitt, *op. cit.* pp. 455, 470.
[4] A. Oldfield, "The Aborigines of Australia," *Transactions of the Ethnological Society of London*, New Series, iii. (1865) p. 245.
[5] A. W. Howitt, *op. cit.* p. 455.
[6] J. Dawson, *Australian Aborigines*, pp. 50 *sq.*

sacrificed : these were inherited by the next of kin.[1]   The
Wurunjerri also interred the personal property of the dead
with him ; if the deceased was a man, his spear-thrower
was stuck in the ground at the head of the grave ; if
the deceased was a woman, the same thing was done with
her digging-stick.   That these implements were intended
for the use of the ghost and not merely as headstones
to mark the situation of the tomb and the sex of the
departed, is clear from a significant exception to the custom.
When the departed brother was a man of violent temper,
who had been quarrelsome and a brawler in his life, no
weapons were buried with him, obviously lest in a fit of
ill-temper he should sally from the grave and assault
people with them.[2]   Similarly the Turrbal tribe, who
deposited their dead in the forks of trees, used to leave
a spear and club near the corpse " that the spirit of the
dead might have weapons wherewith to kill game for his
sustenance in the future state.   A yam-stick was placed in
the ground at a woman's grave, so that she might go away
at night and seek for roots." [3]   The Wolgal tribe were very
particular about burying everything that belonged to a
dead man with him ; spears and nets, though valuable
articles of property, were thus sacrificed ; even a canoe has
been known to be cut up in order that the pieces of it
might be deposited in the grave.   In fact " everything
belonging to a dead man was put out of sight." [4]   Similarly
in the Geawe-gal tribe all the implements and inanimate
property of a warrior were interred with him.[5]   In the
Gringai country not only was all a man's property buried
with him, but every native present at the burial contributed
something, and these contributions were piled together at
the head of the corpse before the grave was filled in.[6]
Among the tribes of Southern Victoria, when the grave
has been dug and lined with fresh leaves and twigs so as
to make a soft bed, the dead man's property is brought in
two bags, and the sorcerer shakes out the contents.   They

[1] J. Dawson, *op. cit.* p. 63.
[2] A. W. Howitt, *Native Tribes of South-East Australia*, p. 458.
[3] A. W. Howitt, *op. cit.* p. 470.
[4] A. W. Howitt, *op. cit.* pp. 461 sq.
[5] A. W. Howitt, *op. cit.* p. 464.
[6] A. W. Howitt, *op. cit.* p. 464.

consist of such small articles as pieces of hard stone suitable for cutting or paring skins, bones for boring holes, twine made of opossum wool, and so forth. These are placed in the grave, and the bags and rugs of the deceased are torn up and thrown in likewise. Then the sorcerer asks whether the dead man had any other property, and if he had, it is brought forward and laid beside the torn fragments of the bags and rugs. Everything that a man owned in life must be laid beside him in death.[1] Again, among the tribes of the Lower Murray, Lachlan, and Darling rivers in New South Wales, all a dead man's property, including his weapons and nets, was buried with his body in the grave.[2] Further, we are told that among the natives of Western Australia the weapons and personal property of the deceased are placed on the grave, "so that when he rises from the dead they may be ready to his hand."[3] In the Boulia district of Queensland the things which belonged to a dead man, such as his boomerangs and spears, are either buried with him, destroyed by fire, or sometimes, though rarely, distributed among his tribal brothers, but never among his children.[4]

Thus among certain tribes of Australia, especially in the south-eastern part of the continent, it appears that the custom of burying or destroying a dead man's property has been very common. That the intention of the custom in some cases is to supply the supposed needs of the ghost, seems to be fairly certain ; but we may doubt whether this explanation would apply to the practice of burning or otherwise destroying the things which had belonged to the deceased. More probably such destruction springs from an overpowering dread of the ghost and a wish to sever all connexion with him, so that he may have no excuse for returning and haunting the survivors, as he might do if his

Intention of destroying the property of the dead.

[1] R. Brough Smyth, *The Aborigines of Victoria*, i. 104.

[2] P. Beveridge, "Of the Aborigines inhabiting the Great Lacustrine and Riverine Depression of the Lower Murray, Lower Murrumbidgee, Lower Lachlan, and Lower Darling," *Journal and Proceedings of the Royal Society of New South Wales*, xvii. (1883) p. 29.

[3] A. Oldfield, "The Aborigines of Australia," *Transactions of the Ethnological Society of London*, New Series, iii. (1865) p. 245.

[4] W. E. Roth, *Ethnological Studies among the North-West-Central Queensland Aborigines* (Brisbane and London, 1897), p. 164.

property were either kept by them or deposited in the

The
property
of the
dead not
destroyed
in Central
Australia.

grave. Whatever the motive for the burial or destruction of a dead man's property may be, the custom appears not to prevail among the tribes of Central Australia. In the eastern Arunta tribe, indeed, it is said that sometimes a little wooden vessel used in camp for holding small objects may be buried with the man, but this is the only instance which Messrs. Spencer and Gillen could hear of in which any article of ordinary use is buried in the grave. Far from wasting property in that way, these economical savages preserve even a man's personal ornaments, such as his necklaces, armlets, and the fur string which he wore round his head ; indeed, as we have seen, they go so far as to cut off the hair from the head of the deceased and to keep it for magical uses.[1] In the Warramunga tribe all the belongings of a dead man go to the tribal brothers of his mother.[2]

Property of
the dead
hung up on
trees, then
washed and
distributed.

The difference in this respect between the practice of the Central tribes and that of the tribes nearer the sea, especially in Victoria and New South Wales, is very notable. A custom intermediate between the two is observed by some tribes of the Darling River, who hang up the weapons, nets, and other property of the deceased on trees for about two months, then wash them, and distribute them among the relations.[3] The reason for hanging the things up and washing them is no doubt to rid them of the infection of death in order that they may be used with safety by the survivors. Such a custom points clearly to a growing fear of the dead ; and that fear or reverence comes out still more clearly in the practice of either burying the property of the dead with them or destroying it altogether, which is observed by the aborigines of Victoria and other parts of Australia who live under more favourable conditions of life than the inhabitants of the Central deserts. This confirms the conclusion which we have reached on other grounds, that among the aboriginal population of Australia favourable natural conditions in

---

[1] Spencer and Gillen, *Native Tribes of Central Australia*, pp. 466, 497 *sq.*, 538 *sq.* See above, p. 138.

[2] Spencer and Gillen, *Northern Tribes of Central Australia*, p. 524.

[3] F. Bonney, "On some Customs of the Aborigines of the River Darling, New South Wales," *Journal of the Anthropological Institute*, xiii. (1884) p. 135.

respect of climate, food, and water have exercised a most important influence in stimulating social progress in many directions, and not least in the direction of religion.   At the same time, while we recognise that the incipient tendency to a worship of the dead which may be detected in these regions marks a step forward in religious development, we must acknowledge that the practice of burying or destroying the property of the dead, which is one of the ways in which the tendency manifests itself, is, regarded from the side of economic progress, a decided step backward.   It marks, in fact, the beginning of a melancholy aberration of the human mind, which has led mankind to sacrifice the real interests of the living to the imaginary interests of the dead.   With the general advance of society and the accompanying accumulation of property these sacrifices have at certain stages of evolution become heavier and heavier, as the demands of the ghosts became more and more exacting.   The economic waste which the belief in the immortality of the soul has entailed on the world is incalculable.   When we contemplate that waste in its small beginnings among the rude savages of Australia it appears insignificant enough ; the world is not much the poorer for the loss of a parcel of boomerangs, spears, fur string, and skin rugs.   But when we pass from the custom in this its feeble source and follow it as it swells in volume through the nations of the world till it attains the dimensions of a mighty river of wasted labour, squandered treasure, and spilt blood, we cannot but wonder at the strange mixture of good and evil in the affairs of mankind, seeing in what we justly call progress so much hardly earned gain side by side with so much gratuitous loss, such immense additions to the substantial value of life to be set off against such enormous sacrifices to the shadow of a shade.

Economic loss entailed by sacrifices to the dead.

LECTURE VII

THE BELIEF IN IMMORTALITY AMONG THE ABORIGINES OF AUSTRALIA (*concluded*)

IN the last lecture I shewed that in the maritime regions of Australia, where the conditions of life are more favourable than in the Central deserts, we may detect the germs of a worship of the dead in certain attentions which the living pay to the spirits of the departed, for example by kindling fires on the grave for the ghost to warm himself at, by leaving food and water for him to eat and drink, and by depositing his weapons and other property in the tomb for his use in the life after death. Another mark of respect shewn to the dead is the custom of erecting a hut on the grave for the accommodation of the ghost. Thus among the tribes of South Australia we are told that "upon the mounds, or tumuli, over the graves, huts of bark, or boughs, are generally erected to shelter the dead from the rain; they are also frequently wound round with netting." [1] Again, in Western Australia a small hut of rushes, grass, and so forth is said to have been set up by the natives over the grave.[2] Among the tribes of the Lower Murray, Lower Lachlan, and Lower Darling rivers, when a person died who had been highly esteemed in life, a neat hut was erected over his grave so as to cover it entirely. The hut was of oval shape, about five feet high, and roofed with thatch, which was firmly tied to the framework by cord many hundreds of yards in length.

[1] E. J. Eyre, *Journals of Expeditions of Discovery into Central Australia* (London, 1845), ii. 349.
[2] A. Oldfield, "The Aborigines of Victoria," *Transactions of the Ethnological Society of London*, N.S. iii. (1865) p. 245.

Sometimes the whole hut was enveloped in a net. At the eastern end of the hut a small opening was left just large enough to allow a full-grown man to creep in, and the floor was covered with grass, which was renewed from time to time as it became withered. Each of these graves was enclosed by a fence of brushwood forming a diamond-shaped enclosure, within which the tomb stood exactly in the middle. All the grass within the fence was neatly shaved off and the ground swept quite clean. Sepulchres of this sort were kept up for two or three years, after which they were allowed to fall into disrepair, and when a few more years had gone by the very sites of them were forgotten.[1] The intention of erecting huts on graves is not mentioned in these cases, but on analogy we may conjecture that they are intended for the convenience and comfort of the ghost. This is confirmed by an account given of a native burial on the Vasse River in Western Australia. We are told that when the grave had been filled in, the natives piled logs on it to a considerable height and then constructed a hut upon the logs, after which one of the male relations went into the hut and said, "I sit in his house."[2] Thus it would seem that the hut on the grave is regarded as the house of the dead man. If only these sepulchral huts were kept up permanently, they might develop into something like temples, in which the spirits of the departed might be invoked and propitiated with prayer and sacrifice. It is thus that the great round huts, in which the remains of dead kings of Uganda are deposited, have grown into sanctuaries or shrines, where the spirits of the deceased monarchs are consulted as oracles through the medium of priests.[3] But in Australia this development is prevented by the simple forgetfulness of the savages. A few years suffice with them to wipe out the memory of the deceased and with it his chance of developing into an ancestral deity. Like most savages, the Australian aborigines seem to fear only the ghosts of the recently departed ; one writer tells us that they have no

---

[1] P. Beveridge, in *Journal and Proceedings of the Royal Society of New South Wales*, xvii. (1883) pp. 29 *sq.* Compare R. Brough Smyth, *Aborigines of Victoria*, i. 100 note.

[2] (Sir) G. Grey, *Journals of Two Expeditions of Discovery*, ii. 332 *sq.*

[3] Rev. J. Roscoe, *The Baganda* (London, 1911), pp. 109 *sqq.*

fear of the ghost of a man who has been dead say forty years.[1]

Fear of the dead and precautions taken by the living against them. The burial customs of the Australian aborigines which I have described betray not only a belief in the existence of the ghost, but also a certain regard for his comfort and convenience. However, we may suspect that in most, if not in all, cases the predominant motive of these attentions is fear rather than affection. The survivors imagine that any want of respect for the dead, any neglect of his personal comforts in the grave, would excite his resentment and draw down on them his vengeance. That these savages are really actuated by fear of the dead is expressly affirmed of some tribes. Thus we are told that the Yuin " were always afraid that the dead man might come out of the grave and follow them."[2] After burying a body the Ngarigo were wont to cross a river in order to prevent the ghost from pursuing them;[3] obviously they shared the common opinion that ghosts for some reason are unable to cross water. The Wakelbura took other measures to throw the poor ghost off the scent. They marked all the trees in a circle round the place where the dead man was buried; so that when he emerged from the grave and set off in pursuit of his retiring relations, he would follow the marks on the trees in a circle and always come back to the point from which he had started. And to make assurance doubly sure they put coals in the dead man's ears, which, by bunging up these apertures, were supposed to keep his ghost in the body till his friends had got a good start away from him. As a further precaution they lit fires and put bushes in the forks of trees, with the idea that the ghost would roost in the bushes and warm himself at the fires, while they were hastening away.[4] Here, therefore, we see that the real motive for kindling fires for the use of the dead is fear, not affection. In this respect the burial customs of the tribes at the Herbert River are still more significant. These savages buried with the dead man his weapons, his ornaments, and indeed everything he had used in life; moreover,

---

[1] E. M. Curr, *The Australian Race* (Melbourne and London, 1886–1887), i. 87.

[2] A. W. Howitt, *Native Tribes of South-East Australia*, p. 463.

[3] A. W. Howitt, *op. cit.* p. 461.

[4] A. W. Howitt, *op. cit.* p. 473.

they built a hut on the grave, put a drinking-vessel in the hut, and cleared a path from it down to the water for the use of the ghost ; and often they placed food and water on the grave.   So far, these measures might be interpreted as marks of pure and disinterested affection for the soul of the departed.   But such an interpretation is totally excluded by the ferocious treatment which these savages meted out to the corpse.   To frighten the spirit, lest he should haunt the camp, the father or brother of the deceased, or the husband, if it was a woman, took a club and mauled the body with such violence that he often smashed the bones ; further, he generally broke both its legs in order to prevent it from wandering of nights ; and as if that were not enough, he bored holes in the stomach, the shoulders, and the lungs, and filled the holes with stones, so that even if the poor ghost should succeed by a desperate effort in dragging his mangled body out of the grave, he would be so weighed down by this ballast of stones that he could not get very far.   However, after roaming up and down in this pitiable condition for a time in their old haunts, the spirits were supposed at last to go up aloft to the Milky Way.[1]   The Kwearriburra tribe, on the Lynd River, in Queensland, also took forcible measures to prevent the resurrection of the dead.   Whenever a person died, they cut off his or her head, roasted it in a fire on the grave, and when it was thoroughly charred they smashed it in bits and left the fragments among the hot coals.   They calculated that when the ghost rose from the grave with the view of following the tribe, he would miss his head and go groping blindly about for it till he scorched himself in the embers of the fire and was glad to shrink back into his narrow bed.[2]

Thus even among those Australian tribes which have progressed furthest in the direction of religion, such approaches as they have made towards a worship of the dead appear to be determined far more by fear than by affection and reverence.   And we are told that it is the nearest relations and the most influential men whose ghosts are most dreaded.[3]

[1] A. W. Howitt, *op. cit.* p. 474.

[2] F. C. Urquhart, " Legends of the Australian Aborigines," *Journal of the* *Anthropological Institute*, xiv. (1885) p. 88.

[3] E. M. Curr, *The Australian Race*, i. 87.

Cuttings
and
brandings
of the
flesh of
the living
in honour
of the dead.
There is another custom observed by the Australian aborigines in mourning which deserves to be mentioned. We all know that the Israelites were forbidden to make cuttings in their flesh for the dead.[1] The custom was probably practised by the heathen Canaanites, as it has been by savages in various parts of the world. Nowhere, perhaps, has the practice prevailed more generally or been carried out with greater severity than in aboriginal Australia. For example, with regard to the tribes in the central part of Victoria we are told that "the parents of the deceased lacerate themselves fearfully, especially if it be an only son whose loss they deplore. The father beats and cuts his head with a tomahawk until he utters bitter groans. The mother sits by the fire and burns her breasts and abdomen with a small fire-stick till she wails with pain; then she replaces the stick in the fire, to use again when the pain is less severe. This continues for hours daily, until the time of lamentation is completed; sometimes the burns thus inflicted are so severe as to cause death."[2] It is especially the women, and above all the widows, who torture themselves in this way. Speaking of the tribes of Victoria, a writer tells us that on the death of her husband a widow, "becoming frantic, seizes fire-sticks and burns her breasts, arms, legs, and thighs. Rushing from one place to another, and intent only on injuring herself, and seeming to delight in the self-inflicted torture, it would be rash and vain to interrupt her. She would fiercely turn on her nearest relative or friend and burn him with her brands. When exhausted, and when she can scarcely walk, she yet endeavours to kick the embers of the fire, and to throw them about. Sitting down, she takes the ashes in her hands, rubs them into her wounds, and then scratches her face (the only part not touched by the fire-sticks) until the blood mingles with the ashes which partly hide her cruel wounds."[3] Among the Kurnai of South-eastern Victoria the relations of the dead would cut and gash themselves with sharp stones and toma-

---

[1] Leviticus xix. 28; Deuteronomy xiv. 1.

[2] W. Stanbridge, "Tribes in the Central Part of Victoria," *Transactions of the Ethnological Society of London,* N.S. i. (1861) p. 298.

[3] R. Brough Smyth, *Aborigines of Victoria,* i. 105.

hawks until their heads and bodies streamed with blood.[1] In the Mukjarawaint tribe, when a man died, his kinsfolk wept over him and slashed themselves with tomahawks and other sharp instruments for about a week.[2]   In the tribes of the Lower Murray and Lower Darling rivers mourners scored their backs and arms, sometimes even their faces, with red-hot brands, which raised hideous ulcers; afterwards they flung themselves prone on the grave, tore out their hair by handfuls, rubbed earth over their heads and bodies in great profusion, and ripped up their green ulcers till the mingled blood and grime presented a ghastly spectacle.   These self-inflicted sores remained long unhealed.[3]   Among the Kamilaroi, a large tribe of eastern New South Wales, the mourners, and especially the women, used to cut their heads with tomahawks and allow the blood to dry on them.[4] Speaking of a native burial on the Murray River, a writer says that "around the bier were many women, relations of the deceased, wailing and lamenting bitterly, and lacerating their thighs, backs, and breasts, with shells or flint, until the blood flowed copiously from the gashes."[5]   In the Boulia district of Queensland women in mourning score their thighs, both inside and outside, with sharp stones or bits of glass, so as to make a series of parallel cuts; in neighbouring districts of Queensland the men make much deeper cross-shaped cuts on their thighs.[6]   In the Arunta tribe of Central Australia a man is bound to cut himself on the shoulder in mourning for his father-in-law; if he does not do so, his wife may be given away to another man in order to appease the wrath of the ghost at his undutiful son-in-law.   Arunta men regularly bear on their shoulders the raised scars which shew that they have done their duty by their dead fathers-in-law.[7]   The female relations of a dead man in the Arunta tribe also cut and hack themselves in token of sorrow, working themselves up into a sort of frenzy as they do so;

[1] A. W. Howitt, *Native Tribes of South-East Australia*, p. 459.

[2] A. W. Howitt, *op. cit.* p. 453.

[3] P. Beveridge, in *Journal and Proceedings of the Royal Society of New South Wales*, xvii. (1883) pp. 28, 29.

[4] A. W. Howitt, *op. cit.* p. 466.

[5] E. J. Eyre, *Journals of Expedi-* tions of Discovery into Central Australia (London, 1845), ii. 347.

[6] W. E. Roth, *Studies among the North-West-Central Queensland Aborigines* (Brisbane and London, 1897), p. 164; compare p. 165.

[7] Spencer and Gillen, *Native Tribes of Central Australia*, p. 500.

yet in all their apparent excitement they take care never to wound a vital part, but vent their fury on their scalps, their shoulders, and their legs.[1]

Cuttings for the dead among the Warramunga.

In the Warramunga tribe of Central Australia Messrs. Spencer and Gillen witnessed the mourning for a dead man. Even before the sufferer had breathed his last the lamentations and self-inflicted wounds began.   When it was known that the end was near, all the native men ran at full speed to the spot, and Messrs. Spencer and Gillen followed them to see what was to be seen.   What they saw, or part of what they saw, was this.   Some of the women, who had gathered from all directions, were lying prostrate on the body of the dying man, while others were standing or kneeling around, digging the sharp ends of yam-sticks into the crown of their heads, from which the blood streamed down over their faces, while all the time they kept up a loud continuous wail.   Many of the men, rushing up to the scene of action, flung themselves also higgledy-piggledy on the sufferer, the women rising and making way for them, till nothing was to be seen but a struggling mass of naked bodies all mixed up together.   Presently up came a man yelling and brandishing a stone knife.   On reaching the spot he suddenly gashed both his thighs with the knife, cutting right across the muscles, so that, unable to stand, he dropped down on the top of the struggling bodies, till his mother, wife, and sisters dragged him out of the scrimmage, and immediately applied their mouths to his gaping wounds, while he lay exhausted and helpless on the ground.   Gradually the struggling mass of dusky bodies untwined itself, disclosing the unfortunate sick man, who was the object, or rather the victim, of this well-meant demonstration of affection and sorrow.   If he had been ill before, he was much worse when his friends left him : indeed it was plain that he had not long to live.   Still the weeping and wailing went on ; the sun set, darkness fell on the camp, and later in the evening the man died.   Then the wailing rose louder than before, and men and women, apparently frantic with grief, rushed about cutting themselves with knives and sharp-pointed sticks, while the women battered each other's heads with

[1] Spencer and Gillen, *op. cit.* p. 510.

clubs, no one attempting to ward off either cuts or blows. An hour later a funeral procession set out by torchlight through the darkness, carrying the body to a wood about a mile off, where it was laid on a platform of boughs in a low gum-tree. When day broke next morning, not a sign of human habitation was to be seen in the camp where the man had died. All the people had removed their rude huts to some distance, leaving the place of death solitary ; for nobody wished to meet the ghost of the deceased, who would certainly be hovering about, along with the spirit of the living man who had caused his death by evil magic, and who might be expected to come to the spot in the outward form of an animal to gloat over the scene of his crime. But in the new camp the ground was strewed with men lying prostrate, their thighs gashed with the wounds which they had inflicted on themselves with their own hands. They had done their duty by the dead and would bear to the end of their life the deep scars on their thighs as badges of honour. On one man Messrs. Spencer and Gillen counted the dints of no less than twenty-three wounds which he had inflicted on himself at various times. Meantime the women had resumed the duty of lamentation. Forty or fifty of them sat down in groups of five or six, weeping and wailing frantically with their arms round each other, while the actual and tribal wives, mothers, wives' mothers, daughters, sisters, mothers' mothers, sisters' husbands' mothers, and grand-daughters, according to custom, once more cut their scalps open with yam-sticks, and the widows afterwards in addition seared the scalp wounds with red-hot fire-sticks.

In these mourning customs, wild and extravagant as the expression of sorrow appears to be, everything is regulated by certain definite rules ; and a woman who did not thus maul herself when she ought to do so would be severely punished, or even killed, by her brother. Similarly with the men, it is only those who stand in certain relationships to the deceased who must cut and hack themselves in his honour, and these relationships are determined by the particular exogamous class to which the dead man happened to belong. Of such classes there are eight in the Warramunga tribe. On the occasion described by Messrs. Spencer and

Cuttings for the dead strictly regulated by custom.

Gillen it was a man of the Tjunguri class who died ; and the men who gashed their thighs stood to him in one or other of the following relationships : grandfather on the mother's side, mother's brother, brother of the dead man's wife, and her mother's brother.[1]

The cuttings and brandings which mourners inflict on themselves may be intended to convince the ghost of the sincerity of their sorrow.We naturally ask, What motive have these savages for inflicting all this voluntary and, as it seems to us, wholly superfluous suffering on themselves ?   It can hardly be that these wounds and burns are merely a natural and unfeigned expression of grief.   We have seen that by experienced observers such extravagant demonstrations of sorrow are set down rather to fear than to affection.   Similarly Messrs. Spencer and Gillen suggest that at least one motive is a fear entertained by the native lest, if he does not make a sufficient display of grief, the ghost of the dead man will be offended and do him a mischief.[2]   In the Kaitish tribe of Central Australia it is believed that if a woman does not keep her body covered with ashes from the camp fire during the whole time of mourning, the spirit of her deceased husband, who constantly follows her about, will kill her and strip all the flesh from her bones.[3]   Again, in the Arunta tribe mourners smear themselves with white pipeclay, and the motive for this custom is said to be to render themselves more conspicuous, so that the ghost may see and be satisfied that he is being properly mourned for.[4]   Thus the fear of the ghost, who, at least among the Australian aborigines, is commonly of a jealous temper and stands very firmly on his supposed rights, may suffice to explain the practice of self-mutilation at mourning.

Custom of allowing the blood of mourners to drip on the corpse or into the grave.But it is possible that another motive underlies the drawing of blood on these occasions.   For it is to be observed that the blood of the mourners is often allowed to drop directly either on the dead body or into the grave. Thus, for example, among the tribes on the River Darling several men used to stand by the open grave and cut each other's heads with a boomerang ; then they held their bleeding heads over the grave so that the blood dripped on the

---

[1] Spencer and Gillen, *Northern Tribes of Central Australia*, pp. 516-522.

[2] Spencer and Gillen, *Native Tribes*, p. 510.

[3] Spencer and Gillen, *Northern Tribes*, p. 507.

[4] Spencer and Gillen, *Native Tribes*, p. 511.

corpse lying in it.   If the deceased was highly esteemed, the
bleeding was repeated after some earth had been thrown on
the body.[1]   Among the Arunta it is customary for the women
kinsfolk of the dead to cut their own and each other's heads
so severely with clubs and digging-sticks that blood streams
from them on the grave.[2]   Again, at a burial on the Vasse
River, in Western Australia, a writer describes how, when
the grave was dug, the natives placed the corpse beside it,
then "gashed their thighs, and at the flowing of the blood
they all said, 'I have brought blood,' and they stamped the
foot forcibly on the ground, sprinkling the blood around
them ; then wiping the wounds with a wisp of leaves, they
threw it, bloody as it was, on the dead man."[3]   With these
Australian practices we may compare a custom observed by
the civilised Greeks of antiquity.   Every year the Pelopon-
nesian lads lashed themselves on the grave of Pelops at
Olympia, till the blood ran down their backs as a libation
in honour of the dead man.[4]

Now what is the intention of thus applying the blood of
the living to the dead or pouring it into the grave ?   So far
as the ancient Greeks are concerned the answer is not
doubtful.   We know from Homer that the ghosts of the
dead were supposed to drink the blood that was offered to
them and to be strengthened by the draught.[5]   Similarly with
the Australian savages, their object can hardly be any other
than that of strengthening the spirit of the dead ; for these
aborigines are in the habit of giving human blood to the
sick and the aged to drink for the purpose of restoring them
to health and strength ;[6] hence it would be natural for
them to imagine that they could refresh and fortify the feeble
ghost in like manner.   Perhaps the blood was intended
specially to strengthen the spirits of the dead for the
new birth or reincarnation, to which so many of these
savages look forward.

The blood intended to strengthen the dead.

[1] F. Bonney, "On some Customs of
the Aborigines of the River Darling,"
*Journal of the Anthropological Insti-
tute*, xiii. (1884) pp. 134 *sq.*
[2] Spencer and Gillen, *Native Tribes
of Central Australia*, pp. 507, 509 *sq.*
[3] (Sir) G. Grey, *Journals of Two*

Expeditions of Discovery, ii. 332,
quoting Mr. Bussel.
[4] Scholiast on Pindar, *Olymp.* i.
146.
[5] Homer, *Odyssey*, xi. 23 *sqq.*
[6] *The Magic Art and the Evolution
of Kings*, i. 91 *sq.*

Custom of burying people in the place where they were born.

The same motive may possibly explain the custom observed by some Australian tribes of burying people, as far as possible, at the place where they were born. Thus in regard to the tribes of Western Victoria we are informed that " dying persons, especially those dying from old age, generally express an earnest desire to be taken to their birthplace, that they may die and be buried there. If possible, these wishes are always complied with by the relatives and friends. Parents will point out the spot where they were born, so that when they become old and infirm, their children may know where they wish their bodies to be disposed of." [1]   Again, some tribes in the north and north-east of Victoria " are said to be more than ordinarily scrupulous in interring the dead. If practicable, they will bury the corpse near the spot where, as a child, it first drew breath. A mother will carry a dead infant for weeks, in the hope of being able to bury it near the place where it was born ; and a dead man will be conveyed a long distance, in order that the last rites may be performed in a manner satisfactory to the tribe." [2]   Another writer, speaking of the Australian aborigines in general, says : "By what I could learn, it is considered proper by many tribes that a black should be buried at or near the spot where he or she was born, and for this reason, when a black becomes seriously ill, the invalid is carried a long distance to these certain spots to die, as in this case. They apparently object to place a body in strange ground." The same writer mentions the case of a blackfellow, who began digging a grave close beside the kitchen door of a Mr. Campbell. When Mr. Campbell remonstrated with him, the native replied that he had no choice, for the dead man had been born on that very spot. With much difficulty Mr. Campbell persuaded him to bury his deceased friend a little further off from the kitchen door. [3]   A practice of this sort would be intelligible on the theory of the Central Australians, who imagine that the spirits of all the dead return to the very spots where they entered into

---

[1] J. Dawson, *Australian Aborigines*, p. 62.
[2] R. Brough Smyth, *Aborigines of Victoria*, i. 108.

[3] J. F. Mann, "Notes on the Aborigines of Australia," *Proceedings of the Geographical Society of Australasia*, i. (Sydney, 1885) p. 48.

their mothers' wombs, and that they wait there until another The custom
opportunity presents itself to them of being born again into perhaps intended
the world.   For if people really believe, as do many to facilitate
Australian tribes, that when they die they will afterwards the rebirth of the soul.
come to life again as infants, it is perfectly natural that they
should take steps to ensure and facilitate the new birth. The
Unmatjera and Kaitish tribes of Central Australia do this
in the case of dead children.   These savages draw a sharp
distinction between young children and very old men and
women.   When very old people die, their bodies are at once
buried in the ground, but the bodies of children are placed
in wooden troughs and deposited on platforms of boughs in
the branches of trees, and the motive for treating a dead
child thus is, we are informed, the hope " that before very
long its spirit may come back again and enter into the body
of a woman—in all probability that of its former mother." [1]
The reason for drawing this distinction between the young
and the old by disposing of their bodies in different fashions,
is explained with great probability by Messrs. Spencer and
Gillen as follows : " In the Unmatjera and Kaitish tribes,
while every old man has certain privileges denied to the
younger men, yet if he be decidedly infirm and unable
to take his part in the performance of ceremonies which
are often closely concerned — or so at least the natives
believe them to be — with the general welfare of the tribe,
then the feeling undoubtedly is that there is no need to pay
any very special respect to his remains.   This feeling is
probably vaguely associated with the idea that, as his body
is infirm, so to a corresponding extent will his spirit part be,
and therefore they have no special need to consider or
propitiate this, as it can do them no harm.   On the other
hand they are decidedly afraid of hurting the feelings of any
strong man who might be capable of doing them some
mischief unless he saw that he was properly mourned for.
Acting under much the same feeling they pay respect to the
bodies of dead children and young women, in the hope that
the spirit will soon return and undergo reincarnation.   It is
also worth noticing that they do not bury in trees any young
man who has violated tribal law by taking as wife a woman

[1] Spencer and Gillen, *Northern Tribes of Central Australia*, p. 506.

who is forbidden to him; such an individual is always buried directly in the ground."[1]   Apparently these law-abiding savages are not anxious that members of the criminal classes should be born again and should have the opportunity of troubling society once more.

Different modes of disposing of the dead adopted in the same tribe.   I would call your attention particularly to the different modes of burial thus accorded by these two tribes to different classes of persons.   It is too commonly assumed that each tribe has one uniform way of disposing of all its dead, say either by burning or by burying, and on that assumption certain general theories have been built as to the different views taken of the state of the dead by different tribes.   But in point of fact the assumption is incorrect.   Not infrequently the same tribe disposes of different classes of dead people in quite different ways; for instance, it will bury some and burn others.   Thus amongst the Angoni of British Central Africa the corpses of chiefs are burned with all their household belongings, but the bodies of commoners are buried with all their belongings in caves.[2]   In various castes or tribes of India it is the custom to burn the bodies of married people but to bury the bodies of the unmarried.[3]   With some peoples of India the distinction is made, not between the married and the unmarried, but between adults and children, especially children under two years old; in such cases the invariable practice appears to be to burn the old and bury the young. Thus among the Malayalis of Malabar the bodies of men and women are burned, but the bodies of children under two years are buried, and so are the bodies of all persons who have died of cholera or small-pox.[4]   The same distinctions are observed by the Nayars, Kadupattans, and

[1] Spencer and Gillen, *Northern Tribes*, p. 512.
[2] R. Sutherland Rattray, *Some Folklore Stories and Songs in Chinyanja* (London, 1907), pp. 99-101, 182.
[3] F. Fawcett, "The Kondayamkottai Maravars, a Dravidian Tribe of Tinnevelly, Southern India," *Journal of the Anthropological Institute*, xxxiii. (1903) p. 64; Captain Wolsley Haig, "Notes on the Rangārī Caste in

Barar," *Journal of the Asiatic Society of Bengal*, lxx. Part iii. (1901) p. 8; E. Thurston, *Castes and Tribes of Southern India* (Madras, 1909), iv. 226 (as to the Lambadis), vi. 244 (as to the Raniyavas); compare *id., Ethnographic Notes in Southern India* (Madras, 1906), p. 155.

[4] E. Thurston, *Ethnographic Notes in Southern India*, p. 207.

other castes or tribes of Cochin.[1] The old rule laid down
in the ancient Hindoo law-book *The Grihya-Sutras* was that
children who died under the age of two should be buried,
not burnt.[2] The Bhotias of the Himalayas bury all children
who have not yet obtained their permanent teeth, but
they burn all other people.[3] Among the Komars the young
are buried, and the old cremated.[4] The Coorgs bury the
bodies of women and of boys under sixteen years of age,
but they burn the bodies of men.[5] The Chukchansi Indians
of California are said to have burned only those who died a
violent death or were bitten by snakes, but to have buried
all others.[6] The Minnetaree Indians disposed of their dead
differently according to their moral character.   Bad and
quarrelsome men they buried in the earth that the Master of
Life might not see them ; but the bodies of good men they
laid on scaffolds, that the Master of Life might behold
them.[7] The Kolosh or Tlingit Indians of Alaska burn their
ordinary dead on a pyre, but deposit the bodies of shamans
in large coffins, which are supported on four posts.[8] The
ancient Mexicans thought that all persons who died of
infectious diseases were killed by the rain-god Tlaloc ; so
they painted their bodies blue, which was the rain-god's
colour, and buried instead of burning them.[9]

These examples may suffice to illustrate the different
ways in which the same people may dispose of their dead
according to the age, sex, social rank, or moral character of
the deceased, or the manner of his death.   In some cases
the special mode of burial adopted seems clearly intended

*Special
modes of
burial
adopted
to prevent
or facilitate
the return
of the
spirit.*

[1] L. K. Anantha Krishna Iyer, *The
Cochin Tribes and Castes* (Madras,
1909–1912), ii. 91, 112, 157, 360,
378.

[2] *The Grihya Sutras*, translated
by H. Oldenberg, Part i. p. 355
(*Sacred Books of the East*, vol. xxix.).
Compare W. Crooke, *Popular Religion
and Folk-lore of Northern India* (Westminster, 1896), i. 245.

[3] Ch. A. Sherring, *Western Tibet
and the British Borderland* (London,
1906), pp. 123 *sq.*

[4] P. N. Bose, "Chhattisgar,"*Journal
of the Asiatic Society of Bengal*, lix.,
Part i. (1891) p. 290.

[5] E. Thurston, *Ethnographic Notes
in Southern India*, p. 205.

[6] S. Powers, *Tribes of California*
(Washington, 1877), p. 383.

[7] Maximilian Prinz zu Wied, *Reise
in das Innere Nord-America* (Coblenz,
1839–1841), ii. 235.

[8] T. de Pauly, *Description Ethno-
graphique des Peuples de la Russie,
Peuples de l'Amérique Russe* (St.
Petersburg, 1862), p. 13.

[9] E. Seler,*Altmexikanische Studien*,
ii. (Berlin, 1899) p. 42 (*Veröffent-
lichungen aus dem Königlichen Museum
für Völkerkunde*, vi. 2/4).

to guard against the return of the dead, whether in the form of ghosts or of children born again into the world. Such, for instance, was obviously the intention of the old English custom of burying a suicide at a cross-road with a stake driven through his body.   And if some burial customs are plainly intended to pin down the dead in the earth, or at least to disable him from revisiting the survivors, so others appear to be planned with the opposite intention of facilitating the departure of the spirit from the grave, in order that he may repair to a more commodious lodging or be born again into the tribe. For example, the Arunta of Central Australia always bury their dead in the earth and raise a low mound over the grave ; but they leave a depression in the mound on the side which faces towards the spot where the spirit of the deceased is supposed to have dwelt in the intervals between his successive reincarna- tions ; and we are expressly told that the purpose of leaving this depression is to allow the spirit to go out and in easily ; for until the final ceremony of mourning has been performed at the grave, the ghost is believed to spend his time partly in watching over his near relations and partly in the company of its *arumburinga* or spiritual double, who lives at the old *nanja* spot, that is, at the place where the dis- embodied soul tarries waiting to be born again.[1] Thus the Arunta imagine that for some time after death the spirit of the deceased is in a sort of intermediate state, partly hovering about the abode of the living, partly visiting his own proper spiritual home, to which on the completion of the mourning ceremonies he will retire to await the new birth.   The final mourning ceremony, which marks the close of this intermediate state, takes place some twelve or eighteen months after the death.   It consists mainly in nothing more or less than a ghost hunt ; men armed with shields and spear-throwers assemble and with loud shouts beat the air, driving the invisible ghost before them from the spot where he died, while the women join in the shouts and buffet the air with the palms of their hands to chase away the dead man from the old camp which he loves to

[1] Spencer and Gillen, *Native Tribes of Central Australia*, p. 497 ; *id.*, *Northern Tribes of Central Australia*, p. 506.

haunt.   In this way the beaters gradually advance towards
the grave till they have penned the ghost into it, when they
immediately dance on the top of it, beating the air downwards as if to drive the spirit down, and stamping on the
ground as if to trample him into the earth.   After that, the
women gather round the grave and cut each other's heads
with clubs till the blood streams down on it.   This brings the
period of mourning to an end ; and if the deceased was a man,
his widow is now free to marry again.   In token that the days
of her sorrow are over, she wears at this final ceremony the
gay feathers of the ring-neck parrot in her hair.   The spirit
of her dead husband, lying in the grave, is believed to
know the sign and to bid her a last farewell.   Even after he
has thus been hunted into the grave and trampled down in it,
his spirit may still watch over his friends, guard them from
harm, and visit them in dreams.[1]

We may naturally ask, Why should the spirit of the
dead be supposed at first to dwell more or less intermittently
near the spot where he died, and afterwards to take up his
abode permanently at his *nanja* spot till the time comes
for him to be born again ?   A good many years ago I
conjectured [2] that this idea of a change in the abode of the
ghost may be suggested by a corresponding change which
takes place, or is supposed to take place, about the same
time in the state of the body ; in fact, that so long as the
flesh adheres to the bones, so long the soul of the dead man
may be thought to be detained in the neighbourhood of the
body, but that when the flesh has quite decayed, the soul is
completely liberated from its old tabernacle and is free to
repair to its true spiritual home.   In confirmation of this
conjecture I pointed to the following facts.   Some of the
Indians of Guiana bring food and drink to their dead so
long as the flesh remains on the bones ; but when it has
mouldered away, they conclude that the man himself has
departed.[3]   The Matacos Indians of the Gran Chaco in
Argentina believe that the soul of a dead man does not

Departure of the ghost supposed to coincide with the disappearance of the flesh from his bones.

---

[1] Spencer and Gillen, *Native Tribes
of Central Australia*, pp. 503-508.
The name of the final mourning ceremony among the Arunta is *urpmil-
chima*.

[2] *The Golden Bough*, Second Edition
(London, 1900), i. 434 *sq.*
[3] A. Biet, *Voyage de la France
Equinoxiale en l'Isle de Cayenne* (Paris,
1664), p. 392.

pass down into the nether world until his body is decomposed or burnt.[1] Further, the Alfoors of Central Celebes suppose that the spirits of the departed cannot enter the spirit-land until all the flesh has been removed from their bones ; for until that has been done, the gods (*lamoa*) in the other world could not bear the stench of the corpse. Accordingly at a great festival the bodies of all who have died within a certain time are dug up and the decaying flesh scraped from the bones.[2]   Comparing these ideas, I suggested that they may explain the widespread custom of a second burial, that is, the practice of disinterring the dead after a certain time and disposing of their bones otherwise.[3]

Second burial of the bones among the tribes of Central Australia. Now so far as the tribes of Central Australia are concerned, my conjecture has been confirmed by the subsequent researches of Messrs. Spencer and Gillen in that region.   For they have found that the tribes to the north of the Arunta regularly give their dead a second burial, that a change in the state of the ghosts is believed to coincide with the second burial, and apparently also, though this is not so definitely stated, that the time for the second burial is determined by the disappearance of the flesh from the bones.   Amongst the tribes which practise a second burial the custom is first to deposit the dead on platforms among the branches of trees, till the flesh has quite mouldered away, and then to bury the bones in the earth : in short, they practise tree-burial first and earth-burial afterwards.[4] For example, in the Unmatjera and Kaitish tribes, when a man dies, his body is carried by his relations to a tree distant a mile or two from the camp.   There it is laid on a platform by itself for some months.   When the flesh has disappeared from the bones, a kinsman of the deceased, in strictness a younger brother (*itia*), climbs up into the tree,

[1] J. Pelleschi, *Los Indios Mataco* (Buenos Ayres, 1897), p. 102.

[2] A. C. Kruijt, " Een en ander aangaande het geestelijk en maatschappelijk leven van den Poso-Alfoer," *Mededeelingen van wege het Nederlandsche Zendelinggenootschap*, xxxix. (1895) pp. 26, 32 *sqq.*

[3] *The Golden Bough*, Second Edition, i. 434 note [2].   Similarly the Tami

of German New Guinea believe that the soul of the deceased only departs to the lower world when the maggots swarm from his decaying body. See G. Bamler, " Tami," in R. Neuhauss, *Deutsch Neu-Guinea*, iii. (Berlin, 1911) p. 519.

[4] Spencer and Gillen, *Northern Tribes of Central Australia*, pp. 505 *sqq.*

dislocates the bones, places them in a wooden vessel, and hands them down to a female relative.   Then the bones are laid in the grave with the head facing in the direction in which his mother's brother is supposed to have camped in days of old.   After the bones have been thus interred, the spirit of the dead man is believed to go away and to remain in his old *alcheringa* home until such time as he once more undergoes reincarnation.[1]   But in these tribes, as we saw, very old men and women receive only one burial, being at once laid in an earthy grave and never set up on a platform in a tree ; and we have seen reason to think that this difference in the treatment of the aged springs from the indifference or contempt in which their ghosts are held by comparison with the ghosts of the young and vigorous.   In the Warramunga tribe, who regularly deposit their dead in trees first and in the earth afterwards, so long as the corpse remains in the tree and the flesh has not completely disappeared from the bones, the mother of the deceased and the women who stand to him or her in the relation of tribal motherhood are obliged from time to time to go to the tree, and sitting under the platform to allow its putrid juices to drip down on their bodies, into which they rub them as a token of sorrow.   This, no doubt, is intended to please the jealous ghost ; for we are told that he is believed to haunt the tree and even to visit the camp, in order, if he was a man, to see for himself that his widows are mourning properly.   The time during which the moulder-ing remains are left in the tree is at least a year and may be more.[2]   The final ceremony which brings the period of mourning to an end is curious and entirely different from the one observed by the Arunta on the same occasion.   When the bones have been taken down from the tree, an arm-bone is put carefully apart from the rest.   Then the skull is smashed, and the fragments together with all the rest of the bones except the arm-bone, are buried in a hollow ant-hill near the tree.   Afterwards the arm-bone is wrapt up in paper-bark and wound round with fur-string, so as to

Final burial ceremony among the Warra-munga.

[1] Spencer and Gillen, *Northern Tribes of Central Australia*, pp. 506-508.

[2] Spencer and Gillen, *Northern Tribes of Central Australia*, p. 530.

make a torpedo-shaped parcel, which is kept by a tribal mother of the deceased in her rude hovel of branches, till, after the lapse of some days or weeks, the time comes for the last ceremony of all. On that day a design emblematic of the totem of the deceased is drawn on the ground, and beside it a shallow trench is dug about a foot deep and fifteen feet long. Over this trench a number of men, elaborately decorated with down of various colours, stand straddle-legged, while a line of women, decorated with red and yellow ochre, crawl along the trench under the long bridge made by the straddling legs of the men. The last woman carries the arm-bone of the dead in its parcel, and as soon as she emerges from the trench, the bone is snatched from her by a kinsman of the deceased, who carries it to a man standing ready with an uplifted axe beside the totemic drawing. On receiving the bone, the man at once smashes it, hastily buries it in a small pit beside the totemic emblem of the departed, and closes the opening with a large flat stone, signifying thereby that the season of mourning is over and that the dead man or woman has been gathered to his or her totem. The totemic design, beside which the arm-bone is buried, represents the spot at which the totemic ancestor of the deceased finally went down into the earth. When once the arm-bone has thus been broken and laid in its last resting-place, the soul of the dead person, which they describe as being of about the size of a grain of sand, is supposed to go back to the place where it camped long ago in a previous incarnation, there to remain with the souls of other men and women of the same totem until the time comes for it to be born again.[1]

General conclusion as to the belief in immortality and the worship of the dead among the Australian aborigines.

This must conclude what I have to say as to the belief in immortality and the worship of the dead among the aborigines of Australia. The evidence I have adduced is sufficient to prove that these savages firmly believe both in the existence of the human soul after death and in the power which it can exert for good or evil over the survivors. On the whole the dominant motive in their treatment of the dead appears to be fear rather than affection. Yet the attention which many tribes pay to the comfort of the

[1] Spencer and Gillen, *Northern Tribes of Central Australia,* pp. 530-543.

departed by providing them with huts, food, water, fire, clothing, implements and weapons, may not be dictated by purely selfish motives ; in any case they are clearly intended to please and propitiate the ghosts, and therefore contain the germs of a regular worship of the dead.

LECTURE VIII

THE BELIEF IN IMMORTALITY AMONG THE NATIVES
OF THE TORRES STRAITS ISLANDS

The
Islanders
of Torres
Straits.

IN the last lecture I concluded my account of the belief in immortality and the worship of the dead, or rather of the elements out of which such a worship might have grown, among the aborigines of Australia. To-day we pass to the consideration of a different people, the islanders of Torres Straits. As you may know, Torres Straits are the broad channel which divides Australia on the south from the great island of New Guinea on the north. The small islands which are scattered over the strait fall roughly into two groups, a Western and an Eastern, of which the eastern is at once the more isolated and the more fertile. In appearance, character, and customs the inhabitants of all these islands belong to the Papuan family, which inhabits the western half of New Guinea, but in respect of language there is a marked difference between the natives of the two groups; for while the speech of the Western Islanders is akin to that of the Australians, the speech of the Eastern Islanders is akin to that of the Papuans of New Guinea. The conclusion to be drawn from these facts appears to be that the Western Islands of Torres Straits were formerly inhabited by aborigines of the Australian family, and that at a later time they were occupied by immigrants from New Guinea, who adopted the language of the aboriginal inhabitants, but gradually extinguished the aboriginal type and character either by peaceful absorption or by conquest and extermination.[1]   Hence   the   Western   Islanders   of

[1] S. H. Ray, in *Reports of the Cambridge Anthropological Expedition* to *Torres Straits*, iii. (Cambridge, 1907) pp. 509-511; A. C. Haddon,

Torres Straits form a transition both geographically and ethnographically between the aborigines of Australia on the one side and the aborigines of New Guinea on the other side. Accordingly in our survey of the belief in immortality among the lower races we may appropriately consider the Islanders of Torres Straits immediately after the aborigines of Australia and before we pass onward to other and more distant races. These Islanders have a special claim on the attention of a Cambridge lecturer, since almost all the exact knowledge we possess of them we owe to the exertions of Cambridge anthropologists and especially to Dr. A. C. Haddon, who on his first visit to the islands in 1888 perceived the urgent importance of procuring an accurate record of the old beliefs and customs of the natives before it was too late, and who never rested till that record was obtained, as it happily has been, first by his own unaided researches in the islands, and afterwards by the united researches of a band of competent enquirers. In the history of anthropology the Cambridge Expedition to Torres Straits in 1898 will always hold an honourable place, to the credit of the University which promoted it and especially to that of the zealous and devoted investigator who planned, organised, and carried it to a successful conclusion. Practically all that I shall have to tell you as to the beliefs and practices of the Torres Straits Islanders is derived from the accurate and laborious researches of Dr. Haddon and his colleagues.

The Cambridge Anthropological Expedition to Torres Straits.

While the natives of Torres Straits are, or were at the time of their discovery, in the condition which we call savagery, they stand on a far higher level of social and intellectual culture than the rude aborigines of Australia. To indicate roughly the degree of advance we need only say that, whereas the Australians are nomadic hunters and fishers, entirely ignorant of agriculture, and destitute to a great extent not only of houses but even of clothes, the natives of Torres Straits live in settled villages and diligently till the soil, raising a variety of crops, such as yams, sweet potatoes, bananas, sugar-cane, and tobacco.[1] Of the two

Social culture of the Torres Straits Islanders.

"The Religion of the Torres Straits Islanders," *Anthropological Essays presented to E. B. Tylor* (Oxford, 1907), p. 175.

[1] *Cambridge Anthropological Expedition to Torres Straits*, iv. 92 *sqq.*, 144 *sqq.*, v. 346, vi. 207 *sqq.*

groups of islands the eastern is the more fertile and the inhabitants are more addicted to agriculture than are the natives of the western islands, who, as a consequence of the greater barrenness of the soil, have to eke out their subsistence to a considerable extent by fishing.[1]   And there is other evidence to shew that the Eastern Islanders have attained to a somewhat higher stage of social evolution than their Western brethren ;[2] the more favourable natural conditions under which they live may possibly have contributed to raise the general level of culture.   One of the most marked distinctions in this respect between the inhabitants of the two groups is that, whereas a regular system of totemism with its characteristic features prevails among the Western Islanders, no such system nor even any very clear evidence of its former existence is to be found among the Eastern Islanders, whether it be that they never had it or, what is more likely, that they once had but have lost it.[3]

Belief of the Torres Straits Islanders in the existence of the human spirit after death.

On the other hand, so far as regards our immediate subject, the belief in immortality and the worship of the dead, a general resemblance may be traced between the creed and customs of the Eastern and Western tribes. Both of them, like the Australian aborigines, firmly believe in the existence of the human spirit after death, but unlike the Australians they seem to have no idea that the souls of the departed are ever born again into the world ; the doctrine of reincarnation, so widespread among the natives of Australia, appears to have no place in the creed of their near neighbours the Torres Straits Islanders, whose dead, like our own, though they may haunt the living for a time, are thought to depart at last to a distant spirit-land and to return no more.   At the same time neither in the one group nor in the other is there any clear evidence of what may be called a worship of the dead in the strict sense of the word, unless we except the cults of certain more or less mythical heroes. On this point the testimony of Dr. Haddon is definite as to the Western Islanders.   He says : " In no case have I obtained

[1] A. C. Haddon, in *Anthropological Essays presented to E. B. Tylor*, p. 186.

[2] *Cambridge Anthropological Ex-*
pedition to Torres Straits, vi. 254 *sq.*

[3] *Cambridge Anthropological Expedition to Torres Straits*, vi. 254 *sqq.*

in the Western Islands an indication of anything approaching a worship of deceased persons ancestral or otherwise, with the exception of the heroes shortly to be mentioned ; neither is there any suggestion that their own ancestors have been in any way apotheosized." [1]

But if these savages have not, with the possible exception of the cult of certain heroes, any regular worship of the dead, they certainly have the germ out of which such a worship might be developed, and that is a firm belief in ghosts and in the mischief which they may do to the living.   The word for a ghost is *mari* in the West and *mar* in the East : it means also a shadow or reflection,[2] which seems to shew that these savages, like many others, have derived their notion of the human soul from the observation of shadows and reflections cast by the body on the earth or on water.   Further, the Western Islanders appear to distinguish the ghosts of the recently departed (*mari*) from the spirits of those who have been longer dead, which they call *markai* ;[3] and if we accept this distinction " we may assert," according to Dr. Haddon, " that the Torres Straits Islanders feared the ghosts but believed in the general friendly disposition of the spirits of the departed." [4]   Similarly we saw that the Australian aborigines regard with fear the ghosts of those who have just died, while they are either indifferent to the spirits of those who have died many years ago or even look upon them as beings of higher powers than their descendants, whom they can benefit in various ways. This sharp distinction between the spirits of the dead, according to the date at which they died, is widespread, perhaps universal among mankind.   However truly the dead were loved in their lifetime, however bitterly they were mourned at their death, no sooner have they passed beyond our ken than the thought of their ghosts seems to inspire the generality of mankind with an instinctive fear and horror, as if the character of even the best friends and

Fear of the ghosts of the recently departed.

---

[1] A. C. Haddon, in *Anthropological Essays presented to E. B. Tylor*, p. 181.

[2] *Cambridge Anthropological Expedition to Torres Straits*, v. 355 *sq.*, vi. 251 ; A. C. Haddon, in *Anthro-pological Essays presented to E. B. Tylor*, p. 179.

[3] For authorities see the references in the preceding note.

[4] *Cambridge Anthropological Expedition to Torres Straits*, vi. 253.

nearest relations underwent a radical change for the worse as soon as they had shuffled off the mortal coil.   But among savages this belief in the moral deterioration of ghosts is certainly much more marked than among civilised races. Ghosts are dreaded both by the Western and the Eastern tribes of Torres Straits.   Thus in Mabuiag, one of the Western Islands, the corpse was carried out of camp feet foremost, else it was thought that the ghost would return and trouble the survivors.   Further, when the body had been laid upon a stage or platform on clear level ground away from the dwelling, the remains of any food and water of which the deceased might have been partaking in his last moments were carried out and placed beside the corpse lest the ghost should come back to fetch them for himself, to the annoyance and terror of his relations.   This is the reason actually alleged by the natives for what otherwise might have been interpreted as a delicate mark of affection and thoughtful care for the comfort of the departed.   If next morning the food was found scattered, the people said that the ghost was angry and had thrown it about.[1]   Further, on the day of the death the mourners went into the gardens, slashed at the taro, knocked down coco-nuts, pulled up sweet potatoes, and destroyed bananas.   We are told that "the food was destroyed for the sake of the dead man, it was 'like good-bye.'"[2]   We may suspect that the real motive for the destruction was the same as that for laying food and water beside the corpse, namely, a wish to give the ghost no excuse for returning to haunt and pester his surviving relatives.   How could he have the heart to return to the desolated garden which in his lifetime it had been his pride and joy to cultivate?

Fear of the ghosts of the recently departed among the Murray Islanders.   In Murray Island, also, which belongs to the Eastern group, the ghost of a recently deceased person is much dreaded; it is supposed to haunt the neighbourhood for two or three months, and the elaborate funeral ceremonies which these savages perform appear to be based on this belief and to be intended, in fact, to dismiss the ghost from the land of the living, where he is a very unwelcome visitor,

[1] *Cambridge Anthropological Expedition to Torres Straits*, v. 248, 249.
[2] *Id.*, p. 250.

to his proper place in the land of the dead.[1] " The Murray
Islanders," says Dr. Haddon, " perform as many as possible
of the necessary ceremonies in order that the ghost of the
deceased might not feel slighted, for otherwise it was sure
to bring trouble on the relatives by causing strong winds to
destroy their gardens and break down their houses." [2] These
islanders still believe that a ghost may feel resentment when
his children are neglected or wronged, or when his lands or
goods are appropriated by persons who have no claim to
them.   And this fear of the wrath of the ghost, Dr. Haddon
tells us, no doubt in past times acted as a wholesome deter-
rent on evil-doers and helped to keep the people from crime,
though now-a-days they look rather to the law than to
ghosts for the protection of their rights and the avenging
of their wrongs.[3]   Yet here, as in so many places, it would
seem that superstition has proved a useful crutch on which
morality can lean until it is strong enough to walk alone.
In the absence of the police the guardianship of law and
morality may be provisionally entrusted to ghosts, who, if
they are too fickle and uncertain in their temper to make
ideal constables, are at least better than nothing.   With this
exception it does not appear that the moral code of the
Torres Straits Islanders derived any support or sanction
from their religion.   No appeal was made by them to
totems, ancestors, or heroes ; no punishment was looked for
from these quarters for any infringement of the rules and
restraints which hold society together.[4]

The land of the dead to which the ghosts finally depart The island
is, in the opinion of the Torres Straits Islanders, a mythical home of
the dead.
island in the far west or rather north-west.   The Western
Islanders name it Kibu ; the Eastern Islanders call it Boigu.
The name Kibu means " sundown."   It is natural enough
that islanders should place the home of the dead in some
far island of the sea to which no canoe of living men has
ever sailed, and it is equally natural that the fabulous island
should lie to westward where the sun goes down ; for it

[1] *Cambridge Anthropological Expedition to Torres Straits*, vi. 253 ;
A. C. Haddon, in *Anthropological
Essays presented to E. B. Tylor*, p.
180.

[2] A. C. Haddon, *l.c.*
[3] A. C. Haddon, *op. cit.* pp. 182
sq. ; *Cambridge Anthropological Expedition to Torres Straits*, vi. 127.
[4] A. C. Haddon, *op. cit.* p. 183.

seems to be a common thought that the souls of the dead
are attracted by the great luminary, like moths by a candle,
and follow him when he sinks in radiant glory into the sea.
To take a single example, in the Maram district of Assam
it is forbidden to build houses facing westward, because that
is the direction in which the spirits of the dead go to their
long home.[1]　But the Torres Straits Islanders have a special
reason, as Dr. Haddon has well pointed out, for thinking
that the home of the dead is away in the north-west; and the
reason is that in these latitudes the trade wind blows steady
and strong from the south-east for seven or eight months of
the year; so that for the most part the spirits have only to
let themselves go and the wind will sweep them away on its
pinions to their place of rest.　How could the poor fluttering
things beat up to windward in the teeth of the blast?[2]

Elaborate
funeral
ceremonies
observed
by the
Torres
Straits
Islanders.　The funeral ceremonies observed by the Torres Straits
Islanders were numerous and elaborate, and they present
some features of special interest.　They succeeded each
other at intervals, sometimes of months, and amongst the
Eastern Islanders in particular there were so many of them
that, were it not that the bodies of the very young and the
very old were treated less ceremoniously, the living would
have been perpetually occupied in celebrating the obsequies
of the dead.[3]　The obsequies differed somewhat from each
other in the East and the West, but they had two characteristics in common : first, the skulls of the dead were commonly
preserved apart from the bodies and were consulted as
oracles ; and, second, the ghosts of the recently deceased
were represented in dramatic ceremonies by masked men,
who mimicked the gait and gestures of the departed and
were thought by the women and children to be the very
ghosts themselves.　But in details there were a good many
variations between the practice of the Eastern and the
Western Islanders.　We will begin with the customs of the
Western Islanders.

[1] T. C. Hodson, *The Naga Tribes
of Manipur* (London, 1911), p. 43.
[2] *Cambridge Anthropological Expedition to Torres Straits*, v. 355 *sq.*,
vi. 252. In the former passage Dr.
Haddon seems to identify Boigu with
the island of that name off the south
coast of New Guinea ; in the latter
he prefers to regard it as mythical.

[3] *Cambridge Anthropological Expedition to Torres Straits*, vi. 127.

When a death had taken place, the corpse was carried
out of the house and set on a staging supported by four
forked posts and covered by a roof of mats. The office of
attending to the body devolved properly on the brothers-in-
law (*imi*) of the deceased, who, while they were engaged in
the duties of the office, bore the special title of *mariget* or
"ghost-hand." It deserves to be noticed that these men
were always of a different totem from the deceased; for if
the dead person was a man, the *mariget* were his wife's
brothers and therefore had the same totem as the dead
man's wife, which, on account of the law of exogamy, always
differed from the totem of her husband. And if the dead
person was a woman, the *mariget* were her husband's brothers
and therefore had his totem, which necessarily differed from
hers. When they had discharged the preliminary duties to
the corpse, the brothers-in-law went and informed the relations and friends. This they did not in words but by a
prescribed pantomime. For example, if the deceased had
had the crocodile for his totem, they imitated the ungainly
gait of crocodiles waddling and resting, if the deceased had
the snake for his totem, they in like manner mimicked the
crawling of a snake. The relations then painted their bodies
with white coral mud, cut their hair, plastered mud over their
heads, and cut off their ear ornaments or severed the dis-
tended lobe of the ear as a sign of mourning. Then, armed
with bows and arrows, they came out to the stage where the
corpse was lying and let fly arrows at the men who were
in attendance on it, that is, at the brothers-in-law of the
deceased, who warded off the shafts as best they could.[1]
The meaning of this sham attack on the men who were
discharging the last offices of respect to the dead comes
out clearly in another ceremony which was performed some
time afterwards, as we shall see presently. For five or six
days the corpse remained on the platform or bier watched
by the brothers-in-law, who had to prevent certain large
lizards from devouring it and to frighten away any prowling
ghosts that might be lured to the spot by the stench. After
the lapse of several days the relations returned to the body,
mourned, and beat the roof of the bier, while they raised a

Funeral
ceremonies
observed
by the
Western
Islanders.

[1] *Cambridge Anthropological Expedition to Torres Straits*, v. 248 *sq.*

shout to drive off any part of the dead man's spirit that
might be lingering about his mouldering remains.   The
reason for doing so was, that the time had now arrived
for cutting off the head of the corpse, and they thought that
the head would not come off easily if the man's spirit were
still in the body ; he might reasonably be expected to hold
on tight to it and not to resign, without a struggle, so
valuable a part of his person.   When the poor ghost had
thus been chased away with shouts and blows, the principal
brother-in-law came forward and performed the amputation
by sawing off the head.   Having done so, he usually placed
it in a nest of termites or white ants in order that the insects
might pick it clean ; but sometimes for the same purpose he
deposited it in a creek.   When it was thoroughly clean, the
grinning white skull was painted red all over and placed in
a decorated basket.   Then followed the ceremony of formally
handing over this relic of the dead to the relations.   The
brothers-in-law, who had been in attendance on the body,
painted themselves black all over, covered their heads with
leaves, and walked in solemn procession, headed by the chief
brother-in-law, who carried the skull in the basket.   Meantime the male relatives were awaiting them, seated on a large
mat in the ceremonial ground, while the women grouped
themselves in the background.   As the procession of men
approached bearing the skull, the mourners shot arrows over
their heads as a sign of anger at them for having decapitated
their relation.   But this was a mere pretence, probably intended to soothe and flatter the angry ghost: the arrows
flew over the men without hurting them.[1]   Similarly in
ancient Egypt the man who cut open a corpse for embalm-
ment had no sooner done his office than he fled precipitately,
pursued by the relations with stones and curses, because he
had wounded and mangled the body of their kinsman.[2]
Sometimes the skull was made up to resemble the head
of a living man : an artificial nose of wood and beeswax
supplied the place of a nose of flesh ; pearl-shells were
inserted in the empty eye-balls ; and any teeth that might
be missing were represented by pieces of wood, while the

[1] *Cambridge Anthropological Expedition to Torres Straits,* v. 250 *sq.*
[2] Diodorus Siculus, i. 91.

lower jaw was lashed firmly to the cranium.[1]   Whether thus Skulls
used in
divination.
decorated or not, the skulls of the dead were preserved and
used in divination.   Whenever a skull was to be thus consulted, it was first cleaned, repainted, and either anointed
with certain plants or placed upon them.   Then the
enquirer enjoined the skull to speak the truth, and placing
it on his pillow at night went to sleep.   The dream which
he dreamed that night was the answer of the skull, which
spoke with a clappering noise like that of teeth chattering
together.   When people went on voyages, they used to take a
divining skull with them in the stern of the canoe.[2]

The great funeral ceremony, or rather death-dance, of Great
death-
dance
of the
Western
Islanders.
the Western Islanders took place in the island of Pulu.
When the time came for it, a few men would meet and
make the necessary preparations.   The ceremony was
always performed on the sacred or ceremonial ground
(*kwod*), and the first thing to do was to enclose this
ground, for the sake of privacy, with a screen of mats
hung on a framework of wood and bamboos.   When the
screen had been erected, the drums which were to be used
by the orchestra were placed in position beside it.   Then
the relations were summoned to attend the performance.
The ceremony might be performed for a number of recently
deceased people at once, and it varied in importance and
elaboration according to the importance and the number
of the deceased whose obsequies were being celebrated.
The chief differences were in the number of the performers
and the greater or less display of scenic apparatus.   The The dead
personated
by masked
actors.
head-dresses or leafy masks worn by the actors in the
sacred drama were made secretly in the bush ; no woman
or uninitiated man might witness the operation.   When
all was ready, and the people were assembled, the men
being stationed in front and the women and children in
the background, the disguised actors appeared on the
scene and played the part of the dead, each one of them
mimicking the gait and actions of the particular man or
woman whom he personated ; for all the parts were played
by men, no woman might act in these ceremonies.   The

[1] *Cambridge Anthropological Expedition to Torres Straits*, v. 258.
[2] *Id.*, p. 362.

order in which the various ghosts were to appear on the
scene was arranged beforehand ; so that when the actors
came forward from behind the screen, the spectators knew
which of the dead they were supposed to have before them.
The performers usually danced in pairs, and vanished behind
the screen when their dance was finished.   Thus one pair
would follow another till the play was over.   Besides the
actors who played the serious and solemn part of the dead,
there was usually a clown who skipped about and cut capers,
tumbling down and getting up again, to make the spectators
laugh and so to relieve the strain on their emotions, which
were deeply stirred by this dance of death.   The beat of
the drums proclaimed that the sacred drama was at an end.
Then followed a great feast, at which special portions of food
were assigned by the relatives of the deceased to the actors
who had personated them.[1]

Intention of the ceremonies.

As to the intention of these curious dramatic performances we have no very definite information.   Dr. Haddon
says : " The idea evidently was to convey to the mourners
the assurance that the ghost was alive and that in the person
of the dancer he visited his friends ; the assurance of his life
after death comforted the bereaved ones." [2]

Funeral ceremonies observed by the Eastern Islanders.

In the Eastern Islands of Torres Straits the funeral ceremonies seem to have been even more numerous and elaborate.
The body was at first laid on the ground on a mat outside the
house, if the weather were fine.   There friends wept and wailed
over it, the nearest relations, such as the wife and mother,
sitting at the head of the corpse.   About an hour after the
sun had set, the drummers and singers arrived.   All night
the drums beat and the people sang, but just as the dawn was
breaking the wild music died away into silence.   The wants
of the living were now attended to : the assembled people
breakfasted on green coco-nuts ; and then, about an hour
after sunrise, they withdrew from the body and took up a
position a little further off to witness the next act of the
drama of death.   The drums now struck up again in quicker
time to herald the approach of an actor, who could be heard,
but not seen, shaking his rattle in the adjoining forest.

[1] *Cambridge Anthropological Expedition to Torres Straits*, v. 252-256.

[2] *Cambridge Anthropological Expedition to Torres Straits*, v. 256.

Faster and faster beat the drums, louder and louder rose the singing, till the spectators were wound up to a pitch of excitement bordering on frenzy.   Then at last a strange figure burst from the forest and came skipping and posturing towards the corpse.   It was Terer, a spirit or mythical being who had come to fetch the soul of the departed and to bear it far away to its place of rest in the island beyond the sea. On his head he wore a wreath of leaves : a mask made of the mid-ribs of coco-nut leaves or of croton leaves hid his face : a long feather of the white tern nodded on his brow ; and a mantle of green coco-nut leaves concealed his body from the shoulders to the knees.   His arms were painted red : round his neck he wore a crescent of pearl-shell : in his left hand he carried a bow and arrows, and in his mouth a piece of wood, to which were affixed two rings of green coco-nut leaf.   Thus attired he skipt forwards, rattling a bunch of nuts in his right hand, bending his head now to one side and now to another, swaying his body backwards and forwards, but always keeping time to the measured beat of the drums.   At last, after a series of rapid jumps from one foot to the other, he ended his dance, and turning round fled away westward along the beach.   He had taken the soul of the dead and was carrying it away to the spirit-land.   The excitement of the women now rose to the highest pitch.   They screamed and jumped from the ground raising their arms in air high above their heads.   Shrieking and wailing all pursued the retreating figure along the beach, the mother or widow of the dead man casting herself again and again prostrate on the sand and throwing it in handfuls over her head.   Among the pursuers was another masked man, who represented Aukem, the mother of Terer.   She, or rather he, was dressed in dried banana leaves : long tufts of grass hung from her head over her face and shoulders ; and in her mouth she carried a lighted bundle of dry coco-nut fibre, which emitted clouds of smoke.   With an unsteady rickety gait the beldame hobbled after her rapidly retreating son, who turned round from time to time, skipping and posturing derisively as if to taunt her, and then hurrying away again westward.   Thus the two quaint figures retreated further and further, he in front and she behind, till they were

The soul of the dead carried away by a masked actor.

lost to view.   But still the drums continued to beat and the singers to chant their wild song, when nothing was to be seen but the deserted beach with the sky and the drifting clouds above and the white waves breaking on the strand. Meantime the two actors in the sacred drama made their way westward till their progress was arrested by the sea. They plunged into it and swimming westward unloosed their leafy envelopes and let them float away to the spirit-land in the far island beyond the rolling waters.   But the men themselves swam back to the beach, resumed the dress of ordinary mortals, and quietly mingled with the assembly of mourners.[1]

Person-
ation of
ghosts by
masked
men.

Such was the first act of the drama. The second followed immediately about ten o'clock in the morning. The actors in it were twenty or thirty men disguised as ghosts or spirits of the dead (*zera markai*). Their bodies were blackened from the neck to the ankles, but the lower part of their faces and their feet were dyed bright red, and a red triangle was painted on the front of their bodies. They wore head-dresses of grass with long projecting ribs of coco-nut leaves, and a long tail of grass behind reaching down to the level of the knees. In their hands they held long ribs of coco-nut leaf. They were preceded by a curious figure called *pager*, a man covered from head to foot with dry grass and dead banana leaves, who sidled along with an unsteady rolling gait in a zigzag course, keeping his head bowed, his red-painted hands clasped in front of his face, and his elbows sticking out from both sides of his body. In spite of his erratic course and curious mode of progression he drew away from the troop of ghosts behind him and came on towards the spectators, jerking his head from side to side, his hands shaking, and wailing as he went. Behind him marched the ghosts, with their hands crossed behind their backs and their faces looking out to sea. When they drew near to the orchestra, who were singing and drumming away, they halted and formed in two lines facing the spectators. They now all assumed the familiar attitude of a fencer on guard, one foot and arm advanced, the other foot and arm drawn back, and lunged to right and left as if they were stabbing some-

[1] *Cambridge Anthropological Expedition to Torres Straits*, vi. 129-133.

thing with the long ribs of the coco-nut leaves which they held in their hands.   This manœuvre they repeated several times, the orchestra playing all the time.   Then they retreated into the forest, but only to march out again, form in line, stand on guard, and lunge again and again at the invisible foe.   This appears to have been the whole of the second act of the drama.   No explanation of it is given. We can only conjecture that the band of men, who seem from their name (*zera markai*) to have represented the ghosts or spirits of the dead, came to inform the living that the departed brother or sister had joined the majority, and that any attempt to rescue him or her would be vain.   That perhaps was the meaning of the solemn pantomime of the lines of actors standing on guard and lunging again and again towards the spectators.   But I must acknowledge that this is a mere conjecture of my own.[1]

Be that as it may, when this act of the drama was over, the mourners took up the body and with weeping and wailing laid it on a wooden framework resting on four posts at a little distance from the house of the deceased.   Youths who had lately been initiated, and girls who had attained to puberty, now had the lobes of their ears cut.   The blood streamed down over their faces and bodies and was allowed to drip on the feet of the corpse as a mark of pity or sorrow.[2] The other relatives cut their hair and left the shorn locks in a heap under the body.   Blood and hair were probably regarded as offerings made to the departed kinsman or kins-woman.   We saw that the Australian aborigines in like manner cut themselves and allow the blood to drip on the corpse ; and they also offer their hair to the dead, cutting off parts of their beards, singeing them, and throwing them on the corpse.[3]   Having placed the body on the stage and deposited their offerings of hair under it, the relatives took some large yams, cut them in pieces, and laid the pieces beside the body in order to serve as food for the ghost, who was supposed to eat it at night.[4]   This notion seems

Marginal note: Blood and hair offered to the dead.

[1] *Cambridge Anthropological Expedition to Torres Straits*, vi. 133 *sq.*

[2] *Id.*, pp. 135, 154.

[3] (Sir) George Grey, *Journals of*

Two Expeditions of Discovery in North-West and Western Australia (London, 1841), ii. 335.

[4] *Cambridge Anthropological Expedition to Torres Straits*, vi. 135.

inconsistent with the belief that the soul of the departed had already been carried off to Boigu, the island of the dead ; but consistency in such matters is as little to be looked for among savages as among ourselves.

Mummifi- cation of the corpse.　　When the body had remained a few days on the stage in the open air, steps were taken to convert it into a mummy. For this purpose it was laid in a small canoe manned by some young people of the same sex as the deceased. They paddled it across the lagoon to the reef and there rubbed off the skin, extracted the bowels from the abdomen and the brain from the skull, and having sewed up the hole in the abdomen and thrown the bowels into the sea, they brought the remains back to land and lashed them to the wooden framework with string, while they fixed a small stick to the lower jaw to keep it from drooping. The framework with its ghastly burden was fastened vertically to two posts behind the house, where it was concealed from public view by a screen of coco-nut leaves. Holes were pricked with an arrow between the fingers and toes to allow the juices of decomposition to escape, and a fire was kindled and kept burning under the stage to dry up the body.[1]

Garb of mourners.　　About ten days after the death a feast of bananas, yams, and germinating coco-nuts was partaken of by the relations and friends, and portions were distributed to the assembled company, who carried them home in baskets. It was on this occasion that kinsfolk and friends assumed the garb of mourners. Their faces and bodies were smeared with a mixture of greyish earth and water : the ashes of a wood fire were strewn on their heads ; and fringes of sago leaves were fastened on their arms and legs. A widow wore besides a special petticoat made of the inner bark of the fig-tree ; the ends of it were passed between her legs and tucked up before and behind. She had to leave her hair unshorn during the whole period of her widowhood ; and in time it grew into a huge mop of a light yellow colour in consequence of the ashes with which it was smeared. This coating of ashes, as well as the grey paint on her face and body, she was expected to renew from time to time.[2] It was also on the occasion of this feast, on or about the tenth

[1] *Op. cit.* p. 136.　　　　[2] *Op. cit.* pp. 138, 153, 157 *sq.*

day after death, that young kinsfolk of the deceased had Cuttings
certain patterns cut in their flesh by a sharp shell. The for the
dead.
persons so operated on were young adults of both sexes
nearly related to the dead man or woman. Women generally operated on women and men on men. The patients
were held down during the operation, which was painful, and
they sometimes fainted under it. The patterns were first
drawn on the skin in red paint and then cut in with the
shell. They varied a good deal in shape. Some consisted
of arrangements of lines and scrolls ; a favourite one, which
was only carved on women, represented a centipede. The
blood which flowed from the wounds was allowed to drip on
the corpse, thus forming a sacrifice or tribute to the dead.[1]

When the body had remained some time, perhaps The Dance
four or six months, on the scaffold, and the process of of Death.
mummification was far advanced, a dance of death was
held to celebrate the final departure of the spirit for its
long home. Several men, seldom exceeding four in
number, were chosen to act the part of ghosts, including
the ghost of him or her in whose honour the performance
was specially held. Further, about a dozen men were
selected to form a sort of chorus ; their business was
to act as intermediaries between the living and the dead,
summoning up the shades, serving as their messengers,
and informing the people of their presence. The costume
of the ghosts was simple, consisting of nothing but a head-
dress and shoulder-band of leaves. The chorus, if we
may call them so, wore girdles of leaves round their
waists and wreaths of leaves on their heads. When The
darkness had fallen, the first act of the drama was played. nocturnal
dance.
The chorus stood in line opposite the mummy. Beyond
them stood or sat the drummers, and beyond them again
the audience was crowded on the beach, the women
standing furthest from the mummy and nearest to the sea.
The drummers now struck up, chanting at the same time
to the beat of the drums. This was the overture. Then
a shrill whistle in the forest announced the approach of
a ghost. The subdued excitement among the spectators,
especially among the women, was intense. Meantime the

---

[1] *Op. cit.* pp. 154 *sq.*

chorus, holding each other's hands, advanced sidelong towards the mummy with strange gestures, the hollow thud of their feet as they stamped on the ground being supposed to be the tread of the ghosts. Thus they advanced to the red-painted mummy with its grinning mouth. Behind it by this time stood one of the ghosts, and between him and the chorus a dialogue ensued. "Whose ghost is there?" called out the chorus; and a strident voice answered from the darkness, "The ghost of so and so is here." At that the chorus retreated in the same order as they had advanced, and again the hollow thud of their feet sounded in the ears of the excited spectators as the tramp of the dead. On reaching the drummers in their retreat the chorus called out some words of uncertain meaning, which have been interpreted, "Spirit of so-and-so, away at sea, loved little." At all events, the name of a dead person was pronounced, and at the sound the women, thrilled with excitement, leaped from the ground, holding their hands aloft; then hurled themselves prone on the sand, throwing it over their heads and wailing. The drums now beat faster and a wild weird chant rose into the air, then died away and all was silent, except perhaps for the lapping of the waves on the sand or the muffled thunder of the surf afar off on the barrier reef. Thus one ghost after another was summoned from the dusty dead and vanished again into the darkness. When all had come and gone, the leader of the chorus, who kept himself invisible behind the screen save for a moment when he was seen by the chorus to glide behind the mummy on its stage, blew a whistle and informed the spectators in a weird voice that all the ghosts that had been summoned that night would appear before them in broad day light on the morrow. With that the audience dispersed. But the men who had played the parts of the ghosts came forward and sat down with the chorus and the drummers on mats beside the body. There they remained singing to the beat of the drums till the first faint streaks of dawn glimmered in the east.

The noonday dance.

Next morning the men assembled beside the body to inspect the actors who were to personate the ghosts,

in order to make sure that they had learned their parts
well and could mimick to the life the figure and gait of
the particular dead persons whom they represented.   By
the time that these preparations were complete, the
morning had worn on to noon.   The audience was already
assembled on the beach and on the long stretch of sand
left by the ebbing tide ; for the hour of the drama was
always fixed at low water so as to allow ample space for
the spectators to stand at a distance from the players,
lest they should detect the features of the living under
the masks of the dead.   All being ready, the drummers
marched in and took up their position just above the
beach, facing the audience.   The overture having been
concluded, the first ghost was seen to glide from the forest
and come dancing towards the beach.   If he represented
a woman, his costume was more elaborate than it had
been under the shades of evening the night before.   His
whole body was painted red.   A petticoat of leaves
encircled his waist : a mask of leaves, surmounted by tufts
of cassowary and pigeon feathers, concealed his head ;
and in his hands he carried brooms of coco-nut palm leaf.
If he personated a man, he held a bow in one hand and
an arrow in the other, and his costume was the usual
dress of a dancer, with the addition of a head-dress
of leaves and feathers and a diamond-shaped ornament
of bamboo, which he held in his teeth and which entirely
concealed his features.   He approached dancing and
mimicking the gestures of the person whom he represented.
At the sight the women wailed, and the widow would cry
out, " That's my husband," the mother would cry out,
" That's my son."   Then suddenly the drummers would
call out, " Ah ! Ah ! Ai ! Ai ! " at which the women would fall
to the ground, while the dancer retreated into the forest.
In this way one ghost after the other would make his
appearance, play his part, and vanish.   Occasionally two
of them would appear and dance together.   The women
and children, we are told, really believed that the actors
were the ghosts of their dead kinsfolk.   When the first
dancer had thus danced before the people, he advanced
with the drummers towards the framework on which the

The ghosts
represented
by masked
actors.

mummy was stretched, and there he repeated his dance before it. But the people were not allowed to witness this mystery ; they remained wailing on the beach, for this was the moment at which the ghost of the dead man or woman was supposed to be departing for ever to the land of shades.[1]

Some days afterwards the mummy was affixed to a new framework of bamboo and carried into the hut. In former times the huts were of a beehive shape, and the framework which supported the mummy was fastened to the central post on which the roof rested. The body thus stood erect within the house. Its dried skin had been painted red. The empty orbits of the eyes had been filled with pieces of pearl-shell of the nautilus to imitate eyes, two round spots of black beeswax standing for the pupils. The ears were decorated with shreds of the sago-palm or with grey seeds. A frontlet of pearl-shell nautilus adorned the head, and a crescent of pearl-shell the breast. In the darkness of the old-fashioned huts the body looked like a living person. In course of time it became almost completely mummified and as light as if it were made of paper. Swinging to and fro with every breath of wind, it turned its gleaming eyes at each movement of the head. The hut was now surrounded by posts and ropes to prevent the ghost from making his way into it and taking possession of his old body. Ghosts were supposed to appear only at night, and it was imagined that in the dark they would stumble against the posts and entangle themselves in the ropes, till in despair they desisted from the attempt to penetrate into the hut. In time the mummy mouldered away and fell to pieces. If the deceased was a male, the head was removed and a wax model of it made and given to the brother, whether blood or tribal brother, of the dead man. The head thus prepared or modelled in wax, with eyes of pearl-shell, was used in divination. The decaying remains of the body were taken to the beach and placed on a platform supported by four posts. That was their last resting-place.[2]

Preservation of the mummy.

[1] *Cambridge Anthropological Expedition to Torres Straits,* vi. 139-141.
[2] *Cambridge Anthropological Expe-* *dition to Torres Straits,* vi. 148 *sq.* As to divination with skulls or waxen models, see *id.,* pp. 266 *sqq.*

To sum up the foregoing evidence, we may say that if the beliefs and practices of the Torres Straits Islanders which I have described do not amount to a worship of the dead, they contain the elements out of which such a worship might easily have been developed.   The preservation of the bodies of the dead, or at least their skulls, in the houses, and the consultation of them as oracles, prove that the spirits of the dead are supposed to possess knowledge which may be of great use to the living ; and the custom suggests that in other countries the images of the gods may perhaps have been evolved out of the mummies of the dead.   Further, the dramatic representation of the ghosts in a series of striking and impressive performances indicates how a sacred and in time a secular drama may elsewhere have grown out of a purely religious celebration concerned with the souls of the departed.   In this connexion we are reminded of Professor Ridgeway's theory that ancient Greek tragedy originated in commemorative songs and dances performed at the tomb for the purpose of pleasing and propitiating the ghost of the mighty dead.[1]   Yet the mortuary dramas of the Torres Straits Islanders can hardly be adduced to support that theory by analogy so long as we are ignorant of the precise significance which the natives themselves attached to these remarkable performances.   There is no clear evidence that the dramas were acted for the amusement and gratification of the ghost rather than for the edification of the spectators.   One important act certainly represented, and might well be intended to facilitate, the final departure of the spirit of the deceased to the land of souls.   But the means taken to effect that departure might be adopted in the interests of the living quite as much as out of a tender regard for the welfare of the dead, since the ghost of the recently departed is commonly regarded with fear and aversion, and his surviving relations resort to many expedients for the purpose of ridding themselves of his unwelcome presence.

General summary

Dramas of the dead.

---

[1] W. Ridgeway, *The Origin of Tragedy, with special reference to the*   *Greek Tragedians* (Cambridge, 1910), pp. 26 *sqq.*

LECTURE IX

THE BELIEF IN IMMORTALITY AMONG THE NATIVES
OF BRITISH NEW GUINEA

The two races of New Guinea, the Papuan and the Melanesian.

IN my last lecture I dealt with the islanders of Torres Straits, and shewed that these savages firmly believe in the existence of the human soul after death, and that if their beliefs and customs in this respect do not always amount to an actual worship of the departed, they contain at least the elements out of which such a worship might easily be developed. To-day we pass from the small islands of Torres Straits to the vast neighbouring island, almost continent, of New Guinea, the greater part of which is inhabited by a race related by physical type and language to the Torres Straits Islanders, and exhibiting approximately the same level of social and intellectual culture. New Guinea, roughly speaking, appears to be occupied by two different races, to which the names of Papuan and Melanesian are now given; and it is to the Papuan race, not to the Melanesian, that the Torres Straits Islanders are akin. The Papuans, a tall, dark-skinned, frizzly-haired race, inhabit apparently the greater part of New Guinea, including the whole of the western and central portions of the island. The Melanesians, a smaller, lighter-coloured, frizzly-haired race, inhabit the long eastern peninsula, including the southern coast from about Cape Possession eastward,[1] and tribes speaking a Melanesian language are also settled about Finsch Harbour and Huon Gulf in German New Guinea.[2] These Melanesians are most probably immigrants who have settled in New

[1] C. G. Seligmann, *The Melanesians of British New Guinea* (Cambridge, 1910), pp. 1 *sq.*

[2] See below, pp. 242, 256, 261 *sq.*, 291.

Guinea from the north and east, where the great chain
of islands known as Melanesia stretches in an immense
semicircle from New Ireland on the north to New
Caledonia on the south-east. The natives of this chain of
islands or series of archipelagoes are the true Melanesians;
their kinsmen in New Guinea have undergone admixture
with the Papuan aborigines, and accordingly should rather
be called Papuo-Melanesians than Melanesians simply. Their
country appears to be wholly comprised within the limits of
British and German New Guinea; so far as I am aware,
the vast area of Dutch New Guinea is inhabited solely by
tribes of the Papuan race. In respect of material culture
both races stand approximately on the same level : they live
in settled villages, they practise agriculture, they engage in
commerce, and they have a fairly developed barbaric art.
Thus they have made some progress in the direction of
civilisation ; certainly they have far outstripped the wandering savages of Australia, who subsist entirely on the products
of the chase and on the natural fruits of the earth.

But although the natives of New Guinea have now
been under the rule of European powers, Britain, Germany,
and Holland, for many years, we unfortunately possess little
detailed information as to their mental and social condition.
It is true that the members of the Cambridge Anthropological Expedition to Torres Straits visited some parts
of the southern coasts of British New Guinea, and several
years later, in 1904, Dr. Seligmann was able to devote
somewhat more time to the investigation of the same region
and has given us the results of his enquiries in a valuable
book. But the time at his disposal did not suffice for a
thorough investigation of this large region ; and accordingly his information, eked out though it is by that of
Protestant and Catholic missionaries, still leaves us in the
dark as to much which we should wish to know. Among the
natives of British New Guinea our information is especially
defective in regard to the Papuans, who occupy the greater
part of the possession, including the whole of the western
region ; for Dr. Seligmann's book, which is the most detailed
and systematic work yet published on the ethnology of British
New Guinea, deals almost exclusively with the Melanesian

Scantiness of our information as to the natives of New Guinea.

portion of the population.   Accordingly I shall begin what
I have to say on this subject with the Melanesian or rather
Papuo-Melanesian tribes of south-eastern New Guinea.

The Motu,
their
beliefs and
customs
concerning
the dead.

Amongst these people the best known are the Motu, a
tribe of fishermen and potters, who live in and about Port
Moresby in the Central District of British New Guinea.
Their language conforms to the Melanesian type.   They
are immigrants, but the country from which they came is
unknown.[1]   In their opinion the spirits of the dead dwell in
a happy land where parted friends meet again and never
suffer hunger.   They fish, hunt, and plant, and are just like
living men, except that they have no noses.   When they first
arrive in the mansions of the blest, they are laid out to dry on
a sort of gridiron over a slow fire in order to purge away the
grossness of the body and make them ethereal and light, as
spirits should be.   Yet, oddly enough, though they have no
noses they cannot enter the realms of bliss unless their noses
were pierced in their lifetime.   For these savages bore holes
in their noses and insert ornaments, or what they regard as
such, in the holes.   The operation is performed on children
about the age of six years ; and if children die before it has
been performed on them, the parents will bore a hole in the
nose of the corpse in order that the spirit of the child may
go to the happy land.   For if they omitted to do so, the
poor ghost would have to herd with other whole-nosed ghosts
in a bad place called Tageani, where there is little food to
eat and no betelnuts to chew.   The spirits of the dead are
very powerful and visit bad people with their displeasure.
Famine and scarcity of fish and game are attributed to the
anger of the spirits.   But they hearken to prayer and appear
to their friends in dreams, sometimes condescending to give
them directions for their guidance in time of trouble.[2]

[1] A. C. Haddon, *Headhunters,
Black, White, and Brown* (London,
1901), pp. 249 *sq.*   As to the Motu
and their Melanesian or Polynesian
affinities, see Rev. W. Y. Turner,
" The Ethnology of the Motu,"*Journal
of the Anthropological Institute*, vii.
(1878) pp. 470 *sqq.*

[2] Rev. J. Chalmers, *Pioneering in*

New Guinea (London, 1887), pp. 168-
170.   Compare Rev. W. Y. Turner,
" The Ethnology of the Motu," *Journal
of the Anthropological Institute*, vii.
(1878) pp. 484 *sqq.* ; Rev. W. G.
Lawes, " Ethnological Notes on the
Motu, Koitapu and Koiari Tribes of
New Guinea," *Journal of the Anthropological Institute*, viii. (1879) pp.
370 *sq.*

Side by side with the Motu live the Koita or Koitapu, who appear to be the aboriginal inhabitants of the country and to belong to the Papuan stock.   Their villages lie scattered for a distance of about forty miles along the coast, from a point about seven miles south-east of Port Moresby to a point on Redscar Bay to the north-west of that settlement.   They live on friendly terms with the Motu and have intermarried with them for generations.   The villages of the two tribes are usually built near to or even in direct continuity with each other.   But while the Motu are mainly fishers and potters, the Koita are mainly tillers of the soil, though they have learned some arts or adopted some customs from their neighbours.   They say to the Motu, " Yours is the sea, the canoes, the nets ; ours the land and the wallaby. Give us fish for our flesh, and pottery for our yams and bananas."   The Motu look down upon the Koita, but fear their power of sorcery, and apply to them for help in sickness and for the weather they happen to require ; for they imagine that the Koita rule the elements and can make rain or sunshine, wind or calm by their magic.   Thus, as in so many cases, the members of the immigrant race confess their inability to understand and manage the gods or spirits of the land, and have recourse in time of need to the magic of the aboriginal inhabitants.   While the Koita belong to the Papuan stock and speak a Papuan language, most of the men understand the Motu tongue, which is one of the Melanesian family.   Altogether these two tribes, the Koita and the Motu, may be regarded as typical representatives of the mixed race to which the name of Papuo-Melanesian is now given.[1]

The Koita believe that the human spirit or ghost, which they call *sua*, leaves the body at death and goes away to live with other ghosts on a mountain called Idu.   But they think that the spirit can quit the body and return to it during life ;

---

[1] A. C. Haddon, *Headhunters, Black, White, and Brown*, pp. 249 *sq.* ; C. G. Seligmann, *The Melanesians of British New Guinea*, pp. 16, 41. As to the Koita (or Koitapu) and the Motu, see further the Rev. W. Y. Turner, " The Ethnology of the Motu," *Journal of the Anthropological Institute*, vii. (1878) pp. 470 *sqq.* ; Rev. W. G. Lawes, " Ethnological Notes on the Motu, Koitapu and Koiari Tribes of New Guinea," *Journal of the Anthropological Institute*, viii. (1879) pp. 369 *sqq.*

it goes away, for example, in dreams, and if a sleeper should unfortunately waken before his soul has had time to return, he will probably fall sick. Sneezing is a sign that the soul has returned to the body, and if a man does not sneeze for many weeks together, his friends look on it as a grave symptom ; his soul, they imagine, must be a very long way off.[1] Moreover, a man's soul may be enticed from his body and detained by a demon or *tabu*, as the Koita call it. Thus, when a man who has been out in the forest returns home and shakes with fever, it is assumed that he has fallen down and been robbed of his soul by a demon. In order to recover that priceless possession, the sufferer and his friends repair to the exact spot in the forest where the supposed robbery was perpetrated. They take with them a long bamboo with some valuable ornaments tied to it, and two men support it horizontally over a pot which is filled with grass. A light is put to the grass, and as it crackles and blazes a number of men standing round the pot strike it with stones till it breaks, whereat they all groan. Then the company returns to the village, and the sick man lies down in his house with the bamboo and its ornaments hung over him. This is supposed to be all that is needed to effect a perfect cure ; for the demon has kindly accepted the soul of the ornaments and released the soul of the sufferer, who ought to recover accordingly.[2]

Beliefs of the Koita concerning the state of the dead.

However, at death the soul goes away for good and all ; at least there appears to be no idea that it will ever return to life in the form of an infant, as the souls of the Central Australian aborigines are supposed to do. All Koita ghosts live together on Mount Idu, and their life is very like the one they led here on earth. There is no distinction between the good and the bad, the righteous and the wicked, the strong and the weak, the young and the old; they all fare alike in the spirit-land, with one exception. Like the Motu, the Koita are in the habit of boring holes in their noses and inserting ornaments in the holes ; and they think that if any person were so unfortunate as to be buried with his nose whole and entire, his ghost would have to go about in the

[1] C. G. Seligmann, *op. cit.* pp. 189-191. [2] C. G. Seligmann, *op. cit.* pp. 185 *sq.*

other world with a creature like a slow-worm depending
from his nostrils on either side. Hence, when anybody dies
before the operation of nose-boring has been performed on
him or her, the friends take care to bore a hole in the nose of
the corpse in order that the ghost may not appear disfigured
among his fellows in dead man's land. There the ghosts
dwell in houses, cultivate gardens, marry wives, and amuse
themselves just as they did here on earth. They live a
long time, but not for ever; for they grow weaker and
weaker and at last die the second death, never to revive
again, not even as ghosts. The exact length of time they
live in the spirit-land has not been accurately ascertained; but there seems to be a notion that they survive
only so long as their names and their memories survive
among the living. When these are utterly forgotten, the
poor ghosts cease to exist. If that is so, it is obvious that
the dead depend for their continued existence upon the
recollection of the living; their names are in a sense their
souls, so that oblivion of the name involves extinction of
the soul.[1] But though the spirits of the dead go away to
live for a time on Mount Idu, they often return to their
native villages and haunt the place of their death. On these
visits they shew little benevolence or lovingkindness to their
descendants. They punish any neglect in the performance
of the funeral rites and any infringement of tribal customs,
and the punishment takes the form of sickness or of bad
luck in hunting or fishing. This dread of the ghost commonly leads the Koita to desert a house after a death and
to let it fall into decay; but sometimes the widow, or in rare
cases a brother or sister, will continue to inhabit the house
of the deceased. Children who play near dwellings which
have been deserted on account of death may fall sick; and
if people who are not members of the family partake of
food which has been hung up in such houses, they also may
sicken. It is in dreams that the ghosts usually appear to
the survivors; but occasionally they may be seen or at least
felt by people in the waking state. Some years ago four
Motuan girls persuaded many natives of Port Moresby that
they could evoke the spirit of a youth named Tamasi, who

Alleged communications with the dead by means of mediums.

[1] C. G. Seligmann, *op. cit.* p. 192.

had died three years before.   The mother and other sorrowing relatives of the deceased paid a high price to the principal medium, a young woman named Mea, for an interview with the ghost.   The meeting took place in a house by night. The relations and friends squatted on the ground in expectation ; and sure enough the ghost presented himself in the darkness and went round shaking hands most affably with the assembled company.   However, a sceptic who happened to assist at this spiritual sitting, had the temerity to hold on tight to the proffered hand of the ghost, while another infidel assisted him to obtain a sight as well as a touch of the vanished hand by striking a light.   It then turned out that the supposed apparition was no spirit but the medium Mea herself.   She was brought before a magistrate, who sentenced her to a short term of imprisonment and relieved her of the property which she had amassed by the exercise of her spiritual talents.[1]   It is hardly for us, or at least for some of us, to cast stones at the efforts of ignorant savages to communicate by means of such intermediaries with their departed friends.   Similar attempts have been made in our own country within our lifetime, and I believe that they are still being made, in perfect good faith, by educated ladies and gentlemen, who like their black brethren and sisters in the faith are sometimes made the dupes of designing knaves.   If New Guinea has its Meas, Europe has its Eusapias.   Human credulity and vulgar imposture are much the same all the world over.

Fear of the dead.

The fear of the dead is strongly marked in some funeral customs which are observed by the Roro-speaking tribes who occupy a territory at the mouth of the St. Joseph river in British New Guinea.[2]   When a death takes place, the female relations of the deceased lacerate their skulls, faces, breasts, bellies, arms, and legs with sharp shells, till they stream with blood and fall down exhausted.   Moreover, a fire is

[1] C. G. Seligmann, *op. cit.* pp. 190-192. As to the desertion of the house after death, see *id.*, pp. 89 *sq.*

[2] The territory of the Roro-speaking tribes extends from Kevori, east of Waimatuma (Cape Possession), to Hiziu in the neighbourhood of Galley Reach.

Inland of these tribes lies a region called by them Mekeo, which is inhabited by two closely related tribes, the Biofa and Vee. Off the coast lies Yule Island, which is commonly called Roro. See C. G. Seligmann, *op. cit.* p. 195.

kindled on the grave and kept up almost continually for months for the purpose, we are told, of warming the ghost.[1] These attentions might be interpreted as marks of affection rather than of fear ; but in other customs of these people the dread of the ghost is unmistakable. For when the corpse has been placed in the grave a near kinsman strokes it twice with a branch from head to foot in order to drive away the dead man's spirit; and in Yule Island, when the ghost has thus been brushed away from the body, he is pursued by two men brandishing sticks and torches from the village to the edge of the forest, where with a last curse they hurl the sticks and torches after him.[2]

Among these people the visits of ghosts, though frequent, are far from welcome, for all ghosts are supposed to be mischievous and to take no delight but in injuring the living. Hence, for example, a widower in mourning goes about everywhere armed with an axe to defend himself against the spirit of his dead wife, who might play him many an ill turn if she caught him defenceless and off his guard. And he is subject to many curious restrictions and has to lead the life of an outcast from society, apparently because people fear to come into contact with a man whose steps are dogged by so dangerous a spirit.[3] This account of the terrors of ghosts we owe to a Catholic missionary. But according to the information collected by Dr. Seligmann among these people the dread inspired by the souls of the dead is not so absolute. He tells us, indeed, that ghosts are thought to make people ill by stealing their souls ; that the natives fear to go alone outside the village in the dark lest they should encounter a spectre ; and that if too many quarrels occur among the women, the spirits of the dead may manifest their displeasure by visiting hunters and fishers with bad luck, so that it may be necessary to conjure their souls out of the village. On the other hand, it is said

Ghost of dead wife feared by widower.

[1] V. Jouet, *La Société des Missionnaires du Sacré Cœur dans les Vicariats Apostoliques de la Mélanésie et de la Micronésie* (Issoudun, 1887), p. 30 ; Father Guis, "Les Canaques : Mort-deuil," *Missions Catholiques*, xxxiv. (1902) pp. 186, 200.

[2] C. G. Seligmann, *op. cit.* pp. 274 *sq.*

[3] Father Guis, "Les Canaques : Mort-deuil," *Missions Catholiques*, xxxiv. (1902) pp. 208 *sq.* See *Psyche's Task*, pp. 75 *sq.*

that if the ghosts abandoned a village altogether, the luck of the villagers would be gone, and if such a thing is supposed to have happened, measures are taken to bring back the spirits of the departed to the old home.[1]

Beliefs of the Mafulu concerning the dead.

Inland from the Roro-speaking tribes, among the mountains at the head of the St. Joseph River, there is a tribe known to their neighbours as the Mafulu, though they call themselves Mambule. They speak a Papuan language, but their physical characteristics are believed to indicate a strain of Negrito blood.[2] The Mafulu hold that at death the human spirit leaves the body and becomes a malevolent ghost. Accordingly they drive it away with shouts. It is supposed to go away to the tops of the mountains there to become, according to its age, either a shimmering light on the ground or a large sort of fungus, which is found only on the mountains. Hence natives who come across such a shimmering light or such a fungus are careful not to tread on it; much less would they eat the fungus. However, in spite of their transformation into these things, the ghosts come down from the mountains and prowl about the villages and gardens seeking what they may devour, and as their intentions are always evil their visits are dreaded by the people, who fill up the crevices and openings, except the doors, of their houses at night in order to prevent the incursions of these unquiet spirits. When a mission station was founded in their country, the Mafulu were amazed that the missionaries should sleep alone in rooms with open doors and windows, through which the ghosts might enter.[3]

Burial customs of the Mafulu.

Common people among the Mafulu are buried in shallow graves in the village, and pigs are killed at the funeral for the purpose of appeasing the ghost. Mourners wear necklaces of string and smear their faces, sometimes also their bodies, with black, which they renew from time to time. Instead of wearing a necklace, a widow, widower, or other near relative may abstain during the period of mourning from eating a favourite food of the deceased. A woman

[1] C. G. Seligmann, *op. cit.* p. 310.
[2] R. W. Williamson, *The Mafulu Mountain People of British New* *Guinea* (London, 1912), pp. 2 *sq.*, 297 *sqq.*
[3] R. W. Williamson, *op. cit.* pp. 243 *sq.*, 246, 266-269.

who has lost a child, especially a first-born or dearly loved child, will often amputate the first joint of one of her fingers with an adze ; and she may repeat the amputation if she suffers another bereavement.   A woman has been seen with three of her fingers mutilated in this fashion.[1]   The corpses of chiefs, their wives, and other members of their families are not buried in graves but laid in rude coffins, which are then deposited either on rough platforms in the village or in the fork of a species of fig-tree.   This sort of tree, called by the natives *gabi*, is specially used for such burials ; one of them has been seen supporting no less than six coffins, one above the other.   The Mafulu never cut down these trees, and in seeking a new site for a village they will often choose a place where one of them is growing.   So long as the corpse of a chief is rotting and stinking on the platform or the tree, the village is deserted by the inhabitants ; only two men, relatives of the deceased, remain behind exposed to the stench of the decaying body and the blood of the pigs which were slaughtered at the funeral feast.   When decomposition is complete, the people return to the village.   Should the coffin fall to the ground through the decay of the platform or the tree on which it rests, the people throw away all the bones except the skull and the larger bones of the arms and legs ; these they bury in a shallow grave under the platform, or put in a box on a burial tree, or hang up in the chief's house.[2]

The skulls and leg and arm bones of chiefs, their wives, and other members of their families, which have thus been preserved, play a prominent part in the great feasts which the inhabitants of a Mafulu village celebrate at intervals of perhaps fifteen or twenty years.   Great preparations are made for such a celebration.   A series of tall posts, one for each household, is erected in the open space which intervenes between the two rows of the village houses.   Yams and taro are fastened to the upper parts of the posts ; and below them are hung in circles the skulls and arm and leg bones of dead chiefs, their wives, and kinsfolk, which have been preserved in the manner described.   Any skulls

Use made of the skulls and bones at a great festival.

[1] R. W. Williamson, *op. cit.* pp. 245-250.   [2] R. W. Williamson, *op. cit.* pp. 256-258, 261-263.

and bones that remain over when all the posts have been thus decorated are placed on a platform, which has either served for the ordinary exposure of a chief's corpse or has been specially erected for the purpose of the festival. At a given moment of the ceremony the chief of the clan cuts down the props which support the platform, so that the skulls and bones roll on the ground. These are picked up and afterwards distributed, along with some of the skulls and bones from the posts, by the chief of the clan to the more important of the invited guests, who wear them as ornaments on their arms in a great dance. None but certain of the male guests take part in the dance; the villagers themselves merely look on. All the dancers are arrayed in full dancing costume, including heavy head-dresses of feathers, and they carry drums and spears, some-times also clubs or adzes. The dance lasts the whole night. When it is over, the skulls and bones are hung up again on the tall posts. Afterwards the fruits and vegetables which have been collected in large quantities are divided among the guests. On a subsequent morning a large number of pigs are killed, and certain of the hosts take some of the human bones from the posts and dip them in the blood which flows from the mouths of the slaughtered pigs. With these blood-stained bones they next touch the skulls and all the other bones on the posts, which include all the skulls and arm and leg bones of all the chiefs and members of their families and other prominent persons who have been buried in the village or in any other village of the community since the last great feast was held. These relics of mortality may afterwards be kept in the chief's house, or hung on a tree, or simply thrown away in the forest; but in no case are they ever again used for purposes of ceremony. The slaughtered pigs are cut up and the portions distributed among the guests, who carry them away for consumption in their own villages.[1]

Trace of ancestor worship among the Mafulu.

This preservation of the skulls and bones of chiefs and other notables for years, and the dipping of them in the blood of pigs at a great festival, must apparently be designed to propitiate or influence in some way the ghosts of the

[1] R. W. Williamson, op. cit. pp. 125-152.

persons to whom the skulls and bones belonged in their lifetime. But Mr. R. W. Williamson, to whom we are indebted for the description of this interesting ceremony, was not able to detect any other clear indications of ancestor worship among the people.[1]

However, a real worship of the dead, or something approaching to it, is reported to exist among some of the natives of the Aroma district in British New Guinea. Each family is said to have a sacred place, whither they carry offerings for the spirits of dead ancestors, whom they terribly fear. Sickness in the family, death, famine, scarcity of fish, and so forth, are all set down to the anger of these dreadful beings, who must accordingly be propitiated. On certain occasions the help of the spirits is especially invoked and their favour wooed by means of offerings. Thus, when a house is being built and the central post has been erected, sacrifices of wallaby, fish, and bananas are presented to the souls of the dead, and a prayer is put up that they will be pleased to keep the house always full of food and to prevent it from falling down in stormy weather. Again, when the natives begin to plant their gardens, they first take a bunch of bananas and sugar-cane and standing in the middle of the garden call over the names of dead members of the family, adding, " There is your food, your bananas and sugar-cane ; let our food grow well, and let it be plentiful. If it does not grow well and plentifully, you all will be full of shame, and so shall we." Again, before the people set out on a trading expedition, they present food to the spirits at the central post of the house and pray them to go before the traders and prepare the people, so that the trade may be good. Once more, when there is sickness in the family, a pig is killed and its carcase carried to the sacred place, where the spirits are asked to accept it. Sins, also, are confessed, such as that people have gathered bananas or coco-nuts without offering any of them to their dead ancestors. In presenting the pig they say, " There is a pig ; accept it, and remove the sickness." But if prayers and sacrifices are vain, and the patient dies, then, while the relatives all stand round the open grave, the chief's sister or cousin calls out in a loud

Worship of the dead among the natives of the Aroma district.

[1] R. W. Williamson, *op. cit.* pp. 270 *sq.*

voice : "You have been angry with us for the bananas or the coco-nuts which we have gathered, and in your anger you have taken away this child. Now let it suffice, and bury your anger." So saying they lower the body into the grave and shovel in the earth on the top of it. The spirits of the departed, on quitting their bodies, paddle in canoes across the lagoon and go away to the mountains, where they live in perfect bliss, with no work to do and no trouble to vex them, chewing betel, dancing all night and resting all day.[1]

The Hood Peninsula.

Between the Aroma District in the south-east and Port Moresby on the north-west is situated the Hood Peninsula in the Central District of British New Guinea. It is inhabited by the Bulaa, Babaka, Kamali, and Kalo tribes, which all speak dialects of one language.[2] The village or town of Kalo, built at the base of the peninsula, close to the mouth of the Vanigela or Kemp Welch River, is said to be the wealthiest village in British New Guinea. It includes some magnificent native houses, all built over the water on piles, some of which are thirty feet high. The sight of these great houses perched on such lofty and massive props is very impressive. In front of each house is a series of large platforms like gigantic steps. Some of the posts and under-surfaces of the houses are carved with figures of crocodiles and so forth. The labour of cutting the huge planks for the flooring of the houses and the platforms must be immense, and must have been still greater in the old days, when the natives had only stone tools to work with. Many of the planks are cut out of the slab-like buttresses of tall forest trees which grow inland. So hard is the wood that the boards are handed down as heirlooms from father to son, and the piles on which the houses are built last for generations. The inhabitants of Kalo possess gardens, where the rich alluvial soil produces a superabundance of coco-nuts, bananas, yams, sweet potatoes, and taro. Areca palms also flourish and produce the betel

The town of Kalo.

[1] J. Chalmers and W. Wyatt Gill, *Work and Adventure in New Guinea* (London, 1885), pp. 84-86.
[2] R. E. Guise, "On the Tribes in-habiting the Mouth of the Wanigela River, New Guinea," *Journal of the Anthropological Institute*, xxviii. (1899) p. 205.

nuts, which are in great demand for chewing with quick-lime and so constitute a source of wealth.   Commanding the mouth of the Vanigela River, the people of Kalo absorb the trade with the interior ; and their material prosperity is said to have rendered them conceited and troublesome.[1]

The tribes inhabiting the Hood Peninsula are reported to have no belief in any good spirit but an unlimited faith in bad spirits, amongst whom they include the souls of their dead ancestors.   At death the ghosts join their fore-fathers in a subterranean region, where they have splendid gardens, houses, and so forth.   Yet not content with their life in the underworld, they are always on the watch to deal out sickness and death to their surviving friends and relations, who may have the misfortune to incur their displeasure.   So the natives are most careful to do nothing that might offend these touchy and dangerous spirits.   Like many other savages, they do not believe that anybody dies a natural death ; they think that all the deaths which we should call natural are brought about either by an ancestral ghost (*palagu*) or by a sorcerer or witch (*wara*). Even when a man dies of snake-bite, they detect in the dis-coloration of the body the wounds inflicted upon him by the fell art of the magician.[2]   On the approach of death the house of the sick man is filled by anxious relatives and friends, who sit around watching for the end.   When it comes, there is a tremendous outburst of grief.   The men beat their faces with their clenched fists ; the women tear their cheeks with their nails till the blood streams down.   They usually bury their dead in graves, which among the inland tribes are commonly dug near the houses of the deceased.   The maritime tribes, who live in houses built on piles over the water, sometimes inter the corpse in the forest.   But at other times they place it in a canoe, which they anchor off the village.   Then, when the body has dried up, they lay it on a platform in a tree. Finally, they collect and clean the bones, tie them in a bundle, and place them on the roof of the house.   When the corpse is buried, a temporary hut is erected over the grave,

Beliefs and customs concerning the dead among the natives of the Hood Peninsula.

---

[1] A. C. Haddon, *Headhunters, Black, White, and Brown*, p. 213.

[2] R. E. Guise, *op. cit.* pp. 216 *sq.*

and in it the widow or widower lives in seclusion for two or
three months. During her seclusion the widow employs
herself in fashioning her widow's weeds, which consist of a
long grass petticoat reaching to the ankles. She wears a
large head-dress made of shells ; her head is shaved, and her
body blackened. Further, she wears round her neck the
waistband of her deceased husband with his lower jaw-bone
attached to it. The costume of a widower is somewhat
similar, though he does not wear a long grass petticoat.
Instead of it he has a graceful fringe, which hangs from his
waist half way to the knees. On his head he wears an
elaborate head-dress made of shells, and on his arms he has
armlets of the same material. His hair is cut off and his
whole skin blackened. Round his neck is a string, from
which depends his dead wife's petticoat. It is sewn up into
small bulk and hangs under his right arm. While the
widow or widower is living in seclusion on the grave, he or
she is supplied with food by relations. At sundown on the
day of the burial, a curious ceremony is performed. An old
woman or man, supposed to be gifted with second-sight, is
sent for. Seating herself at the foot of the grave she peers
into the deepening shadows under the coco-nut palms. At
first she remains perfectly still, while the relations of the
deceased watch her with painful anxiety. Soon her look
becomes more piercing, and lowering her head, while she still
gazes into the depth of the forest, she says in low and
solemn tones, " I see coming hither So-and-So's grandfather "
(mentioning the name of the dead person). " He says he is
glad to welcome his grandson to his abode. I see now his
father and his own little son also, who died in infancy."
Gradually, she grows more and more excited, waving her
arms and swaying her body from side to side. " Now they
come," she cries, " I can see all our forefathers in a fast-
gathering crowd. They are coming closer and yet closer.
Make room, make room for the spirits of our departed
ancestors." By this time she has worked herself up into a
frenzy. She throws herself on the ground, beating her head
with her clenched fists. Foam flies from her lips, her eyes
become fixed, and she rolls over insensible. But the fit
lasts only a short time. She soon comes to herself ;

the vision is past, and the visionary is restored to common life.[1]

Some of the inland tribes of this district have a peculiar way of disposing of their dead. A double platform about ten feet high is erected near the village. On the upper platform the corpse is placed, and immediately below it the widow or widower sleeps on the lower platform, allowing the juices of the decaying body to stream down on her or him. This application of the decomposing juices of a corpse to the persons of the living is not uncommon among savages; it appears to be a form of communion with the dead, the survivors thus in a manner identifying themselves with their departed kinsfolk by absorbing a portion of their bodily substance. Among the tribes in question a widower marks his affection for his dead wife by never washing himself during the period of mourning; he would not rid himself of those products of decomposition which link him, however sadly, with her whom he has lost. Every day, too, reeking with these relics of mortality, he solemnly stalks through the village.[2]

But there is a distinction between ghosts. If all of them are feared, some are more dreadful than others, and amongst the latter may naturally be reckoned the ghosts of slain enemies. Accordingly the slayer has to observe special precautions to guard against the angry and vengeful spirit of his victim. Amongst these people, we are told, a man who has taken life is held to be impure until he has undergone certain ceremonies. As soon as possible after the deed is done, he cleanses himself and his weapon. Then he repairs to his village and seats himself on the logs of sacrificial staging. No one approaches him or takes any notice whatever of him. Meantime a house is made ready, in which he must live by himself for several days, waited on only by two or three small boys. He may eat nothing but toasted bananas, and only the central parts of them; the ends are thrown away. On the third day a small feast is prepared for him by his friends, who also provide him with some new waistbands. Next day, arrayed in all his finery and wearing the badges which mark him as

Applica-tion of the juices of the dead to the persons of the living.

Precau-tions taken by man-slayers against the ghosts of their victims.

---

[1] R. E. Guise, *op. cit.* pp. 210 *sq.*   [2] R. E. Guise, *op. cit.* p. 211.

a homicide, he sallies forth fully armed and parades the village. Next day a hunt takes place, and from the game captured a kangaroo is selected. It is cut open, and with its spleen and liver the back of the homicide is rubbed. Then he walks solemnly down to the nearest water and standing straddle-legs in it washes himself. All young untried warriors then swim between his legs, which is supposed to impart his courage and strength to them. Next day at early dawn he dashes out of his house fully armed and calls aloud the name of his victim. Having satisfied himself that he has thoroughly scared the ghost of the dead man, he returns to his house. Further, floors are beaten and fires kindled for the sake of driving away the ghost, lest he should still be lingering in the neighbourhood. A day later the purification of the homicide is complete and he is free to enter his wife's house, which he might not do before.[1] This account of the purification of a homicide suggests that the purificatory rites, which have been observed in similar cases by many peoples, including the ancient Greeks, are primarily intended to free the slayer from the dangerous ghost of his victim, which haunts him and seeks to take his life. Such rites in fact appear designed, not to restore the homicide to a state of moral innocence, but merely to guard him against a physical danger; they are protective, not reformatory, in character; they are exorcisms, not purifications in the sense which we attach to the word. This interpretation of the ceremonies observed by manslayers among many peoples might be supported by a large array of evidence; but to go into the matter fully would lead me into a long digression. I have collected some of the evidence elsewhere.[2]

Beliefs and customs concerning the dead among the Massim of south-eastern New Guinea.

We now pass to that branch of the Papuo-Melanesian race which occupies the extreme south-eastern part of British New Guinea, and to which Dr. Seligmann gives the name of Massim. These people have been observed more especially at three places, namely Bartle Bay, Wagawaga, and Tubetube, a small island of the Engineer group lying off the south-eastern extremity of New Guinea.

[1] R. E. Guise, op. cit. pp. 213 sq.   and the Perils of the Soul, pp. 167
[2] Psyche's Task, pp. 52 sqq. ; Taboo   sqq.

Among them the old custom was to bury the dead
on the outskirts of the hamlet and sometimes within
a few yards of the houses, and apparently the remains
were afterwards as a rule left undisturbed ; there was no
general practice of exhuming the bones and depositing
them elsewhere.[1]   At Wagawaga the name for the spirit
or soul of a dead person is *arugo*, which also signifies a
man's shadow or reflection in a glass or in water; and
though animals and trees are not supposed to have spirits,
their reflections bear the same name *arugo*.[2]   The souls of   Hiyoyoa,
the dead are believed to depart to the land of Hiyoyoa,   the land of
                                                           the dead.
which is under the sea, near Maivara, at the head of Milne
Bay.   The land of the dead, as usual, resembles in all
respects the land of the living, except that it is day there
when it is night at Wagawaga, and the dead speak of
the upper world in the language of Milne Bay instead of
in that of Wagawaga.   A certain being called Tumudurere
receives the ghosts on their arrival and directs them where
to make their gardens.   The souls of living men and
women can journey to the land of the dead and return
to earth ; indeed this happens not unfrequently.   There
is a man at Wagawaga who has often gone thither and
come back ; whenever he wishes to make the journey, he
has nothing to do but to smear himself with a magical
stuff and to fall asleep, after which he soon wakes up in
Hiyoyoa.   At first the ghosts whom he met in the other
world did not invite him to partake of their food, because
they knew that if he did so he could not return to the
land of the living ; but apparently practice has rendered
him immune to the usually fatal effects of the food of
the dead.[3]   Though Hiyoyoa, at the head of Milne Bay,
lies to the west of Wagawaga, the dead are buried in a
squatting posture with their faces turned to the east, in
order that their souls may depart to the other world.[4]
Immediately after the funeral the relations who have taken   Mourners
part in the burial go down to the sea and bathe, and so   bathe and
                                                            shave their
do the widow and children of the deceased because they   heads.

[1] C. G. Seligmann, *The Melanesians*   [3] C. G. Seligmann, *op. cit.* pp.
of British New Guinea, p. 607.   655 *sq.*
[2] C. G. Seligmann, *op. cit.* p. 655.   [4] C. G. Seligmann, *op. cit.* p. 610.

supported the dying husband and father in his extremity. After bathing in the sea the widow and children shave their heads.[1] Both the bathing and the shaving are doubtless forms of ceremonial purification; in other words, they are designed to rid the survivors of the taint of death, or perhaps more definitely to remove the ghost from their persons, to which he may be supposed to cling like a burr. At Bartle Bay the dead are buried on their sides with their heads pointing in the direction from which the totem clan of the deceased is said to have come origin-

Food deposited in the grave.

ally; and various kinds of food, of which the dead man had partaken in his last illness, are deposited, along with some paltry personal ornaments, in the grave. Apparently the food is intended to serve as provision for the ghost on his journey to the other world. Curiously enough, the

Dietary restrictions imposed on mourners.

widow is forbidden to eat of the same kinds of food of which her husband ate during his last illness, and the prohibition is strictly observed until after the last of the funeral feasts.[2] The motive of the prohibition is not obvious; perhaps it may be a fear of attracting the ghost back to earth through the savoury food which he loved in the body. At Wagawaga, after the relatives who took part in the burial have bathed in the sea, they cut down several of the coco-nut trees which belonged to the deceased, leaving both nuts and trees to rot on the ground. During the first two or three weeks after the funeral these same relatives may not eat boiled food, but only roast; they may not drink water, but only the milk of young coco-nuts made hot, and although they may eat yams they must abstain from bananas and sugar-cane.[3] A man may not eat coco-nuts grown in his dead father's hamlet, nor pigs and areca-nuts from it during the whole remainder of his life.[4] The reasons for these dietary restrictions are not mentioned, but no doubt the abstinences are based on a fear of the ghost, or at all events on a dread of the contagion of death, to which all who had a share in the burial are especially exposed.

[1] C. G. Seligmann, *op. cit.* p. 611.
[2] C. G. Seligmann, *op. cit.* pp. 616 *sq.*
[3] C. G. Seligmann, *op. cit.* p. 611.
[4] C. G. Seligmann, *op. cit.* pp. 618 *sq.*

At Tubetube, in like manner, immediately after a Funeral customs at Tubetube. funeral a brother of the deceased cuts down two or three of the dead man's coco-nut trees. There, also, the children of the deceased may not eat any coco-nuts from their father's trees nor even from any trees grown in his hamlet; nay, they may not partake of any garden produce grown in the vicinity of the hamlet; and similarly they must abstain from the pork of all pigs fattened in their dead father's village. But these prohibitions do not apply to the brothers, sisters, and other relatives of the departed. The relations who have assisted at the burial remain at the grave for five or six days, being fed by the brothers or other near kinsfolk of the deceased. They may not quit the spot even at night, and if it rains they huddle into a shelter built over the grave. During their vigil at the tomb they may not drink water, but are allowed a little heated coco-nut milk; they are supposed to eat only a little yam and other vegetable food.[1] On the day when The fire on the grave. the body is buried a fire is kindled at the grave and kept burning night and day until the feast of the dead has been held. " The reason for having the fire is that the spirit may be able to get warm when it rises from the grave. The natives regard the spirit as being very cold, even as the body is when the life has departed from it, and without this external warmth provided by the fire it would be unable to undertake the journey to its final home. The feast for the dead is celebrated when the flesh has decayed, and in some places the skull is taken from the grave, washed and placed in the house, being buried again when the feast is over. At Tubetube this custom of taking the skull from the grave is not regularly followed, in some instances it is, but the feast is always held, and on the night of the day on which the feast takes place, the fire, which has been in some cases kept burning for over a month, is allowed to burn out, as the spirit, being now safe and happy in the spirit-land, has no further need of it." [2] " In this spirit-land eternal youth The happy land. prevails, there are no old men nor old women, but all

---

[1] C. G. Seligmann, *op. cit.* pp. 613 *sq.*

[2] The Rev. J. T. Field of Tubetube

(Slade Island), quoted by George Brown, D.D., *Melanesians and Polynesians* (London, 1910), pp. 442 *sq.*

are in the full vigour of the prime of life, or are attaining thereto, and having reached that stage never grow older. Old men and old women, who die as such on Tubetube, renew their youth in this happy place, where there are no more sickness, no evil spirits, and no death. Marriage, and giving in marriage, continue ; if a man dies, his widow, though she may have married again, is at her death re-united to her first husband in the spirit-land, and the second husband when he arrives has to take one of the women already there who may be without a mate, unless he marries again before his death, in which case he would have to wait until his wife joins him. Children are born, and on arriving at maturity do not grow older. Houses are built, canoes are made but they are never launched, and gardens are planted and yield abundantly. The spirits of their animals, dogs, pigs, etc., which have died on Tubetube, precede and follow them to the spirit-land. Fighting and stealing are unknown, and all are united in a common brotherhood." [1]

The names of the dead not mentioned.
In the south-eastern part of New Guinea the fear of the dead is further manifested by the common custom of avoiding the mention of their names. If their names were those of common objects, the words are dropped from the language of the district so long as the memory of the departed persists, and new names are substituted for them. For example, when a man named Binama, which means the hornbill, died at Wagawaga, the name of the bird was changed to *ambadina*, which means "the plasterer." [2] In this way many words are either permanently lost or revived with modified or new meanings. Hence the fear of the dead is here, as in many other places, a fertile source of change in language. Another indication of the terror inspired by ghosts is the custom of abandoning or destroying the house in which a death has taken place ; and this custom used to be observed in certain cases at Tubetube and Wagawaga. [3]

[1] Rev. J. T. Field, *op. cit.* pp. 443 *sq.*
[2] C. G. Seligmann, *op. cit.* pp. 629-631. Dr. Seligmann seems to think that the custom is at present dictated by courtesy and a reluctance to grieve the relatives of the deceased ; but the original motive can hardly have been any other than a fear of the ghost.
[3] C. G. Seligmann, *op. cit.* pp. 631 *sq.*

Thus far I have dealt mainly with the beliefs and
practices of the Papuo-Melanesians in the eastern part of
British New Guinea. With regard to the pure Papuan
population in the western part of the possession our information is much scantier. However, we learn that in
Kiwai, a large island at the mouth of the Fly River, the
dead are buried in the villages and the ghosts are supposed
to live in the ground near their decaying bodies, but to
emerge from time to time into the upper air and look about
them, only, however, to return to their abode beneath the
sod. Nothing is buried with the corpse ; but a small
platform is made over the grave, or sticks are planted in
the ground along its sides, and on these are placed sago,
yams, bananas, coco-nuts, and cooked crabs and fish, all for
the spirit of the dead to eat. A fire is also kindled beside
the grave and kept up by the friends for nine days in order
that the poor ghost may not shiver with cold at night.
These practices prove not merely a belief in the survival
of the soul after death but a desire to make it comfortable.
Further, when the deceased is a man, his bow and arrows
are stuck at the head of the grave ; when the deceased is
a woman, her petticoat is hung upon a stick. No doubt
the weapons and the garment are intended for the use of
the ghost, when he or she revisits the upper air. On the
ninth day after the burial a feast is prepared, the drum is
beaten, the conch shell blown, and the chief mourner
declares that no more fires need be lighted and no more
food placed on the grave.[1]

According to the natives of Kiwai the land of the dead
is called Adiri or Woibu. The first man to go thither and
to open up a road for others to follow him, was Sido, a
popular hero about whom the people tell many tales. But
whereas in his lifetime Sido was an admired and beneficent
being, in his ghostly character he became a mischievous elf
who played pranks on such as he fell in with. His adventures after death furnish the theme of many stories.
However, it is much to his credit that, finding the land of

Beliefs and customs concerning the dead in the island of Kiwai.

Adiri, the land of the dead, and Sido, the first man who went thither.

[1] Rev. J. Chalmers, "Notes on the
Natives of Kiwai Island, Fly River,
British New Guinea," *Journal of the*
Anthropological Institute, xxxiii. (1903)
pp. 119, 120.

the dead a barren region without vegetation of any sort, he, by an act of generation, converted it into a garden, where bananas, yams, taro, coco-nuts and other fruits and vegetables grew and ripened in a single night. Having thus fertilised the lower region, he announced to Adiri, the lord of the subterranean realm, that he was the precursor of many more men and women who would descend thereafter into the spirit world. His prediction has been amply fulfilled; for ever since then everybody has gone by the same road to the same place.[1] However, when a person dies, his or her spirit may linger for a few days in the neighbourhood of its old home before setting out for the far country. During that time the spirit may occasionally be seen by ordinary people, and accordingly the natives are careful not to go out in the dark for fear of coming bolt on the ghost; and they sometimes adopt other precautions against the prowling spectre, who might otherwise haunt them and carry them off with him to deadland. Some classes of ghosts are particularly dreaded on account of their malignity; such, for example, are the spirits of women who have died in childbed, and of people who have hanged themselves or been devoured by crocodiles. Such ghosts loiter for a long time about the places where they died, and they are very dangerous, because they are for ever luring other people to die the same death which they died themselves. Yet another troop of evil ghosts are the souls of those who were beheaded in battle; for they kill and devour people, and at night you may see the blood shining like fire as it gushes from the gaping gashes in their throats.[2]

The road to Adiri or deadland is fairly well known, and the people can point to many landmarks on it. For example, in the island of Paho there is a tree called *dani*, under which the departing spirits sit down and weep. When they have cried their fill and rubbed their poor tear-bedraggled faces with mud, they make little pellets of clay and throw them at the tree, and anybody can see for himself the pellets sticking to the branches. It is true that

The fear of ghosts.

The path of the ghosts to Adiri.

[1] G. Landtman, "Wanderings of the Dead in the Folk-lore of the Kiwai-speaking Papuans," *Festskrift tillägnad Edvard Westermarck* (Helsingfors, 1912), pp. 59-66.

[2] G. Landtman, *op. cit.* pp. 67 *sq.*

the pellets resemble the nests of insects, but this resemblance
is only fortuitous.   Near the tree is a rocking stone, which
the ghosts set in motion, and the sound that they make in
so doing is like the muffled roll of a drum.   And while the
stone rocks to and fro with a hollow murmur, the ghosts
dance, the men on one side of the stone and the women on
the other.   Again at Mabudavane, where the Mawata people
have gardens, you may sometimes hear, in the stillness of
night, the same weird murmur, which indicates the presence
of a ghost.   Then everybody keeps quiet, the children are
hushed to silence, and all listen intently.   The murmur
continues for a time and then ends abruptly in a splash,
which tells the listeners that the ghost has leaped over the
muddy creek.   Further on, the spirits come to Boigu, where
they swim in the waterhole and often appear to people in
their real shape.   But after Boigu the track of the ghosts is
lost, or at least has not been clearly ascertained.   The spirit Adiri, the
world lies somewhere away in the far west, but the living land of
are not quite sure of the way to it, and they are somewhat vague in their accounts of it.   There is no difference
between the fate of the good and the fate of the bad
in the far country ; the dead meet the friends who died
before them ; and people who come from the same village
probably live together in the same rooms of the long
house of the ghosts.   However, some native sceptics even
doubt whether there is such a place as Adiri at all, and
whether death may not be the end of consciousness to the
individual.[1]

The dead often appear to the living in dreams, warning Appear-
them of danger or furnishing them with useful information ance of
with regard to the cultivation of their gardens, the practice of to the
witchcraft, and so on.   In order to obtain advice from his dead living in
parents a man will sometimes dig up their skulls from the dreams.
grave and sleep beside them ; and to make sure of receiving
their prompt attention he will not infrequently provide himself
with a cudgel, with which he threatens to smash their skulls
if they do not answer his questions.   Some persons possess
a special faculty of communicating with the departing spirit
of a person who has just died.   Should they desire to

[1] G. Landtman, *op. cit.* pp. 68-71.

question it they will lurk beside the road which ghosts are known to take ; and in order not to be betrayed by their smell, which is very perceptible to a ghost, they will chew the leaf or bark of a certain tree and spit the juice over their bodies. Then the ghost cannot detect them, or rather he takes them to be ghosts like himself, and accordingly he may in confidence impart to them most valuable information, such for example as full particulars with regard to the real cause of his death. This priceless intelligence the ghost-seer hastens to communicate to his fellow tribesmen.[1]

Offerings to the dead.

When a man has just died and been buried, his surviving relatives lay some of his weapons and ornaments, together with presents of food, upon his grave, no doubt for the use of the ghost ; but some of these things they afterwards remove and bring back to the village, probably considering, with justice, that they will be more useful to the living than to the dead. But offerings to the dead may be presented to them at other places than their tombs. "The great power," says Dr. Landtman, "which the dead represent to the living has given rise to a sort of simple offering to them, almost the only kind of offering met with among the Kiwai Papuans. The natives occasionally lay down presents of food at places to which spirits come, and utter some request for assistance which the spirits are supposed to hear."[2] In such offerings and prayers we may detect the elements of a regular worship of the dead.

Dreams as a source of the belief in immortality.

With regard to the source of these beliefs among the Kiwai people Dr. Landtman observes that "undoubtedly dreams have largely contributed in supplying the natives with ideas about Adiri and life after death. A great number of dreams collected by me among the Kiwai people tell of wanderings to Adiri or of meetings with spirits of dead men, and as dreams are believed to describe the real things which the soul sees while roaming about outside the body, we understand that they must greatly influence the imagination of the people."[3]

That concludes what I have to say as to the belief in

[1] G. Landtman, *op. cit.* pp. 77 *sq.*   [2] G. Landtman, *op. cit.* pp. 78 *sq.*
[3] G. Landtman, *op. cit.* p. 71.

immortality and the worship of the dead among the natives of British New Guinea. In the following lectures I shall deal with the same rudimentary aspect of religion as it is reported to exist among the aborigines of the vast regions of German and Dutch New Guinea.

LECTURE X

THE BELIEF IN IMMORTALITY AMONG THE NATIVES
OF GERMAN NEW GUINEA

Andrew
Lang. I FEEL that I cannot begin my second course of lectures without referring to the loss which the study of primitive religion
has lately sustained by the death of one of my predecessors in
this chair, one who was a familiar and an honoured figure in
this place, Mr. Andrew Lang. Whatever may be the judgment
of posterity on his theories—and all our theories on these
subjects are as yet more or less tentative and provisional—
there can be no question but that by the charm of his
writings, the wide range of his knowledge, the freshness and
vigour of his mind, and the contagious enthusiasm which he
brought to bear on whatever he touched, he was a great
power in promoting the study of primitive man not in this
country only, but wherever the English language is spoken,
and that he won for himself a permanent place in the
history of the science to which he devoted so much of his
remarkable gifts and abilities. As he spent a part of every
winter in St. Andrews, I had thought that in the course on
which I enter to-day I might perhaps be honoured by his
presence at some of my lectures. But it was not to be.
Yet a fancy strikes me to which I will venture to give utter-
ance. You may condemn, but I am sure you will not smile
at it. It has been said of Macaulay that if his spirit ever
revisited the earth, it might be expected to haunt the
flagged walk beside the chapel in the great court of Trinity
College, Cambridge, the walk which in his lifetime he loved
to pace book in hand. And if Andrew Lang's spirit could
be seen flitting pensively anywhere, would it not be just

here, in " the college of the scarlet gown," in the "little city worn and grey," looking out on the cold North Sea, the city which he knew and loved so well?   Be that as it may, his memory will always be associated with St. Andrews ; and if the students who shall in future go forth from this ancient university to carry St. Andrew's Cross, if I may say so, on their banner in the eternal warfare with falsehood and error, —if they cannot imitate Andrew Lang in the versatility of his genius, in the variety of his accomplishments, in the manifold graces of his literary art, it is to be hoped that they will strive to imitate him in qualities which are more within the reach of us all, in his passionate devotion to knowledge, in his ardent and unflagging pursuit of truth.

In my last course of lectures I explained that I pro- Review of posed to treat of the belief in immortality from a purely $\underset{\text{lectures.}}{\text{preceding}}$ historical point of view.   My intention is not to discuss the truth of the belief or to criticise the grounds on which it has been maintained.   To do so would be to trench on the province of the theologian and the philosopher.   I limit myself to the far humbler task of describing, first, the belief as it has been held by some savage races, and, second, some of the practical consequences which these primitive peoples have deduced from it for the conduct of life, whether these consequences take the shape of religious rites or moral precepts.   Now in such a survey of savage creed and practice it is convenient to begin with the lowest races of men about whom we have accurate information and to pass from them gradually to higher and higher races, because we thus start with the simplest forms of religion and advance by regular gradations to more complex forms, and we may hope in this way to render the course of religious evolution more intelligible than if we were to start from the most highly developed religions and to work our way down from them to the most embryonic.   In pursuance of this plan I commenced my survey with the aborigines of Australia, because among the races of man about whom we are well informed these savages are commonly and, I believe, justly supposed to stand at the foot of the human scale.   Having given you some account of their beliefs and practices concerning the dead I attempted to do the same for the islanders of Torres Straits and next for the natives of British New Guinea. There I broke off, and to-day I shall resume the thread of my discourse at the broken end by describing the beliefs and practices concerning the dead, as these beliefs are entertained and these practices observed by the natives of German New Guinea.

German
New
Guinea.

As you are aware, the German territory of New Guinea skirts the British territory on the north throughout its entire length and comprises roughly a quarter of the whole island, the British and German possessions making up together the eastern half of New Guinea, while the western half belongs to Holland.

Informa-
tion as to
the natives
of German
New
Guinea.

Our information as to the natives of German New Guinea is very fragmentary, and is confined almost entirely to the tribes of the coast. As to the inhabitants of the interior we know as yet very little. However, German missionaries and others have described more or less fully the customs and beliefs of the natives at various points of this long coast, and I shall extract from their descriptions some notices of that particular aspect of the native religion with which in these lectures we are specially concerned. The points on the coast as to which a certain amount of ethnographical information is forthcoming are, to take them in the order from west to east, Berlin Harbour, Potsdam Harbour, Astrolabe Bay, the Maclay Coast, Cape King William, Finsch Harbour, and the Tami Islands in Huon Gulf. I propose to say something as to the natives at each of these points, beginning with Berlin Harbour, the most westerly of them.

The island
of Tumleo.

Berlin Harbour is formed by a group of four small islands, which here lie off the coast. One of the islands bears the name of Tumleo or Tamara, and we possess an excellent account of the natives of this island from the pen of a Catholic missionary, Father Mathias Josef Erdweg,[1] which I shall draw upon in what follows. We have also

---

[1] P. Mathias Josef Erdweg, "Die Bewohner der Insel Tumleo, Berlinhafen, Deutsch-Neu-Guinea," *Mitthei-* *lungen der Anthropologischen Gesellschaft in Wien,* xxxii. (1902) pp. 274-310, 317-399.

a paper by a German ethnologist, the late Mr. R. Parkinson, on the same subject,[1] but his information is in part derived from Father Erdweg and he appears to have erred by applying too generally the statements which Father Erdweg strictly limited to the inhabitants of Tumleo.[2]

The island of Tumleo lies in 142° 25″ of East Longitude and 3° 15″ of South Latitude, and is distant about sixty sea-miles from the westernmost point of German New Guinea. It is a coral island, surrounded by a barrier reef and rising for the most part only a few feet above the sea.[3] In stature the natives fall below the average European height; but they are well fed and strongly built. Their colour varies from black to light brown. Their hair is very frizzly. Women and children wear it cut short; men wear it done up into wigs. They number less than three hundred, divided into four villages. The population seems to have declined through wars, disease, and infanticide.[4] Like the Papuans generally, they live in settled villages and engage in fishing, agriculture, and commerce. The houses are solidly built of wood and are raised above the ground upon piles, which consist of a hard and durable timber, sometimes iron-wood.[5] The staple food of the people is sago, which they obtain from the sago-palm. These stately palms, with their fan-like foliage, are rare on the coral island of Tumleo, but grow abundantly in the swampy lowlands of the neighbouring mainland. Accordingly in the months of May and June, when the sea is calm, the natives cross over to the mainland in their canoes and obtain a supply of sago in exchange for the products of their island. The sago is eaten in the form both of porridge and of bread.[6] Other vegetable foods are furnished by sweet potatoes, taro, yams, bananas, sugar-cane, and coco-nuts, all of which the natives cultivate.[7] Fishing is a principal industry of the people; it is plied by both sexes and by old and young,

The natives of Tumleo, their material and artistic culture.

[1] R. Parkinson, "Die Berlinhafen Section, ein Beitrag zur Ethnographie der Neu-Guinea-Küste," *Internationales Archiv für Ethnographie,* xiii. (1900) pp. 18-54.
[2] See the note of Father P. W. Schmidt on Father Erdweg's paper, *op. cit.* p. 274.

[3] Erdweg, *op. cit.* p. 274.
[4] Erdweg, *op. cit.* pp. 277 *sq.* The frizzly character of the hair is mentioned by Mr. R. Parkinson, *op. cit.*
[5] Erdweg, *op. cit.* pp. 355 *sqq.*
[6] Erdweg, *op. cit.* pp. 342-346.
[7] Erdweg, *op. cit.* pp. 335 *sqq.*

with nets, spears, and bows and arrows.[1]   Pottery is another flourishing industry.   As among many other savages, it is practised only by women, but the men take the pots to market ;   for these islanders do a good business in pots with the neighbouring tribes.[2]   They build large outrigger canoes, which sail well before the wind, but can hardly beat up against it, being heavy to row.   In these canoes the natives of Tumleo make long voyages along the coast ; but as the craft are not very seaworthy they never stand out to sea, if they can help it, but hug the shore in order to run for safety to the beach in stormy weather.[3]   In regard to art the natives display some taste and skill in wood-carving. For example, the projecting house-beams are sometimes carved in the shape of crocodiles, birds, and grotesque human figures ; and their canoes, paddles, head-rests, drums, drumsticks, and vessels are also decorated with carving.   Birds, fish, crocodiles, foliage, and scroll-work are the usual patterns.[4]

The temples (*paraks*) of Tumleo.   A remarkable feature in the villages of Tumleo and the neighbouring islands and mainland consists of the *paraks* or temples, the high gables of which may be seen rising above the bushes in all the villages of this part of the coast.   No such buildings exist elsewhere in this region.   They are set apart for the worship of certain guardian spirits, and on them the native lavishes all the resources of his elementary arts of sculpture and painting.   They are built of wood in two storeys and raised on piles besides.   The approach to one of them is always by one or two ladders provided on both sides with handrails or banisters.   These banisters are elaborately decorated with carving, which is always of the same pattern. One banister is invariably carved in the shape of a crocodile holding a grotesque human figure in its jaws, while on the other hand the animal's tail is grasped by one or more human figures.   The other banister regularly exhibits a row of human or rather ape-like effigies seated one behind the other, each of them resting his arms on the shoulders of the figure in front.   Often there are seven such

---

[1] Erdweg, *op. cit.* pp. 330 *sqq.*
[2] Erdweg, *op. cit.* pp. 350 *sqq.*
[3] Erdweg, *op. cit.* pp. 363 *sqq.*
[4] Erdweg, *op. cit.* p. 374.

figures in a row. The natives are so shy in speaking of
these temples that it is difficult to ascertain the meaning
of the curious carvings by which they are adorned. Mr.
Parkinson supposed that they represent spirits, not apes.
He tells us that there are no apes in New Guinea. The
interior of the temple (*parak*) is generally empty. The
only things to be seen in its two rooms, the upper and
lower, are bamboo flutes and drums made out of the hollow
trunks of trees. On these instruments men concealed in
the temple discourse music in order to signify the presence
of the spirit.[1]

Different from these *paraks* or temples are the *alols*,
which are bachelors' houses and council-houses in one.
Like the temples, they are raised above the ground and
approached by a ladder, but unlike the temples they have
only one storey. In them the unmarried men live and the
married men meet to take counsel and to speak of things
which may not be mentioned before women. On a small
stand or table in each of these *alols* or men's clubhouses
are kept the skulls of dead men. And as the temple
(*parak*) is devoted to the worship of spirits, so the men's
clubhouse (*alol*) is the place where the dead ancestors are
worshipped. Women and children may not enter it, but it
is not regarded with such superstitious fear as the temple.
The dead are buried in their houses or beside them. Afterwards the bones are dug up and the skulls of grown men
are deposited, along with one of the leg bones, on the
stand or table in the men's clubhouse (*alol*). The skulls of
youths, women, and children are kept in the houses where
they died. When the table in the clubhouse is quite full of
grinning trophies of mortality, the old skulls are removed
to make room for the new ones and are thrown away in a
sort of charnel-house, where the other bones are deposited
after they have been dug up from the graves. Such a
charnel-house is called a *tjoll páru*. There is one such

The
bachelors'
houses
(*alols*) of
Tumleo.

---

[1] R. Parkinson, " Die Berlinhafen
Section, ein Beitrag zur Ethnographie
der Neu - Guinea - Küste," *Internationales Archiv für Ethnographie*,
xiii. (1900) pp. 33-35. Father
Erdweg speaks of the *parak* as a
spirit-temple or spirit-house in which
the deities of the Tumleo dwell (*op.
cit.* p. 377) : he tells us that as a rule
each village has only one *parak*. As
to the spirits which dwell in these
temples, see below, pp. 226 *sq.*

place for the bones of grown men and another for the bones of women and children. Some bones, however, are kept and used as ornaments or as means to work magic with. For the dead are often invoked, for example, to lay the wind or for other useful purposes ; and at such invocations the bones play a part.[1]

Spirits of the dead thought to be the causes of sickness and disease. But while the spirits of the dead are thus invited to help their living relations and friends, they are also feared as the causes of sickness and disease. Any serious ailment is usually attributed to magic or witchcraft, and the treatment which is resorted to aims rather at breaking the spell which has been cast on the sick man than at curing his malady by the application of physical remedies. In short the remedy is exorcism rather than physic. Now the enchantment under which the patient is supposed to be labouring is often, though not always, ascribed to the malignant arts of the spirits of the dead, or the *mōs*, as the natives of Tumleo call them. In such a case the ghosts are thought to be clinging to the body of the sufferer, and the object of the medical treatment is to detach them from him and send them far away. With this kindly intention some men will go into the forest and collect a number of herbs, including a kind of peppermint. These are tied into one or more bundles according to the number of the patients and then taken to the men's clubhouse (*alol*), where they are heated over a fire. Then the patient is brought, and two men strike him lightly with the packet of herbs on his body and legs, while they utter an incantation, inviting the ancestral spirits who are plaguing him to leave his body and go away, in order that he may be made whole. One such incantation, freely translated, runs thus : " Spirit of the great-grandfather, of the father, come out ! We give thee coco-nuts, sago-porridge, fish. Go away (from the sick man). Let him be well. Do no harm here and there. Tell the people of Leming (O spirit) to give us tobacco. When the waves are still, we push off from the land, sailing northward (to Tumleo). It is the time of the north-west wind (when the surf is heavy). May the billows calm down in the south, O in the south, on the coast of Leming, that we may sail

[1] R. Parkinson, *op. cit.* pp. 35, 42 *sq.* ; Erdweg, *op. cit.* pp. 292 *sq.*, 306.

to the south, to Leming! Out there may the sea be calm,
that we may push off from the land for home!" In this
incantation a prayer to the spirit of the dead to relax his
hold on the sufferer appears to be curiously combined with
a prayer or spell to calm the sea when the people sail across
to the coast of Leming to fetch a cargo of tobacco. When
the incantation has been recited and the patient stroked
with the bundle of herbs, one of his ears and both his arm-
pits are moistened with a blood-red spittle produced by the
chewing of betel-nut, pepper, and lime. Then they take
hold of his fingers and make each of them crack, one after
the other, while they recite some of the words of the preceding
incantation. Next three men take each of them a branch
of the *volju* tree, bend it into a bow, and stroke the sick
man from head to foot, while they recite another incantation,
in which they command the spirit to let the sick man alone
and to go away into the water or the mud. Often when a
man is seriously ill he will remove from his own house to
the house of a relation or friend, hoping that the spirit who
has been tormenting him will not be able to discover him at
his new address.[1]

If despite of all these precautions the patient should die, he or she is placed in a wooden coffin and buried with little delay in a grave, which is dug either in the house or close beside it. The body is smeared all over with clay and decked with many rings or ornaments, most of which, however, are removed in a spirit of economy before the lid of the coffin is shut down. Sometimes arrows, sometimes a rudder, sometimes the bones of dead relations are buried with the corpse in the grave. When the grave is dug outside of the house, a small hut is erected over it, and a fire is kept burning on it for a time. In the house of mourning the wife, sister, or other female relative of the deceased must remain strictly secluded for a period which varies from a few weeks to three months. In token of mourning the widow's body is smeared with clay, and from time to time she is heard to chant a dirge in a whining, melancholy tone. This seclusion lasts so long as the ghost is supposed to be still on his way to the other world. When he has reached

Burial and mourning customs in Tumleo.

---

[1] Erdweg, *op. cit.* pp. 284-287.

his destination, the fire is suffered to die down on the grave, and his widow or other female relative is free to quit the house and resume her ordinary occupations. Through her long seclusion in the shade her swarthy complexion assumes a lighter tint, but it soon deepens again when she is exposed once more to the strong tropical sunshine.[1]

Beliefs of the Tumleo people as to the fate of the human soul after death. The people of Tumleo firmly believe in the existence of the human soul after death, though their notions of the disembodied soul or *mōs*, as they call it, are vague. They think that on its departure from the body the soul goes to a place deep under ground, where there is a great water. Over that water every soul must pass on a ladder to reach the abode of bliss. The ladder is in the keeping of a spirit called *Su asin tjakin* or "the Great Evil," who takes toll of the ghosts before he lets them use his ladder. Hence an ear-ring and a bracelet are deposited with every corpse in the grave in order that the dead man may have wherewithal to pay the toll to the spirit at the great water. When the ghost arrives at the place of passage and begs for the use of the ladder, the spirit asks him, " Shall I get my bracelet if I let you pass ? " If he receives it and happens to be in a good humour, he will let the ghost scramble across the ladder to the further shore. But woe to the stingy ghost, who should try to sneak across the ladder without paying toll. The ghostly tollkeeper detects the fraud in an instant and roars out, " So you would cheat me of my dues ? You shall pay for that." So saying he tips the ladder up, and down falls the ghost plump into the deep water and is drowned. But the honest ghost, who has paid his way like a man and arrived on the further shore, is met by two other ghosts who ferry him in a canoe across to Sisano, which is a place on the mainland a good many miles to the north of Tumleo. A great river flows there and in the river are three cities of the dead, in one of which the newly arrived ghost takes up his abode. Then it is that the fire on his grave is allowed to go out and his widow may mingle with her fellows again. However, the ghosts are not strictly confined to the spirit-land. They can come back to earth and roam about working good or evil for the living and especially for their friends and relations.[2]

---

[1] Erdweg, *op. cit.* pp. 288-291.　　　　[2] Erdweg, *op. cit.* pp. 297 *sq.*

It is perhaps this belief not only in the existence but in the return of the spirits of the dead which induces the survivors to erect monuments or memorials to them. In Tumleo these monuments consist for the most part of young trees, which are cut down, stripped of their leaves, and set up in the ground beside the house of the deceased. The branches of such a memorial tree are hung with fruits, coco-nuts, loin-cloths, pots, and personal ornaments, all of which we may suppose are intended for the comfort and convenience of the ghost when he returns from deadland to pay his friends a visit.[1] But the remains of the dead are not allowed to rest quietly in the grave for ever. After two or three years they are dug up with much ceremony at the point of noon, when the sun is high overhead. The skull of the deceased, if he was a man, is then deposited, as we saw, with one of the thigh bones in the men's clubhouse, while of the remaining bones some are kept by the relations and the others thrown away in a charnel-house. Among the relics which the relations preserve are the lower arm bones, the shoulder-blades, the ribs, and the vertebra. The vertebra is often fastened to a bracelet ; a couple of ribs are converted into a necklace ; and the shoulder-blades are used to decorate baskets. The lower arm bones are generally strung on a cord, which is worn on solemn occasions round the neck so that the bones hang down behind. They are especially worn thus in war, and they are made use of also when their owner desires to obtain a favourable wind for a voyage. No doubt, though this is not expressly affirmed, the spirit of the departed is supposed to remain attached in some fashion to his bones and so to help the possessor of these relics in time of need. When the bones have been dug up and disposed of with all due ceremony, several men who were friends or relations of the deceased must keep watch and ward for some days in the men's clubhouse, where his grinning skull now stands amid similar trophies of mortality on a table or shelf. They may not quit the building except in case of necessity, and they must always speak in a whisper for fear of disturbing the ghost, who is very naturally lurking in the neighbourhood of his skull.

Monuments to the dead in Tumleo.

Disinterment of the bones.

[1] Erdweg, *op. cit.* p. 291.

However, in spite of these restrictions the watchers enjoy themselves; for baskets of sago and fish are provided abundantly for their consumption, and if their tongues are idle their jaws are very busy.[1]

Propitia-
tion of
the souls
of the dead
and other
spirits.
The people think that if they stand on a good footing with the souls of the departed and with other spirits, these powerful beings will bring them good luck in trade and on their voyages. Now the time when trade is lively and the calm sea is dotted with canoes plying from island to island or from island to mainland, is the season when the gentle south-east monsoon is blowing. On the other hand, when the waves run high under the blast of the strong north-west monsoon, the sea is almost deserted and the people stay at home;[2] the season is to these tropical islanders what winter is to the inhabitants of northern latitudes. Accordingly it is when the wind is shifting round from the stormy north-west to the balmy south-east that the natives set themselves particularly to win the favour of ghosts and spirits, and this they do by repairing the temples and club-houses in which the spirits and ghosts are believed to dwell, and by cleaning and tidying up the open spaces around them. These repairs are the occasion of a festival accompanied by dances and games. Early in the morning of the festive day the shrill notes of the flutes and the hollow rub-a-dub of the drums are heard to proceed from the interior of the temple, proclaiming the arrival of the guardian spirit and his desire to partake of fish and sago. So the men assemble and the feast is held in the evening. Festivals are also held both in the temples and in the men's club-houses on the occasion of a successful hunt or fishing. Out of gratitude for the help vouchsafed them by the ancestral spirits, the hunters or fishers bring the larger game or fish to the temples or clubhouses and eat them there; and then hang up some parts of the animals or fish, such as the skeletons, the jawbones of pigs, or the shells of turtles, in the clubhouses as a further mark of homage to the spirits of the dead.[3]

So far as appears, the spirits who dwell in the temples

---

[1] Erdweg, *op. cit.* pp. 291-293.
[2] Erdweg, *op. cit.* pp. 298, 371.
[3] Erdweg, *op. cit.* pp. 295 *sqq.*, 299 *sq.*, 334 *sq.*

are not supposed to be ancestors. Father Erdweg describes Guardian spirits (*tapum*) in Tumleo. them as guardian spirits or goddesses, for they are all of the female sex. Every village has several of them; indeed in the village of Sapi almost every family has its own guardian spirit. The name for these guardian spirits is *tapum*, which seems to be clearly connected with the now familiar word *tapu* or taboo, in the sense of sacred, which is universally understood in the islands of the Pacific. On the whole the *tapum* are kindly and beneficent spirits, who bring good luck to such as honour them. A hunter or a fisherman ascribes his success in the chase or in fishing to the protection of his guardian spirit; and when he is away from home trading for sago and other necessaries of life, it is his guardian spirit who gives him favour in the eyes of the foreigners with whom he is dealing. Curiously enough, though these guardian spirits are all female, they have no liking for women and children. Indeed, no woman or child may set foot in a temple, or even loiter in the open space in front of it. And at the chief festivals, when the temples are being repaired, all the women and children must quit the village till the evening shadows have fallen and the banquet of their husbands, fathers, and brothers at the temple is over.[1]

On the whole, then, we conclude that a belief in the continued existence of the spirits of the dead, and in their power to help or harm their descendants, plays a considerable part in the life of the Papuans of Tumleo. Whether the guardian spirits or goddesses, who are worshipped in the temples, were originally conceived as ancestral spirits or not, must be left an open question for the present.

Passing eastward from Tumleo along the northern coast The Monumbo of Potsdam Harbour. of German New Guinea we come to Monumbo or Potsdam Harbour, situated about the 145th degree of East Longitude. The Monumbo are a Papuan tribe numbering about four hundred souls, who inhabit twelve small villages close to the seashore. Their territory is a narrow but fertile strip of country, well watered and covered with luxuriant vegetation, lying between the sea and a range of hills. The bay is sheltered by an island from the open sea, and the natives

[1] Erdweg, *op. cit.* pp. 295-297.

can paddle their canoes on its calm water in almost any weather. The villages, embowered on the landward side in groves of trees of many useful sorts and screened in front by rows of stately coco-nut palms, are composed of large houses solidly built of timber and are kept very clean and tidy. The Monumbo are a strongly-built people, of the average European height, with what is described as a remarkably Semitic type of features. The men wear their hair plaited about a long tube, decorated with shells and dogs' teeth, which sticks out stiffly from the head. The women wear their hair in a sort of mop, composed of countless plaits, which hang down in tangle. In disposition the Monumbo are cheerful and contented, proud of themselves and their country ; they think they are the cleverest and most fortunate people on earth, and look down with pity and contempt on Europeans. According to them the business of the foreign settlers in their country is folly, and the teaching of the missionaries is nonsense. They subsist by agriculture, hunting, and fishing. Their well-kept plantations occupy the level ground and in some places extend up the hill-sides. Among the plants which they cultivate are taro, yams, sweet potatoes, bananas, various kinds of vegetables, and sugar-cane. Among their fruit-trees are the sago-palm, the coco-nut palm, and the bread-fruit tree. They make use both of earthenware and of wooden vessels. Their dances, especially their masked dances, which are celebrated at intervals of four or five years, have excited the warm admiration of the despised European.[1]

Beliefs of the Monumbo concerning the spirits of the dead. With regard to their religion and morality I will quote the evidence of a Catholic missionary who has laboured among them. "The Monumbo are acquainted with no Supreme Being, no moral good or evil, no rewards, no place of punishment or joy after death, no permanent immortality. . . . When people die, their souls go to the land of spirits, a place where they dwell without work or suffering, but which they can also quit. Betel-chewing, smoking,

---

[1] P. Franz Vormann, "Dorf und Hausanlage bei den Monumbo, Deutsch-Neuguinea," *Anthropos*, iv. (1909) pp. 660 *sqq.*; *id.*, "Zur Psychologie, Religion, Soziologie und Geschichte der Monumbo-Papua, Deutsch-Neuguinea," *Anthropos*, v. (1910) pp. 407-409.

dancing, sleeping, all the occupations that they loved on earth, are continued without interruption in the other world.   They converse with men in dreams, but play them many a shabby trick, take possession of them and even, it may be, kill them.   Yet they also help men in all manner of ways in war and the chase.   Men invoke them, pray to them, make statues in their memory, which are called *dva* (plural *dvaka*), and bring them offerings of food, in order to obtain their assistance.   But if the spirits of the dead do not help, they are rated in the plainest language.   Death makes no great separation.   The living converse with the dead very much as they converse with each other.   Time alone brings with it a gradual oblivion of the departed. Falling stars and lightning are nothing but the souls of the dead, who stick dry banana leaves in their girdles, set them on fire, and then fly through the air.   At last when the souls are old they die, but are not annihilated, for they are changed into animals and plants.   Such animals are, for example, the white ants and a rare kind of wild pig, which is said not to allow itself to be killed.   Such a tree, for example, is the *barimbar*.   That, apparently, is the whole religion of the Monumbo.   Yet they are ghost-seers of the most arrant sort.   An anxious superstitious fear pursues them at every step.   Superstitious views are the motives that determine almost everything that they do or leave undone."[1]   Their dread of ghosts is displayed in their custom of doing no work in the plantations for three days after a death, lest the ghost, touched to the quick by their heartless indifference, should send wild boars to ravage the plantations.   And when a man has slain an enemy in war, he has to remain a long time secluded in the men's club-house, touching nobody, not even his wife and children, while the villagers celebrate his victory with song and dance.   He is believed to be in a state of ceremonial impurity (*bolobolo*) such that, if he were to touch his wife and children, they would be covered with sores.   At the end of his seclusion he is purified by washings and other purgations and is clean once more.[2]   The reason of this

Dread of ghosts.

---

[1] P. Franz Vormann, in *Anthropos*, v. (1910) pp. 409 *sq*.

[2] P. Franz Vormann, in *Anthropos*, v. (1910) pp. 410, 411.

uncleanness of a victorious warrior is not mentioned, but analogy makes it nearly certain that it is a dread of the vengeful ghost of the man whom he has slain. A similar fear probably underlies the rule that a widower must abstain from certain foods, such as fish and sauces, and from bathing for a certain time after the death of his wife.[1]

The Tamos of Astrolabe Bay.

Leaving Potsdam Harbour and the Monumbo, and moving still eastward along the coast of German New Guinea, we come to a large indentation known as Astrolabe Bay. The natives of this part of the coast call themselves Tamos. The largest village on the bay bears the name of Bogadyim and in 1894 numbered about three hundred inhabitants.[2] Our principal authority on the natives is a German ethnologist, Dr. B. Hagen, who spent about eighteen months at Stefansort on Astrolabe Bay. Unfortunately he has mixed up his personal observations of these particular people not merely with second-hand accounts of natives of other parts of New Guinea but with discussions of general theories of the origin and migrations of races and of the development of social institutions; so that it is not altogether easy to disentangle the facts for which he is a first-hand witness, from those which he reports at second,

Mistake of attempting to combine descriptive with comparative anthropology.

third, or fourth hand. Scarcely anything, I may observe in passing, more impairs the value and impedes the usefulness of personal observations of savage races than this deplorable habit of attempting to combine the work of description with the work of comparison and generalisation. The two kinds of work are entirely distinct in their nature, and require very different mental qualities for their proper performance; the one should never be confused with the other. The task of descriptive anthropology is to record observations, without any admixture of theory; the task of comparative anthropology is to compare the observations made in all parts of the world, and from the comparison to deduce theories, more or less provisional, of the origin and growth of beliefs and institutions, always subject to modification and correction by facts which may afterwards be brought to light. There is no harm, indeed there is

[1] P. Franz Vormann, *ibid.* p. 412.
[2] B. Hagen, *Unter den Papua's* (Wiesbaden, 1899), pp. 143, 221.

great positive advantage, in the descriptive anthropologist making himself acquainted with the theories of the comparative anthropologist, for by so doing his attention will probably be called to many facts which he might otherwise have overlooked and which, when recorded, may either confirm or refute the theories in question. But if he knows these theories, he should keep his knowledge strictly in the background and never interlard his descriptions of facts with digressions into an alien province. In this way descriptive anthropology and comparative anthropology will best work hand in hand for the furtherance of their common aim, the understanding of the nature and development of man.

Like the Papuans in general, the Tamos of Astrolabe Bay are a settled agricultural people, who dwell in fixed villages, subsist mainly by the produce of the ground which they cultivate, and engage in a commerce of barter with their neighbours.[1] Their material culture thus does not differ essentially from that of the other Papuans, and I need not give particulars of it. With regard to their religious views Dr. Hagen tells us candidly that he has great hesitation in expressing an opinion. " Nothing," he says very justly, " is more difficult for a European than to form an approximately correct conception of the religious views of a savage people, and the difficulty is infinitely increased when the enquirer has little or no knowledge of their language." Dr. Hagen had, indeed, an excellent interpreter and intelligent assistant in the person of a missionary, Mr. Hoffmann ; but Mr. Hoffmann himself admitted that he had no clear ideas as to the religious views of the Tamos ; however, in his opinion they are entirely destitute of the conception of God and of a Creator. Yet among the Tamos of Bogadyim Dr. Hagen tells us, a belief in the existence of the soul after death is proved by their assertion that after death the soul (*gunung*) goes to *buka kure*, which seems to mean the village of ghosts. This abode of the dead appears to be situated somewhere in the earth, and the Tamos speak of it with a shudder. They tell of a man in the village of Bogadyim

The religion of the Tamos.

Beliefs of the Tamos as to the souls of the dead.

---

[1] For the evidence see B. Hagen, *op. cit.* pp. 193 *sqq.* As to barter he tells us (p. 216) that all articles in use at Bogadyim are imported, nothing is made on the spot.

who died and went away to the village of the ghosts. But
as he drew near to the village, he met the ghost of his dead
brother who had come forth with bow and arrows and spear
to hunt a wild boar. This boar-hunting ghost was very
angry at meeting his brother, who had just died, and drove
him back to the land of the living. From this narrative it
would seem that in the other world the ghosts are thought
to pursue the same occupations which they followed in life.
The natives are in great fear of ghosts (*buka*). Travelling
alone with them in the forest at nightfall you may mark
their timidity and hear them cry anxiously, " Come, let us
be going ! The ghost is roaming about." The ghosts of
those who have perished in battle do not go to the Village
of Ghosts (*buka kure*); they repair to another place called
bopa kure. But this abode of the slain does not seem to be
a happy land or Valhalla ; the natives are even more afraid
of it than of the Village of Ghosts (*buka kure*). They will
hardly venture at night to pass a spot where any one has
been slain. Sometimes fires are kindled by night on such
spots ; and the sight of the flames flickering in the distance
inspires all the beholders with horror, and nothing in the
world would induce them to approach such a fire. The
souls of men who have been killed, but whose death has not
been avenged, are supposed to haunt the village. For some
time after death the ghost is believed to linger in the
neighbourhood of his deserted body. When Mr. Hoffmann
went with some Tamos to another village to bring back the
body of a fellow missionary, who had died there, and darkness had fallen on them in the forest, his native companions
started with fear every moment, imagining that they saw
the missionary's ghost popping out from behind a tree.[1]

Treatment
of the
corpse.

When death has taken place, the corpse is first exposed
on a scaffold in front of the house, where it is decked with
ornaments and surrounded with flowers. If the deceased
was rich, a dog is hung on each side of the scaffold, and
the souls of the animals are believed to accompany the
ghost to the spirit-land. Taros, yams, and coco-nuts are
also suspended from the scaffold, no doubt for the refreshment of the ghost. Then the melancholy notes of a horn are

[1] B. Hagen, *Unter den Papua's* (Wiesbaden, 1899), pp. 264-266.

heard in the distance, at the sound of which all the women rush away. Soon the horn-blower appears, paints the corpse white and red, crowns it with great red hibiscus roses, then blows his horn, and vanishes.[1] He is a member of a secret society, called *Asa*, which has its lodge standing alone in the forest. Only men belong to the society; women and children are excluded from it and look upon it with fear and awe. If any one raises a cry, "*Asa* is coming," or the sound of the musical instruments of the society is heard in the distance, all the women and children scamper away. The natives are very unwilling to let any stranger enter one of the lodges of the society. The interior of such a building is usually somewhat bare, but it contains the wooden masks which are worn in the ceremonial dances of the society, and the horns and flutes on which the members discourse their awe-inspiring music. In construction it scarcely differs from the ordinary huts of the village; if anything it is worse built and more primitive. The secrets of the society are well kept; at least very little seems to have been divulged to Europeans. The most important of its ceremonies is that of the initiation of the young men, who on this occasion are circumcised before they are recognised as full-grown men and members of the secret society. At such times the men encamp and feast for weeks or even months together on the open space in front of the society's lodge, and masked dances are danced to the accompaniment of the instrumental music. These initiatory ceremonies are held at intervals of about ten or fifteen years, when there are a considerable number of young men to be initiated together.[2] Although we are still in the dark as to the real meaning of this and indeed of almost all similar secret societies among savages, the solemn part played by a member of the society at the funeral rites seems very significant. Why should he come mysteriously to the melancholy music of the horn, paint the corpse red and white, crown it with red roses, and then

Secret Society called Asa.

---

[1] B. Hagen, *op. cit.* pp. 258 *sq.*

[2] B. Hagen, *op. cit.* pp. 270 *sq.*

As to the period and details of the circumcision ceremonies see *id.*, pp. 234-238.

vanish again to music as he had come? It is scarcely rash to suppose that this ceremony has some reference to the state of the dead man's soul, and we may conjecture that just as the fruits hung on the scaffold are doubtless intended for the consumption of the ghost, and the souls of the dogs are expressly said to accompany him to the spirit-land, so the painting of the corpse and the crown of red roses may be designed in some way to speed the parting spirit on the way to its long home. In the absence of exact information as to the beliefs of these savages touching the state of the dead we can only guess at the meaning which they attach to these symbols. Perhaps they think that only ghosts who are painted red and white and who wear wreaths of red roses on their heads are admitted to the Village of the Ghosts, and that such as knock at the gate with no paint on their bodies and no wreath of roses on their brows are refused admittance and must turn sorrowfully away, to haunt their undutiful friends on earth who had omitted to pay the last marks of respect and honour to the dead.

Burial customs of the Tamos. When the corpse has lain in all its glory, with its ornaments, its paint and its flowers, for a short time on the scaffold, it is removed and buried. The exposure never lasts more than a day. If the man died in the morning, he is buried at night. The grave is dug in the house itself. It is only about three feet deep and four feet long. If the corpse is too long for the grave, as usually happens, the legs are remorselessly doubled up and trampled in. It is the relations on the mother's side who dig the grave and lower the body, shrouded in mats or leaves, into its narrow bed. Before doing so they take care to strip it of its ornaments, its rings, necklaces, boar's teeth, and so forth, which no doubt are regarded as too valuable to be sacrificed. Yet a regard for the comfort of the dead is shewn by the custom of covering the open grave with wood and then heaping the mould on the top, in order, we are told, that the earth may not press heavy on him who sleeps below. *Sit tibi terra levis!* After some months Removal of the lower jawbone. the grave is opened and the lower jaw removed from the corpse and preserved. This removal of the jaw is the

occasion of solemnities and ceremonial washings, in which
the whole male population of the village takes part.
But as to the meaning of these ceremonies, and as to
what is done with the jawbone, we have no exact information.[1]   According to the Russian traveller, Baron N.
von Miklucho-Maclay, who has also given us an account
of the Papuans of Astrolabe Bay,[2] though not apparently
of the villages described by Dr. Hagen, the whole skull
is dug up and separated from the corpse after the lapse of
about a year, but only the lower jawbone is carefully kept by
the nearest kinsman as a memorial of the deceased.   Baron
Miklucho-Maclay had great difficulty in inducing a native
to part with one of these memorials of a dead relation.[3]
In any case the preservation of this portion of the deceased
may be supposed to have for its object the maintenance of
friendly relations between the living and the dead.   Similarly
in Uganda the jawbone is the only part of the body of a
deceased king which, along with his navel-string, is carefully
preserved in his temple-tomb and consulted oracularly.[4]
We may conjecture that the reason for preserving this
part of the human frame rather than any other is that the
jawbone is an organ of speech, and that therefore it appears
to the primitive mind well fitted to maintain intercourse
with the dead man's spirit and to obtain oracular communications from him.

The Russian traveller, Baron Miklucho-Maclay, has
described a curious funeral ceremony which is observed by
some of the Papuans of Astrolabe Bay.   I will give the first
part of his description in his own words, which I translate from
the German.   He says : " The death of a man is announced to
the neighbouring villages by a definite series of beats on the
drum.   On the same day or the next morning the whole male
population assembles in the vicinity of the village of the
deceased.   All the men are in full warlike array.   To the
beat of drum the guests march into the village, where a crowd

Sham fight
as a funeral
ceremony
at Astro-
labe Bay.

[1] B. Hagen, *op. cit.* p. 260.
[2] N. von Miklucho-Maclay, "Ethno-
logische Bemerkungen über die Papuas
der Maclay-Küste in Neu-Guinea,"
*Natuurkundig Tijdschrift voor Neder-
landsch Indie*, xxxv. (1875) pp. 66-93 ;

id., xxxvi. (1876) pp. 294-333.
[3] N. von Miklucho-Maclay, *op. cit.*
xxxvi. (1876) p. 302.
[4] Rev. J. Roscoe, *The Baganda*
(London, 1911), pp. 109 *sqq.* ; *Totemism and Exogamy*, ii. 470.

of men, also armed for war, await the new-comers beside the dead man's hut.   After a short parley the men divide into two opposite camps, and thereupon a sham fight takes place. However, the combatants go to work very gingerly and make no use of their spears.   But dozens of arrows are continually discharged, and not a few are wounded in the sham fight, though not seriously.   The nearest relations and friends of the deceased appear especially excited and behave as if they were frantic.   When all are hot and tired and all arrows have been shot away, the pretended enemies seat themselves in a circle and in what follows most of them act as simple spectators."   Thereupon the nearest relations bring out the corpse and deposit it in a crouching position, with the knees drawn up to the chin, on some mats and leaves of the sago-palm, which had previously been spread out in the middle of the open space.   Beside the corpse are laid his things, some presents from neighbours, and some freshly cooked food.   While the men sit round in a circle, the women, even the nearest relatives of the deceased, may only look on from a distance.   When all is ready, some men step out from the circle to help the nearest of kin in the next proceedings, which consist in tying the corpse up tightly into a bundle by means of rattans and creepers. Then the bundle is attached to a stout stick and carried back into the house.   There the corpse in its bundle is fastened under the roof by means of the stick, and the dead man's property, together with the presents of the neighbours and the food, are left beside it.   After that the house is abandoned, and the guests return to their own villages.   A few days later, when decomposition is far advanced, the corpse is taken down and buried in a grave in the house, which continues to be inhabited by the family.   After the lapse of about a year, the body is dug up, the skull separated from it, and the lower jawbone preserved by the nearest relation, as I have already mentioned.[1]

The sham fight perhaps intended to deceive the ghost.

What is the meaning of this curious sham fight which among these people seems to be regularly enacted after a death ?   The writer who reports the custom offers no explanation of it.   I would conjecture with all due caution

[1] N. von Miklucho-Maclay, *op. cit.* xxxvi. (1876) pp. 300-302.

that it may possibly be intended as a satisfaction to the ghost in order to make him suppose that his death has been properly avenged.   In a former lecture I shewed that natural deaths are regularly imagined by many savages to be brought about by the magical practices of enemies, and that accordingly the relations of the deceased take vengeance on some innocent person whom for one reason or another they regard as the culprit.   It is possible that these Papuans of Astrolabe Bay, instead of actually putting the supposed sorcerer to death, have advanced so far as to abandon that cruel and unjust practice and content themselves with throwing dust in the eyes of the ghost by a sham instead of a real fight.   But that is only a conjecture of my own, which I merely suggest for what it is worth.

Altogether, looking over the scanty notices of the beliefs and practices of these Papuans of Astrolabe Bay concerning the departed, we may say in general that while the fear of ghosts is conspicuous enough among them, there is but little evidence of anything that deserves to be called a regular worship of the dead.

LECTURE XI

THE BELIEF IN IMMORTALITY AMONG THE NATIVES
OF GERMAN NEW GUINEA (*continued*)

The Papuans of Cape King William.

IN my last lecture I gave you some account of the beliefs and practices concerning the dead which have been recorded among the Papuans of German New Guinea. To-day I resume the subject and shall first speak of the natives on the coast about Cape King William, at the foot of Mount Cromwell. We possess an account of their religion and customs from the pen of a German missionary, Mr. Stolz, who has lived three years among them and studied their language.[1] His description applies to the inhabitants of two villages only, namely Lamatkebolo and Quambu, or Sialum and Kwamkwam, as they are generally called on the maps, who together number about five hundred souls. They belong to the Papuan stock and subsist chiefly by the cultivation of yams, which they plant in April or May and reap in January or February. But they also cultivate sweet potatoes and make some use of bananas and coco-nuts. They clear the land for cultivation by burning down the grass and afterwards turning up the earth with digging-sticks, a labour which is performed chiefly by the men. The land is not common property ; each family tills its own fields, though sometimes one family will aid another in the laborious task of breaking up the soil. Moreover they trade with the natives of the interior, who, inhabiting a more fertile and better-watered country, are able to export a portion of their superfluities, especially taro, sweet potatoes, betel-nuts, and

---

[1] Stolz, "Die Umgebung von Kap König Wilhelm," in R. Neuhauss's *Deutsch Neu-Guinea* (Berlin, 1911), iii. 243-286.

tobacco, to the less favoured dwellers on the sea-coast, receiving mostly dried fish in return. Curiously enough the
traffic is chiefly in the hands of old women.[1]

With regard to the religion of these people Mr. Stolz
tells us that they know nothing of a deity who should
receive the homage of his worshippers; they recognise only
spirits and the souls of the dead. To these last they bring
offerings, not because they feel any need to do them reverence, but simply out of fear and a desire to win their favour.
The offerings are presented at burials and when they begin
to cultivate the fields. Their purpose is to persuade the
souls of the dead to ward off all the evil influences that
might thwart the growth of the yams, their staple food.
The ghosts are also expected to guard the fields against
the incursions of wild pigs and the ravages of locusts. At
a burial the aim of the sacrifice is to induce the soul of the
departed brother or sister to keep far away from the village
and to do no harm to the people. Sacrifices are even
offered to the souls of animals, such as dogs and pigs, to
prevent them from coming back and working mischief.
However, the ghosts of these creatures are not very exacting; a few pieces of sugar-cane, a coco-nut shell, or a taro
shoot suffice to content their simple tastes and to keep them
quiet. Amongst the spirits to whom the people pay a sort
of worship there is one named Mate, who seems to be
closely akin to Balum, a spirit about whom we shall hear
more among the Yabim further to the east. However, not
very much is known about Mate; his worship, if it can be
called so, flourishes chiefly among the inland tribes, of whom
the coast people stand so much in awe that they dare not
speak freely on the subject of this mysterious being. Some
of them indeed are bold enough to whisper that there is no
such being as Mate at all, and that the whole thing is a
cheat devised by sly rogues for the purpose of appropriating
a larger share of roast pork at their religious feasts, from
which women are excluded. Whatever may be thought of
these sceptical views, it appears to be certain that the name
of Mate is also bestowed on a number of spirits who disport
themselves by day in open grassy places, while they retire

*Propitia-
tion of
ghosts and
spirits.*

*The spirit
Mate.*

[1] Stolz, *op. cit.* pp. 252-254.

by night to the deep shades of the forest ; and the majority
of these spirits are thought to be the souls of ancestors or
of the recently departed.   Again, there is another class
of spirits called *Nai*, who unlike all other spirits are on
friendly terms with men.   These are the souls of dead
villagers, who died far away from home.   They warn people
of danger and very obligingly notify them of the coming
of trading steamers.   When a man dies in a foreign land,
his soul appears as a *Nai* to his sorrowing relatives and
announces his sad fate to them.   He does so always at night.
When the men are gathered round the fire on the open
square of the village, the ghost climbs the platform which
usually serves for public meetings and banquets, and from
this coin of vantage, plunged in the deep shadow, he lifts up
his voice and delivers his message of warning, news, or
prediction, as the case may be.[1]

However, ghosts of the dead are not the only spiritual
beings with whom these people are acquainted.   They know
of a much higher being, of the name of Nemunemu, endowed
with superhuman power, who made the heaven and the
earth with the assistance of two brothers ; the elder brother
constructed the mainland of New Guinea, while the younger
fashioned the islands and the sea.   When the natives first
saw a steamer on the horizon they thought it was Nemunemu's
ship, and the smoke at the funnel they took to be the
tobacco-smoke which he puffed to beguile the tedium of the
voyage.[2]   They are also great believers in magic and witchcraft, and cases of sickness and death, which are not attributed
to the malignity of ghosts and spirits, are almost invariably
set down to the machinations of sorcerers.   Only the deaths
of decrepit old folks are regarded as natural.   When a man
has died, and his death is believed to have been caused by
magic, the people resort to divination in order to discover
the wicked magician who has perpetrated the crime.   For
this purpose they place the corpse on a bier, cover it with a
mat, and set it on the shoulders of four men, while a fifth
man taps lightly with an arrow on the mat and enquires of
the departed whether such and such a village has bewitched
him to death.   If the bier remains still, it means " No " ; but

Spirits
called *Nai*.

The
creator
Nemu-
nemu.

Sickness
and death
often
regarded
as the
effects of
sorcery.

---

[1] Stolz, *op. cit.* pp. 245-247.   [2] Stolz, *op. cit.* pp. 247 *sq.*

if it rocks backward and forward, it means " Yes," and the avengers of blood must seek their victim, the guilty sorcerer, in that village.   The answer is believed to be given by the dead man's ghost, who stirs his body at the moment when his murderer's village is named.   It is useless for the inhabitants of that village to disclaim all knowledge of the sickness and death of the deceased.   The people repose implicit faith in this form of divination.   " His soul itself told us," they say, and surely he ought to know.   Another form of divination which they employ for the same purpose is to put the question to the ghost, while two men hold a bow which belonged to him and to which some personal articles of his are attached.   The answer is again yes or no according as the bow moves or is still.[1]

When the author of the death has been discovered in one way or another, the corpse is decked with all the orna- ments that can be collected from the relatives and prepared for burial.   A shallow grave is dug under the house and lined with mats.   Then the body is lowered into the grave : one of the sextons strikes up a lament, and the shrill voices of the women in the house join in the melancholy strain. When he lies in his narrow bed, the ornaments are removed from his person, but some of his tools, weapons, and other belongings are buried with him, no doubt for his use in the life hereafter.   The funeral celebration, in which the whole village commonly takes part, lasts several days and consists in the bringing of offerings to the dead and the abstinence from all labour in the fields.   Yams are brought from the field of the departed and cooked.   A small pot filled with yams and a vessel of water are placed on the grave ; the rest of the provisions is consumed by the mourners.   The next of kin, especially the widow or widower, remain for about a week at the grave, watching day and night, lest the body should be dug up and devoured by a certain foul fiend with huge wings and long claws, who battens on corpses. The mourning costume of men consists in smearing the face with black and wearing a cord round the neck and a netted cap on the head.   Instead of such a cap a woman in mourning wraps herself in a large net and a great apron of

Funeral and mourning customs.

---

[1] Stolz, *op. cit.* pp. 248-250.

grass. While the other ensigns of woe are soon discarded or disappear, the cord about the neck is worn for a longer time, generally till next harvest. The sacrifice of a pig brings the period of mourning to an end and after it the cord may be laid aside. If any one were so hard-hearted as not to wear that badge of sorrow, the people believe that the angry ghost would come back and fetch him away. He would die.[1] Thus among these savages the mourning costume is regarded as a protection against the dangerous ghost of the departed; it soothes his wounded feelings and prevents him from making raids on the living.

Fate of the souls of the dead.

As to the place to which the souls of the dead repair and the fate that awaits them there, very vague and contradictory ideas prevail among the natives of this district. Some say that the ghosts go eastward to Bukaua on Huon Gulf and there lead a shadowy life very like their life on earth. Others think that the spirits hover near the village where they lived in the flesh. Others again are of opinion that they transmigrate into animals and prolong their life in one or other of the bodies of the lower creatures.[2]

The Yabim and Bukaua tribes.

Leaving Cape King William we pass eastward along the coast of German New Guinea and come to Finsch Harbour. From a point some miles to the north of Finsch Harbour as far as Samoa Harbour on Huon Gulf the coast is inhabited by two kindred tribes, the Yabim and the Bukaua, who speak a Melanesian language. I shall deal first with the Yabim tribe, whose customs and beliefs have been described for us with a fair degree of fulness by two German missionaries, Mr. Konrad Vetter and Mr. Heinrich Zahn.[3] The following account is based chiefly on the writings of Mr. Vetter, whose mission station is at the village of Simbang.

Material and artistic culture of the Yabim.

Like the other natives of New Guinea the Yabim build permanent houses, live in settled villages, and till the ground. Every year they make a fresh clearing in the forest by

[1] Stolz, *op. cit.* p. 258.

[2] Stolz, *op. cit.* p. 259.

[3] K. Vetter, in *Komm herüber und hilf uns! oder die Arbeit der Neuen-Dettelsauer Mission,* Nos. 1-4 (Barmen, 1898); *id.,* in *Nachrichten über Kaiser Wilhelms-Land,* 1897, pp. 86-102;

id. [? J. Vetter], in *Mitteilungen der Geographischen Gesellschaft zu Jena,* xi. (Jena, 1892) pp. 102-106; *id.,* in *Mitteilungen der Geographischen Gesellschaft zu Jena,* xii. (Jena, 1893) pp. 95-97; H. Zahn, "Die Jabim," in R. Neuhauss's *Deutsch Neu-Guinea,* iii (Berlin, 1911) pp. 287-394.

cutting down the trees, burning the fallen timber, and planting taro, bananas, sugar-cane, and tobacco in the open glade. When the crops have been reaped, the place is abandoned, and is soon overgrown again by the rank tropical vegetation, while the natives move on to another patch, which they clear and cultivate in like manner. This rude mode of tillage is commonly practised by many savages, especially within the tropics. Cultivation of this sort is migratory, and in some places, though apparently not in New Guinea, the people shift their habitations with their fields as they move on from one part of the forest to another. Among the Yabim the labour of clearing a patch for cultivation is performed by all the men of a village in common, but when the great trees have fallen with a crash to the ground, and the trunks, branches, foliage and underwood have been burnt, with a roar of flames and a crackling like a rolling fire of musketry, each family appropriates a portion of the clearing for its own use and marks off its boundaries with sticks. But they also subsist in part by fishing, and for this purpose they build outrigger canoes. They display considerable skill and taste in wood-carving, and are fond of ornamenting their houses, canoes, paddles, tools, spears, and drums with figures of crocodiles, fish, and other patterns.[1]

The villages are divided into wards, and every ward contains its clubhouse for men, called a *lum*, in which young men and lads are obliged to pass the night. It consists of a bedroom above and a parlour with fireplaces below. In the parlour the grown men pass their leisure hours during the day, and here the councils are held. The wives cook the food at home and bring it for their husbands to the clubhouse. The bull-roarers which are used at the initiatory ceremonies are kept in the principal clubhouse of the village. Such a clubhouse serves as an asylum ; men fleeing from the avenger of blood who escape into it are safe. It is said that the spirit (*balum*) has swallowed or concealed them. But if they steal out of it and attempt to make their way to another village, they carry their life in their hand.[2]

Men's clubhouses (lum).

[1] K. Vetter, *Komm herüber und hilf uns!* ii. (Barmen, 1898) pp. 6-12.
[2] K. Vetter, *op. cit.* ii. 8; H.

Zahn, " Die Jabim," in R. Neuhauss's *Deutsch Neu-Guinea*, iii. 291, 308, 311.

Among the Yabim, according to Mr. Zahn, religion in the proper sense does not exist, but on the other hand the whole people is dominated by the fear of witchcraft and of the spirits of the dead.[1] The following is the account which Mr. Vetter gives of the beliefs and customs of these people concerning the departed.

Beliefs of the Yabim concerning the state of the dead.

They do not believe that death is the end of all things for the individual; they think that his soul survives and becomes a spirit or ghost, which they call a *balum*. The life of human spirits in the other world is a shadowy continuation of the life on earth, and as such it has little attraction for the mind of the Papuan. Of heaven and hell, a place of reward and a place of punishment for the souls of the good and bad respectively, he has no idea. However, his world of the dead is to some extent divided into compartments. In one of them reside the ghosts of people who have been slain, in another the ghosts of people who have been hanged, and in a third the ghosts of people who have been devoured by a shark or a crocodile. How many more compartments there may be for the accommodation of the souls, we are not told. The place is in one of the islands of Siasi. No living man has ever set foot in the island, for smoke and mist hang over it perpetually; but from out the mist you may hear the sound of the barking of dogs, the grunting of swine, and the crowing of cocks, which seems to shew that in the opinion of these people animals have immortal souls as well as men. The natives of the Siasi islands say that the newly arrived ghosts may often be seen strolling on the beach; sometimes the people can even recognise the familiar features of friends with whom they did business in the flesh. The mode in which the spirits of the dead arrive at their destination from the mainland is naturally by a ferry: indeed, the prow of the ghostly ferry-boat may be seen to this day in the village of Bogiseng. The way in which it came to be found there was this. A man of the village lay dying, and on his deathbed he promised to give his friends a sign of his continued existence after death by appearing as a ghost in their midst. Only he stipulated that in order to enable him to do so they would place a stone club in the hand of his corpse. This was done. He

The ghostly ferry.

---

[1] H. Zahn, *op. cit.* iii. 291.

died, the club was placed in his cold hand, and his sorrowing but hopeful relations awaited results.   They had not very long to wait.   For no sooner had the ghost, armed with the stone club, stepped down to the sea-shore than he called imperiously for the ferry-boat.   It soon hove in sight, with the ghostly ferryman in it paddling to the beach to receive the passenger.   But when the prow grated on the pebbles, the artful ghost, instead of stepping into it as he should have done, lunged out at it with the stone club so forcibly that he broke the prow clean off.   In a rage the ferryman roared out to him, " I won't put you across !   You and your people shall be kangaroos."   The ghost had gained his point.   He turned back from the ferry and brought to his friends as a trophy the prow of the ghostly canoe, which is treasured in the village to this day.   I should add that the prow in question bears a suspicious resemblance to a powder-horn which has been floating about for some time in the water ; but no doubt this resemblance is purely fortuitous and without any deep significance.

From this veracious narrative we gather that sometimes the souls of the dead, instead of going away to the spirit-land, transmigrate into the bodies of animals.   The case of the kangaroos is not singular.   In the village of Simbang Mr. Vetter knows two families, of whom the ghosts pass at death into the carcases of crocodiles and a species of fabulous pigs respectively.   Hence members of the one family are careful not to injure crocodiles, lest the souls of their dead should chance to be lodged in the reptiles ; and the members of the other family would be equally careful not to hurt the fabulous pigs if ever they fell in with them.   However, the crocodile people, not to be behind their neighbours, assert that after death their spirits can also roam about the wood as ghosts and go to the spirit-land.   In explanation they say that every human being has two souls ; one of them is his reflection on the water, the other is his shadow on the land.   No doubt it is the water-soul which goes to the island of Siasi, while the land-soul is free to occupy the body of a crocodile, a kangaroo, or some other animal.[1]

Transmigration of human souls into animals.

---

[1] K. Vetter, *Komm herüber und hilf uns !* iii. 21 *sq.*   According to Mr. H. Zahn (*op. cit.* p. 324) every village has its own entrance into the spirit-land.

Return of
the ghosts. But even when the ghosts have departed to their island home, they are by no means strictly confined to it. They can return, especially at night, to roam about the woods and the villages, and the living are very much afraid of them, for the ghosts delight in doing mischief. It is especially in the first few days after a death that the ghost is an object of terror, for he is then still loitering about the village. During these days everybody is afraid to go alone into the forest for fear of meeting him, and if a dog or a pig strays in the wood and is lost, the people make sure that the ghost has made off with the animal, and the aggrieved owners roundly abuse the sorrowing family, telling them that their old father or mother, as the case may be, is no better than a thief. They are also very unwilling to mention the names of dead persons, imagining that were the ghost to hear his name pronounced he might fancy he was being called for and might accordingly suspend his habitual occupation of munching sour fruits in the forest to come and trouble the living.

Offerings
to ghosts. Hence in order to keep the short-tempered ghost in good humour by satisfying his wants, lest he should think himself neglected and wreak his vexation on the survivors, the people go a-fishing after a death, or they kill a pig or a dog; sometimes also they cut down a fruit-tree. But it is only the souls of the animals which are destined for the consumption of the ghost; their bodies are roasted and eaten by the living. On a grave you may sometimes see a small basket suspended from a stick; but if you look into it you will find nothing but a little soot and some fish scales, which is all that remains of the fried fish.

Ghosts
provided
with fire. The Yabim also imagine that the ghost has need of fire to guide him to the door of the man who has done him to death by sorcery. Accordingly they provide the spirit with this necessary as follows. On the evening of the day on which the body has been buried, they kindle a fire on a potsherd and heap dry leaves on it. As they do so they mention the names of all the sorcerers they can think of, and he at whose name the smouldering leaves burst into a bright flame is the one who has done the deed. Having thus ascertained the true cause of death, beyond reach of

cavil, they proceed to light up the ghost to the door of his
murderer. For this purpose a procession is formed. A
man, holding the smouldering fire in the potsherd with one
hand and a bundle of straw with the other, leads the way.
He is followed by another who draws droning notes from
a water-bottle of the deceased, which he finally smashes.
After these two march a number of young fellows who
make a plumping sound by smacking their thighs with the
hollow of their hands. This solemn procession wends its
way to a path in the neighbouring forest. By this time the
shades of night have fallen. The firebearer now sets the
fire on the ground and calls on the ghost to come and take
it. They firmly believe that he does so and that having
got it he hies away to cast the glowing embers down at the
door of the man who has done him to death. They even
fancy they see the flickering light carried by the invisible
hand retreating through the shadows into the depth of the
forest ; and in order to follow it with their eyes they will
sometimes climb tall trees or launch a canoe and put out to
sea, gazing intently at the glimmering ray till it vanishes
from their sight in the darkness. Perhaps the gleam of
fire-flies, which abound in these tropical forests, or the
flashing of a meteor, as it silently drops from the starry
heaven into the sea, may serve to feed this superstitious
fancy.[1]

But the spirits of the dead are supposed to be able to
help as well as harm the living. Good crops and a successful hunt are attributed to their influence. It is especially the
spirits of the ancient owners of the land who are credited with
the power of promoting the growth of the crops. Hence
when a clearing has been made in the forest and planted
with taro, and the plants are shewing a good head of leaves,
preparations are made to feast the ghosts of the people to
whom the land belonged in days gone by. For this purpose
a sago-palm is cut down, sago-porridge made, and a wild
boar killed. Then the men arrayed in all their finery march
out in solemn procession by day to the taro field ; and the
leader invites the spirits in a loud voice to come to the

Ghosts
thought to
help in the
cultivation
of the land.

[1] K. Vetter, *Komm herüber und hilf uns!* iii. 19-24 ; *id.*, in *Mittei- lungen der Geographischen Gesellschaft zu Jena,* xii. (1893) pp. 96 *sq.*

village and partake of the sago-porridge and pork that have
been made ready for them.   But the invisible guests content
themselves as usual with snuffing up the fragrant smell of
the roast pork and the steam of the porridge ; the substance
of these dainties is consumed by the living.   Yet the help
which the ghosts give in the cultivation of the land would
seem to be conceived as a purely negative one ; the offerings
are made to them for the purpose of inducing them to keep
away and not injure the growing crops.   It is also believed
that the ghosts of the dead make communications to the
living in dreams or by whistling, and even that they can
bring things to their friends and relations.   But on the
whole, Mr. Vetter tells us, the dominant attitude of the
living to the dead is one of fear ; the power of the ghosts
is oftener exerted for evil than for good.[1]   The ghost of a
murdered man in particular is dreaded, because he is believed
to haunt his murderer and to do him a mischief.   Hence
they drive away such a dangerous ghost with shouts and
the beating of drums ; and by way of facilitating his
departure they launch a model of a canoe, laden with taro
and tobacco, in order to transport him with all comfort to
the land of souls.[2]

Burial and
mourning
customs
among the
Yabim.

Among the Yabim the dead are usually buried in shallow
graves close to the houses where they died.   Some trifles
are laid with the body in the grave, in order that the dead
man or woman may have the use of them in the other
world.   But any valuables that may be deposited with the
corpse are afterwards dug up and appropriated by the
survivors.   If the deceased was the householder himself or
his wife, the house is almost always deserted, however solidly
it may be built.   The reason for thus abandoning so valuable a piece of property is not mentioned ; but we may
assume that the motive is a fear of the ghost, who is
supposed to haunt his old home.   A temporary hut is built
on the grave, and in it the family of the deceased take up
their abode for six weeks or more ; here they cook, eat, and
sleep.   A widower sits in a secluded corner by himself,

[1] K. Vetter, *Komm herüber und
hilf uns!* ii. 7, iii. 24 ; *id.,* in *Nachrichten über Kaiser Wilhelms-Land und*
den *Bismarck-Archipel,* 1897, p. 94.
[2] K. Vetter, in *Nachrichten über
Kaiser Wilhelms-Land,* 1897, p. 94.

invisible to all and unwashed; during the period of full
mourning he may not shew himself in the village. When
he does come forth again, he wears a mourning hat made of
bark in the shape of a cylinder without crown or brim; a
widow wears a great ugly net, which wraps her up almost
completely from the head to the knees. Sometimes in
memory of the deceased they wear a lock of his hair or a
bracelet. Other relations wear cords round their necks in
sign of mourning. The period of mourning varies greatly;
it may last for months or even years. Sometimes the
bodies of beloved children or persons who have been much
respected are not buried but tied up in bundles and set up
in a house until the flesh has quite mouldered away; then
the skull and the bones of the arms and legs are anointed,
painted red, and preserved for a time. Mr. Vetter records
the case of a chief whose corpse was thus preserved in the
assembly-house of the village, after it had been dried over a
fire. When it had been reduced to a mummy, the skull and
the arm-bones and leg-bones were detached, oiled, and
reddened, and then kept for some years in the house of the
chief's eldest son, till finally they were deposited in the
grave of a kinsman. In some of the inland villages of this
part of New Guinea the widow is sometimes throttled by
her relations at the death of her husband, in order that she
may accompany him to the other world.[1]

The Yabim believe that except in the case of very old
people every death is caused by sorcery; hence when anybody has departed this life, his relations make haste to
discover the wicked sorcerer who has killed their kinsman.
For that purpose they have recourse to various forms of
divination. One of them has been already described, but
they have others. For example, they put a powder like
sulphur in a piece of bamboo tube and kindle a fire under
it. Then an old man takes a bull-roarer and taps with
it on the bamboo tube, naming all the sorcerers in the
neighbouring villages. He at the mention of whose name
the fire catches the powder and blazes up is the guilty

Deaths attributed by the Yabim to sorcery.

[1] K. Vetter, in *Nachrichten über Kaiser Wilhelms-Land*, 1897, pp. 94 sq.; *id.*, *Komm herüber und hilf uns!* iii. 15-19. Compare H. Zahn, "Die Jabim," in R. Neuhauss's *Deutsch Neu-Guinea*, iii. 320 sq.

man. Another way of detecting the culprit is to attach the feather of a bird of paradise to a staff and give the staff to two men to hold upright between the palms of their right hands. Then somebody names the sorcerers, and he at whose name the staff turns round and the feather points downwards is the one who caused the death. When the avengers of blood, wrought up to a high pitch of fury, fall in with the family of the imaginary criminal, they may put the whole of them to death lest the sons should afterwards avenge their father's murder by the black art. Sometimes a dangerous and dreaded sorcerer will be put out of the way with the connivance of the chief of his own village ; and after a few days the murderers will boldly shew themselves in the village where the crime was perpetrated and will reassure the rest of the people, saying, " Be still. The wicked man has been taken off. No harm will befall you." [1]

Bull-roarers (*balum*).

It is very significant that the word *balum*, which means a ghost, is applied by the Yabim to the instrument now generally known among anthropologists as a bull-roarer. It is a small fish-shaped piece of wood which, being tied to a string and whirled rapidly round, produces a humming or booming sound like the roaring of a bull or the muttering of distant thunder. Instruments of this sort are employed by savages in many parts of the world at their mysteries ; the weird sound which the implement makes when swung is supposed by the ignorant and uninitiated to be the voice of a spirit and serves to impress them with a sense of awe and mystery. So it is with the Papuans about Finsch Harbour, with whom we are at present concerned. At least one such bull-roarer is kept in the *lum* or bachelors' clubhouse of every village, and the women and uninitiated boys are forbidden to

Initiation of young men.

see it under pain of death. The instrument plays a great part in the initiation of young men, which takes place at intervals of several years, when there are a number of youths ready to be initiated, and enough pigs can be procured to furnish forth the feasts which form an indispensable part of the ceremony. The principal initiatory rite consists of circumcision, which is performed on all youths before they

[1] H. Zahn, "Die Jabim," in R. Neuhauss's *Deutsch Neu-Guinea*, iii. 318-320.

are admitted to the rank of full-grown men. The age of
the candidates varies considerably, from four years up to
twenty. Many are married before they are initiated. The
operation is performed in the forest, and the procession of
the youths to the place appointed is attended by a number
of men swinging bull-roarers. As the procession sets out,
the women look on from a distance, weeping and howling,
for they are taught to believe that the lads, their sons and
brothers, are about to be swallowed up by a monster called
a *balum* or ghost, who will only release them from his belly
on condition of receiving a sufficient number of roast pigs.
How, then, can the poor women be sure that they will ever
see their dear ones again? So amid the noise of weeping
and wailing the procession passes into the forest, and the
booming sound of the bull-roarers dies away in the
distance.

The place where the operation is performed on the lads
is a long hut, about a hundred feet in length, which
diminishes in height towards the rear. This represents the
belly of the monster which is to swallow up the candidates.
To keep up the delusion a pair of great eyes are painted
over the entrance, and above them the projecting roots of
a betel-palm represent the monster's hair, while the trunk of
the tree passes for his backbone. As the awe-struck lads
approach this imposing creature, he is heard from time to
time to utter a growl. The growl is in fact no other than
the humming note of bull-roarers swung by men, who are
concealed within the edifice. When the procession has
come to a halt in front of the artificial monster, a loud
defiant blast blown on shell-trumpets summons him to
stand forth. The reply follows in the shape of another
muffled roar of the bull-roarers from within the building. At
the sound the men say that "Balum is coming up," and they
raise a shrill song like a scream and sacrifice pigs to the
monster in order to induce him to spare the lives of the
candidates. When the operation has been performed on
the lads, they must remain in strict seclusion for three or
four months, avoiding all contact with women and even the
sight of them. They live in the long hut, which represents
the monster's belly, and their food is brought them by elder

The rite
of circum-
cision ; the
lads sup-
posed to be
swallowed
by a
monster
(*balum*).

men. Their leisure time is spent in weaving baskets and playing on certain sacred flutes, which are never used except at such seasons. The instruments are of two patterns. One is called the male and the other the female, and they are supposed to be married to each other. No woman may see these mysterious flutes; if she did she would die. Even if she hears their shrill note in the distance, she will hasten to hide herself in a thicket. When the initiatory ceremonies are over, the flutes are carefully kept in the men's clubhouse of the village till the next time they are wanted for a similar occasion. On the other hand, if the women are obliged to go near the place where the lads are living in seclusion, they beat on certain bamboo drums in order to warn them to keep out of the way. Sometimes, though perhaps rarely, one of the lads dies under the operation; in that case the men explain his disappearance to the women by saying that the monster has a pig's stomach as well as a human stomach, and that unfortunately the deceased young man slipped by mistake into the wrong stomach and so perished miserably. But as a rule the candidates pass into the right stomach and after a sufficient period has been allowed for digestion, they come forth safe and sound, the monster having kindly consented to let them go free in consideration of the roast pigs which have been offered to him by the men. Indeed he is not very exacting, for he contents himself with devouring the souls of the pigs, while he leaves their bodies to be consumed by his worshippers. This is a kindly and considerate way of dealing with sacrifice, which our New Guinea ghost or monster shares with many deities of much higher social pretensions. However, lest he should prove refractory and perhaps run away with the poor young men in his inside, or possibly make a dart at any women or children who might be passing, the men take the precaution of tying him down tight with ropes. When the time of seclusion is up, one of the last acts in the long series of ceremonies is to cast off the ropes and let the monster go free. He avails himself of his liberty to return to his subterranean abode, and the young men are brought back to the village with much solemnity.

An eye-witness has described the ceremony. The lads, now ranking as full-grown men, were first bathed in the sea and then elaborately decorated with paint and so forth. In marching back to the village they had to keep their eyes tightly shut, and each of them was led by a man who acted as a kind of god-father. As the procession moved on, an old bald-headed man touched each boy solemnly on the chin and brow with a bull-roarer. In the village preparations for a banquet had meanwhile been made, and the women and girls were waiting in festal attire. The women were much moved at the return of the lads; they sobbed and tears of joy ran down their cheeks. Arrived in the village the newly-initiated lads were drawn up in a row and fresh palm leaves were spread in front of them. Here they stood with closed eyes, motionless as statues. Then a man passed behind them, touching each of them in the hams with the handle of an axe and saying, " O circumcised one, sit down." But still the lads remained standing, stiff and motionless. Not till another man had knocked repeatedly on the ground with the stalk of a palm-leaf, crying, " O circumcised ones, open your eyes!" did the youths, one after another, open their eyes as if awaking from a profound stupor. Then they sat down on the mats and partook of the food brought them by the men. Young and old now ate in the open air. Next morning the circumcised lads were bathed in the sea and painted red instead of white. After that they might talk to women. This was the end of the ceremony.[1]

The meaning of these curious ceremonies observed on the return of the lads to the village is not explained by the writer who describes them; but the analogy of similar ceremonies observed at initiation by many other races allows us to divine it with a fair degree of probability. As I have already observed in a former lecture,

The return of the novices to the village.

The essence of the initiatory rites seems to be a simulation of death and resurrection; the novice is supposed to be killed and to come to life or be born again.

[1] K. Vetter, in *Nachrichten über Kaiser Wilhelms-Land und den Bismarck-Archipel*, 1897, pp. 92 *sq.*; *id.*, in *Mitteilungen der Geographischen Gesellschaft zu Jena*, xi. (1892) p. 105; *id.*, *Komm herüber und hilf uns!* ii. (1898) p. 18; *id.*, cited by M. Krieger, *Neu-Guinea*, pp. 167-170; O. Schellong, " Das Barlum (*sic*)-fest der Gegend Finsch-hafens (Kaiserwilhelmsland), ein Beitrag zur Kenntniss der Beschneidung der Melanesier," *Internationales Archiv für Ethnographie*, ii. (1889) pp. 145-162; H. Zahn, " Die Jabim," in R. Neuhauss's *Deutsch Neu-Guinea*, iii. 296-298.

the ceremony of initiation at puberty is very often regarded
as a process of death and resurrection ; the candidate is
supposed to die or to be killed and to come to life again or
be born again ; and the pretence of a new birth is not uncommonly kept up by the novices feigning to have forgotten
all the most common actions of life and having accordingly
to learn them all over again like newborn babes. We may
conjecture that this is why the young circumcised Papuans,
with whom we are at present concerned, march back to their
village with closed eyes ; this is why, when bidden to sit
down, they remain standing stiffly, as if they understood
neither the command nor the action ; and this, too, we may
surmise, is why their mothers and sisters receive them with
a burst of emotion, as if their dead had come back to them

The
new birth
among the
Akikuyu
of British
East
Africa.
from the grave. This interpretation of the ceremony is confirmed by a curious rite which is observed by the Akikuyu
of British East Africa. Amongst them every boy or girl at
or about the age of ten years has solemnly to pretend to be
born again, not in a moral or religious, but in a physical
sense. The mother of the child, or, if she is dead, some
other woman, goes through an actual pantomime of bringing
forth the boy or girl. I will spare you the details of the
pantomime, which is very graphic, and will merely mention
that the bouncing infant squalls like a newborn babe.
Now this ceremony of the new birth was formerly enacted
among the Akikuyu at the rite of circumcision, though the
two ceremonies are now kept distinct.[1] Hence it is not
very rash to conjecture that the ceremony performed by the
young Papuans of Finsch Harbour on their return to the
village after undergoing circumcision is merely a way of
keeping up the pretence of being born again and of being
therefore as ignorant and helpless as babes.

The mock
death of
the novices
as a pre-
liminary to
the mock
birth.
But if the end of the initiation is a mock resurrection, or
rather new birth, as it certainly seems to be, we may infer
with some confidence that the first part of it, namely the
act of circumcision, is a mock death. This is borne out by

[1] W. S. Routledge and K. Routledge, *With a Prehistoric People, the
Akikuyu of British East Africa*
(London, 1910), pp. 151 *sq.* Compare *Totemism and Exogamy*, iv.

228 ; C. W. Hobley, "Kikuyu Customs and Beliefs," *Journal of the
Royal Anthropological Institute*, xl.
(1910) pp. 440 *sq.*

the explicit statement of a very good authority, Mr. Vetter, that "the circumcision is designated as a process of being swallowed by the spirit, out of whose stomach (represented by a long hut) the release must take place by means of a sacrifice of pigs."[1] And it is further confirmed by the observation that both the spirit which is supposed to operate on the lads, and the bull-roarer, which apparently represents his voice, are known by the name of *balum*, which means the ghost or spirit of a dead person. Similarly, among the Tugeri or Kaya-Kaya, a large Papuan tribe on the south coast of Dutch New Guinea, the name of the bull-roarer, which they call *sosom*, is given to a mythical giant, who is supposed to appear every year with the south-east monsoon. When he comes, a festival is held in his honour and bull-roarers are swung. Boys are presented to the giant, and he kills them, but brings them to life again.[2] Thus the initiatory rite of circumcision, to which all lads have to submit among the Yabim, seems to be closely bound up with their conception of death and with their belief in a life after death ; since the whole ceremony apparently consists in a simulation of dying and coming to life again. That is why I have touched upon these initiatory rites, which at first sight might appear to have no connexion with our immediate subject, the belief in immortality and the worship of the dead.

On the whole we may say that the Yabim have a very firm and practical belief in a life after death, and that while their attitude to the spirits of the departed is generally one of fear, they nevertheless look to these spirits also for information and help on various occasions. Thus their beliefs and practices contain at least in germ the elements of a worship of the dead. General summary as to the Yabim.

---

[1] K. Vetter, in *Nachrichten über Kaiser Wilhelmsland und den Bismarck-Archipel*, 1897, p. 93.

[2] R. Pöch, "Vierter Bericht über meine Reise nach Neu-Guinea," *Sit-* zungsberichte der mathematisch-naturwissenschaftlichen Klasse der Kaiserlichen Akademie der Wissenschaften (Vienna), cxv. (1906) Abteilung I, pp. 901, 902.

LECTURE XII

THE BELIEF IN IMMORTALITY AMONG THE NATIVES OF GERMAN NEW GUINEA (*continued*)

The Bukaua of German New Guinea.

IN the last lecture I described the beliefs and practices concerning the dead as they are to be found among the Yabim of German New Guinea. To-day we begin with the Bukaua, a kindred and neighbouring tribe, which occupies the coast lands of the northern portion of Huon Gulf from Schollenbruch Point to Samoa Harbour. The language which the Bukaua speak belongs, like the language of the Yabim, to the Melanesian, not to the Papuan family. Their customs and beliefs have been reported by a German missionary, Mr. Stefan Lehner, whose account I follow.[1] In many respects they closely resemble those of their neighbours the Yabim.

Means of subsistence of the Bukaua.

The Bukaua are an agricultural people who subsist mainly on the crops of taro which they raise. But they also cultivate many kinds of bananas and vegetables, together with sugar-cane, sago, and tobacco. From time to time they cut down and burn the forest in order to obtain fresh fields for cultivation. The land is not held in common. Each family has its own fields and patches of forest, and would resent the intrusion of others on their hereditary domain. Hunting and fishing supply them with animal food to eke out the vegetable nourishment which they draw from their fields and plantations.[2] Every village contains one or more of the men's clubhouses which are a common feature in the social life of the tribes on this coast. In these club-

Men's clubhouses.

---

[1] Stefan Lehner, " Bukaua," in R. Neuhauss's *Deutsch Neu-Guinea*, iii. (Berlin, 1911) pp. 395-485.

[2] S. Lehner, *op. cit.* pp. 399, 433 *sq.*, 437 *sqq.*

houses the young men are obliged to sleep, and on the platforms in front of them the older men hold their councils. Such a clubhouse is called a *lum*.[1]

The Bukaua have a firm belief in the existence of the human soul after death. They think that a man's soul can even quit his body temporarily in his lifetime during sleep or a swoon, and that in its disembodied state it can appear to people at a distance; but such apparitions are regarded as omens of approaching death, when the soul will depart for good and all. The soul of a dead man is called a *balum*. The spirits of the departed are believed to be generally mischievous and spiteful to the living, but they can be appeased by sacrifice, and other measures can be taken to avert their dangerous influence.[2] They are very touchy, and if they imagine that they are not honoured enough by their kinsfolk, and that the offerings made to them are insufficient, they will avenge the slight by visiting their disrespectful and stingy relatives with sickness and disease. Among the maladies which the natives ascribe to the anger of ghosts are epilepsy, fainting fits, and wasting decline.[3] When a man suffers from a sore which he believes to have been inflicted on him by a ghost, he will take a stone from the fence of the grave and heat it in the fire, saying: "Father, see, thou hast gone, I am left, I must till the land in thy stead and care for my brothers and sisters. Do me good again." Then he dips the hot stone in a puddle on the grave, and holds his sore in the steam which rises from it. His pain is eased thereby and he explains the alleviation which he feels by saying, "The spirit of the dead man has eaten up the wound." [4]

But like most savages the Bukaua attribute many illnesses and many deaths not to the wrath of ghosts but to the malignant arts of sorcerers; and in such cases they usually endeavour by means of divination to ascertain the culprit and to avenge the death of their friend by taking the life of his imaginary murderer.[5] If they fail to exact vengeance, the ghost is believed to be very angry, and they

Marginal notes:
Beliefs of the Bukaua concerning the souls of the dead.

Sickness and disease attributed to ghostly agency.

Sickness and death often ascribed by the Bukaua to sorcery.

[1] S. Lehner, *op. cit.* p. 399.
[2] S. Lehner, *op. cit.* p. 414.
[3] S. Lehner, *op. cit.* pp. 466, 468.
[4] S. Lehner, *op. cit.* p. 469.
[5] S. Lehner, *op. cit.* pp. 462 *sqq.*, 466, 467, 471 *sqq.*

must be on their guard against him. He may meet them anywhere, but is especially apt to dog the footsteps of the sorcerer who killed him. Hence when on the occasion of a great feast the sorcerer comes to the village of his victim, the surviving relatives of the dead man are at particular pains to protect themselves and their property against the insidious attacks of the prowling ghost. For this purpose they bury a creeper with white blossoms in the path leading to the village ; the ghost is thought to be filled with fear at the sight of it and to turn back, leaving his kinsfolk, their dogs, and pigs in peace.[1]

Fear of the ghosts of the slain.   Another class of ghosts who are much dreaded are the spirits of slain foes. They are believed to pursue their slayers to the village and to blind them so that sooner or later they fall an easy prey to their enemies. Hence when a party of warriors has returned home from a successful attack on a village, in which they have butchered all on whom they could lay their hands, they kindle a great fire, dance wildly about it, and hurl burning brands in the direction of the battlefield in order to keep the ghosts of their slaughtered foes at bay. Phosphorescent lights seen under the houses throw the inmates into great alarm, for they are thought to be the souls of the slain. Sometimes the vanquished in battle resort to a curious ruse for the purpose of avenging themselves on the victors by means of a ghost. They take the sleeping-mat of one of the slain, roll it up in a bundle along with his loin-cloth, apron, netted bag, or head-rest, and give the bundle to two cripples to carry. Then they steal quietly to the landing-place of their foes, peering warily about lest they should be observed. The bundle represents the dead man, and the cripples who carry it reel to and fro, and finally sink to the ground with their burden. In this way the ghost of the victim, whose things are carried in the bundle, is supposed to make their enemies weak and tottery. Strong young men are not given the bundle to carry, lest the ghost should spoil their manly figures ; whereas if he should wound or maim a couple of poor cripples, no great harm is done.[2]

However, the Bukaua also look on the ghosts of their

---

[1] S. Lehner, *op. cit.* p. 462.   [2] S. Lehner, *op. cit.* pp. 444 *sq*

ancestors in a more amiable light as beings who, if properly
appealed to, can and will help them in the affairs of life,
especially by procuring for them good crops.   Hence when
they are planting their fields, which are formed in clearings
of the forest, they take particular care to insert shoots of
all their crops in the ground near the tree stumps which
remain standing, because the souls of their dead grandfathers
and great-grandfathers are believed to be sitting on the
stumps watching their descendants at their work.   Accordingly in the act of planting they call out the names of
these forefathers and pray them to guard the field in order
that their living children may have food and not suffer
from hunger.   And at harvest, when the first-fruits of the
taro, bananas, sugar-cane, and so forth have been brought
back from the fields, a portion of them is offered in a bowl
to the spirits of the forefathers in the house of the landowner,
and the spirits are addressed in prayer as follows : " O ye
who have guarded our field as we prayed you to do, there
is something for you ; now and henceforth behold us with
favour."   While the family are feasting on the rest of the
first - fruits, the householder will surreptitiously stir the
offerings in the bowl with his finger, and will then shew
the bowl to the others as a proof that the souls of the dead
have really partaken of the good things provided for them.[1]
A hunter will also pray to his dead father to drive the
wild pigs into his net.[2]

The Bukaua bury their dead in shallow graves, which
are sometimes dug under the houses but more usually in front
of or beside them.   Along with the corpses are deposited bags
of taro, nuts, drinking-vessels, and other articles of daily use.
Only the stone axes are too valuable to be thus sacrificed.
Over the grave is erected a rude hut in which the widower,
if the deceased was a married woman, remains for a time
in seclusion.   A widow on the death of her husband
remains in the house.   Widow and widower may not shew
themselves in public until they have prepared their mourning
costume.   The widower wears a black hat made of bark,
cords round his neck, wicker work on his arms and feet, and

---

[1] S. Lehner, *op. cit.* pp. 434 *sqq.* ; compare *id.*, pp. 478 *sq.*
[2] S. Lehner, *op. cit.* p. 462.

a torn old bracelet of his wife in a bag on his breast. A widow is completely swathed in nets, one over the other, and she carries about with her the loincloth of her deceased husband. The souls of the dead dwell in a subterranean region called *lamboam,* and their life there seems to resemble life here on earth ; but the ideas of the people on the subject are very vague.[1]

Initiation of young men among the Bukaua.

The customs and beliefs of the Bukaua in regard to the initiation of young men are practically identical with those of their neighbours the Yabim. Indeed the initiatory ceremonies are performed by the tribes jointly, now in the territory of the Bukaua, now in the territory of the Yabim, or in the land of the Kai, a tribe of mountaineers, or again in the neighbouring Tami islands. The intervals between the ceremonies vary from ten to eighteen years.[2] The central feature of the initiatory rites is the circumcision of the novices.

Lads at circumcision supposed to be swallowed by a monster.

It is given out that the lads are swallowed by a ferocious monster called a *balum,* who, however, is induced by the sacrifice of many pigs to vomit them up again. In spewing them out of his maw he bites or scratches them, and the wound so inflicted is circumcision. This explanation of the rite is fobbed off on the women, who more or less believe it and weep accordingly when their sons are led away to be committed to the monster's jaws. And when the time for the ceremony is approaching, the fond mothers busy themselves with rearing and fattening young pigs, so that they may be able with them to redeem their loved ones from the belly of the ravenous beast ; for he must have a pig for every boy. When a lad bleeds to death from the effect of the operation, he is secretly buried, and his sorrowful mother is told that the monster swallowed him and refused to bring him up again. What really happens is that the youths are shut up for several months in a house specially built for the purpose in the village. During their seclusion they are under the charge of guardians, usually two young men, and must observe strictly a rule of fasting and chastity. When they are judged to be ready to undergo the rite, they are led forth and circumcised in front of the house amid a

[1] S. Lehner, *op. cit.* pp. 430, 470, 472 *sq.*, 474 *sq.*
[2] S. Lehner, *op. cit.* p. 403.

prodigious uproar made by the swinging of bull-roarers. The noise is supposed to be the voice of the monster who swallows and vomits up the novice at circumcision. The bull-roarer as well as the monster bears the name of *balum*, and the building in which the novices are lodged before and after the operation is called the monster's house (*balumslum*). After they have been circumcised the lads remain in the house for several months till their wounds are healed; then, painted and bedizened with all the ornaments that can be collected, they are brought back and restored to their joyful mothers. Women must vacate the village for a long time while the initiatory ceremonies are being performed.[1]

The meaning of the whole rite, as I pointed out in dealing with the similar initiatory rite of the Yabim, appears to be that the novices are killed and then restored to a new and better life; for after their initiation they rank no longer as boys but as full-grown men, entitled to all the privileges of manhood and citizenship, if we can speak of such a thing as citizenship among the savages of New Guinea. This interpretation of the rite is supported by the notable fact that the Bukaua, like the Yabim, give the name of *balum* to the souls of the dead as well as to the mythical monster and to the bull-roarer; this shews how intimately the three things are associated in their minds. Indeed not only is the bull-roarer in general associated with the souls of the dead by a community of name, but among the Bukaua each particular bull-roarer bears in addition the name of a particular dead man and varies in dignity and importance with the dignity and importance of the deceased person whom it represents. The most venerated of all are curiously carved and have been handed down for generations; they bear the names of famous warriors or magicians of old and are supposed to reproduce the personal peculiarities of the celebrated originals in their shape and tones. And there are smaller bull-roarers which emit shriller notes and are thought to represent the shrill-voiced wives of the ancient heroes.[2]

The Bukaua and the Yabim, the two tribes with which I have been dealing in this and the last lecture, inhabit, as

Novices at circumcision supposed to be killed and then restored to a new and higher life.

[1] S. Lehner, *op. cit.* pp. 402-410.   [2] S. Lehner, *op. cit.* pp. 410-414.

The Kai
tribe of
Saddle
Mountain
in German
New
Guinea.

The land
of the Kai.

Their
mode of
cultivation.

I have said, the coast about Finsch Harbour and speak a
Melanesian language. We now pass from them to the
consideration of another people, belonging to a different
stock and speaking a different language, who inhabit the
rugged and densely wooded mountains inland from Finsch
Harbour. Their neighbours on the coast call these
mountaineers by the name of Kai, a word which signifies
forest or inland in opposition to the seashore ; and this
name of the tribe we may adopt, following the example of
a German missionary, Mr. Ch. Keysser, who has laboured
among them for more than eleven years and has given us
an excellent description of their customs and beliefs. His
account applies particularly to the natives of what is called
Saddle Mountain, the part of the range which advances
nearest to the coast and rises to the height of about three
thousand feet. It is a rough, broken country, cleft by many
ravines and covered with forest, bush, or bamboo thickets ;
though here and there at rare intervals some brown patches
mark the clearings which the sparse inhabitants have made
for the purpose of cultivation. Water is plentiful. Springs
gush forth everywhere in the glens and valleys, and rushing
streams of crystal-clear water pour down the mountain sides,
and in the clefts of the hills are lonely tarns, the undisturbed
haunts of wild ducks and other water fowl. During the
wet season, which extends from June to August, the rain
descends in sheets and the mountains are sometimes covered
for weeks together with so thick a mist that all prospect is
cut off at the distance of a hundred yards. The natives
are then loth to leave their huts and will spend the day
crouching over a fire. They are a shorter and sturdier race
than the tribes on the coast ; the expression of their face
is less frank and agreeable, and their persons are very much
dirtier. They belong to the aboriginal Papuan stock,
whereas the Yabim and Bukaua on the coast are probably
immigrants from beyond the sea, who have driven the
indigenous population back into the mountains.[1] Their
staple foods are taro and yams, which they grow in their
fields. A field is cultivated for only one year at a time ;

[1] Ch. Keysser, "Aus dem Leben der Kaileute," in R. Neuhauss's *Deutsch
Neu-Guinea,* iii. 3-6.

it is then allowed to lie fallow and is soon overgrown with
rank underwood. Six or eight years may elapse before
it is again cleared and brought under cultivation. Game
and fish abound in the woods and waters, and the Kai
make free use of these natural resources. They keep pigs
and dogs, and eat the flesh of both. Pork is indeed a
favourite viand, figuring largely in the banquets which are
held at the circumcision festivals.[1] The people live in small Their
villages, each village comprising from two to six houses. villages.
The houses are raised on piles and the walls are usually
constructed of pandanus leaves, though many natives now
make them of boards. After eighteen months or two years
the houses are so rotten and tumble-down that the village
is deserted and a new one built on another site. Assembly-
houses are erected only for the circumcision ceremonies, and
the bull-roarers used on these occasions are kept in them.
Husband and wife live together, often two couples in one
hut ; but each family has its own side of the house and
its own fireplace. In times of insecurity the Kai used to
build their huts for safety among the spreading boughs
of great trees. A whole village, consisting of three or
four huts, might thus be quartered on a single tree. Of
late years, with the peace and protection for life introduced by German rule, these tree-houses have gone out of
fashion.[2]

After describing the manners and customs of the Kai Observa-
people at some length, the German missionary, who knows tions of a
German
them intimately, proceeds to give us a very valuable account missionary
of their old native religion or superstition. He prefaces his on the
animistic
account with some observations, the fruit of long experience, beliefs of
which deserve to be laid to heart by all who attempt to the Kai.
penetrate into the inner life, the thoughts, the feelings, the
motives of savages. As his remarks are very germane to
the subject of these lectures, I will translate them. He
says : " In the preceding chapters I have sketched the
daily life of the Kai people. But I have not attempted to
set forth the reasons for their conduct, which is often very
peculiar and unintelligible. The explanation of that conduct

[1] Ch. Keysser, *op. cit.* pp. 12 *sq.*, 17-20.
[2] Ch. Keysser, *op. cit.* pp. 9-12.

lies in the animistic view which the Papuan takes of the world. It must be most emphatically affirmed that nobody can judge the native aright who has not gained an insight into what we may call his religious opinions. The native must be described as very religious, although his ideas do not coincide with ours. His feelings, thoughts, and will are most intimately connected with his belief in souls. With that belief he is born, he has sucked it in with his mother's milk, and from the standpoint of that belief he regards the things and occurrences that meet him in life ; by that belief he regulates his behaviour. An objective way of looking at events is unknown to him ; everything is brought by him into relation to his belief, and by it he seeks to explain everything that to him seems strange and rare."[1] " The labyrinth of animistic customs at first sight presents an appearance of wild confusion to him who seeks to penetrate into them and reduce them to order ; but on closer inspection he will soon recognise certain guiding lines. These guiding lines are the laws of animism, which have passed into the flesh and blood of the Papuan and influence his thought and speech, his acts and his omissions, his love and hate, in short his whole life and death. When once we have discovered these laws, the whole of the superstitious nonsense falls into an orderly system which compels us to regard it with a certain respect that increases in proportion to the contempt in which we had previously held the people. We need not wonder, moreover, that the laws of animism partially correspond to general laws of nature."[2]

The essential rationality of the savage. Thus according to Mr. Keysser, who has no theory to maintain and merely gives us in this passage the result of long personal observation, the Kai savages are thinking, reasoning men, whose conduct, however strange and at first sight unintelligible it may appear to us, is really based on a definite religious or if you please superstitious view of the world. It is true that their theory as well as their practice differs widely from ours ; but it would be false and unjust to deny that they have a theory and that on the whole their practice squares with it. Similar testimony is borne to other savage races by men who have lived long

[1] Ch. Keysser, *op. cit.* p. 111. [2] Ch. Keysser, *op. cit.* p. 113.

among them and observed them closely;[1] and on the
strength of such testimony I think we may lay it down as
a well-established truth that savages in general, so far as
they are known to us, have certain more or less definite
theories, whether we call them religious or philosophical, by
which they regulate their conduct, and judged by which
their acts, however absurd they may seem to the civilised
man, are really both rational and intelligible. Hence it is,
in my opinion, a profound mistake hastily to conclude that
because the behaviour of the savage does not agree with
our notions of what is reasonable, natural, and proper, it
must therefore necessarily be illogical, the result of blind
impulse rather than of deliberate thought and calculation.
No doubt the savage like the civilised man does often act
purely on impulse ; his passions overmaster his reason, and
sweep it away before them. He is probably indeed much

---

[1] Compare Ch. Hose and W.
McDougall, *The Pagan Tribes of
Borneo* (London, 1912), ii. 221 *sq.* :
" It has often been attempted to exhibit
the mental life of savage peoples as
profoundly different from our own ; to
assert that they act from motives, and
reach conclusions by means of mental
processes, so utterly different from our
own motives and processes that we
cannot hope to interpret or understand
their behaviour unless we can first, by
some impossible or at least by some
hitherto undiscovered method, learn
the nature of these mysterious motives
and processes. These attempts have
recently been renewed in influential
quarters. If these views were applied
to the savage peoples of the interior of
Borneo, we should characterise them
as fanciful delusions natural to the
anthropologist who has spent all the
days of his life in a stiff collar and a
black coat upon the well-paved ways
of civilised society. We have no
hesitation in saying that, the more
intimately one becomes acquainted with
these pagan tribes, the more fully one
realises the close similarity of their
mental processes to one's own. Their
primary impulses and emotions seem
to be in all respects like our own. It
is true that they are very unlike the
typical civilised man of some of the
older philosophers, whose every action
proceeded from a nice and logical
calculation of the algebraic sum of
pleasures and pains to be derived from
alternative lines of conduct ; but we
ourselves are equally unlike that purely
mythical personage. The Kayan or
the Iban often acts impulsively in ways
which by no means conduce to further
his best interests or deeper purposes ;
but so do we also. He often reaches
conclusions by processes that cannot be
logically justified ; but so do we also.
He often holds, and upon successive
occasions acts upon, beliefs that are
logically inconsistent with one another;
but so do we also." For further testimonies to the reasoning powers of
savages, which it would be superfluous
to affirm if it were not at present a
fashion with some theorists to deny, see
Taboo and the Perils of the Soul, pp.
420 *sqq.* And on the tendency of the
human mind in general, not of the
savage mind in particular, calmly to
acquiesce in inconsistent and even contradictory conclusions, I may refer to
a note in *Adonis, Attis, Osiris*, Second
Edition, p. 4. But indeed to observe
such contradictions in practice the
philosopher need not quit his own
study.

more impulsive, much more liable to be whirled about by gusts of emotion than we are ; yet it would be unfair to judge his life as a whole by these occasional outbursts rather than by its general tenour, which to those who know him from long observation reveals a groundwork of logic and reason resembling our own in its operations, though differing from ours in the premises from which it sets out. I think it desirable to emphasise the rational basis of savage life because it has been the fashion of late years with some writers to question or rather deny it. According to them, if I understand them aright, the savage acts first and invents his reasons, generally very absurd reasons, for so doing afterwards. Significantly enough, the writers who argue in favour of the essential irrationality of savage conduct have none of them, I believe, any personal acquaintance with savages. Their conclusions are based not on observation but on purely theoretical deductions, a most precarious foundation on which to erect a science of man or indeed of anything. As such, they cannot be weighed in the balance against the positive testimony of many witnesses who have lived for years with the savage and affirm emphatically the logical basis which underlies and explains his seeming vagaries. At all events I for one have no hesitation in accepting the evidence of such men to matters of fact with which they are acquainted, and I unhesitatingly reject all theories which directly contradict that evidence. If there ever has been any race of men who invariably acted first and thought afterwards, I can only say that in the course of my reading and observation I have never met with any trace of them, and I am apt to suppose that, if they ever existed anywhere but in the imagination of bookish dreamers, their career must have been an exceedingly short one, since in the struggle for existence they would surely succumb to adversaries who tempered and directed the blind fury of combat with at least a modicum of reason and sense. The myth of the illogical or prelogical savage may safely be relegated to that museum of learned absurdities and abortions which speculative anthropology is constantly enriching with fresh specimens of misapplied ingenuity and wasted industry. But enough of these fantasies. Let us return to facts.

The life of the Kai people, according to Mr. Keysser, is dominated by their conception of the soul. That concep- tion differs greatly from and is very much more ex- tensive than ours. The Kai regards his reflection and his shadow as his soul or parts of it ; hence you should not tread on a man's shadow for fear of injuring his soul. The soul likewise dwells in his heart, for he feels it beating. Hence if you give a native a friendly poke in the ribs, he protests, saying, " Don't poke me so ; you might drive my soul out of my body, and then I should die." The soul moreover resides in the eye, where you may see it twinkling ; when it departs, the eye grows dim and vacant. Moreover, the soul is in the foot as much as in the head ; it lurks even in the spittle and the other bodily excretions. The soul in fact pervades the body just as warmth does ; everything that a man touches he infects, so to say, with his soul ; that mysterious entity exists in the very sound of his voice. The sorcerer catches a man's soul by his magic, shuts it up tight, and destroys it. Then the man dies. He dies because the sorcerer has killed his soul. Yet the Kai believes, whether consistently or not, that the soul of the dead man continues to live. He talks to it, he makes offerings to it, he seeks to win its favour in order that he may have luck in the chase ; he fears its ill-will and anger ; he gives it food to eat, liquor to drink, tobacco to smoke, and betel to chew. What could a reasonable ghost ask for more ? [1]

Thus, according to Mr. Keysser, whose exposition I am simply reproducing, the Kai believes not in one nor yet in many souls belonging to each individual ; he implicitly assumes that there are two different kinds of souls. One of these is the soul which survives the body at death ; in all respects it resembles the man himself as he lived on earth, except that it has no body. It is not indeed absolutely incorporeal, but it is greatly shrunken and attenuated by death. That is why the souls of the dead are so angry with the living ; they repine at their own degraded condition ; they envy the full-blooded life which the living enjoy and which the dead have lost. The second kind of soul is distinguished by Mr. Keysser from the former as a spiritual

---

[1] Ch. Keysser, *op. cit.* pp. 111 *sq.*

essence or soul-stuff, which pervades the body as sap
pervades the tree, and which diffuses itself like corporeal
warmth over everything with which the body is brought
into contact.[1]   In these lectures we are concerned chiefly
with the former kind of soul, which is believed to survive
the death of the body, and which answers much more
nearly than the second to the popular European conception
of the soul.   Accordingly in what follows we shall confine
our attention mainly to it.

Death
thought
by the Kai
to be
commonly
caused by
sorcery.

Like many other savages, the Kai do not believe in the
possibility of a natural death ; they think that everybody
dies through the maleficent arts of sorcerers or ghosts.
Even in the case of old people, we are told, they assume
the cause of death to be sorcery, and to sorcery all misfortunes are ascribed.   If a man falls on the path and
wounds himself to death, as often happens, on the jagged
stump of a bamboo, the natives conclude that he was
bewitched.   The way in which the sorcerer brought about
the catastrophe was this.   He obtained some object which
was infected with the soul-stuff or spiritual essence of his
victim ; he stuck a pile in the ground, he spread the soul-
stuff on the pile ; then he pretended to wound himself on
the pile and to groan with pain.   Anybody can see for
himself that by a natural and necessary concatenation of
causes this compelled the poor fellow to stumble over that
jagged bamboo stump and to perish miserably.   Again,
take the case of a hunter in the forest who is charged and
ripped up by a wild boar.   On a superficial view of the
circumstances it might perhaps occur to you that the cause
of death was the boar.   But you would assuredly be
mistaken.   The real cause of death was again a sorcerer,
who pounded up the soul-stuff of his victim with a boar's
tooth.   Again, suppose that a man is bitten by a serpent
and dies.   A shallow rationalist might say that the man
died of the bite ; but the Kai knows better.   He is aware
that what really killed him was the sorcerer who took a
pinch of his victim's soul and bunged it up tight in a tube
along with the sting of a snake.   Similarly, if a woman
dies in childbed, or if a man hangs himself, the cause of

---

[1] Ch. Keysser, *op. cit.* p. 112.

death is still a sorcerer operating with the appropriate means and gestures. Thus to make a man hang himself all that the sorcerer has to do is to get a scrap of his victim's soul—and the smallest scrap is quite enough for his purpose, it may be a mere shred or speck of soul adhering to a hair of the man's head, to a drop of his sweat, or to a crumb of his food,—I say that the sorcerer need only obtain a tiny little bit of his victim's soul, clap it in a tube, set the tube dangling at the end of a string, and go through a pantomime of gurgling, goggling and so forth, like a man in the last stage of strangulation, and his victim is thereby physically compelled to put his neck in the noose and hang himself in good earnest.[1]

Where these views of sorcery prevail, it is no wonder that the sorcerer is an unpopular character. He naturally therefore shrinks from publicity and hides his somewhat lurid light under a bushel. Not to put too fine a point on it, he carries his life in his hand and may be knocked on the head at any moment without the tedious formality of a trial. Once his professional reputation is established, all the deaths in the neighbourhood may be set down at his door. If he gets wind of a plot to assassinate him, he may stave off his doom for a while by soothing the angry passions of his enemies with presents, but sooner or later his fate is sealed.[2] *Danger incurred by the sorcerer.*

However, the Kai savage is far from attributing all deaths without distinction to sorcerers.[3] In many hurts and maladies he detects the cold clammy hand of a ghost. If a man, for example, wounds himself in the forest, perhaps in the pursuit of a wild beast, he may imagine that he has been speared or clubbed by a malignant ghost. And when a person falls ill, the first thing to do is naturally to *Many hurts and maladies attributed by the Kai to the action of ghosts.*

---

[1] Ch. Keysser, *op. cit.* p. 140. As to the magical tubes in which the sorcerer seals up some part of his victim's soul, see *id.*, p. 135.

[2] Ch. Keysser, *op. cit.* pp. 140 *sq.*

[3] Mr. Keysser indeed affirms that in the mind of the Kai sorcery "is regarded as the cause of all deaths" (*op. cit.* p. 102), and again that "all men without exception die in consequence of the baneful arts of these sorcerers and their accomplices" (p. 134); and again that "even in the case of old people they assume sorcery to be the cause of death; to sorcery, too, all misfortunes whatever are ascribed" (p. 140). But that these statements are exaggerations seems to follow from Mr. Keysser's own account of the wounds, sicknesses, and deaths which these savages attribute to ghosts and not to sorcerers.

ascertain the cause of the illness in order that it may be treated properly. In all such enquiries, Mr. Keysser tells us, suspicion first falls on the ghosts ; they are looked upon as even worse than the sorcerers.[1] So when a doctor is called in to see a patient, the only question with him is whether the sickness is caused by a sorcerer or a ghost. To decide this nice point he takes a boiled taro over which he has pronounced a charm. This he bites, and if he finds a small stone in the fruit, he decides that ghosts are the cause of the malady ; but if on the other hand he detects a minute roll of leaves, he knows that the sufferer is bewitched. In the latter case the obvious remedy is to discover the sorcerer and to induce him, for an adequate consideration, to give up the magic tube in which he has bottled up a portion of the sick man's soul. If, however, the magician turns a deaf ear alike to the voice of pity and the allurement of gain, the resources of the physician are not yet exhausted. He now produces his whip or scourge for souls. This valuable instrument consists, like a common whip, of a handle with a lash attached to it, but what gives it the peculiar qualities which distinguish it from all other whips is a small packet tied to the end of the lash. The packet contains a certain herb, and the sick man and his friends must all touch it in order to impregnate it with the volatile essence of their souls. Armed with this potent implement the doctor goes by night into the depth of the forest ; for the darkness of night and the solitude of the woods are necessary for the success of the delicate operation which this good physician of souls has now to perform. Finding himself alone he whistles for the lost soul of the sufferer, and if only the sorcerer by his infernal craft has not yet brought it to death's door, the soul appears at the sound of the whistle ; for it is strongly attracted by the soul-stuff of its friends in the packet. But the doctor has still to catch it, a feat which is not so easily accomplished as might be supposed. It is now that the whip of souls comes into play. Suddenly the doctor heaves up his arm and lashes out at the truant soul with all his might. If only he hits it, the business is done, the soul is captured, the doctor carries it back to the

In other cases the sickness is traced to witchcraft.

Capturing a lost soul.

[1] Ch. Keysser, *op. cit.* p. 141.

house in triumph, and restores it to the body of the poor sick man, who necessarily recovers.[1]

But suppose that the result of the diagnosis is different, and that on mature consideration the doctor should decide that a ghost and not a sorcerer is at the bottom of the mischief. The question then naturally arises whether the sick man has not of late been straying on haunted ground and infected himself with the very dangerous soul-stuff or spiritual essence of the dead. If he remembers to have done so, some leaves are fetched from the place in the forest where the mishap occurred, and with them the whole body of the sufferer or the wound, as the case may be, is stroked or brushed down. The healing virtue of this procedure is obvious. The ghosts who are vexing the patient are attracted by the familiar smell of the leaves which come from their old home ; and yielding in a moment of weakness to the soft emotions excited by the perfume they creep out of the body of the sick man and into the leaves. Quick as thought the doctor now whisks the leaves away with the ghosts in them ; he belabours them with a cudgel, he hangs them up in the smoke, or he throws them into the fire. Such powerful disinfectants have their natural results ; if the ghosts are not absolutely destroyed they are at least disarmed, and the sick is made whole.

Extracting ghosts from a sick man.

Another equally effective cure for sickness caused by ghosts is this. You take a stout stick, cleave it down the middle so that the two ends remain entire, and give it to two men to hold. Then the sick man pokes his head through the cleft ; after that you rub him with the stick from the crown of his head to the soles of his feet. In this way you obviously scrape off the bloodsucking ghosts who are clinging like flies or mosquitoes to his person, and having thus transferred them to the cleft stick you throw it away or otherwise destroy it. The cure is now complete, and if the patient does not recover, he cannot reasonably blame the doctor, who has done all that humanly speaking could be done to bring back the bloom of health to the poor sick man.[2]

Scraping ghosts from the patient's body.

If, however, the sick man obstinately persists in dying, there is a great uproar in the village. For the fear of his

---

[1] Ch. Keysser, *op. cit.* pp. 133 *sq.*   [2] Ch. Keysser, *op. cit.* pp. 141 *sq.*

Extrava-
gant
demonstra-
tions of
grief at
the death
of a sick
man.

ghost has now fallen like a thunderclap on all the people. His disembodied spirit is believed to be hovering in the air, seeing everything that is done, hearing every word that is spoken, and woe to the unlucky wight who does not display a proper degree of sorrow for the irreparable loss that has just befallen the community. Accordingly shrieks of despair begin to resound, and crocodile tears to flow in cataracts. The whole population assemble and give themselves up to the most frantic demonstrations of grief. Cries are raised on all sides, "Why must he die?" "Wherefore did they bewitch him?" "Those wicked, wicked men!" "I'll do for them!" "I'll hew them in pieces!" "I'll destroy their crops!" "I'll fell all their palm-trees!" "I'll stick all their pigs!" "O brother, why did you leave me?" "O friend, how can I live without you?" To make good these threats one man will be seen prancing wildly about and stabbing with a spear at the invisible sorcerers; another catches up a cudgel and at one blow shivers a water-pot of the deceased into atoms, or rushes out like one demented and lays a palm-tree level with the ground. Some fling themselves prostrate beside the corpse and sob as if their very hearts would break. They take the dead man by the hand, they stroke him, they straighten out the poor feet which are already growing cold. They coo to him softly, they lift up the languid head, and then lay it gently down. Then in a frenzy of grief one of them will leap to his feet, shriek, bellow, stamp on the floor, grapple with the roof beams, shake the walls, as if he would pull the house down, and finally hurl himself on the ground and roll over and over howling as if his distress was more than he could endure. Another looks wildly about him. He sees a knife. He grasps it. His teeth are set, his mind is made up. "Why need he die?" he cries, "he, my friend, with whom I had all things in common, with whom I ate out of the same dish?" Then there is a quick movement of the knife, and down he falls. But he is not dead. He has only slit the flap of one of his ears, and the trickling blood bedabbles his body. Meantime with the hoarse cries of the men are mingled the weeping and wailing, the shrill screams and lamentations of the women; while above all the din and uproar rises the booming sound of the shell trumpets blown to carry the tidings of death to all the villages in' the neighbourhood.   But gradually the wild tumult dies away into silence.   Grief or the simulation of it has exhausted itself: the people grow calm ; they sit down, they smoke or chew betel, while some engage in the last offices of attention to the dead.[1]

A civilised observer who witnessed such a scene of boisterous lamentation, but did not know the natives well, might naturally set down all these frantic outbursts to genuine sorrow, and might enlarge accordingly on the affectionate nature of savages, who are thus cut to the heart by the death of any one of their acquaintance.   But the missionary who knows them better assures us that most of these expressions of mourning and despair are a mere blind to deceive and soothe the dreaded ghost of the deceased into a comfortable persuasion that he is fondly loved and sadly missed by his surviving relatives and friends. This view of the essential hypocrisy of the lamentations is strongly confirmed by the threats which sick people will sometimes utter to their attendants.   " If you don't take better care of me," a man will sometimes say, " and if you don't do everything you possibly can to preserve my valuable life, my ghost will serve you out."   That is why friends and relations are so punctilious in paying visits of respect and condolence to the sick.   Sometimes the last request which a dying man addresses to his kinsfolk is that they will kill this or that sorcerer who has killed him ; and he enforces the injunction by threats of the terrible things he will do to them in his disembodied state if they fail to avenge his death on his imaginary murderer.   As all the relatives of a dead man stand in fear of his ghost, the body may not be buried until all of them have had an opportunity of paying their respects to it.   If, as sometimes happens, a corpse is interred before a relative can arrive from a distance, he will on arrival break out into reproaches and upbraidings against the grave-diggers for exposing him to the wrath of the departed spirit.[2]

When all the relations and friends have assembled and

Marginal note: Hypo-critical character of these demonstrations, which are intended to deceive the ghost.

---

[1] Ch. Keysser, *op. cit.* pp. 80 *sq*., 142.   [2] Ch. Keysser, *op. cit.* p. 142.

Burial and mourning customs of the Kai.

testified their sorrow, the body is buried on the second or third day after death. The grave is usually dug under the house and is so shallow that even when it has been closed the stench is often very perceptible. The ornaments which were placed on the body when it was laid out are removed before it is lowered into the grave, and the dead takes his last rest wrapt in a simple leaf-mat. Often a dying man expresses a wish not to be buried. In that case his corpse, tightly bandaged, is deposited in a corner of the house, and the products of decomposition are allowed to drain through a

Preservation of the lower jawbone.

tube into the ground. When they have ceased to run, the bundle is opened and the bones taken out and buried, except the lower jawbone, which is preserved, sometimes along with one of the lower arm bones. The lower jawbone reminds the possessor of the duty of blood revenge which he owes to the deceased, and which the dying man may have inculcated on him with his last breath. The lower arm bone brings luck in the chase, especially if the departed relative was a mighty hunter. However, if the hunters have a long run of bad luck, they conclude that the ghost has departed to the under world and accordingly bury the lower arm bone and the lower jawbone with the rest of the skeleton. The length of the period of mourning is similarly determined by the good or bad fortune of the huntsmen. If the ghost provides them with game in abundance for a long time after his death, the days of mourning are proportionately extended ; but when the game grows scarce or fails altogether, the mourning comes to an end and the memory of the deceased soon fades away.[1] The savage is a thoroughly practical man and is not such a fool as to waste his sorrow over a ghost who gives him nothing in return. Nothing for nothing is his principle. His relations to the dead stand on a strictly commercial basis.

Mourning costume.

The mourning costume consists of strings round the neck, bracelets of reed on the arms, and a cylindrical hat of bark on the head. A widow is swathed in nets. The intention of the costume is to signify to the ghost the sympathy which the mourner feels for him in his disembodied state. If the man in his lifetime was wont to crouch shivering

---

[1] Ch. Keysser, *op. cit.* pp. 82, 83.

over the fire, a little fire will be kept up for a time at the foot of the grave in order to warm his homeless spirit.[1] The widow or widower has to discharge the disagreeable duty of living day and night for several weeks in a hovel built directly over the grave. Not unfrequently the lot of a widow is much harder. At her own request she is some-times strangled and buried with her husband in the grave, in order that her soul may accompany his on the journey to the other world. The other relations have no interest in encouraging the woman to sacrifice herself, rather the contrary ; but if she insists they fear to balk her, lest they should offend the ghost of her husband, who would punish them in many ways for keeping his wife from him. But even such voluntary sacrifices, if we may believe Mr. Ch. Keysser, are dictated rather by a selfish calculation than by an impulse of disinterested affection. He mentions the case of a man named Jabu, both of whose wives chose thus to attend their husband in death. The deceased was an industrious man, a skilful hunter and farmer, who provided his wives with abundance of food. As such men are believed to work hard also in the other world, tilling fields and killing game just as here, the widows thought they could not do better than follow him as fast as possible to the spirit land, since they had no prospect of getting such another husband here on earth. " How firmly convinced," adds the missionary admiringly, " must these people be of the reality of another world when they sacrifice their earthly existence, not for the sake of a better life hereafter, but merely in order to be no worse off there than they have been on earth." And he adds that this consideration explains why no man ever chooses to be strangled at the death of his wife. The labour market in the better land is apparently not recruited from the ranks of women.[2]

The house in which anybody has died is deserted, because the ghost of the dead is believed to haunt it and make it unsafe at night. If the deceased was a chief or a man of importance, the whole village is abandoned and a new one built on another site.[3]

Widows strangled to accompany their dead husbands.

House or village deserted after a death.

[1] Ch. Keysser, *op. cit.* pp. 82, 142 *sq.*
[2] Ch. Keysser, *op. cit.* pp. 83 *sq.*, 143.   [3] Ch. Keysser, *op. cit.* p. 83.

LECTURE XIII

THE BELIEF IN IMMORTALITY AMONG THE NATIVES OF
GERMAN NEW GUINEA (*continued*)

Offerings
to appease
ghosts. IN the last lecture I gave you some account of the fear and awe which the Kai of German New Guinea entertain for the spirits of the dead. Believing that the ghost is endowed with all the qualities and faculties which distinguished the man in his lifetime, they naturally dread most the ghosts of warlike, cruel, violent, and passionate men, and take the greatest pains to soothe their anger and win their favour. For that purpose they give the departed spirit all sorts of things to take with him to the far country. And in order that he may have the use of them it is necessary to smash or otherwise spoil them. Thus the spear that is given him must be broken, the pot must be shivered, the bag must be torn, the palm-tree must be cut down. Fruits are offered to the ghost by dashing them in pieces or hanging a bunch of them over the grave. Objects of value, such as boars' tusks or dogs' teeth, are made over to him by being laid on the corpse ; but the economical savage removes these precious things from the body at burial. All such offerings and sacrifices, we are told, are made simply out of fear of the ghost. It is no pleasure to a man to cut down a valuable palm-tree, which might have helped to nourish himself and his family for years ; he does it only lest a worse thing should befall him at the hands of the departed spirit.[1]

But the greatest service that the Kai can render to a dead man is to take vengeance on the sorcerer who caused

---

[1] Ch. Keysser, *op. cit.* pp. 142 *sq.*

his death by witchcraft.   The first thing is to discover the
villain, and in the search for him the ghost obligingly
assists his surviving kinsfolk.   Sometimes, however, it is
necessary to resort to a stratagem in order to secure his
help.   Thus, for example, one day while the ghost, blinded
by the strong sunlight, is cowering in a dark corner or
reposing at full length in the grave, his relatives will set up
a low scaffold in a field, cover it with leaves, and pile up
over it a mass of the field fruits which belonged 'to the dead
man, so that the whole erection may appear to the eye of
the unsuspecting ghost a heap of taro, yams, and so forth,
and nothing more.   But before the sun goes down, two or
three men steal out from the house, and ensconce themselves
under the scaffold, where they are completely concealed
by the piled-up fruits.   When darkness has fallen, out
comes the ghost and prowling about espies the heap of
yams and taro.   At sight of the devastation wrought in his
field he flies into a passion, and curses and swears in the
feeble wheezy whisper in which ghosts always speak.   In
the course of his fluent imprecations he expresses a wish
that the miscreants who have wasted his substance may
suffer so and so at the hands of the sorcerer.   That is just
what the men in hiding have been waiting for.   No sooner
do they hear the name of the sorcerer than they jump up
with a great shout; the startled ghost takes to his heels;
and all the people in the village come pouring out of the
houses.   Very glad they are to know that the murderer
has been found out, and sooner or later they will have his
blood.[1]

Another mode of eliciting the requisite information from
the ghost is this.   In order to allow him to communicate
freely with his mouldering body, his relations insert a tube
through the earth of the grave down to the corpse; then
they sprinkle powdered lime on the grave.   At night the
ghost comes along, picks up the powdered lime, and makes off
in a bee line for the village where the sorcerer who bewitched
him resides.   On the way he drops some of the powder
here and there, so that next morning, on the principle of the
paper-chase, his relatives can trace his footsteps to the

Mode of discovering the sorcerer who caused a death.

Another way of detecting the sorcerer.

---

[1] Ch. Keysser, *op. cit.* p. 143.

very door of his murderer. In many districts the people
tie a packet of lime to the knee of a corpse so that his
ghost may have it to hand when he wants it.[1]

Cross-
question-
ing the
ghost by
means of
fire.

But the favourite way of cross-questioning the ghost on
the subject of his decease is by means of fire. A few men
go out before nightfall from the village and sit down in a
row, one behind the other, on the path. The man in front
has a leaf-mat drawn like a hood over his head and back
in order that the ghost may not touch him from behind
unawares. In his hand he holds a glowing coal and some
tinder, and as he puts the one to the other he calls to the
ghost, " Come, take, take, take ; come, take, take, take," and
so on. Meantime his mates behind him are reckoning up
the names of all the men near and far who are suspected of
sorcery, and a portion of the village youth have clambered
up trees and are on the look-out for the ghost. If they do
not see his body they certainly see his eye twinkling in the
gloom, though the uninstructed European might easily
mistake it for a glow-worm. No sooner do they catch sight
of it than they bawl out, " Come hither, fetch the fire, and
burn him who burnt thee." If the tinder blazes up at the
name of a sorcerer, it is flung towards the village where the
man in question dwells. And if at the same time a glow-
worm is seen to move in the same direction, the people
entertain no doubt that the ghost has appeared and fetched
the soul of the fire.[2]

Necessity
of destroy-
ing the
sorcerer
who caused
a death.

In whichever way the author of the death may be
detected, the avengers of blood set out for the village of
the miscreant and seek to take his life. Almost all the
wars between villages or tribes spring from such expeditions.
The sorcerer or sorcerers must be extirpated, nay all their
kith and kin must be destroyed root and branch, if the
people are to live in peace and quiet. The ghost of the
dead calls, nay clamours for vengeance, and if he does not
get it, he will wreak his spite on his negligent relations.
Not only will he give them no luck in the chase, but he
will drive the wild swine into the fields to trample down
and root up the crops, and he will do them every mischief
in his power. If rain does not fall, so that the freshly

[1] Ch. Keysser, *l.c.*   [2] Ch. Keysser, *op. cit.* pp. 143 *sq.*

planted root crops wither ; or if sickness is rife, the people recognise in the calamity the wrath of the ghost, who can only be appeased by the slaughter of the wicked magician or of somebody else.   Hence the avengers of blood often do not set out until a fresh death, an outbreak of sickness, failure in the chase, or some other misfortune reminds the living of the duty they owe to the dead.   The Kai is not by nature warlike, and he might never go to war if it were not that he dreads the vengeance of ghosts more than the wrath of men.[1]

If the expedition has been successful, if the enemy's village has been surprised and stormed, the men and old women butchered, and the young women taken prisoners, the warriors beat a hasty retreat with their booty in order to be safe at home, or at least in the shelter of a friendly village, before nightfall.   Their reason for haste is the fear of being overtaken in the darkness by the ghosts of their slaughtered foes, who, powerless by day, are very dangerous and terrible by night.   Restlessly through the hours of darkness these unquiet spirits follow like sleuth-hounds in the tracks of their retreating enemies, eager to come up with them and by contact with the bloodstained weapons of their slayers to recover the spiritual substance which they have lost.   Not till they have done so can they find rest and peace. That is why the victors are careful not at first to bring back their weapons into the village but to hide them somewhere in the bushes at a safe distance.   There they leave them for some days until the baffled ghosts may be supposed to have given up the chase and returned, sad and angry, to their mangled bodies in the charred ruins of their old home. The first night after the return of the warriors is always the most anxious time ; all the villagers are then on the alert for fear of the ghosts ; but if the night passes quietly, their terror gradually subsides and gives place to the dread of their surviving enemies.[2]

As the victors in a raid are supposed to have more or less of the soul-stuff or spiritual essence of their slain foes adhering to their persons, none of their friends will venture to touch them for some time after their return to the village.

Slayers dread the ghosts of the slain.

Seclusion of man-slayers from fear of their victims' ghosts.

[1] Ch. Keysser, *op. cit.* pp. 62 *sq.*   [2] Ch. Keysser, pp. 64 *sqq.*, 147 *sq.*

Everybody avoids them and goes carefully out of their way. If during this time any of the villagers suffers from a pain in his stomach, he thinks that he must have inadvertently sat down where one of the warriors had sat before him. If somebody endures the pangs of toothache, he makes sure that he must have eaten a fruit which had been touched by one of the slayers. All the refuse of the meals of these gallant men must be most carefully put away lest a pig should devour it; for if it did do so, the animal would certainly die, which would be a serious loss to the owner. Hence when the warriors have satisfied their hunger, any food that remains over is burnt or buried. The fighting men themselves are not very seriously incommoded, or at all events endangered, by the ghosts of their victims; for they have taken the precaution to disinfect themselves by the sap of a certain creeper, which, if it does not render them absolutely immune to ghostly influence, at least fortifies their constitution to a very considerable extent.[1]

Sometimes, instead of sending forth a band of warriors to ravage, burn, and slaughter the whole male population of the village in which the wicked sorcerer resides, the people of one village will come to a secret understanding with the people of the sorcerer's village to have the miscreant quietly put out of the way. A hint is given to the scoundrel's next of kin, it may be his brother, son, or nephew, that if he will only wink at the slaughter of his obnoxious relative, he will receive a handsome compensation from the slayers. Should he privately accept the offer, he is most careful to conceal his connivance at the deed of blood, lest he should draw down on his head the wrath of his murdered kinsman's ghost. So, when the deed is done and the murder is out, he works himself up into a state of virtuous sorrow and indignation, covers his head with the leaves of a certain plant, and chanting a dirge in tones of heart-rending grief, marches straight to the village of the murderers. There, on the public square, surrounded by an attentive audience, he opens the floodgates of his eloquence and pours forth the torrent of an aching heart. "You have slain my kinsman," says he, "you are wicked men! How could you kill so

---

[1] Ch. Keysser, *op. cit.* p. 132.

good a man, who conferred so many benefits on me in his
lifetime? I knew nothing of the plot. Had I had an
inkling of it, I would have foiled it. How can I now
avenge his death? I have no property with which to hire
men of war to go and punish his murderers. Yet in spite
of everything my murdered kinsman will not believe in my
innocence! He will be angry with me, he will pay me out, he
will do me all the harm he can. Therefore do you declare
openly whether I had any share whatever in his death,
and come and strew lime on my head in order that he may
convince himself of my innocence." This appeal of injured
innocence meets with a ready response. The people dust
the leaves on his head with powdered lime; and so, decorated
with the white badge of spotless virtue, and enriched with a
boar's tusk or other valuable object as the price of his compliance, he returns to his village with a conscience at peace
with all the world, reflecting with satisfaction on the profit-
able transaction he has just concluded, and laughing in his
sleeve at the poor deluded ghost of his murdered relative.[1]

Sometimes the worthy soul who thus for a valuable
consideration consents to waive all his personal feelings,
will even carry his self-abnegation so far as to be present
and look on at the murder of his kinsman. But true to his
principles he will see to it that the thing is done decently
and humanely. When the struggle is nearly over and the
man is down, writhing on the ground with the murderers
busy about him, his loving kinsman will not suffer them to
take an unfair advantage of their superior numbers to cut
him up alive with their knives, to chop him with their axes,
or to smash him with their clubs. He will only allow them
to stab him with their spears, repeating of course the stabs
again and again till the victim ceases to writhe and
quiver, and lies there dead as a stone. Then begins the
real time of peril for the virtuous kinsman who has been
a spectator and director of the scene; for the ghost of the
murdered man has now deserted its mangled body, and,
still blinded with blood and smarting with pain, might
easily and even excusably misunderstand the situation.
It is essential, therefore, in order to prevent a painful

Comedy acted to deceive the ghost of a murdered kinsman.

[1] Ch. Keysser, *op. cit.* p. 148.

misapprehension, that the kinsman should at once and emphatically disclaim any part or parcel in the murder. This he accordingly does in language which leaves no room for doubt or ambiguity. He falls into a passion: he rails at the murderers: he proclaims his horror at their deed. All the way home he refuses to be comforted. He upbraids the assassins, he utters the most frightful threats against them; he rushes at them to snatch their weapons from them and dash them in pieces. But they easily wrench the weapons from his unresisting hands. For the whole thing is only a piece of acting. His sole intention is that the ghost may see and hear it all, and being convinced of the innocence of his dear kinsman may not punish him with bad crops, wounds, sickness, and other misfortunes. Even when he has reached the village, he keeps up the comedy for a time, raging, fretting and fuming at the irreparable loss he has sustained by the death of his lamented relative.[1]

Pretence of avenging the ghost of a murdered sorcerer.

Similarly when a chief has among his subjects a particular sorcerer whom he fears but with whom he is professedly on terms of friendship, he will sometimes engage a man to murder him. No sooner, however, is the murder perpetrated than the chief who bespoke it hastens in seeming indignation with a band of followers to the murderer's village. The assassin, of course, has got a hint of what is coming, and he and his friends take care not to be at home when the chief arrives on his mission of vengeance. Balked by the absence of their victim the avengers of blood breathe out fire and slaughter, but content themselves in fact with smashing an old pot or two, knocking down a deserted hut, and perhaps felling a banana-tree or a betel-palm. Having thus given the ghost of the murdered man an unequivocal proof of the sincerity of their friendship, they return quietly home.[2]

The Kai afraid of ghosts.

The habits of Kai ghosts are to some extent just the contrary of those of living men. They sleep by day and go about their business by night, when they frighten people and play them all kinds of tricks. Usually they appear in the form of animals. As light has the effect of blinding or at

[1] Ch. Keysser, *op. cit.* pp. 148 *sq.*   [2] Ch. Keysser, *op. cit.* p. 149.

least dazzling them, they avoid everything bright, and hence it is easy to scare them away by means of fire. That is why no native will go even a short way in the dark without a bamboo torch. If it is absolutely necessary to go out by night, which he is very loth to do, he will hum and haw loudly before quitting the house so as to give notice to any lurking ghost that he is coming with a light, which allows the ghost to scuttle out of his way in good time. The people of a village live in terror above all so long as a corpse remains unburied in it; after nightfall nobody would then venture out of sight of the houses. When a troop of people go by night to a neighbouring village with flaring torches in their hands, nobody is willing to walk last on the path; they all huddle together for safety in the middle, till one man braver than the rest consents to act as rearguard. The rustling of a bush in the evening twilight startles them with the dread of some ghastly apparition; the sight of a pig in the gloaming is converted by their fears into the vision of a horrible spectre. If a man stumbles, it is because a ghost has pushed him, and he fancies he perceives the frightful thing in a tree-stump or any chance object. No wonder a Kai man fears ghosts, since he believes that the mere touch of one of them may be fatal. People who fall down in fits or in faints are supposed to have been touched by ghosts; and on coming to themselves they will tell their friends with the most solemn assurance how they felt the death-cold hand of the ghost on their body, and how a shudder ran through their whole frame at contact with the uncanny being.[1]

But it would be a mistake to imagine that the ghosts of the dead are a source of danger, annoyance, and discomfort, and nothing more. That is not so. They may and do render the Kai the most material services in everyday life, particularly by promoting the supply of food both vegetable and animal. I have said that these practical savages stand towards their departed kinsfolk on a strictly commercial footing; and I will now illustrate the benefits which the Kai hope to receive from the ghosts in return for all the respect and attention lavished on them. In the first

Services rendered to the living by ghosts of the dead.

[1] Ch. Keysser, *op. cit.* p. 147.

place, then, so long as a ghost remains in the neighbourhood of the village, it is expected of him that he shall make the crops thrive and neither tread them down himself nor allow wild pigs to do so. The expectation is reasonable, yet the conduct of the ghost does not always answer to it. Occasionally, whether out of sheer perverseness or simple absence of mind, he will sit down in a field ; and wherever he does so, he makes a hollow where the fruits will not grow. Indeed any fruit that he even touches with his foot in passing, shrivels up. Where these things have happened, the people offer boiled taro and a few crabs to the ghosts to induce them to keep clear of the crops and to repose their weary limbs elsewhere than in the tilled fields.[1]

Ghosts help Kai hunters to kill game.

But the most important service which the dead render to the living is the good luck which they vouchsafe to hunters. Hence in order to assure himself of the favour of the dead the hunter hangs his nets on a grave before he uses them. If a man was a good and successful hunter in his lifetime, his ghost will naturally be more than usually able to assist his brethren in the craft after his death. For that reason when such a man has just died, the people, to adopt a familiar proverb, hasten to make hay while the sun shines by hunting very frequently, in the confident expectation of receiving ghostly help from the deceased hunter. In the evening, when they return from the chase, they lay a small portion of their bag near his grave, scatter a powder which possesses the special virtue of attracting ghosts, and call out, "So-and-so, come and eat ; here I set down food for you, it is a part of all we have." If after such an offering and invocation the night wind rustles the tops of the trees or shakes the thatch of leaves on the roofs, they know that the ghost is in the village. The twinkle of a glow-worm near his grave is the glitter of his eye. In the morning, too, before they sally forth to the woods, one of the next of kin to the dead huntsman will go betimes to his grave, stamp on it to waken the sleeper below, and call out, "So-and-so, come ! we are now about to go out hunting. Help us to a good bag !" If they have luck, they praise the deceased as a good spirit and in the evening supply

[1] Ch. Keysser, *op. cit.* p. 145.

his wants again with food, tobacco, and betel. The sacrifice, as usually happens in such cases, does not call for any great exercise of self-denial; since the spirit consumes only the spiritual essence of the good things, while he leaves their material substance to be enjoyed by the living.[1]

However, it sometimes happens that the ghost dis- *Ill-treat-*
appoints them, and that the hunters return in the evening *ment of*
a ghost
hungry and empty-handed. This may even be repeated *who fails*
day after day, and still the people will not lose hope. They *to help*
hunters.
think that the ghost is perhaps busy working in his field, or that he has gone on a visit and will soon come home. To give him time to do his business or see his friends at leisure, they will remain in the village for several days. Then, when they imagine that he must surely have re- turned, they go out into the woods and try their luck again. But should there still be no ghost and no game, they begin to be seriously alarmed. They think that some evil must have befallen him. But if time goes on and still he gives no sign and the game continues scarce and shy, their feelings towards the ghost undergo a radical alteration. Passion getting the better of prudence, they will even re- proach him with ingratitude, taunt him with his uselessness, and leave him to starve. Should he after that still remain deaf to their railing and regardless of the short commons to which they have reduced him, they will discharge a volley of abuse at his grave and trouble themselves about him no more. However, if, not content with refusing his valuable assistance in the chase, the ghost should actually blight the crops or send wild boars into the fields to trample them down, the patience of the long-suffering people is quite exhausted: the vials of their wrath overflow; and snatching up their cudgels in a fury they belabour his grave till his bones ache, or even drive him with blows and curses altogether from the village.[2]

Such an outcast ghost, if he does not seek his revenge *The*
by prowling in the neighbourhood and preying on society *journey of*
ghosts to
at large, will naturally bethink himself of repairing to his *the spirit*
long home in the under world. For sooner or later the *land.*
spirits of the dead congregate there. It is especially when

[1] Ch. Keysser, *op. cit.* p. 145.   [2] Ch. Keysser, *op. cit.* pp. 145 *sq.*

the flesh has quite mouldered away from his bones that the ghost packs up his little traps and sets out for the better land. The entrance to the abode of bliss is a cave to the west of Saddle Mountain. Here in the gully there is a projecting tree-stump on which the ghosts perch waiting for a favourable moment to jump into the mouth of the cavern. When a slight earthquake is felt, a Kai man will often say, "A ghost has just leaped from the tree into the cave; that is why the earth is shaking." Down below the ghosts are received by Tulmeng, lord of the nether world. Often he appears in a canoe to ferry them over to the further shore. "Blood or wax?" is the laconic question which he puts to the ghost on the bank. He means to say, "Were you killed or were you done to death by magic?" For it is with wax that the sorcerer stops up the fatal little tubes in which he encloses the souls of his enemies. And the reason why the lord of the dead puts the question to the newcomer is that the ghosts of the slain and the ghosts of the bewitched dwell in separate places. Right in front of the land of souls rises a high steep wall, which cannot be climbed even by ghosts. The spirits have accordingly to make their way through it and thereupon find themselves in their new abode. According to some Kai, before the ghosts are admitted to ghost land they must swing to and fro on a rope and then drop into water, where they are washed clean of bloodstains and all impurity; after which they ascend, spick and span, the last slope to the village of ghosts.

Life of ghosts in the other world.

Tulmeng has the reputation of being a very stern ruler in his weird realm, but the Kai really know very little about him. He beats refractory souls, and it is essential that every ghost should have his ears and nose bored. The operation is very painful, and to escape it most people take the precaution of having their ears and noses bored in their lifetime. Life in the other world goes on just like life in this one. Houses are built exactly like houses on earth, and there as here pigs swarm in the streets. Fields are tilled and crops are got in; ghostly men marry ghostly women, who give birth to ghostly children. The same old round of love and hate, of quarrelling and fighting, of battle, murder and sudden death goes on in the shadowy realm below ground just as in the more solid world above ground. Sorcerers are there also, and they breed just as bad blood among the dead as among the living. All things indeed are the same except for their shadowy unsubstantial texture.[1]

But the ghosts do not live for ever in the nether world. They die the second death and turn into animals, generally into cuscuses. In the shape of animals they haunt the wildest, deepest, darkest glens of the rugged mountains. No one but the owner has the right to set foot on such haunted ground. He may even kill the ghostly animals. Any one else who dared to disturb them in their haunts would do so at the peril of his life. But even the owner of the land who has killed one of the ghostly creatures is bound to appease the spirit of the dead beast. He may not cut up the carcase at once, but must leave it for a time, perhaps for a whole night, after laying on it presents which are intended to mollify and soothe the injured spirit. In placing the gifts on the body he says, " Take the gifts and leave us that which was a game animal, that we may eat it." When the animal's ghost has appropriated the spiritual essence of the offerings, the hunter and his family may eat the carcase. Should one of these ghostly creatures die or be killed, its spirit turns either into an insect or into an ant-hill. Children who would destroy such an ant-hill or throw little darts at it, are warned by their elders not to indulge in such sacrilegious sport. When the insect also dies, the series of spiritual transformations is at an end.[2]

Ghosts die and turn into animals.

The ghosts whose help is invoked by hunters and farmers are commonly the spirits of persons who have lately died, since such spirits linger for a time in the neighbourhood, or rather in the memory of the people. But besides these spirits of the recent dead there are certain older ghosts who may be regarded as permanent patrons of hunting and other departments of life and nature, because their fame has survived long after the men or women themselves were gathered to their fathers. For example, men who were bold and resolute in battle during their

Ghosts of persons eminent for good or evil in their lives are remembered and appealed to for help long after their deaths.

---

[1] Ch. Keysser, *op. cit.* pp. 149 *sq.*   [2] Ch. Keysser, *op. cit.* pp. 112, 150 *sq.*

life will be invoked long after their death, whenever a stout heart is needed for some feat of daring. And men who were notorious thieves and villains in the flesh will be invited, long after their bodies have mouldered in the grave, to lend their help when a deed of villainy is to be done. The names of men or women who were eminent for good or evil in their lives survive indefinitely in the memory of the tribe. Thus before a battle many a Kai warrior will throw something over the enemy's village and as he does so he will softly call on two ghosts, " We and Gunang, ye two heroes, come and guard me and keep the foes from me, that they may not be able to hurt me ! But stand by me that I may be able to riddle them with spears ! " Again, when a magician wishes to cause an earthquake, he will take a handful of ashes, wrap them in certain leaves, and pronounce the following spell over the packet: "Thou man Sâiong, throw about everything that exists ; houses, villages, paths, fields, bushes and tall forest trees, yams, and taro, throw them all hither and thither ; break and smash everything, but leave me in peace ! " While he utters this incantation or prayer, the sorcerer's body itself twitches and quivers more and more violently, till the hut creaks and cracks and his strength is exhausted. Then he throws the packet of ashes out of the hut, and after that the earthquake is sure to follow sooner or later. So when they want rain, the Kai call upon two ghostly men named Balong and Batu, or Dinding and Bojang, to drive away a certain woman named Yondimi, so that the rain which she is holding up may fall upon the earth. The prayer for rain addressed to the ghosts is combined with a magical spell pronounced over a stone. And when rain has fallen in abundance and the Kai wish to make it cease, they strew hot ashes on the stone or lay it in a wood fire. On the principle of homoeopathic magic the heat of the ashes or of the fire is supposed to dry up the rain. Thus in these ceremonies for the production or cessation of rain we see that religion, represented by the invocation of the ghosts, goes hand in hand with magic, represented by the hocus-pocus with the stone. Again, certain celebrated ghosts are invoked to promote the growth

Prayers to ghosts for rain, a good crop of yams, and so forth.

of taro and yams.   Thus to ensure a good crop of taro,
the suppliant will hold a bud of taro in his hand and pray,
" O Mrs. Zewanong, may my taro leaves unfold till they
are as broad as the petticoat which covers thy loins!"
When they are planting yams, they pray to two women
named Tendung and Molewa that they would cause the
yams to put forth as long suckers as the strings which the
women twist to make into carrying-nets.   Before they dig
up the yams, they take a branch and drive with it the evil
spirits or ghosts from the house in which the yams are to
be stored.   Having effected this clearance they stick the
branch in the roof of the house and appoint a certain
ghostly man named Ehang to act as warden.   Again,
fowlers invoke a married pair of ghosts called Mânze and
Tâmingoka to frighten the birds from the trees and drive
them on the limed twigs.   Or they pray to a ghostly
woman named Lâne, saying, " In all places of the neighbourhood shake the betel-nuts from the palms, that they may
fall down to me on this fruit-tree and knock the berries
from the boughs!"   But by the betel-nuts the fowler in
veiled language means the birds, which are to come in flocks
to the fruit-tree and be caught fast by the lime on the
branches.   Again, when a fisherman wishes to catch eels,
he prays to two ghosts called Yambi and Ngigwâli, saying:
" Come, ye two men, and go down into the holes of the
pool; smite the eels in them, and draw them out on the
bank, that I may kill them!"   Once more, when a child
suffers from enlarged spleen, which shews as a swelling on
its body, the parent will pray to a ghost named Aidolo for
help in these words: " Come and help this child!   It is
big with a ball of sickness.   Cut it up and squeeze and
squash it, that the blood and pus may drain away and my
child may be made whole!"   To give point to the prayer
the petitioner simultaneously pretends to cut a cross on the
swelling with a knife.[1]

From this it appears that men and women who impressed their contemporaries by their talents, their virtues,

[1] Ch. Keysser, *op. cit.* pp. 151-154. In this passage the ghosts are spoken of simply as spirits (*Geister*); but the context proves that the spirits in question are those of the dead.

Possible
develop-
ment of
depart-
mental
gods out
of ghosts.

or their vices in their lifetime, are sometimes remembered long after their death and continue to be invoked by their descendants for help in the particular department in which they had formerly rendered themselves eminent either for good or for evil. Such powerful and admired or dreaded ghosts might easily grow in time into gods and goddesses, who are worshipped as presiding over the various departments of nature and of human life. There is good reason to think that among many tribes and nations of the world the history of a god, if it could be recovered, would be found to be the history of a spirit who served his apprenticeship as a ghost before he was promoted to the rank of deity.

Kai lads
at circum-
cision
supposed
to be
swallowed
by a
monster.

Before quitting the Kai tribe I will mention that they, like the other tribes on this coast, practise circumcision and appear to associate the custom more or less vaguely with the spirits of the dead. Like their neighbours, they impress women with the belief that at circumcision the lads are swallowed by a monster, who can only be induced to disgorge them by the bribe of much food and especially of pigs, which are accordingly bred and kept nominally for this purpose, but really to furnish a banquet for the men alone. The ceremony is performed at irregular intervals of several years. A long hut, entered through a high door at one end and tapering away at the other, is built in a lonely part of the forest. It represents the monster which is to swallow the novices in its capacious jaws. The process of deglutition is represented as follows. In front of the entrance to the hut a scaffold is erected and a man mounts it. The novices are then led up one by one and passed under the scaffold. As each comes up, the man overhead makes a gesture of swallowing, while at the same time he takes a great gulp of water from a coco-nut flask. The trembling novice is now supposed to be in the maw of the monster; but a pig is offered for his redemption, the man on the scaffold, as representative of the beast, accepts the offering, a gurgling sound is heard, and the water which he had just gulped descends in a jet on the novice, who now goes free. The actual circumcision follows immediately on this impressive pantomime. The monster who swallows the lads is named Ngosa, which means "Grandfather"; and the same name is given to the bull-roarers which are swung at the festival. The Kai bull-roarer is a lance-shaped piece of palm-wood, more or less elaborately carved, which being swung at the end of a string emits the usual droning, booming sound. When they are not in use, the instruments are kept, carefully wrapt up, in the men's house, which no woman may enter. Only the old men have the right to undo these precious bundles and take out the sacred bull-roarers. Women, too, are strictly excluded from the neighbourhood of the circumcision ground; any who intrude on it are put to death. The mythical monster who is supposed to haunt the ground is said to be very dangerous to the female sex. When the novices go forth to be swallowed by him in the forest, the women who remain in the village weep and wail; and they rejoice greatly when the lads come back safe and sound.[1]

The last tribe of German New Guinea to which I shall invite your attention are the Tami. Most of them live not on the mainland but in a group of islands in Huon Gulf, to the south-east of Yabim. They are of a purer Melanesian stock than most of the tribes on the neighbouring coast of New Guinea. The German missionary Mr. G. Bamler, who lived amongst them for ten years and knows the people and their language intimately, thinks that they may even contain a strong infusion of Polynesian blood.[2] They are a seafaring folk, who extend their voyages all along the coast for the purpose of trade, bartering mats, pearls, fish, coconuts, and other tree-fruits which grow on their islands for taro, bananas, sugar-cane, and sago, which grow on the mainland.[3]

In the opinion of these people every man has two souls, a long one and a short one. The long soul is identified with the shadow. It is only loosely attached to its owner, wandering away from his body in sleep and returning to it when he wakes with a start. The seat of the long soul is

Bull-roarers.

The Tami Islanders of Huon Gulf.

The long soul and the short soul.

[1] Ch. Keysser, *op. cit.* pp. 34-40.
[2] G. Bamler, "Tami," in R. Neuhauss's *Deutsch Neu-Guinea*, iii. (Berlin, 1911) p. 489; compare *ib.* p. vii.
[3] H. Zahn, "Die Jabim," in R. Neuhauss's *Deutsch Neu-Guinea*, iii. 315 *sq.*

in the stomach. When the man dies, the long soul quits
his body and appears to his relations at a distance, who
thus obtain the first intimation of his decease. Having
conveyed the sad intelligence to them, the long soul departs
by way of Maligep, on the west coast of New Britain, to a
village on the north coast, the inhabitants of which recognise
the Tami ghosts as they flit past.[1]

Departure
of the short
soul to
Lamboam,
the nether
world. The short soul, on the other hand, never leaves the
body in life but only after death. Even then it tarries for
a time in the neighbourhood of the body before it takes its
departure for Lamboam, which is the abode of the dead in
the nether world. The Tami bury their dead in shallow
graves under or near the houses. They collect in a coco-
nut shell the maggots which swarm from the decaying
corpse ; and when the insects cease to swarm, they know
that the short soul has gone away to its long home. It is
the short soul which receives and carries away with it the
offerings that are made to the deceased. These offerings
serve a double purpose ; they form the nucleus of the
dead man's property in the far country, and they ensure
him a friendly reception on his arrival. For example, the
soul shivers with cold, when it first reaches the subterranean
realm, and the other ghosts, the old stagers, obligingly heat
stones to warm it up.[2]

Dilemma
of the
Tami. However, the restless spirit returns from time to time
to haunt and terrify the sorcerer, who was the cause of its
death. But its threats are idle ; it can really do him very
little harm. Yet it keeps its ghostly eye on its surviving
relatives to see that they do not stand on a friendly footing
with the wicked sorcerer. Strictly speaking the Tami
ought to avenge his death, but as a matter of fact they do
not. The truth of it is that the Tami do a very good
business with the people on the mainland, among whom
the sorcerer is usually to be found ; and the amicable relations which are essential to the maintenance of commerce
would unquestionably suffer if a merchant were to indulge
his resentment so far as to take his customer's head instead
of his sago and bananas. These considerations reduce the
Tami to a painful dilemma. If they gratify the ghost

[1] G. Bamler, *op. cit.* p. 518.   [2] G. Bamler, *l.c.*

they lose a customer; if they keep the customer they must bitterly offend the ghost, who will punish them for their disrespect to his memory. In this delicate position the Tami endeavour to make the best of both worlds. On the one hand, by loudly professing their wrath and indignation against the guilty sorcerer they endeavour to appease the ghost; and on the other hand, by leaving the villain unmolested they do nothing to alienate their customers.[1]

But if they do not gratify the desire for vengeance of the blood-thirsty ghost, they are at great pains to testify their respect for him in all other ways. The whole village takes part in the mourning and lamentation for a death. The women dance death dances, the men lend a hand in the preparations for the burial. All festivities are stopped: the drums are silent. As the people believe that when anybody has died, the ghosts of his dead kinsfolk gather in the village and are joined by other ghosts, they are careful not to leave the mourners alone, exposed to the too pressing attentions of the spectral visitors; they keep the bereaved family company, especially at night; indeed, if the weather be fine, the whole population of the village will encamp round the temporary hut which is built on the grave. This watch at the grave lasts about eight days. The watchers are supported and comforted in the discharge of their pious duty by a liberal allowance of food and drink. Nor are the wants of the ghost himself forgotten. Many families offer him taro broth at this time. The period of mourning lasts two or three years. During the first year the observances prescribed by custom are strictly followed, and the nearest relations must avoid publicity. After a year they are allowed more freedom; for example, the widow may lay aside the heavy net, which is her costume in full mourning, and may replace it by a lighter one; moreover, she may quit the house. At the end of the long period of mourning, dances are danced in honour of the deceased. They begin in the evening and last all night till daybreak. The mourners on these occasions smear their heads, necks, and breasts with black earth. A great quantity of food,

Funeral and mourning customs of the Tami.

---

[1] G. Bamler, *op. cit.* pp. 518 *sq.*

particularly of pigs and taro broth, has been made ready ;
for the whole village, and perhaps a neighbouring village
also, has been invited to share in the festivity, which
may last eight or ten days, if the provisions suffice. The
dances begin with a gravity and solemnity appropriate to a
memorial of the dead ; but towards the close the performers
indulge in a lighter vein and act comic pieces, which so
tickle the fancy of the spectators, that many of them roll
on the ground with laughter. Finally, the temporary hut
erected on the grave is taken down and the materials
burned. As the other ghosts of the village are believed
to be present in attendance on the one who is the guest of
honour, all the villagers bring offerings and throw them
into the fire. However, persons who are not related to the
ghosts may snatch the offerings from the flames and convert
them to their own use. Precious objects, such as boars'
tusks and dogs' teeth, are not committed to the fire but
merely swung over it in a bag, while the name of the
person who offers the valuables in this economical fashion
is proclaimed aloud for the satisfaction of the ghost. With
these dances, pantomimes, and offerings the living have
discharged the last duties of respect and affection to the
dead. Yet for a while his ghost is thought to linger as a
domestic or household spirit ; but the time comes when he
is wholly forgotten.[1]

Bones of
the dead
dug up and
kept in the
house for
a time.

Many families, however, not content with the observance of these ordinary ceremonies, dig up the bodies of
their dead when the flesh has mouldered away, redden the
bones with ochre, and keep them bundled up in the house
for two or three years, when these relics of mortality are
finally committed to the earth. The intention of thus
preserving the bones for years in the house is not mentioned,
but no doubt it is to maintain a closer intimacy with the
departed spirit than seems possible if his skeleton is left to
rot in the grave. When he is at last laid in the ground,
the tomb is enclosed by a strong wooden fence and planted
with ornamental shrubs. Yet in the course of years, as
the memory of the deceased fades away, his grave is
neglected, the fence decays, the shrubs run wild ; another

[1] G. Bamler, *op. cit.* pp. 519-522.

generation, which knew him not, will build a house on the
spot, and if in digging the foundations they turn up his
bleached and mouldering bones, it is nothing to them : why
should they trouble themselves about the spirit of a man
or woman whose very name is forgotten?[1]

[1] G. Bamler, *op. cit.* p. 518.

LECTURE XIV

THE BELIEF IN IMMORTALITY AMONG THE NATIVES OF GERMAN AND DUTCH NEW GUINEA

The Tami
doctrine
of souls
and gods. AT the close of the last lecture I dealt with the Tami, a people of Melanesian stock who inhabit a group of islands off the mainland of New Guinea. I explained their theory of the human soul. According to them, every man has two distinct souls, a long one and a short one, both of which survive his death, but depart in different directions, one of them repairing to the lower world, and the other being last sighted off the coast of New Britain. But the knowledge which these savages possess of the spiritual world is not limited to the souls of men; they are acquainted with several deities (*buwun*), who live in the otherwise uninhabited island of Djan. They are beings of an amorous disposition, and though their real shape is that of a fish's body with a human head, they can take on the form of men in order to seduce women. They also cause epidemics and earthquakes; yet the people shew them no respect, for they believe them to be dull-witted as well as lecherous. At most, if a fearful epidemic is raging, they will offer the gods a lean little pig or a mangy cur; and should an earthquake last longer than usual they will rap on the ground, saying, "Hullo, you down there! easy a little! We men are still here." They also profess acquaintance with a god named Anuto, who created the heaven and the earth together with the first man and woman. He is a good being; nobody need be afraid of him. At festivals and meat markets the Tami offer him the first portion in a little basket, which a lad

carries away into the wood and leaves there. As usual,
the deity consumes only the soul of the offering ; the bearer
eats the material substance.[1] The Tami further believe
in certain spirits called Tago which are very old, having
been created at the same time as the village. Every
family or clan possesses its own familiar spirits of this
class. They are represented by men who disguise their
bodies in dense masses of sago leaves and their faces in
grotesque masks with long hooked noses. In this costume
the maskers jig it as well as the heavy unwieldy disguise
allows them to do. But the dance consists in little more
than running round and round in a circle, with an occasional
hop ; the orchestra stands in the middle, singing and
thumping drums. Sometimes two or three of the masked
men will make a round of the village, pelting the men
with pebbles or hard fruits, while the women and children
scurry out of their way. When they are not in use the
masks are hidden away in a hut in the forest, which women
and children may not approach. Their secret is sternly
kept : any betrayal of it is punished with death. The
season for the exhibition of these masked dances recurs
only once in ten or twelve years, but it extends over a
year or thereabout. During the whole of the dancing-
season, curiously enough, coco-nuts are strictly tabooed ;
no person may eat them, so that the unused nuts
accumulate in thousands. As coco-nuts ordinarily form
a daily article of diet with the Tami, their prohibition
for a year is felt by the people as a privation. The
meaning of the prohibition and also of the masquerades
remains obscure.[2]

But while the Tami believe in gods and spirits of
various sorts, the superhuman beings with whom they chiefly
concern themselves are the souls of the dead. On this
subject Mr. Bamler writes : " All the spirits whom we have
thus far described are of little importance in the life and
thought of the Tami ; they are remembered only on
special occasions. The spirits who fill the thoughts and
attract the attention of the Tami are the *kani*, that is,

The Tago spirits, represented by masked men.

The superhuman beings with whom the Tami are chiefly concerned are the souls of the dead.

[1] G. Bamler, "Tami," in R. Neu-hauss's *Deutsch Neu-Guinea*, iii. (Berlin, 1911) pp. 489-492.
[2] G. Bamler, *op. cit.* pp. 507-512.

the souls of the departed. The Tami therefore practise the worship of ancestors. Yet the memory of ancestors does not reach far back; people occupy themselves only with the souls of those relatives whom they have personally known. Hence the worship seldom extends beyond the grandfather, even when a knowledge of more remote progenitors survives. An offering to the ancestors takes the form of a little dish of boiled taro, a cigar, betel-nuts, and the like; but the spirits partake only of the image or soul of the things offered, while the material substance falls to the share of mankind. There is no fixed rule as to the manner or time of the offering. It is left to the caprice or childlike affection of the individual to decide how he will make it. With most natives it is a simple matter of business, the throwing of a sprat to catch a salmon; the man brings his offering only when he needs the help of the spirits. There is very little ceremony about it. The offerer will say, for example, 'There, I lay a cigar for you; smoke it and hereafter drive fish towards me'; or, 'Accompany me on the journey, and see to it that I do good business.' The place where the food is presented is the shelf for pots and dishes under the roof. Thus they imagine that the spirits exert a tolerably far-reaching influence over all created things, and it is their notion that the spirits take possession of the objects. In like manner the spirits can injure a man by thwarting his plans, for example, by frightening away the fish, blighting the fruits of the fields, and so forth. If the native is forced to conclude that the spirits are against him, he has no hesitation about deceiving them in the grossest manner. Should the requisite sacrifices be inconvenient to him, he flatly refuses them, or gives the shabbiest things he can find. In all this the native displays the same craft and cunning which he is apt to practise in his dealings with the whites. He fears the power which the spirit has over him, yet he tries whether he cannot outwit the spirit like an arrant block-head." [1]

Offerings to the dead.

Crude motives for sacrifice.

This account of the crude but quite intelligible motives which lead these savages to sacrifice to the spirits of their

---

[1] G. Bamler, *op. cit.* pp. 513 *sq.*

dead may be commended to the attention of writers on the history of religion who read into primitive sacrifice certain subtle and complex ideas which it never entered into the mind of primitive man to conceive and which, even if they were explained to him, he would in all probability be totally unable to understand.

According to the Tami, the souls of the dead live in the nether world. The spirit-land is called Lamboam ; the entrance to it is by a cleft in a rock. The natives of the mainland also call Hades by the name of Lamboam ; but whereas according to them every village has its own little Lamboam, the Tami hold that there is only one big Lamboam for everybody, though it is subdivided into many mansions, of which every village has one to itself. In Lamboam everything is fairer and more perfect than on earth. The fruits are so plentiful that the blessed spirits can, if they choose, give themselves up to the delights of idleness ; the villages are full of ornamental plants. Yet on the other hand we are informed that life beneath the ground is very like life above it : people work and marry, they squabble and wrangle, they fall sick and even die, just as people do on earth. Souls which die the second death in Lamboam are changed into vermin, such as ants and worms ; however, others say that they turn into wood-spirits, who do men a mischief in the fields. It is not so easy as is commonly supposed to effect an entrance into the spirit-land. You must pass a river, and even when you have crossed it you will be very likely to suffer from the practical jokes which the merry old ghosts play on a raw newcomer. A very favourite trick of theirs is to send him up a pandanus tree to look for fruit. If he is simple enough to comply, they catch him by the legs as he is swarming up the trunk and drag him down, so that his whole body is fearfully scratched, if not quite ripped up, by the rough bark. That is why people put valuable things with the dead in the grave, in order that their ghosts on arrival in Lamboam may have the wherewithal to purchase the good graces of the facetious old stagers.[1]

However, even when the ghosts have succeeded in effecting a lodgment in Lamboam, they are not strictly confined

Lamboam, the land of the dead.

[1] G. Bamler, *op. cit.* pp. 514 *sq.*

Return of
the ghosts
to earth,
sometimes
in the form
of serpents. to it.   They can break bounds at any moment and return
to the upper air.   This they do particularly when any of
their surviving relations is at the point of death.   Ghosts of
deceased kinsfolk and of others gather round the parting soul
and attend it to the far country.   Yet sometimes, apparently,
the soul sets out alone, for the anxious relatives will call out
to it, " Miss not the way."   But ghosts visit their surviving
friends at other times than at the moment of death.   For
example, some families possess the power of calling up spirits
in the form of serpents from the vasty deep.   The spirits
whom they evoke are usually those of persons who have died
quite lately ; for such ghosts cannot return to earth except
in the guise of serpents.   In this novel shape they naturally
feel shy and hide under a mat.   They come out only in the
dusk of the evening or the darkness of night and sit on the
shelf for pots and dishes under the roof.   They have lost
the faculty of speech and can express themselves only in
whistles.   These whistles the seer, who is generally a woman,
understands perfectly and interprets to his or her less gifted
fellows.   In this way a considerable body of information,
more or less accurate in detail, is collected as to life in the
other world.   More than that, it is even possible for men,
and especially for women, to go down alive into the nether
world and prosecute their enquiries at first hand among the
ghosts.   Women who possess this remarkable faculty trans-
mit it to their daughters, so that the profession is hereditary.
When anybody wishes to ascertain how it fares with one of
his dead kinsfolk in Lamboam, he has nothing to do but to
engage the services of one of these professional mediums,
giving her something which belonged to his departed friend.
The medium rubs her forehead with ginger, muttering an
incantation, lies down on the dead man's property, and falls
asleep.   Her soul then goes down in a dream to deadland
and elicits from the ghosts the required information, which
on waking from sleep she imparts to the anxious enquirer.[1]

Sickness
caused by
a spirit.   Sickness accompanied by fainting fits is ascribed to the
action of a spirit, it may be the ghost of a near relation, who
has carried off the " long soul " of the sufferer.   The truant
soul is recalled by a blast blown on a triton-shell, in which

---

[1] G. Bamler, *op. cit.* pp. 515 *sq.*

some chewed ginger or *massoi* bark has been inserted.   The booming sound attracts the attention of the vagrant spirit, while the smell of the bark or of the ginger drives away the ghost.[1]

The name which the Tami give to the spirits of the dead is *kani*; but like other tribes in this part of New Guinea they apply the same term to the bull-roarer and also to the mythical monster who is supposed to swallow the lads at circumcision.   The identity of the name for the three things seems to prove that in the mind of the Tami the initiatory rites, of which circumcision is the principal feature, are closely associated with their conception of the state of the human soul after death, though what the precise nature of the association may be still remains obscure.   Like their neighbours on the mainland of New Guinea, the Tami give out that the novices at initiation are swallowed by a monster or dragon, who only consents to disgorge his prey in consideration of a tribute of pigs, the rate of the tribute being one novice one pig.   In the act of disgorging the lad the dragon bites him, and the bite is visible to all in the cut called circumcision.   The voice of the monster is heard in the hum of the bull-roarers, which are swung at the ceremony in such numbers and with such force that in still weather the booming sound may be heard across the sea for many miles.   To impress women and children with an idea of the superhuman strength of the dragon deep grooves are cut in the trunks of trees and afterwards exhibited to the uninitiated as the marks made by the monster in tugging at the ropes which bound him to the trees.   However, the whole thing is an open secret to the married women, though they keep their knowledge to themselves, fearing to incur the penalty of death which is denounced upon all who betray the mystery.

Tami lads supposed to be swallowed by a monster at circumcision; the monster and the bull-roarer are both called kani.

The initiatory rites are now celebrated only at intervals of many years.   When the time is come for the ceremony, women are banished from the village and special quarters prepared for them elsewhere ; for they are strictly forbidden to set foot in the village while the monster or spirit who swallows the lads has his abode in it.   A special hut is then built for the accommodation of the novices during the many

The rite of circumcision.

[1] G. Bamler, *op. cit.* p. 516.

months which they spend in seclusion before and after the
operation of circumcision.   The hut represents the monster ;
it consists of a framework of thin poles covered with palm-
leaf mats and tapering down at one end.   Looked at from a
distance it resembles a whale.   The backbone is composed
of a betel-nut palm, which has been grubbed up with its
roots.   The root with its fibres represents the monster's head
and hair, and under it are painted a pair of eyes and a great
mouth in red, white, and black.   The passage of the novices
into the monster's belly is represented by causing them to
defile past a row of men who hold bull-roarers aloft over the
heads of the candidates.   Before this march past takes place,
each of the candidates is struck by the chief with a bull-
roarer on his chin and brow.   The operation of circumcising
the lads is afterwards performed behind a screen set up near
the monster-shaped house.   It is followed by a great feast
on swine's flesh.   After their wounds are healed the circumcised lads have still to remain in seclusion for three or four
months.   Finally, they are brought back to the village with
great pomp.   For this solemn ceremony their faces, necks,
and breasts are whitened with a thick layer of chalk, while
red stripes, painted round their mouths and eyes and prolonged to the ears, add to the grotesqueness of their appearance.   Their eyes are closed with a plaster of chalk, and
thus curiously arrayed and blindfolded they are led back to
the village square, where leave is formally given them to
open their eyes.   At the entrance to the village they are
received by the women, who weep for joy and strew boiled
field-fruits on the way.   Next morning the newly initiated lads
wash off the crust of chalk, and have their hair, faces, necks,
and breasts painted bright red.   This ends their time of
seclusion, which has lasted five or six months ; they now
rank as full-grown men.[1]

Seclusion and return of the newly circum- cised lads.

Simulation of death and re- surrection.
    In these initiatory rites, as in the similar rites of the
neighbouring tribes on the mainland of New Guinea, we may
perhaps detect a simulation of death and of resurrection to a
new and higher life.   But why circumcision should form
the central feature of such a drama is a question to which
as yet no certain or even very probable answer can be given.

[1] G. Bamler, *op. cit.* pp. 493-507.

IN GERMAN AND DUTCH NEW GUINEA 303

The bodily mutilations of various sorts, which in many savage tribes mark the transition from boyhood to manhood, remain one of the obscurest features in the life of uncultured races. That they are in most cases connected with the great change which takes place in the sexes at puberty seems fairly certain ; but we are far from understanding the ideas which primitive man has formed on this mysterious subject.

That ends what I have to say as to the notions of death and a life hereafter which are entertained by the natives of German New Guinea. We now turn to the natives of Dutch New Guinea, who occupy roughly speaking the western half of the great island. Our information as to their customs and beliefs on this subject is much scantier, and accordingly my account of them will be much briefer. The natives of Dutch New Guinea.

Towards the western end of the Dutch possession there is on the northern coast a deep and wide indentation known as Geelvink Bay, which in its north-west corner includes a very much smaller indentation known as Doreh Bay. Scattered about in the waters of the great Geelvink Bay are many islands of various sizes, such as Biak or Wiak, Jappen or Jobi, Run or Ron, Noomfor, and many more. It is in regard to the natives who inhabit the coasts or islands of Geelvink Bay that our information is perhaps least imperfect, and it is accordingly with them that I shall begin. In physical appearance, expression of the face, mode of wearing the hair, and still more in manners and customs these natives of the coast and islands differ from the natives of the mountains in the interior. The name given to them by Dutch and German writers is Noofoor or Noomfor. Their original home is believed to be the island of Biak or Wiak, which lies at the northern entrance of the bay, and from which they are supposed to have spread southwards and south-westwards to the other islands and to the mainland of New Guinea.[1] They are a handsomely built race. Their colour is usually dark brown, but in some individuals it Geelvink Bay and Doreh Bay. The Noofoor or Noomfor people.

[1] J. L. van Hasselt, " Die Papua-stämme an der Geelvinkbai (Neu-guinea)," *Mitteilungen der geographischen Gesellschaft zu Jena*, ix. (1890) p. 1 ; F. S. A. de Clercq, " De West en Noordkust van Nederlandsch Nieuw-Guinea," *Tijdschrift van het Kon. Nederlandsch Aardrijkskundig Genootschap*, Tweede Serie, x. (1893) pp. 587 *sq.*

shades off to light-brown, while in others it deepens into black-brown. The forehead is high and narrow ; the eye is dark brown or black with a lively expression ; the nose broad and flat, the lips thick and projecting. The cheek-bones are not very high. The facial angle agrees with that of Europeans. The hair is abundant and frizzly. The people live in settled villages and subsist by agriculture, hunting, and fishing. Their large communal houses are raised above the ground on piles ; on the coast they are built over the water. Each house has a long gallery, one in front and one behind, and a long passage running down the middle of the dwelling, with the rooms arranged on either side of it. Each room has its own fireplace and is occupied by a single family. One such communal house may contain from ten to twenty families with a hundred or more men, women, and children, besides dogs, fowls, parrots, and other creatures. When the house is built over the water, it is commonly connected with the shore by a bridge ; but in some places no such bridge exists, and at high water the inmates can only communicate with the shore by means of their canoes. The staple food of the people is sago, which they extract from the sago-palm ; but they also make use of bread-fruit, together with millet, rice, and maize, whenever they can obtain these cereals. Their flesh diet includes wild pigs, birds, fish, and trepang. While some of them subsist mainly by fishing and commerce, others devote themselves almost exclusively to the cultivation of their gardens, which they lay out in clearings of the dense tropical forest, employing chiefly axes and chopping-knives as their instruments of tillage. Of ploughs they, like most savages, seem to know nothing. The rice and other plants which they raise in these gardens are produced by the dry method of cultivation. In hunting birds they employ chiefly bows and arrows, but sometimes also snares. The arrows with which they shoot the birds of paradise are blunted so as not to injure the splendid plumage of the birds. Turtle-shells, feathers of the birds of paradise, and trepang are among the principal articles which they barter with traders for cotton-goods, knives, swords, axes, beads and so forth. They display some skill and taste in wood-carving. The art of working in iron has been introduced among them from abroad and is now extensively practised by the men. They make large dug-out canoes with outriggers, which seem to be very seaworthy, for they accomplish long voyages even in stormy weather. The making of pottery, basket-work, and weaving, together with pounding rice and cooking food, are the special business of women. The men wear waistbands or loin-cloths made of bark, which is beaten till it becomes as supple as leather. The women wear petticoats or strips of blue cotton round their loins, and as ornaments they have rings of silver, copper, or shell on their arms and legs.[1] Thus the people have attained to a fair degree of barbaric culture.

Now it is significant that among these comparatively advanced savages the fear of ghosts and the reverence entertained for them have developed into something which might almost be called a systematic worship of the dead. As to their fear of ghosts I will quote the evidence of a Dutch missionary, Mr. J. L. van Hasselt, who lived for many years among them and is the author of a grammar and dictionary of their language. He says: "That a great fear of ghosts prevails among the Papuans is intelligible. Even by day they are reluctant to pass a grave, but nothing would induce them to do so by night. For the dead are then roaming about in their search for gambier and tobacco, and they may also sail out to sea in a canoe. Some of the departed, above all the so-called *Mambrie* or heroes, inspire them with especial fear. In such cases for some days after the burial you may hear about sunset a simultaneous and horrible din in all the houses of all the villages, a yelling, screaming, beating and throwing of sticks ; happily the uproar does not last long : its intention is to compel the ghost to take himself off : they have given him all that befits him, namely, a grave, a funeral banquet, and funeral ornaments ; and now they beseech him not to thrust himself on their observation any more, not to breathe any sickness upon the survivors, and not to kill them or 'fetch' them, as the Papuans put it. Their ideas of the spirit-world are very vague. Their usual answer to such questions is,

[marginal notes:] Fear of ghosts.

Ideas of the spirit-world.

---

[1] J. L. van Hasselt, *op. cit.* pp. 2, 3, 5 *sq.* ; A. Goudswaard, *De Papoewa's*   *van de Geelvinksbaai* (Schiedam, 1863), pp. 28 *sqq.*, 33 *sqq.*, 42 *sq.*, 47 *sqq.*

'We know not.' If you press them, they will commonly say that the spirit realm is under the earth or under the bottom of the sea. Everything there is as it is in the upper world, only the vegetation down below is more luxuriant, and all plants grow faster. Their fear of death and their helpless wailing over the dead indicate that the misty kingdom of the shades offers but little that is consolatory to the Papuan at his departure from this world."[1]

Fear of ghosts in general and of the ghosts of the slain in particular. Again, speaking of the natives of Doreh, a Dutch official observes that "superstition and magic play a principal part in the life of the Papuan. Occasions for such absurdities he discovers at every step. Thus he cherishes a great fear of the ghosts of slain persons, for which reason their bodies remain unburied on the spot where they were murdered. When a murder has taken place in the village, the inhabitants assemble for several evenings in succession and raise a fearful outcry in order to chase away the soul, in case it should be minded to return to the village. They set up miniature wooden houses here and there on trees in the forest for the ghosts of persons who die of disease or through accidents, believing that the souls take up their abode in them."[2] The same writer remarks that these savages have no priests, but that they have magicians (*kokinsor*), who practise exorcisms, work magic, and heal the sick, for which they receive a small payment in articles of barter or food.[3] Speaking of the Papuans of Dutch New Guinea in general another writer informs us that "they honour the memory of the dead in every way, because they ascribe to the spirits of the departed a great influence on the life of the survivors. . . . Whereas in life all good and evil comes from the soul, after death, on the other hand, the spirit works for the most part only evil. It loves especially to haunt by night the neighbourhood of its old dwelling and the grave ; so the people particularly avoid the neighbourhood of graves at night, and when darkness has fallen they will not go out except with a burning brand. . . . According to the belief

[1] J. L. van Hasselt, " Die Papua-stämme an der Geelvinkbai (Neu-guinea)," *Mitteilungen der Geographischen Gesellschaft zu Jena*, ix. (1891) p. 101.

[2] H. van Rosenberg, *Der Malayische Archipel* (Leipsic, 1878), p. 461.

[3] H. van Rosenberg, *op. cit.* p. 462.

of the Papuans the ghosts cause sickness, bad harvests, war, and in general every misfortune. From fear of such evils and in order to keep them in good humour, the people make provision for the spirits of the departed after death. Also they sacrifice to them before every important undertaking and never fail to ask their advice." [1]

A Dutch writer, who has given us a comparatively full account of the natives of Geelvink Bay, describes as follows their views in regard to the state of the dead : " According to the Papuans the soul, which they imagine to have its seat in the blood, continues to exist at the bottom of the sea, and every one who dies goes thither. They imagine the state of things there to be much the same as that in which they lived on earth. Hence at his burial the dead man is given an equipment suitable to his rank and position in life. He is provided with a bow and arrow, armlets and body-ornaments, pots and pans, everything that may stand him in good stead in the life hereafter. This provision must not be neglected, for it is a prevalent opinion that the dead continue always to maintain relations with the world and with the living, that they possess superhuman power, exercise great influence over the affairs of life on earth, and are able to protect in danger, to stand by in war, to guard against shipwreck at sea, and to grant success in fishing and hunting. For such weighty reasons the Papuans do all in their power to win the favour of their dead. On undertaking a journey they are said never to forget to hang amulets about themselves in the belief that their dead will then surely help them ; hence, too, when they are at sea in rough weather, they call upon the souls of the departed, asking them for better weather or a favourable breeze, in case the wind happens to be contrary." [2]

In order to communicate with these powerful spirits and to obtain their advice and help in time of need, the Papuans of Geelvink Bay make wooden images of their dead, which they keep in their houses and consult from time to time.

Papuan ideas as to the state of the dead.

Wooden images of the dead (korwar).

---

[1] M. Krieger, *Neu-Guinea* (Berlin, N.D., preface dated 1899), pp. 401, 402.

[2] A. Goudswaard, *De Papoewa's van* *de Geelvinksbaai* (Schiedam, 1863), p. 77. Compare O. Finsch, *Neu-Guinea und seine Bewohner* (Bremen, 1865), p. 105.

Every family has at least one such ancestral image, which forms the medium whereby the soul of the deceased communicates with his or her surviving relatives. These images or Penates, as we may call them, are carved of wood, about a foot high, and represent the deceased person in a standing, sitting, or crouching attitude, but commonly with the hands folded in front. The head is disproportionately large, the nose long and projecting, the mouth wide and well furnished with teeth; the eyes are formed of large green or blue beads with black dots to indicate the pupils. Sometimes the male figures carry a shield in the left hand and brandish a sword in the right; while the female figures are represented grasping with both hands a serpent which stands on its coiled tail. Rags of many colours adorn these figures, and the hair of the deceased, whom they represent, is placed between their legs. Such an ancestral image is called a *korwar* or *karwar*. The natives identify these effigies with the deceased persons whom they portray, and accordingly they will speak of one as their father or mother or other relation. Tobacco and food are offered to the images, and the natives greet them reverentially by bowing to the earth before them with the two hands joined and raised to the forehead.

Such images carried on voyages and consulted as oracles.

Such images are kept in the houses and carried in canoes on voyages, in order that they may be at hand to help and advise their kinsfolk and worshippers. They are consulted on many occasions, for example, when the people are going on a journey, or about to fish for turtles or trepang, or when a member of the family is sick, and his relations wish to know whether he will recover. At these consultations the enquirer may either take the image in his hands or crouch before it on the ground, on which he places his offerings of tobacco, cotton, beads, and so forth. The spirit of the dead is thought to be in the image and to pass from it into the enquirer, who thus becomes inspired by the soul of the deceased and acquires his superhuman knowledge. As a sign of his inspiration the medium shivers and shakes. According to some accounts, however, this shivering and shaking of the medium is an evil omen; whereas if he remains tranquil, the omen is good. It is especially in cases of sickness that the images are consulted. The mode of consultation has been described as follows by a Dutch writer : "When any one is sick and wishes to know the means of cure, or when any one desires to avert misfortune or to discover something unknown, then in presence of the whole family one of the members is stupefied by the fumes of incense or by other means of producing a state of trance. The image of the deceased person whose advice is sought is then placed on the lap or shoulder of the medium in order to cause the soul to pass out of the image into his body. At the moment when that happens, he begins to shiver ; and, encouraged by the bystanders, the soul speaks through the mouth of the medium and names the means of cure or of averting the calamity. When he comes to himself, the medium knows nothing of what he has been saying. This they call *kor karwar*, that is, 'invoking the soul' ; and they say *karwar iwos*, 'the soul speaks.'" The writer adds : "It is sometimes reported that the souls go to the underworld, but that is not true. The Papuans think that after death the soul abides by the corpse and is buried with it in the grave ; hence before an image is made, if it is necessary to consult the soul, the enquirer must betake himself to the grave in order to do so. But when the image is made, the soul enters into it and is supposed to remain in it so long as satisfactory answers are obtained from it in consultation. But should the answers prove disappointing, the people think that the soul has deserted the image, on which they throw the image away as useless. Where the soul has gone, nobody knows, and they do not trouble their heads about it, since it has lost its power." [1] The person who acts as medium in consulting the spirit may be either the house-father himself or a magician (*konoor*).[2]

The images consulted in sickness.

---

[1] F. S. A. de Clercq, "De West- en Noordkust van Nederlandsch Nieuw-Guinea," *Tijdschrift van het Kon. Nederlandsch Aardrijkskundig Genootschap,* Tweede Serie, x. (1893) p. 631. On these *korwar* or *karwar* (images of the dead) see further A. Goudswaard, *De Papoewa's van de Geelvinksbaai,* pp. 72 *sq.,* 77-79; O. Finsch, *Neu-Guinea und seine Bewohner,* pp. 104-106 ; H.

von Rosenberg, *Der Malayische Archipel,* pp. 460 *sq.* ; J. L. van Hasselt, "Die Papuastämme an der Geelvinkbaai (Neu-Guinea)" *Mitteilungen der Geographischen Gesellschaft zu Jena,* ix. (1891) p. 100 ; M. Krieger, *Neu-Guinea,* pp. 400 *sq.,* 402 *sq.,* 498 *sqq.* In the text I have drawn on these various accounts.

[2] J. L. van Hasselt, *l.c.*

Example
of the con-
sultation
of an
ancestral
image.

As an example of these consultations we may take
the case of a man who was suffering from a painful sore on
his finger and wished to ascertain the cause of the trouble.
So he set one of the ancestral images before him and
questioned it closely. At first the image made no reply ;
but at last the man remembered that he had neglected his
duty to his dead brother by failing to marry his widow, as,
according to native custom, he should have done. Now the
natives believe that the dead can punish them for any
breach of customary law ; so it occurred to our enquirer that
the ghost of his dead brother might have afflicted him with
the sore on his finger for not marrying his widow. Accordingly
he put the question to the image, and in doing so the com-
punction of a guilty conscience caused him to tremble. This
trembling he took for an answer of the image in the affirmative, wherefore he went off and took the widow to wife and
provided for her maintenance.[1]

Ancestral
images
consulted
as to the
cause of
death.

Again, the ancestral images are often consulted to ascertain
the cause of a death ; and if the image attributes the death to
the evil magic of a member of another tribe, an expedition
will be sent to avenge the wrong by slaying the supposed
culprit. For the souls of the dead take it very ill and wreak
their spite on the survivors, if their death is not avenged on
their enemies. Not uncommonly the consultation of the
images merely furnishes a pretext for satisfying a grudge
against an individual or a tribe.[2] The mere presence of
these images appears to be supposed to benefit the sick ; a
woman who was seriously ill has been seen to lie with four
or five ancestral figures fastened at the head of her bed. On
enquiry she explained that they did not all belong to her,
but that some of them had been kindly lent to her by
relations and friends.[3] Again, the images are taken by the
natives with them to war, because they hope thereby to
secure the help of the spirits whom the images represent.

Offerings
to the
images.

Also they make offerings from time to time to the effigies
and hold feasts in their honour.[4] They observe, indeed,

[1] A. Goudswaard, *De Papoewa's
van de Geelvinksbaai*, pp. 78 *sq.* ;
O. Finsch, *Neu-Guinea und seine
Bewohner*, pp. 105 *sq.*

[2] A. Goudswaard, *op. cit.* p. 79 ;
O. Finsch, *op. cit.* p. 106.
[3] J. L. van Hasselt, *op. cit.* p. 100.
[4] A. Goudswaard, *op. cit.* p. 78.

that the food which they present to these household idols remains unconsumed, but they explain this by saying that the spirits are content to snuff up the savour of the viands, and to leave their gross material substance alone.[1]

In general, images are only made of persons who have died at home. But in the island of Ron or Run they are also made of persons who have died away from home or have fallen in battle. In such cases the difficulty is to compel the soul to quit its mortal remains far away and come to animate the image. However, the natives of Ron have found means to overcome this difficulty. They first carve the wooden image of the dead person and then call his soul back to the village by setting a great tree on fire, while the family assemble round it and one of them, holding the image in his hand, acts the part of a medium, shivering and shaking and falling into a trance after the approved fashion of mediums in many lands. After this ceremony the image is supposed to be animated by the soul of the deceased, and it is kept in the house with as much confidence as any other.[2] *(sidenote: Images of persons who have died away from home.)*

Sometimes the head of the image consists of the skull of the deceased, which has been detached from the skeleton and inserted in a hole at the top of the effigy. In such cases the body of the image is of wood and the head of bone. It is especially men who have distinguished themselves by their bravery or have earned a name for themselves in other ways who are thus represented. Apparently the notion is that as a personal relic of the departed the skull is better fitted to retain his soul than a mere head of wood. But in the island of Ron or Run, and perhaps elsewhere, skull-topped images of this sort are made for all first-born children, whether male or female, young or old, at least for all who die from the age of twelve years and upward. These images have a special name, *bemar boo*, which means "head of a corpse." They are kept in the room of the parents who have lost the child.[3] *(sidenote: Sometimes the head of the image is composed of the skull of the deceased.)*

The mode in which such images are prepared is as

[1] F. S. A. de Clercq, *op. cit.* p. 632.
[2] F. S. A. de Clercq, *op. cit.* p. 632.
[3] F. S. A. de Clercq, *op. cit.* p. 632.

follows. The body of the firstborn child, who dies at the
age of twelve years or upwards, is laid in a small canoe,
which is deposited in a hut erected behind the dwelling-
house. Here the mother is obliged to keep watch night
and day beside the corpse and to maintain a blazing fire
till the head drops off the body, which it generally does
about twenty days after the death. Then the trunk is
wrapped in leaves and buried, but the head is brought
into the house and carefully preserved. Above the spot
where it is deposited a small opening is made in the roof,
through which a stick is thrust bearing some rags or flags
to indicate that the remains of a dead body are in the
house. When, after the lapse of three or four months,
the nose and ears of the head have dropped off, and
the eyes have mouldered away, the relations and friends
assemble in the house of mourning. In the middle of the
assembly the father of the child crouches on his hams with
downcast look in an attitude of grief, while one of the
persons present begins to carve a new nose and a new pair
of ears for the skull out of a piece of wood. The kind of
wood varies according as the deceased was a male or a
female. All the time that the artist is at work, the rest of
the company chant a melancholy dirge. When the nose
and ears are finished and have been attached to the skull,
and small round fruits have been inserted in the hollow
sockets of the eyes to represent the missing orbs, a banquet
follows in honour of the deceased, who is now represented
by his decorated skull set up on a block of wood on the
table. Thus he receives his share of the food and of the
cigars, and is raised to the rank of a domestic idol or
korwar. Henceforth the skull is carefully kept in a corner
of the chamber to be consulted as an oracle in time of need.
The bodies of fathers and mothers are treated in the same
way as those of firstborn children. On the other hand the
bodies of children who die under the age of two years are
never buried. The remains are packed in baskets of rushes
covered with lids and tightly corded, and the baskets are
then hung on the branches of tall trees, where no more
notice is taken of them. Four or five such baskets containing the mouldering bodies of infants may sometimes be seen

hanging on a single tree.[1]   The reason for thus disposing
of the remains of young children is said to be as follows.
A thick mist hangs at evening over the top of the dense
tropical forest, and in the mist dwell two spirits called
Narwur and Imgier, one male and the other female, who
kill little children, not out of malice but out of love, because
they wish to have the children with them.   So when a
child dies, the parents fasten its little body to the branches
of a tall tree in the forest, hoping that the spirit pair will
take it and be satisfied, and will spare its small brothers and
sisters.[2]

In some parts of Geelvink Bay, however, the bodies of
the dead are treated differently.   For example, on the
south coast of the island of Jobi or Jappen and elsewhere
the corpses are reduced to mummies by being dried on a
bamboo stage over a slow fire; after which the mummies,
wrapt in cloth, are kept in the house, being either laid along
the wall or hung from the ceiling.   When the number of
these relics begins to incommode the living inmates of the
house, the older mummies are removed and deposited in the
hollow trunks of ancient trees.   In some tribes who thus
mummify their dead the juices of corruption which drip
from the rotting corpse are caught in a vessel and given to
the widow to drink, who is forced to gulp them down under
the threat of decapitation if she were to reject the loathsome
beverage.[3]

The family in which a death has taken place is subject
for a time to certain burdensome restrictions, which are
probably dictated by a fear of the ghost.   Thus all the
time till the effigy of the deceased has been made and a
feast given in his honour, they are obliged to remain in the
house without going out for any purpose, not even to bathe

Mummi-
fication of
the dead.

Restric-
tions ob-
served by
mourners.

[1] A. Goudswaard, *De Papoewa's van de Geelvinksbaai*, pp. 70-73; O. Finsch, *Neu-Guinea und seine Bewohner*, pp. 104 *sq.*; M. Krieger, *Neu-Guinea*, p. 398.

[2] J. L. van Hasselt, in *Mitteilungen der Geographischen Gesellschaft zu Jena*, iv. (1886) pp. 118 *sq.* As to the spirit or spirits who dwell in tree tops and draw away the souls of the living to themselves, see further "Eenige

bijzonderheden betreffende de Papoeas van de Geelvinksbaai van Nieuw-Guinea," *Bijdragen tot de Taal- Land- en Volkenkunde van Neêrlandsch-Indië*, ii. (1854) pp. 375 *sq.*

[3] A. Goudswaard, *De Papoewa's van de Geelvinksbaai*, p. 73; J. L. van Hasselt, in *Mitteilungen der Geographischen Gesellschaft zu Jena*, iv. (1886) p. 118; M. Krieger, *Neu-Guinea*, pp. 398 *sq.*

or to fetch food and drink. Moreover they must abstain from the ordinary articles of diet and confine themselves to half-baked cakes of sago and other unpalatable viands. As these restrictions may last for months they are not only irksome but onerous, especially to people who have no slaves to fetch and carry for them. However, in that case the neighbours come to the rescue and supply the mourners with wood, water, and the other necessaries of life, until custom allows them to go out and help themselves. After the effigy of the dead has been made, the family go in state to a sacred place to purify themselves by bathing. If the journey is made by sea, no other canoe may meet or sail past the canoe of the mourners under pain of being confiscated to them and redeemed at a heavy price. On their return from the holy place, the period of mourning is over, and the family is free to resume their ordinary mode of life and their ordinary victuals.[1] That the seclusion of the mourners in the house for some time after the death springs from a fear of the ghost is not only probable on general grounds but is directly suggested by a custom which is observed at the burial of the body. When it has been laid in the earth along with various articles of daily use, which the ghost is supposed to require for his comfort, the mourners gather round the grave and each of them picks up a leaf, which he folds in the shape of a spoon and holds several times over his head as if he would pour out the contents upon it. As they do so, they all murmur, " *Rur i rama*," that is, " The spirit comes." This exclamation or incantation is supposed to prevent the ghost from troubling them. The gravediggers may not enter their houses till they have bathed and so removed from their persons the contagion of death, in order that the soul of the deceased may have no power over them.[2] Mourners sometimes tattoo themselves in honour of the dead. For a father, the marks are tattooed on the cheeks and under the eyes ; for a grandfather, on the breast ; for a mother, on the shoulders and arms ; for a brother, on the back. On the death of a father or mother,

Tattooing in honour of the dead.

[1] A. Goudswaard, *De Papoewa's van de Geelvinksbaai*, pp. 75 *sq.*

[2] J. L. van Hasselt, in *Mitteilungen* *der Geographischen Gesellschaft zu Jena*, iv. (1886) 117 *sq.* ; M. Krieger, *op. cit.* pp. 397 *sq.*

the eldest son or, if there is none such, the eldest daughter Teeth of the dead worn by relatives.
wears the teeth and hair of the deceased. When the teeth
of old people drop out, they are kept on purpose to be thus
strung on a string and worn by their sons or daughters
after their death. Similarly, a mother wears as a permanent
mark of mourning the teeth of her dead child strung on a
cord round her neck, and as a temporary mark of mourning
a little bag on her throat containing a lock of the child's
hair.[1] The intention of these customs is not mentioned.
Probably they are not purely commemorative but designed
in some way either to influence for good the spirit of the
departed or to obtain its help and protection for the living.

Thus far we have found no evidence among the natives Rebirth of parents in their children.
of New Guinea of a belief that the dead are permanently
reincarnated in their human descendants. However, the
inhabitants of Ayambori, an inland village about an hour
distant to the east of Doreh, are reported to believe that
the soul of a dead man returns in his eldest son, and that
the soul of a dead woman returns in her eldest daughter.[2]
So stated the belief is hardly clear and intelligible ; for if a
man has several sons, he must evidently be alive and not
dead when the eldest of them is born, and similarly with a
woman and her eldest daughter. On the analogy of similar
beliefs elsewhere we may conjecture that these Papuans
imagine every firstborn son to be animated by the soul of
his father, whether his father be alive or dead, and every
firstborn daughter to be animated by the soul of her
mother, whether her mother be alive or dead.

Beliefs and customs concerning the dead like those which Customs concerning the dead observed in the islands off the western end of New Guinea.
we have found among the natives of Geelvink Bay are
reported to prevail in other parts of Dutch New Guinea, but
our information about them is much less full. Thus, off the
western extremity of New Guinea there is a group of small
islands (Waaigeoo, Salawati, Misol, Waigama, and so on),
the inhabitants of which make *karwar* or wooden images of
their dead ancestors. These they keep in separate rooms
of their houses and take with them as talismans to war.
In these inner rooms are also kept miniature wooden houses

---

[1] A. Goudswaard, *op. cit.* pp. 74 *sq.*
[2] *Nieuw Guinea ethnographisch en* *natuurkundig onderzocht en beschreven* (Amsterdam, 1862), p. 162.

in which their ancestors are believed to reside, and in which even Mohammedans (for some of the natives profess Islam) burn incense on Fridays in honour of the souls of the dead. These souls are treated like living beings, for in the morning some finely pounded sago is placed in the shrines ; at noon it is taken away, but may not be eaten by the inmates of the house. Curiously enough, women are forbidden to set food for the dead in the shrines : if they did so, it is believed that they would be childless. Further, in the chief's house there are shrines for the souls of all the persons who have died in the whole village. Such a house might almost be described as a temple of the dead. Among the inhabitants of the Negen Negorijen or " Nine Villages " the abodes of the ancestral spirits are often merely frameworks of houses decorated with coloured rags. These frameworks are called *roem seram.* On festal occasions they are brought forth and the people dance round them to music. The mountain tribes of these islands to the west of New Guinea seldom have any such little houses for the souls of the dead. They think that the spirits of the departed dwell among the branches of trees, to which accordingly the living attach strips of red and white cotton, always to the number of seven or a multiple of seven. Also they place food on the branches or hang it in baskets on the boughs,[1] no doubt in order to feed the hungry ghosts. But among the tribes on the coast, who make miniature houses for the use of their dead, these little shrines form a central feature of the religious life of the people. At festivals, especially on the occasion of a marriage or a death, the shrines are brought out from the side chamber and are set down in the central room of the house, where the people dance round them, singing and making music for days together with no interruption except for meals.[2]

Wooden images of the dead.   According to the Dutch writer, Mr. de Clercq, whose account I am reproducing, this worship of the dead, represented by wooden images (*karwar*) and lodged in miniature

---

[1] F. S. A. de Clercq, " De West- en Noordkust van Nederlandsch Nieuw-Guinea," *Tijdschrift van het Kon. Nederlandsch Aardrijkskundig Genoot-* *schap,* Tweede Serie, x. (1893) pp. 198 *sq.*

[2] F. S. A. de Clercq, *op. cit.* p. 201.

houses, is, together with a belief in good and bad spirits, the only thing deserving the name of religion that can be detected among these people. It is certain that the wooden images represent members of the family who died a natural death at home ; they are never, as in Ansoes and Waropen, images of persons who have been murdered or slain in battle. Hence they form a kind of Penates, who are supposed to lead an invisible life in the family circle. The natives of the Negen Negorijen, for example, believe that these wooden images (*karwar*), which are both male and female, contain the souls of their ancestors, who protect the house and household and are honoured at festivals by having portions of food set beside their images.[1] The Seget Sélé, who occupy the extreme westerly point of New Guinea, bury their dead in the island of Lago and set up little houses in the forest for the use of the spirits of their ancestors. But these little houses may never be entered or even approached by members of the family.[2] A traveller, who visited a hut occupied by members of the Seget tribe in Princess Island, or Kararaboe, found a sick man in it and observed that before the front and back door were set up double rows of roughly hewn images painted with red and black stripes. He was told that these images were intended to keep off the sickness ; for the natives thought that it would not dare to run the gauntlet between the double rows of figures into the house.[3] We may conjecture that these rude images represented ancestral spirits who were doing sentinel duty over the sick man.

Among the natives of the Macluer Gulf, which penetrates deep into the western part of Dutch New Guinea, the souls of dead men who have distinguished themselves by bravery or in other ways are honoured in the shape of wooden images, which are sometimes wrapt in cloth and decorated with shells about the neck. In Sekar, a village on the south side of the gulf, small bowls, called *kararasa* after the spirits of ancestors who are believed to lodge in them, are hung up in the houses;

Customs concerning the dead among the natives of the Macluer Gulf.

---

[1] F. S. A. de Clercq, *op. cit.* pp. 202, 205.

[2] F. S. A. de Clercq, *op. cit.* p. 211.

[3] J. W. van Hille, "Reizen in West-Nieuw - Guinea," *Tijdschrift van het Kon. Nederlandsch Aardrijkskundig Genootschap*, Tweede Serie, xxiii. (1906) p. 463.

on special occasions food is placed in them. In some of the
islands of the Macluer Gulf the dead are laid in hollows of
the rocks, which are then adorned with drawings of birds,
hands, and so forth. The hands are always painted white
or yellowish on a red ground. The other figures are drawn
with chalk on the weathered surface of the rock. But the
natives either cannot or will not give any explanation of the
custom.[1]

Burial and
mourning
customs in
the Mimika
district.

The Papuans of the Mimika district, on the southern
coast of Dutch New Guinea, sometimes bury their dead in
shallow graves near the huts ; sometimes they place them
in coffins on rough trestles and leave them there till decomposition is complete, when they remove the skull and preserve
it in the house, either burying it in the sand of the floor
or hanging it in a sort of basket from the roof, where it
becomes brown with smoke and polished with frequent handling. The people do not appear to be particularly attached
to these relics of their kinsfolk and they sell them readily
to Europeans. Mourners plaster themselves all over with
mud, and sometimes they bathe in the river, probably as a
mode of ceremonial purification. They believe in ghosts,
which they call *niniki*; but beyond that elementary fact
we have no information as to their beliefs concerning the
state of the dead.[2]

Burial
customs at
Windessi.

The natives of Windessi in Dutch New Guinea generally
bury their dead the day after the decease. As a rule the
corpse is wrapt in mats and a piece of blue cloth and laid
on a scaffold ; few are coffined. All the possessions of the
dead, including weapons, fishing-nets, wooden bowls, pots,
and so forth, according as the deceased was a man or a woman,

---

[1] F. S. A. de Clercq, *op. cit.* pp. 459
sq., 461 *sq.* A German traveller, Mr.
H. Kühn, spent some time at Sekar
and purchased a couple of what he
calls "old heathen idols," which are
now in the ethnological Museum at
Leipsic. One of them, about a foot
high, represents a human head and
bust ; the other, about two feet high,
represents a squat sitting figure. They
are probably ancestral images (*korwar*
or *karwar*). The natives are said to
have such confidence in the protection

of these "idols" that they leave their
jewellery and other possessions un-
guarded beside them, in the full belief
that nobody would dare to steal anything from spots protected by such
mighty beings. See H. Kühn, "Mein
Aufenthalt in Neu-Guinea," *Festschrift
des 25jährigen Bestehens des Vereins
für Erdkunde zu Dresden* (Dresden,
1888), pp. 143 *sq.*
[2] A. F. R. Wollaston, *Pygmies and
Papuans* (London, 1912), pp. 132 *sq.*,
136-140.

are placed beside him or her.   If the death is attributed to the influence of an evil spirit, they take hold of a lock of hair of the corpse and mention various places.   At the mention of each place, they tug the hair ; and if it comes out, they conclude that the death was caused by somebody at the place which was mentioned at the moment.   But if the hair does not come out, they infer that evil spirits had no hand in the affair.   Before the body is carried away, the family bathes, no doubt to purify themselves from the contagion of death.   Among the people of Windessi it is a common custom to bury the dead in an island.   At such a burial the bystanders pick up a fallen leaf, tear it in two, and stroke the corpse with it, in order that the ghost of the departed may not kill them.   When the body has been disposed of either in a grave or on a scaffold, they embark in the canoe and sit listening for omens.   One of the men in a loud voice bids the birds and the flies to be silent ; and all the others sit as still as death in an attitude of devotion. At last, after an interval of silence, the man who called out tells his fellows what he has heard.   If it was the buzz of the blue flies that he heard, some one else will die.   If it was the booming sound of a triton shell blown in the distance, a raid must be made in that direction to rob and murder.   Why it must be so, is not said, but we may suppose that the note of the triton shell is believed to betray the place of the enemy who has wrought the death by magic, and that accordingly an expedition must be sent to avenge the supposed crime on the supposed murderer.   If the note of a bird called *kohwi* is heard, then the fruit-trees will bear fruit.   Though all the men sit listening in the canoe, the ominous sounds are heard only by the man who called out.[1]

When the omens have thus been taken, the paddles again dip in the water, and the canoe returns to the house of mourning.   Arrived at it, the men disembark, climb up the ladder (for the houses seem to be built on piles over the water) and run the whole length of the long house with their paddles on their shoulders.   Curiously enough, they never do this at any other time, because they imagine that it would

Mourning customs at Windessi.

[1] J. L. D. van der Roest, "Uit the leven der bevolking van Windessi," *Tijdschrift voor Indische Taal- Land- en Volkenkunde*, xl. (1898) pp. 159 *sq.*

cause the death of somebody.   Meantime the women have
gone into the forest to get bark, which they beat into
bark-cloth and make into mourning caps for themselves.
The men busy themselves with plaiting armlets and leglets
of rattan, in which some red rags are stuck.   Large blue and
white beads are strung on a red cord and worn round the
neck.   Further, the hair is shorn in sign of mourning.
Mourners are forbidden to eat anything cooked in a pot.
Sago-porridge, which is a staple food with some of the natives
of New Guinea, is also forbidden to mourners at Windessi.
If they would eat rice, it must be cooked in a bamboo.   The
doors and windows of the house are closed with planks or
mats, just as with us the blinds are lowered in a house after
a death.   The surviving relatives make as many long sago-
cakes as there are houses in the village and send them to the
inmates ; they also prepare a few for themselves.   All who
do not belong to the family now leave the house of mourning.
Then the eldest brother or his representative gets up and all
follow him to the back verandah, where a woman stands
holding a bow and arrows, an axe, a paddle, and so forth.
Every one touches these implements.   Since the death, there
has been no working in the house, but this time of inactivity
is now over and every one is free to resume his usual occupations.   This ends the preliminary ceremonies of mourning,
which go by the name of *djawarra*.

A month afterwards round cakes of sago are baked on
the fire, and all the members of the family, their friends, and
the persons who assisted at the burial receive three such
cakes each.   Only very young children are now allowed to
eat sago-porridge.   This ceremony is called *djawarra baba*.

Festival of
the dead.

When a year or more has elapsed, the so-called festival
of the dead takes place.   Often the festival is held for
several dead at the same time, and in that case the cost is
borne in common.   From far and near the people have
collected sago, coco-nuts, and other food.   For two nights
and a day they dance and sing, but without the accompaniment of drums (? *tifa*) and gongs.   The first night, the
signs of mourning are still worn, hence no sago-porridge
may be eaten ; only friends who are not in mourning are
allowed to partake of it.   The night is spent in eating,

drinking, smoking, singing and dancing. Next day many people make *korwars* of their dead, that is, grotesque wooden images carved in human form, which are regarded as the representatives of the departed. Some people fetch the head of the deceased person, and having made a wooden image with a large head and a hole in the back of it, they insert the skull into the wooden head from behind. After that friends feed the mourners with sago-porridge, putting it into their mouths with the help of the chopsticks which are commonly used in eating sago. When that is done, the period of mourning is at an end, and the signs of mourning are thrown away. A dance on the beach follows, at which the new wooden images of the dead make their appearance. But still the drums and gongs are silent. Dancing and singing go on till the next morning, when the whole of the ceremonies come to an end.[1]

The exact meaning of all these ceremonies is not clear, but we may conjecture that they are based in large measure on the fear of the ghost. That fear comes out plainly in the ceremony of stroking the corpse with leaves in order to prevent the ghost from killing the survivors. The writer to whom we are indebted for an account of these customs tells us in explanation of them that among these people death is ascribed to the influence of evil spirits called *manoam*, who are supposed to be incarnate in some human beings. Hence they often seek to avenge a death by murdering somebody who has the reputation of being an evil spirit incarnate. If they succeed in doing so, they celebrate the preliminary mourning ceremonies called *djawarra* and *djawarra baba*, but the festival of the dead is changed into a memorial festival, at which the people dance and sing to the accompaniment of drums (? *tifa*), gongs, and triton shells ; and instead of carving a wooden image of the deceased, they make marks on the fleshless skull of the murdered man.[2]

The natives of Windessi are said to have the following belief as to the life after death, though we are told that the creed is now known to very few of them ; for their old beliefs and customs are fading away under the influence of a

Wooden images of the dead.

Fear of the ghost.

Beliefs of the natives of Windessi as to the life after death.

[1] J. L. D. van der Roest, *op. cit.* pp. 161 *sq.*

[2] J. L. D. van der Roest, *op. cit.* p. 162.

mission station which is established among them.   According
to their ancient creed, every man and every woman has two
spirits, and in the nether world, called *sarooka*, is a large house
where there is room for all the people of Windessi.   When
a woman dies, both her spirits always go down to the
nether world, where they are clothed with flesh and bones,
need do no work, and live for ever.   But when a man dies,
only one of his spirits must go to the under world ; the
other may pass or transmigrate into a living man or, in rare
Medicine-
men in-
spired by
the spirits
of the dead. cases, into a living woman ; the person so inspired by a
dead man's spirit becomes an *inderri*, that is, a medicine-
man or medicine-woman and has power to heal the sick.
When a person wishes to become a medicine-man or
medicine-woman, he or she acts as follows.   If a man has
died, and his friends are sitting about the corpse lamenting,
the would-be medicine-man suddenly begins to shiver and
to rub his knee with his folded hands, while he utters a
monotonous sound.   Gradually he falls into an ecstasy, and
if his whole body shakes convulsively, the spirit of the dead
man is supposed to have entered into him, and he becomes
a medicine-man.   Next day or the day after he is taken
into the forest ; some hocus-pocus is performed over him,
and the spirits of lunatics, who dwell in certain thick
trees, are invoked to take possession of him.   He is now
himself called a lunatic, and on returning home behaves
as if he were half-crazed.   This completes his training
as a medicine-man, and he is now fully qualified to kill
or cure the sick.   His mode of cure depends on the
native theory of sickness.   These savages think that sickness
is caused by a malicious or angry spirit, apparently the
spirit of a dead person ; for a patient will say, " The *korwar* "
(that is, the wooden image which represents a particular
dead person) " is murdering me, or is making me sick."   So
the medicine-man is called in, and sets to work on the
sufferer, while the *korwar*, or wooden image of the spirit who
is supposed to be doing all the mischief, stands beside him.
The principal method of cure employed by the doctor is
massage.   He chews a certain fruit fine and rubs the
patient with it ; also he pinches him all over the body as if
to drive out the spirit.   Often he professes to extract a

stone, a bone, or a stick from the body of the sufferer.   At last he gives out that he has ascertained the cause of the sickness; the sick man has done or has omitted to do something which has excited the anger of the spirit.[1]

From all this it would seem that the souls of the dead are more feared than loved and reverenced by the Papuans of Windessi.   Naturally the ghosts of enemies who have perished at their hands are particularly dreaded by them. That dread explains some of the ceremonies which are observed in the village at the return of a successful party of head-hunters.   As they draw near the village, they announce their approach and success by blowing on triton shells. Their canoes also are decked with branches.   The faces of the men who have taken a head are blackened with charcoal ; and if several have joined in killing one man, his skull is divided between them.   They always time their arrival so as to reach home in the early morning.   They come paddling to the village with a great noise, and the women stand ready to dance in the verandahs of the houses.   The canoes row past the *roem sram* or clubhouse where the young men live ; and as they pass, the grimy-faced slayers fling as many pointed sticks or bamboos at the house as they have killed enemies.   The rest of the day is spent very quietly.   But now and then they drum or blow on the conch, and at other times they beat on the walls of the houses with sticks, shouting loudly at the same time, to drive away the ghosts of their victims.[2]

That concludes what I have to say as to the fear and worship of the dead in Dutch New Guinea.

Ghosts of slain enemies dreaded.

---

[1] J. L. D. van der Roest, *op. cit.* pp. 164-166.

[2] J. L. D. van der Roest, *op. cit.* pp. 157 *sq.*

LECTURE XV

THE BELIEF IN IMMORTALITY AMONG THE NATIVES
OF SOUTHERN MELANESIA (NEW CALEDONIA)

Melanesia and the Melanesians. IN the last lecture I concluded our survey of the beliefs and practices concerning death and the dead which are reported to prevail among the natives of New Guinea. We now pass to the natives of Melanesia, the great archipelago or rather chain of archipelagoes, which stretches round the north-eastern and eastern ends of New Guinea and southward, parallel to the coast of Queensland, till it almost touches the tropic of Capricorn. Thus the islands lie wholly within the tropics and are for the most part characterised by tropical heat and tropical luxuriance of vegetation. Only New Caledonia, the most southerly of the larger islands, differs somewhat from the rest in its comparatively cool climate and scanty flora.[1] The natives of the islands belong to the Melanesian race. They are dark-skinned and woolly-haired and speak a language which is akin to the Polynesian language. In material culture they stand roughly on the same level as the natives of New Guinea, a considerable part of whom in the south-eastern part of the island, as I pointed out before, are either pure Melanesians or at all events exhibit a strong infusion of Melanesian blood. They cultivate the ground, live in settled villages, build substantial houses, construct outrigger - canoes, display some aptitude for art, possess strong commercial instincts, and even employ various mediums of exchange, of which shell-money is the most notable.[2]

[1] F. H. H. Guillemard, *Australasia*, II. *Malaysia and the Pacific Archipelagoes* (London, 1894), p. 458.

[2] J. Deniker, *The Races of Man* (London, 1900), pp. 498 *sq.* As to the mediums of exchange, particularly

We shall begin our survey of these islands with New The New
Caledon-
ians. Caledonia in the south, and from it shall pass northwards through the New Hebrides and Solomon Islands to the Bismarck Archipelago, which consists chiefly of the two great islands of New Britain and New Ireland with the group of the Admiralty Islands terminating it to the westward. For our knowledge of the customs and religion of the New Caledonians we depend chiefly on the evidence of a Catholic missionary, Father Lambert, who has worked among them since 1856 and has published a valuable book on the subject.[1] To be exact, his information applies not to the natives of New Caledonia itself, but to the inhabitants of a group of small islands, which lie immediately off the northern extremity of the island and are known as the Belep group. Father Lambert began to labour among the Belep at a time when no white man had as yet resided among them. At a later time circumstances led him to transfer his ministry to the Isle of Pines, which lies off the opposite or southern end of New Caledonia. A comparative study of the natives at the two extremities of New Caledonia revealed to him an essential similarity in their beliefs and customs ; so that it is not perhaps very rash to assume that similar customs prevail among the aborigines of New Caledonia itself, which lies intermediate between the two points observed by Father Lambert.[2] The assumption is confirmed by evidence which was collected by Dr. George Turner from the mainland of New Caledonia so long ago as 1845.[3] Accordingly in what follows I shall commonly speak of the New Caledonians in general, though the statements for the most part apply in particular to the Belep tribe.

The souls of the New Caledonians, like those of most savages, are supposed to be immortal, at least to survive

---

the shell-money, see R. H. Codrington, *The Melanesians* (Oxford, 1891), pp. 323 *sqq.* ; R. Parkinson, *Dreissig Jähre in der Südsee* (Stuttgart, 1907), pp. 82 *sqq.*

[1] Le Père Lambert, *Mœurs et Superstitions des Néo-Calédoniens* (Nouméa, 1900). This work originally appeared as a series of articles in the Catholic

missionary journal *Les Missions Catholiques.*

[2] Lambert, *Mœurs et Superstitions des Néo-Calédoniens*, pp. ii., iv. *sq.* ; 255.

[3] George Turner, LL.D., *Samoa a Hundred Years Ago and long before* (London, 1884), pp. 340 *sqq.*

Beliefs of
the New
Caledon-
ians as to
the land of
the dead. death for an indefinite period. They all go, good and bad
alike, to dwell in a very rich and beautiful country situated
at the bottom of the sea, to the north-east of the island
of Pott. The name of the land of souls is Tsiabiloum.
But before they reach this happy land they must run the
gauntlet of a grim spirit called Kiemoua, who has his abode
on a rock in the island of Pott. He is a fisherman of
souls; for he catches them as they pass in a net and after
venting his fury on them he releases them, and they pursue
their journey to Tsiabiloum, the land of the dead. It is
a country more fair and fertile than tongue can tell. Yams,
taros, sugar-canes, bananas all grow there in profusion and
without cultivation. There are forests of wild orange-trees,
also, and the golden fruits serve the blessed spirits as
playthings. You can tell roughly how long it is since a
spirit quitted the upper world by the colour of the orange
which he plays with; for the oranges of those who have
just arrived are green; the oranges of those who have been
longer dead are ripe; and the oranges of those who died
long ago are dry and wizened. There is no night in that
blessed land, and no sleep; for the eyes of the spirits are
never weighed down with slumber. Sorrow and sickness,
decrepitude and death never enter; even boredom is
unknown. But it is only the nights, or rather the hours
corresponding to nights on earth, which the spirits pass
in these realms of bliss. At daybreak they revisit their old
home on earth and take up their posts in the cemeteries
where they are honoured; then at nightfall they flit away
back to the spirit-land beneath the sea, there to resume
their sport with oranges, green, golden, or withered, till dawn
of day. On these repeated journeys to and fro they have
nothing to fear from the grim fisherman and his net; it
is only on their first passage to the nether world that he
catches and trounces them.[1]

Burial
customs
of the New
Caledon-
ians.   The bodies of the dead are buried in shallow graves,
which are dug in a sacred grove. The corpse is placed in
a crouching attitude with the head at or above the surface
of the ground, in order to allow of the skull being easily
detached from the trunk at a subsequent time. In token

---

[1] Lambert, *op. cit.* pp. 13-16.

of sorrow the nearest relations of the deceased tear the
lobes of their ears and inflict large burns on their arms and
breasts.   The houses, nets, and other implements of the
dead are burnt; his plantations are ravaged, his coco-nut
palms felled with the axe.   The motive for this destruction
of the property of the deceased is not mentioned, but the
custom points to a fear of the ghost; the people probably
make his old home as unattractive as possible in order to
offer him no temptation to return and haunt them.   The
same fear of the ghost, or at all events of the infection of
death, is revealed by the stringent seclusion and ceremonial
pollution of the grave-diggers.   They are two in number;
no other persons may handle the corpse.   After they have
discharged their office they must remain near the corpse for
four or five days, observing a rigorous fast and keeping
apart from their wives.   They may not shave or cut their
hair, and they are obliged to wear a tall pyramidal and very
cumbersome head-dress.   They may not touch food with
their hands.   If they help themselves to it, they must pick
it up with their mouths alone or with a stick, not with their
fingers.   Oftener they are fed by an attendant, who puts the
victuals into their mouths as he might do if they were
palsied.   On the other hand they are treated by the people
with great respect; common folk will not pass near them
without stooping.[1]

A curious ceremony which the New Caledonians observe
at a certain period of mourning for the dead is a sham fight.
Father Lambert describes one such combat which he witnessed.   A number of men were divided into two parties;
one party was posted on the beach, the other and much
larger party was stationed in the adjoining cemetery, where
food and property had been collected.   From time to time
a long piercing yell would be heard; then a number of men
would break from the crowd in the cemetery and rush
furiously down to the beach with their slings and stones
ready to assail their adversaries.   These, answering yell
with yell, would then plunge into the sea, armed with
battle-axes and clubs, while they made a feint of parrying
the stones hurled at them by the other side.   But neither

Sham fight as a mourning ceremony.

[1] Lambert, *op. cit.* pp. 235-239.

the shots nor the parries appeared to be very seriously meant.   Then when the assailants retired, the fugitives pretended to pursue them, till both parties had regained their original position.   The same scene of alternate attack and retreat was repeated hour after hour, till at last, the pretence of enmity being laid aside, the two parties joined in a dance, their heads crowned with leafy garlands.   Father Lambert, who describes this ceremony as an eye-witness, offers no explanation of it.   But as he tells us that all deaths are believed by these savages to be an effect of sorcery, we may conjecture that the sham fight is intended to delude the ghost into thinking that his death is being avenged on the sorcerer who killed him.[1]   In former lectures I shewed that similar pretences are made, apparently for a similar purpose, by some of the natives of Australia and New Guinea.[2]   If the explanation is correct, we can hardly help applauding the ingenuity which among these savages has discovered a bloodless mode of satisfying the ghost's craving for blood.

Preservation of the skulls of the dead.   About a year after the death, when the flesh of the corpse is entirely decayed, the skull is removed and placed solemnly in another burying-ground, or rather charnel-house, where all the skulls of the family are deposited.   Every family has such a charnel-house, which is commonly situated near the dwelling.   It appears to be simply an open space in the forest, where the skulls are set in a row on the ground.[3]   Yet in a sense it may be called a temple for the worship of ancestors ; for recourse is had to the skulls on various occasions in order to obtain the help of the spirits of the dead.   " The true worship of the New Caledonians," says Father Lambert, " is the worship of ancestors.   Each family has its own ; it religiously preserves their name ; it is proud of them and has confidence in them.   Hence it has its burial-place and its pious hearth for the sacrifices to be offered to their ghosts.   It is the most inviolable piece of property ; an encroachment on such a spot by a neighbour is a thing unheard of." [4]

A few examples may serve to illustrate the ancestor-

<hr/>

[1] Lambert, *op. cit.* pp. 238, 239 *sq.*
[2] Above, pp. 136 *sq.*, 235 *sq.*
[3] Lambert, *op. cit.* pp. 24, 240.
[4] Lambert, *op. cit.* p. 274.

worship of the New Caledonians. When a person is sick, a member of the family, never a stranger, is appointed to heal him by means of certain magical insufflations. To enable him to do so with effect the healer first repairs to the family charnel-house and lays some sugar-cane leaves beside the skulls, saying, "I lay these leaves on you that I may go and breathe upon our sick relative, to the end that he may live." Then he goes to a tree belonging to the family and lays other sugar-cane leaves at its foot, saying, "I lay these leaves beside the tree of my father and of my grandfather, in order that my breath may have healing virtue." Next he takes some leaves of the tree or a piece of its bark, chews it into a mash, and then goes and breathes on the patient, his breath being moistened with spittle which is charged with particles of the leaves or the bark.[1] Thus the healing virtue of his breath would seem to be drawn from the spirits of the dead as represented partly by their skulls and partly by the leaves and bark of the tree which belonged to them in life, and to which their souls appear in some manner to be attached in death.

Again, when a shoal of fish has made its appearance on the reef, a number of superstitious ceremonies have to be performed before the people may go and spear them in the water. On the eve of the fishing-day the medicine-man of the tribe causes a quantity of leaves of certain speci-fied plants to be collected and roasted in the native ovens. Next day the leaves are taken from the ovens and deposited beside the ancestral skulls, which have been arranged and decorated for the ceremony. All the fishermen, armed with their fishing-spears, repair to the holy ground or sacred grove where the skulls are kept, and there they draw them-selves up in two rows, while the medicine-man chants an invocation or prayer for a good catch. At every verse the crowd raises a cry of approval and assent. At its conclusion the medicine-man sets an example by thrusting with his spear at a fish, and all the men immediately plunge into the water and engage in fishing.[2]

Again, in order that a sugar plantation may flourish, the medicine-man will lay a sugar-cane beside the ancestral

---

[1] Lambert, *op. cit.* pp. 24, 26.   [2] Lambert, *op. cit.* p. 211.

skulls, saying, " This is for you.　We beg of you to ward off all curses, all tricks of wicked people, in order that our plantations may prosper." [1]

Prayers for yams. Again, when the store of yams is running short and famine is beginning to be felt, the New Caledonians celebrate a festival called *moulim* in which the worship of their ancestors is the principal feature.　A staff is wreathed with branches, apparently to represent a yam, and a hedge of coco-nut leaves is made near the ancestral skulls.　The decorated staff is then set up there, and prayers for the prosperity of the crops are offered over and over again. After that nobody may enter a yam-field or a cemetery or touch sea-water for three days.　On the third day a man stationed on a mound chants an invocation or incantation in a loud voice.　Next all the men go down to the shore, each of them with a firebrand in his hand, and separating into two parties engage in a sham fight.　Afterwards they bathe and repairing to the charnel-house deposit coco-nut leaves beside the skulls of their ancestors.　They are then free to partake of the feast which has been prepared by the women. [2]

Caverns used by the natives as charnel-houses in the Isle of Pines. While the beliefs and customs of the New Caledonians in regard to the dead bear a general resemblance to each other, whether they belong to the north or to the south of the principal island, a special feature is introduced into the mortuary customs of the natives of the Isle of Pines by the natural caves and grottoes with which the outer rim of the island, to the distance of several miles from the shore, is riddled ; for in these caverns the natives in the old heathen days were wont to deposit the bones and skulls of their dead and to use the caves as sanctuaries or chapels for the worship of the spirits of the departed.　Some of the caves are remarkable both in themselves and in their situation. Most of those which the natives turned into charnel-houses are hidden away, sometimes at great distances, in the rank luxuriance of the tropical forests.　Some of them open straight from the level of the ground ; to reach others you must clamber up the rocks ; to explore others you must descend into the bowels of the earth.　A glimmering

---

[1] Lambert, *op. cit.* p. 218.　　　[2] Lambert, *op. cit.* pp. 224 *sq.*

twilight illumines some; thick darkness veils others, and it
is only by torchlight that you can explore their mysterious
depths.   Penetrating into the interior by the flickering
gleam of flambeaus held aloft by the guides, and picking
your steps among loose stones and pools of water, you
might fancy yourself now in the great hall of a ruined
castle, now in the vast nave of a gothic cathedral with its
chapels opening off it into the darkness on either hand.
The illusion is strengthened by the multitude of stalactites
which hang from the roof of the cavern and, glittering in the
fitful glow of the torches, might be taken for burning cressets
kindled to light up the revels in a baronial hall, or for holy
lamps twinkling in the gloom of a dim cathedral aisle before
holy images, where solitary worshippers kneel in silent
devotion.   In the shifting play of the light and shadow cast
by the torches the fantastic shapes of the incrustations which
line the sides or rise from the floor of the grotto appear to
the imagination of the observer now as the gnarled trunks
of huge trees, now as statues or torsos of statues, now as
altars, on which perhaps a nearer approach reveals a row of
blanched and grinning skulls.   No wonder if such places,
chosen for the last resting-places of the relics of mortality,
have fed the imagination of the natives with weird notions
of a life after death, a life very different from that which the
living lead in the glowing sunshine and amid the rich tropical
verdure a few paces outside of these gloomy caverns.   It is
with a shiver and a sense of relief that the visitor escapes
from them to the warm outer air and sees again the ferns
and creepers hanging over the mouth of the cave like a
green fringe against the intense blue of the sky.[1]

While this is the general character of the caves which Sea-caves.
are to be found hidden away in the forests, many of those
near the shore consist simply of apertures hollowed out in
the face of the cliffs by the slow but continuous action of
the waves in the course of ages.   On the beach itself sea-
caves are found in which the rising tide precipitates itself
with a hollow roar as of subterranean thunder; and at a
point, some way back from the strand, where the roof of
one of these caves has fallen in, the salt water is projected

[1] Lambert, *op. cit.* pp. 275 *sqq.*

into the air in the form of intermittent jets of spray, which
vary in height with the force of the wind and tide.[1]

Prayers
and
sacrifices
offered to
the dead
by the New
Caledon-
ians.

With regard to the use which the natives make of these
caves as charnel - houses and mortuary chapels, Father
Lambert tells us that any one of them usually includes
three compartments, a place of burial, a place of skulls, and
a place of sacrifice. But often the place of skulls is also the
place of sacrifice ; and in no case is the one far from the
other. The family priest, who is commonly the senior
member of the family, may address his prayers to the
ancestors in the depth of the cavern, in the place of skulls,
or in the place of sacrifice, whenever circumstances call for
a ritual of unusual solemnity. Otherwise with the help
of his amulets he may pray to the souls of the forefathers
anywhere ; for these amulets consist of personal and portable
relics of the dead, such as locks of hair, teeth, and so forth ; or
again they may be leaves or other parts of plants which are
sacred to the family ; so that a wizard who is in possession
of them can always and anywhere communicate with the
ancestral spirits. The place of sacrifice would seem to be
more often in the open air than in a cave, for Father
Lambert tells us that in the centre of it a shrub, always of
the same species, is planted and carefully cultivated. Beside
it may be seen the pots and stones which are used in
cooking the food offered to the dead. In this worship of
the dead a certain differentiation of functions or division of
labour obtains between the various families. All have not
the same gifts and graces. The prayers of one family
offered to their ancestral ghosts are thought to be powerful
in procuring rain in time of drought ; the prayers of another
will cause the sun to break through the clouds when the
sky is overcast ; the supplications of a third will produce a
fine crop of yams ; the earnest entreaties of a fourth will
ensure victory in war ; and the passionate pleadings of a
fifth will guard mariners against the perils and dangers of
the deep. And so on through the whole gamut of human
needs, so far as these are felt by savages. If only wrestling
in prayer could satisfy the wants of man, few people should
be better provided with all the necessaries and comforts of

---

[1] Lambert, *op. cit.* p. 276.

life than the New Caledonians. And according to the
special purpose to which a family devotes its spiritual
energies, so will commonly be the position of its oratory.
For example, if rain-making is their strong point, their
house of prayer will be established near a cultivated field,
in order that the crops may immediately experience the
benefit to be derived from their orisons. Again, if they
enjoy a high reputation for procuring a good catch of fish,
the family skulls will be placed in the mouth of a cave
looking out over the great ocean, or perhaps on a bleak
little wind-swept isle, where in the howl of the blast, the
thunder of the waves on the strand, and the clangour of
the gulls overhead, the fancy of the superstitious savage
may hear the voices of his dead forefathers keeping watch
and ward over their children who are tossed on the heaving
billows.[1] Thus among these fortunate islanders religion
and industry go hand in hand ; piety has been reduced to
a co-operative system which diffuses showers of blessings
on the whole community.

As it is clearly impossible even for the most devout Prayer-
to pray day and night without cessation, the weakness of posts.
the flesh requiring certain intervals for refreshment and
repose, the New Caledonians have devised an ingenious
method of continuing their orisons at the shrine in their
own absence. For this purpose they make rods or poles
of various lengths, carve and paint them rudely, wind
bandages of native cloth about them, and having fastened
large shells to the top, set them up either in the sepulchral
caves or in the place of skulls. In setting up one of these
poles the native will pray for the particular favour which
he desires to obtain from the ancestors for himself or his
family ; and he appears to think that in some way the pole
will continue to recite the prayer in the ears of the ghosts,
when he himself has ceased to speak and has returned to
his customary avocations. And when members of his
family visit the shrine and see the pole, they will be reminded
of the particular benefit which they are entitled to expect
from the souls of the departed. A certain rude symbolism
may be traced in the materials and other particulars of

[1] Lambert, *op. cit.* pp. 288 *sq.*

these prayer-posts. A hard wood signifies strength; a tall pole overtopping all the rest imports a wish that he for whose sake it was erected may out-top all his rivals; and so on.[1]

Religion combined with magic in the ritual of the New Caledonians.

We may assume with some probability that in the mind of the natives such resemblances are not purely figurative or symbolic, but that they are also magical in intention, being supposed not merely to represent the object of the supplicant's prayer, but actually, on the principle of homoeopathic or imitative magic, to contribute to its accomplishment. If that is so, we must conclude that the religion of these savages, as manifested in their prayers to the spirits of the dead, is tinctured with an alloy of magic; they do not trust entirely to the compassion of the spirits and their power to help them; they seek to reinforce their prayers by a certain physical compulsion acting through the natural properties of the prayer-posts. This interpretation is confirmed by a parallel use which these people make of

Sacred stones endowed with special magical virtues.

certain sacred stones, which apart from their possible character as representatives of the ancestors, seem to be credited with independent magical virtues by reason of their various shapes and appearances. For example, there is a

The "stone of famine."

piece of polished jade which is called "the stone of famine," because it is supposed capable of causing either dearth or abundance, but is oftener used by the sorcerer to create, or at least to threaten, dearth, in order thereby to extort presents from his alarmed fellow tribesmen. This stone is kept in a burial-ground and derives its potency from the dead. The worshipper or the sorcerer (for he combines the two characters) who desires to cause a famine repairs to the burial-ground, uncovers the stone, rubs it with certain plants, and smears one half of it with black pigment. Then he makes a small hole in the ground and inserts the blackened end of the stone in the hole. Next he prays to the ancestors that nothing may go well with the country. If this malevolent rite should be followed by the desired effect, the sorcerer soon sees messengers arriving laden with presents, who entreat him to stay the famine. If his cupidity is satisfied, he rubs the stone again, inserts it upside down

[1] Lambert, *op. cit.* pp. 290, 292.

in the ground, and prays to his ancestors to restore plenty
to the land.[1]

Again, certain rough unhewn stones, which are kept
in the sacred places, are thought to possess the power of
driving people mad. To effect this purpose the sorcerer
has only to strike one of them with the branches of a
certain tree and to pray to the ancestral spirits that they
would deprive so-and-so of his senses.[2]

Again, there is a stone which they use in cursing a
plantation of coco-nut palms. The stone resembles a
blighted coco-nut, and no doubt it is this resemblance
which is supposed to endow it with the magical power to
blight coco-nut trees. In order to effect his malicious
purpose the sorcerer rubs the stone in the cemetery with
certain leaves and then deposits it in a hole at the foot
of a coco-nut tree, covers it up, and prays that all the
trees of the plantation may be barren. This ceremony
combines the elements of magic and religion. The prayer,
which is no doubt addressed to the spirits of the dead,
though this is not expressly affirmed, is purely religious;
but the employment of a stone resembling a blighted coco-
nut for the purpose of blighting the coco-nut palms is a
simple piece of homoeopathic or imitative magic, in which,
as usual, the desired effect is supposed to be produced by
an imitation of it. Similarly, in order to make a bread-
fruit tree bear fruit they employ two stones, one of which
resembles the unripe and the other the ripe fruit. These
are kept, as usual, in a cemetery; and when the trees begin
to put forth fruit, the small stone resembling the unripe fruit
is buried at the foot of one of the trees with the customary
prayers and ceremonies; and when the fruits are more
mature the small stone is replaced by the larger stone
which resembles the ripe fruit. Then, when the fruits on
the tree are quite ripe, the two stones are removed and
deposited again in the cemetery: they have done their work
by bringing to maturity the fruits which they resemble.
This again is a piece of pure homoeopathic or imitative
magic working by means of mimicry; but the magical
virtue of the stones is reinforced by the spiritual power

Stones to
drive
people
mad.

Stones to
blight
coco-nut
palms.

Stones
to make
bread-fruit
trees bear
fruit.

---

[1] Lambert, *op. cit.* pp. 292 *sq.*   [2] Lambert, *op. cit.* pp. 293 *sq.*

of the dead, for the stones have been kept in a cemetery and prayers have been addressed to the souls of the departed.[1]

The "stone of the sun."

Again, the natives have two disc-shaped stones, each with a hole in the centre, which together make up what they call "the stone of the sun." No doubt it is regarded as a symbol of the sun, and as such it is employed to cause drought in a ceremony which, like the preceding, combines the elements of magic and religion. The sun-stone is kept in one of the sacred places, and when a sorcerer wishes to make drought with it, he brings offerings to the ancestral spirits in the sacred place. These offerings are purely religious, but the rest of the ceremony is purely magical. At the moment when the sun rises from the sea, the magician or priest, whichever we choose to call him (for he combines both characters), passes a burning brand in and out of the hole in the sun-stone, while he says, " I kindle the sun, in order that he may eat up the clouds and dry up our land, so that it shall no longer bear fruit." Here the putting of fire to the sun-stone is a piece of pure homoeopathic or imitative magic, designed to increase the burning heat of the sun by mimicry.[2]

Stones to make rain.

On the contrary, when a wizard desires to make rain, he proceeds as follows. The place of sacrifice is decorated and enclosed with a fence, and a large quantity of provisions is deposited in it to be offered to the ancestors whose skulls stand there in a row. Opposite the skulls the wizard places a row of pots full of a medicated water, and he brings a number of sacred stones of a rounded form or shaped like a skull. Each of these stones, after being rubbed with the leaves of a certain tree, is placed in one of the pots of water. Then the wizard recites a long litany or series of invocations to the ancestors, which may be summarised thus : " We pray you to help us, in order that our country may revive and live anew." Then holding a branch in his hand he climbs a tree and scans the horizon if haply he may descry a cloud, be it no larger than a man's hand. Should he be fortunate enough to see one, he waves the branch to and fro to make the cloud mount up in the sky, while he also stretches out his arms to right and left to enlarge it so

[1] Lambert, *op. cit.* p. 294.   [2] Lambert, *op. cit.* pp. 296 *sq.*

that it may hide the sun and overcast the whole heaven.[1]
Here again the prayers and offerings are purely religious ;
while the placing of the skull-shaped stones in pots full
of water, and the waving of the branch to bring up the
clouds, are magical ceremonies designed to produce rain by
mimicry and compulsion.

Again, the natives have a stone in the shape of a canoe, Stones to
which they employ in ceremonies for the purpose of favour- make or
ing or hindering navigation. If the sorcerer desires to make voyages.
a voyage prosperous, he places the canoe-shaped stone before
the ancestral skulls with the right side up ; but if he wishes
to cause his enemy to perish at sea, he places the canoe-
shaped stone bottom upwards before the skulls, which, on
the principles of homoeopathic or imitative magic, must
clearly make his enemy's canoe to capsize and precipitate
its owner into the sea. Whichever of these ceremonies he
performs, the wizard accompanies the magical rite, as usual,
with prayers and offerings of food to the ancestral spirits
who are represented by the skulls.[2]

The natives of the Isle of Pines subsist mainly by Stones
fishing ; hence they naturally have a large number of to help
fishermen.
sacred stones which they use for the purpose of securing
the blessing of the ancestral spirits on the business of the
fisherman.   Indeed each species of fish has its own special
sacred stone.   These stones are kept in large shells in a
cemetery. A wizard who desires to make use of one of
them paints the stone with a variety of colours, chews
certain leaves, and then breathes on the stone and moistens
it with his spittle. After that he sets up the stone before
the ancestral skulls, saying, "Help us, that we may be
successful in fishing." The sacrifices to the spirits consist
of bananas, sugar-cane, and fish, never of taros or yams.
After the fishing and the sacrificial meal, the stone is put
back in its place, and covered up respectfully.[3]

Lastly, the natives of the Isle of Pines cultivate many Stones to
different kinds of yams, and they have a correspondingly make yams
grow.
large number of sacred stones destined to aid them in the
cultivation by ensuring the blessing of the dead upon the

---

[1] Lambert, *op. cit.* pp. 297 *sq.*   [2] Lambert, *op. cit.* p. 298.
[3] Lambert, *op. cit.* p. 300.

work. In shape and colour these stones differ from each other, each of them bearing a resemblance, real or fanciful, to the particular species of yam which it is supposed to quicken. But the method of operating with them is much the same for all. The stone is placed before the skulls, wetted with water, and wiped with certain leaves. Yams and fish, cooked on the spot, are offered in sacrifice to the dead, the priest or magician saying, "This is your offering in order that the crop of yams may be good." So saying he presents the food to the dead and himself eats a little of it. After that the stone is taken away and buried in the yam field which it is designed to fertilise.[1] Here, again, the prayer and sacrifice to the dead are purely religious rites intended to propitiate the spirits and secure their help; while the burying of the yam-shaped stone in the yam-field to make the yams grow is a simple piece of homoeopathic or imitative magic. Similarly in order to cultivate taros and bananas, stones resembling taros and bananas are buried in the taro field or the banana grove, and their magical virtue is reinforced by prayers and offerings to the dead.[2]

The religion of the New Caledonians is mainly a worship of the dead tinctured with magic. On the whole we may conclude that among the natives of New Caledonia there exists a real worship of the dead, and that this worship is indeed the principal element in their religion. The spirits of the dead, though they are supposed to spend part of their time in a happy land far away under the sea, are nevertheless believed to be near at hand, hovering about in the burial-grounds or charnel-houses and embodied apparently in their skulls. To these spirits the native turns for help in all the important seasons and emergencies of life; he appeals to them in prayer and seeks to propitiate them by sacrifice. Thus in his attitude towards his dead ancestors we perceive the elements of a real religion. But, as I have just pointed out, many rites of this worship of ancestors are accompanied by magical ceremonies. The religion of these islanders is in fact deeply tinged with magic; it marks a transition from an age of pure magic in the past to an age of more or less pure religion in the future.

[1] Lambert, *op. cit.* pp. 301 *sq.*		[2] Lambert, *op. cit.* pp. 217 *sq.*, 300.

Thus far I have based my account of the beliefs and customs of the New Caledonians concerning the dead on the valuable information which we owe to the Catholic missionary Father Lambert. But, as I pointed out, his evidence refers not so much to the natives of the mainland as to the inhabitants of certain small islands at the two extremities of the great island. It may be well, therefore, to supplement his description by some notes which a distinguished Protestant missionary, the Rev. Dr. George Turner, obtained in the year 1845 from two native teachers, one a Samoan and the other a Rarotongan, who lived in the south-south-eastern part of New Caledonia for three years.[1] Their evidence, it will be observed, goes to confirm Father Lambert's view as to the general similarity of the religious beliefs and customs prevailing throughout the island.

Evidence as to the religion of the New Caledonians furnished by Dr. G. Turner.

The natives of this part of New Caledonia were divided into separate districts, each with its own name, and war, perpetual war, was the rule between the neighbouring communities. They cultivated taro, yams, coco-nuts, and sugar-cane ; but they had no intoxicating *kava* and kept no pigs. They cooked their food in earthenware pots manufactured by the women. In former days their only edge-tools were made of stone, and they felled trees by a slow fire smouldering close to the ground. Similarly they hollowed out the fallen trees by means of a slow fire to make their canoes. Their villages were not permanent. They migrated within certain bounds, as they planted. A village might comprise as many as fifty or sixty round houses. The chiefs had absolute power of life and death. Priests did not meddle in political affairs.[2]

Material culture of the New Caledonians.

At death they dressed the corpse with a belt and shell armlets, cut off the nails of the fingers and toes, and kept them as relics. They spread the grave with a mat, and buried all the body but the head. After ten days the friends twisted off the head, extracted the teeth to be kept as relics, and preserved the skull also. In cases of sickness and other calamities they presented offerings of food to the skulls of

Burial customs ; preservation of the skulls and teeth.

[1] George Turner, LL.D., *Samoa a Hundred Years Ago and long before* (London, 1884), pp. 340 *sqq.*

[2] G. Turner, *op. cit.* pp. 340, 341, 343, 344.

the dead.   The teeth of the old women were taken to the yam plantations and were supposed to fertilise them ; and their skulls were set up on poles in the plantations for the same purpose.   When they buried a chief, they erected spears at his head, fastened a spear-thrower to his fore-finger, and laid a club on the top of his grave,[1] no doubt for the convenience of the ghost.

Prayers to ancestors.

"Their gods," we are told, "were their ancestors, whose relics they kept up and idolised.   At one place they had wooden idols before the chiefs' houses.   The office of the priest was hereditary.   Almost every family had its priest. To make sure of favours and prosperity they prayed not only to their own gods, but also, in a general way, to the gods of other lands.   Fishing, planting, house - building, and everything of importance was preceded by prayers to their guardian spirits for success.   This was especially the case before going to battle.   They prayed to one for the eye, that they might see the spear as it flew towards them. To another for the ear, that they might hear the approach of the enemy.   Thus, too, they prayed for the feet, that they might be swift in pursuing the enemy ; for the heart, that they might be courageous ; for the body, that they might not be speared ; for the head, that it might not be clubbed ; and for sleep, that it might be undisturbed by an attack of the enemy.   Prayers over, arms ready, and equipped with their relic charms, they went off to battle."[2]

"Grand concert of spirits."

The spirits of the dead were believed to go away into the forest.   Every fifth month they had a "spirit night" or "grand concert of spirits."   Heaps of food were prepared for the occasion.   The people assembled in the afternoon round a certain cave.   At sundown they feasted, and then one stood up and addressed the spirits in the cave, saying, "You spirits within, may it please you to sing a song, that all the women and men out here may listen to your sweet voices."   Thereupon a strange unearthly concert of voices burst on their ears from the cave, the nasal squeak of old men and women forming the dominant note.   But the hearers outside listened with delight to the melody, praised the sweet voices of the singers, and then got up and danced

---

[1] G. Turner, *op. cit.* pp. 342 *sq.*   [2] G. Turner, *op. cit.* p. 345.

to the music.   The singing swelled louder and louder as the
dance grew faster and more furious, till the concert closed
in a nocturnal orgy of unbridled license, which, but for the
absence of intoxicants, might compare with the worst of the
ancient bacchanalia.   The singers in the cave were the old
men and women who had ensconced themselves in it
secretly during the day; but the hoax was not suspected
by the children and young people, who firmly believed
that the spirits of the dead really assembled that night in
the cavern and assisted at the sports and diversions of the
living.[1]

The souls of the departed also kindly bore a hand in the
making of rain.   In order to secure their co-operation for
this beneficent purpose the human rain-maker proceeded as
follows.   He blackened himself all over, exhumed a dead
body, carried the bones to a cave, jointed them, and suspended the skeleton over some taro leaves.   After that
he poured water on the skeleton so that it ran down and
fell on the leaves underneath.   They imagined that the soul
of the deceased took up the water, converted it into rain, and
then caused it to descend in refreshing showers.   But the
rain-maker had to stay in the cavern fasting till his efforts
were crowned with success, and when the ghost was tardy in
executing his commission, the rain-maker sometimes died of
hunger.   As a rule, however, they chose the showery months
of March and April for the operation of rain-making, so that
the wizard ran little risk of perishing a martyr to the cause
of science.   When there was too much rain, and they wanted
fine weather, the magician procured it by a similar process,
except that instead of drenching the skeleton with water he
lit a fire under it and burned it up,[2] which naturally induced
or compelled the ghost to burn up the clouds and let the sun
shine out.

Another class of magicians were the maleficent sorcerers
who caused people to fall ill and die by burning their personal rubbish.   When one of these rascals was convicted
of repeated offences of that sort, he was formally tried and
condemned.   The people assembled and a great festival was
held.   The condemned man was decked with a garland

*Making
rain by
means of
the bones
of the dead.*

*Execution
of
maleficent
sorcerers.*

[1] G. Turner, *op. cit.* pp. 346 *sq.*   [2] G. Turner, *op. cit.* pp. 345 *sq.*

of red flowers ; his arms and legs were covered with flowers and shells, and his face and body painted black. Thus arrayed he came dashing forward, rushed through the people, plunged from the rocks into the sea, and was seen no more. The natives also ascribed sickness to the arts of white men, whom they identified with the spirits of the dead ; and assigned this belief as a reason for their wish to kill the strangers.[1]

Reincar-
nation of
the dead
in white
people.

[1] G. Turner, *op. cit.* p. 342.

LECTURE XVI

THE BELIEF IN IMMORTALITY AMONG THE NATIVES OF CENTRAL MELANESIA

IN our survey of savage beliefs and practices concerning the dead we now pass from New Caledonia, the most southerly island of Melanesia, to the groups of islands known as the New Hebrides, the Banks' Islands, the Torres Islands, the Santa Cruz Islands, and the Solomon Islands, which together constitute what we may call Central Melanesia. These groups of islands may themselves be distinguished into two archipelagoes, a western and an eastern, of which the Western comprises the Solomon Islands and the Eastern includes all the rest. Corresponding to this geographical distinction there is a religious distinction ; for while the religion of the Western islanders (the Solomon Islanders) consists chiefly in a fear and worship of the ghosts of the dead, the religion of the Eastern islanders is characterised mainly by the fear and worship of spirits which are not supposed ever to have been incarnate in human bodies. Both groups of islanders, the Western and the Eastern, recognise indeed both classes of spirits, namely ghosts that once were men and spirits who never were men ; but the religious bias of the one group is towards ghosts rather than towards pure spirits, and the religious bias of the other group is towards pure spirits rather than towards ghosts. It is not a little remarkable that the islanders whose bent is towards ghosts have carried the system of sacrifice and the arts of life to a higher level than the islanders whose bent is towards pure spirits ; this applies particularly to the sacrificial system, which is much more developed in the west than in the

The islands of Central Melanesia.

Distinction between the religion of the Eastern and Western Islanders.

east.[1]   From this it would seem to follow that if a faith in ghosts is more costly than a faith in pure spirits, it is at the same time more favourable to the evolution of culture.

Dr. R. H. Codrington on the Melanesians.

For the whole of this region we are fortunate in possessing the evidence of the Rev. Dr. R. H. Codrington, one of the most sagacious, cautious, and accurate of observers, who laboured as a missionary among the natives for twenty-four years, from 1864 to 1887, and has given us a most valuable account of their customs and beliefs in his book *The Melanesians*, which must always remain an anthropological classic.   In describing the worship of the dead as it is carried on among these islanders I shall draw chiefly on the copious evidence supplied by Dr. Codrington ; and I shall avail myself of his admirable researches to enter into considerable details on the subject, since details recorded by an accurate observer are far more instructive than the vague generalities of superficial observers, which are too often all the information we possess as to the religion of savages.

Melanesian theory of the soul.

In the first place, all the Central Melanesians believe that man is composed of a body and a soul, that death is the final parting of the soul from the body, and that after death the soul continues to exist as a conscious and more or less active being.[2]   Thus the creed of these savages on this profound subject agrees fundamentally with the creed of the average European ; if my hearers were asked to state their beliefs as to the nature of life and death, I imagine that most of them would formulate them in substantially the same way. However, when the Central Melanesian savage attempts to define the nature of the vital principle or soul, which animates the body during life and survives it after death, he finds himself in a difficulty ; and to continue the parallel I cannot help thinking that if my hearers in like manner were invited to explain their conception of the soul, they would similarly find themselves embarrassed for an answer.   But an examination of the Central Melanesian theory of the soul would lead us too far from our immediate subject ; we must be content to say that, " whatever word the Melanesian

[1] R. H. Codrington, *The Melanesians* (Oxford, 1891), pp. 122, 123, 124, 180 *sq.*

[2] R. H. Codrington, *The Melanesians* (Oxford, 1891), pp. 247, 253.

people use for soul, they mean something essentially belonging to each man's nature which carries life to his body with it, and is the seat of thought and intelligence, exercising therefore power which is not of the body and is invisible in its action."[1] However the soul may be defined, the Melanesians are universally of opinion that it survives the death of the body and goes away to some more or less distant region, where the spirits of all the dead congregate and continue for the most part to live for an indefinite time, though some of them, as we shall see presently, are supposed to die a second death and so to come to an end altogether. In Western Melanesia, that is, in the Solomon Islands, the abode of the dead is supposed to be in certain islands, which differ in the creed of different islanders; but in Eastern Melanesia the abode of the dead is thought to be a subterranean region called Panoi.[2]

But though the souls of the departed go away to the spirit land, nevertheless, with a seeming or perhaps real inconsistency, their ghosts are also supposed to haunt their graves and their old homes and to exercise great power for good or evil over the living, who are accordingly often obliged to woo their favour by prayer and sacrifice. According to the Solomon Islanders, however, among whom ghosts are the principal objects of worship, there is a great distinction to be drawn among ghosts. "The distinction," says Dr. Codrington, "is between ghosts of power and ghosts of no account, between those whose help is sought and their wrath deprecated, and those from whom nothing is expected and to whom no observance is due. Among living men there are some who stand out distinguished for capacity in affairs, success in life, valour in fighting, and influence over others; and these are so, it is believed, because of the supernatural and mysterious powers which they have, and which are derived from communication with those ghosts of the dead gone before them who are full of those same powers. On the death of a distinguished man his ghost retains the powers that belonged to him in life, in greater activity and with stronger force; his ghost therefore

Distinction between ghosts of power and ghosts of no account.

---

[1] R. H. Codrington, *op. cit.* p. 248.
[2] R. H. Codrington, *op. cit.* pp. 255 *sqq.*, 264 *sqq.*

is powerful and worshipful, and so long as he is remembered the aid of his powers is sought and worship is offered him ; he is the *tindalo* of Florida, the *lio'a* of Saa. In every society, again, the multitude is composed of insignificant persons, '*numerus fruges consumeri nati,*' of no particular account for valour, skill, or prosperity. The ghosts of such persons continue their insignificance, and are nobodies after death as before ; they are ghosts because all men have souls, and the souls of dead men are ghosts ; they are dreaded because all ghosts are awful, but they get no worship and are soon only thought of as the crowd of the nameless population of the lower world." [1]

Ghosts of the great and of the recently dead are chiefly regarded.

From this account of Dr. Codrington we see that it is only the ghosts of great and powerful people who are worshipped ; the ghosts of ordinary people are indeed feared, but no worship is paid to them. Further, we are told that it is the ghosts of those who have lately died that are deemed to be most powerful and are therefore most regarded ; as the dead are forgotten, their ghosts cease to be worshipped, their power fades away,[2] and their place in the religion of the people is taken by the ghosts of the more recently departed. In fact here, as elsewhere, the existence of the dead seems to be dependent on the memory of the living ; when they are forgotten they cease to exist. Further, it deserves to be noticed that in the Solomon Islands what we should call a man's natural powers and capacities are regarded as supernatural endowments acquired by communication with a mighty ghost. If a man is a great warrior, it is not because he is strong of arm, quick of eye, and brave of heart ; it is because he is supported by the ghost of a dead warrior, whose power he has drawn to himself through an amulet of stone tied round his neck, or a tuft of leaves in his belt, or a tooth attached to one of his fingers, or a spell by the recitation of which he can enlist the aid of the ghost.[3] And similarly with all other pre-eminent capacities and virtues ; in the mind of the Solomon Islanders, they are all super-

Supernatural power (*mana*) acquired through ghosts.

[1] R. H. Codrington, *op. cit.* pp.   125, 130.
253 *sq.*
[2] R. H. Codrington, *op. cit.* pp.   [3] R. H. Codrington, *op. cit.* pp.
254, 258, 261 ; compare *id.*, pp.   120, 254.

natural gifts and graces bestowed on men by ghosts. This
all-pervading supernatural power the Central Melanesian
calls *mana*.[1] Thus for these savages the whole world teems
with ghostly influences; their minds are filled, we may
almost say, obsessed, with a sense of the unseen powers
which encompass and determine even in its minute
particulars the life of man on earth : in their view the
visible world is, so to say, merely a puppet-show of which
the strings are pulled and the puppets made to dance by
hands invisible. Truly the attitude of these savages to
the universe is deeply religious.

We may now consider the theory and practice of the
Central Melanesians on this subject somewhat more in
detail ; and in doing so we shall begin with their funeral
customs, which throw much light on their views of death and
the dead.

Thus, for example, in Florida, one of the Solomon
Islands, the corpse is usually buried. Common men are
buried in their gardens or plantations, chiefs sometimes in
the village, a chief's child sometimes in the house. If the
ghost of the deceased is worshipped, his grave becomes a
sanctuary (*vunuhu*) ; the skull is often dug up and hung
in the house. On the return from the burial the mourners
take a different road from that by which they carried the
corpse to the grave ; this they do in order to throw the
ghost off the scent and so prevent him from following them
home. This practice clearly shews the fear which the
natives feel for the ghosts of the newly dead. A man
is buried with money, porpoise teeth, and some of his
personal ornaments ; but, avarice getting the better of
superstition, these things are often secretly dug up again and
appropriated by the living. Sometimes a dying man will
express a wish to be cast into the sea ; his friends will
therefore paddle out with the corpse, tie stones to the feet,
and sink it in the depths. In the island of Savo, another of
the Solomon Islands, common men are generally thrown
into the sea and only great men are buried.[2] The same
distinction is made at Wango in San Cristoval, another of

Burial customs in the Solomon Islands.

Land burial and sea burial.

[1] R. H. Codrington, *op. cit.* pp.
118 *sqq.*   [2] R. H. Codrington, *op. cit.* pp. 254
sq.

the same group of islands ; there also the bodies of common folk are cast into the sea, but men of consequence are buried, and some relic of them, it may be a skull, a tooth, or a finger-bone, is preserved in a shrine at the village. From this difference in burial customs flows a not unimportant religious difference. The souls of the great people who are buried on land turn into land-ghosts, and the souls of commoners who are sunk in the sea turn into sea-ghosts. The land-ghosts are seen to hover about the villages, haunting their graves and their relics ; they are also heard to speak in hollow whispers. Their aid can be obtained by such as know them. The sea-ghosts have taken a great hold on the imagination of the natives of the south-eastern Solomon Islands ; and as these people love to illustrate their life by sculpture and painting, they shew us clearly what they suppose these sea-ghosts to be like. At Wango there used to be a canoe-house full of sculptures and paintings illustrative of native life ; amongst others there was a series of scenes like those which are depicted on the walls of Egyptian tombs. One of the scenes represented a canoe attacked by sea-ghosts, which were portrayed as demons compounded partly of human limbs, partly of the bodies and tails of fishes, and armed with spears and arrows in the form of long-bodied garfish and flying-fish. If a man falls ill on returning from a voyage or from fishing on the rocks, it is thought that one of these sea-ghosts has shot him. Hence when men are in danger at sea, they seek to propitiate the ghosts by throwing areca-nuts and fragments of food into the water and by praying to the ghosts not to be angry with them. Sharks are also supposed to be animated by the ghosts of the dead.[1] It is interesting and instructive to find that in this part of the world sea-demons, who might be thought to be pure spirits of nature, are in fact ghosts of the dead.

Land-ghosts and sea-ghosts.

In the island of Florida, two days after the death of a chief or of any person who was much esteemed, the relatives and friends assemble and hold a funeral feast, at which they throw a bit of food into the fire for the ghost, saying, " This is for you." [2]   In other of the Solomon Islands morsels of

Burnt offerings in honour of the dead.

---

[1] R. H. Codrington, *op. cit.* pp. 258 *sq.*   [2] R. H. Codrington, *op. cit.* p. 255.

food are similarly thrown on the fire at the death-feasts as
the dead man's share.[1]   Thus, in the Shortlands Islands,
when a famous chief named Gorai died, his body was burnt
and his relatives cast food, beads, and other property into
the fire.   The dead chief had been very fond of tea, so one
of his daughters threw a cup of tea into the flames.   Women
danced a funeral dance round the pyre till the body was
consumed.[2]   Why should the dead man's food and property
be burnt?   No explanation of the practice is given by our
authorities, so we are left to conjecture the reason of it.   Is
it that by volatilising the solid substance of the food you
make it more accessible to the thin unsubstantial nature
of the ghost?   Is it that you destroy the property of the
ghost lest he should come back in person to fetch it and
so haunt and trouble the survivors?   Is it that the spirits
of the dead are supposed to reside in the fire on the hearth,
so that offerings cast into the flames are transmitted to
them directly?   Whether it is with any such ideas that the
Solomon Islanders throw food into the fire for ghosts, I
cannot say.   The whole question of the meaning of burnt
sacrifice is still to a great extent obscure.

At the funeral feast of a chief in the island of Florida   Funeral
the axes, spears, shield and other belongings of the deceased   customs in the
are hung up with great lamentations in his house ; everything   island of
remains afterwards untouched and the house falls into ruins,   Florida.
which as time goes on are thickly mantled with the long
tendrils of the sprouting yams.   But we are told that the
weapons are not intended to accompany the ghost to the
land of souls ; they are hung up only as a memorial of a
great and valued man.   " With the same feeling they cut
down a dead man's fruit-trees as a mark of respect and
affection, not with any notion of these things serving him in
the world of ghosts ; he ate of them, they say, when he was
alive, he will never eat again, and no one else shall have
them."   However, they think that the ghost benefits by
burial ; for if a man is killed and his body remains unburied,
his restless ghost will haunt the place.[3]   The ghosts of such

[1] R. H. Codrington, *op. cit.* p.   *Polynesians* (London, 1910), pp. 214,
259.   217.
[2] G. Brown, D.D., *Melanesians and*   [3] R. H. Codrington, *op. cit.* p. 255.

The
ghostly
ferry.

Florida people as have been duly buried depart to Betindalo,
which seems to be situated in the south-eastern part of the
great island of Guadalcanar. A ship waits to ferry them
across the sea to the spirit-land. This is almost the only
example of a ferry-boat used by ghosts in Melanesia. On
their way to the ferry the ghosts may be heard twittering ;
and again on the shore, while they are waiting for the ferry-
boat, a sound of their dancing breaks the stillness of night ;
but no man can see the dancers. It is not until they land
on the further shore that they know they are dead. There
they are met by a ghost, who thrusts a rod into their noses
to see whether the cartilage is pierced as it should be ; ghosts
whose noses have been duly bored in life follow the onward
path with ease, but all others have pain and difficulty in
making their way to the realm of the shades. Yet though
the souls of the dead thus depart to Betindalo, nevertheless
their ghosts as usual not only haunt their burial-places, but
come to the sacrifices offered to them and may be heard
disporting themselves at night, playing on pipes, dancing,
and shouting.[1]

Belief of the
Solomon
Islanders
that the
souls of
the dead
live in
islands.

Similarly at Bugotu in the island of Ysabel (one of the
Solomon Islands) the ghosts of the dead are supposed to go
away to an island, and yet to haunt their graves and shew
themselves to the survivors by night. In the island of the
dead there is a pool with a narrow tree-trunk lying across it.
Here is stationed Bolafagina, the ghostly lord of the place.
Every newly arrived ghost must appear before him, and he
examines their hands to see whether they bear the mark
of the sacred frigate-bird cut on them ; if they have the
mark, the ghosts pass across the tree-trunk and mingle
with the departed spirits in the world of the dead. But
ghosts who have not the mark on their hands are cast into
the gulf and perish out of their ghostly life : this is the
second death.[2] The same notion of a second death meets
us in a somewhat different form among the natives of Saa
in Malanta, another of the Solomon Islands. All the ghosts
of these people swim across the sea to two little islands
called Marapa, which lie off Marau in Guadalcanar. There

[1] R. H. Codrington, *op. cit.* pp. 255
sq.   [2] R. H. Codrington, *op. cit.* pp. 256
sq.

the ghosts of children live in one island and the ghosts of grown-up people in another ; for the older people would be plagued by the chatter of children if they all dwelt together in one island.   Yet in other respects the life of the departed spirits in these islands is very like life on earth.   There are houses, gardens, and canoes there just as here, but all is thin and unsubstantial.   Living men who land in the islands see nothing of these things ; there is a pool where they hear laughter and merry cries, and where the banks are wet with invisible bathers.   But the life of the ghosts in these islands The second is not eternal.   The spirits of common folk soon turn into ^(death.) the nests of white ants, which serve as food for the more robust ghosts.   Hence a living man will say to his idle son, " When I die, I shall have ants' nests to eat, but then what will you have ? "   The ghosts of persons who were powerful on earth last much longer.   So long as they are remembered and worshipped by the living, their natural strength remains unabated ; but when men forget them, and turn to worship some of the more recent dead, then no more food is offered to them in sacrifice, so they pine away and change into white ants' nests just like common folk.   This is the second death.   However, while the ghosts survive they can return from the islands to Saa and revisit their village and friends. The living can even discern them in the form of dim and fleeting shadows.   A man who wishes for any reason to see a ghost can always do so very simply by taking a pinch of lime from his betel-box and smearing it on his forehead. Then the ghost appears to him quite plainly.[1]

In Saa the dead are usually buried in a common cemetery ; Burial but when the flesh has decayed the bones are taken up and customs heaped on one side.   But if the deceased was a very great man or a beloved father, his body is preserved for a time in his son's house, being hung up either in a canoe or in the carved effigy of a sword-fish.   Very favourite children are treated in the same way.   The corpse may be kept in this way for years.   Finally, there is a great funeral feast, at Preserva- which the remains are removed to the common burial-ground, tion of the but the skull and jawbone are detached from the skeleton jawbone. and kept in the house enclosed in the hollow wooden figure

---

[1] R. H. Codrington, *op. cit.* pp. 260 *sq.*

of a bonito-fish. By means of these relics the survivors think that they can secure the aid of the powerful ghost. Sometimes the corpse and afterwards the skull and jaw-bone are preserved, not in the house of the deceased, but in the *oha* or public canoe-house, which so far becomes a sort of shrine or temple of the dead.[1] At Santa Cruz in the Solomon Islands the corpse is buried in a very deep grave in the house. Inland they dig up the bones again to make arrow-heads ; also they detach the skull and keep it in a chest in the house, saying that it is the man himself. They even set food before the skull, no doubt for the use of the ghost. Yet they imagine that the ghosts of the dead go to the great volcano Tamami, where they are burnt in the crater and thus being renewed stay in the fiery region. Nevertheless the souls of the dead also haunt the forests in Santa Cruz ; on wet and dark nights the natives see them twinkling in the gloom like fire-flies, and at the sight they are sore afraid.[2] So little consistent with itself is the creed of these islanders touching the state of the dead. At Bugotu in the island of Ysabel (one of the Solomon Islands) a chief is buried with his head near the surface and a fire is kept burning over the grave, in order that the skull may be taken up and preserved in the house of his successor. The spirit of the dead chief has now become a worshipful ghost, and an expedition is sent out to cut off and bring back human heads in his honour. Any person, not belonging to the place, whom the head-hunters come across will be killed by them and his or her skull added to the collection, which is neatly arranged on the shore. These ghastly trophies are believed to add fresh spiritual power (*mana*) to the ghost of the dead chief. Till they have been procured, the people of the place take care not to move about. The grave of the chief is built up with stones and sacrifices are offered upon it.[3]

Burial customs in Santa Cruz.

Burial customs in Ysabel.

Thus far we have been considering the beliefs and practices concerning the dead which prevail among the Western Melanesians of the Solomon Islands and Santa

[1] R. H. Codrington, *op. cit.* pp. 261 *sq.*

[2] R. H. Codrington, *op. cit.* pp. 257.

[3] R. H. Codrington, *op. cit.* p. 263 *sq.*

Cruz. We now turn to those of the Eastern Melanesians,
who inhabit the Torres Islands, the Banks' Islands, and the
New Hebrides. A broad distinction exists between the
ghosts of these two regions in as much as the ghosts of the
Western Melanesians all live in islands, but the ghosts of all
Eastern Melanesians live underground in a subterranean
region which commonly bears the name of Panoi. The
exact position of Panoi has not been ascertained ; all that is
regarded as certain is that it is underground. However,
there are many entrances to it and some of them are well
known. One of them, for example, is a rock on the
mountain at Mota, others are at volcanic vents which belch
flames on the burning hill of Garat over the lake at Gaua,
and another is on the great mountain of Vanua Lava. The
ghosts congregate on points of land before their departure,
as well as at the entrances to the underworld, and there on
moonlight nights you may hear the ghostly crew dancing,
singing, shouting, and whistling on the claws of land-crabs.
It is not easy to extract from the natives a precise and consistent account of the place of the dead and the state of the
spirits in it ; nor indeed, as Dr. Codrington justly observes,
would it be reasonable to expect full and precise details on a
subject about which the sources of information are perhaps
not above suspicion. However, as far as can be made out,
Panoi or the abode of the dead is on the whole a happy
region. In many respects it resembles the land of the living ;
for there are houses there and villages, and trees with red
leaves, and day and night. Yet all is hollow and unreal.
The ghosts do nothing but talk and sing and dance ; there
is no clubhouse there, and though men and women live
together, there is no marrying or giving in marriage. All is
very peaceful, too, in that land ; for there is no war and no
tyrant to oppress the people. Yet the ghost of a great man
goes down like a great man among the ghosts, resplendent in
all his trinkets and finery ; but like everything else in the
underworld these ornaments, for all the brave show they
make, are mere unsubstantial shadows. The pigs which
were killed at his funeral feast and the food that was heaped
on his grave cannot go down with him into that far country ;
for none of these things, not even pigs, have souls. How

then could they find their way to the spirit world? It is clearly impossible. The ghosts in the nether world do not mix indiscriminately. There are separate compartments for such as died violent deaths. There is one compartment for those who were shot, there is another for those who were clubbed, and there is another for those who were done to death by witchcraft. The ghosts of those who were shot keep rattling the reeds of the arrows which dealt them their fatal wounds. Ghosts in the nether world have no knowledge of things out of their sight and hearing ; yet the living call upon them in time of need and trouble, as if they could hear and help. Life, too, in the kingdom of shadows is not eternal. The ghosts die the second death. Yet some say that there are two such kingdoms, each called Panoi, the one over the other ; and that when the dead die the second death in the upper realm they rise again from the dead in the nether realm, where they never die but only turn into white ants' nests.[1]

Distinction between the fate of the good and the fate of the bad in the other world.

It is interesting and not unimportant to observe that some of these islanders make a distinction between the fate of good people and the fate of bad people after death. The natives of Motlav, one of the Banks' Islands, think that Panoi is a good place and that only the souls of the good can enter it. According to them the souls of murderers, sorcerers, thieves, liars, and adulterers are not suffered to enter the happy land. The ghost of a murderer, for example, is met at the entrance by the ghost of his victim, who withstands him and turns him back. All the bad ghosts go away to a bad place, where they live, not indeed in physical pain, but in misery : they quarrel, they are restless, homeless, pitiable, malignant : they wander back to earth : they eat the foulest food, their breath is noisome : they harm the living out of spite, they eat men's souls, they haunt graves and woods. But in the true Panoi the souls of the good live in peace and harmony.[2] Thus these people believe that the state of the soul after death depends on the kind of life a man led on earth ; if he was good, he will be happy ; if he was bad, he will be miserable. If this creed

[1] R. H. Codrington, *op. cit.* pp. 264, 273 *sq.*, 275-277.

[2] R. H. Codrington, *op. cit.* pp. 274 *sq.*

is of purely native origin, and Dr. Codrington seems to entertain no doubt that it is so, it marks a considerable ethical advance among those who accept it.

The Eastern Melanesians think that living people can go down to the land of the dead and return alive to the upper world. Sometimes they do this in the body, but at other times only in the spirit, when they are asleep or in a faint; for at such times their souls quit their bodies and can wander away down to Panoi. When the living thus make their way to the spirit land, they are sometimes cautioned by friendly ghosts to eat nothing there, no doubt lest by partaking of ghostly food they should be turned to ghosts and never return to the land of the living.[1]

We will now consider the various modes in which the Eastern Melanesians dispose of their dead; for funeral customs commonly furnish some indication of the ideas which a people entertain as to the state of the soul after death. The Banks' Islanders generally buried their dead in the forest not far from the village; but if the deceased was a great man or died a remarkable death, they might inter him in the village near the men's clubhouse (*gamal*). A favourite son or child might be buried in the house itself; but in such cases the grave would be opened after fifty or a hundred days and the bones taken up and hidden in the forest, though some of them might be hung up in the house. However, in some places there was, and indeed still is, a custom of keeping the putrefying corpse unburied in the house as a mark of affection. At Gaua, in Santa Maria, the body was dried over slow fires for ten days or more, till nothing but skin and bones remained; and the women who watched over it during these days drank the juices of putrefaction which dripped from the decaying flesh. The same thing used formerly to be done in Mota, another of the Banks' Islands. The corpses of great men in these islands were adorned in all their finery and laid out on the open space in the middle of the village. Here bunches of coconuts, yams, and other food were heaped up beside the body; and an orator of fluent speech addressed the ghost telling him that when he had gone down to Panoi, the spirit land,

Descent of the living to the world of the dead.

Disposal of the dead among the Eastern islanders.

Burial customs of the Banks' Islanders.

[1] R. H. Codrington, *op. cit.* pp. 266, 276, 277, 286.

and the ghosts asked him after his rank, he was to give them a list of all the things heaped beside his dead body ; then the ghosts would know what a great man he was and would treat him with proper deference. The orator dealt very candidly with the moral character of the deceased. If he had been a bad man, the speaker would say, " Poor ghost, will you be able to enter Panoi ? I think not." The food which is piled up beside the body while the orator is pronouncing the eulogium or the censure of the departed is afterwards heaped up on the grave or buried in it. At Gaua they kill pigs and hang up the carcases or parts of them at the grave. The object of all this display is to make a favourable impression on the ghosts in the spirit land, in order that they may give the newly deceased man a good reception. When the departed was an eminent warrior or sorcerer, his friends will sometimes give him a sham burial and hide his real grave, lest people should dig up his bones and his skull to make magic with them ; for the relics of such a man are naturally endowed with great magical virtue.[1]

Ghosts driven away from the village.

In these islands the ghost does not at once leave the neighbourhood of his old body ; he shews no haste to depart to the nether world. Indeed he commonly loiters about the house and the grave for five or ten days, manifesting his presence by noises in the house and by lights upon the grave. By the fifth day his relations generally think that they have had quite enough of him, and that it is high time he should set out for his long home. Accordingly they drive him away with shouts and the blowing of conch-shells or the booming sound of bull-roarers.[2] At Ureparapara the mode of expelling the ghost from the village is as follows. Missiles to be hurled at the lingering spirit are collected in the shape of small stones and pieces of bamboo, which have been charmed by wizards so as to possess a ghost-expelling virtue. The artillery having been thus provided, the people muster at one end of the village, armed with bags of enchanted stones and pieces of enchanted bamboos. The signal to march is given by two men, who sit in the dead man's house, one on either side, holding two white stones in their hands,

[1] R. H. Codrington, *The Melanesians*, pp. 267-270.
[2] R. H. Codrington, *op. cit.* p. 269.

which they clink together.   At the sound of the clinking the
women begin to wail and the men to march; tramp, tramp
they go like one man through the village from end to end,
throwing stones into the houses and all about and beating
the bamboos together.   Thus they drive the reluctant ghost
step by step from the village into the forest, where they
leave him to find his own way down to the land of the dead.
Till that time the widow of the deceased was bound to remain
on his bed without quitting it for a moment except on
necessity; and if she had to leave it for a few minutes she
always left a coco-nut on the bed to represent her till she
came back.   The reason for this was that her husband's
ghost was believed to be lingering in the house all these
days, and he would naturally expect to see his wife in the
nuptial chamber.   At Motlav the people are not so hard
upon the poor ghosts: they do not drive away all ghosts
from their old homes, but only the ghosts of such as had in
their lifetime the misfortune to be afflicted with grievous
sores and ulcers.   The expulsion of such ghosts may therefore be regarded as a sanitary precaution designed to prevent the spirits from spreading the disease.   When a man
who suffers severely from sores or ulcers lies dying, the
people of his village, taking time by the forelock, send word
to the inhabitants of the next village westwards, warning
them to be in readiness to give the ghost a warm reception.
For it is well known that at their departure from the body
ghosts always go westward towards the setting sun.   So
when the poor man is dead, they bury his diseased body in
the village and devote all their energies to the expulsion of
his soul.   By blowing blasts on shell-trumpets and beating
the ground with the stalks of coco-nut fronds they chase the
ghost clean away from their own village and on to the next.
The inhabitants of that village meantime are ready to receive
their unwelcome visitor, and beating their bounds in the most
literal sense they soon drive him onwards to the land of their
next neighbours.   So the chase goes on from village to
village, till the ghost has been finally hunted into the sea at
the point of the shore which faces the setting sun.   There
at last the beaters throw away the stalks which have served
to whack the ghost, and return home in the perfect assurance

Expulsion of the ghosts of persons who suffered from sores and ulcers.

that he has left the island and gone to his own place down below, so that he cannot afflict anybody with the painful disease from which he suffered. But as for his ulcerated corpse rotting in the grave, they do not give a thought to it. Their concern is with the spiritual and the unseen ; they do not stoop to regard the material and carnal.[1]

Special treatment of the ghosts of women who died in childbed.

A special treatment is accorded to the ghosts of women who died in childbed. If the mother dies and the child lives, her ghost will not go away to the nether world without taking the infant with her. Hence in order to deceive the ghost, they wrap a piece of a banana-trunk loosely in leaves and lay it on the bosom of the dead mother when they lower her into the grave. The ghost clasps the bundle to her breast, thinking it is her baby, and goes away contentedly to the spirit land. As she walks, the banana-stalk slips about in the leaves and she imagines it is the infant stirring ; for she has not all her wits about her, ghosts being naturally in a dazed state at first on quitting their familiar bodies. But when she arrives in deadland and finds she has been deceived, and when perhaps some heartless ghosts even jeer at her wooden baby, back she comes tearing to earth in grief and rage to seek and carry off the real infant. However, the survivors know what to expect and have taken the precaution of removing the child to another house where the mother will never find it ; but she keeps looking for it always, and a sad and angry ghost is she.[2]

Funeral feasts.

After the funeral follows a series, sometimes a long series, of funeral feasts, which form indeed one of the principal institutions of these islands. The number of the feasts and the length of time during which they are repeated vary much in the different islands, and depend also on the consideration in which the deceased was held. The days on which the feasts are celebrated are the fifth and the tenth after the death, and afterwards every tenth day up to the hundredth or even it may be, in the case of a father, a mother, or a wife, up to the thousandth day. These feasts appear now to be chiefly commemorative, but they also benefit the dead ; for the ghost is naturally gratified by

[1] R. H. Codrington, *The Melanesians*, pp. 270 *sq.*

[2] R. H. Codrington, *The Melanesians*, p. 275.

seeing that his friends remember him and do their duty by him so handsomely.   At these banquets food is put aside for the dead with the words " This is for thee."   The practice of thus setting aside food for the ghost at a series of funeral feasts appears at first sight, as Dr. Codrington observes, inconsistent with the theory that the ghosts live underground.[1]   But the objection thus suggested is rather specious than real ; for we must always bear in mind that, to judge from the accounts given of them in all countries, ghosts experience no practical difficulty in obtaining temporary leave of absence from the other world and coming to this one, so to say, on furlough for the purpose of paying a surprise visit to their sorrowing friends and relations.   The thing is so well known that it would be at once superfluous and tedious to illustrate it at length ; many examples have incidentally met us in the course of these lectures.

The natives of Vaté or Efat, one of the New Hebrides, set up a great wailing at a death and scratched their faces till they streamed with blcod.   Bodies of the dead were buried.   When a corpse was laid in the grave, a pig was brought to the place and its head was chopped off and thrown into the grave to be buried with the body.   This, we are told, "was supposed to prevent disease spreading to other members of the family."   Probably, in the opinion of the natives, the pig's head was a sop thrown to the ghost to keep him from coming and fetching away other people to deadland.   With the same intention, we may take it, they buried with the dead the cups, pillows, and other things which he had used in his lifetime.   On the top of the grave they kindled a fire to enable the soul of the deceased to rise to the sun.   If that were not done, the soul went to the wretched regions of Pakasia down below.   The old were buried alive at their own request.   It was even deemed a disgrace to the family of an aged chief if they did not bury him alive.   When an old man felt sick and weak and thought that he was dying, he would tell his friends to get all ready and bury him.   They yielded to his wishes, dug a deep round pit, wound a number of fine mats round his body, and

Funeral customs in Vaté or Efat.

Old people buried alive.

[1] R. H. Codrington, *The Melanesians*, pp. 271 *sq.*

lowered him into the grave in a sitting posture. Live pigs were then brought to the brink of the grave, and each of them was tethered by a cord to one of the old man's arms. When the pigs had thus, as it were, been made over to him, the cords were cut, and the animals were led away to be killed, baked, and eaten at the funeral feast; but the souls of the pigs the old man took away with him to the spirit land, and the more of them he took the warmer and more gratifying was the reception he met with from the ghosts. Having thus ensured his eternal welfare by the pig strings which dangled at his arms, the old man was ready; more mats were laid over him, the earth was shovelled in, and his dying groans were drowned amid the weeping and wailing of his affectionate kinsfolk.[1]

Burial and mourning customs in Aurora, one of the New Hebrides.

At Maewo in Aurora, one of the New Hebrides, when a death has taken place, the body is buried in a grave near the village clubhouse. For a hundred days afterwards the female mourners may not go into the open and their faces may not be seen; they stay indoors and in the dark and cover themselves with a large mat reaching to the ground. But the widow goes every day, covered with her mat, to weep at the grave; this she does both in the morning and in the afternoon. During this time of mourning the next of kin may not eat certain succulent foods, such as yams, bananas, and caladium; they eat only the gigantic caladium, bread-fruit, coco-nuts, mallows, and so forth; "and all these they seek in the bush where they grow wild, not eating those which have been planted." They count five days after the death and then build up great heaps of stones over the grave. After that, if the deceased was a very great man, who owned many gardens and pigs, they count fifty days and then kill pigs, and cut off the point of the liver of each pig; and the brother of the deceased goes toward

---

[1] G. Turner, *Samoa a Hundred Years Ago and long before* (London, 1884), pp. 335 *sq.* This account is based on information furnished by Suālo, a Samoan teacher, who lived for a long time on the island. The statement that the fire kindled on the grave was intended "to enable the soul of the departed to rise to the sun" may be doubted; it may be a mere inference of Dr. Turner's Samoan informant. More probably the fire was intended to warm the shivering ghost. I do not remember any other evidence that the souls of the Melanesian dead ascend to the sun; certainly it is much more usual for them to descend into the earth.

the forest and calls out the dead man's name, crying, " This is for you to eat." They think that if they do not kill pigs for the benefit of their departed friend, his ghost has no proper existence, but hangs miserably on tangled creepers. After the sacrifice they all cry again, smear their bodies and faces all over with ashes, and wear cords round their necks for a hundred days in token that they are not eating good food.[1] They imagine that as soon as the soul quits the body at death, it mounts into a tree where there is a bird's nest fern, and sitting theré among the fronds it laughs and mocks at the people who are crying and making great lamentations ovèr his deserted tabernacle. " There he sits, wondering at them and ridiculing them. ' What are they crying for ? ' he says ; ' whom are they sorry for ? Here am I.' For they think that the real thing is the soul, and that it has gone away from the body just as a man throws off his clothes and leaves them, and the clothes lie by themselves with nothing in them.".[2] This estimate of the comparative value of soul and body is translated from the words of a New Hebridean native ; it singularly resembles that which is sometimes held up to our admiration as one of the finest fruits of philosophy and religion. So narrow may be the line that divides the meditations of the savage and the sage.

Behaviour of the soul at death.

When a Maewo ghost has done chuckling at the folly of his surviving relatives, who sorrow as those who have no hope, he turns his back on his old home and runs along the line of hills till he comes to a place where there are two rocks with a deep ravine between them. He leaps the chasm, and if he lands on the further side, he is dead indeed ; but if he falls short, he returns to life. At the land's end, where the mountains descend into the sea, all the ghosts of the dead are gathered to meet him. If in his lifetime he had slain any one by club or arrow, or done any man to death by magic, he must now run the gauntlet of the angry ghosts of his victims, who beat and tear him and stab him with daggers such as people stick pigs with ; and as they do so, they taunt him, saying, "While you were still in the world you thought yourself a valiant man ; but now

Journey of the ghost to the other world.

[1] R. H. Codrington, *op. cit.* pp. 281 *sq.*   [2] R. H. Codrington, *op. cit.* pp. 278 *sq.*

we will take our revenge on you." At another point in
the path there is a deep gully, where if a ghost falls he is
inevitably dashed to pieces ; and if he escapes this peril,
there is a ferocious pig waiting for him further on, which
devours the ghosts of all persons who in their life on earth
omitted to plant pandanus trees, from which mats are
made. But the wise man, who planted pandanus betimes,
now reaps the fruit of his labours ; for when the pig makes
a rush at his departed spirit, the ghost nimbly swarms up
the pandanus tree and so escapes his pursuer. That is why
everybody in Maewo likes to plant pandanus trees. And
if a man's ears were not pierced in his life, his ghost will
not be allowed to drink water ; if he was not tattooed, his
ghost may not eat good food. A thoughtful father will
provide for the comfort of his children in the other world
by building a miniature house for each of them in his garden
when the child is a year old ; if the infant is a boy, he puts
a bow, an arrow, and a club in the little house ; if the child
is a girl, he plants pandanus for her beside the tiny dwelling.[1]

Only ghosts of powerful men are worshipped.

So much for the fate of common ghosts in Central
Melanesia. We have now to consider the position of the
more powerful spirits, who after death are believed to exercise
great influence over the living, especially over their surviving
relations, and who have accordingly to be propitiated with
prayer and sacrifice. This worship of the dead, as we saw,
forms the principal feature in the religion of the Solomon
Islanders. "But it must not be supposed," says Dr.
Codrington, "that every ghost becomes an object of worship.
A man in danger may call upon his father, his grandfather,
or his uncle : his nearness of kin is sufficient ground for it.
The ghost who is to be worshipped is the spirit of a man
who in his lifetime had *mana* [supernatural or magical power]
in him ; the souls of common men are the common herd of
ghosts, nobodies alike before and after death. The supernatural power abiding in the powerful living man abides in
his ghost after death, with increased vigour and more ease
of movement. After his death, therefore, it is expected
that he should begin to work, and some one will come
forward and claim particular acquaintance with the ghost ;

[1] R. H. Codrington, *op. cit.* pp. 279 *sq.*

if his power should shew itself, his position is assured as one worthy to be invoked, and to receive offerings, till his cultus gives way before the rising importance of one newly dead, and the sacred place where his shrine once stood and his relics were preserved is the only memorial of him that remains; if no proof of his activity appears, he sinks into oblivion at once." [1]

From this instructive account we learn that worship is paid chiefly to the recent and well-remembered dead, to the men whom the worshippers knew personally and feared or respected in their lifetime. On the other hand, when men have been long dead, and all who knew them have also been gathered to their fathers, their memory fades away and with it their worship gradually falls into complete desuetude. Thus the spirits who receive the homage of these savages were real men of flesh and blood, not mythical beings conjured up by the fancy of their worshippers, which some legerdemain of the mind has foisted into the shrine and encircled with the halo of divinity. Not that the Melanesians do not also worship beings who, so far as we can see, are purely mythical, though their worshippers firmly believe in their reality. But "they themselves make a clear distinction between the existing, conscious, powerful disembodied spirits of the dead, and other spiritual beings that never have been men at all. It is true that the two orders of beings get confused in native language and thought, but their confusion begins at one end and the confusion of their visitors at another; they think so much and constantly of ghosts that they speak of beings who were never men as ghosts; Europeans take the spirits of the lately dead for gods; less educated Europeans call them roundly devils." [2]

As an example of the way in which the ghost of a real man who has just died may come to be worshipped Dr. Codrington tells us the story of Ganindo, which he had from Bishop Selwyn. This Ganindo was a great fighting man of Honggo in Florida, one of the Solomon Islands. He went with other warriors on a head-hunting expedition against Gaeta; but being mortally wounded with an arrow

Marginal notes:
Worship paid chiefly to the recent and well-remembered dead.

Way in which a dead warrior came to be worshipped as a martial ghost.

[1] R. H. Codrington, *The Melanesians*, pp. 124 *sq.*

[2] R. H. Codrington, *The Melanesians*, p. 121.

near the collar-bone he was brought back by his comrades to the hill of Bonipari, where he died and was buried. His friends cut off his head, put it in a basket, built a house for it, and said that he was a worshipful ghost (*tindalo*). Afterwards they said, " Let us go and take heads." So they embarked on their canoe and paddled away to seek the heads of enemies. When they came to quiet water, they stopped paddling and waited till they felt the canoe rock under them, and when they felt it they said, " That is a ghost." To find out what particular ghost it was they called out the names of several, and when they came to the name of Ganindo, the canoe rocked again. So they knew that it was he who was making the canoe to rock. In like manner they learned what village they were to attack. Returning victorious with the heads of the foe they threw a spear into the roof of Ganindo's house, blew conch-shells, and danced round it, crying, " Our ghost is strong to kill ! " Then they sacrificed fish and other food to him. Also they built him a new house, and made four images of him for the four corners, one of Ganindo himself, two of his sisters, and another. When it was all ready, eight men translated the relics to the new shrine. One of them carried Ganindo's bones, another his betel-nuts, another his lime-box, another his shell-trumpet. They all went into the shrine crouching down, as if burdened by a heavy weight, and singing in chorus, " Hither, hither, let us lift the leg ! " At that the eight legs went up together, and then they sang, " Hither, hither ! " and at that the eight legs went down together. In this solemn procession the relics were brought and laid on a bamboo platform, and sacrifices to the new martial ghost were inaugurated. Other warlike ghosts revered in Florida are known not to have been natives of the island but famous warriors of the western isles, where supernatural power is believed to be stronger.[1]

Offerings to the dead. Throughout the islands of Central Melanesia prayers and offerings are everywhere made to ghosts or spirits or to both. The simplest and commonest sacrificial act is that of throwing a small portion of food to the dead ; this is probably a universal practice in Melanesia. A morsel of

[1] R. H. Codrington, *The Melanesians*, pp. 125 *sqq.*

food ready to be eaten, for example of yam, a leaf of mallow, or a bit of betel-nut, is thrown aside ; and where they drink kava, a libation is made of a few drops, as the share of departed friends or as a memorial of them with which they will be pleased.   At the same time the offerer may call out the name of some one who either died lately or is particularly remembered at the time ; or without the special mention of individuals he may make the offering generally to the ghosts of former members of the community. To set food on a burial-place or before some memorial image is a common practice, though in some places, as in Santa Cruz, the offering is soon taken away and eaten by the living.[1]

In the Solomon Islands the sacrificial ritual is more highly developed.   It may be described in the words of a native of San Cristoval.   " In my country," he wrote, " they think that ghosts are many, very many indeed, some very powerful, and some not.   There is one who is principal in war ; this one is truly mighty and strong.   When our people wish to fight with any other place, the chief men of the village and the sacrificers and the old men, and the elder and younger men, assemble in the place sacred to this ghost ; and his name is Harumae.   When they are thus assembled to sacrifice, the chief sacrificer goes and takes a pig ; and if it be not a barrow pig they would not sacrifice it to that ghost, he would reject it and not eat of it.   The pig is killed (it is strangled), not by the chief sacrificer, but by those whom he chooses to assist, near the sacred place. Then they cut it up ; they take great care of the blood lest it should fall upon the ground ; they bring a bowl and set the pig in it, and when they cut it up the blood runs down into it.   When the cutting up is finished, the chief sacrificer takes a bit of flesh from the pig, and he takes a cocoa-nut shell and dips up some of the blood.   Then he takes the blood and the bit of flesh and enters into the house (the shrine), and calls that ghost and says, ' Harumae ! Chief in war ! we sacrifice to you with this pig, that you may help us to smite that place ; and whatsoever we shall carry away shall be your property, and we also will be yours.'   Then

[1] R. H. Codrington, *The Melanesians*, pp. 127, 128.

he burns the bit of flesh in a fire upon a stone, and pours down the blood upon the fire. Then the fire blazes greatly upwards to the roof, and the house is full of the smell of pig, a sign that the ghost has heard. But when the sacrificer went in he did not go boldly, but with awe; and this is the sign of it; as he goes into the holy house he puts away his bag, and washes his hands thoroughly, to shew that the ghost shall not reject him with disgust." The pig was afterwards eaten. It should be observed that this Harumae who received sacrifices as a martial ghost, mighty in war, had not been dead many years when the foregoing account of the mode of sacrificing to him was written. The elder men remembered him alive, nor was he a great warrior, but a kind and generous man, believed to be plentifully endowed with supernatural power. His shrine was a small house in the village, where relics of him were preserved.[1] Had the Melanesians been left to themselves, it seems possible that this Harumae might have developed into the war-god of San Cristoval, just as in Central Africa another man of flesh and blood is known to have developed into the war-god of Uganda.[2]

[1] R. H. Codrington, *The Melanesians*, pp. 129 *sq.*

[2] Rev. J. Roscoe, "Kibuka, the War God of the Baganda," *Man*, vii. (1907) pp. 161-166; *id., The Baganda* (London, 1911), pp. 301 *sqq.* The history of this African war-god is more or less mythical, but his personal relics, which are now deposited in the Ethnological Museum at Cambridge, suffice to prove his true humanity.

LECTURE XVII

THE BELIEF IN IMMORTALITY AMONG THE NATIVES
OF CENTRAL MELANESIA (*concluded*)

AT the close of last lecture I described the mode in which sacrifices are offered to a martial ghost in San Cristoval, one of the Solomon Islands. We saw that the flesh of a pig is burned in honour of the ghost and that the victim's blood is poured on the flames. Similarly in Florida, another of the Solomon Islands, food is conveyed to worshipful ghosts by being burned in the fire. Some ghosts are known by name to everybody, others may be known only to individuals, who have found out or been taught how to approach them, and who accordingly regard such ghosts as their private property. In every village a public ghost is worshipped, and the chief is the sacrificer. He has learned from his predecessor how to throw or heave the sacrifice, and he imparts this knowledge to his son or nephew, whom he intends to leave as his successor. The place of sacrifice is an enclosure with a little house or shrine in which the relics are kept; it is new or old according as the man whose ghost is worshipped died lately or long ago. When a public sacrifice is performed, the people assemble near but not in the sacred place; boys but not women may be present. The sacrificer alone enters the shrine, but he takes with him his son or other person whom he has instructed in the ritual. Muttering an incantation he kindles a fire of sticks, but may not blow on the holy flame. Then from a basket he takes some prepared food, such as a mash of yams, and throws it on the fire, calling out the name of the ghost and bidding him take his food, while at the same time he prays for whatever is desired. If the fire blazes up and consumes the food, it is a good sign ; it proves that the ghost is present and that he is blowing up the flame. The remainder of the food the sacrificer takes back to the assembled people ; some of it he eats himself and some of it he gives to his assistant to eat. The people receive their portions of the food at his hands and eat it or take it away. While the sacrificing is going on, there is a solemn silence. If a pig is killed, the portion burned in the sacrificial fire is the heart in Florida, but the gullet at Bugotu. One ghost who is commonly known and worshipped is called Manoga. When the sacrificer invokes this ghost, he heaves the sacrifice round about and calls him, first to the east, where rises the sun, saying, " If thou dwellest in the east, where rises the sun, Manoga ! come hither and eat thy *tutu* mash ! " Then turning he lifts it towards where sets the sun, and says, " If thou dwellest in the west, where sets the sun, Manoga ! come hither and eat thy *tutu* ! " There is not a quarter to which he does not lift it up. And when he has finished lifting it he says, " If thou dwellest in heaven above, Manoga ! come hither and eat thy *tutu* ! If thou dwellest in the Pleiades or Orion's belt ; if below in Turivatu ; if in the distant sea ; if on high in the sun, or in the moon ; if thou dwellest inland or by the shore, Manoga ! come hither and eat thy *tutu* ! " [1]

First-fruits of the canarium nuts sacrificed to ghosts. Twice a year there are general sacrifices in which the people of a village take part. One of these occasions is when the canarium nut, so much used in native cookery, is ripe. None of the nuts may be eaten till the first-fruits have been offered to the ghost. " Devil he eat first ; all man he eat behind," is the lucid explanation which a native gave to an English enquirer. The knowledge of the way in which the first-fruits must be offered is handed down from generation to generation, and the man who is learned in this lore has authority to open the season. He observes the state of the crop, and early one morning he is heard to shout. He climbs a tree, picks some nuts, cracks them, eats, and puts some on the stones in his sacred place for the ghost. Then the rest of the people may gather the

[1] R. H. Codrington, *The Melanesians*, pp. 130-132.

nuts for themselves. The chief himself sacrifices the new nuts, mixed with other food, to the public ghost on the stones of the village sanctuary; and every man who has a private ghost of his own does the same in his own sacred place. About two months afterwards there is another public sacrifice when the root crops generally have been dug; pig or fish is then offered; and a man who digs up his yams, or whatever it may be, offers his private sacrifice besides.[1]

In like manner the natives of Tanna, one of the Southern New Hebrides, offered the first-fruits to the deified spirits of their ancestors. On this subject I will quote the evidence of the veteran missionary, the Rev. Dr. George Turner, who lived in Tanna for seven months in 1841. He says: "The general name for gods seemed to be *aremha*; that means a *dead man*, and hints alike at the origin and nature of their religious worship. The spirits of their departed ancestors were among their gods. Chiefs who reach an advanced age were after death deified, addressed by name, and prayed to on various occasions. They were supposed especially to preside over the growth of the yams and the different fruit trees. The first-fruits were presented to them, and in doing this they laid a little of the fruit on some stone, or shelving branch of the tree, or some more temporary altar of a few rough sticks from the bush, lashed together with strips of bark, in the form of a table, with its four feet stuck in the ground. All being quiet, the chief acted as high priest, and prayed aloud thus: 'Compassionate father! here is some food for you; eat it; be kind to us on account of it.' And, instead of an *amen*, all united in a shout. This took place about mid-day, and afterwards those who were assembled continued together feasting and dancing till midnight or three in the morning."[2]

In addition to the public ghosts, each of whom is revered by a whole village, many a man keeps, so to say, a private or

Sacrifice of first-fruits to ancestral spirits in Tanna.

Private ghosts.

[1] R. H. Codrington, *The Melanesians*, pp. 132 *sq.*; C. M. Woodford, *A Naturalist among the Head-hunters* (London, 1890), pp. 26-28.
[2] G. Turner, LL.D., *Samoa a Hundred Years Ago and long before* (London, 1884), pp. 318 *sq.* Yams are the principal fruits cultivated by the Tannese, who bestow a great deal of labour on the plantations and keep them in fine order. See G. Turner, *op. cit.* pp. 317 *sq.*

tame ghost of his own on leash. The art of taming a ghost consists in knowing the leaves, bark, and vines in which he delights and in treating him accordingly. This knowledge a man may acquire by the exercise of his natural faculties or he may learn it from somebody else. However he may obtain the knowledge, he uses it for his own personal advantage, sacrificing to the ghost in order to win his favour and get something from him in return. The mode of sacrificing to a private ghost is the same as to a public ghost. The owner has a sacred place or private chapel of his own, where he draws near to the ghost in prayer and burns his bit of food in the fire. A man often keeps a fighting ghost (*keramo*), who helps him in battle or in slaying his private enemy. Before he goes out to commit homicide, he pulls up his ginger-plant and judges from the ease or difficulty with which the plant yields to or resists his tug, whether he will succeed in the enterprise or not. Then he sacrifices to the ghost, and having placed some ginger and leaves on his shield, and stuffed some more in his belt and right armlet, he sallies forth. He curses his enemy by his fighting ghost, saying, " Siria (if that should be the name of the ghost) eats thee, and I shall slay thee " ; and if he kills him, he cries to the ghost, " Thine is this man, Siria, and do thou give me supernatural power ! " No prudent Melanesian would attempt to commit man-slaughter without a ghost as an accomplice ; to do so would be to court disaster, for the slain man's ghost would have power over the slayer ; therefore before he imbrues his hands in blood he deems it desirable to secure the assistance of a valiant ghost who can, if need be, overcome the ghost of his victim in single combat. If he cannot procure such a useful auxiliary in any other way, he must purchase him. Further, he fortifies himself with some personal relic, such as a tooth or lock of hair of the deceased warrior, whose ghost he has taken into his service ; this relic he wears as an amulet in a little bag round the neck, when he is on active service ; at other times it is kept in the house.[1]

Fighting ghosts kept as auxiliaries.

Garden ghosts.

Different from these truculent spirits are the peaceful

[1] R. H. Codrington, *The Melanesians*, pp. 133 *sq.*

ghosts who cause the garden to bear fruit. If the gardener happens to know such a ghost, he can pray and sacrifice to him on his own account; but if he has no such friend in the spirit world, he must employ an expert. The man of skill goes into the midst of the garden with a little mashed food in his left hand, and smiting it with his right hand he calls on the ghost to come and eat. He says: "This produce thou shalt eat; give supernatural power (*mana*) to this garden, that food may be good and plentiful." He digs holes at the four corners of the garden, and in them he buries such leaves as the ghost loves, so that the garden may have ghostly power and be fruitful. And when the yams sprout, he twines them with the particular creeper and fastens them with the particular wood to which the ghost is known to be partial. These agricultural ghosts are very sensitive; if a man enters the garden, who has just eaten pork or cuscus or fish or shell-fish, the ghost of the garden manifests his displeasure by causing the produce of the garden to droop; but if the eater lets three or four days go by after his meal, he may then enter the garden with impunity, for the food has left his stomach. For a similar reason, apparently, when the yam vines are being trained, the men sleep near the gardens and never approach their wives; for should they tread the garden after conjugal intercourse, the yams would be blighted.[1]

Sometimes the favour of a ghost is obtained by human sacrifices. On these occasions the flesh of the victim does not, like the flesh of a pig, furnish the materials of a sacrificial banquet; but little bits of it are eaten by young men to improve their fighting power and by elders for a special purpose. Such sacrifices are deemed more effectual than the sacrifices of less precious victims; and advantage was sometimes taken of a real or imputed crime to offer the criminal to some ghost. So, for example, within living memory Dikea, chief of Ravu, convicted a certain man of stealing tobacco, and sentenced him to be sacrificed; and the grown lads ate pieces of him cooked in the sacrificial fire. Again, the same chief offered another human sacrifice in the year 1886. One of his wives had proved false, and

Human sacrifices to ghosts.

---

[1] R. H. Codrington, *The Melanesians*, p. 134.

he sent her away vowing that she should not return till he had offered a human sacrifice to Hauri. Also his son died, and he vowed to kill a man for him. The vow was noised abroad, and everybody knew that he would pay well for somebody to kill. Now the Savo people had bought a captive boy in Guadalcanar, but it turned out a bad bargain, for the boy was lame and nearly blind. So they brought him to Dikea, and he gave them twenty coils of shell money for the lad. Then the chief laid his hand on the victim's breast and cried, "Hauri! here is a man for you," and his followers killed him with axes and clubs. The cripple's skull was added to the chief's collection, and his legs were sent about the country to make known what had been done. In Bugotu of Ysabel, when the people had slain an enemy in fight, they used to bring back his head in triumph, cut slices off it, and burn them in sacrifice. And if they took a prisoner alive, they would bring him to the sacred place, the grave of the man whose ghost was to be honoured. There they bound him hand and foot and buffeted him till he died, or if he did not die under the buffets they cut his throat. As they beat the man with their fists, they called on the ghost to take him, and when he was dead, they burned a bit of him in the fire for the ghost.[1]

Sacrifices to ghosts in Saa.

At Saa in Malanta, one of the Solomon Islands, sacrifices are offered to ghosts on various occasions. Thus on his return from a voyage a man will put food in the case which contains the relics of his dead father; and in the course of his voyage, if he should land in a desert isle, he will throw food and call on father, grandfather, and other deceased friends. Again, when sickness is ascribed to the anger of a ghost, a man of skill is sent for to discover what particular ghost is doing the mischief. When he has ascertained the culprit, he is furnished by the patient's relatives with a little pig, which he is to sacrifice to the ghost as a substitute for the sick man. Provided with this vicarious victim he repairs to the haunt of the ghost, strangles the animal, and burns it whole in a fire along with grated yam, coco-nut, and fish. As he does so, he calls out the names of all the

---

[1] R. H. Codrington, op. cit. pp. 135 sq.

ghosts of his family, his ancestors, and all who are deceased, down even to children and women, and he names the man who furnished the pig for the ghostly repast. A portion of the mixed food he preserves unburnt, wraps it in a dracaena leaf, and puts it beside the case which contains the relics of the man to whose ghost the sacrifice has been offered. Sometimes, however, instead of burning a pig in the fire, which is an expensive and wasteful form of sacrifice, the relatives of the sick man content themselves with cooking a pig or a dog in the oven, cutting up the carcase, and laying out all the parts in order. Then the sacrificer comes and sits at the animal's head, and calls out the names of all the dead members of the ghost's family in order downwards, saying, " Help, deliver this man, cut short the line that has bound him." Then the pig is eaten by all present except the women ; nothing is burnt.[1]

The last sort of sacrifices to ghosts at Saa which we need notice is the sacrifice of first-fruits. Thus, when the yams are ripe the people fetch some of them from each garden to offer to the ghosts. All the male members of the family assemble at the holy place which belongs to them. Then one of them enters the shrine, lays a yam beside the skull which lies there, and cries with a loud voice to the ghost, " This is yours to eat." The others call quietly on the names of all the ancestors and give their yams, which are very many in number, because one from each garden is given to each ghost. If any man has besides a relic of the dead, such as a skull, bones, or hair, in his house, he takes home a yam and sets it beside the relic. Again, the first flying-fish of the season are sacrificed to ghosts, who may take the form of sharks ; for we shall see presently that Melanesian ghosts are sometimes supposed to inhabit the bodies of these ferocious monsters. Some ghost-sharks have sacred places ashore, where figures of sharks are set up. In that case the first flying-fish are cooked and set before the shark images. But it may be that a shark ghost has no sacred place on land, and then there is nothing for it but to take the flying-fish out to sea and shred them into the water, while the sacrificer calls

Sacrifices of first-fruits to ghosts in Saa.

[1] R. H. Codrington, *The Melanesians*, pp. 137 *sq.*

out the name of the particular ghost whom he desires to summon to the feast.[1]

Vicarious sacrifices for the sick. Vicarious sacrifices for the sick are offered in San Cristoval to a certain malignant ghost called Tapia, who is believed to seize a man's soul and tie it up to a banyan tree. When that has happened, a man who knows how to manage Tapia intercedes with him. He takes a pig or fish to the sacred place and offers it to the grim ghost, saying, "This is for you to eat in place of that man ; eat this, don't kill him." With that he can loose the captive soul and take it back to the sick man, who thereupon recovers.[2]

Sacrifices to ghosts in Santa Cruz. In Santa Cruz the sacrifices offered to ghosts are very economical; for if the offering is of food, the living eat it up after a decent interval ; if it is a valuable, they remove it and resume the use of it themselves. The principle of this spiritual economy probably lies in the common belief that ghosts, being immaterial, absorb the immaterial essence of the objects, leaving the material substance to be enjoyed by **The dead represented by a stock.** men. When a man of mark dies in Santa Cruz, his relations set up a stock of wood in his house to represent him. This is renewed from time to time, till after a while the man is forgotten or thrown into the shade by the attractions of some newer ghost, so that the old stock is neglected. But when the stock is first put up, a pig is killed and two strips of flesh from the back bone are set before the stock as food for the ghost, but only to be soon taken away and eaten by the living. Similar offerings may be repeated from time to time, as when the stock is renewed. Again, when a garden is planted, they spread feather-money and red native cloth round it for the use of the ghost ; but his enjoyment of these riches is brief and precarious.[3]

Native account of sacrifices to ghosts in Santa Cruz. To supplement the foregoing account of sacrifices to ghosts in Santa Cruz, I will add a description of some of them which was given by a native of Santa Cruz in his own language and translated for us by a missionary. It runs thus : "When anyone begins to fall sick he seeks a doctor (*meduka*), and when the doctor comes near the sick man he

[1] R. H. Codrington, *The Melanesians*, p. 138.
[2] R. H. Codrington, *op. cit.* pp.

138 *sq.*
[3] R. H. Codrington, *op. cit.* p. 139.

stiffens his body, and all those in the house think a ghost has entered into the doctor, and they are all very quiet. Some doctors tell the sick man's relatives to kill a pig for the ghost who has caused the sickness. When they have killed the pig they take it into the ghost-house and invite some other men, and they eat with prayers to the ghost ; and the doctor takes a little piece and puts it near the base of the ghost-post, and says to it : ' This is thy food ; oh, deliver up again the spirit of thy servant, that he may be well again.' The little portion they have offered to the ghost is then eaten ; but small boys may not eat of it." [1] " Every year the people plant yams and tomagos ; and when they begin to work and have made ready the place and begun to plant, first, they offer to the ghost who they think presides over foods. There is an offering place in the bush, and they go there and take much food, and also feather money. Men, women, and children do this, and they think the ghost notices if there are many children, and gives much food at harvest ; and the ghost to whom they offer is named Ilene. When the bread-fruit begins to bear they take great care lest anyone should light a fire near the bole of the tree, or throw a stone at the tree. The ghost, who they think protects the bread-fruit, is called Duka-Kane or Kae Tuabia, who has two names ; they think this ghost has four eyes." [2] " The heathen thinks a ghost makes the sun to shine and the rain. If it is continual sunshine and the yams are withering the people assemble together and contribute money, and string it to the man with whom the rain-ghost abides, and food also, and beseech him not to do the thing he was doing. That man will not wash his face for a long time, he will not work lest he perspire and his body be wet, for he thinks that if his body be wet it will rain. Then this man, with whom the rain-ghost is, takes water and goes into the ghost-house and sprinkles it at the head of the ghost-post (*duka*), and if there are many ghost-posts in the house he pours water over them all that it may rain." [3]

[1] " Native Stories of Santa Cruz and Reef Islands," translated by the Rev. W. O'Ferrall, *Journal of the Anthropological Institute*, xxxiv. (1904) p. 223.

[2] " Native Stories from Santa Cruz and Reef Islands," *op. cit.* p. 224.

[3] " Native Stories from Santa Cruz and Reef Islands," *op. cit.* p. 225.

Combination of magic with religion.

In these ceremonies for the making of rain we see a combination of magic with religion. The appeal to the rain-ghost is religious ; but the pouring of the water on the ghost-post is magical, being an imitation of the result which the officiating priest or magician, whichever we choose to call him, desires to produce. The taboos observed by the owner of the rain-ghost so long as he wishes to prevent the rain from falling are also based on the principle of homoeopathic or imitative magic : he abstains from washing his face or working, lest the water or the sweat trickling down his body should mimick rain and thereby cause it to fall.[1]

Prayers to the dead.

The natives of Aneiteum, one of the Southern New Hebrides, worshipped the spirits of their ancestors, chiefly on occasions of sickness.[2] Again, the people of Vaté or Efat, another of the New Hebrides, worshipped the souls of their forefathers and prayed to them over the *kava*-bowl for health and prosperity.[3] As an example of prayers offered to the dead we may take the petition which the natives of Florida put up at sea to Daula, a well-known ghost, who is associated with the frigate-bird. They say : " Do thou draw the canoe, that it may reach the land ; speed my canoe, grandfather, that I may quickly reach the shore whither I am bound. Do thou, Daula, lighten the canoe, that it may quickly gain the land and rise upon the shore." They also invoke Daula to help them in fishing. " If thou art powerful, O Daula," they say, " put a fish or two into this net and let them die there." After a good catch they praise him, saying, " Powerful is the ghost of the net." And when the natives of Florida are in danger on the sea, they call upon their immediate forefathers ; one will call on his grandfather, another on his father, another on some dead friend, calling with reverence and saying, " Save us on the deep ! Save us from the tempest ! Bring us to the shore ! " In San Cristoval people apply to ghosts for victory in battle, health in sickness, and good crops ; but the word which they use to signify such an application conveys the notion of charm rather than of prayer. However, in the Banks' Islands

---

[1] Compare *The Magic Art and the Evolution of Kings*, i. 269 *sqq.*

[2] G. Turner, *Samoa a Hundred Years Ago and long before* (London, 1884), p. 326.

[3] G. Turner, *op. cit.* p. 334.

what may be called prayer is strictly speaking an invocation
of the dead ; indeed the very word for prayer (*tataro*) seems
to be identical with that for a powerful ghost (*'ataro* in San
Cristoval).   A man in peril on the sea will call on his dead
friends, especially on one who was in his lifetime a good
sailor.   And in Mota, when an oven is opened, they throw
in a leaf of cooked mallow for a ghost, saying to him, " This
is a lucky bit for your eating ; they who have charmed your
food or clubbed you (as the case may be), take hold of their
hands, drag them away to hell, let them be dead."   So
when they pour water on the oven, they pray to the ghost,
saying, " Pour it on the head of him down there who has
laid plots against me, has clubbed me, has shot me, has
stolen things of mine (as the case may be), he shall die."
Again, when they make a libation before drinking, they
pray, saying, " Grandfather ! this is your lucky drop of
kava ; let boars come in to me ; the money I have spent
let it come back to me ; the food that is gone, let it come
back hither to the house of you and me."   And on starting
for a voyage they will say, " Uncle ! father ! plenty of boars
for you, plenty of money ; kava for your drinking, lucky
food for your eating in the canoe.   I pray you with this,
look down upon me, let me go on a safe sea."   Or when
the canoe labours with a heavy freight, they will pray,
" Take off your burden from us, that we may speed on a
safe sea." [1]

In the island of Florida, the sanctuary of a powerful Sanctuaries
ghost is called a *vunuhu*.   Sometimes it is in the village, of ghosts
sometimes in the garden-ground, sometimes in the forest. in Florida.
If it is in the village, it is fenced about, lest the foot of any
rash intruder should infringe its sanctity.   Sometimes the
sanctuary is the place where the dead man is buried ; sometimes it merely contains his relics, which have been translated thither.   In some sanctuaries there is a shrine and in
some an image.   Generally, if not always, stones may be
seen lying in such a holy place.   The sight of one of them
has probably struck the fancy of the man who founded the
worship ; he thought it a likely place for the ghost to
haunt, and other smaller stones and shells have been

[1] R. H. Codrington, *The Melanesians*, pp. 145-148.

subsequently added. Once a sanctuary has been established, everything within it becomes sacred (*tambu*) and belongs to the ghost. Were a tree growing within it to fall across the path, nobody would step over it. When a sacrifice is to be offered to the ghost on the holy ground, the man who knows the ghost, and whose duty it is to perform the sacrifice, enters first and all who attend him follow, treading in his footsteps. In going out no one will look back, lest his soul should stay behind. No one would pass such a sanctuary when the sun was so low as to cast his shadow into it; for if he did the ghost would seize his shadow and so drag the man himself into his den. If there were a shrine in the sanctuary, nobody but the sacrificer might enter it. Such a shrine contained the weapons and other properties which belonged in his lifetime to the man whose ghost was worshipped on the spot.[1]

Sanctuaries of ghosts in Malanta. At Saa in Malanta, another of the Solomon Islands, all burial-grounds where common people are interred are so far sacred that no one will go there without due cause; but places where the remains of nobles repose, and where sacrifices are offered to their ghosts, are regarded with very great respect, they may indeed be called family sanctuaries. Some of them are very old, the powerful ghosts who are worshipped in them being remote ancestors. It sometimes happens that the man who used to sacrifice in such a place dies without having instructed his son in the proper chant of invocation with which the worshipful ghost should be approached. In such a case the young man who succeeds him may fear to go to the old sanctuary, lest he should commit a mistake and offend the ghost; so he will take some ashes from the old sacrificial fire-place and found a new sanctuary. It is not common in that part of Malanta to build shrines for the relics of the dead, but it is sometimes done. Such shrines, on the other hand, are common in the villages of San Cristoval and in the sacred places of that island where great men lie buried. To trespass on them would be likely to rouse the anger of the ghosts, some of whom are known to be of a malignant disposition.[2]

[1] R. H. Codrington, *The Melanesians*, pp. 175 *sq.*

[2] R. H. Codrington, *The Melanesians*, pp. 176 *sq.*

But burial-grounds are not the only sanctuaries in the Sanctuaries which are not burial-grounds. Solomon Islands. There are some where no dead man is known to be interred, though in Dr. Codrington's opinion there are probably none which do not derive their sanctity from the presence of a ghost. In the island of Florida the appearance of something wonderful will cause any place to become a sanctuary, the wonder being accepted as proof of a ghostly presence. For example, in the forest near Olevuga a man planted some coco-nut and almond trees and died not long afterwards. Then there appeared among the trees a great rarity in the shape of a white cuscus. The people took it for granted that the animal was the dead man's ghost, and therefore they called it by his name. The place became a sanctuary ; no one would gather the coco-nuts and almonds that grew there, till two Christian converts set the ghost at defiance and appropriated his garden, with the coco-nuts and almonds. Through the same part of the forest ran a stream full of eels, one of which was so big that the people were quite sure it must be a ghost ; so nobody would bathe in that stream or drink from it, except at one pool, which for the sake of convenience was considered not to be sacred. Again, in Bugotu, a district of Ysabel, which is another of the Solomon Islands, there is a pool known to be the haunt of a very old ghost. When a man has an enemy whom he wishes to harm he will obtain some scraps of his food and throw them into the water. If the food is at once devoured by the fish, which swarm in the pool, the man will die, but otherwise his life may be saved by the intervention of a man who knows the habits of the ghost and how to propitiate him. In these sacred places there are stones, on which people place food in order to obtain good crops, while for success in fishing they deposit morsels of cooked fish. Such stones are treated with reverence and seem to be in a fair way to develop into altars. However, when the old ghost is superseded, as he often is, by younger rivals, the development of an altar out of the stones is arrested.[1]

From some of these instances we learn that Melanesian ghosts can sometimes take up their abode in animals, such

[1] R. H. Codrington, *op. cit.* pp. 177 *sq.*

Ghosts in
animals,
such as
sharks,
alligators,
snakes,
bonitos,
and frigate-
birds.
as cuscuses, eels, and fish. The creatures which are oftenest
used as vehicles by the spirits of the dead are sharks,
alligators, snakes, bonitos, and frigate-birds. Snakes which
haunt a sacred place are themselves sacred, because they
belong to or actually embody the ghost. Sharks, again, in
all these islands are very often thought to be the abode of
ghosts ; for men before their death will announce that they
will appear as sharks, and afterwards any shark remarkable
for size or colour which haunts a certain shore or coast is
taken to be somebody's ghost and receives the name of the
deceased. At Saa certain food, such as coco-nuts from
particular trees, is reserved to feed such a ghost-shark ;
and men of whom it is known for certain that they will
be sharks after their death are allowed to anticipate the
posthumous honours which await them by devouring such
food in the sacred place, just as if they were real sharks.
Sharks are very commonly believed to be the abode of
ghosts in Florida and Ysabel, and in Savo, where they are
particularly numerous ; hence, though all sharks are not
venerated, there is no living creature so commonly held
sacred by the Central Melanesians as a shark ; and shark-
ghosts seem even to form a class of powerful supernatural
beings. Again, when a lizard was seen frequenting a house
after a death, it would be taken for the ghost returning to
its old home ; and many ghosts, powerful to aid the mariner
at sea, take up their quarters in frigate-birds.[1]

The belief
in ghosts
underlies
the Melan-
esian
conception
of magic.
Again, a belief in powerful ghosts underlies to a great
extent the Melanesian conception of magic, as that conception
is expounded by Dr. Codrington. " That invisible power,"
he tells us, " which is believed by the natives to cause all
such effects as transcend their conception of the regular
course of nature, and to reside in spiritual beings, whether
in the spiritual part of living men or in the ghosts of the
dead, being imparted by them to their names and to various
things that belong to them, such as stones, snakes, and
indeed objects of all sorts, is that generally known as *mana*.
Without some understanding of this it is impossible to
understand the religious beliefs and practices of the
Melanesians ; and this again is the active force in all they

[1] R. H. Codrington, *The Melanesians*, pp. 178-180.

do and believe to be done in magic, white or black. By means of this men are able to control or direct the forces of nature, to make rain or sunshine, wind or calm, to cause sickness or remove it, to know what is far off in time and space, to bring good luck and prosperity, or to blast and curse. No man, however, has this power of his own ; all that he does is done by the aid of personal beings, ghosts or spirits." [1]

Thus, to begin with the medical profession, which is a branch of magic long before it becomes a department of science, every serious sickness is believed to be brought about by ghosts or spirits, but generally it is to the ghosts of the dead that illness is ascribed both by the Eastern and by the Western islanders. Hence recourse is had to ghosts for aid both in causing and in curing sickness. They are thought to inflict disease, not only because some offence, such as trespass, has been committed against them, or because one who knows their ways has instigated them thereto by sacrifice and spells, but because there is a certain malignity in the feeling of all ghosts towards the living, who offend them simply by being alive. All human faculties, apart from the mere bodily functions, are supposed to be enhanced by death ; hence the ghost of a powerful and ill-natured man is only too ready to take advantage of his increased powers for mischief.[2] Thus in the island of Florida illness is regularly laid at the door of a ghost ; the only question that can arise is which particular ghost is doing the mischief. Sometimes the patient imagines that he has offended his dead father, uncle, or brother, who accordingly takes his revenge by stretching him on a bed of sickness. In that case no special intercessor is required ; the patient himself or one of his kinsfolk will sacrifice and beg the ghost to take the sickness away ; it is purely a family affair. Sometimes the sick man thinks that it is his own private or tame ghost who is afflicting him ; so he will leave the house in order to escape his tormentor. But if the cause of sickness remains obscure, a professional doctor or medicine-man will be consulted. He always knows, or at least can ascertain, the ghost who is causing all the trouble, and he

Illness generally thought to be caused by ghosts.

[1] R. H. Codrington, *op. cit.* p. 191.   [2] R. H. Codrington, *op. cit.* p. 194.

takes his measures accordingly. Thus he will bind on the sick man the kind of leaves that the ghost loves; he will chew ginger and blow it into the patient's ears and on that part of the skull which is soft in infants; he will call on the name of the ghost and entreat him to remove the sickness. Should all these remedies prove vain, the doctor is by no means at the end of his resources. He may shrewdly suspect that somebody, who has an ill-will at the patient, has set his private ghost to maul the sick man and do him a grievous bodily injury. If his suspicions are confirmed and he discovers the malicious man who is egging on the mischievous ghost, he will bribe him to call off his ghost; and if the man refuses, the doctor will hire another ghost to assault and batter the original assailant. At Wango in San Cristoval regular battles used to be fought by the invisible champions above the sickbed of the sufferer, whose life or death depended on the issue of the combat. Their weapons were spears, and sometimes more than one ghost would be engaged on either side.[1]

Diagnosis of ghosts who have caused illness.

In Ysabel the doctor employs an ingenious apparatus for discovering the cause of sickness and ascertaining its cure. He suspends a stone at one end of a string while he holds the other end in his hand. Then he recites the names of all the people who died lately, and when the stone swings at anybody's name, he knows that the ghost of that man has caused the illness. It remains to find out what the ghost will take to relax his clutch on the sick man, it may be a mash of yams, a fish, a pig, or perhaps a human substitute. The question is put and answered as before; and whatever the oracle declares to be requisite is offered on the dead man's grave. Thus the ghost is appeased and the sufferer is made whole.[2] In these islands a common cause of illness is believed to be an unwarrantable intrusion on premises occupied by a ghost, who punishes the trespasser by afflicting him with bodily pains and ailments, or it may be by carrying off his soul. At Maewo in Aurora, one of the New Hebrides, when there is reason to think that a sickness is due to ghostly agency, the friends of the sick man send

[1] R. H. Codrington, *The Melanesians*, pp. 194-196.
[2] R. H. Codrington, *op. cit.* p. 196.

for a professional dreamer, whose business it is to ascertain
what particular ghost has been offended and to make it up
with him.   So the dreamer falls asleep and in his sleep he
dreams a dream.   He seems to himself to be in the place
where the patient was working before his illness ; and there
he spies a queer little old man, who is really no other than
the ghost.   The dreamer falls into conversation with him,
learns his name, and winning his confidence extracts from
him a true account of the whole affair.   The fact is that in
working at his garden the man encroached, whether wittingly
or not is no matter, on land which the ghost regards as his
private preserve ; and to punish the intrusion the ghost
carried off the intruder's soul and impounded it in a magic
fence in his garden, where it still languishes in durance vile.
The dreamer at once tenders a frank and manly apology on
behalf of his client ; he assures the ghost that the trespass
was purely inadvertent, that no personal disrespect whatever
was intended, and he concludes by requesting the ghost to
overlook the offence for this time and to release the imprisoned soul.   This appeal to the better feelings of the
ghost has its effect ; he pulls up the fence and lets the soul
out of the pound ; it flies back to the sick man, who thereupon recovers.   Sometimes an orphan child is made sick by
its dead mother, whose ghost draws away the soul of the
infant to keep her company in the spirit land.   In such a
case, again, a dreamer is employed to bring back the lost
soul from the far country ; and if he can persuade the
mother's ghost to relinquish the tiny soul of her baby, the
child will be made whole.[1]   Once more certain long stones
in the Banks' Islands are inhabited by ghosts so active and
robust that if a man's shadow so much as falls on one of
them, the ghost in the stone will clutch the shadow and pull
the soul clean out of the man, who dies accordingly.   Such
stones, dangerous as they unquestionably are to the chance
passer-by, nevertheless for that very reason possess a valuable
property which can be turned to excellent account.   A man,
for example, will put one of these stones in his house to

[1] R. H. Codrington, *The Melanesians*, pp. 208 *sq.*   As to sickness supposed to be caused by trespass on the premises of a ghost see further *id.*, pp. 194, 195, 218.

guard it like a watch-dog in his absence ; and if he sends a friend to fetch something out of it which he has forgotten, the messenger, on approaching the house, will take good care to call out the owner's name, lest the ghost in the stone, mistaking him for a thief and a robber, should pounce out on him and do him a mischief before he had . time to explain.[1]

Contrast between Melanesian and European medicine.

Thus it appears that for a medical practitioner in Melanesia the first requisite is an intimate acquaintance, not with the anatomy of the human frame and the properties of drugs, but with ghosts, their personal peculiarities, habits, and haunts.   Only by means of the influence which such a knowledge enables him to exert on these powerful and dangerous beings can the good physician mitigate and assuage the sufferings of poor humanity.   His professional skill, while it certainly aims at the alleviation of physical evils, attains its object chiefly, if not exclusively, by a direct appeal to those higher, though invisible, powers which encompass the life of man, or at all events of the Melanesian. The firm faith in the spiritual and the unseen which these sable doctors display in their treatment of the sick presents a striking contrast to the procedure of their European colleagues, who trust exclusively to the use of mere physical remedies, such as drugs and lancets, now carving the body of the sufferer with knives, and now inserting substances, about which they know little, into places about which they know nothing.   Has not science falsely so called still much to learn from savagery ?

The weather believed to be regulated by ghosts and spirits.

But it is not the departments of medicine and surgery alone, important as these are to human welfare, which in Melanesia are directed and controlled by spiritual forces.   The weather in those regions is also regulated by ghosts and spirits.   It is they who cause the wind to blow or to be still, the sun to shine forth or to be overcast with clouds, the rain to descend or the earth to be parched with drought ; hence fertility and abundance or dearth and famine prevail alternately at the will of these spiritual directors.   From this it follows that men who stand on a footing of intimacy with ghosts and spirits can by judicious

[1] R. H. Codrington, *The Melanesians*, p. 184.

management induce them to adapt the weather to the varying needs of mankind.   But it is to be observed that the
supernatural beings, who are the real sources of atmospheric
phenomena, have delegated or deputed a portion of their
powers not merely to certain material objects, such as stones
or leaves, but to certain set forms of words, which men call
incantations or spells ; and accordingly all such objects and
formulas do, by virtue of this delegation, possess in themselves a real and we may almost say natural influence over
the weather, which is often manifested in a striking congruity
or harmony between the things themselves and the effects
which they are calculated to produce.   This adaptation of
means to end in nature may perhaps be regarded as a
beautiful proof of the existence of spirits and ghosts working
their purposes unseen behind the gaily coloured screen or
curtain of the physical universe.   At all events men who are   Weather-
acquainted with the ghostly properties of material objects and   doctors.
words can turn them to account for the benefit of their friends
and the confusion of their foes, and they do so very readily if
only it is made worth their while.   Hence it comes about that
in these islands there are everywhere weather-doctors or
weather-mongers, who through their familiarity with ghosts
and spirits and their acquaintance with the ghostly or
spiritual properties of things, are able to control the weather
and to supply their customers with wind or calm, rain or
sunshine, famine or abundance, at a reasonable rate and a
moderate figure.[1]   The advantages of such a system over our
own blundering method of managing the weather, or rather
of leaving it to its own devices, are too obvious to be insisted
on.   To take a few examples.   In the island of Florida,
when a calm is wanted, the weather-doctor takes a bunch of
leaves, of the sort which the ghost loves, and hides the bunch
in the hollow of a tree where there is water, at the same
time invoking the ghost with the proper charm.   This
naturally produces rain and with the rain a calm.   In the
seafaring life of the Solomon Islanders the maker of calms is
a really valuable citizen.[2]   The Santa Cruz people are also

---

[1] R. H. Codrington, *The Melan-*
esians, p. 200.

[2] R. H. Codrington, *The Melan-*

esians, pp. 200, 201.   The spirit whom
the Florida wizard appeals to for good
or bad weather is called a *vigona* ; and

great voyagers, and their wizards control the weather on their
expeditions, taking with them the stock or log which represents
their private or tame ghost and setting it up on a stage in
the cabin.   The presence of the familiar ghost being thus
secured, the weather-doctor will undertake to provide wind
or calm according to circumstances.[1]   We have already seen
how in these islands the wizard makes rain by pouring water
on the wooden posts which represent the rain-ghosts.[2]

Black
magic
working
through
personal
refuse or
rubbish of
the victim.

Such exercises of ghostly power for the healing of the sick
and the improvement of the weather are, when well directed
and efficacious, wholly beneficial.   But ghostly power is a two-
edged weapon which can work evil as well as good to mankind.   In fact it can serve the purpose of witchcraft.   The
commonest application of this pernicious art is one which is
very familiar to witches and sorcerers in many parts of the
world.   The first thing the wizard does is to obtain a fragment of food, a bit of hair, a nail-clipping, or indeed anything
that has been closely connected with the person of his
intended victim.   This is the medium through which the
power of the ghost or spirit is brought to bear; it is, so to
say, the point of support on which the magician rests the
whole weight of his infernal engine.   In order to give effect
to the charm it is very desirable, if not absolutely necessary,
to possess some personal relic, such as a bone, of the dead
man whose ghost is to set the machinery in motion.   At all
events the essential thing is to bring together the man who
is to be injured and the ghost or spirit who is to injure him;
and this can be done most readily by placing the personal
relics or refuse of the two men, the living and the dead, in
contact with each other; for thus the magic circuit, if we
may say so, is complete, and the fatal current flows from the
dead to the living.   That is why it is most dangerous to
leave any personal refuse or rubbish lying about; you never
can tell but that some sorcerer may get hold of it and work
your ruin by means of it.   Hence the people are naturally most
careful to hide or destroy all such refuse in order to prevent it

the natives believe it to be always the
ghost of a dead man. But it seems very
doubtful whether this opinion is strictly
correct.   See R. H. Codrington, *op.
cit.* pp. 124, 134.

[1] R. H. Codrington, *op. cit.* p. 201.
The Santa Cruz name for such a ghost
is *duka* (*ibid.* p. 139).

[2] Above, p. 375.

from falling into the hands of witches and wizards ; and this
sage precaution has led to habits of cleanliness which the
superficial European is apt to mistake for what he calls enlightened sanitation, but which a deeper knowledge of native
thought would reveal to him in their true character as far-
seeing measures designed to defeat the nefarious art of the
sorcerer.[1]

Unfortunately, however, an adept in the black art can
work his fell purpose even without any personal relic of his
victim.   In the Banks' Islands, for example, he need only
procure a bit of human bone or a fragment of some lethal
weapon, it may be a splinter of a club or a chip of an arrow,
which has killed somebody.   This he wraps up in the proper
leaves, recites over it the appropriate charm, and plants it
secretly in the path along which his intended victim is expected to pass.   The ghost of the man who owned the bone
in his life or perished by the club or the arrow, is now lurking
like a lion in the path ; and if the poor fellow strolls along it
thinking no evil, the ghost will spring at him and strike him
with disease.   The charm is perfectly efficient if the man
does come along the path, but clearly it misses fire if he does
not.   To remedy this defect in the apparatus a sorcerer sometimes has recourse to a portable instrument, a sort of pocket
pistol, which in the Banks' Islands is known as a ghost-
shooter.   It is a bamboo tube, loaded not with powder and
shot, but with a dead man's bone and other magical in-
gredients, over which the necessary spell has been crooned.
Armed with this deadly weapon the sorcerer has only to step
up to his unsuspecting enemy, whip out the pocket pistol,
uncork the muzzle by removing his thumb from the orifice,
and present it at the victim ; the fatal discharge follows in
an instant and the man drops to the ground.   The ghost in
the pistol has done his work.   Sometimes, however, an
accident happens.   The marksman misses his victim and
hits somebody else.   This occurred, for example, not very
many years ago in the island of Mota.   A man named
Isvitag was waiting with his ghost-shooter to pop at his
enemy, but in his nervous excitement he let fly too soon,
just as a woman with a child on her hip stepped across the

Black magic working without any personal relic of the victim.

The ghost-shooter.

[1] R. H. Codrington, *The Melanesians*, pp. 202-204.

path. The shot, or rather the ghost, hit the child point-blank, and it was his sister's child, his own next of kin ! You may imagine the distress of the affectionate uncle at this deplorable miscarriage. To prevent inflammation of the wound he, with great presence of mind, plunged his pocket pistol in water, and this timely remedy proved so efficacious that the child took no hurt.[1]

Prophecy inspired by ghosts.

Another department of Melanesian life in which ghosts figure very prominently is prophecy. The knowledge of future events is believed to be conveyed to the people by a ghost or spirit speaking with the voice of a man, who is himself unconscious while he speaks. The predictions which emanate from the prophet under these circumstances are in the strictest sense inspired. His human personality is for the time being in abeyance, and he is merely the mouthpiece of the powerful spirit which has temporarily taken possession of his body and speaks with his voice. The possession is indeed painfully manifest. His eyes glare, foam bursts from his mouth, his limbs writhe, his whole body is convulsed. These are the workings of the mighty spirit shaking and threatening to rend the frail tabernacle of flesh. This form of inspiration is not clearly distinguishable from what we call madness ; indeed the natives do not attempt to distinguish between the two things ; they regard the madman and the prophet as both alike inspired by a ghost or spirit, and a man will sometimes pretend to be mad in order that he may get the reputation of being a prophet. At Saa a man will speak with the voice of a powerful man deceased, while he twists and writhes under the influence of the ghost ; he calls himself by the name of the deceased who speaks through him, and he is so addressed by others ; he will eat fire, lift enormous weights, and foretells things to come. When the inspiration, or insanity, is particularly violent, and the Banks' Islanders think they have had quite enough of it, the friends of the prophet or of the madman will sometimes catch him and hold him struggling and roaring in the smoke of strong-smelling leaves, while they call out the names of the dead men whose ghosts

[1] R. H. Codrington, *The Melanesians*, pp. 205 *sq.*

are most likely to be abroad at the time, for as soon as
the right name is mentioned the ghost departs from the
man, who then returns to his sober senses. But this
method of smoking out a ghost is not always successful.[1]

There are many methods by which ghosts and spirits
are believed to make known to men who employ them
the secret things which the unassisted human intelligence
could not discover ; and some of them hardly perhaps
need the intervention of a professional wizard.   These
methods of divination differ very little in the various
islands.   In the Solomon Islands, for instance, when an
expedition has started in a fleet of canoes, there is sometimes a hesitation whether they shall proceed, or a doubt
as to what direction they should take.   Thereupon a
diviner may declare that he has felt a ghost step on
board ; for did not the canoe tip over to the one side ?
Accordingly he asks the invisible passenger, " Shall we go
on ?   Shall we go to such and such a place ? "   If the
canoe rocks, the answer is yes ; if it lies on an even
keel, the answer is no.   Again, when a man is sick and
his friends wish to know what ghost is vexing or, as they
say, eating him, a diviner or wizard is sent for.   He comes
bringing an assistant, and the two sit down, the wizard
in front and the assistant at his back, and they hold a
stick or bamboo by the two ends.   The wizard then begins
to slap the end of the bamboo he holds, calling out one
after another the names of men not very long deceased, and
when he names the one who is afflicting the sick man the
stick of itself becomes violently agitated.[2]   We are not
informed, but we may probably assume, that it is the ghost
and not the man who really agitates the stick.   A somewhat different mode of divination was occasionally employed
at Motlav in the Banks' Islands in order to discover a thief
or other criminal.   After a burial they would take a bag,
put some Tahitian chestnut and scraped banana into it, and
tie it to the end of a hollow bamboo tube about ten feet long
in such a way that the end of the tube was inserted in the
mouth of the bag.   Then the bag was laid on the dead

Divination by means of ghosts.

[1] R. H. Codrington, *The Melan-esians*, pp. 209 *sq.*, 218-220.   [2] R. H. Codrington, *The Melan-esians*, p. 210.

man's grave, and the diviners grasped the other end of the bamboo.   The names of the recently dead were then called over, and while this was being done the men felt the bamboo grow heavy in their hands, for a ghost was scrambling up from the bag into the hollow of the bamboo.   Having thus secured him they carried the imprisoned ghost in the bamboo into the village, where the roll of the recent dead was again called over in order to learn whose ghost had been caught in the trap.   When wrong names were mentioned, the free end of the bamboo moved from side to side, but at the mention of the right name it revolved briskly.   Having thus ascertained whom they had to deal with, they questioned the entrapped ghost, "Who stole so and so?   Who was guilty in such a case?"   Thereupon the bamboo, moved no doubt by the ghost inside, pointed at the culprit, if he was present, or made signs as before when the names of the suspected evildoers were mentioned.[1]

Taboo based on a fear of ghosts.

Of the many departments of Central Melanesian life which are permeated by a belief in ghostly power the last which I shall mention is the institution of taboo.   In Melanesia, indeed, the institution is not so conspicuous as it used to be in Polynesia;   yet even there it has been a powerful instrument in the consolidation of the rights of private property, and as such it deserves the attention of historians who seek to trace the evolution of law and morality.   As understood in the Banks' Islands and the New Hebrides the word taboo (*tambu* or *tapu*) signifies a sacred and unapproachable character which is imposed on certain things by the arbitrary will of a chief or other powerful man.   Somebody whose authority with the people gives him confidence to make the announcement will declare that such and such an object may not be touched, that such and such a place may not be approached, and that such and such an action may not be performed under a certain penalty, which in the last resort will be inflicted by ghostly or spiritual agency.   The object, place, or action in question becomes accordingly taboo or sacred.   Hence in these islands taboo may be defined as a prohibition with a curse expressed or implied.   The sanction or power at the back

[1] R. H. Codrington, *The Melanesians*, pp. 211 *sq.*

of the taboo is not that of the man who imposes it ; rather
it is that of the ghost or spirit in whose name or in reliance
upon whom the taboo is imposed.   Thus in Florida a chief
will forbid something to be done or touched under a penalty;
he may proclaim, for example, that any one who violates
his prohibition must pay him a hundred strings of shell
money.   To a European such a proclamation seems a proof
of the chief's power ; but to the native the chief's power, in
this and in everything, rests on the persuasion that the chief
has his mighty ghost at his back.   The sense of this in the
particular case is indeed remote, the fear of the chief's anger
is present and effective, but the ultimate sanction is the
power of the ghost.   If a common man were to take upon
himself to taboo anything he might do so ; people would
imagine that he would not dare to make such an announcement unless he knew he could enforce it ; so they would
watch, and if anybody violated the taboo and fell sick afterwards, they would conclude that the taboo was supported by
a powerful ghost who punished infractions of it.   Hence the
reputation and authority of the man who imposed the taboo
would rise accordingly ; for it would be seen that he had a
powerful ghost at his back.   Every ghost has a particular
kind of leaf for his badge ; and in imposing his taboo a man
will set the leaf of his private ghost as a mark to warn tres-
passers of the spiritual power with which they have to
reckon ; when people see a leaf stuck, it may be, on a tree, a
house, or a canoe, they do not always know whose it is ; but
they do know that if they disregard the mark they have to
deal with a ghost and not with a man,[1] and the knowledge is
a more effectual check on thieving and other crimes than the
dread of mere human justice.   Many a rascal fears a ghost
who does not fear the face of man.

The life of the Central Melanesians deeply influenced by their belief in the survival of the human soul after death.

What I have said may suffice to impress you with a
sense of the deep practical influence which a belief in the
survival of the human soul after death exercises on the life
and conduct of the Central Melanesian savage.   To him the
belief is no mere abstract theological dogma or speculative
tenet, the occasional theme of edifying homilies and pious
meditation ; it is an inbred, unquestioning, omnipresent

---

[1] R. H. Codrington, *The Melanesians*, pp. 215 *sq.*

conviction which affects his thoughts and actions daily and at every turn ; it guides his fortunes as an individual and controls his behaviour as a member of a community, by inculcating a respect for the rights of others and enforcing a submission to the public authorities.   With him the fear of ghosts and spirits is a bulwark of morality and a bond of society ; for he firmly believes in their unseen presence everywhere and in the punishments which they can inflict on wrongdoers.   His whole theory of causation differs fundamentally from ours and necessarily begets a fundamental difference of practice.   Where we see natural forces and material substances, the Melanesian sees ghosts and spirits.   A great gulf divides his conception of the world from ours ; and it may be doubted whether education will ever enable him to pass the gulf and to think and act like us.   The products of an evolution which has extended over many ages cannot be forced like mushrooms in a summer day ; it is vain to pluck the fruit of the tree of knowledge before it is ripe.

LECTURE XVIII

THE BELIEF IN IMMORTALITY AMONG THE NATIVES
OF NORTHERN AND EASTERN MELANESIA

IN the last lecture I concluded my account of the belief in immortality and the worship of the dead among the natives of Central Melanesia. To-day we pass to what may be called Northern Melanesia, by which is to be understood the great archipelago lying to the north-east of New Guinea. It comprises the two large islands of New Britain and New Ireland, now called New Pomerania and New Mecklenburg, with the much smaller Duke of York Island lying between them, and the chain of New Hanover and the Admiralty Islands stretching away westward from the north-western extremity of New Ireland. The whole of the archipelago, together with the adjoining island of Bougainville in the Solomon Islands, is now under German rule. The people belong to the same stock and speak the same language as the natives of Central and Southern Melanesia, and their level of culture is approximately the same. They live in settled villages and subsist chiefly by the cultivation of the ground, raising crops of taro, yams, bananas, sugar-cane, and so forth. Most of the agricultural labour is performed by the women, who plant, weed the ground, and carry the produce to the villages. The ground is, or rather used to be, dug by sharp-pointed sticks. The men hunt cassowaries, wallabies, and wild pigs, and they catch fish by both nets and traps. Women and children take part in the fishing and many of them become very expert in spearing fish. Among the few domestic animals which they keep are pigs, dogs, and fowls. The villages are generally situated in

(margin notes) Northern Melanesia.

Material culture of the North Melanesians.

393

4

the midst of a dense forest ; but on the coast the natives build their houses not far from the beach as a precaution against the attacks of the forest tribes, of whom they stand greatly in fear. A New Britain village generally consists of a number of small communities or families, each of which dwells in a separate enclosure. The houses are very small and badly built, oblong in shape and very low. Between the separate hamlets which together compose a village lie stretches of virgin forest, through which run irregular and often muddy foot-tracks, scooped out here and there into mud-holes where the pigs love to wallow during the heat of the tropical day. As the people of any one district used generally to be at war with their neighbours, it was necessary that they should live together for the sake of mutual protection.[1]

Commercial habits of the North Melanesians.

Nevertheless, in spite of their limited intercourse with surrounding villages, the natives of the New Britain or the Bismarck Archipelago were essentially a trading people. They made extensive use of shell money and fully recognised the value of any imported articles as mediums of exchange or currency. Markets were held on certain days at fixed places, where the forest people brought their yams, taro, bananas and so forth and exchanged them for fish, tobacco, and other articles with the natives of the coast. They also went on long trading expeditions to procure canoes, cuscus teeth, pigs, slaves, and so forth, which on their return they generally sold at a considerable profit. The shell which they used as money is the *Nassa immersa* or *Nassa calosa*, found on the north coast of New Britain. The shells were perforated and threaded on strips of cane, which were then joined together in coils of fifty to two hundred fathoms.[2] The rights of private property were fully recognised. All lands belonged to certain families, and husband and wife had each the exclusive right to his or her goods and chattels. But while in certain directions the people had made some progress, in others they remained

Their backwardness in other respects.

[1] G. Brown, D.D., *Melanesians and Polynesians* (London, 1910), pp. 23 sq., 125, 320 sqq.
[2] G. Brown, *op. cit.* pp. 294 sqq. ; P. A. Kleintitschen, *Die Küstenbe-* wohner *der Gazellehalbinsel* (Hiltrup bei Münster, N.D.), pp. 90 sqq. The shell money is called *tambu* in New Britain, *diwara* in the Duke of York Island, and *aringit* in New Ireland.

very backward.   Pottery and the metals were unknown ; no metal or specimen of metal-work has been found in the archipelago ; on the other hand the natives made much use of stone implements, especially adzes and clubs.   In war they never used bows and arrows.[1]   They had no system of government, unless that name may be given to the power wielded by the secret societies and by chiefs, who exercised a certain degree of influence principally by reason of the reputation which they enjoyed as sorcerers and magicians. They were not elected nor did they necessarily inherit their office ; they simply claimed to possess magical powers, and if they succeeded in convincing the people of the justice of their claim, their authority was recognised.   Wealth also contributed to establish their position in the esteem of the public.[2]

With regard to the religious ideas and customs of the natives we are not fully informed, but so far as these have been described they appear to agree closely with those of their kinsfolk in Central Melanesia.   The first European to settle in the archipelago was the veteran missionary, the Rev. George Brown, D.D., who resided in the islands from 1875 to 1880 and has revisited them on several occasions since ; he reduced the language to writing for the first time,[3] and is one of our best authorities on the people.   In what follows I shall make use of his valuable testimony along with that of more recent observers.

The natives of the archipelago believe that every person is animated by a soul, which survives his death and may afterwards influence the survivors for good or evil.   Their word for soul is *nio* or *niono*, meaning a shadow.   The root is *nio*, which by the addition of personal suffixes becomes *niong* " my soul or shadow," *niom* " your soul or shadow," *niono* " his soul or shadow."   They think that the soul is like the man himself, and that it always stays inside of his body, except when it goes out on a ramble during sleep or a faint. A man who is very sleepy may say, " My soul wants to go away."   They believe, however, that it departs for ever at

The Rev. George Brown on the Melanesians.

North Melanesian theory of the soul.

---

[1] Rev. G. Brown, *op. cit.* pp. 307, 313, 435, 436.
[2] Rev. G. Brown, *op. cit.* pp. 270

sq., compare pp. 127, 200.
[3] Rev. G. Brown, *op. cit.* pp. v., 18.

death; hence when a man is sick, his friends will offer prayers to prevent its departure. There is only one kind of soul, but it can appear in many shapes and enter into animals, such as rats, lizards, birds, and so on. It can hear, see, and speak, and present itself in the form of a wraith or apparition to people at the moment of or soon after death. On being asked why he thought that the soul does not perish with the body, a native said, "Because it is different; it is not of the same nature at all." They believe that the souls of the dead occasionally visit the living and are seen by them, and that

Fear of ghosts, especially the ghosts of persons who have been killed and eaten.

they haunt houses and burial-places. They are very much afraid of the ghosts and do all they can to drive or frighten them away. Above all, being cannibals, they stand in great fear of the ghosts of the people whom they have killed and eaten. The man who is cutting up a human body takes care to tie a bandage over his mouth and nose during the operation of carving in order to prevent the enraged soul of the victim from entering into his body by these apertures; and for a similar reason the doors of the houses are shut while the cannibal feast is going on inside. And to keep the victim's ghost quiet while his body is being devoured, a cut from a joint is very considerately placed on a tree outside of the house, so that he may eat of his own flesh and be satisfied. At the conclusion of the banquet, the people shout, brandish spears, beat the bushes, blow horns, beat drums, and make all kinds of noises for the purpose of chasing the ghost or ghosts of the murdered and eaten men away from the village. But while they send away the souls, they keep the skulls and jawbones of the victims; as many as thirty-five jawbones have been seen hanging in a single house in New Ireland. As for the skulls, they are, or rather were placed on the branch of a dead tree and so preserved on the beach or near the house of the man who had taken them.[1]

Offerings to the souls of the dead.

With regard to the death of their friends they deem it very important to obtain the bodies and bury them. They offer food to the souls of their departed kinsfolk for a long time after death, until all the funeral feasts are over; but they do not hold annual festivals in honour of dead ancestors. The food offered to the dead is laid every day

[1] G. Brown, *op. cit.* pp. 141 *sq.*, 144, 145, 190-193.

on a small platform in a tree ; but the natives draw a distinction between offerings to the soul of a man who died a
natural death and offerings to the soul of a man who was
killed in a fight ; for whereas they place the former on a
living tree, they deposit the latter on a dead tree. Moreover,
they lay money, weapons, and property, often indeed the
whole wealth of the family, near the corpse of their friend,
in order that the soul of the deceased may carry off the
souls of these valuables to the spirit land. But when the
body is carried away to be buried, most of the property is
removed by its owners for their own use. However, the
relations will sometimes detach a few shells from the coils of
shell money and a few beads from a necklace and drop them
in a fire for the behoof of the ghost. But when the deceased
was a chief or other person of importance, some of his
property would be buried with him. And before burial his
body would be propped up on a special chair in front of his
house, adorned with necklaces, wreaths of flowers and feathers,
and gaudy with war-paint. In one hand would be placed a
large cooked yam, and in the other a spear, while a club
would be put on his shoulder. The yam was to stay the
pangs of hunger on his long journey, and the weapons were
to enable him to fight the foes who might resist his entrance
into the spirit land. In the Duke of York Island the corpse
was usually disposed of by being sunk in a deep part of the
lagoon ; but sometimes it was buried in the house and a fire
kept burning on the spot.[1]

In New Ireland the dead were rolled up in winding-
sheets made of pandanus leaves, then weighted with stones
and buried at sea. However, at some places they were
deposited in deep underground watercourses or caverns.
Towards the northern end of New Ireland corpses were
burned on large piles of firewood in an open space of the
village. A number of images curiously carved out of wood
or chalk were set round the blazing pyre, but the meaning of
these strange figures is uncertain. Men and women uttered
the most piteous wailings, threw themselves on the top of the
corpse, and pulled at the arms and legs. This they did not
merely to express their grief, but because they thought that

Burial customs in New Ireland and New Britain.

[1] G. Brown, *op. cit.* pp. 142, 192, 385, 386 *sq.*

if they saw and handled the dead body while it was burning, the ghost could not or would not haunt them afterwards.[1] Amongst the natives of the Gazelle Peninsula in New Britain the dead are generally buried in shallow graves in or near their houses. Some of the shell money which belonged to a man in life is buried with him. Women with blackened bodies sleep on the grave for weeks.[2] When the deceased was a great chief, his corpse, almost covered with shell money, is placed in a canoe, which is deposited in a small house. Thereupon the nearest female relations are led into the house, and the door being walled up they are obliged to remain there with the rotting body until all the flesh has mouldered away. Food is passed in to them through a hole in the wall, and under no pretext are they allowed to leave the hut before the decomposition of the corpse is complete. When nothing of the late chief remains but a skeleton, the hut is opened

Preservation of the skull.

and the solemn funeral takes place. The bones of the dead are buried, but his skull is hung up in the taboo house in order, we are told, that his ghost may remain in the neighbourhood of the village and see how his memory is honoured. After the burial of the headless skeleton feasting and dancing go on, often for more than a month, and the expenses are defrayed out of the riches left by the deceased.[3] Even in the case of eminent persons who have been buried whole and entire in the usual way, a special mark of respect is sometimes paid to their memory by digging up their skulls after a year or more, painting them red and white, decorating them with feathers, and setting them up on a scaffold constructed for the purpose.[4]

Somewhat similar is the disposal of the dead among the Sulka, a tribe of New Britain who inhabit a mountainous and

---

[1] G. Brown, *op. cit.* p. 390. The custom of cremating the dead in New Ireland is described more fully by Mr. R. Parkinson, who says that the life-sized figures which are burned with the corpse represent the deceased (*Dreissig Jahre in der Südsee*, pp. 273 *sqq.*). In the central part of New Ireland the dead are buried in the earth; afterwards the bones are dug up and thrown into the sea. See Albert Hahl, "Das mittlere Neumecklenburg," *Globus*, xci.

(1907) p. 314.

[2] R. Parkinson, *Dreissig Jahre in der Südsee* (Stuttgart, 1907) p. 78; P. A. Kleintitschen, *Die Küstenbewohner der Gazellehalbinsel* (Hiltrup bei Münster, N.D.), p. 222.

[3] Mgr. Couppé, "En Nouvelle-Poméranie," *Les Missions Catholiques*, xxiii. (1891) pp. 364 *sq.*; J. Graf Pfeil, *Studien und Beobachtungen aus der Südsee* (Brunswick, 1899), p. 79.

[4] R. Parkinson, *op. cit.* p. 81.

well-watered country to the south of the Gazelle Peninsula.
When a Sulka dies, his plantation is laid waste, and the
young fruit-trees cut down, but the ripe fruits are first
distributed among the living.   His pigs are slaughtered and
their flesh in like manner distributed, and his weapons are
broken.   If the deceased was a rich man, his wife or wives
will sometimes be killed.   The corpse is usually buried next
morning.   A hole is dug in the house and the body deposited
in it in a sitting posture.   The upper part of the corpse
projects from the grave and is covered with a tower-like
structure of basket-work, which is stuffed with banana-leaves.
Great care is taken to preserve the body from touching the
earth.   Stones are laid round about the structure and a fire
kindled.   Relations come and sleep for a time beside the
corpse, men and women separately.   Some while afterwards
the soul of the deceased is driven away.   The time for
carrying out the expulsion is settled by the people in whispers,
lest the ghost should overhear them and prepare for a stout
resistance.   The evening before the ceremony takes place
many coco-nut leaves are collected.   Next morning, as soon
as a certain bird (*Philemon coquerelli*) is heard to sing, the
people rise from their beds and set up a great cry.   Then
they beat the walls, shake the posts, set fire to dry coco-nut
leaves, and finally rush out into the paths.   At that moment,
so the people think, the soul of the dead quits the hut.
When the flesh of the corpse is quite decayed, the bones are
taken from the grave, sewed in leaves, and hung up.   Soon
afterwards a funeral feast is held, at which men and women
dance.   For some time after a burial taro is planted beside
the house of death and enclosed with a fence.   The Sulka
think that the ghost comes and gathers the souls of the taro.
The ripe fruit is allowed to rot.   Falling stars are supposed
to be the souls of the dead which have been hurled up aloft
and are now descending to bathe in the sea.   The trail of
light behind them is thought to be a tail of coco-nut leaves
which other souls have fastened to them and set on fire.   In
like manner the phosphorescent glow on the sea comes from
souls disporting themselves in the water.   Persons who at
their death left few relations, or did evil in their life, or were
murdered outside of the village, are not buried in the house.

Their corpses are deposited on rocks or on scaffolds in the forest, or are interred on the spot where they met their death. The reason for this treatment of their corpses is not mentioned; but we may conjecture that their ghosts are regarded with contempt, dislike, or fear, and that the survivors seek to give them a wide berth by keeping their bodies at a distance from the village. The corpses of those who died suddenly are not buried but wrapt up in leaves and laid on a scaffold in the house, which is then shut up and deserted. This manner of disposing of them seems also to indicate a dread or distrust of their ghosts.[1]

Disposal of the dead among the Moanus of the Admiralty Islands.

Among the Moanus of the Admiralty Islands the dead are kept in the houses unburied until the flesh is completely decayed and nothing remains but the bones. Old women then wash the skeleton carefully in sea-water, after which it is disjointed and divided. The backbone, together with the bones of the legs and upper arms, is deposited in one basket and put away somewhere; the skull, together with the ribs and the bones of the lower arms, is deposited in another basket, which is sunk for a time in the sea. When the bones are completely cleaned and bleached in the water, they are laid with sweet-smelling herbs in a wooden vessel and placed in the house which the dead man inhabited during his life. But the teeth have been previously extracted from the skull and converted into a necklace for herself by the sister of the deceased. After a time the ribs are distributed by the son among the relatives. The principal widow gets two, other near kinsfolk get one apiece, and they wear these relics under their arm-bands. The distribution of the ribs is the occasion of a great festival, and it is followed some time afterwards by a still greater feast, for which extensive preparations are made long beforehand. All who intend to be present at the ceremony send vessels of coco-nut oil in advance; and if the deceased was a great chief the number of the oil vessels and of the guests may amount to two thousand. Meantime the giver of the feast causes a scaffold to be erected for the reception of the skull, and the whole art of the wood-carver

Prayers offered to the skull of a dead chief.

[1] P. Rascher, M.S.C., "Die Sulka, ein Beitrag zur Ethnographie Neu-Pommern," Archiv für Anthropologie, xxix. (1904) pp. 214 sq., 216; R. Parkinson, Dreissig Jahre in der Südsee, pp. 185-187.

is exhausted in decorating the scaffold with figures of turtles, birds, and so forth, while a wooden dog acts as sentinel at either end.   When the multitude has assembled, and the orchestra of drums, collected from the whole neighbourhood, has sent forth a far-sounding crash of music, the giver of the feast steps forward and pronounces a florid eulogium on the deceased, a warm panegyric on the guests who have honoured him by their presence, and a fluent invective against his absent foes.   Nor does he forget to throw in some delicate allusions to his own noble generosity in providing the assembled visitors with this magnificent entertainment.   For this great effort of eloquence the orator has been primed in the morning by the sorcerer.   The process of priming consists in kneeling on the orator's shoulders and tugging at the hair of his head with might and main, which is clearly calculated to promote the flow of his rhetoric.   If none of the hair comes out in the sorcerer's hands, a masterpiece of oratory is confidently looked forward to in the afternoon. When the speech, for which such painful preparations have been made, is at last over, the drums again strike up.   No sooner have their booming notes died away over land and sea, than the sorcerer steps up to the scaffold, takes from it the bleached skull, and holds it in both his hands.   Then the giver of the feast goes up to him, dips a bunch of dracaena leaves in a vessel of oil, and smites the skull with it, saying, "Thou art my father!"   At that the drums again beat loudly.   Then he strikes the skull a second time with the leaves, saying, "Take the food that has been made ready in thine honour!"   And again there is a crash of drums. After that he smites the skull yet again and prays saying, "Guard me!   Guard my people!   Guard my children!" And every prayer of the litany is followed by the solemn roll of the drums.   When these impressive invocations to the spirit of the dead chief are over, the feasting begins. The skull is thenceforth carefully preserved.[1]

In the Kaniet Islands, a small group to the north-west of the Admiralty Islands, the dead are either sunk in the sea or buried in shallow graves, face downward, near the house. All the movable property of the deceased is piled on the

Disposal of the dead in the Kaniet Islands.

R. Parkinson, *Dreissig Jahre in der Südsee*, pp. 404-406.

Preservation of the skull.

grave, left there for three weeks, and then burnt. Afterwards the skull is dug up, placed in a basket, and having been decorated with leaves and feathers is hung up in the house. Thus adorned it not only serves to keep the dead in memory, but is also employed in many conjurations to defeat the nefarious designs of other ghosts, who are believed to work most of the ills that afflict humanity.[1] Apparently these islanders employ a ghost to protect them against ghosts on the principle of setting a thief to catch a thief.

Death attributed to witchcraft.

Amongst the natives of the Bismarck Archipelago few persons, if any, are believed to die from natural causes alone; if they are not killed in war they are commonly supposed to perish by witchcraft or sorcery, even when the cause of death might seem to the uninstructed European to be sufficiently obvious in such things as exposure to heavy rain, the carrying of too heavy a burden, or remaining too long a time under water. So when a man has died, his friends are anxious to discover who has bewitched him to death. In this enquiry the ghost is expected to lend his assistance. Thus on the night after the decease the friends will assemble outside the house, and a sorcerer will address the ghost and request him to name the author of his death. If the ghost, as sometimes happens, makes no reply, the sorcerer will jog his memory by calling out the name of some suspected person; and should the ghost still be silent, the wizard will name another and another, till at the mention of one name a tapping sound is heard like the drumming of fingers on a board or on a mat. The sound may proceed from the house or from a pearl shell which the sorcerer holds in his hand; but come from where it may, it is taken as a certain proof that the man who has just been named did the deed, and he is dealt with accordingly. Many a poor wretch in New Britain has been killed and eaten on no other evidence than that of the fatal tapping.[2]

[1] R. Parkinson, *op. cit.* pp. 441 *sq.*

[2] G. Brown, *op. cit.* pp. 176, 183, 385 *sq.* As to the wide-spread belief in New Britain that what we call natural deaths are brought about by sorcery, see further P. Rascher, *M.S.C.,* "Die Sulka, ein Beitrag zur Ethnographie Neu-Pommern," *Archiv für Ethnographie,* xxix. (1904) pp. 221 *sq.*; R. Parkinson, *Dreissig Jahre in der Südsee,* pp. 117 *sq.*, 199-201; P. A. Kleintitschen, *Die Küstenbewohner der Gazellehalbinsel* (Hiltrup bei Münster, N.D.), p. 215.

When a man of mark is buried in the Duke of York Island, the masters of sorcery take leaves, spit on them, and throw them, with a number of poisonous things, into the grave, uttering at the same time loud imprecations on the wicked enchanter who has killed their friend. Then they go and bathe, and returning they fall to cursing again ; and if the miscreant survived the first imprecations, it is regarded as perfectly certain that he will fall a victim to the second. Sometimes, when the deceased was a chief distinguished for bravery and wisdom, his corpse would be exposed on a high platform in front of his house and left there to rot, while his relatives sat around and inhaled the stench, conceiving that with it they absorbed the courage and skill of the departed worthy. Some of them would even anoint their bodies with the drippings from the putrefying corpse for the same purpose. The women also made fires that the ghost might warm himself at them. When the head became detached from the trunk, it was carefully preserved by the next of kin, while the other remains were buried in a shallow grave in the house. All the female relatives blackened their dusky faces for a long time, after which the skull was put on a platform, a great feast was held, and dances were performed for many nights in its honour. Then at last the spirit of the dead man, which till that time was supposed to be lingering about his old abode, took his departure, and his friends troubled themselves about him no more.[1]

The souls of the dead are always regarded by these people as beings whose help can be invoked on special occasions, such as fighting or fishing or any other matter of importance ; and since the spirits whom they invoke are always those of their own kindred they are presumed to be friendly to the petitioners. The objects for which formal prayers are addressed to the souls of ancestors appear to be always temporal benefits, such as victory over enemies and plenty of food ; prayers for the promotion of moral virtue are seemingly unknown. For example, if a woman laboured hard in childbirth, she was thought to be bewitched, and prayers would be offered to the spirits of dead ancestors to counteract the spell. Again, young men are instructed by

[1] G. Brown, *op. cit.* pp. 387-390.

their elders in the useful art of cursing the enemies of the tribe ; and among a rich variety of imprecations an old man will invoke the spirit of his brother, father, or uncle, or all of them, to put their fingers into the ears of the enemy that he may not hear, to cover his eyes that he may not see, and to stop his mouth that he may not cry for help, but may fall an easy prey to the curser and his friends.[1] More amiable and not less effectual are the prayers offered to the spirits of the dead over a sick man. At the mention of each name in the prayer the supplicants make a chirping or hissing sound, and rub lime over the patient. Before administering medicine they pray over it to the spirits of the dead ; then the patient gulps it down, thus absorbing the virtue of the medicine and of the prayer in one. In New Britain they reinforce the prayers to the dead in time of need by wearing the jawbone of the deceased ; and in the Duke of York Island people often wear a tooth or some hair of a departed relative, not merely as a mark of respect, but as a magical means of obtaining supernatural help.[2]

North Melanesian views as to the land of the dead.

Sooner or later the souls of all the North Melanesian dead take their departure for the spirit land. But the information which has reached the living as to that far country is at once vague and inconsistent. They call it *Matana nion*, but whereabout it lies they cannot for the most part precisely tell. All they know for certain is that it is far away, and that there is always some particular spot in the neighbourhood from which the souls take their departure ; for example, the Duke of York ghosts invariably start from the little island of Nuruan, near Mioko. Wherever it may be, the land of souls is divided into compartments ; people who have died of sickness or witchcraft go to one place, and people who have been killed in battle go to another. They do not go unattended ; for when a man dies two friends sleep beside his corpse the first night, one on each side, and their spirits are believed to accompany the soul of the dead man to the spirit land. They say that on their arrival in the far country, betel-nut is presented to them all, but the two living men refuse to partake of it,

---

[1] G. Brown, *op. cit.* pp. 35, 89, 196, 201.

[2] G. Brown, *op. cit.* pp. 177, 183, 184.

because they know that were they to eat it they would return no more to the land of the living. When they do return, they have often, as might be expected, strange tales to tell of what they saw among the ghosts. The principal personage in the other world is called the " keeper of souls." It is said that once on a time the masterful ghost of a dead chief attempted to usurp the post of warden of the dead ; in pursuance of this ambitious project he attacked the warden with a tomahawk and cut off one of his legs, but the amputated limb immediately reunited itself with the body ; and a second amputation was followed by the same disappointing result. Life in the other world is reported to be very like life in this world. Some people find it very dismal, and others very beautiful. Those who were rich here will be rich there, and those who were poor on earth will be poor in Hades. As to any moral retribution which may overtake evil-doers in the life to come, their ideas are very vague ; only they are sure that the ghosts of the niggardly will be punished by being dumped very hard against the buttress-roots of chestnut-trees. They say, too, that all breaches of etiquette or of the ordinary customs of the country will meet with certain appropriate punishments in the spirit land. When the soul has thus done penance, it takes possession of the body of some animal, for instance, the flying-fox. Hence a native is much alarmed if he should be sitting under a tree from which a flying-fox has been frightened away. Should anything drop from the bat or from the tree on which it was hanging, he would look on it as an omen of good or ill according to the nature of the thing which fell on or near him. If it were useless or dirty, he would certainly apprehend some serious misfortune. Sometimes when a man dies and his soul arrives in the spirit land, his friends do not want him there and drive him back to earth, so he comes to life again. That is the explanation which the natives give of what we call the recovery of consciousness after a faint or swoon.[1]

Some of the natives of the Gazelle Peninsula in New Britain imagine that the home of departed spirits is in Nakanei, the part of the coast to which they sail to get

The land of the dead.

[1] G. Brown, *op. cit.* pp. 192-195.

their shell money. Others suppose that it is in the islands off Cape Takes. So when they are sailing past these islands they dip the paddles softly in the water, and observe a death-like stillness, cowering down in the canoes, lest the ghosts should spy them and do them a mischief. At the entrance to these happy isles is posted a stern watchman to see that no improper person sneaks into them. To every ghost that arrives he puts three questions, "Who are you? Where do you come from? How much shell money did you leave behind you?" On his answers to these three questions hangs the fate of the ghost. If he left much money, he is free to enter the realm of bliss, where he will pass the time with other happy souls smoking and eating and enjoying other sensual delights. But if he left little or no money, he is banished the earthly paradise and sent home to roam like a wild beast in the forest, battening on leaves and filth. With bitter sighs and groans he prowls about the villages at night and seeks to avenge himself by scaring or plaguing the survivors. To stay his hunger and appease his wrath relatives or friends will sometimes set forth food for him to devour. Yet even for such an impecunious soul there is hope; for if somebody only takes pity on him and gives a feast in his honour and distributes shell money to the guests, the ghost may return to the islands of the blest, and the door will be thrown open to him.[1]

So much for the belief in immortality as it is reported to exist among the Northern Melanesians of New Britain and the Bismarck Archipelago. We now pass to the consideration of a similar belief among another people of the same stock, who have been longer known to Europe, the Fijians. The archipelago which they occupy lies to the east of the New Hebrides and forms in fact the most easterly outpost of the black Melanesian race in the Pacific. Beyond it to the eastward are situated the smaller archipelagoes of Samoa and Tonga, inhabited by branches of the brown Polynesian race, whose members are scattered over the islands of the Pacific Ocean from Hawaii in the north to New Zealand in the south. Of all the branches of the

State of the dead in the other world supposed to depend on the amount of money they left in this one.

Fiji and the Fijians.

---

[1] P. A. Kleintitschen, *Die Küsten-bewohner der Gazellehalbinsel*, pp. 225 *sq.* Compare R. Parkinson, *Dreissig Jahre in der Südsee*, p. 79.

Melanesian stock the Fijians at the date of their discovery
by Europeans appear to have made the greatest advance in
culture, material, social, and political. " The Fijian," says
one who knew him long and intimately, " takes no mean
place among savages in the social scale. Long before the
white man visited his shores he had made very considerable
progress towards civilisation. His intersexual code had
advanced to the ' patriarchal stage ' : he was a skilful and
diligent husbandman, who carried out extensive and laborious
agricultural operations : he built good houses, whose interior
he ornamented with no little taste, carved his weapons in
graceful and intricate forms, manufactured excellent pottery,
beat out from the inner bark of a tree a serviceable papyrus-
cloth, upon which he printed, from blocks either carved or
ingeniously pieced together, elegant and elaborate patterns
in fast colours ; and, with tools no better than a stone
hatchet, a pointed shell, and a firestick, he constructed large
canoes capable of carrying more than a hundred warriors
across the open sea." [1]

Politically the Fijians shewed their superiority to all the
other Melanesians in the advance they had made towards a
regular and organised government. While among the other
branches of the same race government can hardly be said
to exist, the power of chiefs being both slender and precarious, in Fiji the highest chiefs exercised despotic sway
and received from Europeans the title of kings. The people
had no voice in the state ; the will of the king was generally
law, and his person was sacred. Whatever he touched or
wore became thereby holy and had to be made over to him ;
nobody else could afterwards touch it without danger of
being struck dead on the spot as if by an electric shock.
One king took advantage of this superstition by dressing up
an English sailor in his royal robes and sending him about
to throw his sweeping train over any article of food, whether
dead or alive, which he might chance to come near. The
things so touched were at once conveyed to the king without
a word of explanation being required or a single remonstrance
uttered. Some of the kings laid claim to a divine origin
and on the strength of the claim exacted and received from

Political superiority of the Fijians over the other Melanesians.

---

[1] Lorimer Fison, *Tales from Old Fiji* (London, 1904), p. xiv.

their subjects the respect due to deities.   In these exorbitant pretensions they were greatly strengthened by the institution of taboo, which lent the sanction of religion to every exertion of arbitrary power.[1]   Corresponding with the growth of monarchy was the well-marked gradation of social ranks which prevailed in the various tribes from the king downwards through chiefs, warriors, and landholders, to slaves. The resulting political constitution has been compared to the old feudal system of Europe.[2]

Means of subsistence of the Fijians.

Like the other peoples of the Melanesian stock the Fijians subsist chiefly by agriculture, raising many sorts of esculent fruits and roots, particularly yams, taro, plantains, bread-fruit, sweet potatoes, bananas, coco-nuts, ivi nuts, and sugar-cane ; but the chief proportion of their food is derived from yams (*Dioscorea*), of which they cultivate five or six varieties.[3]   It has been observed that " the increase of cultivated plants is regular on receding from the Hawaiian group up to Fiji, where roots and fruits are found that are unknown on the more eastern islands." [4]   Yet the Fijians in their native state, like all other Melanesian and Polynesian peoples, were entirely ignorant of the cereals ; and in the opinion of a competent observer the consequent defect in their diet has contributed to the serious defects in their national character.   The cereals, he tells us, are the staple food of all races that have left their mark in history ; and on the other hand " the apathy and indolence of the Fijians arise from their climate, their diet and their communal institutions.   The climate is too kind to stimulate them to exertion, their food imparts no staying power.   The soil gives the means of existence for every man without effort, and the communal institutions destroy the instinct of accumulation." [5]   Nor are apathy and indolence the only or

---

[1] Thomas Williams, *Fiji and the Fijians*, Second Edition (London, 1860), i. 22-26.

[2] Charles Wilkes, *Narrative of the United States Exploring Expedition*, New Edition (New York, 1851), iii. 77 ; Th. Williams, *op. cit.* i. 18.

[3] Charles Wilkes, *Narrative of the United States Exploring Expedition*,

New Edition (New York, 1851), iii. 332 *sqq.* ; Thomas Williams, *Fiji and the Fijians*, Second Edition (London, 1860), i. 60 *sqq.* ; Berthold Seeman, *Viti* (Cambridge, 1862), pp. 279 *sqq.* ; Basil Thomson, *The Fijians* (London, 1908), pp. 335 *sq.*

[4] Th. Williams, *op. cit.* i. 60 *sq.*

[5] Basil Thomson, *The Fijians*, pp. 338, 389 *sq.*   The Fijians are in the

the worst features in the character of these comparatively
advanced savages. Their ferocity, cruelty, and moral
depravity are depicted in dark colours by those who had
the best opportunity of knowing them in the old days before
their savagery was mitigated by contact with a milder
religious faith and a higher civilisation. "In contemplating
the character of this extraordinary portion of mankind,"
says one observer, "the mind is struck with wonder and
awe at the mixture of a complicated and carefully conducted
political system, highly finished manners, and ceremonious
politeness, with a ferocity and practice of savage vices which
is probably unparalleled in any other part of the world."[1]
One of the first civilised men to gain an intimate acquaintance
with the Fijians draws a melancholy contrast between the
baseness and vileness of the people and the loveliness of the
land in which they live.[2]

For the Fijian islands are exceedingly beautiful. They
are of volcanic origin, mostly high and mountainous, but
intersected by picturesque valleys, clothed with woods, and
festooned with the most luxuriant tropical vegetation.
"Among their attractions," we are told, "are high mountains,
abrupt precipices, conical hills, fantastic turrets and crags of
rock frowning down like olden battlements, vast domes,
peaks shattered into strange forms ; native towns on eyrie
cliffs, apparently inaccessible ; and deep ravines, down which
some mountain stream, after long murmuring in its stony

Ferocity and depravity of the Fijians.

Scenery of the Fijian islands.

---

main vegetarians, but the vegetables
which they cultivate "contain a large
proportion of starch and water, and
are deficient in proteids. Moreover,
the supply of the principal staples is
irregular, being greatly affected by
variable seasons, and the attacks of
insects and vermin. Very few of them
will bear keeping, and almost all of
them must be eaten when ripe. As
the food is of low nutritive value, a
native always eats to repletion. In
times of plenty a full-grown man will
eat as much as ten pounds' weight of
vegetables in the day ; he will seldom
be satisfied with less than five. A
great quantity, therefore, is required
to feed a very few people, and as
everything is transported by hand, a

disproportionate amount of time is
spent in transporting food from the
plantation to the consumer. The time
spent in growing native food is also out
of all proportion to its value" (Basil
Thomson, *op. cit.* pp. 334 *sq.*). The
same writer tells us (p. 335) that it has
never occurred to the Fijians to dry any
of the fruits they grow and to grind
them into flour, as is done in Africa.

[1] Capt. J. E. Erskine, *Journal of
a Cruise among the Islands of the
Western Pacific* (London, 1853), pp.
272 *sq.*

[2] Ch. Wilkes, *op. cit.* iii. 46, 363.
As to the cruelty and depravity of the
Fijians in the old days see further
Lorimer Fison, *Tales from Old Fiji*
(London, 1904), pp. xv. *sqq.*

bed, falls headlong, glittering as a silver line on a block of jet, or spreading like a sheet of glass over bare rocks which refuse it a channel.   Here also are found the softer features of rich vales, cocoa-nut groves, clumps of dark chestnuts, stately palms and bread-fruit, patches of graceful bananas or well-tilled taro-beds, mingling in unchecked luxuriance, and forming, with the wild reef-scenery of the girdling shore, its beating surf, and far-stretching ocean beyond, pictures of surpassing beauty."[1]   Each island is encircled by a reef of white coral, on which the sea breaks, with a thunderous roar, in curling sheets of foam ; while inside the reef stretches the lagoon, a calm lake of blue crystalline water revealing in its translucent depths beautiful gardens of seaweed and coral which fill the beholder with delighted wonder.   Great and sudden is the contrast experienced by the mariner when he passes in a moment from the tossing, heaving, roaring billows without into the unbroken calm of the quiet haven within the barrier reef.[2]

Fijian doctrine of souls.

Like most savages, the Fijians believed that man is animated by a soul which quits his body temporarily in sleep and permanently at death, to survive for a longer or a shorter time in a disembodied state thereafter.   Indeed, they attributed souls to animals, vegetables, stones, tools, houses, canoes, and many other things, allowing that all of them may become immortal.[3]   On this point I will quote the evidence

[1] Th. Williams, *Fiji and the Fijians*, i. 6 *sq.* As to the scenery of the Fijian archipelago see further *id.*, i. 4 *sqq.* ; Ch. Wilkes, *op. cit.* iii. 46, 322 ; *Stanford's Compendium of Geography and Travel, Australasia*, vol. ii. *Malaysia and the Pacific Archipelago*, edited by F. H. H. Guillemard (London, 1894), pp. 467 *sqq.* ; Miss Beatrice Grimshaw, *From Fiji to the Cannibal Islands* (London, 1907), pp. 43 *sq.*, 54 *sq.*, 76-78, 106, 109 *sq.*

[2] Th. Williams, *Fiji and the Fijians*, i. 5 *sq.*, 11 ; Ch. Wilkes, *op. cit.* iii. 46 *sq.*   However, there is a remarkable difference not only in climate but in appearance between the windward and the leeward sides of these islands.   The windward side, watered by abundant showers, is covered with luxuriant tropical vegetation ; the leeward side, receiving little rain, presents a comparatively barren and burnt appearance, the vegetation dying down to the grey hues of the boulders among which it struggles for life.   Hence the dry leeward side is better adapted for European settlement. See Ch. Wilkes, *op. cit.* iii. 320 *sq.* ; Th. Williams, *op. cit.* i. 10 ; B. Seeman, *Viti, an Account of a Government Mission to the Vitian or Fijian Islands in the years 1860-1861* (Cambridge, 1862), pp. 277 *sq.*

[3] Th. Williams, *op. cit.* i. 241 ; J. E. Erskine, *op. cit.* p. 249 ; B. Seeman, *Viti* (Cambridge, 1862), p. 398.

of one of the earliest and best authorities on the customs and beliefs of the South Sea Islanders. "There seems," says William Mariner, "to be a wide difference between the opinions of the natives in the different clusters of the South Sea islands respecting the future existence of the soul. Whilst the Tonga doctrine limits immortality to chiefs, *matabooles*, and at most, to *mooas*, the Fiji doctrine, with abundant liberality, extends it to all mankind, to all brute animals, to all vegetables, and even to stones and mineral substances. If an animal or a plant die, its soul immediately goes to Bolotoo ; if a stone or any other substance is broken, immortality is equally its reward ; nay, artificial bodies have equal good luck with men, and hogs, and yams. If an axe or a chisel is worn out or broken up, away flies its soul for the service of the gods. If a house is taken down, or any way destroyed, its immortal part will find a situation on the plains of Bolotoo ; and, to confirm this doctrine, the Fiji people can show you a sort of natural well, or deep hole in the ground, at one of their islands, across the bottom of which runs a stream of water, in which you may clearly perceive the souls of men and women, beasts and plants, of stocks and stones, canoes and houses, and of all the broken utensils of this frail world, swimming or rather tumbling along one over the other pell-mell into the regions of immortality. Such is the Fiji philosophy, but the Tonga people deny it, unwilling to think that the residence of the gods should be encumbered with so much useless rubbish. The natives of Otaheite entertain similar notions respecting these things, viz. that brutes, plants, and stones exist hereafter, but it is not mentioned that they extend the idea to objects of human invention." [1]

According to one account, the Fijians imagined that every man has two souls, a dark soul, consisting of his shadow, and a light soul, consisting of his reflection in water or a looking-glass : the dark soul departs at death to Hades, while the light soul stays near the place where he died or was

Reported Fijian doctrine of two human souls, a light one and a dark one.

[1] William Mariner, *An Account of the Natives of the Tonga Islands*, Second Edition (London, 1818), ii. 129 *sq.* The *matabooles* were a sort of honourable attendants on chiefs and ranked next to them in the social hierarchy ; the *mooas* were the next class of people below the *matabooles*. See W. Mariner, *op. cit.* ii. 84, 86. Bolotoo or Bulu was the mythical land of the dead.

killed. "Probably," says Thomas Williams, "this doctrine of shadows has to do with the notion of inanimate objects having spirits. I once placed a good-looking native suddenly before a mirror. He stood delighted. 'Now,' said he, softly, 'I can see into the world of spirits.'"[1] However, according to another good authority this distinction of two human souls rests merely on a misapprehension of the Fijian word for shadow, *yaloyalo*, which is a reduplication of *yalo*, the word for soul.[2] Apparently the Fijians pictured to themselves the human soul as a miniature of the man himself. This may be inferred from the customs observed at the death of a chief among the Nakelo tribe. When a chief dies, certain men who are the hereditary undertakers call him, as he lies, oiled and ornamented, on fine mats, saying, "Rise, sir, the chief, and let us be going. The day has come over the land." Then they conduct him to the river side, where the ghostly ferryman comes to ferry Nakelo ghosts across the stream. As they attend the chief on his last journey, they hold their great fans close to the ground to shelter him, because, as one of them explained to a missionary, "His soul is only a little child."[3]

Absence of the soul in sleep.   The souls of some men were supposed to quit their bodies in sleep and enter into the bodies of other sleepers, troubling and disturbing them. A soul that had contracted this bad habit was called a *yalombula*. When any one fainted or died, his vagrant spirit might, so the Fijians thought, be induced to come back by calling after it. Sometimes, on awaking from a nap, a stout man might be seen lying at full length and bawling out lustily for the return of his own soul.[4] In the windward islands of Fiji there used to be an ordeal called *yalovaki* which was much dreaded by evil-doers. When the evidence was strong against suspected criminals, and they stubbornly refused to confess, the chief, who was also the judge, would call for a scarf, with which "to

Catching the soul of a rascal in a scarf.

[1] Th. Williams, *Fiji and the Fijians*, i. 241.

[2] This is the opinion of my late friend, the Rev. Lorimer Fison, which he communicated to me in a letter dated 26th August, 1898.

[3] Communication of the late Rev.

Lorimer Fison in a letter to me dated 3rd November, 1898. I have already published it in *Taboo and the Perils of the Soul*, pp. 29 *sq*.

[4] Th. Williams, *op. cit.* i. 242; Lorimer Fison, *Tales from Old Fiji*, pp. 163 *sq.*; *Taboo and the Perils of the Soul*, pp. 39 *sq*.

catch away the soul of the rogue." A threat of the rack could not have been more effectual. The culprit generally confessed at the sight and even the mention of the light instrument; but if he did not, the scarf would be waved over his head until his soul was caught in it like a moth or a fly, after which it would be carefully folded up and nailed to the small end of a chief's canoe, and for want of his soul the suspected person would pine and die.[1]

Further, the Fijians, like many other savages, stood in great terror of witchcraft, believing that the sorcerer had it in his power to kill them by the practice of his nefarious art. "Of all their superstitions," says Thomas Williams, "this exerts the strongest influence on the minds of the people. Men who laugh at the pretensions of the priest tremble at the power of the wizard; and those who become christians lose this fear last of all the relics of their heathenism."[2] Indeed "native agents of the mission who, in the discharge of their duty, have boldly faced death by open violence, have been driven from their posts by their dread of the sorcerer; and my own observation confirms the statement of more than one observer that savages not unfrequently die of fear when they think themselves bewitched."[3] Professed practitioners of witchcraft were dreaded by all classes, and by destroying mutual confidence they annulled the comfort and shook the security of society. Almost all sudden deaths were set down to their machinations. A common mode of effecting their object was to obtain a shred of the clothing of the man they intended to bewitch, some refuse of his food, a lock of his hair, or some other personal relic; having got it they wrapped it up in certain leaves, and then cooked or buried it or hung it up in the forest; whereupon the victim was supposed to die of a wasting disease. Another way was to bury a coco-nut, with the eye upward, beneath the hearth of the temple, on which a fire was kept constantly burning; and as the life of the nut was destroyed, so the health of the person whom the nut represented would fail till death put an end to his sufferings. "The native imagination," we are told, "is so

Fijian dread of sorcery and witchcraft.

---

[1] Th. Williams, *op. cit.* i. 250. [2] Th. Williams, *op. cit.* i. 248.
[3] Lorimer Fison, *op. cit.* p. xxxii.

absolutely under the control of fear of these charms, that persons, hearing that they were the object of such spells, have lain down on their mats, and died through fear." [1]   To guard against the fell craft of the magician the people resorted to many precautions.   A man who suspected another of plotting against him would be careful not to eat in his presence or at all events to leave no morsel of food behind, lest the other should secrete it and bewitch him by it ; and for the same reason people disposed of their garments so that no part could be removed ; and when they had their hair cut they generally hid the clippings in the thatch of their own houses.   Some even built themselves a small hut and surrounded it with a moat, believing that a little water had power to neutralise the charms directed against them.[2]

The fear of sorcery has had the beneficial effect of enforcing habits of personal cleanliness.

" In the face of such instances as these," says one who knows the Fijians well, " it demands some courage to assert that upon the whole the belief in witchcraft was formerly a positive advantage to the community.   It filled, in fact, the place of a system of sanitation.   The wizard's tools consisting in those waste matters that are inimical to health, every man was his own scavenger.   From birth to old age a man was governed by this one fear ; he went into the sea, the graveyard or the depths of the forest to satisfy his natural wants ; he burned his cast-off *malo* ; he gave every fragment left over from his food to the pigs ; he concealed even the clippings of his hair in the thatch of his house. This ever-present fear even drove women in the western districts out into the forest for the birth of their children, where fire destroyed every trace of their lying-in.   Until Christianity broke it down, the villages were kept clean ; there were no festering rubbish-heaps nor filthy *raras*." [3]

Fijian dread of ghosts.

Of apparitions the Fijians used to be very much afraid. They believed that the ghosts of the dead appeared often and afflicted mankind, especially in sleep.   The spirits of slain men, unchaste women, and women who died in childbed were most dreaded.   After a death people have

[1] Th. Williams, *op. cit.* i. 248 *sq.* ; Lorimer Fison, *op. cit.* pp. xxxi. *sq.*
[2] Th. Williams, *op. cit.* i. 249.
[3] Basil Thomson, *The Fijians* (London, 1908), p. 166.   A *rārā* is a public square (Rev. Lorimer Fison, in *Journal of the Anthropological Institute*, xiv. (1885) p. 17).

been known to hide themselves for a few days, until they supposed the soul of the departed was at rest.   Also they shunned the places where people had been murdered, particularly when it rained, because then the moans of the ghost could be heard as he sat up, trying to relieve his pain by resting his poor aching head on the palms of his hands. Some however said that the moans were caused by the soul of the murderer knocking down the soul of his victim, whenever the wretched spirit attempted to get up.[1]   When Fijians passed a spot in the forest where a man had been clubbed to death, they would sometimes throw leaves on it as a mark of homage to his spirit, believing that they would soon be killed themselves if they failed in thus paying their respects to the ghost.[2]   And after they had buried a man alive, as they very often did, these savages used at nightfall to make a great din with large bamboos, trumpet-shells, and so forth, in order to drive away his spirit and deter him from loitering about his old home.   " The uproar is always held in the late habitation of the deceased, the reason being that as no one knows for a certainty what reception he will receive in the invisible world, if it is not according to his expectations he will most likely repent of his bargain and wish to come back.   For that reason they make a great noise to frighten him away, and dismantle his former habitation of everything that is attractive, and clothe it with everything that to their ideas seems repulsive. "[3]

Uproar made to drive away ghosts.

However, stronger measures were sometimes resorted to. It was believed to be possible to kill a troublesome ghost. Once it happened that many chiefs feasted in the house of Tanoa, King of Ambau.   In the course of the evening one of them related how he had slain a neighbouring chief. That very night, having occasion to leave the house, he saw, as he believed, the ghost of his victim, hurled his club at him, and killed him stone dead.   On his return to the house he roused the king and the rest of the inmates from their slumbers, and recounted his exploit.   The matter was deemed of high importance, and they all sat on it in solemn

Killing a ghost.

---

[1] Th. Williams, *op. cit.* i. 241.
[2] Ch. Wilkes, *op. cit.* iii. 50.
[3] Narrative of John Jackson, in

Capt. J. E. Erskine's *Journal of a Cruise among the Islands of the Western Pacific* (London, 1853), p. 477.

conclave.   Next morning a search was made for the club
on the scene of the murder; it was found and carried with
great pomp and parade to the nearest temple, where it was
laid up for a perpetual memorial.   Everybody was firmly
persuaded that by this swashing blow the ghost had been
not only killed but annihilated.[1]

Dazing
the ghost
of a grand-
father.

A more humane method of dealing with an importunate
ghost used to be adopted in Vanua-levu, the largest but one
of the Fijian islands.   In that island, as a consequence,
it is said, of reckoning kinship through the mother, a child
was considered to be more closely related to his grandfather
than to his father.   Hence when a grandfather died, his
ghost naturally desired to carry off the soul of his grandchild with him to the spirit land.   The wish was credit-
able to the warmth of his domestic affection, but if the
survivors preferred to keep the child with them a little
longer in this vale of tears, they took steps to baffle
grandfather's ghost.   For this purpose when the old man's
body was stretched on the bier and raised on the shoulders
of half-a-dozen stout young fellows, the mother's brother
would take the grandchild in his arms and begin running
round and round the corpse.   Round and round he ran,
and grandfather's ghost looked after him, craning his neck
from side to side and twisting it round and round in the
vain attempt to follow the rapid movements of the runner.
When the ghost was supposed to be quite giddy with this
unwonted exercise, the mother's brother made a sudden
dart away with the child in his arms, the bearers fairly
bolted with the corpse to the grave, and before he could
collect his scattered wits grandfather was safely landed in
his long home.[2]

Special
relation of
grand-
father to
grandchild.

Mr. Fison, who reports this quaint mode of bilking a
ghost, explains the special attachment of the grandfather
to his grandchild by the rule of female descent which survives in Vanua-levu; and it is true that where exogamy
prevails along with female descent, a child regularly belongs
to the exogamous class of its grandfather and not of its
father and hence may be regarded as more closely akin to
the grandfather than to the father.   But on the other hand

[1] Ch. Wilkes, *op. cit.* iii. 85.   [2] Lorimer Fison, *op. cit.* pp. 168 *sq.*

it is to be observed that exogamy at present is unknown in Fiji, and at most its former prevalence in the islands can only be indirectly inferred from relics of totemism and from the existence of the classificatory system of relationship.[1] Perhaps the real reason why in Vanua-levu a dead grandfather is so anxious to carry off the soul of his living grandchild lies nearer to hand in the apparently widespread belief that the soul of the grandfather is actually reborn in his grandchild. For example, in Nukahiva, one of the Marquesas Islands, every one " is persuaded that the soul of a grandfather is transmitted by nature into the body of his grandchildren ; and that, if an unfruitful wife were to place herself under the corpse of her deceased grandfather, she would be sure to become pregnant." [2]   Again, the Kayans of Borneo " believe in the reincarnation of the soul, although this belief is not clearly harmonised with the belief in the life in another world. It is generally believed that the soul of a grandfather may pass into one of his grandchildren, and an old man will try to secure the passage of his soul to a favourite grandchild by holding it above his head from time to time. The grandfather usually gives up his name to his eldest grandson, and reassumes the original name of his childhood with the prefix or title *Laki*, and the custom seems to be connected with this belief or hope." [3]

Soul of a grandfather reborn in his grandchild.

Now where such a belief is held, it seems reasonable enough that a dead grandfather should reclaim his own soul for his personal use before he sets out for the spirit land ; else how could he expect to be admitted to that blissful abode if on arriving at the portal he were obliged to explain to the porter that he had no soul about him, having left that indispensable article behind in the person of his grandchild ?   " Then you had better go back and fetch it. There is no admission at this gate for people without souls." Such might very well be the porter's retort ; and foreseeing it any man of ordinary prudence would take the precaution of recovering his lost spiritual property before presenting

A dead grandfather may reasonably reclaim his own soul from his grandchild.

[1] W. H. R. Rivers, " Totemism in Fiji," *Man*, viii. (1908) pp. 133 *sqq.* ; *Totemism and Exogamy*, ii. 134 *sqq.*
[2] U. Lisiansky, *A Voyage Round the World* (London, 1814), p. 89.
[3] Ch. Hose and W. McDougall, *The Pagan Tribes of Borneo* (London, 1912), ii. 47.

himself to the Warden of the Dead. This theory would sufficiently account for the otherwise singular behaviour of grandfather's ghost in Vanua-levu. At the same time it must be admitted that the theory of the reincarnation of a grandfather in a grandson would be suggested more readily in a society where the custom of exogamy was combined with female descent than in one where the same custom coexisted with male descent; since, given exogamy and female descent, grandfather and grandson regularly belong to the same exogamous class, whereas father and son never do so.[1] Thus Mr. Fison may after all be right in referring the partiality of a Fijian grandfather for his grandson in the last resort to a system of exogamy and female kinship.

[1] Compare *Totemism and Exogamy*, iii. 297-299.

LECTURE XIX

THE BELIEF IN IMMORTALITY AMONG THE NATIVES
OF EASTERN MELANESIA (FIJI) (*continued*)

AT the close of last lecture I illustrated the unquestioning belief which the Fijians entertain with regard to the survival of the human soul after death. " The native superstitions with regard to a future state," we are told, " go far to explain the apparent indifference of the people about death ; for, while believing in an eternal existence, they shut out from it the idea of any moral retribution in the shape either of reward or punishment. The first notion concerning death is that of simple rest, and is thus contained in one of their rhymes :— *Fijian indifference to death.*

> *Death is easy :*
> *Of what use is life ?*
> *To die is rest.*" [1]

Again, another writer, speaking of the Fijians, says that " in general, the passage from life to death is considered as one from pain to happiness, and I was informed that nine out of ten look forward to it with anxiety, in order to escape from the infirmities of old age, or the sufferings of disease." [2]

The cool indifference with which the Fijians commonly regarded their own death and that of other people might be illustrated by many examples. I will give one in the words of an English eye-witness, who lived among these savages for some time like one of themselves. At a place on the coast of Viti Levu, the largest of the Fijian Islands, he says, *John Jackson's account of the burying alive of a young Fijian man.*

---

[1] Th. Williams, *Fiji and the Fijians,* Second Edition (London, 1860), i. 242 *sq.*

[2] Charles Wilkes, *Narrative of the United States Exploring Expedition,* New Edition (New York, 1851), iii. 86.

419

" I walked into a number of temples, which were very plentiful, and at last into a *bure theravou* (young man's *bure*), where I saw a tall young man about twenty years old. He appeared to be somewhat ailing, but not at all emaciated. He was rolling up the mat he had been sleeping upon, evidently preparing to go away somewhere. I addressed him, and asked him where he was going, when he immediately answered that he was going to be buried. I observed that he was not dead yet, but he said he soon should be dead when he was put under ground. I asked him why he was going to be buried? He said it was three days since he had eaten anything, and consequently he was getting very thin ; and that if he lived any longer he would be much thinner, and then the women would call him a *lila* (skeleton), and laugh at him. I said he was a fool to throw himself away for fear of being laughed at ; and asked him what or who his private god was, knowing it to be no use talking to him about Providence, a thing he had never heard of. He said his god was a shark, and that if he were cast away in a canoe and was obliged to swim, the sharks would not bite him. I asked him if he believed the shark, his god, had any power to act over him? He said yes. ' Well then,' said I, ' why do you not live a little longer, and trust to your god to give you an appetite ? ' Finding that he could not give me satisfactory answers, and being determined to get buried to avoid the jeers of the ladies, which to a Feejeean are intolerable, he told me I knew nothing about it, and that I must not compare him to a white man, who was generally insensible to all shame, and did not care how much he was laughed at. I called him a fool, and said the best thing he could do was to get buried out of the way, because I knew that most of them work by the rules of contrary ; but it was all to no purpose. By this time all his relations had collected round the door. His father had a kind of wooden spade to dig the grave with, his mother a new suit of *tapa* [bark-cloth], his sister some vermilion and a whale's tooth, as an introduction to the great god of Rage-Rage. He arose, took up his bed and walked, not for life, but for death, his father, mother, and sister following after, with several other distant relations,

whom I accompanied. I noticed that they seemed to follow
him something in the same way that they follow a corpse in
Europe to the grave (that is, as far as relationship and
acquaintance are concerned), but, instead of lamenting, they
were, if not rejoicing, acting and chatting in a very un-
concerned way. At last we reached a place where several
graves could be seen, and a spot was soon selected by the
man who was to be buried. The old man, his father, began
digging his grave, while his mother assisted her son in
putting on a new *tapa* [bark-cloth], and the girl (his sister)
was besmearing him with vermilion and lamp-black, so as to
send him decent into the invisible world, he (the victim)
delivering messages that were to be taken by his sister to
people then absent. His father then announced to him and
the rest that the grave was completed, and asked him,
in rather a surly tone, if he was not ready by this time.
The mother then *nosed* him, and likewise the sister. He
said, 'Before I die, I should like a drink of water.' His
father made a surly remark, and said, as he ran to fetch it
in a leaf doubled up, 'You have been a considerable trouble
during your life, and it appears that you are going to trouble
us equally at your death.' The father returned with the
water, which the son drank off, and then looked up into
a tree covered with tough vines, saying he should prefer
being strangled with a vine to being smothered in the grave.
His father became excessively angry, and, spreading the mat
at the bottom of the grave, told the son to die *faka tamata*
(like a man), when he stepped into the grave, which was
not more than four feet deep, and lay down on his back
with the whale's tooth in his hands, which were clasped
across his belly. The spare sides of the mats were lapped
over him so as to prevent the earth from getting to his
body, and then about a foot of earth was shovelled in
upon him as quickly as possible. His father stamped it
immediately down solid, and called out in a loud voice,
'*Sa tiko, sa tiko* (You are stopping there, you are stopping
there),' meaning 'Good-bye, good-bye.' The son answered
with a very audible grunt, and then about two feet more
earth was shovelled in and stamped as before by the loving
father, and '*Sa tiko*' called out again, which was answered

Son buried alive by his father.

by another grunt, but much fainter. The grave was then
completely filled up, when, for curiosity's sake, I said myself,
' *Sa tiko*,' but no answer was given, although I fancied, or
really did see, the earth crack a little on the top of the
grave. The father and mother then turned back to back on
the middle of the grave, and, having dropped some kind
of leaves from their hands, walked away in opposite
directions towards a running stream of water hard by, where
they and all the rest washed themselves, and made me wash
myself, and then we returned to the town, where there was
a feast prepared. As soon as the feast was over (it being
then dark), began the dance and uproar which are always
carried on either at natural or violent deaths." [1]

The readi-
ness of the
Fijians to
die seems
to have
been partly
a conse-
quence of
their belief
in immor-
tality.

The readiness with which the Fijians submitted to or
even sought death appears to have been to some extent
a direct consequence of their belief in immortality and of
their notions as to the state of the soul hereafter. Thus we
are informed by an early observer of this people that " self-
immolation is by no means rare, and they believe that as
they leave this life, so will they remain ever after. This
forms a powerful motive to escape from decrepitude, or
from a crippled condition, by a voluntary death." [2] Or,
as another equally early observer puts it more fully, " the
custom of voluntary suicide on the part of the old men,
which is among their most extraordinary usages, is also
connected with their superstitions respecting a future life.
They believe that persons enter upon the delights of their
elysium with the same faculties, mental and physical, that
they possess at the hour of death, in short, that the spiritual
life commences where the corporeal existence terminates.
With these views, it is natural that they should desire to
pass through this change before their mental and bodily
powers are so enfeebled by age as to deprive them of their
capacity for enjoyment. To this motive must be added
the contempt which attaches to physical weakness among
a nation of warriors, and the wrongs and insults which await

[1] John Jackson's Narrative, in Capt.
J. E. Erskine's *Journal of a Cruise
among the Islands of the Western
Pacific* (London, 1853), pp. 475-477.
The narrator, John Jackson, was an
English seaman who resided alone
among the Fijians for nearly two
years and learned their language.

[2] Ch. Wilkes, *op. cit.* iii. 96.

those who are no longer able to protect themselves. When therefore a man finds his strength declining with the advance of age, and feels that he will soon be unequal to discharge the duties of this life, and to partake in the pleasures of that which is to come, he calls together his relations, and tells them that he is now worn out and useless, that he sees they are all ashamed of him, and that he has determined to be buried." So on a day appointed they met and buried him alive.[1]

The proposal to put the sick and aged to death did not always emanate from the parties principally concerned ; when a son, for example, thought that his parents were growing too old and becoming a burden to him, he would give them notice that it was time for them to die, a notice which they usually accepted with equanimity, if not alacrity. As a rule, it was left to the choice of the aged and infirm to say whether they would prefer to be buried alive or to be strangled first and buried afterwards ; and having expressed a predilection one way or the other they were dealt with accordingly. To strangle parents or other frail and sickly relatives with a rope was considered a more delicate and affectionate way of dispatching them than to knock them on the head with a club. In the old days the missionary Mr. Hunt witnessed several of these tender partings. " On one occasion, he was called upon by a young man, who desired that he would pray to his spirit for his mother, who was dead. Mr. Hunt was at first in hopes that this would afford him an opportunity of forwarding their great cause. On inquiry, the young man told him that his brothers and himself were just going to bury her. Mr. Hunt accompanied the young man, telling him he would follow in the procession, and do as he desired him, supposing, of course, the corpse would be brought along ; but he now met the procession, when the

The sick and aged put to death by their relatives.

---

[1] *United States Exploring Expedition, Ethnology and Philology*, by H. Hale (Philadelphia, 1846), p. 65. Compare Capt. J. E. Erskine, *op. cit.* p. 248 : "It would also seem that a belief in the resurrection of the body, in the exact condition in which it leaves the world, is one of the causes that induce, in many instances, a desire for death in the vigour of manhood, rather than in the decrepitude of old age"; Th. Williams, *op. cit.* i. 183 : "The heathen notion is, that, as they die, such will their condition be in another world; hence their desire to escape extreme infirmity."

young man said that this was the funeral, and pointed out
his mother, who was walking along with them, as gay and
lively as any of those present, and apparently as much
pleased. Mr. Hunt expressed his surprise to the young
man, and asked him how he could deceive him so much
by saying his mother was dead, when she was alive and
well. He said, in reply, that they had made her death-
feast, and were now going to bury her ; that she was old ;
that his brother and himself had thought she had lived long
enough, and it was time to bury her, to which she had
willingly assented, and they were about it now. He had
come to Mr. Hunt to ask his prayers, as they did those of
the priest. He added, that it was from love for his mother
that he had done so ; that, in consequence of the same love,
they were now going to bury her, and that none but themselves could or ought to do so sacred an office ! Mr. Hunt
did all in his power to prevent so diabolical an act ; but
the only reply he received was, that she was their mother,
and they were her children, and they ought to put her to
death. On reaching the grave, the mother sat down, when
they all, including children, grandchildren, relations, and
friends, took an affectionate leave of her ; a rope, made of
twisted *tapa* [bark-cloth], was then passed twice around her
neck by her sons, who took hold of it, and strangled her ;
after which she was put into her grave, with the usual
ceremonies. They returned to feast and mourn, after which
she was entirely forgotten as though she had not existed." [1]

Wives strangled or buried alive at their husbands' funerals.

Again, wives were often strangled, or buried alive, at
the funeral of their husbands, and generally at their own
instance. Such scenes were frequently witnessed by white
residents in the old days. On one occasion a Mr. David
Whippy drove away the murderers, rescued the woman,
and carried her to his own house, where she was resuscitated.
But far from feeling grateful for her preservation, she loaded
him with reproaches and ever afterwards manifested the
most deadly hatred towards him. "That women should
desire to accompany their husbands in death, is by no

[1] Ch. Wilkes, *op. cit.* iii. 94 *sq.*
Compare Th. Williams, *Fiji and the
Fijians*, i. 183-186 ; Lorimer Fison,
Tales from Old Fiji (London, 1904),
pp. xxv. *sq.*

means strange when it is considered that it is one of the articles of their belief, that in this way alone can they reach the realms of bliss, and she who meets her death with the greatest devotedness, will become the favourite wife in the abode of spirits. The sacrifice is not, however, always voluntary; but, when a woman refuses to be strangled, her relations often compel her to submit. This they do from interested motives; for, by her death, her connexions become entitled to the property of her husband. Even a delay is made a matter of reproach. Thus, at the funeral of the late king Ulivou, which was witnessed by Mr. Cargill, his five wives and a daughter were strangled. The principal wife delayed the ceremony, by taking leave of those around her; whereupon Tanoa, the present king, chid her. The victim was his own aunt, and he assisted in putting the rope around her neck, and strangling her, a service he is said to have rendered on a former occasion to his own mother."[1] In the case of men who were drowned at sea or killed and eaten by enemies in war, their wives were sacrificed in the usual way. Thus when Ra Mbithi, the pride of Somosomo, was lost at sea, seventeen of his wives were destroyed; and after the news of a massacre of the Namena people at Viwa in 1839 eighty women were strangled to accompany the spirits of their murdered husbands.[2]

The bodies of women who were put to death for this purpose were regularly laid at the bottom of the grave to serve as a cushion for the dead husband to lie upon; in this capacity they were called grass (*thotho*), being compared to the dried grass which in Fijian houses used to be thickly strewn on the floors and covered with mats.[3] On this point, however, a nice distinction was observed. While wives were commonly sacrificed at the death of their husbands, in order to be spread like grass in their graves, it does not transpire that husbands were ever sacrificed at the death of their wives for the sake of serving as grass to their dead spouses in the grave. The great truth that all flesh is grass appears

Human "grass" for the grave.

[1] Ch. Wilkes, *op. cit.* iii. 96. Compare Th. Williams, *op. cit.* i. 188 *sq.*, 193 *sqq.*, 200-202; Lorimer Fison, *op. cit.* pp. xxv. *sq.*

[2] Th. Williams, *op. cit.* i. 200.

[3] Th. Williams, *op. cit.* i. 189; Lorimer Fison, *op. cit.* p. xvi.

to have been understood by the Fijians as applicable chiefly to the flesh of women. Sometimes a man's mother was strangled as well as his wives. Thus Ngavindi, a young chief of Lasakau, was laid in the grave with a wife at his side, his mother at his feet, and a servant not far off. However, men as well as women were killed to follow their masters to the far country. The confidential companion of a chief was expected as a matter of common decency to die with his lord ; and if he shirked the duty, he fell in the public esteem. When Mbithi, a chief of high rank and greatly esteemed in Mathuata, died in the year 1840, not only his wife but five men with their wives were strangled to form the floor of his grave. They were laid on a layer of mats, and the body of the chief was stretched upon them.[1] There used to be a family in Vanua Levu which enjoyed the high privilege of supplying a hale man to be buried with the king of Fiji on every occasion of a royal decease. It was quite necessary that the man should be hale and hearty, for it was his business to grapple with the Fijian Cerberus in the other world, while his majesty slipped past into the abode of bliss.[2]

Sacrifices of foreskins and fingers in honour of the dead.
    A curious sacrifice offered in honour of a dead chief consisted in the foreskins of all the boys who had arrived at a suitable age ; the lads were circumcised on purpose to furnish them. Many boys had their little fingers chopped off on the same occasion, and the severed foreskins and fingers were placed in the chief's grave. When this bloody rite had been performed, the chief's relatives presented young bread-fruit trees to the mutilated boys, whose friends were bound to cultivate them till the boys could do it for themselves.[3] Women as well as boys had their fingers cut off in mourning. We read of a case when after the death of a king of Fiji sixty fingers were amputated and

---

[1] Th. Williams, op. cit. i. 189.

[2] Th. Williams, op. cit. i. 197.

[3] Ch. Wilkes, op. cit. iii. 100. Williams also says (op. cit. i. 167) that the proper time for performing the rite of circumcision was after the death of a chief, and he tells us that "many rude games attend it. Blind-folded youths strike at thin vessels of water hung from the branch of a tree. At Lakemba, the men arm themselves with branches of the cocoa-nut, and carry on a sham fight. At Ono, they wrestle. At Mbau, they fillip small stones from the end of a bamboo with sufficient force to make the person hit wince again. On Vanua Levu, there is a mock siege."

being each inserted in a slit reed were stuck along the eaves of the king's house.[1] Why foreskins and fingers were buried with a dead chief or stuck up on the roof of his house, we are not informed, and it is not easy to divine. Apparently we must suppose that, when they were buried with the body, they were thought to be of some assistance to the departed spirit in the land of souls. At all events it deserves to be noted that according to a very good authority a similar sacrifice of foreskins used to be made not only for the dead but for the living. When a man of note was dangerously ill, a family council would be held, at which it might be agreed that a circumcision should take place as a propitiatory measure. Notice having been given to the priests, an uncircumcised lad, the sick man's own son or the son of one of his brothers, was then taken by his kinsman to the *Vale tambu* or God's House, and there presented as a *soro*, or offering of atonement, in order that his father or father's brother might be made whole. His escort at the same time made a present of valuable property at the shrine and promised much more in future, should their prayers be answered. The present and the promises were graciously received by the priest, who appointed a day on which the operation was to be performed. In the meantime no food might be taken from the plantations except what was absolutely required for daily use ; no pigs or fowls might be killed, and no coco-nuts plucked from the trees. Everything, in short, was put under a strict taboo ; all was set apart for the great feast which was to follow the performance of the rite. On the day appointed the son or nephew of the sick chief was circumcised, and with him a number of other lads whose friends had agreed to take advantage of the occasion. Their foreskins, stuck in the cleft of a split reed, were taken to the sacred enclosure (*Nanga*) and presented to the chief priest, who, holding the reeds in his hand, offered them to the ancestral gods and prayed for the sick man's recovery. Then followed a great feast, which ushered in a period of indescribable revelry and licence. All distinctions of property were for the time being suspended. Men and women arrayed themselves

Marginal notes: Circumcision performed on a lad as a propitiatory sacrifice to save the life of his father or father's brother.

The rite of circumcision followed by a licentious orgy.

[1] Th. Williams, *op. cit.* i. 198.

in all manner of fantastic garbs, addressed one another in the foulest language, and practised unmentionable abominations openly in the public square of the town. The nearest relationships, even that of own brother and sister, seemed to be no bar to the general licence, the extent of which was indicated by the expressive phrase of an old Nandi chief, who said, "While it lasts, we are just like the pigs." This feasting and orgy might be kept up for several days, after which the ordinary restraints of society and the common decencies of life were observed once more. The rights of private property were again respected; the abandoned revellers and debauchees settled down into staid married couples; and brothers and sisters, in accordance with the regular Fijian etiquette, might not so much as speak to one another. It should be added that these extravagances in connexion with the rite of circumcision appear to have been practised only in certain districts of Viti Levu, the largest of the Fijian Islands, where they were always associated with the sacred stone enclosures which went by the name of *Nanga*.[1]

These orgies were apparently associated with the worship of the dead, to whom offerings were made in the *Nanga* or sacred enclosure of stones.

The meaning of such orgies is very obscure, but from what we know of the savage and his ways we may fairly assume that they were no mere outbursts of unbridled passion, but that in the minds of those who practised them they had a definite significance and served a definite purpose. The one thing that seems fairly clear about them is that in some way they were associated with the worship or propitiation of the dead. At all events we are told on good authority that the *Nanga*, or sacred enclosure of stones, in which the severed foreskins were offered, was "the Sacred Place where the ancestral spirits are to be found by their worshippers, and thither offerings are taken on all occasions

[1] Rev. Lorimer Fison, "The Nanga, or Sacred Stone Enclosure, of Waini-mala, Fiji," *Journal of the Anthropological Institute*, xiv. (1885) pp. 27 *sq.* On the other hand Mr. Basil Thomson's enquiries, made at a later date, did not confirm Mr. Fison's statement that the rite of circumcision was practised as a propitiation to recover a chief from sickness. " I was assured," he says, "on the contrary, that while offerings were certainly made in the *Nanga* for the recovery of the sick, every youth was circumcised as a matter of routine, and that the rite was in no way connected with sacrifice for the sick" (Basil Thomson, *The Fijians*, pp. 156 *sq.*). However, Mr. Fison was a very careful and accurate enquirer, and his testimony is not to be lightly set aside.

when their aid is to be invoked.   Every member of the *Nanga* has the privilege of approaching the ancestors at any time.   When sickness visits himself or his kinsfolk, when he wishes to invoke the aid of the spirits to avert calamity or to secure prosperity, or when he deems it advisable to present a thank-offering, he may enter the *Nanga* with proper reverence and deposit on the dividing wall his whale's tooth, or bundle of cloth, or dish of toothsome eels so highly prized by the elders, and therefore by the ancestors whose living representatives they are : or he may drag into the Sacred *Nanga* his fattened pig, or pile up there his offering of the choicest yams.   And, having thus recommended himself to the dead, he may invoke their powerful aid, or express his thankfulness for the benefits they have conferred, and beg for a continuance of their goodwill." [1]   The first-fruits of the yam harvest were presented with great ceremony to the ancestors in the *Nanga* before the bulk of the crop was dug for the people's use, and no man might taste of the new yams until the presentation had been made.   The yams so offered were piled up in the sacred enclosure and left to rot there.   If any one were impious enough to appropriate them to his own use, it was believed that he would be smitten with madness.   Great feasts were held at the presentation of the first-fruits ; and the sacred enclosure itself was often spoken of as the *Mbaki* or Harvest.[2]

But the most characteristic and perhaps the most important of the rites performed in the *Nanga* or sacred stone enclosure was the periodical initiation of young men, who by participation in the ceremony were admitted to the full privileges of manhood.   According to one account the ceremony of initiation was performed as a rule only once in two years ; according to another account it was observed annually in October or November, when the *ndrala* tree (*Erythrina*) was in flower.   The flowering of the tree

Periodical initiation of young men in the Nanga.

---

[1] Rev. Lorimer Fison, "The Nanga, or Sacred Stone Enclosure, of Waini-mala, Fiji," *Journal of the Anthropological Institute*, xiv. (1885) p. 26. Compare Basil Thomson, *The Fijians*, p. 147 : "The *Nanga* was the 'bed' of the Ancestors, that is, the spot where their descendants might hold communion with them ; the *Mbaki* were the rites celebrated in the *Nanga*, whether of initiating the youths, or of presenting the first-fruits, or of recovering the sick, or of winning charms against wounds in battle."

[2] Rev. Lorimer Fison, *op. cit.* p. 27.

marked the beginning of the Fijian year; hence the novices who were initiated at this season bore the title of *Vilavou*, that is, " New Year's Men."   As a preparation for the feasts which attended the ceremony enormous quantities of yams were garnered and placed under a strict taboo; pigs were fattened in large numbers, and bales of native cloth stored on the tie-beams of the house-roofs.   Spears of many patterns and curiously carved clubs were also provided against the festival.   On the day appointed the initiated men went first into the sacred enclosure and made their offerings, the chief priest having opened the proceedings by libation and prayer.   The heads of the novices were clean shaven, and their beards, if they had any, were also removed. Then each youth was swathed in long rolls of native cloth, and taking a spear in one hand and a club in the other he marched with his comrades, similarly swathed and armed, in procession into the sacred enclosure, though not into its inner compartment, the Holy of Holies.   The procession was headed by a priest bearing his carved staff of office, and it was received on the holy ground by the initiates, who sat chanting a song in a deep murmuring tone, which occasionally swelled to a considerable volume of sound and was thought to represent the muffled roar of the surf break- ing on a far-away coral reef.   On entering the enclosure the youths threw down their weapons before them, and with the help of the initiated men divested themselves of the huge folds of native cloth in which they were enveloped, each man revolving slowly on his axis, while his attendant pulled at the bandage and gathered in the slack.   The weapons and the cloth were the offerings presented by the novices to the ancestral spirits for the purpose of rendering themselves acceptable to these powerful beings.   The offerings were repeated in like manner on four successive days; and as each youth was merely, as it were, the central roller of a great bale of cloth, the amount of cloth offered was con- siderable.   It was all put away, with the spears and clubs, in the sacred storehouse by the initiated men.   A feast concluded each day and was prolonged far into the night.

On the fifth day, the last and greatest of the festival, the heads of the young men were shaven again and their bodies swathed in the largest and best rolls of cloth. Then, taking their choicest weapons in their hands, they followed their leader as before into the sacred enclosure. But the outer compartment of the holy place, where on the previous days they had been received by the grand chorus of initiated men, was now silent and deserted. The procession stopped. A dead silence prevailed. Suddenly from the forest a harsh scream of many parrots broke forth, and then followed a mysterious booming sound which filled the souls of the novices with awe. But now the priest moves slowly forward and leads the train of trembling novices for the first time into the inner shrine, the Holy of Holies, the *Nanga tambu-tambu.* Here a dreadful spectacle meets their startled gaze. In the background sits the high priest, regarding them with a stony stare ; and between him and them lie a row of dead men, covered with blood, their bodies seemingly cut open and their entrails protruding. The leader steps over them one by one, and the awestruck youths follow him until they stand in a row before the high priest, their very souls harrowed by his awful glare. Suddenly he utters a great yell, and at the cry the dead men start to their feet, and run down to the river to cleanse themselves from the blood and filth with which they are besmeared. They are initiated men, who represent the departed ancestors for the occasion ; and the blood and entrails are those of many pigs that have been slaughtered for that night's revelry. The screams of the parrots and the mysterious booming sound were produced by a concealed orchestra, who screeched appropriately and blew blasts on bamboo trumpets, the mouths of which were partially immersed in water.

The dead men having come to life again, the novices offered their weapons and the bales of native cloth in which they were swathed. These were accordingly removed to the storehouse and the young men were made to sit down in front of it. Then the high priest, cheered perhaps by the sight of the offerings, unbent the starched dignity of his demeanour. Skipping from side to side he cried in stridulous tones, "Where are the people of my enclosure ? Are they gone to Tongalevu ? Are they gone to the deep sea?" He had not called long when an answer rang out from the river in a deep-mouthed song, and soon the singers came in view moving rhythmically to the music of their solemn chant. Singing they filed in and took their places in front of the young men; then silence ensued. After that there entered four old men of the highest order of initiates; the first bore a cooked yam carefully wrapt in leaves so that no part of it should touch the hands of the bearer; the second carried a piece of baked pork similarly enveloped; the third held a drinking-cup of coco-nut shell or earthenware . filled with water and wrapt round with native cloth; and the fourth bore a napkin of the same material. Thereupon the first elder passed along the row of novices putting the end of the yam into each of their mouths, and as he did so each of them nibbled a morsel of the sacred food; the second elder did the same with the sacred pork; the third elder followed with the holy water, with which each novice merely wetted his lips; and the rear was brought up by the fourth elder, who wiped all their mouths with his napkin. Then the high priest or one of the elders addressed the young men, warning them solemnly against the sacrilege of divulging to the profane any of the high mysteries they had seen and heard, and threatening all such traitors with the vengeance of the gods.

Presentation of the pig.

That ceremony being over, all the junior initiated men (*Lewe ni Nanga*) came forward, and each man presented to the novices a yam and a piece of nearly raw pork; whereupon the young men took the food and went away to cook it for eating. When the evening twilight had fallen, a huge pig, which had been specially set aside at a former festival, was dragged into the sacred enclosure and there presented to the novices, together with other swine, if they should be needed to furnish a plenteous repast.

Acceptance of the novices by the ancestral spirits.

The novices were now "accepted members of the *Nanga*, qualified to take their place among the men of the community, though still only on probation. As children—their childhood being indicated by their shaven heads—they were presented to the ancestors, and their acceptance was notified by what (looking at the matter from the natives' standpoint) we might, without irreverence, almost call the *sacrament* of food and water, too sacred even for the elders' hands to touch. This acceptance was acknowledged and confirmed on the part of all the *Lewe ni Nanga* [junior initiated men] by their gift of food, and it was finally ratified by the presentation of the Sacred Pig. In like manner, on the birth of an infant, its father acknowledges it as legitimate, and otherwise acceptable, by a gift of food ; and his kinsfolk formally signify approval and confirmation of his decision on the part of the clan by similar presentations."

Next morning the women, their hair dyed red and wearing waistbands of hibiscus or other fibre, came to the sacred enclosure and crawled through it on hands and knees into the Holy of Holies, where the elders were singing their solemn chant. The high priest then dipped his hands into the water of the sacred bowl and prayed to the ancestral spirits for the mothers and for their children. After that the women crawled back on hands and feet the way they had come, singing as they went and creeping over certain mounds of earth which had been thrown up for the purpose in the sacred enclosure. When they emerged from the holy ground, the men and women addressed each other in the vilest language, such as on ordinary occasions would be violently resented ; and thenceforth to the close of the ceremonies some days later very great, indeed almost unlimited, licence prevailed between the sexes. During these days a number of pigs were consecrated to serve for the next ceremony. The animals were deemed sacred, and had the run of the fleshpots in the villages in which they were kept. Indeed they were held in the greatest reverence. To kill one, except for sacrifice at the rites in the *Nanga*, would have been a sacrilege which the Fijian mind refused to contemplate ; and on the other hand to feed the holy swine was an act of piety. Men might be seen throwing down basketfuls of food before the snouts of the worshipful pigs, and at the same time calling the attention of the ancestral spirits to the meritorious deed. "Take knowledge of me," they would cry, "ye who lie buried, our heads ! I am feeding this pig of yours." Finally, all the men who had taken part in the ceremonies bathed together in the river, carefully cleansing themselves

The initiation followed by a period of sexual licence.

Sacred pigs.

from every particle of the black paint with which they had been bedaubed. When the novices, now novices no more, emerged from the water, the high priest, standing on the river bank, preached to them an eloquent sermon on the duties and responsibilities which devolved on them in their new position.[1]

The intention of the initiatory rites seems to be to introduce the young men to the ancestral spirits.

The general intention of these initiatory rites appears to be, as Mr. Fison has said in the words which I have quoted, to introduce the young men to the ancestral spirits at their sanctuary, to incorporate them, so to say, in the great community which embraces all adult members of the tribe, whether living or dead. At all events this interpretation fits in very well with the prayers which are offered to the souls of departed kinsfolk on these occasions, and it is supported by the analogy of the New Guinea initiatory rites which I described in former lectures ; for in these rites, as I pointed out, the initiation of the youths is closely associated with the conceptions of death and the dead, the main feature in the ritual consisting indeed of a simulation of death and subsequent resurrection. It is, therefore, significant that the very same simulation figures prominently in the Fijian cere- mony, nay it would seem to be the very pivot on which the whole ritual revolves. Yet there is an obvious and important difference between the drama of death and resurrection as it is enacted in New Guinea and in Fiji ; for whereas in New

The drama of death and resur- rection.

---

[1] Rev. Lorimer Fison, "The Nanga, or Sacred Stone Enclosure, of Wainimala, Fiji," *Journal of the Anthropological Institute*, xiv. (1885) pp. 14-26. The *Nanga* and its rites have also been described by Mr. A. B. Joske ("The Nanga of Viti-levu," *Internationales Archiv für Ethno- graphie*, ii. (1889) pp. 254-266), and Mr. Basil Thomson (*The Fijians*, pp. 146-156). As to the interval between the initiatory ceremonies Mr. Fison tells us that it was normally two years, but he adds : "This period, however, is not necessarily restricted to two years. There are always a number of youths who are growing to the proper age, and the length of the interval depends upon the decision of the elders. When- ever they judge that there is a sufficient number of youths ready for admission, a *Nanga* is appointed to be held ; and thus the interval may be longer or shorter, according to the supply of novices" (*op. cit.* p. 19). According to Mr. Basil Thomson the rites were cele- brated annually. Mr. Fison's evidence as to the gross licence which prevailed between the sexes after the admission of the women to the sacred enclosure is confirmed by Mr. Basil Thomson, who says, amongst other things, that "a native of Mbau, who lived for some years near the *Nanga*, assured me that the visit of the women to the *Nanga* resulted in temporary promis- cuity ; all tabus were defied, and relations who could not speak to one another by customary law committed incest" (*op. cit.* p. 154).

Guinea it is the novices who pretend to die and come to life again, in Fiji the pretence is carried out by initiated men who represent the ancestors, while the novices merely look on with horror and amazement at the awe-inspiring spectacle. Of the two forms of ritual the New Guinea one is probably truer to the original purpose of the rite, which seems to have been to enable the novices to put off the old, or rather the young, man and to put on a higher form of existence by participating in the marvellous powers and privileges of the mighty dead. And if such was really the intention of the ceremony, it is obvious that it was better effected by compelling the young communicants, as we may call them, to die and rise from the dead in their own persons than by obliging them to assist as mere passive spectators at a dramatic performance of death and resurrection. Yet in spite of this difference between the two rituals, the general resemblance between them is near enough to justify us in conjecturing that there may be a genetic connexion between the one and the other. The conjecture is confirmed, first, by the very limited and definite area of Fiji in which these initiatory rites were practised, and, second, by the equally definite tradition of their origin. With regard to the first of these points, the *Nanga* or sacred stone enclosure with its characteristic rites was known only to certain tribes, who occupied a comparatively small area, a bare third of the island of Viti Levu. These tribes are the Nuyaloa, Vatusila, Mbatiwai, and Mdavutukia. They all seem to have spread eastward and southward from a place of origin in the western mountain district. Their physical type is pure Melanesian, with fewer traces of Polynesian admixture than can be detected in the tribes on the coast.[1] Hence it is natural to enquire whether the ritual of the *Nanga* may not have been imported into Fiji by Melanesian immigrants from the west. The question appears to be answered in the affirmative by native tradition. "This is the word of our fathers concerning the *Nanga*," said an old Wainimala grey-beard to Mr. Fison. "Long, long ago their fathers were

[marginal note: The Fijian rites of initiation seem to have been imported by Melanesian immigrants from the west.]

---

[1] Rev. Lorimer Fison, "The Nanga, or Sacred Stone Enclosure, of Wainimala, Fiji," *Journal of the Anthropological Institute*, xiv. (1885) pp. 14 *sqq.* ; Basil Thomson, *The Fijians*, pp. 147, 149.

ignorant of it ; but one day two strangers were found sitting
in the *rārā* (public square), and they said they had come up
from the sea to give them the *Nanga*. They were little men,
and very dark-skinned, and one of them had his face and
bust painted red, while the other was painted black.
Whether these two were gods or men our fathers did not tell
us, but it was they who taught our people the *Nanga*. This
was in the old old times when our fathers were living in
another land—not in this place, for we are strangers here.
Our fathers fled hither from Navosa in a great war which
arose among them, and when they came there was no *Nanga* in
the land.   So they built one of their own after the fashion
of that which they left behind them." [1]   " Here," says Mr.
Basil Thomson, " we have the earliest tradition of missionary
enterprise in the Pacific.   I do not doubt that the two sooty-
skinned little men were castaways driven eastward by one
of those strong westerly gales that have been known to last
for three weeks at a time.   By Fijian custom the lives of all
castaways were forfeit, but the pretence to supernatural
powers would have saved men full of the religious rites of
their Melanesian home, and would have assured them a
hearing.   The Wainimala tribes can name six generations
since they settled in their present home, and therefore
the introduction of the *Nanga* cannot have been less than
two centuries ago.   During that time it has overspread one
third of the large island." [2]

The general licence associated with the ritual of the *Nanga* may be a temporary revival of primitive communism. A very remarkable feature in the *Nanga* ritual consists
in the temporary licence accorded to the sexes and the
suspension of proprietary rites in general.   What is the
meaning of this curious and to the civilised mind revolting
custom?   Here again the most probable, though merely
conjectural, answer is furnished by Mr. Fison.   " We cannot
for a moment believe," he says, " that it is a mere licentious
outbreak, without an underlying meaning and purpose.   It
is part of a religious rite, and is supposed to be acceptable
to the ancestors.   But why should it be acceptable to them
unless it were in accordance with their own practice in the

[1] Rev. Lorimer Fison, *op. cit.* p.
17. Wainimala is a district in the
centre of Viti Levu, the largest of the
Fijian islands ; Navosa is a district
also in the centre of Viti Levu, but to
the west of Wainimala.

[2] Basil Thomson, *The Fijians*,
p. 150.

far-away past ?   There may be another solution of this difficult problem, but I confess myself unable to find any other which will cover all the corroborating facts." [1]   In other words, Mr. Fison supposes that in the sexual licence and suspension of the rights of private property which characterise these festivals we have a reminiscence of a time when women and property were held in common by the community, and the motive for temporarily resuscitating these obsolete customs was a wish to propitiate the ancestral spirits, who were thought to be gratified by witnessing a revival of that primitive communism which they themselves had practised in the flesh so long ago.   Truly a religious revival of a remarkable kind !

To conclude this part of my subject I will briefly describe the construction of a *Nanga* or sacred stone enclosure, as it used to exist in Fiji.   At the present day only ruins of these structures are to be seen, but by an observation of the ruins and a comparison of the traditions which still survive among the natives on the subject it is possible to reconstruct one of them with a fair degree of exactness.   A *Nanga* has been described as an open-air temple, and the description is just. It consisted of a rough parallelogram enclosed by flat stones set upright and embedded endwise in the earth.   The length of the enclosure thus formed was about one hundred feet and its breadth about fifty feet.   The upright stones which form the outer walls are from eighteen inches to three feet high, but as they do not always touch they may be described as alignments rather than walls.   The long walls or alignments run east and west, the short ones north and south ; but the orientation is not very exact.   At the eastern end are two pyramidal heaps of stones, about five feet high, with square sloping sides and flat tops.   The narrow passage between them is the main entrance into the sacred enclosure.   Internally the structure was divided into three separate enclosures or compartments by two cross-walls of stone running north and south.   These compartments, taking them from east to west, were called respectively the Little Nanga, the Great Nanga, and the Sacred Nanga or Holy of Holies (*Nanga tambu-tambu*).   The partition walls between

Descrip-tion of the Nanga or sacred enclosure of stones.

[1] Rev. Lorimer Fison, *op. cit.* p. 30.

them were built solid of stones, with battering sides, to a height of five feet, and in the middle of each there was an opening to allow the worshippers to pass from one compartment to another.   Trees, such as the candlenut and the red-leaved dracaena, and odoriferous shrubs were planted round the enclosure ; and outside of it, to the west of the Holy of Holies, was a bell-roofed hut called *Vale tambu*, the Sacred House or Temple.   The sacred *kava* bowl stood in the Holy of Holies.[1]   It is said that when the two traditionary founders of the *Nanga* in Fiji were about to erect the first structure of that name in their new home, the chief priest poured a libation of *kava* to the ancestral gods, " and, calling upon those who died long, long ago by name, he prayed that the people of the tribe, both old and young, might live before them." [2]

Comparison of the *Nanga* with the cromlechs and other megalithic monuments of Europe.

The sacred enclosures of stones which I have described have been compared to the alignments of stones at Carnac in Brittany and Merivale on Dartmoor, and it has been suggested that in the olden time these ancient European monuments may have witnessed religious rites like those which were till lately performed in the rude open-air temples of Fiji.[3]   If there is any truth in the suggestion, which I mention for what it is worth, it would furnish another argument in favour of the view that our European cromlechs and other megalithic monuments were erected specially for the worship of the dead.   The mortuary character of Stonehenge, for example, is at least suggested by the burial mounds which cluster thick around and within sight of it ; about three hundred such tombs have been counted within a radius of three miles, while the rest of the country in the neighbourhood is comparatively free from them.[4]

[1] Rev. Lorimer Fison, *op. cit.* pp. 15, 17, with Plate I. ; Basil Thomson, *The Fijians*, pp. 147 *sq.* Mr. Fison had not seen a *Nanga* ; his description is based on information received from natives. Mr. Basil Thomson visited several of these structures and found them so alike that one description would serve for all.   He speaks of only two inner compartments, which he calls the Holy of Holies (*Nanga tambu-tambu*) and the Middle Nanga

(*Loma ni Nanga*), but the latter name appears to imply a third compartment, which is explicitly mentioned and named by Mr. Fison.   The bell-shaped hut or temple to the west of the sacred enclosure is not noticed by Mr. Thomson.

[2] Rev. Lorimer Fison, *op. cit.* p. 17.

[3] Basil Thomson, *The Fijians*, p. 147.

[4] As to these monuments see Sir John Lubbock (Lord Avebury), *Prehistoric Times*, Fifth Edition (London, 1890), p. 127.

LECTURE XX

THE BELIEF IN IMMORTALITY AMONG THE NATIVES OF EASTERN MELANESIA (FIJI) (*concluded*)

IN the last lecture I described the rites of ancestor worship which in certain parts of Fiji used to be celebrated at the sacred enclosures of stones known as *Nangas*. But the worship of ancestral spirits was by no means confined to the comparatively small area in Fiji where such sacred enclosures were erected, nor were these open-air temples the only structures where the homage of the living was paid to the dead. On the contrary we are told by one who knew the Fijians in the old heathen days that among them " as soon as beloved parents expire, they take their place amongst the family gods. *Bures*, or temples, are erected to their memory, and offerings deposited either on their graves or on rudely constructed altars—mere stages, in the form of tables, the legs of which are driven into the ground, and the top of which is covered with pieces of native cloth. The construction of these altars is identical with that observed by Turner in Tanna, and only differs in its inferior finish from the altars formerly erected in Tahiti and the adjacent islands. The offerings, consisting of the choicest articles of food, are left exposed to wind and weather, and firmly believed by the mass of Fijians to be consumed by the spirits of departed friends and relations ; but, if not eaten by animals, they are often stolen by the more enlightened class of their countrymen, and even some of the foreigners do not disdain occasionally to help themselves freely to them. However, it is not only on tombs or on altars that offerings are made ; often, when the natives eat or drink

439

anything, they throw portions of it away, stating them to be for their departed ancestors. I remember ordering a young chief to empty a bowl containing *kava*, which he did, muttering to himself, ' There, father, is some *kava* for you. Protect me from illness or breaking any of my limbs whilst in the mountains.' " [1]

Fijian notion of divinity. Two classes of gods, namely, gods strictly so called, and deified men. " The native word expressive of divinity is *kalou*, which, while used to denote the people's highest notion of a god, is also constantly heard as a qualificative of any thing great or marvellous, or, according to Hazlewood's Dictionary, ' anything superlative, whether good or bad.' . . . Often the word sinks into a mere exclamation, or becomes an expression of flattery. ' You are a *kalou*!' or, 'Your countrymen are gods!' is often uttered by the natives, when hearing of the triumphs of art among civilized nations." [2] The Fijians distinguished two classes of gods : first, *kalou vu*, literally " Root-gods," that is, gods strictly so called, and second, *kalou yalo*, literally, " Soul-gods," that is, deified mortals. Gods of the first class were supposed to be absolutely eternal ; gods of the second class, though raised far above mere humanity, were thought nevertheless to be subject to human passions and wants, to accidents, and even to death. These latter were the spirits of departed chiefs, heroes, and friends ; admission into their number was easy, and any one might secure his own apotheosis who could ensure the services of some one to act as his representative and priest after his death.[3] However, though the Fijians admitted the distinction between the two classes of gods in theory, they would seem to have confused them in practice. Thus we are informed by an early authority that " they have superior and inferior gods and goddesses, more general and local deities, and, were it not an obvious contradiction, we should say they have gods *human*, and gods *divine* ; for they have some gods who were gods originally, and some who were originally men. It is impossible to ascertain with any degree of probability how many gods the Feejeeans

[1] Berthold Seeman, *Viti, an Account of a Government Mission to the Vitian or Fijian Islands* (Cambridge, 1862), pp. 391 *sq.*

[2] Th. Williams, *Fiji and the Fijians*, i. 216.

[3] Th. Williams, *op. cit.* i. 216, 218 *sq.*; Basil Thomson, *The Fijians*, p. 112.

have, as any man who can distinguish himself in murdering his fellow-men may certainly secure to himself deification after death.   Their friends are also sometimes deified and invoked.   I have heard them invoke their friends who have been drowned at sea.   I need not advert to the absurdity of praying to those who could not save themselves from a watery grave.   Tuikilakila, the chief of Somosomo, offered Mr. Hunt a preferment of this sort.   ' If you die first,' said he, ' I shall make you my god.'   In fact, there appears to be no certain line of demarcation between departed spirits and gods, nor between gods and living men, for many of the priests and old chiefs are considered as sacred persons, and not a few of them will also claim to themselves the right of divinity.   ' I am a god,' Tuikilakila would some-times say ; and he believed it too.   They were not merely the words of his lips ; he believed he was something above a mere man." [1]

Writers on Fiji have given us lists of some of the principal gods of the first class,[2] who were supposed never to have been men ; but in their account of the religious ritual they do not distinguish between the worship which was paid to such deities and that which was paid to deified men. Accordingly we may infer that the ritual was practically the same, and in the sequel I shall assume that what is told us of the worship of gods in general holds good of the worship of deified men in particular.

Every Fijian town had at least one *bure* or temple, many of them had several.   Significantly enough the spot where a chief had been killed was sometimes chosen for the site of a temple.   The structure of these edifices was somewhat peculiar.   Each of them was built on the top of a mound, which was raised to the height of from three to twenty feet above the ground and faced on its sloping sides with dry rubble-work of stone.   The ascent to the temple was by a thick plank, the upper surface of which was cut into notched steps.   The proportions of the sacred edifice

The Fijian temple (bure).

[1] Hazlewood, quoted by Capt. J. E. Erskine, *Journal of a Cruise among the Islands of the Western Pacific* (London, 1853), pp. 246 *sq.*

[2] Ch. Wilkes, *Narrative of the United States Exploring Expedition,* New Edition (New York, 1851), iii. 83 *sq.* ; Th. Williams, *Fiji and the Fijians,* i. 217 *sqq.*

itself were inelegant, if not uncouth, its height being nearly twice as great as its breadth at the base. The roof was high-pitched; the ridge-pole was covered with white shells (*Ovula cypraea*) and projected three or four feet at each end. For the most part each temple had two doors and a fire-place in the centre. From some temples it was not lawful to throw out the ashes, however much they might accumulate, until the end of the year, which fell in November. The furniture consisted of a few boxes, mats, several large clay jars, and many drinking vessels. A temple might also contain images, which, though highly esteemed as ornaments and held sacred, were not worshipped as idols. From the roof depended a long piece of white bark-cloth; it was carried down the angle so as to hang before the corner-post and lie on the floor. This cloth formed the path down which the god was believed to pass in order to enter and inspire his priest. It marked the holy place which few but he dared to approach. However, the temples were by no means dedicated exclusively to the use of religion. Each of them served also as a council-chamber and town-hall; there the chiefs lounged for hours together; there strangers were entertained; and there the head persons of the village might even sleep.[1] In some parts of Viti Levu the dead were sometimes buried in the temples, " that the wind might not disturb, nor the rain fall upon them," and in order that the living might have the satisfaction of lying near their departed friends. A child of high rank having died under the charge of the queen of Somosomo, the little body was placed in a box and hung from the tie-beam of the principal temple. For some months afterwards the daintiest food was brought daily to the dead child, the bearers approaching with the utmost respect and clapping their hands when the ghost was thought to have finished his meal just as a chief's retainers used to do when he had done eating.[2]

Temples were often unoccupied for months and allowed

[1] Ch. Wilkes, *Narrative of the United States Exploring Expedition*, New Edition (New York, 1851), iii. 49, 86, 351, 352; Th. Williams, *Fiji and the Fijians*, i. 221-223; B. Seeman, *Viti*, pp. 392-394.

[2] Th. Williams, *op. cit.* i. 191 *sq.*

to fall into ruins, until the chief had some request to make Worship at the temples.
to the god, when the necessary repairs were first carried out.
No regular worship was maintained, no habitual reverence
was displayed at the shrines. The principle of fear, we are
told, seemed to be the only motive of religious observances,
and it was artfully fomented by the priests, through whom
alone the people had access to the gods when they desired to
supplicate the favour of the divine beings. The prayers were
naturally accompanied by offerings, which in matters of
importance comprised large quantities of food, together with
whales' teeth ; in lesser affairs a tooth, club, mat, or spear
sufficed. Of the food brought by the worshippers part was
dedicated to the god, but as usual he only ate the soul of it,
the substance being consumed by the priest and old men ;
the remainder furnished a feast of which all might partake.[1]

The office of priest (*mbete*, *bete*) was usually hereditary, The priests.
but when a priest died without male heirs a cunning fellow,
ambitious of enjoying the sacred character and of living in
idleness, would sometimes simulate the convulsive frenzy,
which passed for a symptom of inspiration, and if he
succeeded in the imposture would be inducted into the
vacant benefice. Every chief had his priest, with whom he
usually lived on a very good footing, the two playing into
each other's hands and working the oracle for their mutual
benefit. The people were grossly superstitious, and there
were few of their affairs in which the priest had not a hand.
His influence over them was great. In his own district he
passed for the representative of the deity ; indeed, according
to an early missionary, the natives seldom distinguished
the idea of the god from that of his minister, who was
viewed by them with a reverence that almost amounted to
deification.[2]

The principal duty of the priest was to reveal to men Oracles given by the priest under the inspiration of the god.
the will of the god, and this he always did through the
direct inspiration of the deity. The revelation was usually
made in response to an enquiry or a prayer ; the supplicant
asked, it might be, for a good crop of yams or taro, for

[1] Th. Williams, *Fiji and the Fijians*, i. 223, 231.
[2] Ch. Wilkes, *op. cit.* iii. 87 ; Th.

Williams, *op. cit.* i. 226, 227 ; Basil Thomson, *The Fijians*, pp. 157 *sqq.*

showers of rain, for protection in battle, for a safe voyage, or for a storm to drive canoes ashore, so that the supplicant might rob, murder, and eat the castaways.   To lend force to one or other of these pious prayers the worshipper brought a whale's tooth to the temple and presented it to the priest.   The man of god might have had word of his coming and time to throw himself into an appropriate attitude.   He might, for example, be seen lying on the floor near the sacred corner, plunged in a profound meditation. On the entrance of the enquirer the priest would rouse himself so far as to get up and then seat himself with his back to the white cloth, down which the deity was expected to slide into the medium's body.   Having received the whale's tooth he would abstract his mind from all worldly matters and contemplate the tooth for some time with rapt attention.   Presently he began to tremble, his limbs twitched,

Paroxysm of inspiration.

his features were distorted.   These symptoms, the visible manifestation of the entrance of the spirit into him, gradually increased in violence till his whole frame was convulsed and shook as with a strong fit of ague : his veins swelled : the circulation of the blood was quickened.   The man was now possessed and inspired by the god : his own human personality was for a time in abeyance : all that he said and did in the paroxysm passed for the words and acts of the indwelling deity.   Shrill cries of "*Koi au! Koi au!*" "It is I! It is I!" filled the air, proclaiming the actual presence of the powerful spirit in the vessel of flesh and blood.   In giving the oracular response the priest's eyes protruded from their sockets and rolled as in a frenzy : his voice rose into a squeak : his face was pallid, his lips livid, his breathing depressed, his whole appearance that of a furious madman.   At last sweat burst from every pore, tears gushed from his eyes : the strain on the organism was visibly relieved ; and the symptoms gradually abated. Then he would look round with a vacant stare : the god within him would . cry, "I depart!" and the man would announce the departure of the spirit by throwing himself on his mat or striking the ground with his club, while blasts on a shell-trumpet conveyed to those at a distance the tidings that the deity had withdrawn from mortal sight into the

world invisible.[1] " I have seen," says Mr. Lorimer Fison,
" this possession, and a horrible sight it is.   In one case, after
the fit was over, for some time the man's muscles and nerves
twitched and quivered in an extraordinary way.   He was
naked except for his breech-clout, and on his naked breast
little snakes seemed to be wriggling for a moment or two
beneath his skin, disappearing and then suddenly reappear-
ing in another part of his chest.   When the *mbete* (which
we may translate ' priest' for want of a better word) is
seized by the possession, the god within him calls out his
own name in a stridulous tone, ' It is I ! Katouviere !' or
some other name.   At the next possession some other
ancestor may declare himself." [2]

From this last description of an eye-witness we learn Specimens
that the spirit which possessed a priest and spoke of the
oracular
through him was often believed to be that of a dead utterances
ancestor.   Some of the inspired utterances of these of Fijian
gods.
prophets have been recorded.   Here are specimens of Fijian
inspiration.   Speaking in the name of the great god Ndengei,
who was worshipped in the form of a serpent, the priest
said : " Great Fiji is my small club.   Muaimbila is the
head ; Kamba is the handle.   If I step on Muaimbila, I
shall sink it into the sea, whilst Kamba shall rise to the sky.
If I step on Kamba, it will be lost in the sea, whilst
Muaimbila would rise into the skies.   Yes, Viti Levu is my
small war-club.   I can turn it as I please.   I can turn it
upside down."   Again, speaking by the mouth of a priest,
the god Tanggirianima once made the following observations :
" I and Kumbunavannua only are gods.   I preside over
wars, and do as I please with sickness.   But it is difficult
for me to come here, as the foreign god fills the place.   If I
attempt to descend by that pillar, I find it pre-occupied by
the foreign god.   If I try another pillar, I find it the
same.   However, we two are fighting the foreign god ; and

---

[1] Ch. Wilkes, *op. cit.* iii. 87 *sq.* ;
Th. Williams, *op. cit.* i. 224 *sq.* ;
Capt. J. E. Erskine, *op. cit.* p. 250 ;
Lorimer Fison, *Tales from Old Fiji*
(London, 1904), pp. 166 *sq.*   As for
the treatment of castaways, see J. E.
Erskine, *op. cit.* p. 249; Th. Williams,
op. cit. i. 210.   The latter writer

mentions a recent case in which four-
teen or sixteen shipwrecked persons
were cooked and eaten.
  [2] The Rev. Lorimer Fison, in a
letter to me dated August 26th, 1898.
I have already quoted the passage in
*The Magic Art and the Evolution of
Kings*, i. 378.

if we are victorious, we will save the woman. I *will* save the woman. She will eat food to-day. Had I been sent for yesterday, she would have eaten then," and so on. The woman, about whose case the deity was consulted and whom he announced his fixed intention of saving, died a few hours afterwards.[1]

Human sacrifices in Fiji.

Ferocious and inveterate cannibals themselves, the Fijians naturally assumed that their gods were so too; hence human flesh was a common offering, indeed the most valued of all.[2] Formal human sacrifices were frequent. The victims were usually taken from a distant tribe, and when war and violence failed to supply the demand, recourse was sometimes had to negotiation. However obtained, the victims destined for sacrifice were often kept for a time and fattened to make them better eating. Then, tightly bound in a sitting posture, they were placed on hot stones in one of the usual ovens, and being covered over with leaves and earth were roasted alive, while the spectators roared with laughter at the writhings and contortions of the victims in their agony. When their struggles ceased and the bodies were judged to be done to a nicety, they were raked out of the oven, their faces painted black, and so carried to the temple, where they were presented to the gods, only, however, to be afterwards removed, cut up, and devoured by the people.[3]

Human sacrifices offered when a king's house was built or a great new canoe launched.

However, roasting alive in ovens was not the only way in which men and women were made away with in the service of religion. When a king's house was built, men were buried alive in the holes dug to receive the posts: they were compelled to clasp the posts in their arms, and then the earth was shovelled over them and rammed down. And when a large new canoe was launched, it was hauled down to the sea over the bodies of living men, who were pinioned and laid out at intervals on the beach to serve as rollers on which the great vessel glided smoothly into the water, leaving a row of mangled corpses behind. The theory of both these modes of sacrifice was explained by the Fijians to an Englishman who witnessed them. I will quote their explanation in his

[1] Th. Williams, *Fiji and the Fijians*, i. 225 *sq.*
[2] Th. Williams, *op. cit.* i. 231.
[3] Ch. Wilkes, *op. cit.* iii. 97; Th. Williams, *op. cit.* i. 53.

words. " They said in answer to the questions I put respecting the people being buried alive with the posts, that a
house or palace of a king was just like a king's canoe : if the
canoe was not hauled over men, as rollers, she would not be
expected to float long, and in like manner the palace could
not stand long if people were not to sit down and continually
hold the posts up.   But I said, ' How could they hold the
posts up after they were dead ? '   They said, if they sacrificed
their lives endeavouring to hold the posts in their right
position to their superior's *turanga kai na kalou* (chiefs and
god), that the virtue of the sacrifice would instigate the gods
to uphold the house after they were dead, and that they were
honoured by being considered adequate to such a noble task." [1]
Apparently the Fijians imagined that the souls of the dead
men would somehow strengthen the souls of the houses and
canoes and so prolong the lives of these useful objects ; for
it is to be remembered that according to Fijian theology
houses and canoes as well as men and women were provided
with immortal souls.

Perhaps the same theory of immortality partially accounts
for the high honour in which the Fijian held the act of
murder and for the admiration which he bestowed on all
murderers.   " Shedding of blood," we are told, " to him is no
crime, but a glory.   Whoever may be the victim,—whether
noble or vulgar, old or young, man, woman, or child,—whether
slain in war, or butchered by treachery,—to be somehow an
acknowledged murderer is the object of the Fijian's restless
ambition." [2]   It was customary throughout Fiji to give
honorary names to such as had clubbed to death a human
being, of any age or either sex, during a war.   The new
epithet was given with the complimentary prefix *Koroi*.
Mr. Williams once asked a man why he was called *Koroi*.
" Because," he replied, " I, with several other men, found some

High estimation in which murder was held by the Fijians.

[1] John Jackson's Narrative, in Capt.
J. E. Erskine's *Journal of a Cruise
among the Islands of the Western Pacific*
(London, 1853), pp. 464 *sq.*, 472 *sq.*
The genital members of the men over
whom the canoe was dragged were cut
off and hung on a sacred tree (*akau-
tambu*), "which was already artificially
prolific in fruit, both of the masculine
and feminine gender."   The tree which
bore such remarkable fruit was commonly an ironweed tree standing in a
conspicuous situation.   As to these
sacrifices compare Ch. Wilkes, *op. cit.*
iii. 97 ; Lorimer Fison, *Tales from Old
Fiji*, pp. xvi. *sq.*

[2] Th. Williams, *op. cit.* i. 112.

women and children in a cave, drew them out and clubbed them, and then was consecrated."[1]   Mr. Fison learned from another stout young warrior that he had earned the honourable distinction of *Koroi* by lying in wait among the mangrove bushes at the waterside and killing a miserable old woman of a hostile tribe, as she crept along the mudflat seeking for shellfish.   The man would have been equally honoured, adds Mr. Fison, if his victim had been a child.   The hero of such an exploit, for two or three days after killing his man or woman, was allowed to besmear his face and bust with a mixture of lampblack and oil which differed from the common black war-paint; decorated with this badge of honour he strutted proudly through the town, the cynosure of all eyes, an object of envy to his fellows and of tender interest to the girls.   The old men shouted approval after him, the women would *lulilu* admiringly as he passed by, and the boys looked up to him as a superior being whose noble deeds they thirsted to emulate.   Higher titles of honour still were bestowed on such as had slain their ten, or twenty, or thirty; and Mr. Fison tells us of a chief whose admiring countrymen had to compound all these titles into one in order to set forth his superlative claims to glory.   A man who had never killed anybody was of very little account in this life, and he received the penalty due to his sin in the life hereafter.   For in the spirit land the ghost of such a poor-spirited wretch was sentenced to what the Fijians regarded as the most degrading of all punishments, to beat a heap of muck with his bloodless club.[2]

Ceremony of consecrating a manslayer.

The ceremony of consecrating a manslayer was elaborate. He was anointed with red oil from the hair of his head to the soles of his feet; and when he had been thus incarnadined he exchanged clubs with the spectators, who believed that their weapons acquired a mysterious virtue by passing through his holy hands.   Afterwards the anointed one, attended by the king and elders, solemnly stalked down to the sea and wetted the soles of his feet in the water. Then the whole company returned to the town, while the

[1] Th. Williams, *op. cit.* i. 55.

[2] Lorimer Fison, *Tales from Old Fiji*, pp. xx., xxi. *sq.*; Th. Williams, *op. cit.* i. 247; B. Seeman, *Viti* (Cambridge, 1862), p. 401.

shell-trumpets sounded and the men raised a peculiar hoot. Custom required that a hut should be built in which the anointed man and his companions must pass the next three nights, during which the hero might not lie down, but had to sleep as he sat; all that time he might not change his bark-cloth garment, nor wash the red paint away from his body, nor enter a house in which there was a woman.[1] The reason for observing these curious restrictions is not mentioned, but in the light of similar practices, some of which have been noticed in these lectures,[2] we may conjecture that they were dictated by a fear of the victim's ghost, who among savages generally haunts his slayer and will do him a mischief, if he gets a chance. As it is especially in dreams that the naturally incensed spirit finds his opportunity, we can perhaps understand why the slayer might not lie down for the first three nights after the slaughter; the wrath of the ghost would then be at its hottest, and if he spied his murderer stretched in slumber on the ground, the temptation to take an unfair advantage of him might have been too strong to be resisted. But when his anger had had time to cool down or he had departed for his long home, as ghosts generally do after a reasonable time, the precautions taken to baffle his vengeance might be safely relaxed. Perhaps, as I have already hinted, the reverence which the Fijians felt for any man who had taken a human life, or at all events the life of an enemy, may have partly sprung from a belief that the slayer increased his own strength and valour either by subjugating the ghost of his victim and employing it as his henchman, or perhaps rather by simply absorbing in some occult fashion the vital energy of the slain. This view is confirmed by the permission given to the killer to assume the name of the killed, whenever his victim was a man of distinguished rank;[3] for by taking the name he, according to an opinion common among savages, assumed the personality of his namesake.

The temporary restrictions laid on a manslayer were probably dictated by a fear of his victim's ghost.

---

[1] Th. Williams, *op. cit.* i. 55 *sq.* The writer witnessed what he calls the ceremony of consecration in the case of a young man of the highest rank in Somosomo and he has described what he saw. In this case a special hut was not built for the manslayer, and he was allowed to pass the nights in the temple of the war god.

[2] See above, pp. 205 *sq.*, 229 *sq.*, 258, 279 *sq.*, 323, 396, 415.

[3] Th. Williams, *op. cit.* i. 55.

Other
funeral
customs
based on
a fear of
the ghost.
The same fear of the ghost of the recently departed which manifested itself, if my interpretation of the customs is right, in the treatment of manslayers, seems to have imprinted itself, though in a more attenuated form, on some of the practices observed by Fijian mourners after a natural, not a violent, death.

Persons
who have
handled
a corpse
forbidden
to touch
food.
Thus all the persons who had handled a corpse were forbidden to touch anything for some time afterwards; in particular they were strictly debarred from touching their food with their hands; their victuals were brought to them by others, and they were fed like infants by attendants or obliged to pick up their food with their mouths from the ground. The time during which this burdensome restriction lasted was different according to the rank of the deceased: in the case of great chiefs it lasted from two to ten months; in the case of a petty chief it did not exceed one month; and in the case of a common person a taboo of not more than four days sufficed. When a chief's principal wife did not follow him to the other world by being strangled or buried alive, she might not touch her own food with her hands for three months. When the mourners grew tired of being fed like infants or feeding themselves like dogs, they sent word to the head chief and he let them know that he would remove the taboo whenever they pleased. Accordingly they sent him presents of pigs and other provisions, which he shared among the people. Then the tabooed persons went into a stream and washed themselves; after that they caught some animal, such as a pig or a turtle, and wiped their hands on it, and the animal thereupon became sacred to the chief. Thus the taboo was removed, and the men were free once more to work, to feed themselves, and to live with their wives. Lazy and idle fellows willingly undertook the duty of waiting on the dead, as it relieved them for some time from the painful necessity of earning their own bread.[1] The reason why such persons might not touch food with their hands was probably a fear of the ghost or at all events

---

[1] Ch. Wilkes, *op. cit.* iii. 98, 99 *sq.* Compare Lorimer Fison, *Tales from Old Fiji*, p. 163 : " A person who has defiled himself by touching a corpse is called *yambo*, and is not allowed to touch food with his hands for several days." The custom as to a surviving widow is mentioned by Th. Williams, *op. cit.* i. 198.

of the infection of death; the ghost or the infection might
be clinging to their hands and might so be transferred from
them to their food with fatal effects.   In Great Fiji not every   Seclusion
one might dig a chief's grave.   The office was hereditary in   of grave-
a certain clan.   After the funeral the grave-digger was shut   diggers.
up in a house and painted black from head to foot.   When
he had to make a short excursion, he covered himself with
a large mantle of painted native cloth and was supposed to
be invisible.   His food was brought to the house after dark
by silent bearers, who placed it just within the doorway.
His seclusion might last for a long time;[1] it was probably
intended to screen him from the ghost.

The usual outward sign of mourning was to crop the   Hair
hair or beard, or very rarely both.   Some people merely   cropped
made bald the crown of the head.   Indeed the Fijians were   and finger-
too vain of their hair to part with it lightly, and to conceal   joints cut
the loss which custom demanded of them on these occasions   off in
they used to wear wigs, some of which were very skilfully   mourning.
made.   The practice of cutting off finger-joints in mourning
has already been mentioned; one early authority affirms and
another denies that joints of the little toes were similarly
amputated by the living as a mark of sorrow for the dead.
So common was the practice of lopping off the little fingers
in mourning that till recently few of the older natives could
be found who had their hands intact; most of them indeed
had lost the little fingers of both hands.   There was a Fijian
saying that the fourth finger " cried itself hoarse in vain for
its absent mate " (*droga-droga-wale*).   The mutilation was
usually confined to the relations of the deceased, unless he
happened to be one of the highest chiefs.   However, the
severed joints were often sent by poor people to wealthy
families in mourning, who never failed to reward the senders
for so delicate a mark of sympathy.   Female mourners
burned their skin into blisters by applying lighted rolls of
bark-cloth to various parts of their bodies; the brands so
produced might be seen on their arms, shoulders, necks, and
breasts.[2]   During the mourning for a king people fasted till

[1] Lorimer Fison, *Tales from Old Fiji*, p. 167.
[2] Ch. Wilkes, *op. cit.* iii. 101; Th.

Williams, *op. cit.* i. 197 *sq.*; Lorimer Fison, *Tales from Old Fiji*, p. 168; Basil Thomson, *The Fijians*, p. 375.

evening for ten or twenty days; the coast for miles was tabooed and no one might fish there; the nuts also were made sacred. Some people in token of grief for a bereavement would abstain from fish, fruit, or other pleasant food for months together; others would dress in leaves instead of in cloth.[1]

Though the motive for these observances is not mentioned, we may suppose that they were intended to soothe and please the ghost by testifying to the sorrow felt by the survivors at his decease. It is more doubtful whether the same explanation would apply to another custom which the Fijians used to observe in mourning. During ten days after a death, while the soul of a deceased chief was thought to be still lingering in or near his body, all the women of the town provided themselves with long whips, knotted with shells, and applied them with great vigour to the bodies of the men, raising weals and inflicting bloody wounds, while the men retorted by flirting pellets of clay from splinters of bamboo.[2] According to Mr. Williams, this ceremony was performed on the tenth day or earlier, and he adds: " I have seen grave personages, not accustomed to move quickly, flying with all possible speed before a company of such women. Sometimes the men retaliate by bespattering their assailants with mud; but they use no violence, as it seems to be a day on which they are bound to succumb."[3] As the soul of the dead was believed to quit his body and depart to his destined abode on the tenth day after death,[4] the scourging of the men by the women was probably supposed in some way to speed the parting guest on his long journey.

Men whipped by women in time of mourning for a chief.

When a certain king of Fiji died, the side of the house was broken down to allow the body to be carried out, though there were doorways wide enough for the purpose close at hand. The missionary who records the fact could not learn the reason of it.[5] The custom of taking the dead out of the house by a special opening, which is afterwards closed up, has not been confined to Fiji; on the contrary it has been practised by a multitude of peoples, savage, bar-

The dead taken out of the house by a special opening made in a wall.

[1] Th. Williams, *op. cit.* i. 197, 198.
[2] Ch. Wilkes, *op. cit.* iii. 99.
[3] Th. Williams, *op. cit.* i. 198 *sq.*
[4] Ch. Wilkes, *l.c.*
[5] Th. Williams, *Fiji and the Fijians,* i. 197.

barous, and civilised, in many parts of the world. For example, it was an old Norse rule that a corpse might not be carried out of the house by the door which was used by the living; hence a hole was made in the wall at the back of the dead man's head and he was taken out through it backwards, or a hole was dug in the ground under the south wall and the body was drawn out through it.[1] The custom may have been at one time common to all the Aryan or Indo-european peoples, for it is mentioned in other of their ancient records and has been observed by widely separated branches of that great family down to modern times. Thus, the Zend-Avesta prescribes that, when a death has occurred, a breach shall be made in the wall and the corpse carried out through it by two men, who have first stripped off their clothes.[2] In Russia "the corpse was often carried out of the house through a window, or through a hole made for the purpose, and the custom is still kept up in many parts."[3] Speaking of the Hindoos a French traveller of the eighteenth century says that "instead of carrying the corpse out by the door they make an opening in the wall by which they pass it out in a seated posture, and the hole is closed up after the ceremony."[4] Among various Hindoo castes it is still customary, when a death has occurred on an inauspicious day, to remove the corpse from the house not through the door, but through a temporary hole made in the wall.[5] Old German law required that the corpses of criminals and suicides should be carried out through a hole under the threshold.[6] In the Highlands of Scotland the bodies of suicides were not taken out of the house for burial by the doors, but through an opening made between the wall and the thatch.[7]

of the custom among Aryan peoples.

Examples

---

[1] K. Weinhold, *Altnordisches Leben* (Berlin, 1856), p. 476.

[2] *The Zend-Avesta*, Part i. *The Vendidâd*, translated by James Darmesteter (Oxford, 1880), p. 95 (Fargard, viii. 2. 10) (*Sacred Books of the East*, vol. iv.).

[3] W. R. S. Ralston, *The Songs of the Russian People*, Second Edition (London, 1872), p. 318.

[4] Sonnerat, *Voyage aux Indes Orientales et à la Chine* (Paris, 1782), i. 86.

[5] J. A. Dubois, *Mœurs, Institutions et Cérémonies des Peuples de l'Inde* (Paris, 1825), ii. 225; E. Thurston, *Ethnographic Notes in Southern India* (Madras, 1906), pp. 226 *sq.*

[6] J. Grimm, *Deutsche Rechtsalterthümer*[3] (Göttingen, 1881), pp. 726 *sqq.*

[7] Rev. J. G. Campbell, *Superstitions of the Highlands and Islands of Scotland* (Glasgow, 1900), p. 242.

Examples
of the
custom
among
non-Aryan
peoples.

But widespread as such customs have been among
Indo-european peoples, they have been by no means confined to that branch of the human race.   It was an
ancient Chinese practice to knock down part of the wall of
a house for the purpose of carrying out a corpse.[1]   Some of
the Canadian Indians would never take a corpse out of the
hut by the ordinary door, but always lifted a piece of the
bark wall near which the dead man lay and then drew him
through the opening.[2]   Among the Esquimaux of Bering
Strait a corpse is usually raised through the smoke-hole in
the roof, but is never taken out by the doorway.   Should
the smoke-hole be too small, an opening is made in the rear
of the house and then closed again.[3]   When a Greenlander
dies, " they do not carry out the corpse through the entry of
the house, but lift it through the window, or if he dies in
a tent, they unfasten one of the skins behind, and convey it
out that way.   A woman behind waves a lighted chip backward and forward, and says : ' There is nothing more to be
had here.' "[4]   Similarly the Hottentots, Bechuanas, Basutos,
Marotse, Barongo, and many other tribes of South and
West Africa never carry a corpse out by the door of the hut
but always by a special opening made in the wall.[5]   A similar

---

[1] *The Sacred Books of China*, trans-
lated by James Legge, Part iii. *The
Lî-Kî*, i.-x. (Oxford, 1885) pp. 144 *sq.*
(Bk. ii. Sect. i. Pt. II. 33) (*Sacred
Books of the East*, vol. xxvii.) ; J. F.
Lafitau, *Mœurs des Sauvages Ameri-
quains* (Paris, 1724), ii. 401 *sq.*, citing
Le Comte, *Nouv. Mémoires de la Chine*,
vol. ii. p. 187.

[2] *Relations des Jésuites*, 1633, p. 11 ;
id., 1634, p. 23 (Canadian reprint,
Quebec, 1858) ; J. G. Kohl, *Kitschi-
Gami* (Bremen, 1859), p. 149 note.

[3] E. W. Nelson, "The Eskimo
about Bering Strait," *Eighteenth
Annual Report of the Bureau of
American Ethnology*, Part i. (Washington, 1899), p. 311.

[4] David Crantz, *History of Greenland* (London, 1767), i. 237.   Compare Hans Egede, *Description of
Greenland*, Second Edition (London,
1818), pp. 152 *sq.* ; Captain G. F.
Lyon, *Private Journal* (London, 1824),
p. 370 ; C. F. Hall, *Narrative of the*

Second Arctic Expedition (Washington,
1879), p. 265 (Esquimaux).

[5] P. Kolben, *The Present State of
the Cape of Good Hope* (London, 1731-
1738), i. 316 ; C. P. Thunberg, "An
Account of the Cape of Good Hope,"
in Pinkerton's *Voyages and Travels*,
xvi. (London, 1814) p. 142 ; *Bulletin
de la Société de Géographie* (Paris), ii.
Série, ii. (1834) p. 196 (Bechuanas);
id., vii. Série, vii. (1886) p. 587
(Fernando Po) ; T. Arbousset et F.
Daumas, *Relation d'un Voyage d'Ex-
ploration au Nord-est de la Colonie du
Cap de Bonne-Espérance* (Paris, 1842),
pp. 502 *sq.* ; C. J. Andersson, *Lake
Ngami*, Second Edition (London,
1856), p. 466 ; G. Fritsch, *Die Ein-
geborenen Süd-Afrika's* (Breslau, 1872),
pp. 210, 335 ; R. Moffat, *Missionary
Labours and Scenes in Southern Africa*
(London, 1842), p. 307 ; E. Casalis,
The Basutos (London, 1861), p. 202 ;
Ladislaus Magyar, *Reisen in Süd-
Afrika* (Buda-Pesth and Leipsic, 1859),

custom is observed by the maritime Gajos of Sumatra[1] and by some of the Indian tribes of North-west America, such as the Tlingit and the Haida.[2] Among the Lepchis of Sikhim, whose houses are raised on piles, the dead are taken out by a hole made in the floor.[3] Dwellers in tents who practise this custom remove a corpse from the tent, not by the door, but through an opening made by lifting up an edge of the tent-cover: this is done by European gypsies[4] and by the Koryak of north-eastern Asia.[5]

In all such customs the original motive probably was a fear of the ghost and a wish to exclude him from the house, lest he should return and carry off the survivors with him to the spirit land. Ghosts are commonly credited with a low degree of intelligence, and it appears to be supposed that they can only find their way back to a house by the aperture through which their bodies were carried out. Hence people made a practice of taking a corpse out not by the door, but through an opening specially made for the purpose, which was afterwards blocked

The motive of the custom is a desire to prevent the ghost from returning to the house.

p. 350; Rev. J. Macdonald, *Light in Africa*, Second Edition (London, 1890), p. 166; E. Béguin, *Les Ma-Rotse* (Lausanne and Fontaines, 1903), p. 115; Henri A. Junod, *Les Ba-Ronga* (Neuchâtel, 1898), p. 48; *id.*, *The Life of a South African Tribe*, i. (Neuchâtel, 1912) p. 138; Dudley Kidd, *The Essential Kafir* (London, 1904), p. 247; A. F. Mockler-Ferryman, *British Nigeria* (London, 1902), p. 234; Ramseyer and Kühne, *Four Years in Ashantee* (London, 1875), p. 50; A. B. Ellis, *The Land of Fetish* (London, 1883), p. 13; *id.*, *The Tshi-speaking Peoples of the Gold Coast* (London, 1887), p. 239; E. Perregaud, *Chez les Achanti* (Neuchâtel, 1906), p. 127; J. Spieth, *Die Ewe - Stämme* (Berlin, 1906), p. 756; H. R. Palmer, "Notes on the Korôrofawa and Jukoñ," *Journal of the African Society*, No. 44 (July, 1912), p. 414. The custom is also observed by some tribes of Central Africa. See Miss A. Werner, *The Natives of British Central Africa* (London, 1906), p. 161; B. Gutmann, "Trauer und Begräbnisssitten der Wadschagga," *Globus*, lxxxix. (1906)

p. 200; Rev. N. Stam, "Religious Conceptions of the Kavirondo," *Anthropos*, v. (1910) p. 361.

[1] C. Snouck Hurgronje, *Het Gajō-land en zijne Bewoners* (Batavia, 1903), p. 313.

[2] Aurel Krause, *Die Tlinkit-Indianer* (Jena, 1885), p. 225; Franz Boas, in *Sixth Report of the Committee on the North-western Tribes of Canada*, p. 23 (separate reprint from the *Report of the British Association for the Advancement of Science*, Leeds Meeting, 1890); J. R. Swanton, *Contributions to the Ethnology of the Haida* (Leyden and New York, 1905), pp. 52, 54 (*The Jesup North Pacific Expedition, Memoir of the American Museum of Natural History*).

[3] J. A. H. Louis, *The Gates of Thibet* (Calcutta, 1894), p. 114.

[4] H. von Wlislocki, *Volksglaube und religiöser Brauch der Zigeuner* (Münster i. W., 1891), p. 99.

[5] W. Jochelson, *The Koryak* (New York and Leyden, 1908), pp. 110 *sq.* (*The Jesup North Pacific Expedition, Memoir of the American Museum of Natural History*).

up, so that when the ghost returned from the grave and attempted to enter the house, he found the orifice closed and was obliged to turn away disappointed.   That this was the train of reasoning actually followed by some peoples may be gathered from the explanations which they themselves give of the custom.   Thus among the Tuski of Alaska "those who die a natural death are carried out through a hole cut in the back of the hut or *yaráng*.   This is immediately closed up, that the spirit of the dead man may not find his way back."[1]   Among the Esquimaux of Hudson Bay "the nearest relatives on approach of death remove the invalid to the outside of the house, for if he should die within he must not be carried out of the door but through a hole cut in the side wall, and it must then be carefully closed to prevent the spirit of the person from returning."[2]   Again, "when a Siamese is dead, his relations deposit the body in a coffin well covered. They do not pass it through the door but let it down into the street by an opening which they make in the wall.   They also carry it thrice round the house, running at the top of their speed.   They believe that if they did not take this precaution, the dead man would remember the way by which he had passed, and that he would return by night to do some ill turn to his family."[3]   In Travancore the body of a dead rajah "is taken out of the palace through a breach in the wall, made for the purpose, to avoid pollution of the gate, and afterwards built up again so that the departed spirit may not return through the gate to trouble the survivors."[4]   Among the Kayans of Borneo, whose dwellings are raised on piles above the ground, the coffin is conveyed out of the house by lowering it with rattans either through the floor, planks being taken up for the purpose, or under the eaves at the side of the gallery.   "In

[1] W. H. Dall, *Alaska and its Resources* (London, 1870), p. 382.

[2] Lucien M. Turner, "Ethnology of the Ungava District, Hudson Bay Territory," *Eleventh Annual Report of the Bureau of Ethnology* (Washington, 1894), p. 191.

[3] Mgr. Bruguière, in *Annales de l'Association de la Propagation de la Foi*, v. (Lyons and Paris, 1831) p. 180.   Compare Mgr. Pallegoix, *De-scription du royaume Thai ou Siam* (Paris, 1854), i. 245 ; Adolf Bastian, *Die Völker des östlichen Asien*, iii. (Jena, 1867) p. 258 ; E. Young, *The Kingdom of the Yellow Robe* (Westminster, 1898), p. 246.

[4] S. Mateer, *Native Life in Travancore* (London, 1883), p. 137.   Compare A. Butterworth, "Royal Funerals in Travancore," *Indian Antiquary*, xxxi. (1902) p. 251.

this way they avoid carrying it down the house-ladder ; and it seems to be felt that this precaution renders it more difficult for the ghost to find its way back to the house."[1] Among the Cheremiss of Russia, "old custom required that the corpse should not be carried out by the door but through a breach in the north wall, where there is usually a sash-window. But the custom has long been obsolete, even among the heathen, and only very old people speak of it. They explain it as follows : to carry it out by the door would be to shew the *Asyrèn* (the dead man) the right way into the house, whereas a breach in the wooden wall is immediately closed by replacing the beams in position, and thus the *Asyrèn* would in vain seek for an entrance."[2] The Samoyeds never carry a corpse out of the hut by the door, but lift up a piece of the reindeer-skin covering and draw the body out, head foremost, through the opening. They think that if they were to carry a corpse out by the door, the ghost would soon return and fetch away other members of the family.[3] On the same principle, as soon as the Indians of Tumupasa, in north-west Bolivia, have carried a corpse out of the house, "they shift the door to the opposite side, in order that the deceased may not be able to find it."[4] Once more, in Mecklenburg "it is a law regulating the return of the dead that they are compelled to return by the same way by which the corpse was removed from the house. In the villages of Picher, Bresegard, and others the people used to have movable thresholds at the house-doors, which, being fitted into the door-posts, could be shoved up. The corpse was then carried out of the house under the threshold, and therefore could not return over it."[5]

[1] Ch. Hose and W. McDougall, *The Pagan Tribes of Borneo* (London, 1912), ii. 35.

[2] S. K. Kusnezow, "Über den Glauben vom Jenseits und den Todten-cultus der Tscheremissen," *Internationales Archiv für Ethnographie,* ix. (1896) p. 157.

[3] P. S. Pallas, *Reise durch verschiedene Provinzen des Russischen Reichs* (St. Petersburg, 1771–1776), iii. 75 ; Middendorff, *Reise in den äussersten Norden und Osten Sibiriens,* iv. 1464.

[4] *Exploraciones y Noticias hidrograficas de los Rios del Norte de Bolivia,* publicados por Manuel V. Ballivian, Segunda Parte, *Diario del Viage al Madre de Dios hecho por el P. Fr. Nicolas Armentia, en los años de 1884 y 1885* (La Paz, 1890), p. 20 : " *Cuando muere alguno, apénas sacan el cadáver de la casa, cambian la puerta al lado opuesto, para que no dé con ella el difunto.*"

[5] Karl Bartsch, *Sagen, Märchen und Gebräuche aus Meklenburg* (Vienna, 1879–1880), ii. 100, § 358.

Some people only remove in this manner the bodies of persons whose ghosts are especially feared.

Even without such express testimonies to the meaning of the custom we may infer from a variety of evidence that the real motive for practising it is a fear of the ghost and a wish to prevent his return. For it is to be observed that some peoples do not carry out all their dead by a special opening, but that they accord this peculiar mode of removal only to persons who die under unlucky or disgraceful circumstances, and whose ghosts accordingly are more than usually dreaded. Thus we have seen that some modern Hindoo castes observe the custom only in the case of people who have died on inauspicious days ; and that in Germany and the Highlands of Scotland this mode of removal was specially reserved for the bodies of suicides, whose ghosts are exceedingly feared by many people, as appears from the stringent precautions taken against them.[1]   Again, among the Kavirondo of Central Africa, " when a woman dies without having borne a child, she is carried out of the back of the house. A hole is made in the wall and the corpse is ignominiously pushed through the hole and carried some distance to be buried, as it is considered a curse to die without a child. If the woman has given birth to a child, then her corpse is carried out through the front door and buried in the verandah of the house." [2]   In Brittany a stillborn child is removed from the house, not by the door, but by the window ; " for if by ill-luck it should chance otherwise, the mothers who should pass through that fatal door would bear nothing but stillborn infants." [3]   In Perche, another province of France, the same rule is observed with regard to stillborn children, though the reason for it is not alleged.[4]   But of all ghosts none perhaps inspire such deep and universal terror as the ghosts of women who have died in childbed, and extraordinary measures are accordingly taken to disable these dangerous spirits from returning and doing a mischief to the living.[5]

[1] For some evidence on this subject, see R. Lasch, " Die Behandlung der Leiche des Selbstmörders," *Globus*, lxxxvi. (1899) pp. 63-66 ; Rev. J. Roscoe, *The Baganda* (London, 1911), pp. 20 *sq.* ; A. Karasek, " Beiträge zur Kenntnis der Waschamba," *Baessler-Archiv*, i. (1911) pp. 190 *sq.*
[2] Rev. N. Stam, " The Religious Conceptions of the Kavirondo," *Anthropos*, v. (1910) p. 361.
[3] Alfred de Nore, *Coutumes, Mythes, et Traditions des Provinces de France* (Paris and Lyons, 1846), p. 198.
[4] Félix Chapiseau, *Le Folk-lore de la Beauce et du Perche* (Paris, 1902), ii. 164.
[5] For some evidence on this subject see *Psyche's Task*, pp. 64 *sq.*

Amongst the precautions adopted to keep them at bay is the custom of carrying their corpses out of the house by a special opening, which is afterwards blocked up. Thus in Laos, a province of Siam, "the bodies of women dying in childbirth, or within a month afterwards, are not even taken out of the house in the ordinary way by the door, but are let down through the floor."[1] The Kachins of Burma stand in such fear of the ghosts of women dying in childbed that no sooner has such a death occurred than the husband, the children, and almost all the people in the house take to flight lest the woman's ghost should bite them. "The body of the deceased must be burned as soon as possible in order to punish her for dying such a death, and also in order to frighten her ghost (*minla*). They bandage her eyes with her own hair and with leaves to prevent her from seeing anything; they wrap her in a mat, and they carry her out of the house, not by the ordinary door, but by an opening made for the purpose in the wall or the floor of the room where she breathed her last. Then they convey her to a deep ravine, where no one dares to pass; they lay her in the midst of a great pyre with all the clothes, jewellery, and other objects which belonged to her and of which she made use; and they burn the whole to cinders, to which they refuse the rites of sepulture. Thus they destroy all the property of the unfortunate woman, in order that her soul may not think of coming to fetch it afterwards and to bite people in the attempt."[2] Similarly among the Kayans or Bahaus of Central Borneo "the corpses of women dying in childbed excite a special horror; no man and no young woman may touch them; they are not carried out of the house through the front gallery, but are thrown out of the back wall of the dwelling, some boards having been removed for the purpose."[3] Indeed so great is the alarm felt by the Kayans at a miscarriage of this sort that when a woman labours hard in childbed, the news quickly spreads through the large communal house in which the people dwell; and

[1] Carl Bock, *Temples and Elephants* (London, 1884), p. 262.

[2] Ch. Gilhodes, "Naissance et Enfance chez les Katchins (Birmanie)," *Anthropos*, vi. (1911) pp. 872 *sq.*

[3] A. W. Nieuwenhuis, *Quer durch Borneo* (Leyden, 1901–1907), i. 91.

if the attendants begin to fear a fatal issue, the whole household is thrown into consternation. All the men, from the chief down to the boys, will flee from the house, or, if it is night, they will clamber up among the beams of the roof and there hide in terror; and, if the worst happens, they remain there until the woman's corpse has been removed from the house for burial.[1]

Sometimes the custom is observed when the original motive for it is forgotten.

Sometimes, while the custom continues to be practised, the idea which gave rise to it has either become obscured or has been incorrectly reported. Thus we are told that when a death has taken place among the Indians of North-west America "the body is at once taken out of the house through an opening in the wall from which the boards have been removed. It is believed that his ghost would kill every one if the body were to stay in the house."[2] Such a belief, while it would furnish an excellent reason for hurrying the corpse out of the house as soon as possible, does not explain why it should be carried out through a special opening instead of through the door. Again, when a Queen of Bali died, "the body was drawn out of a large aperture made in the wall to the right-hand side of the door, in the absurd opinion of *cheating the devil*, whom these islanders believe to lie in wait in the ordinary passage."[3] Again, in Mukden, the capital of Manchuria, the corpses of children "must not be carried out of a door or window, but through a new or disused opening, in order that the evil spirit which causes the disease may not enter. The belief is that the Heavenly Dog which eats the sun at an eclipse demands the bodies of children, and that if they are denied to him he will bring certain calamity on the household."[4] These explanations of the custom are probably misinterpretations adopted at a later time when its original meaning was forgotten. For a custom often outlives the memory of the

---

[1] Ch. Hose and W. McDougall, *The Pagan Tribes of Borneo* (London, 1912), ii. 155.

[2] Franz Boas, in *Sixth Report of the Committee on the North-western Tribes of Canada*, p. 23 (separate reprint from the *Report of the British Association for the Advancement of Science*, Leeds Meeting, 1890).

[3] Prevost, quoted by John Crawford, *History of the Indian Archipelago* (Edinburgh, 1820), ii. 245. Compare Adolf Bastian, *Die Völker des östlichen Asien*, v. (Jena, 1869) p. 83.

[4] Mrs. Bishop (Isabella L. Bird), *Korea and her Neighbours* (London, 1898), i. 239 *sq.*

motives which gave it birth.   And as royalty is very conservative of ancient usages, it would be no matter for surprise if the corpses of kings should continue to be carried
out through special openings long after the bodies of
commoners were allowed to be conveyed in commonplace
fashion through the ordinary door.   In point of fact we find
the old custom observed by kings in countries where it
has apparently ceased to be observed by their subjects.
Thus among the Sakalava and Antimerina of Madagascar,
" when a sovereign or a prince of the royal family dies
within the enclosure of the king's palace, the corpse must be
carried out of the palace, not by the door, but by a breach
made for the purpose in the wall ; the new sovereign could
not pass through the door that had been polluted by the
passage of a dead body."[1]   Similarly among the Macassars
and Buginese of Southern Celebes there is in the king's
palace a window reaching to the floor through which on his
decease the king's body is carried out.[2]   That such a custom
is only a limitation to kings of a rule which once applied to
everybody becomes all the more probable, when we learn
that in the island of Saleijer, which lies to the south of
Celebes, each house has, besides its ordinary windows, a
large window in the form of a door, through which, and not
through the ordinary entrance, every corpse is regularly
removed at death.[3]

To return from this digression to Fiji, we may conclude
with a fair degree of probability that when the side of a
Fijian king's house was broken down to allow his corpse to
be carried out, though there were doors at hand wide enough
for the purpose, the original intention was to prevent the
return of his ghost, who might have proved a very unwelcome
intruder to his successor on the throne.   But I cannot offer
any explanation of another Fijian funeral custom.   You may
remember that in Fiji it was customary after the death of a

Another Fijian funeral custom.

---

[1] Arnold van Gennep, *Tabou et
Totémisme à Madagascar* (Paris, 1904),
p. 65, quoting Dr. Catat.
[2] B. F. Matthes, *Bijdragen tot de Ethnologie van Zuid-Celebes* (The Hague,
1875), p. 139 ; *id.*, " Over de *âdâ's* of
gewoonten der Makassaren en Boegineezen," *Verslagen en Mededeelingen*

der Koninklijke Akademie van Wetenschappen, Afdeeling Letterkunde,
Derde Reeks, ii. (Amsterdam, 1885)
p. 142.
[3] W. M. Donselaar, " Aanteekeningen over het eiland Saleijer," *Mededeelingen van wege het Nederlandsche
Zendelinggenootschap,* i. (1857) p. 291.

chief to circumcise such lads as had reached a suitable age.[1] Well, on the fifth day after a chief's death a hole used to be dug under the floor of a temple and one of the newly circumcised lads was secreted in it. Then his companions fastened the doors of the temple securely and ran away. When the lad hidden in the hole blew on a shell-trumpet, the friends of the deceased chief surrounded the temple and thrust their spears at him through the fence.[2] What the exact significance of this curious rite may have been, I cannot even conjecture ; but we may assume that it had something to do with the state of the late chief's soul, which was probably supposed to be lingering in the neighbourhood.

Fijian notions concerning the other world and the way thither. It remains to say a little as to the notions which the Fijians entertained of the other world and the way thither. After death the souls of the departed were believed to set out for Bulu or Bulotu, there to dwell with the great serpent-shaped god Ndengei. His abode seems to have been generally placed in the Nakauvandra mountains, towards the western end of Viti Levu, the largest of the Fijian Islands. But on this subject the ideas of the people were, as might be expected, both vague and inconsistent. Each tribe filled in the details of the mythical land and the mythical journey to suit its own geographical position. The souls had generally to cross water, either the sea or a river, and they were put across it by a ghostly ferryman, who treated the passengers with scant

The River of the Souls. courtesy.[3] According to some people, the River of the Souls (*Waini-yalo*) is what mortals now call the Ndravo River. When the ghosts arrived on the bank, they hailed the ferryman and he paddled his canoe over to receive them. But before he would take them on board they had to state whether they proposed to ship as steerage or as cabin passengers, and he gave them their berths accordingly ; for there was no mixing up of the classes in the ferry-boat ; the ghosts of chiefs kept strictly to themselves at one end of the canoe, and the ghosts of commoners huddled together at the other end.[4] The natives of Kandavu, in Southern Fiji, say that on clear

---

[1] See above, p. 426.

[2] Th. Williams, *Fiji and the Fijians*, Second Edition (London, 1860), i. 167.

[3] Ch. Wilkes, *Narrative of the*

United States Exploring Expedition, New Edition (New York, 1851), iii. 83 ; Basil Thomson, *The Fijians*, p. 117.

[4] Basil Thomson, *op. cit.* p. 121.

days they often see Bulotu, the spirit land, lying away across
the sea with the sun shining sweetly on it ; but they have
long ago given up all hope of making their way to that
happy land.[1] They seem to say with the Demon Lover,

> " *O yonder are the hills of heaven*
> *Where you will never win.*"

Though every island and almost every town had its own
portal through which the spirits passed on their long journey
to the far country, yet there was one called Nai Thombo-
thombo, which appears to have been more popular and
frequented than any of the others as a place of embarcation
for ghosts. It is at the northern point of Mbua Bay, and
the ghosts shew their good taste in choosing it as their port
to sail from, for really it is a beautiful spot. The foreland
juts out between two bays. A shelving beach slopes up to
precipitous cliffs, their rocky face mantled with a thick green
veil of creepers. Further inland the shade of tall forest trees
and the softened gloom cast by crags and rocks lend to the
scene an air of solemnity and hallowed repose well fitted to
impress the susceptible native mind with an awful sense of
the invisible beings that haunt these sacred groves. Natives
have been known to come on pilgrimage to the spot expecting
to meet ghosts and gods face to face.[2]

The place of embarcation for the ghosts.

Many are the perils and dangers that beset the Path of
the Souls (*Sala Ni Yalo*). Of these one of the most celebrated is a certain pandanus tree, at which every ghost must
throw the ghost of the real whale's tooth which was placed
for the purpose in his hand at burial. If he hits the tree, it
is well for him ; for it shews that his friends at home are
strangling his wives, and accordingly he sits down contentedly
to wait for the ghosts of his helpmeets, who will soon come
hurrying to him. But if he makes a bad shot and misses the
tree, the poor ghost is very disconsolate, for he knows that
his wives are not being strangled, and who then will cook for
him in the spirit land ? It is a bitter thought, and he reflects
with sorrow and anger on the ingratitude of men and especially
of women. His reflections, as reported by the best authority,

The ghost and the pandanus tree.

[1] Lorimer Fison, *Tales from Old Fiji*, p. 163.

[2] Th. Williams, *Fiji and the Fijians*, i. 239.

run thus : " How is this ?   For a long time I planted food for my wife, and it was also of great use to her friends : why then is she not allowed to follow me ?   Do my friends love me no better than this, after so many years of toil ?   Will no one, in love to me, strangle my wife ? " [1]

Hard fate of un- married ghosts. But if the lot of a married ghost, whose wives have not been murdered, is hard, it is nevertheless felicity itself com- pared to the fate of bachelor ghosts.   In the first place there is a terrible being called the Great Woman, who lurks in a shady defile, ready to pounce out on him ; and if he escapes her clutches it is only to fall in with a much worse monster, of the name of Nanggananggga, from whom there is, humanly speaking, no escape.   This ferocious goblin lays himself out to catch the souls of bachelors, and so vigilant and alert is he that not a single unmarried Fijian ghost is known to have ever reached the mansions of the blest.   He sits beside a big black stone at high-water mark waiting for his prey.   The bachelor ghosts are aware that it would be useless to attempt to march past him when the tide is in ; so they wait till it is low water and then try to sneak past him on the wet sand left by the retiring billows.   Vain hope ! Nanggananggga, sitting by the stone, only smiles grimly and asks, with withering sarcasm, whether they imagine that the tide will never flow again ?   It does so only too soon for the poor ghosts, driving them with every breaking wave nearer and nearer to their implacable enemy, till the water laps on the fatal stone, and then he grips the shivering souls and dashes them to pieces on the big black block.[2]

The Killer of Souls. Again, there is a very terrible giant armed with a great axe, who lies in wait for all and sundry.   He makes no nice distinction between the married and the unmarried, but strikes out at all ghosts indiscriminately.   Those whom he wounds dare not present themselves in their damaged state to the great God Ndengei ; so they never reach the happy fields, but are doomed to roam the rugged mountains disconsolate. However, many ghosts contrive to slip past him unscathed.

[1] Th. Williams, *op. cit.* i. 243 *sq.* Compare Berthold Seeman, *Viti, an Account of a Government Mission to the Vitian or Fijian Islands in the years 1860-1861* (Cambridge, 1862), p. 399 ; Lorimer Fison, *Tales from Old Fiji*, p. 163 ; Basil Thomson, *The Fijians*, pp. 120 *sq.*, 121 *sq.*

[2] Th. Williams, *op. cit.* i. 244 *sq.*

It is said that after the introduction of fire-arms into the islands the ghost of a certain chief made very good use of a musket which had been providentially buried with his body. When the giant drew near and was about to lunge out with the axe in his usual style, the ghost discharged the blunder-buss in his face, and while the giant was fully engaged in dodging the hail of bullets, the chief rushed past him and now enjoys celestial happiness.[1]   Some lay the scene of this encounter a little beyond the town of Nambanaggatai ; for it is to be remembered that many of the places in the Path of the Souls were identified with real places in the Fijian Islands. And the name of the giant is Samu-yalo, that is, the Killer of Souls.   He artfully conceals himself in some mangrove bushes just beyond the town, from which he rushes out in the nick of time to fell the passing ghosts.   Whenever he kills a ghost, he cooks and eats him and that is the end of the poor ghost.   It is the second death.   The highway to the Elysian fields runs, or used to run, right through the town of Nam-banaggatai ; so all the doorways of the houses were placed opposite each other to allow free and uninterrupted passage to the invisible travellers.   And the inhabitants spoke to each other in low tones and communicated at a little distance by signs.   The screech of a paroquet in the woods was the signal of the approach of a ghost or ghosts ; the number of screeches was proportioned to the number of the ghosts,—one screech, one ghost, and so on.[2]

Souls who escape the Killer of Souls pass on till they come to Naindelinde, one of the highest peaks of the Kauvandra mountains.   Here the path ends abruptly on the brink of a precipice, the foot of which is washed by a deep lake.   Over the edge of the precipice projects a large steer-oar, and the handle is held either by the great god Ndengei himself or, according to the better opinion, by his deputy.   When a ghost comes up and peers ruefully over the precipice, the deputy accosts him.   " Under what circum-stances," he asks, " do you come to us ?   How did you con-duct yourself in the other world ? "   Should the ghost be a man of rank, he may say, " I am a great chief.   I lived as a chief, and my conduct was that of a chief.   I had great

A trap for unwary ghosts.

[1] Ch. Wilkes, *op. cit.* iii. 83.   [2] Th. Williams, *op. cit.* i. 245 *sq.*

wealth, many wives, and ruled over a powerful people.   I
have destroyed many towns, and slain many in war."   " Good,
good," says the deputy, " just sit down on the blade of that
oar, and refresh yourself in the cool breeze."   If the ghost is
unwary enough to accept the invitation, he has no sooner
seated himself on the blade of the oar with his legs dangling
over the abyss, than the deputy-deity tilts up the other end
of the oar and precipitates him into the deep water, far far
below.   A loud smack is heard as the ghost collides with
the water, there is a splash, a gurgle, a ripple, and all is over.
The ghost has gone to his account in Murimuria, a very
second-rate sort of heaven, if it is nothing worse.   But a ghost
who is in favour with the great god Ndengei is warned by
him not to sit down on the blade of the oar but on the
handle.   The ghost takes the hint and seats himself firmly on
the safe end of the oar ; and when the deputy-deity tries to
heave it up, he cannot, for he has no purchase.   So the ghost
remains master of the situation, and after an interval for
refreshment is sent back to earth to be deified.[1]

Murimuria, an inferior sort of heaven.

In Murimuria, which, as I said, is an inferior sort of
heaven, the departed souls by no means lead a life of pure and
unmixed enjoyment.   Some of them are punished for the
sins they committed in the flesh.   But the Fijian notion of
sin differs widely from ours.   Thus we saw that the ghosts
of men who did no murder in their lives were punished for
their negligence by having to pound muck with clubs.   Again,
people who had not their ears bored on earth are forced in
Hades to go about for ever bearing on their shoulders one of
the logs of wood on which bark-cloth is beaten out with
mallets, and all who see the sinner bending under the load
jeer at him.   Again, women who were not tattooed in their life
are chased by the female ghosts, who scratch and cut and tear
them with sharp shells, giving them no respite ; or they scrape
the flesh from their bones and bake it into bread for the gods.
And ghosts who have done anything to displease the gods are

The Fijian Elysium.

laid flat on their faces in rows and converted into taro beds.
But the few who do find their way into the Fijian Elysium are
blest indeed.   There the sky is always cloudless ; the groves
are perfumed with delicious scents ; the open glades in the

---

[1] Th. Williams, *op. cit.* i. 246 *sq.*

forest are pleasant; there is abundance of all that heart can desire.   Language fails to describe the ineffable bliss of the happy land.   There the souls of the truly good, who have murdered many of their fellows on earth and fed on their roasted bodies, are lapped in joy for ever.[1]

Nevertheless the souls of the dead were not universally believed to depart by the Spirit Path to the other world or to stay there for ever.   To a certain extent the doctrines of transmigration found favour with the Fijians.   Some of them held that the spirits of the dead wandered about the villages in various shapes and could make themselves visible or invisible at pleasure.   The places which these vagrant souls loved to haunt were known to the people, who in passing by them were wont to make propitiatory offerings of food or cloth.   For that reason, too, they were very loth to go abroad on a dark night lest they should come bolt upon a ghost. Further, it was generally believed that the soul of a celebrated chief might after death enter into some young man of the tribe and animate him to deeds of valour.   Persons so distinguished were pointed out and regarded as highly favoured ; great respect was paid to them, they enjoyed many personal privileges, and their opinions were treated with much consideration.[2] *Fijian doctrine of transmigration.*

On the whole, when we survey the many perils which beset the way to the Fijian heaven, and the many risks which the souls of the dead ran of dying the second death in the other world or of being knocked on the head by the living in this, we shall probably agree with the missionary Mr. Williams in concluding that under the old Fijian dispensation there were few indeed that were saved.   " Few, comparatively," he says, " are left to inhabit the regions of Mbulu, and the immortality even of these is sometimes disputed.   The belief in a future state is universal in Fiji ; but their superstitious notions often border upon transmigration, and sometimes teach an eventual annihilation." [3] *Few souls saved under the old Fijian dispensation.*

Here I must break off my survey of the natural belief in immortality among mankind.   At the outset I had expected *Concluding observations.*

[1] Th. Williams, *op. cit.* i. 247.   [2] Ch. Wilkes, *op. cit.* iii. 85 *sq.*
[3] Th. Williams, *op. cit.* i. 248.

to carry the survey further, but I have already exceeded the usual limits of these lectures and I must not trespass further on your patience. Yet the enquiry which I have opened seems worthy to· be pursued, and if circumstances should admit of it, I shall hope at some future time to resume the broken thread of these researches and to follow it a little further through the labyrinth of human history. Be that as it may, I will now conclude with a few general observations suggested by the facts which I have laid before you.

Strength and universality of the natural belief in immortality among savages.

In the first place, then, it is impossible not to be struck by the strength, and perhaps we may say the universality, of the natural belief in immortality among the savage races of mankind. With them a life after death is not a matter of speculation and conjecture, of hope and fear ; it is a practical certainty which the individual as little dreams of doubting as he doubts the reality of his conscious existence. He assumes it without enquiry and acts upon it without hesitation, as if it were one of the best-ascertained truths within the limits of human experience. The belief influences his attitude towards the higher powers, the conduct of his daily life, and his behaviour towards his fellows ; more than that, it regulates to a great extent the relations of independent communities to each other. For the state of war, which

Wars between savage tribes spring in large measure from their belief in immortality.

normally exists between many, if not most, neighbouring savage tribes, springs in large measure directly from their belief in immortality ; since one of the commonest motives for hostility is a desire to appease the angry ghosts of friends, who are supposed to have perished by the baleful arts of sorcerers in another tribe, and who, if vengeance is not inflicted on their real or imaginary murderers, will wreak their fury on their undutiful fellow-tribesmen. Thus the belief in immortality has not merely coloured the outlook of the individual upon the world ; it has deeply affected the social and political relations of humanity in all ages ; for the religious wars and persecutions, which distracted and devastated Europe for ages, were only the civilised equivalents of the battles and murders which the fear of ghosts has instigated amongst almost all races of savages of whom we possess a record. Regarded from this point of view, the faith in a life hereafter has been sown like dragons' teeth on the earth and has brought forth crop after crop of armed men, who have turned their swords against each other.   And when we consider further the gratuitous and wasteful destruction of property as well as of life which is involved in sacrifices to the dead, we must admit that with all its advantages the belief in immortality has entailed heavy economical losses upon the races—and they are practically all the races of the world—who have indulged in this expensive luxury.   It is not for me to estimate the extent and gravity of the consequences, moral, social, political, and economic, which flow directly from the belief in immortality. I can only point to some of them and commend them to the serious attention of historians and economists, as well as of moralists and theologians. *Economic loss involved in sacrifices to the dead.*

My second observation concerns, not the practical consequences of the belief in immortality, but the question of its truth or falsehood.   That, I need hardly say, is an even more difficult problem than the other, and as I intimated at the outset of the lectures I find myself wholly incompetent to solve it.   Accordingly I have confined myself to the comparatively easy task of describing some of the forms of the belief and some of the customs to which it has given rise, without presuming to pass judgment upon them.   I must leave it to others to place my collections of facts in the scales and to say whether they incline the balance for or against the truth of this momentous belief, which has been so potent for good or ill in history.   In every enquiry much depends upon the point of view from which the enquirer approaches his subject; he will see it in different proportions and in different lights according to the angle and the distance from which he regards it.   The subject under discussion in the present case is human nature itself; and as we all know, men have formed very different estimates of themselves and their species.   On the one hand, there are those who love to dwell on the grandeur and dignity of man, and who swell with pride at the contemplation of the triumphs which his genius has achieved in the visionary world of imagination as well as in the realm of nature.   Surely, they say, such a glorious creature was not born for mortality, to be snuffed out *How does the savage belief in immortality bear on the question of the truth or falsehood of that belief in general?* *The answer depends to some extent on the view we take of human nature.* *The view of the grandeur and dignity of man.*

like a candle, to fade like a flower, to pass away like a
breath.   Is all that penetrating intellect, that creative fancy,
that vaulting ambition, those noble passions, those far-
reaching hopes, to come to nothing, to shrivel up into a
pinch of dust?   It is not so, it cannot be.   Man is the
flower of this wide world, the lord of creation, the crown and
consummation of all things, and it is to wrong him and his
creator to imagine that the grave is the end of all.   To
those who take this lofty view of human nature it is easy
and obvious to find in the similar beliefs of savages a welcome confirmation of their own cherished faith, and to insist
that a conviction so widely spread and so firmly held must
be based on some principle, call it instinct or intuition or
what you will, which is deeper than logic and cannot be
confuted by reasoning.

The view
of the
pettiness
and in-
significance
of man.
On the other hand, there are those who take a different
view of human nature, and who find in its contemplation a
source of humility rather than of pride.   They remind us
how weak, how ignorant, how short-lived is the individual,
how infirm of purpose, how purblind of vision, how subject
to pain and suffering, to diseases that torture the body
and wreck the mind.   They say that if the few short
years of his life are not wasted in idleness and vice, they are
spent for the most part in a perpetually recurring round
of trivialities, in the satisfaction of merely animal wants,
in eating, drinking, and slumber.   When they survey the
history of mankind as a whole, they find the record
chequered and stained by folly and crime, by broken
faith, insensate ambition, wanton aggression, injustice,
cruelty, and lust, and seldom illumined by the mild radiance
of wisdom and virtue.   And when they turn their eyes
from man himself to the place he occupies in the universe,
how are they overwhelmed by a sense of his littleness and
insignificance!   They see the earth which he inhabits
dwindle to a speck in the unimaginable infinities of space,
and the brief span of his existence shrink into a moment
in the inconceivable infinities of time.   And they ask, Shall
a creature so puny and frail claim to live for ever, to
outlast not only the present starry system but every other
that, when earth and sun and stars have crumbled into dust,

shall be built upon their ruins in the long long hereafter ?
It is not so, it cannot be.   The claim is nothing but the
outcome of exaggerated self-esteem, of inflated vanity ; it is
the claim of a moth, shrivelled in the flame of a candle, to
outlive the sun, the claim of a worm to survive the destruction of this terrestrial globe in which it burrows.   Those
who take this view of the pettiness and transitoriness of
man compared with the vastness and permanence of the
universe find little in the beliefs of savages to alter their
opinion.   They see in savage conceptions of the soul and
its destiny nothing but a product of childish ignorance, the
hallucinations of hysteria, the ravings of insanity, or the
concoctions of deliberate fraud and imposture.   They dismiss the whole of them as a pack of superstitions and lies,
unworthy the serious attention of a rational mind ; and
they say that if such drivellings do not refute the belief in
immortality, as indeed from the nature of things they cannot
do, they are at least fitted to invest its high-flown pretensions with an air of ludicrous absurdity.

Such are the two opposite views which I conceive may
be taken of the savage testimony to the survival of our
conscious personality after death.   I do not presume to
adopt the one or the other.   It is enough for me to have
laid a few of the facts before you.   I leave you to draw
your own conclusion.

The conclusion left open.

NOTE

MYTH OF THE CONTINUANCE OF DEATH [1]

THE following story is told by the Balolo of the Upper Congo to explain the continuance, if not the origin, of death in the world. One day, while a man was working in the forest, a little man with two bundles, one large and one small, went up to him and said, "Which of these bundles will you have? The large one contains knives, looking-glasses, cloth and so forth; and the small one contains immortal life." "I cannot choose by myself," answered the man; "I must go and ask the other people in the town." While he was gone·to ask the others, some women arrived and the choice was left to them. They tried the edges of the knives, decked themselves in the cloth, admired themselves in the looking-glasses, and, without more ado, chose the big bundle. The little man, picking up the small bundle, vanished. So when the man came back from the town, the little man and his bundles were gone. The women exhibited and shared the things, but death continued on the earth. Hence the people often say, "Oh, if those women had only chosen the small bundle, we should not be dying like this!" [2]

[1] See above, p. 77.

[2] Rev. John H. Weeks, "Stories and other Notes from the Upper Congo," *Folk-lore*, xii. (1901) p. 461 ; *id., Among Congo Cannibals* (London, 1913), p. 218. The country of the Balolo lies five miles south of the Equator, on Longitude 18° East.

INDEX

Abinal, Father, 49

Abipones, their belief in sorcery as a cause of death, 35

Abnormal mental states explained by inspiration, 15

Aborigines, magical powers attributed by immigrants to, 193

Abstinence from certain food in mourning, 198, 208, 209, 230, 314, 360, 452

Abundance of food and water favourable to social progress, 90 *sq.*

Action as a clue to belief, 143

Actors personating ghosts and spirits, 176, 179 *sq.*, 180 *sqq.*; 185 *sqq.*

Adiri, the land of the dead, 211, 212, 213, 214

Admiralty Islands, 393, 400, 401

—— Islanders, their myths of the origin of death, 71, 76 *sq.*

Advance of culture among the aborigines of South-Eastern Australia, 141 *sq.*, 148 *sq.*

Africa, aborigines of, their ideas as to the cause of death, 49 *sqq.* ; use of poison ordeal in, 50 *sqq.*

——, British Central, 162

——, British East, 61, 66, 254

Agriculture, rise of, favourable to astronomy, 140 *sq.* ; Fijian, 408

Akamba, their story of the origin of death, 61 *sq.*

Akikuyu, resurrection and circumcision among the, 254

Alcheringa or dream times, 96, 103, 114

—— ancestors, their marvellous powers, 103

—— home of the dead, 167

Alfoors of Celebes, 166

Alligators, ghosts in, 380

Alols, bachelors' houses, 221, 222

Altars, stones used as, 379

Amputation of fingers in mourning, 199, 426 *sq.*, 451

Amulets consisting of relics of the dead, 332, 370

Ancestor, totemic, developing into a god, 113

Ancestor-worship possibly evolved from totemism, 114 *sq.*

Ancestors, reincarnation of, 92 *sqq.* ; marvellous powers ascribed to remote, 103, 114 *sq.* ; totemic, traditions concerning, 115 *sqq.* ; dramatic ceremonies to commemorate the doings of, 118 *sqq.* ; possible evolution of worship of, in Central Australia, 125 *sq.* ; worshipped, 221, 297 *sq.*, 328 *sqq.*, 338, 340 ; ghosts of, appealed to for help, 258 *sq.*; offerings to, 298 ; prayers to, 329 *sq.*, 332 *sqq. See also* Dead

Ancestral gods, foreskins of circumcised lads offered to, 427 ; libations to, 430, 438

—— images, 307 *sqq.*, 315, 316 *sq.*, 321, 322

—— spirits help hunters and fishers, 226 ; shrines for, 316, 317 ; worshipped as gods, 369 ; worshipped in the *Nanga*, 428 *sq.* ; first-fruits offered to, 429 ; cloth and weapons offered to, 430 *sq.* ; novices presented to, at initiation, 432 *sq.*, 434

Angola, the poison ordeal in, 51 *sq.*

Angoni, their burial customs, 162

Animals, souls of sorcerers in, 39 ; spirits of, go to the spirit land, 210 ; sacrifices to the souls of, 239 ; transmigration of dead into, 242, 245 ; ghosts in the form of, 282 ; ghosts turn into, 287 ; ghosts incarnate in, 379 *sq.*

Animistic views of the Papuans, 264

Anjea, a mythical being, 128

Annam, 67, 69

Anointing manslayers, 448

Ant-hills, ghosts turn into, 287

Ant totem, dramatic ceremony concerned with, 120 *sq.*

Ants' nests, ghosts turn into, 351

Anthropology, comparative and descriptive, 230 *sq.*

473

Antimerina of Madagascar, burial custom of the, 461
Anuto, a creator, 296
Apparitions, 396 ; fear of, 414
Appearance of the dead in dreams, 229
Araucanians of Chili, their disbelief in natural death, 35, 53 *sq.*
Arawaks of Guiana, 36 ; their myth of the origin of death, 70
Arm - bone, final burial ceremony performed with the, 167 *sq.* ; lower, of dead preserved, 274
—— -bones, special treatment of the, 199 ; of dead preserved, 225, 249
Aroma district of British New Guinea, 201, 202
Arrow-heads made of bones of the dead, 352
Art, primitive religious, 114 ; Papuan, 220
Arugo, soul of dead, 207
Arumburinga, spiritual double, 164
Arunta, the, of Central Australia, 94 ; ceremonies connected with totems, 119 *sqq.* ; their magical ceremonies for the multiplication of the totems, 122 *sq.* ; their customs as to the hair of the dead, 138 ; their cuttings for the dead, 155 *sq.*, 159 ; burial customs of the, 164 *sq.*, 166
Aryan burial custom, 453
Asa, Secret Society, 233
Ashantee story of the origin of death, 63 *sq.*
Ashes smeared on mourners, 184, 361
Astrolabe Bay in German New Guinea, 218, 230, 235, 237
Astronomy, rise of, favoured by agriculture, 140 *sq.*
Asylums, 243
Asyrèn, dead man, 457
'*Ataro*, a powerful ghost, 377
Atonement for sick chief, 427
Aukem, a mythical being, 181
Aurora, one of the New Hebrides, 360, 382
Australia, causes which retarded progress in, 89 *sq.* ; germs of a worship of the dead in, 168 *sq.* *See also* Central Australia, Western Australia
——, the aborigines of, their ideas as to death from natural causes, 40 *sqq.* ; their primitive character, 88, 91 ; the belief in immortality among, 127 *sqq.* ; thought to be reborn in white people, 130, 131 *sqq.* ; their burial customs, 144 *sqq.* ; their primitive condition, 217
——, South, beliefs as to the dead in, 134 *sqq.*

Australia, South-Eastern, beliefs as to the dead in, 133 *sq.*, 139 ; burial customs among the aborigines of, 145 *sqq.*
——, Western, burial customs in, 147, 150, 151
Authority of chiefs based on their claim to magical powers, 395
Avenging a death, pretence of, 282, 328

Bachelor ghosts, hard fate of, 464
Bachelors' houses, 221
Bad and good, different fate of the, after death, 354
Baganda, the, their ideas as to the causes of death, 56 *n.*[2] ; their myth of the origin of death, 78 *sqq.* *See also* Uganda
Bahaus, the, of Borneo, 459
Bahnars of Cochinchina, 74
Bakairi, the, of Brazil, 35
Bakerewe, the, of the Victoria Nyanza, 50
Bali, burial custom in, 460
Balking ghosts, 455 *sqq.*
Balolo, of the Upper Congo, their myth of the continuance of death, 472
Balum, ghost or spirit of dead, 244 ; name for bull-roarer, 250 ; name for a ghost or monster who swallows lads at initiation, 251, 255, 260, 261 ; soul of a dead man, 257, 261
Bamler, G., 291, 297 *sq.*
Bananas in myths of the origin of death, 60, 70, 72 *sq.*
Bandages to prevent entrance of ghosts, 396
Bandaging eyes of corpse, 459
Banks' Islands, 343, 353, 386 ; myths of the origin of death in, 71, 83 *sq.*
—— Islanders, funeral customs of the, 355 *sqq.*
Bantu family, 60
Baronga, the, 61 ; burial custom of the, 454
Bartle Bay, 206, 208
Basutos, the, 61 ; burial custom of the, 454
Bat in myth of origin of death, 75
Bathing in sea after funeral, 207 *sq.* ; as purification after a death, 314, 319
Battel, Andrew, 51 *sq.*
Bechuanas, the, 61 ; burial custom of the, 454
Beetles in myth of the origin of death, 70
Belep tribe of New Caledonia, 325
Belief, acts as a clue to, 143
Belief in immortality, origin of belief in, 25 *sqq.* ; almost universal among races of mankind, 33 ; among the aborigines of Central Australia, 87 *sqq.* ; among the islanders of Torres Straits, 170 *sqq.* ; among the natives of British New

Guinea, 190 *sqq.* ; among the natives
of German New Guinea, 216 *sqq.* ;
among the natives of Dutch New
Guinea, 303 *sqq.* ; among the natives
of Southern Melanesia, 324 *sqq.* ;
among the natives of Central Melanesia, 343 *sqq.* ; its practical effect on
the life of the Central Melanesians,
391 *sq.* ; among the natives of Northern
Melanesia, 393 *sqq.*; among the Fijians,
406 *sqq.* ; strongly held by savages,
468 ; destruction of life and property
entailed by the, 468 *sq.* ; the question
of its truth, 469 *sqq.*
Belief in sorcery a cause of keeping down
the population, 38, 40
Berkeley, his theory of knowledge, 11 *sq.*
Berlin Harbour in German New Guinea,
218
Bernau, Rev. J. H., 38
Beryl-stone in *Rose Mary*, 130
Betindalo, the land of the dead, 350
Bhotias, the, of the Himalayas, 163
Biak or Wiak, island, 303
Bilking a ghost, 416
Bird in divination as to cause of death,
45
Birds, souls of sorcerers in, 39
Birth, new, at initiation, pretence of, 254
Birthplaces, the dead buried in their,
160
Birth-stones and birth-sticks (*churinga*)
of the Central Australians, 96 *sqq.*
Bismarck Archipelago, 70, 394, 402
Black, mourners painted, 178, 241, 293 ;
gravediggers painted, 451
—— -snake people, 94
Blackened, faces of mourners, 403
Blood of mourners dropped on corpse or
into grave, 158 *sq.*, 183, 185 ; and
hair of mourners offered to the dead,
183 ; of pigs smeared on skulls and
bones of the dead, 200 ; soul thought
to reside in the, 307 ; of sacrificial
victim not allowed to fall on the
ground, 365
—— revenge, duty of, 274, 276 *sq.* ;
discharged by sham fight, 136 *sq.*
Bogadyim, in German New Guinea, 230,
231
Boigu, the island of the dead, 175, 184,
213
Bolafagina, the lord of the dead, 350
Bolotoo, the land of souls, 411
Bones of the dead, second burial of the,
166 *sq.* ; kept in house, 203 ; worn by
survivors, 225 ; disinterred and kept
in house, 225, 294 ; making rain by
means of the, 341
—— and skulls of dead smeared with
blood of pigs, 200
Bonitos, ghosts in, 380

Boollia, magic, 41 *sq.*
" Born of an oak or a rock," 128
Bougainville, island of, 393
Boulia district of Queensland, 147, 155
Bow, divination by, 241
Bread-fruit trees, stones to make them
bear fruit, 335 *sq.*
Breaking things offered to the dead,
276
Breath, vital principle associated with
the, 129 *sq.*
Brett, Rev. W. H., 35 *sqq.*
Brewin, an evil spirit, 45
Brittany, burial custom in, 458
Brothers-in-law in funeral rites, 177
Brown, Rev. Dr. George, 48, 395
Buandik, the, 138
Buckley, the convict, 131
Buginese, burial custom of the, 461
Bugotu, 350, 352 ; in Ysabel, 372, 379
Building king's house, men sacrificed at,
446
Bukaua, the, of German New Guinea,
242, 256 *sqq.*
Bull-roarers, 243 ; used in divination,
249 ; described, 250 ; used at initiation
of young men among the Yabim, 250
sqq. ; among the Kaya-Kaya, 255 ;
at initiation among the Bukaua, 260
sq. ; associated with the spirits of the
dead, 261 ; at initiation among the
Kai, 263, 291 ; at initiation of young
men among the Tami, 301, 302
Bulotu or Bulu, the land of the dead,
462, 463
Bundle, the fatal, 472 ; story of, 77 *sq.*
Bures, Fijian temples, 439
Burial different for old and young,
married and unmarried, etc., 161 *sqq.* ;
and burning of the dead, 162 *sq.* ;
special modes of, intended to prevent
or facilitate the return of the spirit,
163 *sqq.* ; second, custom of, 166 *sq.* ;
in trees, 203 ; in island, 319 ; in the
sea, 347 *sq.*
—— customs of the Australian aborigines, 144 *sqq.* ; in Tumleo, 223 ;
of the Kai, 274 ; of the New Caledonians, 326 *sq.*, 339 *sq.* ; in New
Ireland, 397 *sq.*; in the Duke of York
Island, 403. *See also* Corpse, Grave
—— -grounds, sacred, 378
Buried alive, old people, 359 *sq.*
Burma, 75
Burning and burial of the dead, 162 *sq.*
—— bodies of women who died in
childbed, 459
Burns inflicted on themselves by mourners,
154, 155, 157, 327, 451
Burnt offerings to the dead, 294
—— sacrifices, reasons for, 348 *sq.* ; to
ghosts, 366, 367 *sq.*, 373

Hose, Ch., and McDougall, W., quoted, 265 *n.*, 417

Hottentots, their myth of the origin of death, 65 ; burial custom of the, 454

House deserted after a death, 195, 196 *n.*[1], 248, 275, 349, 400 ; deserted or destroyed after a death, 210 ; dead buried in the, 236, 347, 352, 397, 398, 399 ; dead carried out of, by special opening, 452 *sqq.*

Houses, native, at Kalo, 202 ; communal, 304

Howitt, Dr. A. W., 44 *sq.*, 139, 141

Human gods, 20, 23 *sqq.*

—— nature, two different views of, 469 *sqq.*

—— sacrifices to ghosts, 371 *sq.* ; in Fiji, 446 *sq.*

Hume's analysis of cause, 18 *sq.*

Hunt, Mr., his experience in Fiji, 423 *sq.*

Hunters supposed to be helped by ghosts, 274, 284 *sq.*

Huon Gulf, in German New Guinea, 242, 256

Hut built to represent mythical monster at initiation, 251, 290, 301 *sq.*

Huts erected on graves for use of ghosts, 150 *sq.* ; erected on graves, 203, 223, 248, 259, 275, 293, 294

Hypocritical lamentations at a death, 273

—— indignation of accomplice at a murder, 280 *sqq.*

Idu, mountain of the dead, 193, 194 *sq.*

Iguana in myth of origin of death, 70

Ilene, a worshipful ghost, 373

Ill-treatment of ghost who gives no help, 285

Illusion of the external world, 21

Images of the dead, wooden (*korwar* or *karwar*), 307 *sqq.*, 311, 315, 316 *sq.*, 321, 322 ; of sharks, 373; in temples, 442

Imitation of totems by disguised actors, 119 *sqq.*; of totemic animals, 177

Imitative magic, 335, 336, 338, 376

Immortality, belief in, among the aborigines of Central Australia, 87 *sqq.* ; among the islanders of Torres Straits, 170 *sqq.*; among the natives of British New Guinea, 190 *sqq.*; among the natives of German New Guinea, 216 *sqq.* ; among the natives of Dutch New Guinea, 303 *sqq.* ; among the natives of Southern Melanesia, 324 *sqq.*; among the natives of Central Melanesia, 343 *sqq.*; among the natives of Northern Melanesia, 393 *sqq.*; among the Fijians, 406 *sqq.* ; strongly held by savages, 468

Immortality, limited sense of, 25 ; origin of belief in, 25 *sqq.* ; belief in human, almost universal among races of mankind, 33 ; rivalry between men and animals for gift of, 74 *sq.* ; question of the truth of the belief in, 469 *sqq.*; destruction of life and property entailed by the belief in, 468 *sq.*

—— in a bundle, 77 *sq.*

Impecunious ghosts, hard fate of, 406

Impurity, ceremonial, of manslayer, 229 *sq.*

Im Thurn, Sir Everard F., 38 *sq.*

Incantations or spells, 385

Inconsistencies and contradictions in reasoning not peculiar to savages, 111 *sq.*

Inconsistency of savage thought, 143

Indians of Guiana, their ideas about death, 35 *sqq.*; their beliefs as to the dead, 165

—— of North-West America, burial custom of the, 455, 460

Indifference to death, 419 ; a consequence of belief in immortality, 422 *sq.*

Indo-European burial custom, 453

Infanticide as cause of diminished population, 40

Influence of European teaching on native beliefs, 142 *sq.*

Initiation at puberty regarded as a process of death and resurrection, 254, 261

—— of young men, 233 ; in Central Australia, 100 ; among the Yabim, 250 *sqq.*; among the Bukaua, 260 *sq.*; among the Kai, 290 *sq.*; in Fiji, 429 *sqq.*

Insanity, influence of, in history, 15 *sq.*

—— and inspiration not clearly distinguished, 388

Insect in divination as to cause of death, 44, 46

Inspiration, theory of, 14 *sq.* ; of medium by ancestral spirits, 308 *sqq.*; by spirits of the dead, 322 ; by ghosts in Central Melanesia, 388 *sq.*; attested by frenzy, 443, 444 *sq.*

—— and insanity not clearly distinguished, 388

Insufflations, magical, to heal the sick, 329

Intichiuma, magical ceremonies for the multiplication of totems, 122 *sq.*

Intuition and experience, 11

Invocation of ghosts, 288 *sq.* ; of the dead, 329 *sq.*, 332 *sqq.*, 377, 378, 401, 441

Island, dead buried in, 319

—— of the dead, fabulous, 175

Islands, ghosts live in, 350, 353

Isle of Pines, 325, 330, 337

Sickness and death set down to sorcery, 240, 257
—— and disease recognised by some savages as due to natural causes, 55 *sq. See also* Disease
Sido, his journey to the land of the dead, 211 *sq.*
Sins, confession of, 201
Skin cast as a means of renewing youth, 69 *sqq.*, 74 *sq.*, 83
Skull-shaped stones in rain-making, 336 *sq.*
Skulls, spirits of the dead embodied in their, 338
—— and arm-bones, special treatment of the, 199 *sq.* ; carried by dancers at funeral dance, 200
—— of the dead preserved, 199 *sqq.*, 209, 249, 318, 328, 339, 347, 351 *sq.*, 398, 400 *sq.*, 403 ; preserved and consulted as oracles, 176, 178 *sq.*, 179 ; used in divination, 213 ; kept in men's clubhouses, 221, 225 ; inserted in wooden images, 311 *sq.*, 321 ; religious ceremonies performed with the, 329 *sq.* ; food offered to the, 339 *sq.*, 352 ; used to fertilise plantations, 340 ; used in conjurations, 402
Sky, souls of the dead thought to be in the, 133 *sq.*, 135, 138 *sq.*, 141, 142
Slain, ghosts of the, especially dreaded, 205, 258, 279, 306, 323
Sleep, soul thought to quit body in, 257, 291, 395, 412
Smith, E. R., 53
Smyth, R. Brough, 43 *sq.*
Snakes, ghosts in, 380
Sneezing, omens from, 194
Social progress stimulated by favourable natural conditions, 141 *sq.*, 148 *sq.*
—— ranks, gradation of, in Fiji, 408
Solomon Islands, 343, 346 *sqq.* ; sacrificial ritual in the, 365 *sq.*
Somosomo, one of the Fijian islands, 425, 441, 442
Sorcerers, their importance in history, 16
—— catch and detain souls, 267, 268 *sq.*, 270
—— put to death, 35, 35 *sq.*, 37 *sq.*, 40 *sq.*, 44, 50, 136, 250, 269, 277, 278 *sq.*, 341 *sq. See also* Magician
Sorcery as the supposed cause of natural deaths, 33 *sqq.*, 136, 268, 270, 402 ; sickness and death ascribed to, 257
—— a cause of keeping down the population, belief in, 38, 40, 46 *sq.*, 51 *sqq.*
—— Fijian dread of, 413 *sq. See also* Magic *and* Witchcraft
Sores ascribed to action of ghosts, 257
Soro, atonement, 427
Soul, world-wide belief in survival of soul after death, 24, 25, 33

Soul of sleeper detained by enemy, 49 ; human, associated with shadow or reflection, 173, 267, 395, 412 ; pretence of carrying away the, 181 *sq.* ; detained by demon, 194 ; recovery of a lost, 194, 270 *sq.* ; thought to quit body in sleep, 257, 291, 395, 412 ; resides in the eye, 267 ; thought to pervade the body, 267 ; two kinds of human, 267 *sq.* ; caught and detained by sorcerer, 267, 268 *sq.*, 270 ; long soul and short soul, 291 *sq.* ; of offering consumed by deity or spirit, 297, 298 ; thought to reside in the blood, 307 ; Melanesian theory of the, 344 *sq.* ; of sick tied up by ghost, 374 ; North Melanesian theory of the, 395 *sq.* ; in form of animals, 396 ; Fijian theory of the, 410 *sqq.* ; caught in a scarf, 412 *sq.* ; of grandfather reborn in grandchild, 417 ; of offerings consumed by gods, 443
—— -stuff or spiritual essence, 267 *sq.*, 270, 271, 279. *See also* Spirit
Souls, recovery of lost, 300 *sq.* ; River of the, 462 ; the killer of, 464 *sq.*
—— of animals, sacrifices to the, 239; of animals offered to ghosts, 246
—— attributed by the Fijians to animals, vegetables, and inanimate things, 410 *sq.*
—— of the dead identified with spirits of nature, 130 ; turned into animals, 229 ; as falling stars, 229 ; live in trees, 316
—— carried off by ghosts, 197, 383 ; of sorcerers in animals, 39
—— of noblemen only saved, 33 ; of those who died from home called back, 311
Spells or incantations, 385
Spencer and Gillen, 46 *sq.*, 91 *sq.*, 103, 104, 105, 106, 108, 116 *sqq.*, 123 *sq.*, 140, 148, 156, 157, 158
Spider and Death, 82 *sq.*
Spirit, human, associated with the-heart, 129 ; associated with the shadow, 129, 130. *See also* Soul
Spirits, ancestral, help hunters and fishers, 226 ; worshipped in the *Nanga*, 428 *sq.* ; cloth and weapons offered to, 430 *sq.* ; novices presented to, at initiation, 432 *sq.*, 434
—— of animals go to the spirit land, 210
—— consume spiritual essence of sacrifices, 285, 287, 297, 298
—— of the dead thought to be strengthened by blood, 159 ; reborn in women, 93 *sq.* ; give information to the living, 240 ; give good crops, 247 *sq.* ; thought to be mischievous, 257

END OF VOL. I

RENEWALS 691-4574

DATE DUE

OCT 2 6			
MAY 1 3			
DEC 0 5			

Demco, Inc. 38-293